ONCE THERE WAS A PLACE:
SETTLEMENT ARCHAEOLOGY AT CHAGAR BAZAR, 1999-2002

Augusta McMahon
with Carlo Colantoni, Julia Frane and Arkadiusz Sołtysiak

BRITISH INSTITUTE FOR THE STUDY OF IRAQ

© British Institute for the Study of Iraq
(Gertrude Bell Memorial)
2009

All rights reserved. No part of this publication may be reproduced or stored in a retrieval system or transmitted in any manner or by any means without the prior permission of the publishers in writing.

ISBN 978-0-903472-27-2

Printed by Short Run Press in Exeter

Table of Contents

List of Text Figures	5
List of Plates	7
Acknowledgements	11
Ch. 1 Introduction and Site Biography	13
Ch. 2 Community Buildings: Architecture in Area A	29
Ch. 3 Neighbourhood Dynamics: Area G and Mallowan's Area BD	63
Ch. 4 Chagar Bazar Burial Practices	109
Ch. 4 Appendix Human bones from Chagar Bazar: scientific analyses	129
Ch. 5 Ceramic Assemblage and Social Inference	161
Ch. 6 The Material World: Objects from Areas A and G	193
Ch. 7 Chagar Bazar as a Place in a Landscape	217
References Cited	227
Plates 1-9 Burials	243
Plates 10-68 Pottery	262
Plates 69-88 Objects	380
Summary (in English and Arabic)	423

Text Figures

Chapter 1

Fig. 1	Map of the Upper Khabur with key sites indicated	14
Fig. 2	Taurus Mountains from Chagar Bazar	16
Fig. 3	Chagar Bazar from southwest	16
Fig. 4	Topographic plan of Chagar Bazar with excavation areas indicated	17
Fig. 5	CORONA image of Chagar Bazar and its surroundings (December 1967)	18
Fig. 6	Topographic map of Chagar Bazar's micro-region, with ancient sites and modern villages indicated (from a base map courtesy of J. Ur)	19
Fig. 7	Hollow ways around Chagar Bazar, from CORONA image (December 1967)	22

Chapter 2

Fig. 8	Topographic plan of the northern end of Chagar Bazar with Mallowan and BSAI excavation areas indicated	30
Fig. 9	Area A, Phase II plan	32
Fig. 10	Vaulting of south wall of Building I, Area A Phase II, from west	34
Fig. 11	Baked brick path across courtyard of Building III, Phase II Area A	35
Fig. 12	Detail of cobble edging in courtyard of Building III, Area A Phase II, from north	36
Fig. 13	Assembly room in Building III, Phase II Area A, from northwest	37
Fig. 14	Building III, Area A Phase II, with secondary façade	38
Fig. 15	Building in Mallowan's Area TD (after Mallowan 1936: Fig. 3), at the same scale as Fig. 14 (dashed lines indicate possible original walls)	39
Fig. 16	Area A, Phase III plan (with walls of Phase II indicated)	44
Fig. 17	Barrel vault in Locus 61, Phase III, and "porthole" doorway	45
Fig. 18	Area A Phase I plan (with walls of Phase II indicated as dashed lines)	46

Chapter 3

Fig. 19	Combined plan of Area G (Phase II/2) and Mallowan's Area BD	64
Fig. 20	Plan of Area G Phase IV (Trench G II only); overlying Phase II/2 wall shown as dashed line	68
Fig. 21	Plan of Area G, Phase III	69
Fig. 22	Area G, Phase III, Building BDG 5 from northwest	71
Fig. 23	Area G Phase III, Building BDG 4 from west	72
Fig. 24	Plan of Area G, Phase II/2	74
Fig. 25	Drain 00-34 in courtyard of Building G 2, from west	75
Fig. 26	Oven 00-10 and steps in Locus 16, Building BDG 2, from south	76
Fig. 27	Alley in Area G, from south, with fallen mud-brick in foreground	78
Fig. 28	Plan of Area G, Phase II/1	80
Fig. 29	Courtyard of Building G 2 at right, Building BDG 2 at left, paving 00-47 at rear left, from north	82
Fig. 30	Paving 00-47 in foreground, façade of Building G1 and courtyard of Building G2 at rear, from east	83

Fig. 31	Plan of Area G, Trench II, Sub-phase II/1A	83
Fig. 32	Plan of Area G, Phase I	84

Appendix to Chapter 4

Fig. 33	Average state of preservation in children and adults (see Table 4.2)	130
Fig. 34	T.37, dental calculus on central lower incisor	131
Fig. 35	T.33, cribra orbitalia	132
Fig. 36	T.33, femoral cribra	132
Fig. 37	Frequency of degenerative joint disease in spine (see Tables 4.31, 4.34)	133
Fig. 38	T.10, extreme eburnation of left patella	133
Fig. 39	T.10, degenerative joint disease in cervical vertebrae	133
Fig. 40	T.10, degenerative joint disease in sacrum	134
Fig. 41	T.4, eburnation in first metacarpal	134
Fig. 42	T.37, osteoarthritis in right talus	134
Fig. 43	T.4, osteoporosis in femoral midshaft	134
Fig. 44	T.4, osteoporosis in articular surface of fibula	134
Fig. 45	T.39, osteochondrosis in femoral condyles	134
Fig. 46	Local thickening of femoral cortical bone from L 54.1	135
Fig. 47	T.34, local thinning of parietal bone	135
Fig. 48	T.9, fracture in scapular acromion	135
Fig. 49	T.4, broken and healed rib	135
Fig. 50	T.11, broken and healed rib	135
Fig. 51	T.11, irregular development of interior margin of rib	136
Fig. 52	T.37, dislocated sternal end of rib	136
Fig. 53	T.4, distorted first toe segments	137
Fig. 54	T.10, plantar calcaneal spur	137
Fig. 55	T.39, pinched lateral edge of left navicular	137
Fig. 56	T.11, deltoid tuberosity	137
Fig. 57	T.10, distal articular surfaces of first metacarpals	138
Fig. 58	T.50/1, crooked right first metacarpal	138
Fig. 59	T.10, developed margins in finger segments	138

Chapter 5

Fig. 60	Ceramic typology hierarchy	153
Fig. 61	Paint splash pattern inside a medium barrel (CB 1924)	159
Fig. 62	Rim diameters of Common Ware and Grey Ware bowls, as percentage of excavated sample of bowls of each fabric type	165
Fig. 63	Relative percentages of rim diameters in carinated and plain-sided bowls	167
Fig. 64	Relative percentages of rim diameters in plain-sided common ware, carinated common ware and grey ware bowls	167

Chapter 6

Fig. 65	Distribution of objects, Area A, Phase II	182
Fig. 66	Distribution of objects, Area G, Phase II/2	185
Fig. 67	Distribution of objects, Area G, Phase II/1	187

Plates

Plate 1	Area A Tomb 4
Plate 2	a) Area A Tombs 8 and 9
	b) Area A Tomb 12
	c) Area A Tomb 34
Plate 3	a) Area A Tomb 35
	b) Area A Tomb 38
	c) Area A Tomb 41
Plate 4	a) Area G Tomb 15
	b) Area G Tomb 32
	c) Area G Tomb 49
Plate 5	a) Area G Tomb 18
	b) Area G Tomb 37
Plate 6	a) Area G Tomb 39
	b) Area G Building G 2 courtyard with Tombs 10, 11, 13 & 4.3
	c) Area G Tomb 10
Plate 7	a) Area G Tomb 11
	b) Area G L. 4.3
Plate 8	Area G Tomb 13
Plate 9	a) Area G Tomb 33
	b) Area A Tomb 30
	c) Area A Tomb 7
Plate 10	Small Shallow and Deep Bowls
Plate 11	Medium Shallow Bowls
Plate 12	Medium Deep Bowls
Plate 13	Medium Deep Bowls
Plate 14	Large Shallow and Deep Bowls
Plate 15	Large Deep Bowls
Plate 16	Large Deep Cylindrical Bowls
Plate 17	Large Deep Cylindrical Bowls
Plate 18	Small Shallow and Deep Carinated Bowls
Plate 19	Medium Carinated Shallow Bowls
Plate 20	Medium Carinated Shallow Bowls
Plate 21	Medium Carinated Shallow Bowls
Plate 22	Medium Carinated Shallow Bowls
Plate 23	Medium Carinated Deep Bowls
Plate 24	Medium Carinated Deep Bowls
Plate 25	Large Carinated Shallow Bowls
Plate 26	Large Carinated Shallow and Deep Bowls
Plate 27	Large Carinated Deep Bowls
Plate 28	Small and Medium Grey Ware Bowls
Plate 29	Medium and Large Grey Ware Bowls
Plate 30	Ridged Bowls

Plate 31	Z-Sided Bowls
Plate 32	Medium Barrels
Plate 33	Medium and Large Barrels
Plate 34	Large Barrels
Plate 35	Large Barrels
Plate 36	Large and Very Large Barrels
Plate 37	Small Plain-Sided and Small Fine Ware Ridged Barrels
Plate 38	Small and Medium Ridged Barrels
Plate 39	Medium and Large Ridged Barrels
Plate 40	Large and Very Large Ridged Barrels
Plate 41	Basins
Plate 42	Basins and Stands
Plate 43	Stands
Plate 44	Stands
Plate 45	Cups
Plate 46	Fine Ware Beakers
Plate 47	Grain Measures
Plate 48	Khabur Ware jars
Plate 49	Khabur Ware jars
Plate 50	Khabur Ware jars
Plate 51	Narrow-Mouth Jars
Plate 52	Narrow-Mouth Jars
Plate 53	Narrow-Mouth Jars
Plate 54	Wide-mouth Jars, A Sub-Type, Medium
Plate 55	Wide-mouth Jars, A Sub-Type, Medium
Plate 56	Wide-mouth Jars, A Sub-Type, Medium
Plate 57	Wide-mouth Jars, A Sub-Type, Medium and Large
Plate 58	Wide-mouth Jars, A Sub-Type, Large
Plate 59	Wide-mouth Jars, B Sub-Type, Medium
Plate 60	Wide-mouth Jars, B Sub-Type, Medium and Large
Plate 61	Wide-mouth Jars, B Sub-Type, Large
Plate 62	Cooking Pots
Plate 63	Cooking Pots
Plate 64	Cooking Pots and Bottles
Plate 65	Miscellaneous Vessels
Plate 66	Possible Late 3rd Millennium BC Forms
Plate 67	Bases
Plate 68	Painted Sherds
Plate 69	Animal Figurines–Zebu and Horses
Plate 70	Animal Figurines–Horses and Cattle
Plate 71	Animal Figurines–Miscellaneous
Plate 72	Model Wheels
Plate 73	Model Wagons and Human Figurines
Plate 74	Grinding Stones, Hammer-stones
Plate 75	Grinding Stones, Hammer-stones
Plate 76	Stone mortars, grinding stones and bowls

Plate 77	Whetstones, Burnishing Tools
Plate 78	Spindle Whorls and Loom Weights
Plate 79	Bone Weaving Tools
Plate 80	Seals & Sealings
Plate 81	Seals and Tallies
Plate 82	Sealings, Tokens and Seal
Plate 83	Metal Objects
Plate 84	Metal Objects
Plate 85	Metal Objects
Plate 86	Beads
Plate 87	Beads and Ornaments
Plate 88	Miscellaneous objects

Acknowledgements

I am very grateful to the current and previous Directors-General of Antiquities and Museums in Damascus, Dr. Bassam Jamous, Dr. Moaz Razzaq and Dr. Sultan Muheisin, for their support and interest in our work at Chagar Bazar during 1999-2002. We also must thank the current and previous Directors of Excavations in Damascus, Dr. Michel al-Maqdissi and Dr. Adnan Bounni. Special thanks go to the Chagar Bazar Co-Directors, Mr. Abdul-Massih Baghdo, Director of the Hasseke Department of Antiquities, and Prof. Önhan Tunca, University of Liège.

Financial support for the 1999-2002 British excavations at Chagar Bazar was generously provided by the British School of Archaeology in Iraq (now the British Institute for the Study of Iraq), the McDonald Institute for Archaeological Research in Cambridge and Newnham College, Cambridge.

I am most grateful to all the members of the British team for their high standards of professionalism, skill and commitment. Team members in each season were:
1999: Carlo Colantoni, Julia Frane, Jason Ur, Frank Scheler, Melanie Wasmuth.
2000: Carlo Colantoni, Julia Frane, Lamya Khalidi, Matthew Pritchard, Lauren Ristvet, Jason Ur.
2001: Carlo Colantoni, Julia Frane, Carrie Hritz, Lamya Khalidi, Alexandra Nadin, Jason Ur.
2002: Carlo Colantoni, Keith Dobney, Julia Frane, Miranda Semple.
Although he was not present during excavation, Dr. Arkadiusz Sołtysiak was subsequently able to lend his expertise to analysis of the human remains, and this contribution has been invaluable.

Illustrations in this volume were prepared by Carlo Colantoni, Lamya Khalidi, Jason Ur and Augusta McMahon. David and Joan Oates, Geoff Emberling and the Tell Brak team were the project's good neighbours and good friends. Karl-Erik McCullough provided vital support in the UK and USA. Sir Max Mallowan (the "Armadillo of Assyria") was both an inspiration and an irritant from beyond the grave. The inhabitants of Hittin (Chagar Bazar village) were gracious hosts and enthusiastic co-workers.

This book is dedicated to my parents, Donald and Hylarie McMahon, for their decades of unqualified support.

A. McMahon
Cambridge, UK
1/07/2009

Chapter 1

Settlement Archaeology and Site Biography

A. McMahon

Settlement archaeology has had numerous foster parents since Chang (1958, 1968), Trigger (1967), Willey (1953, 1968) and others unpacked and renovated Kossinna's *Siedlungsarchaologie* as part of the New Archaeology movement. Settlement archaeology embraces activity areas and buildings, households and communities, and landscapes and environments. This approach is still most closely associated with settlement *pattern* studies–broad regional surveys focusing on the relationship of sites to each other and to their environmental setting. But at its centre is settlement. A settlement is both a physical locus and a cultural idea, both a minimum acting unit and a heterogeneous collection of independent households, a home to both actors and systems. In current usage, a settlement may be a "place" with practical and symbolic meanings: "It is place, permanent position both in the social and topographical sense, that gives us our identity" (Jackson 1984: 152).

This study incorporates ideas of place in exploring the settlement of Chagar Bazar, a northern Mesopotamian site with a long and complex biography. The biography begins in the 6th millennium BC, and its final chapters include the 1930s excavations conducted by Sir Max Mallowan and the recent excavations (since 1999) by the British School of Archaeology in Iraq, the University of Liège, and the Syrian Directorate General of Antiquities & Museums. We have taken a contextual approach, isolating and integrating discrete aspects of the settlement's material culture. Our primary focus is the settlement in the early 2nd millennium BC (Old Babylonian Period), its final ancient occupation.

From 1934 to 1937, Chagar Bazar was investigated by Max Mallowan, as one of several sites selected after his extensive survey of the Upper and Lower Khabur regions in Syria. His excavations were part of an ambitious programme aimed at delineation of the settlement history and chronological markers of the Upper Khabur plains in particular, which was then almost-unexplored territory in archaeological terms.[1] Other sites selected by Mallowan were Tell Brak, Tell Arbid, and Gir Mayir (see Fig. 1), but Chagar Bazar and Tell Brak were to become the twin foci of his project. Characteristically, Chagar Bazar was chosen in part for what it was, but almost equally for what it was not:

> "Chagar Bazar was selected as a mound likely to give a cross-section of the main periods of occupation of the Habur region from prehistoric times down to the historical period, and it seemed eminently suitable for our purpose because the top of the mound was not encumbered by any post-Assyrian buildings." (Mallowan 1934: 5)

---

[1] This region was more sparsely settled in the 1930s than currently, being then mostly pasture land gradually undergoing resettlement in the wake of the changing political milieu and the shift in this area from a backwater province of the Ottoman empire to a frontier of three new nations. See Mallowan 1936 for a scholarly account of the survey, Christie 1946 for an impressionistic description of life on the survey and excavation.

Chapter 1

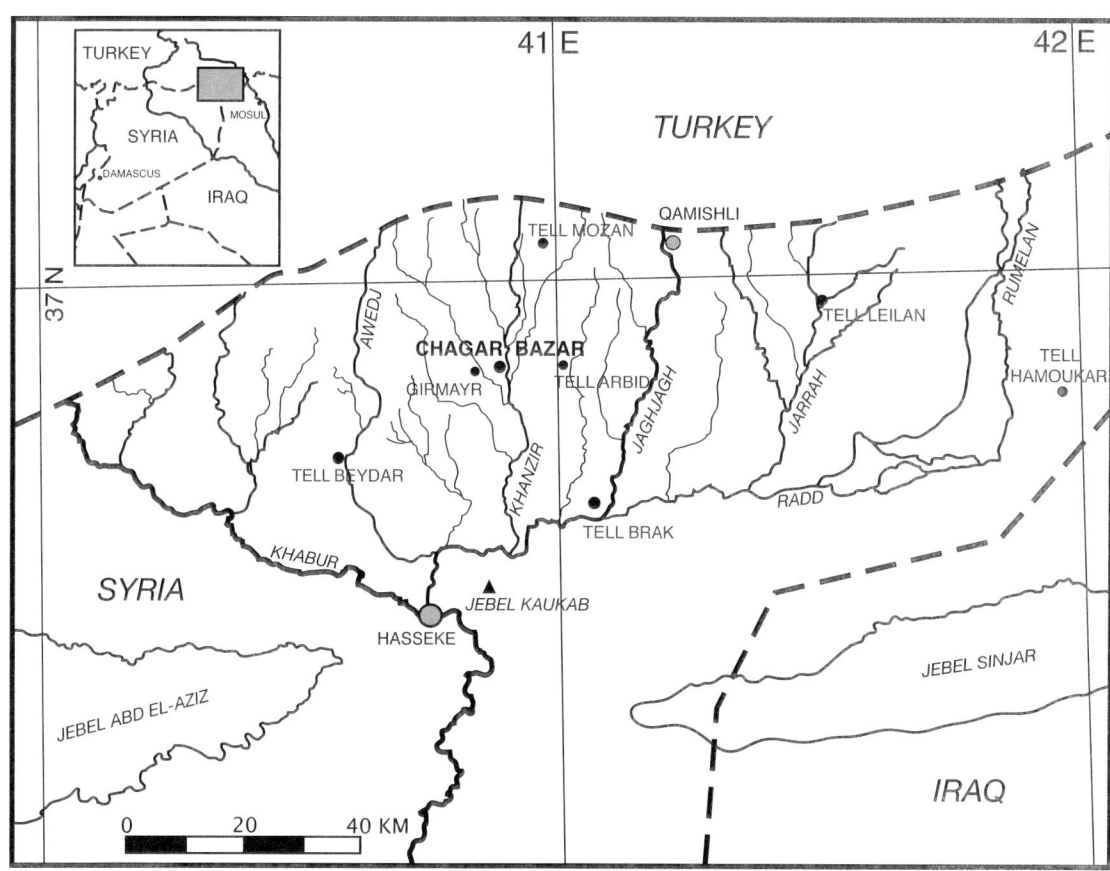

Figure 1: Map of the Upper Khabur with key sites indicated

The three seasons spent at Chagar Bazar served as a trial run and testing ground for Mallowan's subsequent work at the more massive and complex Tell Brak. Yet his Chagar Bazar results are impressive in isolation. His excavations in the Halaf Period levels expanded the evidence for internal variability and regional interconnections during prehistory. For the historic periods, his work is most notable for a significant horizontal exposure of a neighbourhood of houses belonging to the early 2nd millennium BC. He was responsible for the first identification of and date assignment to Khabur Ware, the distinctive pottery with painted horizontal bands and cross-hatched triangles now used as a type-fossil for the early 2nd millennium BC across much of northern Mesopotamia. The archive of early 2nd millennium BC economic tablets found in an administrative building in 1937 supplements information in the contemporary or near-contemporary archives of Mari, Tell Leilan and Tell al Rimah. The Chagar Bazar tablets refer to the existence of a royal estate near Chagar Bazar, linked to the regional state of the king Samsi-Addu[2]. The texts offer valuable information on the ethnic groups and the economic and political dynamics of the Upper Khabur region. Broadly, Mallowan's excavations revealed that Chagar Bazar was occupied from the late 6th through the mid 2nd millennia BC, with apparent episodes of abandonment during the late 5th through the 4th and in the late 3rd millennia

---

[2] The tablets excavated in 1937 are published by Gadd 1937, Gadd 1940, Loretz 1969, Snell 1983 and Talon 1997. A brief note on an archive of tablets regarding beer production found nearby in 2000 and 2001 appears in Tunca & Lacambre 2002 and a fuller publication in Tunca & Baghdo 2008.

BC (see Mallowan 1936, especially his classic schematic section of the Deep Sounding, his Fig. 2).

Mallowan attributed Chagar Bazar's substantial prehistoric size and its great length of near-continuous occupation to its position on a persistent east-west trade route. Yet he made an unusual effort to downplay its significance as opposed to other sites in the region: "There was nothing to suggest that Til-sha-annim [then thought to be the site's ancient name] was of greater importance than any of the hundreds of other small towns which studded the Khabur steppe" (Mallowan 1947: 81). At times, his publications express faint surprise that Chagar Bazar exhibited such relative wealth and sophistication. His trade route node explanation is plausible as one element within the foundation and history of Chagar Bazar, but such a single-factor explanation is no longer entirely valid. Site biographies are inevitably complex; the initial foundation of a site and its subsequent persistence of occupation may have different rationales; cultural traditions and individuals' personal histories may conquer economic concerns.

In 1999, a renewed programme of excavations was initiated at Chagar Bazar, a collaborative project involving the British School of Archaeology in Iraq, the University of Liège, and the Syrian Directorate General of Antiquities & Museums. Research of the British team within this project utilized two inter-related approaches widespread in historical and contextual archaeology. The first was the exploration of the "material systems" of one episode in northern Mesopotamian history, as represented in the site's final occupation in the early 2nd millennium BC. This aspect of our research programme explored spatial use and material culture continuities within the textually-delineated context of growth and collapse of the region's first territorial state. The combination of Mallowan's legacy with our new excavations offers the opportunity for a dense "compositional study" of the settlement layout and material culture assemblage, or the settlement's "microstructure" (Chang 1968: 7). The second approach regarded the role of the site within the Upper Khabur region, as its internal occupation cycle meshes with wider regional developments or "macrostructures" (*ibid.*); soundings in 3rd and 4th millennium BC levels supplemented the larger investigations into the early 2nd millennium BC occupation.

Site and Setting

Chagar Bazar lies on the west bank of the Wadi Khanzir[3], a tributary of the Khabur River in northeast Syria (see Fig. 1). Its surrounding "economic landscape" is richly resourced. The wadi is currently intermittent at best and completely dry from late spring, but its down-cut depth indicates that in the past it must have been a more significant and long-term water source. The Turkish Taurus mountains with their timber, limestone, flint and metals are clearly visible on most days and their foothills are a mere 50 kilometers' journey to the north (Fig. 2). Basalt outcrops are found c 35 kilometers to the south around Jebel Kaukab (near the modern city of Hasseke). The wadi and its banks would have provided the vital resource of clay, plus reeds, small trees such as poplar, and fish at times; the plains on all sides of the site have high agricultural potential and offer good grazing opportunities. The primary limiting factor on settlement in the region is rainfall, with the area around Chagar Bazar generally

---

[3] The wadi's official name, as given on topographic maps, is Wadi Amuda; however, it is locally more commonly known as the Wadi Khanzir and occasionally as the Wadi Dara.

receiving an adequate but variable c 300 mm of rainfall per year, clustered during the months from December through March.

Figure 2: Taurus Mountains from Chagar Bazar

The mounded portion of the site is currently approximately 12 hectares, comprising a smaller and higher south mound (c 5 hectares, reaching 21 m above the plain) and a longer lower north mound (c 7 hectares, maximum 15 m above plain level) (Figs. 3, 4). This internal variable morphology is matched by variability in site size–within the mound's "envelope"–during the site's lifetime. Chagar Bazar was a large prehistoric site; Halaf pottery is found over all 12 hectares of the mounds. During the mid 3rd millennium BC, its absolute size may have been maintained at c 12 hectares, but its relative size compared to other expanding sites in the region would have been reduced. Certainly during the terminal 3rd and early 2nd millennia BC, the site shrank significantly from its prehistoric maximum and would be classed as a large village within a traditional site-size hierarchy. However, the 1930s excavations had already revealed that the site, at least during the 2nd millennium BC, had greater significance than what would be expected of a "village" or low-rank small site. The texts found in Mallowan's excavations indicate that it played a key role within Samsi-Addu's regional administration. The density and variability of occupation revealed by our excavations and the significance of Chagar Bazar's location within the contemporary settlement pattern and landscape both add support to the reconstruction of a substantive role for the settlement within that territorial state, an importance that persisted in the aftermath of that state's collapse.

Figure 3: Chagar Bazar from southwest

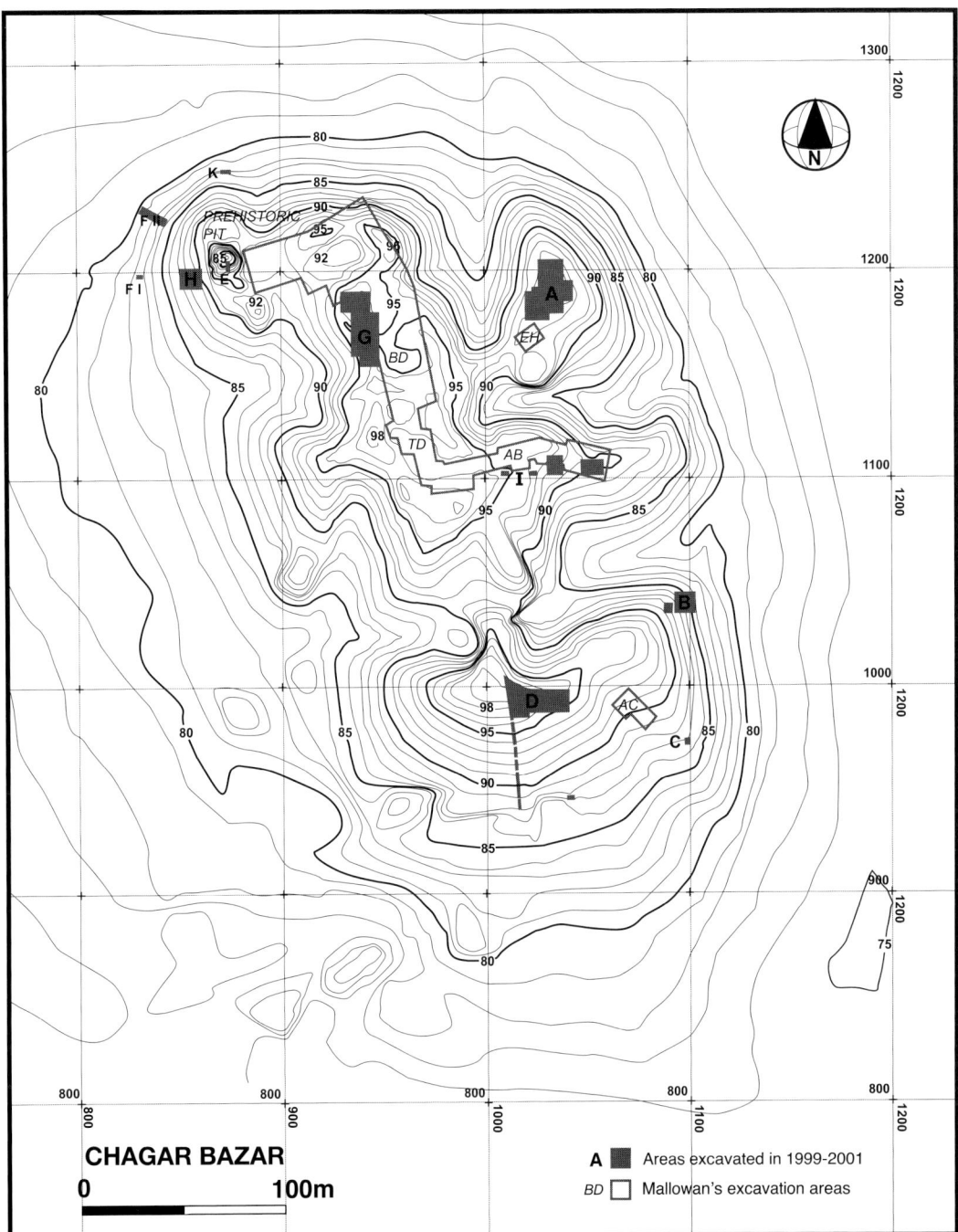

Figure 4: Topographic plan of Chagar Bazar with excavation areas indicated

Our excavations partially filled two of Mallowan's supposed occupational hiatuses (during the late 5th-4th millennium and the late 3rd millennium BC); however, there remains a genuine occupational gap from the very late 3rd millennium to the early 2nd millennium BC (late Post-Akkadian to Early Khabur in ceramic terms, Isin-Larsa in historical terms). Chagar Bazar was then re-occupied, probably in c 1850-1800 BC, at the end of a region-wide episode of higher aridity experienced during 2200-1900 BC (Ristvet & Weiss 2005, Matthews 2003a). A key question for Chagar Bazar's biography is: what factors were considered in the choice of this ancient pre-existing mound as a re-settlement location in the early 2nd millennium? The welcoming economic landscape was certainly a factor. But if the re-occupiers of Chagar Bazar were consciously looking for a mounded site to appropriate, they would have seen Tell

Khanzir, a comparably sized multiple mound, adjacent to a fork in the Wadi Khanzir only four km further south, as well as Tell 'Arus, a slightly smaller mound on the same bank of the wadi, just over five km north. These are but two examples out of many possibilities densely scattered across the region. Micro-variation in environment may have been a factor; even a few kilometers horizontal movement in this region can make a substantial difference to yearly rainfall and to the water table, particularly in years of low rainfall. A relict wadi roughly parallel to Wadi Khanzir visible on CORONA images to the west of Chagar Bazar (Fig. 5) may have continued to affect the micro-regional water table and vegetation and may have added to the spot's economic advantages.[4]

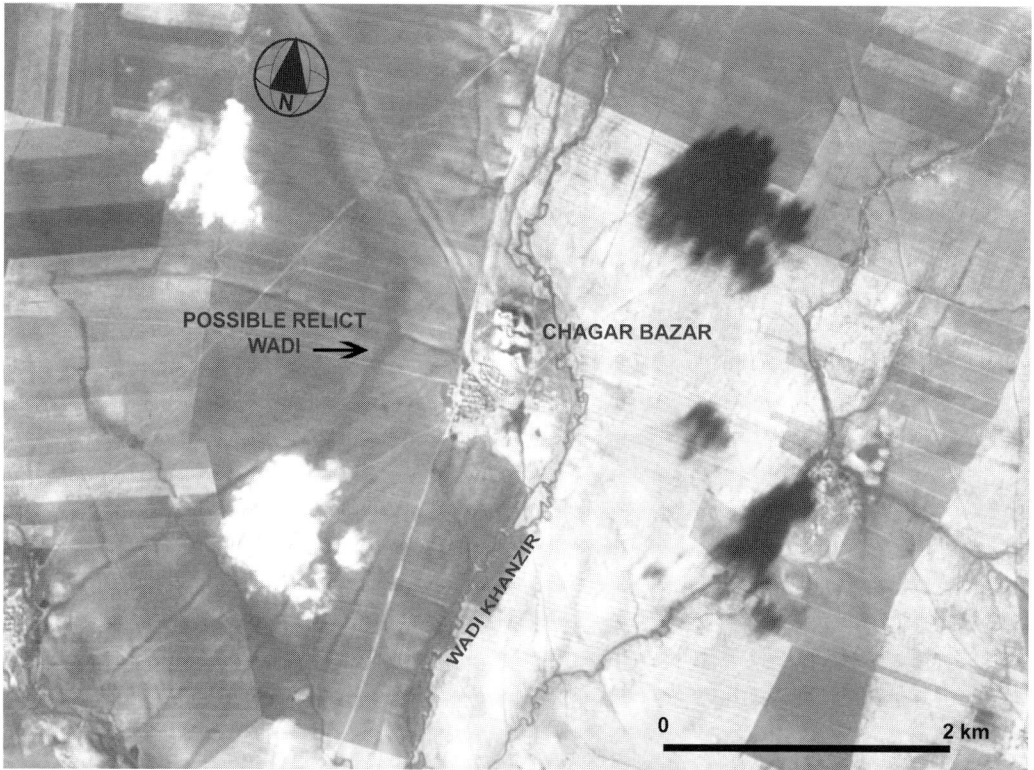

Figure 5: CORONA image of Chagar Bazar and its surroundings (December 1967)

Beyond economic value, issues of sight-lines and visibility, of symbolic meaning and the social or political value of a landscape or place, also come into play in (re)settlement choice. There are significant elevation differences in the plain level near the sites listed: c 365 m near Tell Khanzir, c 375 m near Chagar Bazar and c 385 m near Tel 'Arus (Fig. 6). But more significantly, the area of the plain in which Chagar Bazar lies is noticeably more open and flat than the areas immediately adjacent to both Tell 'Arus and Tell Khanzir. Particularly near Tell 'Arus, but also visibly near Tell Khanzir, the topography presents an elevation rise to the west of each site, cut by multiple wadis. While distant enough to be unrelated to defense or overlook issues, that rise and the down-cut dissection of the landscape might hide or distract the eye from each of these sites. By contrast, the plain surrounding Chagar Bazar on all sides is flatter, and the lines of sight to the mound are unobstructed.

Surveys indicate that the area around Chagar Bazar had low permanent occupation in the early 2nd millennium BC (Wilkinson 1998, 2002; Lyonnet 1996,

---

[4] The dates during which this relict wadi functioned are undetermined.

2000), while texts from Mari indicate a high density of nomadic pastoralists. Visibility and landscape value have differing scales and measures for these contrasted populations. This issue of place and landscape value will be further addressed in Chapter 7.

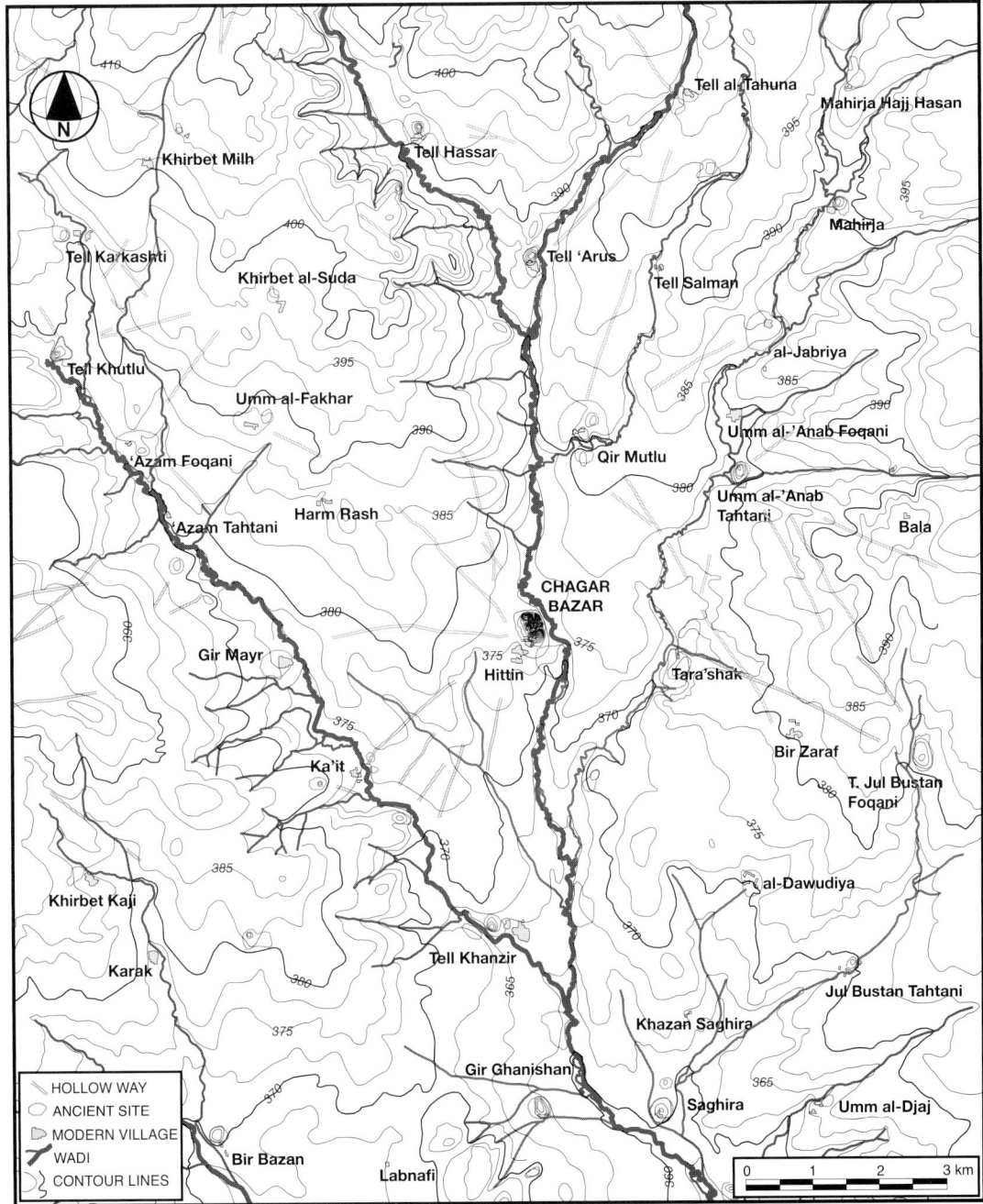

Figure 6: Topographic map of Chagar Bazar's micro-region, with ancient sites and modern villages indicated (from a base map by J. Ur)

Selected Chapters in the Biography of Chagar Bazar

Late Chalcolithic Period, Dynamics of early Social Complexity

Mallowan's excavations did not uncover Late Chalcolithic material in any of his soundings, and the assumption has been that Chagar Bazar was abandoned from the

Late Halaf or early Ubaid Period through to the early 3rd millennium BC[5]. In 1999, an intensive surface sherd collection revealed that the south mound had in fact been occupied during the Late Chalcolithic Period, or the early-mid 4th millennium BC. Late Chalcolithic pottery was found on the surface of the entire south mound, with its greatest concentration on the south and east slopes, below Mallowan's Area AC (see Fig. 4). No Late Chalcolithic pottery was present on the northern mound, and our best estimate of the site size during this key period is three hectares at maximum. This newly-discovered Late Chalcolithic settlement was explored in a small sounding (Area C) in 1999.

During the late 5th-4th millennium BC, the Upper Khabur region experienced a phase of social and economic vitality accompanying early urbanism, followed by vitality of a different nature indicated by the spread of material culture, influence and people from the southern Mesopotamian Late Uruk city-states. From Mallowan's work, it appeared that this dynamic and complicated phase had bypassed Chagar Bazar, which was apparently abandoned in advance of these regional developments. However, following our survey and sounding, we know that the site was occupied during some of these social changes.

The Late Chalcolithic surface collection included pottery types known from Tell Brak (Area CH 9-12, Area TW 14-17, Tell Majnuna), Tepe Gawra (Level VIII) and Hacinebi Tepe (Phases A and B1) to belong to the Late Chalcolithic 3 Period, contemporary with the Early-Middle Uruk Period in South Mesopotamian periodization[6]. It is significant that there were no Southern Mesopotamian ("true Uruk") types present on the surface, not even the near-ubiquitous and easily-identified Beveled-Rim Bowl. A 2 x 3 meter sounding (Area C) was located on the south mound southeast of Mallowan's Area AC, in order to sample the Late Chalcolithic levels. The sounding, which reached c two meters deep, revealed Late Chalcolithic deposits in situ. But this excavated material is mostly earlier than the pottery found on the surface, or Late Chalcolithic 2, contemporary with the Early Uruk Period in South Mesopotamia (full details of the surface survey and Area C excavation will appear in McMahon, in prep.). The earliest Late Chalcolithic occupation was not reached in our sounding, but the absence of Ubaid ceramics on the surface or in any excavated level suggests it was post Late Chalcolithic 1.

This lack of southern presence or influence at the site unfortunately could not be fully explored. The Late Chalcolithic settlement apparently pre-dates any southern influx into the region, and there is a genuine occupational gap on the site contemporary with the southern presence. However, the transition to southern Uruk domination was a process, rather than a single event, and the possibility exists that the arrival of southern Mesopotamian people and/ or influence elsewhere in the region may have contributed to the abandonment of Chagar Bazar.

---

[5] Local Late Chalcolithic, or Northern Uruk, material culture was an utterly unknown quantity in the 1930s, although researchers at Uruk were beginning to come to grips with Southern Uruk culture. However, Mallowan's publications do not show any mis-attributed ceramics or other materials that are now identifiable as Late Chalcolithic.

[6] These types include distinctive angular casseroles, large jars with internal grooves on the neck, fine-ware jars, fine-ware carinated bowls, shallow plates with internally-bevelled rims and "hammerhead" plates. Publication of the Tell Majnuna LC-3 ceramic assemblage (excavated in 2007-8) is in preparation; for Tell Brak see Oates 1985, Oates & Oates 1993; for Tepe Gawra, see Rothman 2002; for Hacinebi, see Pearce 2000, Pollock & Coursey 1995.

Alternatively, purely local processes may offer the explanation for Chagar Bazar's abandonment. Recent research into urbanisation in northern Mesopotamia indicates that urban centres such as Tell Brak expanded as rapidly as did the southern city of Uruk (Ur *et al.* 2007), and it is probable that these urban centres expanded in part by attracting the population of surrounding villages and/or towns, rather than simple internal population growth. The inhabitants of a small site such as Chagar Bazar (c 3 hectares, compared to Tell Brak's c 70+ hectares, for instance) may have been irresistibly attracted or compelled towards the region's most important urbanizing centre.

Surface pottery and excavations confirm that Chagar Bazar was a substantial site (c 10-12 ha.) in the Late Halaf Period. There is Halaf material *in situ* at both the northern end of the site, in Mallowan's Levels 15 through 7 in the Prehistoric Pit, plus the more recent Areas E and F (Tunca, Baghdo & Cruells 2006) as well as in the lowest trench in Area D, at the southern end of the mound. However, it is still not clear whether the Halaf settlement consisted of a large site occupied simultaneously or was a smaller site that gradually shifted over the course of the Halaf Period and created a mound that was ultimately larger than the village's size at any precise moment. There was a genuine abandonment of the site during the Ubaid Period. The subsequent Late Chalcolithic re-occupation of the site only on the southern end of the former Halaf site then surely created the basis for the modern dual morphology of the mound. Its separate south and north mounds were possibly originally created by this strategic reoccupation of only the south end during the Late Chalcolithic Period.

Third Millennium BC, Expansion and Contraction in the urbanized world

Mallowan's Prehistoric Pit and the northern end of his Area BD, at the centre of the north mound, exposed material of the 3rd millennium BC. The published pottery includes Ninevite 5 painted, incised and excised styles, as well as post-Ninevite 5 pottery of "late Early Dynastic" or Early Jezirah III date. As a general point, Chagar Bazar may prove to be an important cultural crossover link between Eastern and Western Jezirah, since both Ninevite 5 pottery (an Eastern category) and Metallic Ware (a Western category) are present in small but significant quantities. Our intensive surface survey of the south mound indicated 3rd millennium ceramics were present over its entirety, with particular concentrations on the top and the north slope; our more random surveys of the northern mound also indicate 3rd millennium material over its whole area. Thus the site was probably approximately the same size as in the Halaf Period, 10-12 hectares.

Radial "hollow ways" associated particularly with 3rd millennium BC intensification of settlement and land use in the region are clearly visible on the 1967 CORONA image of Chagar Bazar and its surroundings (Figs. 5, 7). Some are lengthy cross-country transport routes connecting the site with others in the region, such as the west-east route linking Girmayir, Chagar Bazar, Bir Zaraf, Tell Jul Bustan Foqani and Khirbet Ghazal Foqani. But the majority of Chagar Bazar's hollow ways die out within 2.5-3 km of the site[7]. Utilizing Wilkinson's proposal that the ends of hollow ways correspond to the limits of a site's cultivation zone (1994: 492-3; 2004), the Chagar Bazar hollow ways present a catchment zone of 20-28 km sq (2000 to 2800

---

[7] Most hollow ways in the Jezirah are slightly longer, stopping from three to five km from their associated site (Wilkinson 2003: 116).

hectares)[8]. If this catchment zone could support approximately 1 person per hectare (used in Wilkinson 1994: 496), the potential production would have exceeded the needs of the probable population of the site at the time. At a maximum size of 12 hectares, Chagar Bazar would have had a probable population of just over 1000, needing an agricultural catchment zone only half the size. Issues of fallow and/or small variances in soil fertility may explain the excess.

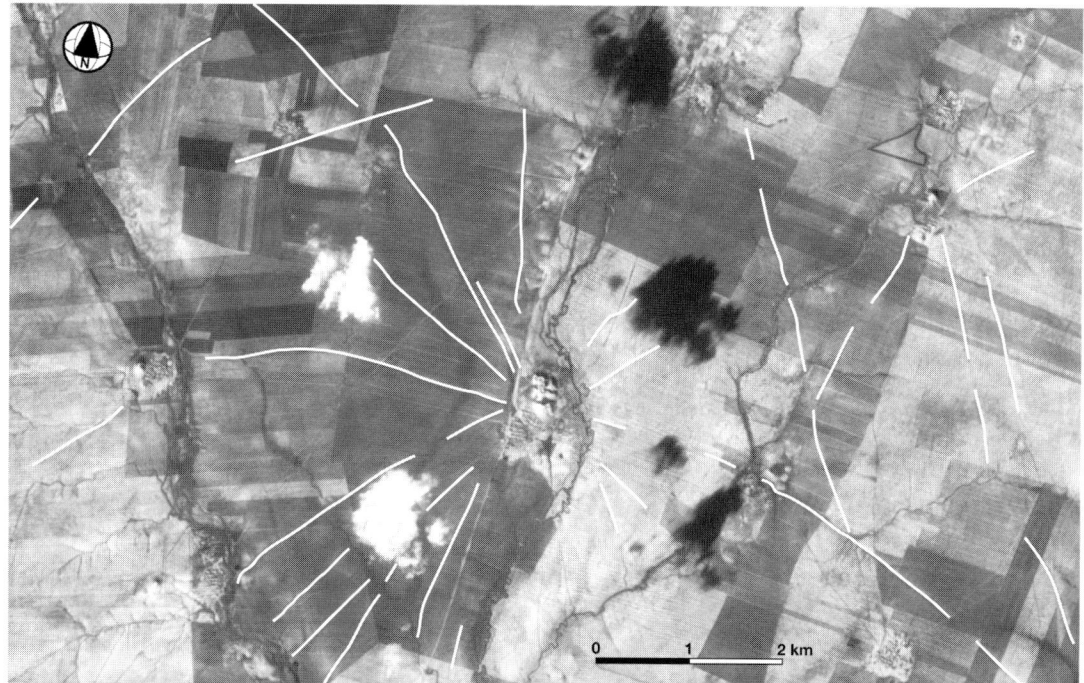

Figure 7: Hollow ways around Chagar Bazar, from CORONA image (December 1967)

The Early Jezirah III occupation was investigated by the British team in 1999 in Area B, a 10 x 10 meter square on the northeast slope of the southern mound, overlooking the gully which separates the north and south mounds. One corner of a building was exposed, and a single room. The building had thick walls, up to 1.5 meters wide, which were preserved to a height of over a meter; but the structure had suffered a great deal of damage after it had fallen out of use. The initial occupational levels were not reached; and the lowest levels exposed consist of later silty deposits that had blown and washed in through the doorways and built up in irregular piles against the walls, once the building was no longer in use. Above this blown-in material, the walls had begun to collapse inwards and sideways, forming exaggerated angles further complicated by strong vertical cracks. The final use of the structure consisted of the construction of two mudbrick cross-walls in the room, which were then packed around with well-laid mudbrick. This may have served as a platform for a structure which has since completely eroded. The pottery from the post-use fill belongs to Early Jezirah III through Khabur Ware.

In the aftermath of the Akkadian empire's collapse, the late 3rd millennium BC, regional settlement disruption occurred in the Upper Khabur, with many sites abandoned, others shrinking, and the nature of many sites' occupation changing. The

---

[8] Issues of potential overlap with the catchment zones of neighboring contemporary sites must remain unexplored until an intensive survey is made of the micro-region.

reconstruction of a total "hiatus" and radical abandonment of the entire region (Weiss *et al.* 1993, Weiss & Bradley 2001) should probably be revised to de-urbanization, given the continued occupation at several sites, but there is no doubt that the nature of the occupation of the Upper Khabur changed. Thus far, the Post-Akkadian Period, or Early Jezirah V, is best represented in the Upper Khabur at Tell Brak and Tell Mozan, both massive and strategically-located urban sites whose survival during a regional settlement disruption is not surprising.

Mallowan's 1930s excavations had not hinted at any terminal 3rd millennium BC levels at Chagar Bazar. But in Area D, at the top of the south mound, the 1999-2000 excavations revealed part of a large public or community building of Post-Akkadian date (Tunca, McMahon & Baghdo 2007). Our surface sherd survey and excavations in Areas C and D indicated that the Post-Akkadian occupation was restricted to the top of the southern mound only. The apparent lack of houses and a supporting settlement for the administrative building is difficult to explain, but the possibility exists that post-Akkadian settlement splintered into very small villages, easily overlooked in surveys or all but eradicated by post-occupational taphonomic processes.

The presence of an administrative building of this date on an otherwise virtually abandoned site may indicate that "second rank" sites such as Chagar Bazar (and the physically similar Tell Khoshi in Iraq, among others) took over some of the administrative roles once held by massive urban centres during the Akkadian Period, as the region's population shifted in the Post-Akkadian Period. The degree to which memory of this key role was responsible for the recurrent administrative importance of the site in the early 2nd millennium under Samsi-Addu is uncertain but holds much potential. The Post-Akkadian structure in Area D, even abandoned, would have been a prominent physical reminder of the site's function into the following millennium.

The positioning of the Post-Akkadian building on the top of the smaller southern mound further articulated the separation between the two mounds. Already significantly higher than the northern extended mound, the southern mound would have increased substantially in height yet again. An occupational gap, or at the very least a retraction of the site, took place within the later Post-Akkadian/ Isin-Larsa Period. The transition from late Post-Akkadian to early 2nd millennium (Khabur Ware) Periods remains unclear here for the moment, as it is also at Tell Brak and other nearby sites.

Early Second Millennium BC, Town and Landscape

In this focus period, major political changes occurred in northern Mesopotamia, specifically the growth and collapse of the region's first indigenous territorial state. One of our primary aims was to investigate the reaction (or non-reaction) at Chagar Bazar–neither an insignificant village nor a major urban centre–to these wider changes. Excavations in early 2nd millennium BC levels in the region have tended to concentrate on key urban centres (i.e., Tell Leilan, Tell Brak, Tell al-Rimah, Mari), and excavations at smaller sites have only partially redressed the balance (i.e., Tell Arbid, Tell Rijm). The exploration of a town, a lower node in the political administration and socio-economic network, offers valuable information about the working of the regional state and its devolution, plus the similarities of regional material culture assemblages and details of economic realities.

The historical record indicates that the first steps towards wider regional hegemony in the early 2nd millennium BC were taken by Yahdun-Lim from Mari, whose control spread from his Middle Euphrates stronghold into the lower Khabur, western Upper Khabur and the Balikh valley (c 1810-1794 BC). Part of this area was under his direct control, while the Upper Khabur was maintained as a network of vassals.[9] From Ekallatum and Ashur on the Tigris, Samsi-Addu (1833-1775 BC[10]) rose to the challenge and began to move westward, establishing a new capital at Shubat Enlil (formerly Shehna/ modern Tell Leilan). The frontier between these two expansionist states seems initially to have formed around the Wadi Jaghjagh, with Yahdun-Lim and Samsi-Addu fighting at one point in front of the gates of ancient Nagar/ modern Tell Brak (Oates *et al.* 1997: 142; Charpin 2004: 138). This frontier would have put Chagar Bazar just barely into the western sector and the orbit of Mari, although it is possible that it was not yet reoccupied at that time.[11] Following Yahdun-Lim's death and in Sumu-Yamam's short reign over Mari, Samsi-Addu moved across the Upper Khabur to absorb areas previously held by Yahdun-Lim and eventually incorporated Mari itself in 1793-2 BC. It is likely that it was in this new geo-political era that Chagar Bazar was reoccupied, or at least more prominently established and expanded, and became a key part of the kingdom. The reoccupation of the Upper Khabur after the Post-Akkadian de-urbanization has been in part attributed to the amelioration of climatic conditions (Weiss *et al.* 2002), but the political reasons for resettlement are equally strong.

Chagar Bazar lies only c 70 km west of and in the same environmental and cultural region as Tell Leilan, and thus it fell under Shubat Enlil's jurisdiction within this territorial state[12]. The texts from the archive recovered in 1937 detail a thriving and diverse economic situation: ration lists refer to (mostly) female employees in textile workshops, male craftsmen (including leatherworkers, blacksmiths, reed workers), scribes, grooms, farmers and herdsmen; an agricultural (?) estate belonging to the "House of Shubat Enlil" was located near the site; and lists of fodder and animals record the presence of horses, donkeys, oxen, cattle, sheep, deer, birds and pigs (Talon 1997). A population census–the preparations for which were recorded in the latest Chagar Bazar texts–occurred in the last few years of Samsi-Addu's reign and dealt with both settled and nomadic groups nearby. A nomadic pastoralist population in the wider area is amply documented in the Mari texts both contemporary with the reign of Samsi-Addu and in Zimri-Lim's subsequent era. Such land use may be

---

[9] The Upper Khabur had already seen cross-traffic from Old Assyrian merchants earlier in the 2nd millennium BC. A raid by Naram-Sin of Eshnunna in c 1818+ BC, which allegedly included the conquest of Ashnakkum and Tarnip in the eastern Khabur basin (Charpin 2004: 131), can be considered a brief event without long-lasting impact but still a symptom of region-wide nascent expansionist politics. For recent political histories of the Kingdom of Upper Mesopotamia, see Charpin *et al.* 2004, Fleming 2004, Charpin & Zeigler 2003.

[10] Traditional Middle Chronology dates will be used here; alternative dates for Samsi-Addu range both earlier and later. The precise length of his reign is in question, as well as the larger complications of connections between astronomical events and king lists, which affect the absolute dates of all rulers in the early 2nd millennium BC.

[11] If Chagar Bazar is ancient Ashnakkum, as has been proposed (Charpin 2004, Tunca & Baghdo 2008, van de Mieroop 2004: 64), this city-state was extant and one of Yahdun-Lim's vassals (Charpin 2004: 144). Qirdahat, an alternative identification for Chagar Bazar (Charpin 2004, Charpin & Zeigler 2003), does not appear to have been mentioned in texts prior to Samsi-Addu. Other alternatives for the ancient name of the site include Hashshum/Habba'um of Membida (Talon 1997, Yuhong 1994, Charpin & Zeigler 2003) and BEshannum (Talon 1997). Other discussions of Chagar Bazar's ancient name include von Koppen 1999/2000, Kupper 1957.

[12] Mari is c 250 km distant; its control may have reached substantially up the Lower Khabur, but the entire Upper Khabur seems to have been linked to Shubat Enlil.

represented by the absence of permanent settlement in survey data for the western Upper Khabur (see Chapter 7). We can assume an economic interdependence between inhabitants of the site and of the adjacent grazing areas that provides one thread in the story of Chagar Bazar's occupation at this time. More immediately, it is probable that the census had an essentially military purpose, assessment of the potential local fighting force–both settled and nomadic–given the need for armies on multiple fronts at the end of Samsi-Addu's reign (Zeigler 2000, Charpin 2004).

Chagar Bazar would have remained under the relatively stable control and effective leadership of Samsi-Addu until his death in 1775 BC. Most military campaigns recorded during this era took place either far to the east of the Upper Habur (i.e., east of the Tigris), well to the south on the mid-Euphrates (against armies from Eshnunna or Babylon) or equally distant to the west (aiding the kings of Qatna against Yamhad/Aleppo) (Zeigler 2000). The Turukkean revolt of 1780 BC (Eidem 1993; Charpin 2004: 177) appears to have taken place slightly nearer, to the north and east of Chagar Bazar; and comparable Bene'iaminite revolts (continued from their beginnings under Yahdun-Lim) may have affected the immediate area of the site. But the archaeological and textual records, although incomplete, do not indicate that these revolts impacted the settlement.

Post-1775 BC and the crumbling of Samsi-Addu's state, Zimri-Lim and Mari again technically controlled the area around Chagar Bazar, but the strength and specifics of that control are questionable. The loosely-integrated tribal territory of Ida-Maras is located to the west of the Wadi Khanzir (or possibly west of the Wadi Jaghjagh), and it is unclear whether Chagar Bazar might not have been part of that territory. A number of small kingdoms re-emerged in the Upper Khabur contemporary with Zimri-Lim's state at Mari (including Kahat and Ashnakkum, among others), while further nomadic revolts took place and armies from first Eshnunna and then Elam encroached. The troops from Eshnunna reached as close to Chagar Bazar as Shubat-Enlil[13], yet this military incursion is not visibly reflected in unusual cultural material nor changes in settlement structure.

For the period after Mari was sacked by Hammurapi of Babylon in c 1760 BC, our reconstruction of political control within the Upper Khabur becomes even more hazy.[14] Babylon's reach does not seem to have extended so far, and Chagar Bazar instead might have fallen under the (surely quite limited) control of Yamhad/Aleppo. Alternatively, at various times during the post-Zimri-Lim era the newly energized kings of Apum/ Tell Leilan or Kahat/ Tell Barri may have included it within their orbit. The fluctuating political scene is documented in the Mari and Leilan texts, with "kings" appearing and disappearing, often seeming to control only a town or two (Eidem 2000, Weiss *et al.* 2002). Ashnakkum is one of the few city-states to have persisted for long enough to register in the post-Samsi-Addu documentation. Nine total "kings" of Ashnakkum are known from texts (Charpin 2004: esp. 392 ff.), as well as details of its political history (Charpin 1993, Kupper 1999). In 1728 BC, Tell Leilan was conquered by Samsu-iluna, and textual documentation of the northern Mesopotamian political situation all but ceased.

Despite radical political changes and genuine military activity during this key century and the less-documented century which followed, evidence of economic or

---

[13] An Eshnunnan army of 3000 may have even headed from Shubat-Enlil towards Ashnakkum (Charpin 2004: 222).

[14] The years used here for Hammurapi's reign are the traditional 1792 to 1750 BC. Alternative chronologies place Hammurapi's reign at 1848-1804 or 1696-1654 BC; see Charpin 2004: 35 for a recent discussion of the issues of absolute chronology and the date determinations of various scholars.

social collapse at Chagar Bazar and in general across the region is non-existent; what is visible in the settlement pattern and archaeological record is simply "the end of a defined state of affairs followed by a different state of affairs" (Meier 2000: 221). Samsi-Addu's archive building at Chagar Bazar may have fallen out of use and the archives certainly ceased abruptly, but alternative administrative buildings were built elsewhere on the site (see Ch. 2). Traditions of vernacular architecture appear largely unchanged in the post-Samsi-Addu era (see Ch. 3). The ceramic assemblage underwent long-term subtle changes during the early 2nd millennium BC, but these are virtually divorced from the political milieu (see Ch. 5). For certain purposes, we are still in a similar situation to that of Mallowan in 1947 when he bemoaned the lack of textual evidence to link the site's final occupation with specific dates or historical figures (Mallowan 1947: 17). But for the purpose of settlement archaeology, our evidence of the cultural trends underlying political events is far more valuable.

Mallowan's excavations uncovered an expanse of early 2nd millennium BC houses at the centre of the north mound (Areas TD and BD, with additional less well-preserved structures in Area AB and the top of the Prehistoric Pit; see Fig. 4 for locations). His plans offer an image of a densely-occupied small town, while the archive of cuneiform tablets in a room of Area TD, a number of relatively rich graves with bronze tools and weapons, and the occasional use of baked brick all indicate a significant degree of prosperity. The primary difficulty with the 1930s excavations is that re-buildings and structural adaptations were masked within the reconstructed stratigraphy and plans, as these were summarized for publication. Mallowan's excavations were appropriate for the era, but the predominant excavation methodology was less detail-oriented than at present. In addition, the current mass of comparative data from other contemporary sites was then virtually unknown. Mallowan's aim, as in many excavations in the Near East during the 1930s, was purely culture-historical: the horizontal exposure of as much architecture as possible, the accumulation of aesthetically-valued material culture, plus the assignment of this material to logical chronological blocks.

Mallowan identified five sub-phases within his Level 1 (early 2nd millennium BC), yet the published plans do not explicitly articulate these distinctions. Major differences from sub-phase to sub-phase were discussed in the text, such as the difference in alignment of the archive building in Area TD (almost exactly north-south) from that of the slightly later Area BD and TD houses (north-northwest to south-southeast). However, the plans do not indicate to which sub-phase specific buildings belong.[15] Mallowan's "Level 1" lasted at minimum one and one-half centuries, and possibly as long as three centuries. Variation of a few years or decades in the date of individual buildings' foundations or structural adaptations is a relatively minor problem when dealing with the larger picture of regional occupation and chronological developments, but the variable use of space, including gradual versus rapid infilling of open areas as a town develops, is key to the understanding of a site's micro-history.

One of our goals in excavating Chagar Bazar was the articulation of diachronic variability within the houses at the central part of the site: did use of space change, and how did the biography of buildings intersect with the stories of other material worlds?

---

[15] In addition, there remain issues of many rooms appearing to lack doorways, occasional spiraling stratigraphy and lack of wall separations, particularly in the Area BD plan. See Ch. 3 for further analysis of these problems.

Thus Area G was placed adjacent to and just west of Mallowan's Area BD. This excavation involved four 10 x 15 meter trenches that ran parallel to and overlapped the western edge of Mallowan's excavations, allowing for architectural connections of our plans to his. Four architectural phases of early 2nd millennium BC houses were identified in Area G, allowing both reinterpretation and some confirmation of Mallowan's findings. Further sub-phases in some of these levels allowed us to write the story of changes within particular rooms or houses, complemented by greater stability of use in others. Unexpectedly, there was a strong axial element to the site plan within the Area G excavations, an alley at least 40 meters long, lined with houses on each side. Such a "logical" feature is uncommon within the generally "organic" settlement format of the region and was not visible in Mallowan's adjacent excavation.

The physical distance between houses in Areas G and BD was notably short; party walls meant immediate contact, and the alley itself was narrow. This short physical distance would have meant limited social distance; but in the absence of texts referring to economic connections, kinship links or political alliances among the houses' inhabitants, we must bring in inference from material culture assemblages. These indicate little to no variation among houses and suggest a tightly-networked economic system[16]. Consistency of burial practice is another unifying factor (see Ch. 4). The temporal depth of this close physical arrangement also speaks to the strong social affinity (see Chapters 3 and 7).

As well as the extensive exposure of early 2nd millennium BC material on the north mound, Mallowan briefly excavated a smaller area on a spur of the mound that extends to the northeast (Area EH, Mallowan 1936: Fig. 29). His brief note on this sounding refers to traces of 2nd millennium BC buildings there (Mallowan 1936: 6); two complete rooms and parts of two others are drawn at a very small scale on the site plan, but no larger plans are available.

A random, non-intensive collection of sherds from the surface of this spur at the beginning of the 1999 season revealed a dense cover of Khabur Ware and other 2nd millennium BC pottery types, as well as 3rd millennium and Halaf sherds. This is where our Area A was located, initially a 10 x 10 meter square north-northeast of the still-visible depression and spoil heap of Mallowan's Area EH. This trench was expanded to the south and west to an eventual size of 26 x 23 meters; this excavation articulated three distinct phases of early 2nd millennium BC occupation. The second phase was particularly well-preserved and comprised a complex of five spacious structures, likely to have been an administrative building and "elite" residences and stables or storage. Ceramic parallels and generalized stratigraphic sequencing indicate this phase was roughly contemporary with the second phase in Area G. The lower, third, phase in Area A was only explored in small soundings but presented the same sort of substantial buildings, deliberately flattened for construction of the next phase. The contrasting architectural arrangements in Areas A and G were crucial to an understanding of the site as a total settlement.

Excavations in Areas A and G did not reach the base of the early 2nd millennium BC occupation and the initial reoccupation of the site. Instead, they fall

---

[16] Analysis of the faunal assemblage from our excavations at Chagar Bazar is ongoing (by Dr. Jill Weber), and the results will appear together with analyses of the Old Babylonian-Mitanni materials from the 2006-2009 excavations at Tell Brak Area HH. This analysis should provide a more detailed reconstruction of the regional subsistence economy, as well as possible variation among contexts; comparable palaeobotanical analyses were regrettably impossible.

entirely into the post-Samsi-Addu era. It is remarkable that despite the collapse of Samsi-Addu's overarching kingdom and the subsequent political devolution and shifts in power, the economic and social situation on the ground seems little changed. As Mallowan had already noted (1947: 17-20), the architectural traditions and modes of production of ceramics and other items were consistent during the early 2nd millennium's spate of political changes. This consistency of production modes played out through the final phase of the site's occupation, beyond the introduction of Nuzi Ware[17].

It should be noted that the final occupation of the site (our Phase I) does exhibit some architectural differences from the previous phases in both Areas A and G: Phase I presents reduced wall thicknesses and less care in construction in both Areas A and G, and a more sparsely occupied site landscape, also in both areas. But this final occupation and the eventual abandonment of the site do not offer evidence of conflict. However, whether the move of the inhabitants from the site was positive, moving towards a new opportunity at another settlement, or was negative, moving in order to avoid a conflict or economic crisis, remains unclear. Abandonment of tells, even those that have significant meaning for their inhabitants, was not necessarily a wrenching experience in the Mesopotamian milieu, where any abandonment was in fact conceptually incomplete, given the continued "occupation" of the site by buried ancestors (see Ch. 4). Mobility and permanence were differently nuanced in the past. The use of the unoccupied Chagar Bazar as a landmark for the neighbouring pastoral communities is probable; settlements do not need to be occupied by a living population to retain value and meaning.

---

[17] Levels with mixed Nuzi and Khabur ware pottery have been identified at Brak and Tell al-Rimah dated to the late 16th century BC. At Chagar Bazar, the latest occupation of the mound is still slightly earlier than this; there are a very few fragments of Nuzi or Nuzi-like pottery at best in our own and Mallowan's excavations, on the surface and in the final phase. Thus the end of the sequence at Chagar Bazar mostly likely dates to within the earlier 16th century, or c 1550 BC at the very latest.

Chapter 2

Community Buildings: Architecture in Area A

A. McMahon

Area A lies on a well-defined spur of the mound that extends northeast of the site's core and towards the Wadi Khanzir (see Figs. 4, 8). Mallowan reported this spur as a "subsidiary hummock" and chose it as the site of his Area EH excavation (Mallowan 1936: 5). This detached north-eastern location would have meant the buildings here were a prominent landmark to travellers coming along the *wadi* from the north in particular (see Chapter 7 for further discussion). Although the spur has been modified on all sides by post-occupation erosion, it is evident that this area was set off from the main settlement core in the early 2nd millennium BC, and that the buildings in Area A were at a lower elevation than their contemporaries in Area G and separated from them by an unused bridging space[1].

Mallowan's characteristically brief note on his results in Area EH describes only "house remains of the same period as 'TD'" (Mallowan 1936: 6; TD refers to the area of the tablet archive). Parts of two buildings, with at least two rooms each, were cleared and presented in a very small and undetailed plan (Mallowan 1936: Fig. 29, reproduced here in Fig. 8).

Area A was chosen for excavation in the expectation that it would comprise houses and in the hopes it would present a contrast in the style and arrangement of those houses from the neighbourhood excavated by Mallowan in Area BD (and our own Area G). The excavation began as a 10 x 10 meter trench in 1999. In 2000, it was expanded to the west by an additional two meters and extended to the south by a second trench of 12 x 16 meters. Further expansions of the southern trench were made on its east (4.5 x 10 m) and southwest (6.5 x 16 m) in the 2001 season, in order to expose specific buildings completely. Three distinct phases of occupation were uncovered in this area, of which Phase II is the best preserved and most important. Phase I, just below the surface, was fairly poorly preserved, while Phase III was only exposed in soundings.

The precise horizontal relationship between Mallowan's EH and our Area A could not be determined and the reconstructed arrangement in Fig. 8 is a compromise; Mallowan's topographic plan of this area of the site is at a slightly different angle when compared to the modern plan and the dimensions are also slightly at odds.

---

[1] The difference in elevation between early 2nd millennium levels in Areas A and G is two to three meters. While the settlement shifts that created the discrete north and south mounds of the site may be outlined, the origins of the northeast spur remain obscure. Ceramics of Halaf, 3rd and early 2nd millennium BC are present on the slopes; Post-Akkadian and Late Chalcolithic ceramics are absent. The base of the erosion cut at the northwest of the spur is well above plain level and at an absolute height that indicates the area was probably enclosed within the contiguous mound in the Halaf Period; it seems probable that the spur was created by settlement spacing in the 3rd millennium BC. However, the possibility exists that erosion wash may obscure a prehistoric separation.

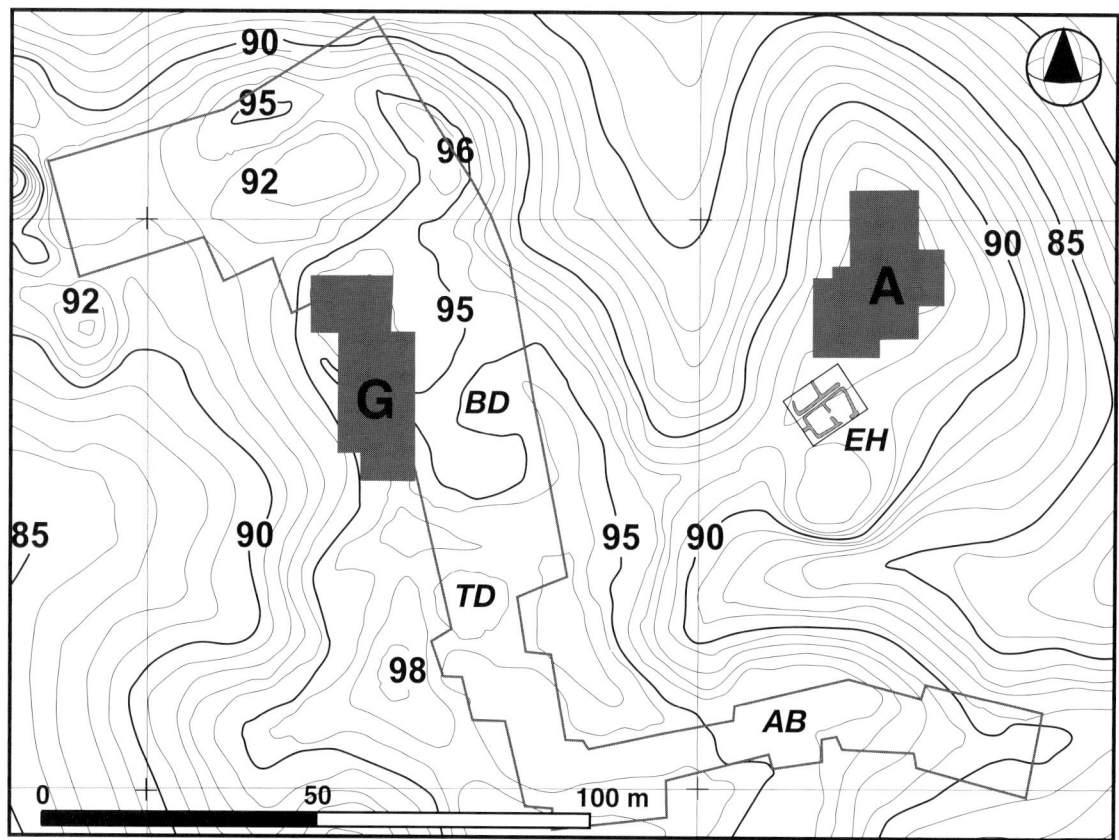

Figure 8: Topographic plan of the northern end of Chagar Bazar with Mallowan and BSAI excavation areas indicated

Our excavations of Phase II defined a cluster of five buildings. The central building (Building III) has similarities in plan to clearly domestic structures elsewhere on the site (Mallowan's Area BD, see below). However, its grand scale, the substantial width of its walls, the care taken in construction and plastering of walls and paving of the courtyard floor, plus the cleanliness of floors and lack of burials below them, all point to this building having a non-domestic function. There were no installations or contents that indicate a religious purpose. Sealings were not common in any of our excavations, but those few recovered come mainly from the alley in front of Building III. Three numerical tallies, two conical stamp seals, the only cylinder seal recovered and the only two items of south Mesopotamian style from our excavations (a sealing with an Old Babylonian style impression and a date-shaped haematite weight; see Ch. 6) all come from Area A. We have used the term "community building" here, borrowed from Willey's classic typology of buildings and settlements in the Virú valley, Peru (1953). As he noted there, some buildings "were of such as size or were situated in such a way that it was most logical to interpret their original use as that of having served community or public functions" (Willey 1953: 55).

Despite its large scale and careful construction, Building III lacks large quantities of administration-linked objects such as sealings, seals and texts. Its ceramic assemblage does not differ greatly from that in the contemporary houses in Area G, although Area A in general had slightly higher percentages of decorated vessels, fine ware and burnished grey ware, and a lower percentage of cooking pot ware than did Area G (see Ch. 5). Metals and luxury items are rare. These aspects combine to create a picture of an elite area but a system of consensus-leading and informally structured political interaction rather than domination. The Mari texts refer to local "tribal" leaders within both the settled and nomadic population (North Mesopotamian *sugagum* 'leader" or *shapitum* 'governor', Fleming 2004; roughly equivalent to South Mesopotamian *rabianum* 'mayor' or 'chief', Stol 1976). Building III may have been the administrative office of such an individual, or alternatively it could be a corporately-owned meeting space for a group of community 'elders', whether from the settlement or from the larger district in which it sits (Akk. *shibutum*; Fleming 2004*)*. The region's co-dependent pastoral and agricultural socio-economic population means that a place such as Building III could have provided the locus for meetings between leaders of the settlement and of nomadic groups occupying the pastoral lands to the west and south of Chagar Bazar.

1999-2001 Excavations in Area A
Phase II

The architecture in Phase II consisted of a tight complex of five buildings, with additional, incompletely-excavated structures to north and east (Fig. 9). The core of this complex was Building III, the largest and most substantially-constructed. At least two buildings (Buildings I and III) and possibly a third (Building IV) open onto an alley that runs NW-SE along the eastern edge of the excavation. Beyond this, further east, traces of a building at the north indicate the extent of site erosion–there was at least one additional structure on the eastern side of the street but it has been almost entirely lost. Two more buildings (Buildings II and V) were entered from what was probably an open space or plaza to the southwest, a space that connects the Area A spur to the rest of the site and persisted as open space in Phase I. The ceramic assemblage indicates a date in the early 2nd millennium BC.

The sequence of construction of the complex was determined from both stratigraphy and plan: the two rectangular structures at north and south, Buildings I and II, were constructed first, after which Building III was inserted into the space between them. This initial group was followed by Building IV to the southeast and Building V to the west. There are no party walls in the complex, but the walls in each case were built directly against the sides of their neighbours.

Buildings I and II are both long narrow rectangles oriented ENE-WSW. Building I was probably a single room (although its western end was poorly preserved), while Building II has a room partitioned-off at its eastern end. Building I shows evidence of having been barrel-vaulted and is c 5.5 meters wide by at least 8 meters long, as preserved[2] (Fig. 10; see also McMahon *et al.* 2001). The vaulting is clear in the southern wall (99-16); its interior face curves inward, while its outer face, along the north wall of Building III (99-6), was vertical, without the gap one would expect if the wall had simply been collapsing. The section through the deposits in this building revealed that its initial use was a period of human occupation, represented by relatively thin ash and rubbish layers. The doorway had a baked brick sill and an older adult female burial was interred in the northeast corner (Tomb 4; see Ch. 4).

---

[2] If the western wall of Building I is reconstructed to the same line as the western wall of Building III, the resulting building length is c 10 m, very close to the preserved length of Building II, of 10.2 m.

Chapter 2

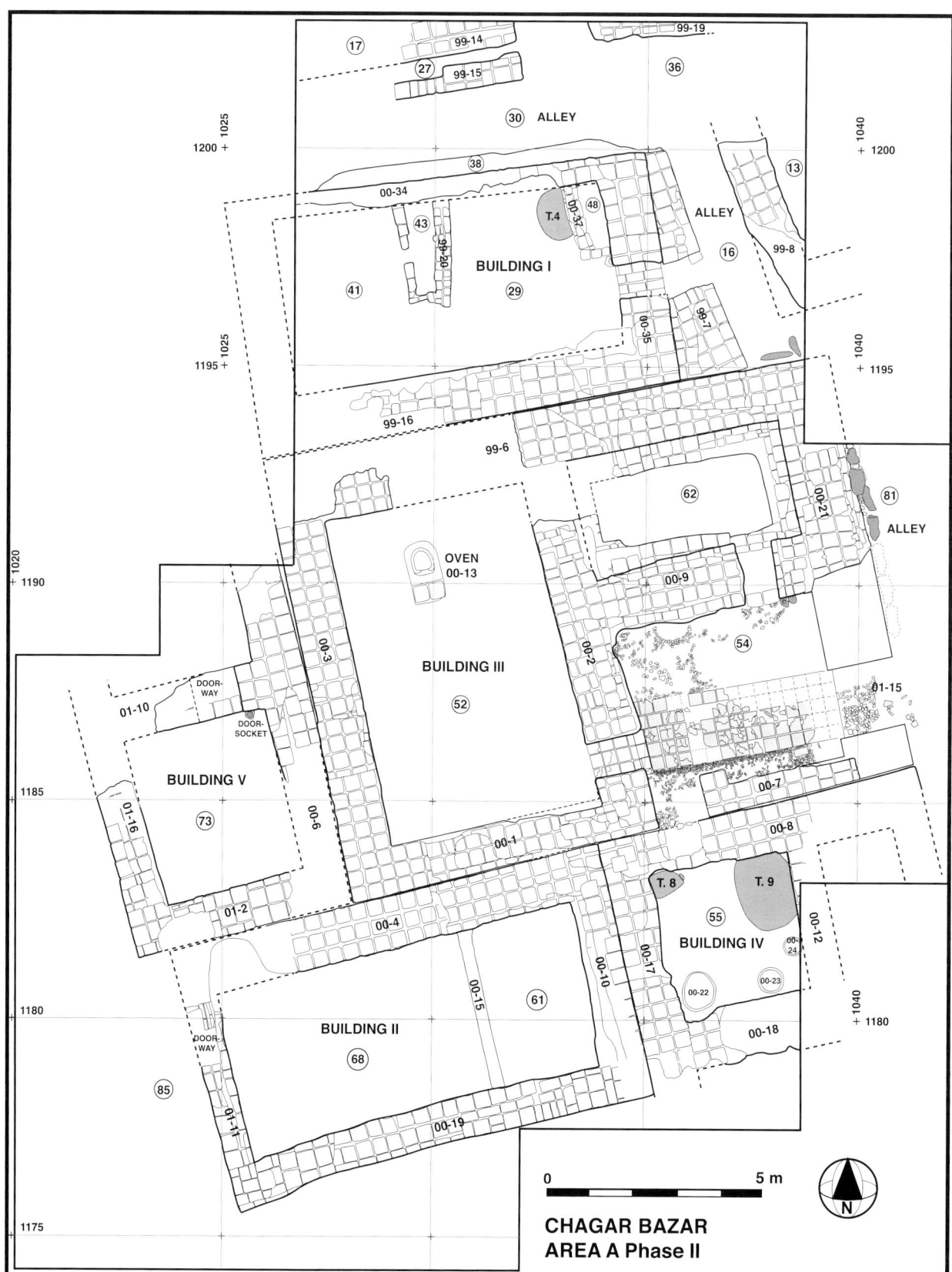

Figure 9: Area A, Phase II plan

Building I underwent a remodelling, possibly at the same time that Building III was modified (see below). After its initial use, the effective alignment of the eastern façade was modified by the addition of a trapezoidal wall (narrower at the north than at the south) along its length (99-7). This created a very deep doorway, two meters deep, and it swung the eastern façade outwards and into parallel alignment with a new wall (99-8), which defined the opposite side of an alley created from what had been an open space[3].

The northern wall of Building I was buttressed at approximately the same time, by the addition of a low solid "bench" of clean yellow-brown *tauf* (Locus 38) against its base. The modification to the façade meant that it was no longer parallel to the façade of Building III, as it had been during the prior sub-phase (although set back to the west). At the same time, the nature of use of Building I changed, and the room deposits indicate possible animal stabling or dung fuel storage. The animal dung is presented as a thick layer of brown-green-grey porous soil with visible plant casts.[4] This dung was particularly concentrated at the corners and edges of the room, as if it had been swept to the sides of the room (or alternatively was not removed when the rest of the room was swept clean). The dung layers spilled out of the doorway and into the alley (Locus 16). The intensity of foot traffic (human and/or animal) in and out of Building I is indicated by the deep trough-sectioned erosion pattern cut into the mud-brick sill in the new doorway. A small mud-brick bin (00-37) in the northeast corner and a second bin near the room centre (99-20) may have held animal fodder.

The long narrow room seems an awkward and unusual space to have kept animals; its size is adequate but the doorway is very narrow. Only the smallest cattle might have fit through the aperture, while sheep and goats would have rarely been stabled within the settlement. The strong possibility exists that it instead was a storage space for dung fuel among other materials. Such storage spaces would have been more appropriate for attachment to a domestic than to an administrative structure (which we assume was the function of Building III). The alignment shift of the façade thus not only emphasizes the change in function to animal stabling or dung fuel storage but probably also signifies the severing of linkage in function or ownership between Buildings I and III. A connection with the unfortunately-eroded eastern building (represented by wall 99-8) or with the unexcavated northern building(s) seems likely.

---

[3] The lowest layer excavated in the eastern alley (L. 16.3) ran against the new Building I façade and below the opposite wall, 99-8, but the time elapse in accumulation of this layer was not great. The material below the new façade and 99-8 was not excavated in the area of the alley, but to the north, an earlier deposit in the northern alley (L. 47) ran below both the façade and wall 99-8 and against the original corner of Building I, wall 00-35.

[4] The presence of animal dung has been confirmed by soil micromorphological analysis (Semple in McMahon *et al.* 2005, Semple, in prep); the deposits from within Building I contain calcareous spherulites typical of herbivore waste. Similar deposits were found in the Phase III building below Building II (see below).

Chapter 2

Figure 10: Vaulting of south wall of Building I, Area A Phase II, from west

Building II closely matches Building I in size, at 5.8 x 10.2 meters, and its side walls are similarly wide and well-built.[5] A thin cross-wall divided the space into a larger western (L. 68) and smaller eastern (L. 61) room. In Phase III, the underlying building in this location (of virtually the same dimensions) was clearly vaulted (see below), but the walls in the Phase II version were not preserved high enough that their construction and any possible vaulting could be determined. We have reconstructed a doorway in the western wall; this wall had been damaged by Phase I trenching and construction but a gap exists near the northwest corner. There is some evidence that Mallowan had articulated and partially emptied this building: there were distinctive fill layers at the eastern end and even the marks of modern pickaxes at its western end. However, it is impossible to connect the plan of our Building II to the plan of Area EH provided by Mallowan, and he may have emptied the building but left it unplanned. There was very little cultural material in the Phase II version of this building. In part this scarcity was due to Mallowan's activities, but areas of intact stratigraphy at wall corners indicate very clean floors and layers of collapsed brick above. Two door-sockets found in the southwest end of the western room (L. 68) may have been discarded by Mallowan's workmen.

Building III has the largest footprint of any building uncovered by our excavations, at 10.4 x 13.6 m[6]. Both external and internal walls were wide and carefully constructed (3 bricks wide with thick mortar and surface plastering). An original construction phase, a remodelling phase and a final abandonment phase were preserved. There is a classic three-room plan in its original version: a front courtyard, a side room and a formal assembly room at the rear (Fig. 9).

The original façade reconstructed here is speculative, but the later adaptations (see below and Fig. 14) were easily distinguishable from the original, and consistency

---

[5] Two similar single-room rectangular buildings were exposed in Area G (Buildings G 1 and G 2; see Ch. 3), also 5.8 meters wide and at least 8 meters long.

[6] The orientations of Buildings I and II were not precisely aligned, so the space between them was slightly irregular; Building III's eastern wall is shorter than its western wall by some 80 cm, at 9.6 m to 10.4 m.

in wall widths and symmetry point to an entrance substantially as shown in Figure 9. The outer face of the wall around the northern corner was edged with irregular basalt slabs, protecting the wall base from erosion in the alley. This basalt edging may have originally continued south up to the doorway. The straight façade had a single entrance, and the width of the front wall provided a small porch. This porch had a paving of rounded cobbles (3-10 cm in diameter) set into a hard clay mortar; a baked-brick doorsill created a step up into the courtyard. This reconstructed entrance is aligned with a baked-brick path leading across the courtyard (L. 54) to the assembly room at the rear (Fig. 11). The door from courtyard to assembly room may have originally been two bricks wider, to match the width of this path. Whole and fragmentary curved baked-bricks re-used in the repair to the courtyard paving may have belonged to an arched doorframe at the original entrance to the building or on the inner wall at the door to the assembly room[7].

The courtyard was edged between the baked-brick walkway and its southern wall by a strip of hard clay with embedded cobbles similar to the paving in the entrance porch (Figs. 11, 12). The northern half of the courtyard may have originally had similar cobble paving, but this was only present in patches, while a more haphazard secondary paving repair of limestone, baked-bricks and reused basalt grindstones covered the rest. There were two floors above the paved floor in the courtyard, both of trampled earth. A small side door initially led out to the south into what must have been an open space at the back of Building II, but this was quickly blocked by a fill of mud-bricks and by the construction of Building IV.

Figure 11: Baked-brick path across courtyard of Building III, Area A Phase II

---

[7] Most of these curved bricks have multiple finger indentations or grooves on one side, and one bears the impression of a dog's paw.

Figure 12: Detail of cobble edging in courtyard of Building III, Area A Phase II, from north

The function of the side room (L. 62) seems to have been storage; there was a mud-brick sill in the doorway between it and the courtyard, and a door-socket on the courtyard side indicated that this room could be closed off. The depth of the doorway encompassed a step down from the courtyard to the room. The walls of this Room 62 were lined on all sides by a continuous low mud-brick ledge, and the plastered floor sloped up and over the top of this ledge. The ledge was one to two bricks wide and would have been appropriate for a storage shelf, either for jars (such as were found on the floor) or for organic containers. The thickness of the walls means that this room would have been relatively cool in summer.

The formal assembly room (L. 52) was reached via an 80 cm wide doorway through wall 00-2; the arrangement of the courtyard path makes it probable that the original doorway was c 1.4 m wide but was narrowed at an intermediate stage of use. Two baked-brick steps within the doorway provide for the 40 cm drop from the courtyard to the room. The walls on all sides of the assembly room were given a thick white plaster, best preserved on the eastern wall (00-2); the floor also retained in places an original orange plaster surface, followed by two white plaster surfaces. A domed hearth at its northern end was made of the same dark red-brown fired clay as the more common circular bread ovens found widely in Area G and in Phase I of Area A, but it was roughly rectangular in plan and set on a low base of mud-bricks (Fig. 13). The top of the hearth sloped inwards slightly on all sides, and an attempt had been made at decoration: parallel vertical finger marks on the sides and a row of five shallow impressions across the front, between the lower fuel access hole and the upper heat aperture. The heat aperture was too small for cooking access and we assume that this hearth was for heating the room. The floors in the assembly room were clean and cultural material was minimal.

Figure 13: Assembly room in Building III, Area A Phase II, from northwest

The façade of Building III underwent a substantial remodelling later in the life of the structure. The original façade was modified by the cutting away of the front wall at the north of the doorway and the creation of a bathroom there, using space that previously had been parts of the courtyard and of the cobbled entrance porch (compare Figs. 9 and 14). Thick chunky deposits of waxy green clay on the floor of this small room (L. 83) together with a drain leading into the alley outside clearly indicate the room's function. The modification is surprisingly clumsy: the previously-straight façade has an odd outward bulge, the walls are irregular and thin, and many of the mud-bricks utilized are small, square, and a distinctive friable orange fabric not seen in the rest of the building.

The final abandonment phase in Building III was best represented in the courtyard and northeast room. There were several broken vessels in the courtyard, and further vessels on the floor in Room 62, with pockets of water-laid yellow silt around them. These vessels included both large storage jars and shallow bowls, implying that both storage and consumption had taken place in the building. The broken vessels are represented by large sherds, as if they had been deliberately broken in situ. Dense silt deposits were also present in the southwest corner and to a lesser extent at the northern edge of the room, along the face of the walls and on the storage ledges. The water-laid silt (presumably from rain) implies that this room was unroofed, but its size and probable use for storage indicate that this was not its original condition. The density of silt at the western end of the room in particular may indicate that the roof had specifically collapsed there, allowing damage from rainfall. The broken pottery and water-laid material in both side room and courtyard were capped by a soil layer including collapsed bricks, and there was a particularly dense pile of mud-bricks, baked bricks, stones and ashy soil in the northeast corner of the courtyard. Further fallen brick was found in the alley (L. 81) at the east of Building III as if part of the eastern wall had eventually collapsed outward.

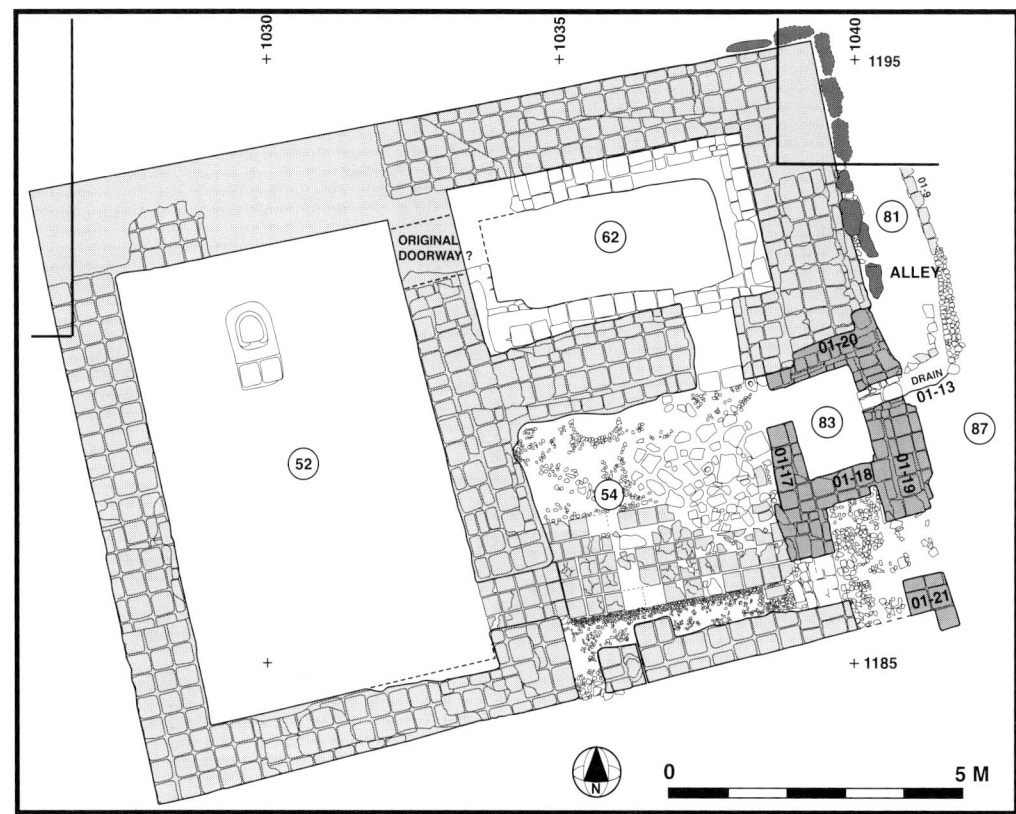

Figure 14: Building III, Area A Phase II, with secondary façade

Building III is similar in plan to an approximately contemporary building in Mallowan's Area TD (Mallowan 1936: 14 and Fig. 3, reproduced here as Fig. 15; see also McMahon *et al.* 2005).[8] Both buildings have a large room at the rear: Room 1 in TD, the assembly room (Locus 52) in Area A. Mallowan called Area TD Room 1 an "open courtyard", and its large size, at c 7.3 x 4.8 meters (internal), suggests an unroofed space. But our comparable room in Building III, slightly larger at 7.5 x 5.0 meters, had white plastered walls that showed no signs of rain damage or frequent re-application, as one would expect of an unroofed space such as a courtyard. The walls in the TD building had "traces of whitewash" (Mallowan 1936: 15), but no details of whether this was confined to a specific room or rooms were given. Both buildings have a courtyard partly paved with clay and pebbles (TD Room 4, Area A Locus 54). Area TD Rooms 2 and 3 correspond to the side room Locus 62 in Area A, and the TD building has a "kitchen" (Room 5) in the place of the probable bathroom in Area A (Locus 83). The inner wall between the assembly room and side room in our Area A building had been cut by an erosion gully, but a door between these two rooms is possible, on analogy with the doorway between TD Rooms 1 and 2.

---

[8] This building also appears at a smaller scale on the plan in Mallowan 1947: Pl. LXXXIII, north of the "tablet building" (Rooms 100-108) and some areas of stone paving.

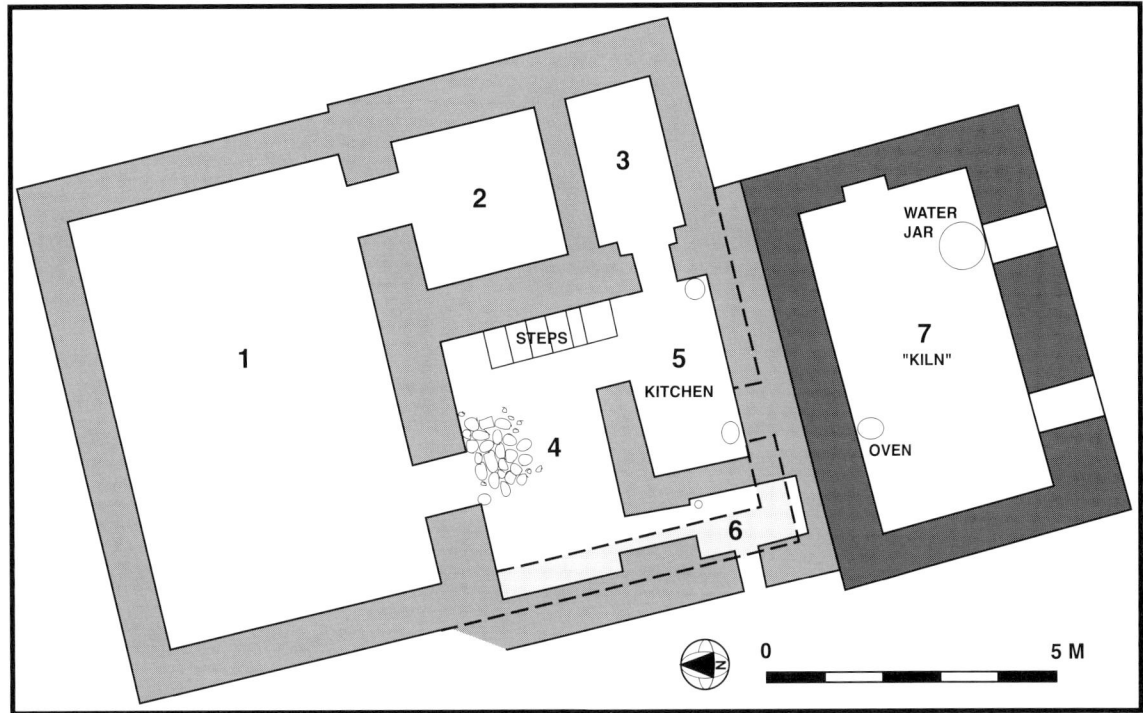

Figure 15: Building in Mallowan's Area TD (after Mallowan 1936: Fig. 3), at same scale as *Figure 14* (dashed lines indicate possible original walls)

In both Areas A and TD, the main building is adjacent to at least one rectangular structure (Buildings I and II in Area A; Room 7 in Area TD), and both TD and A buildings underwent a secondary remodelling. In Area A, Building I is earlier than Building III. The foundations of Building I were lower than those of Building III by c 50 cm[9], but more importantly the slightly trapezoidal plan of Building III indicates it was inserted into a pre-existing space between Buildings I and II. Mallowan does not specify which of his two TD buildings might have been constructed first, or if he determined that there was any time-lag between them. But from the awkward join between the two in the published plan, the most likely scenario is that the multi-roomed building was first, with straight façades on its south and west sides and an entrance in the southern wall (dashed lines on Fig. 15). At a later stage, the vaulted building (Room 7) was added against the south façade, the space between the two buildings was filled; and the west façade of the original building was altered and the entrance shifted to that side. Entrance Room 6 in particular seems to be a later addition rather than an original part of the plan, and it may be that Room 5 was a late partition of an originally larger courtyard. Thus the entrance and façade of this building appear to have been altered in much the same way as that of Area A's Building III. The TD

---

[9] The possibility exists that these 50 cm accumulated gradually and that significant time elapsed between the construction of Building I and of Building III. However, it is more likely that the area below Building III was slightly higher when the construction programme of Phase II began, due to previous Phase III construction and the sloped ancient surfaces of this area of the mound; some further accumulation then took place, but this is likely to have been deliberate fill and levelling material, rather than occupational accumulation. The irregular plan of Building III offers additional support for its place within the sequence of buildings in the complex, indicating that it was built into a remaining space rather than being planned *ab initio*. Building II, although adjacent to Building III, is probably not as closely linked to it as was Building I. The entrances to Buildings I and III are both off the same alley and face east-northeast, while the door into Building II is at the opposite end, facing west-southwest into an open space.

building is shown with a grave in one of Mallowan's plans (1947: Pl. LXXXIII: G. 201 in courtyard 4), but this grave does not appear in the more detailed plan (Mallowan 1936: Fig. 3). It is unlikely that the grave was contemporary, since its location would have interfered with the steps to the roof. It is probable that the grave belonged to a later sub-phase of Level I.[10]

The repetition of this distinctive plan in Area A and Area TD has significance for our reconstruction of building functions and contrasting neighbourhood composition. The lack of graves, care in construction, and large scale of Area A Building III all point to its use as a public space. The different methods of excavation mean that we do not have all points of comparison for the Area TD building, but it was situated just north of Mallowan's Tablet Building and may have been part of an administrative complex there[11]. An alternative explanation is that the TD building was a house (since it is closely surrounded by other houses to its north) and that the semi-public building in Area A utilised a domestic plan. Tribal leadership is strongly dependent on kinship, so it is entirely appropriate for the official headquarters of a tribal leader to have the same plan as a contemporary house. Interactions of the leader(s) with both neighbours and visitors would thus have been physically contained within a space that visually referred to close kinship relations in its house-like access routes and arrangement. Such interactions would have been guided by the plan and thus conceptually constituted within a kin-based system of rights and obligations, by contrast to a formally structured hierarchical relationship, such as that visually presented by a throne room.

The association of Area A's Buildings I and III is paralleled by the pairing of buildings of similar plan in Area TD. In TD, Mallowan identified Room 7 as having begun life as a kiln, on the basis of burned walls and a "chimney" (a niche-like recess) at one end; he determined that it was subsequently used as a kitchen, on the basis of an oven and "kitchen utensils" (Mallowan 1936: 15). The reconstructed use as a kiln seems untenable; the room is too large for anything but a brick kiln, and it is unlikely bricks would have been fired within the settlement. The burned walls in the initial use may have been smoke staining from a kitchen fire.

Contemporary vaulted rooms at other sites offer some comparisons, but our linked pair does not apparently occur elsewhere. Two vaulted rooms at Tell Mohammed Diyab are comparable in construction to Area A Buildings I and II but are on a smaller scale (Sauvage 1992; Castel 1996). A slightly smaller vaulted structure at Tell Brak (Area HH Trenches C4 & D, Level 8) has been identified as a shrine (Oates *et al.* 1997), but any adjacent structure that might match our Building III has not been preserved. A second partly vaulted structure in Area HN at Brak has also been identified as a possible shrine in its initial phase of use (Matthews 2003b: Area HN, Level 2, 275 ff.). In this case the vaulted building is north of and adjacent to a slightly later building with wide walls and a plastered floor; unfortunately not enough of this building was exposed to indicate whether its plan matches that of our Building III, but the scale of construction is suggestive. Both the Brak vaulted structures have niches in

---

[10] Mallowan's graves are frequently shown superimposed on walls or other features in his plans; their horizontal location is reasonably secure, but stratigraphic relationships were omitted, and not all the burials appear on his section drawings.

[11] If contemporary with Mallowan's Tablet Building, the TD building would pre-date Building III in Area A, which belongs to the post-Samsi-Addu occupation.

one short wall that effectively match Mallowan's TD "chimney". Back in our Area A, the only possible location for such a niche in Building I was not preserved due to erosion of its western end, but no niche was present in the similar Building II.

Building IV lies to the south of Building III and east of Building II (Fig. 9). Only two rooms could be defined, although eroded mud-brick extending further south suggests an additional room or rooms in that direction. Its north wall would have blocked the narrow doorway originally leading south out of the courtyard of Building III. This doorway was partially filled by an irregular block of mud-bricks and a re-used basalt door-socket. The walls of Building IV were built of poorer-quality bricks than those in Buildings I, II and III, a crumbly and friable reddish material. The northwest room, unusually, was almost exactly square. Three ovens sunk into the floor at the south of this room (00-22, 00-23 and 00-24) and two burials of a child and an adult (Tombs 8 and 9, respectively) below the floor in its north end indicate that this structure would have had a "normal" domestic function.

Building V lies to the west of Building III (Fig. 9). It was quite poorly preserved, except for its southeast corner, due to its proximity to the erosion gully along the northwest side of the Area A spur. It may be a third example of the long rectangular building plan and had at least two rooms, but not enough was preserved to determine their full extent, nor their nature, whether open or roofed space. However, a door-socket within the southern room (L. 73) indicates that the northern room could be closed off.

Both Buildings IV and V had near-straight wide walls, with well-laid whole bricks, similar to Buildings I, II and III and in contrast to the more haphazard and irregular construction in some of the Area G buildings (see Chapter 3). While Buildings IV and V may have been domestic, their association with the non-domestic Building III may point to their occupation by individuals of a distinct social class or identity. However, the floor areas of the roofed spaces in all the buildings in Area A are, on the whole, no larger than those in Area G (compare Table 2.1 to Table 3.3). The ceramic assemblage of Phase II reinforces the hypothesis of consensus-building administration (see above and Chapter 5). The most common types are wide-mouthed jars and large-diameter bowls, the types of vessels most closely associated with communal meals or "feasting" events. Cooking pots dropped significantly in percentage of the total assemblage from that in Phase III (see below), indicating that cooking for such feasts probably took place elsewhere on site.

The alley that ran along the eastern facades of Buildings I, III and IV was best preserved at its northern end (excavated as Loci 10, 12, 14 and 16–the different locus numbers corresponding to the stratified deposits through its depth). The lower layers (Loci 14 and 16) consisted of water-laid strata of fine silt and small pebbles, dense in pottery sherds and animal bones (the latter particularly in Locus 16). These layers were "trough"-shaped in cross-section, evidence of a great deal of foot traffic along the alley, as well as drainage of water down a gradual slope from north to south. The density of sherds in Locus 16 was so great (more sherds than soil) that it may represent a deliberately-imported and placed paving to cope with water and mud, rather than everyday rubbish discard. These lower layers represent the actual use of the alley, while the final upper layers were a softer brown deposit that probably represents post-use erosion. The west face of wall St. 99/8 was severely eroded at its base, at the same elevation as the densest water-laid deposits in L. 16. Such erosion of foundations from wind and rain is a typical feature of past and modern mud-brick structures and explains the protective facing of basalt blocks applied to Building III in this area.

We have reconstructed the northeast corner of Building III and the angle of the alley around this corner. The alley further south (Locus 81) did not have the same depth of preserved deposit, although the quantities of sherds, grindstone fragments, objects and animal bones remained high. Once Building III had been modified, the drain that led out through the wall from the newly-created bathroom curved to the north and along the side of the building (01-13; Fig. 14); this location makes it probable that the main access route to Building III was then from the south. This access route supports our hypothesis that any original functional or ownership connection between Building I and Building III had shifted when Building I's façade was altered (and the deposits of animal dung accumulated within it). The drain consisted of a clay pipe segment and a stone- and brick-lined cut through the wall which sloped gradually down for about 90 cm beyond the wall face; at that point it was directed in a sharp angle to the north by a line of closely packed cobbles. These cobbles stretched for c 2 meters before being replaced by a line of baked bricks. The range of materials, small scale and casual construction method are at odds with the original grand scale of Building III but match its less formal secondary modification and courtyard paving repairs.

The eastern alley connects to a wider east-west alley at its northern end (Loci 30/36). This space was also characterized by large quantities of ceramics, broken objects and discarded animal bones and appears to have been used as both an access route and a rubbish dump. The southern edge of a final building or buildings lay on the opposite side of this second alley, at the northern edge of our excavation. Very little could be cleared of this northern building, but its orientation is parallel to the other structures of Phase II and the walls were constructed of similar bricks. A gap separates the parallel wall segments 99-14 and 99-19 and may be a wide doorway or actually a further north-south alley between two buildings. Stratigraphic layers in the alley indicate that both the original walls (99-14 and 99-19) were built prior to Building I and thus are slightly earlier than the entire central complex; but a later buttress or repair against 99-14 (99-15) is one of the last modifications in Phase II. This northern area was apparently razed for the construction of the relatively large building of Phase I (see below).

The alleys to north and east of the building complex offer a contrast to the open space to its southwest. This area consisted of deep deposits of overlapping, ephemeral and interleaved ash and rubbish layers (Loci 85, 86), a deposit comparable to that in the subsequent Phase I. These layers sloped down from northeast to southwest, in parallel to the modern slope of the spur. This slope reinforces our reconstruction that the past shape of the mound in this area was roughly the same as at present, with the Area A spur as a genuine projection connected to the main mound by a less intensively-used saddle.

Phase III

Soundings below selected rooms of Phase II explored the architecture that preceded the main complex. In addition to the soundings, the tops of walls belonging to Phase III were visible below the floors of Phase II in some places, although time constraints meant not all areas could be explored. In Phase III, the construction of the walls was equally substantial to that of Phase II; but despite the probable similarity of functions implied, Phase III walls were not always utilized as foundations in Phase II.

The alignments of walls in both Phases III and II were consistent in the southern portion of the area; but the Phase III walls at the northern end of our excavation (below Building I, Phase II) were aligned slightly differently than those in Phase II. In all cases where Phase III was visible, the tops of walls had been deliberately sheared and were perfectly flat. From this feature, it appears that the construction of Phase II was a conscious and simultaneous remodelling of the entire spur, and that the identifiable sub-phasing in terms of building construction sequence within the central complex does not represent any substantial length of time. The ceramic assemblage from Phase III, although limited in size, indicates a date within the early 2nd millennium BC.

The Phase III building at the northern end of the area (below Phase II's Building I) was a multi-roomed structure, in which parts of five rooms could be delineated (see Fig. 16). The main NE-SW wall (99-17) was abutted by at least three perpendicular walls (one on its south, two on its north)[12]. All walls were preserved to approximately one meter high, and the deposits in the rooms (Loci 33, 34 and 44) consisted of horizontally layered occupational strata, including ash-covered surfaces. A collapsed bread oven (00-33), an associated complete pot (CB 1924) and a dense ash deposit were uncovered in the upper layers of L. 44. The probable domestic use of this space in Phase III matches the initially domestic use of Building I, which succeeded it directly in the following Phase II.

The Phase III building at the southern end of our excavation (below Phase II's Building II) corresponds to its plan almost exactly: a narrow rectangular structure divided by a partition wall into a smaller eastern and a larger western room[13]. The walls of this building were preserved 1.25 meters high. The barrel-vaulted roof of this Phase III building was clearly definable in its eastern room: the arch of the northern wall extended just over 50 cm into the room (00-28; dashed line on Fig. 16; see also Fig. 17), although less than 20 cm inward extent of the vault was preserved on the southern wall (00-30; dashed line on Fig. 16). The eastern end wall, 00-29, (and presumably the un-excavated western wall also) was straight rather than vaulted and was offset c 75 cm further west than the comparable wall in the subsequent Phase II.

There were multiple plaster layers on all walls in the eastern room, predominantly white or grey. These plaster layers were particularly well preserved on the eastern and southern walls (00-29, 00-30), where six thin layers of alternating grey and white plaster were identifiable, followed by a thicker tan layer, three or four more white layers, and a final tan layer. Similar sequences appeared on the northern and southern walls, but the partition wall (00-38) had only two white plaster layers, covered by a tan layer. The initial plaster layers on the northern and southern walls ran behind this partition wall where it abutted them, and this wall was clearly a later addition subdividing what had been a single room.

---

[12] This construction technique, a major wall abutted by slightly smaller walls, is distinctively different from and more informal than the bonded construction of all the buildings in the complex in Phase II.

[13] We did not excavate the Phase III western wall of this building, but the use of the Phase III walls as foundations for the other three walls of the building implies that it lies below the western wall of Building II, Phase II.

Chapter 2

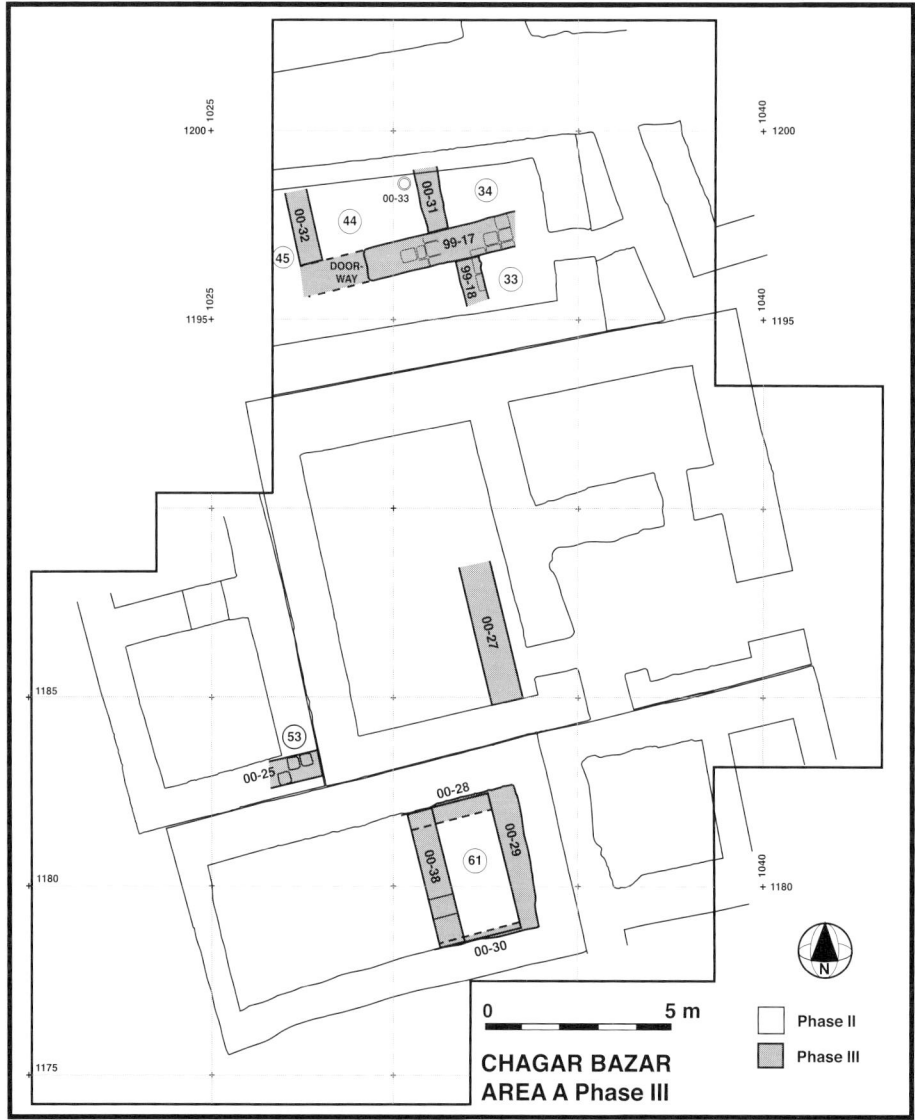

Figure 16: Area A, Phase III plan (with walls of Phase II indicated)

An unusual oval "porthole" doorway had been built in the partition wall, and the plaster continued around its door jambs (Fig. 17). Two substantial surfaces were traced in this room (Locus 61) within multiple accumulated layers of soft ash and greenish soil with white plant casts. This greenish material is very similar to deposits in Building I of Phase II, which soil micromorphological analysis indicates has a high animal dung content (see above, Semple in McMahon *et al.* 2005 and Semple, in prep.). The deposit may be from animal stabling or dung fuel storage. This occupational material was covered by a final layer of fallen mud-bricks and brown soil, deliberate fill added when the walls were flattened for construction of Phase II.

Figure 17: Barrel vault in Locus 61, Phase III, and "porthole" doorway, from east

The tops of two more wall segments were exposed below the central buildings of Phase II: a NW-SE wall (00-27) below the lowest floor in the main room of Building III, parallel to its main internal wall, and a NE-SW wall (00-25) below the southeast corner of Building V and parallel to its southern wall (Fig. 16). These walls indicate that the alignments of Phase III architecture were mirrored in the next phase, although no complete plan was traced.

Although the ceramic sample from Phase III was small, it provides a significant contrast, in percentages of different types, to the type-breakdowns in Phase II (for full discussion, see Chapter 5). Notable differences include a slightly lower percentage of bowls and higher percentage of cups in Phase III than in Phase II. Among jars, narrow-mouthed jars (Khabur Ware jars and similar unpainted forms) took up a larger percent of the assemblage in Phase III than in II, while wide-mouthed jars/pots presented the inverse: a lower percentage in III than in II. Cooking pots, while surprisingly few overall, were still a more significant presence in the assemblage in Phase III than in Phase II. The overall assemblage emphasises cooking, storage biased towards liquids and individual as well as communal consumption.

Phase I

The final occupation in Area A was only preserved at the north and southwest ends of the excavated area. The ruined remains of the Phase II buildings were surely still visible, unused, in the central portion of Area A during Phase I, and there was some re-use of one of those walls at the southwest. The ceramic assemblage indicates that this final phase of occupation still belongs to the early 2nd millennium BC, within Late Khabur Ware, just as Nuzi Ware appeared. There are some clear differences from the Phase II material, but there is also substantial continuity of both types and type frequencies (see Chapter 5).

The erosion damage to Phase I, immediately below the modern surface, was severe; but even so, it was clear that the structures of this phase were more thinly scattered than those in Phase II. The only significant building lies at the north end, while the southwest features were ephemeral and the area between was unused space (Fig. 18). There were several large pits just south of the northern building, the fill of which contained baked-bricks and stones, including broken door-sockets, basalt grindstones, etc. The purpose of these pits remains unclear and the stone fill is likely to be secondary rubbish disposal. The southwest portion of our excavation was used primarily for rubbish dumping and interment of infant burials. The dispersed nature of the final phase in Area G matches that of Phase I in Area A and indicates that there

Chapter 2

was a gradual retraction of settlement at Chagar Bazar at the end of its occupation, rather than a sudden disruption and immediate abandonment.

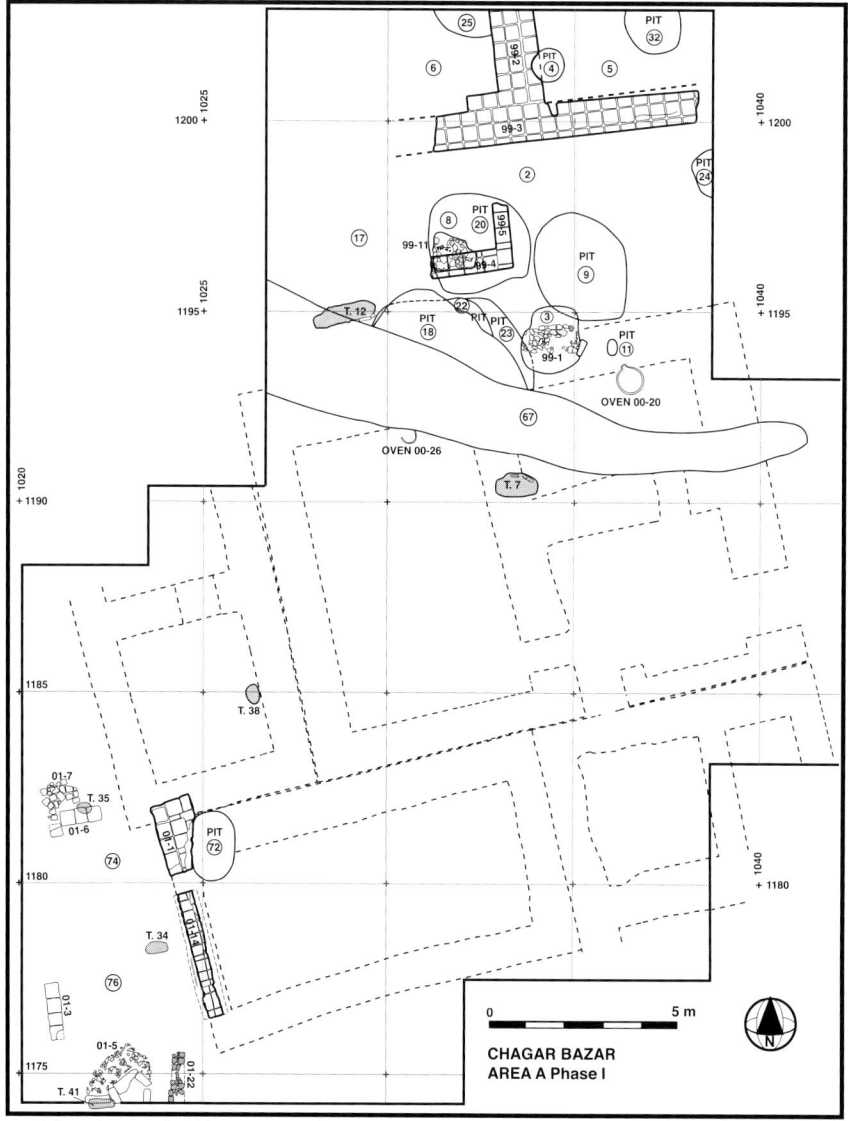

Figure 18: Area A Phase I (with walls of underlying Phase II as dashed lines)

In the southwest corner of Area A, the single Phase I wall rests on top of a wall from Phase II, while further to the east the buildings of Phase II were identified directly below the modern mound surface. This stratigraphic situation makes it difficult to determine whether the structures uncovered by Mallowan in his Area EH would have been contemporary with our Phase II or Phase I. As was mentioned above, the horizontal relationship between the 1930s excavations and our excavations could not be easily determined, given the variance in topographic plans.

The most significant structure of Phase I was a building at the northern end of our excavation; the walls were 2.5 to 3 bricks wide and well-constructed, although not preserved to any great height (Fig. 18). Two rooms (Loci 5 and 6, respectively on east and west) were delineated. Three trampled surfaces were traceable in Locus 5, sloping up slightly at the faces of the walls; the deposit in Locus 6 was more eroded, and comparable use surfaces could not be identified. An ashy lens against the face of western wall 99-2 (L. 25) represents the use of the building in this area. Most of the building lay to the north of our excavation, and its east and west ends were damaged by erosion and pits. The substantial nature of the walls indicates that its function may have matched that of Phase II Building III, administration rather than domestic use. However, its association with pits and burials (although they are somewhat separated) may belie this reconstruction. The ceramic assemblage from Phase I does not differ greatly from that in Phase II (see Chapter 5). But a downward shift in percentage of bowls and an upward shift in percentage of cooking pots support a shift from administration to domestic function.

The cluster of overlapping or neighbouring pits to the south of this building (Loci 9, 18, 20, 22, and 23), together with a single adult burial (Tomb 12), a bread oven (00-26) and a final pit c 2.5 m to the east (L. 24) are all contemporary with the use of the building. Most of these pits were wide shallow trash pits with layered ashy fill; near the centre of pit 9 was the very fragmentary and poorly preserved remains of a newborn infant burial (see Chapter 4, Burial B). Pit 20 contained a "paving" or work area of stones, baked brick fragments, broken basalt grindstones and segments of a bread oven. These features were set into an open space of ephemeral trampled surfaces and accumulated ash layers and lenses (Loci 2 and 17). Slightly later within Phase I are two more pits (Loci 11 and 3), the small wall corner built above pit 20 (walls 99-4 and 99-5 with their associated material L. 8) and another bread oven (00-20)[14]. Pit 3 was shallow and contained a "paving" comparable to that in pit 20: a dense flat deposit of sherds, baked bricks and stones in loose ash fill (99-1); this paving surrounded a very fragmentary bread oven that may have been the predecessor to oven 00-20.

Some of the same range of features was echoed in the southwest, where an open space of overlapping ash and rubbish layers belongs to Phase I (Loci 74, 76). The only substantial feature here was a NW-SE wall (01-1 and 01-14), built in a shallow foundation trench. Generally, it seems that there was a brief period of abandonment of this area after Phase II went out of use, and the re-use in Phase I involved at least some attempt to rebuild on the same lines of earlier architecture— hence the trench was less for foundation stability than it was a pre-build clarification of the earlier wall's location and alignment. Scattered baked-brick and stone pavings (01-5, 01-7 and 01-22) and short lines of mud-brick (01-3 and 01-6) were built in the open area west of the wall. These may have been short-term, small-scale work areas, although in two cases the paved areas covered infant burials (T. 41 and T. 35). This area had persisted as open space from the preceding Phase II and all the layers and lenses here slope down from northeast to southwest, following the general slope of the current (and presumably past) mound surface. Three infant burials (Tombs 34, 35 and 41) were interred in the open southwest area from different surfaces within the accumulation of rubbish. A fourth burial (T. 38; a selection of bones from a foetus and an adult) has also been attributed to this level; the pit for this burial was cut against the face of the eastern wall of Building V of Phase II (00-6) but the level from which it was cut had eroded. The burial may have been cut from a now-missing Phase II floor within that building, but it seems more likely that it was buried within the still-visible ruins of Building V during Phase I.

Very late Phase I surface modifications include two pits cut into the northern Phase I building (Loci 4 and 32) within room 5, both filled with sherds, baked-bricks and broken grindstones. Another late pit (L. 72) filled with ash and mud-brick

---

[14] This bread oven contained the remains of a newborn child; see Chapter 4, Burial A.

Chapter 2

fragments cut into wall 01-1 in the southwest. The final late features comprise a relatively recent (Ottoman Period?) grave of a child (Tomb 7) and a deep, possibly modern, erosion channel (Locus 67) which sloped from southeast to northwest across the centre of Area A, emptying into the main gully to the northwest of the spur on which Area A was sited.

Spatial arrangement and social interaction

Area G has a tight, inward-looking group of houses in a linear arrangement on either side of a central alley (see Chapter 3). By comparison, the building complex in Area A Phase II has an equally tightly-packed but outward-looking plan without the axial feature of Area G[15].

It is something of a paradox that the Area A structures look outwards, while they are also separated from the rest of the settlement. This sends a message of relatively open access but a lack of social integration that is entirely appropriate for an administrative complex. Meanwhile, the visual impact of Area G sends the opposite message, tight social integration but private access to individual spaces.

A brief focus on the assembly room in Building III is also instructive. At 4.9 m wide by 7.6 m long, this space is suited to what Moore (1996) has identified as "public-near interactions"; these involve use of natural facial expressions and gestures but require a raised voice; they take place at a distance of four to nine meters. Distances less than this allow for more intimate interactions, while distances greater than ten meters involve more rigid and un-nuanced speech and a formalized interaction style. Room size may be most directly linked to expected group size, but there may be an unconscious connection to the main type of interaction planned for the space: public and yet still personal, or the previously-mentioned leadership by consensus.

Construction methods and details

The bricks used for walls in Area A were all sun-dried; baked-bricks are restricted to the courtyard paving in Building III, doorsills in Buildings I and III, and re-used fragments in Phase I pits and pavings. Plaster and mortar were of the same clay as the bricks, with chaff inclusions. The white colour in some plaster layers in Building III and the Phase III version of Building II may be due to the addition of lime; grey plaster may have been coloured with ash. Floors in most of the rooms were simply packed earth.

Use of mud-brick dimensions and forms for determination of date has a long tradition within south Mesopotamian archaeology in particular. Brick dimensions are less often used in north Mesopotamia and in recent research programmes, yet widespread brick standardization offers useful information about expectations, traditions and specialization. The overwhelming majority of bricks used in all three phases of Area A were whole square bricks averaging 36-38 x 36-38 x 8-10 cm in dimensions (the range is 34-40 x 34-40 x 8-10 cm). This average size also corresponds to the dimensions of the majority of bricks in Area G (see Chapter 3), although there is greater variety and greater use of half-bricks there. These dimensions also correspond neatly to those identified by Mallowan in Area TD: 37 x 37 x 8.5 or half-bricks of 37 x 17 x 9 cm (Mallowan 1936: 15). Closely comparable brick sizes have also been

---

[15] However, some of this visual impression of Area A may be due to the fact that erosion has removed the eastern edge of this area, making the eastern alley appear to be more "peripheral" and the northern alley shorter than they originally were.

identified in Old Babylonian levels at other north Mesopotamian sites, such as Tell Leilan (34 x 34 x 10 cm and half-bricks of 34 x 16 x 10 cm; Weiss *et al.* 1990: 543)[16], Tell Muhammed Diyab (from 30 x 34 x 8 to 40 x 40 x 9 cm; Bachelot & Sauvage 1992: 21), Tell al-Rimah (38 x 38 cm in a pavement dated to the reign of Samsi-Addu, but replaced in a post-Samsi-Addu pavement by bricks 49 x 49 cm; Postgate *et al.* 1997: 23), and even as far south as Haradum (36 x 37 x 11 cm; Kepinski-Lecomte 1992). The resources for brick production are abundant and local to each site, and transport costs and limits make it unlikely that brick production took place at any great distance from each settlement, but the near-standard brick sizes across the region indicate a degree of semi-specialization in their manufacture and a strong adherence to local building traditions (see Ch. 3 for further discussion).

The sizes of Old Babylonian bricks in south Mesopotamia were conceptually so standardized that specific types were used as examples in mathematical problems (Robson 1999: 57 ff.). The most common square bricks in Old Babylonian south Mesopotamia are significantly smaller than the contemporary north Mesopotamian bricks. Old Babylonian baked bricks average 33 x 33 x 8 cm (Robson 1999: 284), while unbaked half bricks in the Old Babylonian levels at Nippur Area WB are 25 x 16 x 8 cm (Gibson 1978: 56). The thickness of bricks in north and south is the same, 8-10 cm (5-6 "fingers"); thus the moulds were the same height but the brick volumes would have been smaller in the south by 25 percent or more. The implications for raw resources are not impacted, but the labour input in production and construction would have been significantly higher in the south.

Selected Architectural comparanda

The excavators of *Tell Mohammed Diyab* exposed a 3-room building on the acropolis, which bears remarkable similarities to our Area A Phase II Building III. They identify their acropolis building as a temple, through the presence of an altar (Durand & Nicolle 1999). The original plan of this building has a rectangular rear shrine room c 5 x 10 m, with two rooms to the front; the location of doors, the scale of the building and the proportions of the rooms all closely map onto the arrangement of our Building III. The inner doorways of the Muhammed Diyab building are arched, which complements our reconstruction of a possible baked-brick arched doorway in the Chagar Bazar building. We see no evidence of use of Chagar Bazar Building III for religious purposes, however, and the recurrence of the plan for a second non-religious building in Mallowan's Area TD bears out the use of this plan at Chagar Bazar for secular administration[17]. That the plans of both religious and secular public buildings may be similar and may have been ultimately derived from domestic architecture is unsurprising.

Single-room or two-room rectangular buildings like our Phase II Buildings I and II (and Buildings G 1 and G 2 in Area G) are remarkably common across the Upper Khabur and Upper Tigris regions (see Ch. 3). Vaulted versions are less common. At *Tell Brak*, Area HH Trenches D and C4 (Level 8, Late Old Babylonian, end of 17th or early 16th century BC; Oates *et al.* 1997) have revealed a vaulted

---

[16] These brick dimensions were found in Level 1 of the Lower Town Palace. In Level 2, brick sizes were more variable (33 x 33 x 8 cm, 33 x 18 x 8 cm and 33 x 13 x 8 cm), and walls were wider but more poorly constructed (Weiss *et al.* 1990).

[17] A similar plan has also been recovered on the Syrian Euphrates at Tell Halawa A, Planquadrat Q (MBA); but there, the main entrance into the structure is invariably into the largest room, and the smaller rooms are placed at the rear of the building (Meyer 1989: Abb. 6).

rectangular building ca. 11 meters long by ca. 6.5 meters wide, with a niche and platform at the west end. Later structures were built against it on north and south, still within the Old Babylonian Period. This is only slightly larger than our Buildings I and II at Chagar Bazar.

Further excavations at Tell Brak in Area HN, Level 2 revealed another vaulted structure, Room 6/7, possibly another shrine (Matthews 2003b). Again, there is a large building to the south of the vaulted rectangular shrine room, in the same configuration as our Building III lying south of Building I. However, our buildings are unlikely to ever have been shrines, given the burial below the early floor of Building I and the evidence of animal manure build-up thereafter. Our buildings also lack niches or platforms. The early 2nd millennium BC occupation of *Tell Muhammed Diyab* has several vaulted rooms in the "ville haute" area, Niveau 5. Their most clearly vaulted room 991 (only 4.5 x 2 m[18]) was observed to be only 1.55 m high, suggesting its function was storage rather than living space (Sauvage 1992). The fallen brick in nearby rooms (720, 706) suggest the probability of further vaulted buildings in the neighbourhood. Vaults had been an architectural tradition in north Mesopotamia since the 3rd millennium BC (i.e., Tell Hazna, Tell al-Rimah), despite what we assume was reasonable access to roofing timber from Anatolia.

The rectangular single-room building plan also appears in non-vaulted rooms at *Tell Mohammed Diyab*, i.e., in Room 706, of almost identical interior dimensions to Building II (Bachelot & Sauvage 1992: 22). Haus I in Area C at *Tell Mozan* has a similar plan (Schict 5, Old Babylonian/ Alt Gazira II, Dohmann-Pfälzner & Pfälzner 2000: Beilage 1). In both these examples, the rectangular buildings are within a closely packed neighbourhood, with paved courtyards, alleys, open plazas and a generally informal and unplanned appearance. This situation is more reminiscent of Area G at Chagar Bazar. The long rectangular plans even appear at *Haradum* on the mid-Euphrates (Niveau 3, 1775-1628 BC). Although the latter site was politically and culturally more closely linked with Babylonia, the plans of its Bâtiments 11, 12 and 13 suggest a link with north Mesopotamian building traditions, although on a smaller scale (Kepinski-Lecomte 1992: Figs. 28-30).

Among all these rectangular buildings, the key connection is the near 1:2 width-to-length ratio of their inner dimensions; the door placement is a less crucial element. Rectangular, single-room building plans lend themselves easily to both sacred and mundane functions: religious ritual, domestic use, storage and shop-holder activities may all encompass directed movement and, perhaps more crucially, the need or desire to see the entire contents, occupants and features of a room simultaneously.

At *Tell Leilan*, the construction details (although not the building plan or size) of the Lower Town Palace in Operation 3 bear some similarities to our Area A structures. The Palace (Period 1, Level 3) was possibly constructed during the reign of Samsi-Addu but was also used by post-Samsi-Addu rulers (on tablet evidence; Weiss *et al.* 1990). The Leilan palace had straight walls mostly 1-1.5 m wide (3-4 square bricks wide) or in some cases more than 3 meters wide, thickly plastered, and carefully parallel or perpendicular to associated walls. Baked brick in the courtyard indicates a high status for the occupants. In these aspects, there is not a great deal of difference between the Leilan Palace and our Building III, although the scale of the palace is far

---

[18] In general, the average surface area of rooms in Level 5 of the Haute Ville area was 7.1 sq m (Bachelot & Sauvage 1992: 21), less than the average size of Area A rooms (see Table 2.1, below) and closer to that of Area G.

greater (25+ rooms and at least two massive courtyards). Clearly the way to "monumentalize" a building rested not in construction techniques, but in increased scale—the elaboration limits of the basic unit of mud-brick construction were reached very quickly.

Tell Leilan has the classic indicators of hierarchical power still exemplified best in south Mesopotamia: temple, palace, citadel, city walls and a large footprint (even though some of the Lower Town may have been only thinly occupied). But it is probable that the new territorial state would have needed to develop innovative ways of presenting and negotiating power within the countryside. While the state's capital looked essentially south Mesopotamian, the regional sub-loci of power are more likely to have used indigenous and more easily legible iconography. Given the tribal nature of many of the inhabitants of this state (both nomadic and settled), the classic south Mesopotamian urban model of power presentation would not have succeeded. Collaborative power rather than hierarchical control would have been more effective and may explain the house-based administrative buildings we see at Chagar Bazar in Area A, as well as their placement with regard to the rest of the settlement.

Table 2.1 Area A Architectural Geometry

Table 2.1A External measurements of complete or nearly-complete buildings

Building	External dimensions	Area
Building I	5.6 x 10.0 m *(reconstructed)*	56.0 sq m
Building II	5.9 x 10.3 m	60.8 sq m
Building III	10 x 13.6 m	136.0 sq m

Table 2.1B Enclosed, roofed space sizes (floor area, inner wall to inner wall)

Building	Room and Locus	Area and Dimensions
Building II	E room L. 61	8.2 sq m (3.78 x 2.18 m)
	W room L. 68	21.8 sq m (3.78 x 5.76 m)
Building III	Assembly room L. 52	36.9 sq m (4.88 x 7.56 m)
	Side room L. 62	13.6 sq m (2.70 x 5.02 m)
	Bathroom L. 83	1.9 sq m (1.20 x 1.62 m)
Building IV	NW room L. 55	10.3 sq m (3.20 x 3.22 m)
Building V	S room L. 73	13.2 sq m (3.40 x 3.88 m)

Notes:

The average roofed room size is 15.1 square meters; 17.3 square meters if the unusually small and secondary bathroom is omitted.

The area of the assembly room in Building III, at 36.9 square meters, is larger than the average of the main rooms at Haradum, for instance (a functionally quite different site, but a contemporary settlement for which there is significant data for comparison); the average size of the main spaces at the latter site is 25.5 square meters, with a range of 13.75 through 37.0 square meters (Kepinski-Lecomte 1992).

Note on Tables 2.2 and 2.3, Locus and Structure Lists:

Stratigraphic and descriptive information on Loci and Structures is given here by phase. Note that the phasing systems in Area A and Area G (see Ch. 3, Tables 3.4 and 3.5) are not precisely associated: i.e. Phase II in Area A does not correspond exactly to Phase II in Area G. The sequences of Locus and Structure Numbers in these two areas are also independent.

Table 2.2 Area A Loci
Phase IA and Surface

Locus No.	Trench	Description and comments	Layers	Boundary walls
1	A I	Topsoil, = L. 50 in A II	1.1, 1.2, 1.3: surface material	
50	A II	Topsoil, = L. 1 in A I	50.1: eroded material, root disturbance	
4	A I	Pit cut into Phase I architecture near corner of walls 99-2 and 99-3, N building	4.1: ash fill	
32	A I	Pit cut into Phase I architecture, NE corner of trench, cuts 99-19	32.1: dark ash, pottery & stones in fill	
51	A II	Pit for Tomb 7	51.1: fine gray silty fill	
67	A I and A II	Long trough-like erosion channel, cuts Phase II architecture and Phase I pits	67.1-67.8: layers within trough, hard fine material, water-laid, laminated.	
70	A II	Part of erosion channel L. 67	70.1: hard laminated gray-white, fine	
72	A II	Pit cut into Phase I architecture, wall 01-1	72.1: loose crumbly brown-gray deposit, with charcoal, ash, bricky material, root disturbance; 72.2: same, less root disturbance	

Phase I

Locus No.	Trench	Description and comments	Layers	Boundary walls
2	A I	Sealed by topsoil L. 1, unroofed space, = L. 17 to its SW, associated with pits L. 9, 20	2.1: Bricky deposit below topsoil; 2.2: courtyard or open area deposit	99-3
3	A I	Pit with paving/ work area, = L. 57 in A II, cuts pit L. 9	3.1: loose fill around stones	Paving 99-1
5	A I	East room of N building, contemporary with L. 6	5.1: weathered material near centre, intact brown floors near wall faces	99-2, 99-3
6	A I	West room of N building, contemporary with L. 5	6.1: weathered material, bricky above patchy pink floor	99-2, 99-3
7	A I	Eroded brick, = east end of wall St. 99-3, NE corner of trench	7.1: eroded & weathered brick	

Chapter 2

8	A I	Room north and west of walls 99-4 and 99-5	8.1: weathered material	99-4, 99-5
9	A I	Pit, with multiple ash layers, infant burial, cut by pit L. 3, cut into L. 2 and into top of Bldg. I	9.1: ash and brown trash deposits; 9.2: ash layer within pit; 9.3: final cleaning of sides and base of pit	
11	A I	Small pit east of larger set of pits L. 18, 20, 22 and 23, cuts into wall 99-6	11.1: loose ash fill	
17	A I	Open area in W portion of trench, cut by pits L. 18, 20, 22, 23 and burial T. 12, = L. 2 to its NE	17.1, 17.2: bricky layers	
18	A I	Pit, final cut in sequence of pits Loci 20, 22, 23, cut by erosion channel L. 67	18.1: ash fill	
20	A I	Pit, stone and baked-brick paving, cut into Loci 2 and 17	20.1: ash fill; 20.2: cleaning bottom of pit	Paving 99-11
22	A I	Pit, cuts pit L. 23, cut by pit L. 20, cut into L. 17	22.1: ash fill	
23	A I	Pit, cut by pits L. 3 and L. 22, cut into L. 17	23.1: bricky fill	
24	A I	Pit cut into L. 13, E of 99-8	24.1: soft deposit	
25	A I	Ashy lenses at the bottom of L. 6, W room of N bldg = Tomb 12, cuts wall 99-16	25.1: ash lenses, 25.2: ash lenses	
42	A I		42.1: upper soft deposit	
57	A II	Pit with stone and baked-brick paving, S half of L. 3 in A I, on plans as L. 3 only	57.1: soft pit fill, sherds and bones	
58	A I and A II	Below L.57, = part of L.67, cuts N end of 00-2	58.1: ashy material	
69	A II	Small pit cut into 00-15 and L.61	69.1: pebbly brown soil on orange layer at base	
74	A II	Unroofed space W of wall 01-1, = L.76 to S	74.1: Fallen bricks, burned black ashy material, loose brown matrix	01-1
76	A II	Unroofed space, SW corner of trench, = L. 74 to N, seals L. 86	76.1: brown trashy ashy deposit assoc. with 01-3; 76.2: brown trash and ashy deposit; 76.3: compact red-brown layers; 76.4: brown deposit with many sherds and small stones, baked-brick fragments, assoc. with 01-5; 76.5-76.9: harder yellow-brown layers, steeply sloping down from N	01-3, 01-5
78	A II	Narrow strip of material E of wall 01-14, = L. 74	78.1: pinkish crumbly material, eroded and possibly cut by Mallowan	01-14
82	A II	Foundation trench for wall 01-11, cut into 01-14 and L. 86	82.1: loose fine yellow-gray clean fill	01-11
84	A II	Pit for infant burial T. 35	84.1: loose fill	

Area A Architecture

Phase II

Locus No.	Trench	Description and comments	Layers	Boundary walls
10	A I	Upper erosion layer in eastern alley, sealed by L. 2, seals L. 12, approximately contemporary with L. 26	10.1: soft brown deposit; 10.2: hard bricky deposit	99-6, 99-7
12	A I	Lower layer in eastern alley, sealed by L. 10, seals L. 14, = L. 19	12.1: soft brown deposit, 12.2: soft brown with silty patches, 12.3: same	99-6, 99-7, 99-8
13	A I	Occupational material between 99-8 and E section, NE corner of trench, cut by pit L. 24	13.1: weathered material, 13.2: trashy layer	99-8
14	A I	Lower layer in eastern alley, sealed by L. 12, seals L. 16	14.1: street layer, water-laid silt and sand, small pebbles, 14.2, 14.3: street layers	99-6, 99-7, 99-8
15	A I	Eroded and collapsed brick from vault in Bldg I, = 99-12, top of Phase II, also = L. 28	15.1: layer of fallen brick	Collapse from 99-16, 00-34
16	A I	Lowest layer in eastern alley, sealed by L. 14, runs below St. 99/8	16.1, 16.2, 16.3: layers of compact deposit, many sherds, animal bones	99-7
19	A I	Junction of eastern and northern alleys, = L. 12, N of corner 99-7	19.1: greasy layer with charcoal and some eroded brick of 99-7	99-7
21	A I	Doorway in Building I, in wall 99-7	21.1: sloping surfaces above mud-brick pavement, 21. 2: cleaning of wall bases	99-7
26	A I	Top layer of northern alley between 00-34 and 99-15, seals Loci 30 and 38, approx. contemporary with L. 10	26.1: dense brown-grey street layer	99-15, 00-34
27	A I	Soft fill between walls 99-14 and 99-15, northwest corner of trench, = L. 39 to its W	27.1: very soft fine grey-brown material	99-14, 99-15
28	A I	Collapsed vault in Bldg. I, = L. 15	28.1: ashy material & brick collapse	Collapse from 99-16, 00-34
29	A I	Occupational layers in E end of Bldg I, = L. 41 on the W	29.1: loose reddish, large frags broken mud-bricks; 29.2: greenish-grey manure layers	99-16, 00-34, 00-35, 99-7
30	A I	Northern alley deposit north of and running against L. 38 buttress, sealed by L. 26, seals L. 47, grey, pottery-rich	30.1: very hard deposit, grey, many sherds	99-14, 99-19
31	A I	Clean deposit against base of wall 99-7 in eastern alley, possible repair of wind/water erosion	31.1: clean grey clay	99-7
36	A I	Northern alley deposit, NE corner of trench, = L. 30 to its W, contemporary with L. 16	36.1: fallen mud-bricks in upper layers, ash and sherds below	99-19
37	A I	Pit for Tomb 4		
38	A I	Hard yellow *tauf* buttress against N wall of Building I, St. 00/34, sealed by L. 26, abutted by L. 30, rests on L. 47	38.1: dense hard yellow material	99-7, 00-34
39	A I	Soft fill between walls 99-14 and 99-15, northwest corner of	39.1: soft brown fill	99-15

Chapter 2

			trench. = L. 27 to its E	
40	A I	Seals L. 41 at SW end of Building I, mostly collapse layers, upper Phase II, contemporary with Loci 15, 28	40.1: crumbly deposit near surface; 40.2: pinkish deposit with ash lens at bottom; 40.3: compact brown-yellow fill above deposit in room L.41; 40.4: ashy; 40.5: yellow-brown deposit	
41	A I	Occupational layers in Bldg I, W end and E end, = L. 29 in centre of room	41.1: brick collapse layer; 41.2: grey--green striated layer of animal manure, 41.3: ashy deposit within 41.1; 41.4: surface sealed by 41.2	99-16, 00-34, 00-35
43	A I	Occupational material associated with bin 00-20, = L. 41	43.1: striated layer of animal manure; 43.2: striated layer of animal manure, compact	99-20
46	A I	NE of trench, junction of eastern and northern alleys, = L. 26, cut by pit L. 32	46.1: mixed deposit, cut by L.32.	99-8, 99-19
47	A I	Lowest northern alley deposit, sealed by L. 38 and L. 30, runs against 00-34 and 00-35, below 99-7, earlier Phase II	47.1: compact dense grey-brown layer with sparse charcoal: 47.2: similar but with more sherds, extension to W	00-34, 00-35
48	A I	Deposit in bin 00-37 within Bldg I, contemporary with Loci 29, 41	48.1: grey-green striated animal manure lenses	00-34, 00-35, 00-37
49	A I	NW end of northern alley, = L. 30, runs below 99-15, runs up against L. 38, 99-14	49.1: grey ashy deposit	00-34, 99-14
52	A II	Assembly room in Bldg III	52.1: bricky deposit near wall tops; 52.2: fallen mud-brick; 52.3 & 52.4: floor deposits, fine silt compacted into horizontal surfaces; 52.5: W portion of room, upper bricky material	Bounded by 99-6 on N, 00-3 on W, 00-1 on S, 00-2 on E
54	A II	Courtyard in Bldg III	54.1: eroded material near wall tops; 54.2: fallen eroded mud-brick and ashy floors; 54.3: upper fine compact floor deposits; 54.4: fine deposit immediately above pavement St. 00/14; 54.5: E end of locus, in extension to E, eroded brick fall and floor deposits, mixed	Bounded by 00-2 on W, 00-9 on N, 00-21, 01-17 on E, and 00-7 on S
55	A II	NW room of Bldg. IV	55.1: poorly preserved and eroded orange-brown deposit; 55.2: S end of room, near *tanurs*	Bounded by 00-17 on W, 00-8 on N, 00-12 on W, 00-18 on S

56	A II	Pile of ash and broken bricks within L. 54, NE corner	56.1: hard burned red soil and ash, baked bricks and broken grinding stones	00-9, 00-21, 01-17
59	A II	Pit for *tanur* in Bldg IV, SE corner of L. 55	59.1: very ashy loose fill	Oven 00-23
60	A II	Pit for *tanur* in Bldg IV, SW corner of L. 55	60.1: very ashy loose fill	Oven 00-22
61	A II	E room of Bldg II, upper phase emptied by Mallowan, lower phase intact.	61.1: fill near wall tops; 61.2: Mallowan cut fill; 61.3: contemporary with 68.1; 61:4+: Phase III (see below)	Bounded by later versions of 00-15 on W, 00-4 on N, 00-10 on E, 00-19 on S
62	A II	NE room of Bldg III, connected to courtyard L. 54 through doorway L. 65.	62.1: eroded material near wall tops; 62.2: fallen mud-brick and ash floors; 62.3: silty lenses scattered throughout room associated with large sherds, above packed room floor, 62.4: floor deposit	Bounded by 00-2 on W, 99-6 on N, 00-21 on E, 00-9 on S
63	A II	Pit for T. 8, NW corner of L.55	63.1: soft reddish pit fill	
64	A II	Pit for T. 9, NE corner of L.55	64.1: soft fill around skeleton, including sherds W of body; 64.2: eroded soft fill above 64.1 at face of St. 00/12	
65	A II	Doorway in 00-9, between L.54 on S and L. 62 on N	65.1: bricky deposit running over doorsill and down towards L. 62	00-9
66	A II	Doorway in 00-7, between L. 54 on N and exterior space, below Bldg IV on S	66.1: loose fill including sherds which join with those from floor lots of L.54	00-7
68	A II	W room of Bldg II, upper layers possibly fill in Mallowan excavation, seals L. 79	68.1, 68.2: horizontally layered loose fill	Bounded by 00-4 on N, 00-10 on E, 00-19 on S, 01-11 on W
71	A II	Doorway in 00-2, between courtyard L. 54 on E and assembly room L. 52 on W	71.1: fallen mud-bricks directly on baked brick doorsill and step	00-2
73	A II	Room in Bldg V	73.1: crumbly and eroded brown soil, root disturbance; 73.2: less disturbed but still crumbly brown soil, more sherds	N of 01-2, W of 00-6, S of 01-10, E of 01-16, eroded on NW
75	A II	Brick fall in alley E of Bldg III	75.1: red bricky material, alternately crumbly and very solid; 75.2: fallen bricks above L.81	00-21
77	A II	Upper material in bathroom, Bldg III, seals L. 83	77.1: Compact chunky greyish clay deposit	01-17, 01-18
79	A II	W room of Building II, sealed by L. 68	79.1: dark brown ashy, some sherds, esp. at N face of 00-19; 79.2: same	S of 00-4, E of 01-11, N of 00-19, W of 00-15

Chapter 2

80	A I	NE corner of trench, = L. 46	80.1: mixed ashy eroded deposit, many sherds	99-8, 99-19
81	A II	Alley E of Building III	81.1: loose material mixed with fallen bricks, sherds, bones; 81.2: same but below bricks, more sherds and trash	E of 00-21
83	A II	Bathroom in Bldg. III	83.1: thick deposit with some bricky material in upper layer and muddy clay below with many clumps of green waxy clay	S of 01-20, W of 01-19, N of 01-18, E of 01-17, assoc. with drain 01-13
85	A II	SW corner of trench, open space, = L. 86, sealed by L. 74	85.1: grey striated soft layers	
86	A II	SW corner of trench, open space, = L. 85, sealed by L. 76	86.1: grey ashy striated layers	
87	A II	E of alley L. 81, E of small wall 01-9, reddish bricky material in contrast to grey of street, possible wall but very badly eroded off mound slope	87.1: crumbly reddish soil, root disturbance	01-9
88	A II	Brick fall above pavement 01-15 in porch of Bldg. III.	88.1: crumbly reddish brick	

Phase III

Locus No.	Trench	Description and comments	Layers	Boundary walls
33	A I	Southern room, contemporary with L. 34, 44, 45, sealed by L. 29	33.1: soft, clean, brown deposit; 33.2: brown trashier deposit	99-17, 99-18
34	A I	Northeast room, contemporary with L. 34, 44, 45, sealed by L. 29, cut by pit for T. 4	34.1: upper reddish bricky deposit resting on ash lenses, 34.2: layer of occupation debris, ash, 34.3: ash lenses and compact yellow soil	99-17, 00-31
35	A I	Deposit below L. 33, possibly Phase IV	35.1: loose brown deposit	
44	A I	Northwest room, contemporary with L. 34, 35, 45	44.1: some brick collapse with soft brown soil; 44.2: soft brown trash; 44.3: ashy surface; 44.4: ashy area at W edge of room	99-17, 00-31, 00-32
45	A I	Northwest space, contemporary with L. 34, 35, 44	45.1: eroded bricky deposit	00-32
53	A II	Below southern end of wall 00-6	53.1: crumbly yellow deposit	00-25
61	A II	E room of Bldg II, lower phase intact. Upper layers belong to Phase II (see above).	61.4-61.6 striated floor deposits, grey-green animal manure. 61.7-61.9= brown, grey, green layers which may belong to Phase IV	Bounded by earlier versions of 00-15 on W, 00-4 on N, 00-10 on E, 00-19 on S

Table 2.3 Area A Structures (walls and features) *

Phase I

Structure No.	Trench	Description and comments	Associated loci	Associated walls and features
99-1	A I	Stone, sherd and baked-brick paving in pit L. 3	L. 3	
99-2	A I	NW-SE wall, 3 bricks wide, 2 courses high, 38-40 x 38-40 cm, buff-light brown mud-bricks, thick mortar lines, cut by pit L. 4	L. 2, 5, 6	Abuts 99-3
99-3	A I	NE-SW wall, 2.5 bricks wide, 2 courses high, buff-light brown mud-bricks, thick mortar lines, eroded at both ends	L. 2, 5, 6	Abutted by 99-2
99-4	A I	NE-SW wall, 1.5 bricks wide, 2 courses high	2, 8	Bonded with 99-5
99-5	A I	NNW-SSE wall, 1 brick wide, 2 courses high	2, 8	Bonded with 99-4
99-11	A I	"Paving" in pit L. 20, limestone, baked-bricks, basalt grindstone fragments	20	
00-20	A I/II	*Tanur* in section between two trenches, Phase IA		Possibly 00-26
00-26	A II	*Tanur* close to section between two trenches, cut by erosion channel L. 67		Possibly 00-20
01-1	A II	NW-SE wall segment, cut into Phase II walls 00-4 and 01-2, orange mud-bricks, cut by pit L.72	74	01-14
01-3	A II	Ephemeral wall segment at SW corner of trench, 4 bricks long, NW-SE	76	01-5
01-5	A II	Irregular patch of mud-bricks and baked-brick fragments at SW corner of trench	76	01-3
01-6	A II	NE-SW line of four mud-bricks W of 01-1	74	01-7
01-7	A II	Irregular patch of baked-bricks N of 01-6, W of 01-1	74	01-6
01-14	A II	NW-SE wall segment, cut into Phase II walls 01-11	76, 78	01-1
01-22	A II	N-S line of baked-brick fragments at SW corner of trench, earlier than 01-3 and 01-5	76, possibly T. 41	

Phase II

Structure No.	Trench	Description and comments	Associated loci	Associated walls and features
99-6	A I & A II	NE-SW wall, N wall of Building III, 34-38 x 34-38 x 8-10 cm, buff-light brown mud-bricks, built against wall 99-16	L. 10, 12, 14, 16, 62	00-1, 00-2, 00-3, 00-7, 00-9, 00-21
99-7	A I	Façade modification on Bldg I, NW-SE wall, built against wall 00-35, doorway, red-orange mud-bricks, 34-38 x 34-38 x 8-10 cm	L. 10, 12, 14, 16, 21	
99-8	A I	NW-SE wall at E edge of trench, pink-orange mud-bricks, 34-38 x 34-38 x 8-10	L. 10, 12, 13, 14, 16	Slightly later than 99-

Chapter 2

			(L. 16.3 runs below foundation), 36	7;
99-10 and 99-12	A I	Top of collapsed vault in Bldg I, red-orange mud-bricks, end of Phase II		Collapsed from 99-16, 00-34
99-14	A I	NE-SW wall at N section, parallel to 99-19, at least 1.5 bricks wide, eroded at W end, cut by trench for 99-15	L. 30, 47	99-19
99-15	A I	NE-SW wall cut into 99-14, rests on L. 30, later modification within Phase II, 1.5 bricks wide, yellow-brown mud-bricks 34-38 x 34-38 x 8-10 cm and 17 x 34 cm half-bricks	26, 27, 39	
99-16	A I	NE-SW wall, S wall of Bldg. I, 3 bricks wide, brown mud-bricks 34-38 x 34-38 x 8-10 cm.	29, 41	00-34, 00-35
99-19	A I	NE-SW wall at N section, parallel to St. 99/14, cut by pit L. 32	36	99-14
99-20	A I	Partition or bin in Bldg I	29, 41, 43	99-16, 00-34, 00-35
00-1	A II	NE-SW wall, S wall of assembly room in Bldg. III, 3 bricks wide, 34 x 34 x 8 cm, pale yellow mud-bricks, white plaster on N face. Built along pre-existing wall 00-4.	52	99-6, 00-2, 00-3, 00-7, 00-9, 00-21
00-2	A II	NW-SE wall, E wall of assembly room in Bldg. III, W wall of Loci 62 and 54, 34 x 34 x 8 cm., three bricks wide, white plaster on W face	52, 54, 62, 71	99-6, 00-1, 00-3, 00-7, 00-9, 00-21
00-3	A II	NW-SE wall, W wall of assembly room in Bldg. III, pale yellow mud-bricks, 34 x 34 x 8 and 17 x 34 x 8, three bricks wide, white plaster on E face. Wall 00-6 is later built against it.	52	99-6, 00-1, 00-2, 00-7, 00-9, 00-21
00-4	A II	NE-SW wall, N wall of Bldg. II, 3 bricks wide, red mud-bricks, 34 x 34 x 8 cm. Built above Phase III wall 00-28, wall 00-1 was later built against it.	61.1-61.3, 68	00-10, 01-11, 01--12, 00-19
00-6	A II	NW-SE wall, E wall of Bldg V, built along 00-3, 3 bricks wide, brown mud-bricks 34 x 34 x 8 cm	73	01-2, 01-10, 01-16
00-7	A II	NE-SW wall, S wall of courtyard in Bldg. III, pale yellow mud-bricks, 2 bricks wide, 34 x 34 x 8 cm.	54, 66	99-6, 00-1, 00-2, 00-3, 00-9, 00-21
00-8	A II	NE-SW wall, N wall of Bldg IV, built against wall 00-7, 3 bricks wide, red mud-bricks, 34 x 34 x 8 cm	55	00-12, 00-17, 00-18
00-9	A II	NE-SW wall, N wall of courtyard L. 54, S wall of room L. 62 in Bldg III, originally 2.5 bricks wide, with later modifications, pale yellow mud-bricks, 34 x 34 x 8 cm	54, 62, 65	99-6, 00-1, 00-2, 00-3, 00-7, 00-21
00-10	A II	NW-SE wall, E wall of Bldg II, 2.5 to 3 bricks wide, red mud-bricks 34 x 34 x 8-10 cm., built on top of Phase III wall 00-29	61.1-61.3	00-4, 00-19, 01-11
00-12	A II	NW-SE wall, E wall of L. 55 in Bldg IV, 1.5 bricks wide	55	00-8, 00-17, 00-18
00-13	A II	Rectangular domed oven in assembly room L. 52 of Bldg III	52	
00-14	A II	Baked-brick, cobble and stone paving in courtyard of Bldg III	54	
00-15	A II	Cross wall in Bldg II, abuts walls 00-4 and 00-19, built on top of 00-38	61.1-61.3, 68	

00-17	A II	NW-SE wall, W wall of Bldg IV, runs against E face of 00-10, 3 bricks wide, yellow-brown mud-bricks	55	00-8, 00-12, 00-18
00-18	A II	NE-SW wall, S wall of L. 55 in Bldg IV, 3 bricks wide, eroded	55	00-8, 00-12, 00-17
00-19	A II	NE-SW wall, S wall of Bldg II, 2.5 bricks wide	61.1-61.3	00-4, 00-10, 01-11
00-21	A II	NW-SE wall, E wall of Bldg III, originally 3 bricks wide with later modifications, basalt block facing on E, 34 x 34 x 8-10 cm bricks	62, 81, 83	99-6, 00-1, 00-2, 00-3, 00-7, 00-9
00-22	A II	*Tanur* in SW corner of L. 55, Bldg IV	55, 60	00-23, 00-24
00-23	A II	*Tanur* in SE corner of L. 55, Bldg IV	55, 59	00-22, 00-24
00-24	A II	*Tanur* at E wall of L. 55, Bldg IV	55	00-22, 00-23
00-34	A I	N wall of Bldg I, brown mud-bricks, abutted by *tauf* buttress L. 38	29, 41	99-16, 00-35
00-35	A I	Original E wall of Bldg I, doorway, brown mud-bricks 37 x 37 cm	29, 41, 48	99-16, 00-34
00-37	A I	Bin in NE corner of Bldg I, abuts 00-34, 00-35	41, 48	Possibly 99-20
01-2	A II	NE-SW wall, S wall of Bldg V, brown mud-bricks	73	00-6, 01-10, 01-16
01-9	A II	NW-SE line of baked-bricks, sherds and cobbles defining E edge of street L. 81 E of Bldg III	81, 87	Drain 01-13
01-10	A II	NE-SW wall separating two rooms in Bldg V, doorway and door-socket, brown mud-bricks	73	00-6, 01-2, 01-16
01-11	A II	NW-SE wall, W end of Bldg II, orange mud-bricks, cut by trench for 01-14	68, 79	00-4, 00-10, 00-19
01-13	A II	Drain cut through E wall of Bldg III, 01-19-01-20, stones, cobbles and clay pipe in square-sectioned cut	81, 83	01-17, 01-18, 01-19, 01-20, 01-21
01-15	A II	Cobble pavement in porch of Bldg III, 3-10 cm cobbles in hard clay mortar	88	00-14
01-16	A II	NW-SE wall, W wall of Bldg V, 2.5 bricks wide, brown mud-bricks, eroded	73	00-6, 01-2, 01-10
01-17	A II	Part of modification of Bldg III, NW-SE wall separating courtyard and bathroom, mud-bricks, stone and re-used baked bricks	54, 83	01-13, 01-18, 01-19, 01-20, 01-21
01-18	A II	Part of modification of Bldg III, NE-SW, S wall of bathroom, 1.5 bricks wide	83, 88	01-13, 01-17, 01-19, 01-20, 01-21
01-19	A II	Part of modification of Bldg III, NW-SE wall on façade, 2 bricks wide	83, 87, 88	01-13, 01-17, 01-18, 01-20, 01-21
01-20	A II	Part of modification of Bldg III, narrow L-shaped NE-SW, N wall and NE corner of bathroom, small friable orange mud-bricks, abuts cut S end of wall 00-21	83, 88	01-13, 01-17, 01-18, 01-19, 01-21
01-21	A II	Part of modification of Bldg III, wall corner, S part of doorway into porch of Bldg III, 2 bricks wide, brown mud-bricks	81, 87, 88	01-13, 01-17, 01-18, 01-19, 01-20

Phase III

Structure No.	Trench	Description and comments	Associated loci	Associated walls and features
99-17	A I	NE-SW wall below Bldg I, 2.5 bricks wide, 34 x 34 cm, yellow mud-bricks, grey mortar	33, 34, 44	Abutted by 99-18, 00-31, 00-32
99-18	A I	NW-SE wall below Bldg I, 1.5 bricks wide, 34 x 34 cm	33	Abuts 99-17 on N
00-25	A II	NE-SW wall below S corner of Bldg V, not excavated	53	
00-27	A II	NW-SE wall visible below floor of L. 52 assembly room, deliberately flattened for construction of Phase II, 2.5-3 bricks wide, not excavated	N/A	
00-28	A II	NE-SW wall, N wall of Phase III version of Bldg II, below wall 00-4, vaulted	61.4+	00-29, 00-30, 00-38
00-29	A II	NW-SE wall, E wall of Phase II version of Bldg II, below wall 00/10	61.4+	00-28, 00-30, 00-38
00-30	A II	NE-SW wall, S wall of Phase III version of Bldg II, below wall 00/19, vaulted	61.4+	00-28, 00-29, 00-38
00-31	A I	NW-SE wall below Bldg I, 1.5 bricks wide, plastered faces	34, 44	Abuts 99-17 on S
00-32	A I	NW-SE wall below Bldg I, 1.5 bricks wide, plastered faces	44, 45	Abuts 99-17 on S (?)
00-33	A I	Collapsed *tanur* in L. 44	44	
00-38	A II	NW-SE cross-wall in Phase III version of Bldg. II, below 00-15	61.4+	00-28, 00-29, 00-30

* Structure Numbers 99-9, 99-13, 00-5, 00-11, 00-16, 00-36, 01-4, 01-8 and 01-12 were not used or were assigned to wall segments later merged with others.

Chapter 3

Neighbourhood Dynamics:
Area G and Mallowan's Area BD

C. Colantoni & A. McMahon

"The northern half of the mound consists of a ridge over 200 m. in length with a flat top and an average breadth of more than 60 m.: the top of this ridge stands between 14 and 15 m. above the level of the surrounding plough-land." (Mallowan 1936: 5)

The northern ridge at Chagar Bazar appeared much the same in 1999 as it had in 1936, although Mallowan's spoil heaps artificially increased its width and height in places, and his trenches were still visible as partially filled-in hollows. However, the underlying long, wide and flat area of this ridge was still clearly defined. The Area G trenches were placed immediately adjacent to the visible western edge of Mallowan's Area BD, in order to explore the heart of the domestic portion of the settlement in the early 2nd millennium BC and to provide contrastive material to Area A (see Fig. 8). Taken together, the old and new excavations offer a picture of a tightly-grouped neighbourhood with substantial diachronic continuity, yet within which there was identifiable variation in size of rooms and buildings and in construction details.

Mallowan's Areas BD and TD

The majority of the early 2nd millennium BC material excavated by Mallowan was from the large L-shaped excavation across the north mound (Areas BD-TD-AB)[1]. This material was labelled Level 1 and divided into five sub-phases, termed Early, Early Intermediate, Intermediate, Late and Latest (Mallowan 1947: 83-84). Excavations in the principal trench of Area BD consisted of a broad north-south exposure, with a deeper sounding at the northern end. This northern end (Mallowan's Rooms[2] 1-24) was identified as a "Temple-Palace", due to the thickness of walls and care taken in the overall layout. The southern half (Rooms 26-48) was interpreted as an agglomeration of private houses just north of the Tablet Building in TD (Mallowan 1936: 109). The published plan of Area BD (Mallowan 1937: Fig. 5) regrettably included a major error in orientation: Rooms 1-24 were aligned correctly, but Rooms 25-48 were presented at an odd angle to the northern rooms and should actually be parallel/ perpendicular to them. Our correction was made on the basis of walls still visible on the surface east of Area G and is shown in Figure 19.

---

[1] Early 2nd millennium BC occupation was also found in Level 1 in the Prehistoric Pit, northwest of Area BD. The architecture there was poorly preserved, and while it is tempting to reconstruct this situation as being due to that area lying on the edge of the ancient settlement and having only sparse architecture, the presence of at least two vaulted graves implies that the locale of the Prehistoric Pit was substantially occupied. Severe erosion on the northern end of the mound presumably removed most of the structures. Area AB was the "base" of the L along a much narrower and sloping internal ridge; the published plans for this area are notably sketchy.

[2] Mallowan called all spaces delineated by architecture 'rooms'; this designation must be considered to include courtyards and open areas as well as traditional roofed rooms. For the correspondence of Mallowan's 'rooms' and the building labels used in this study, see Table 3.2 at the end of the chapter.

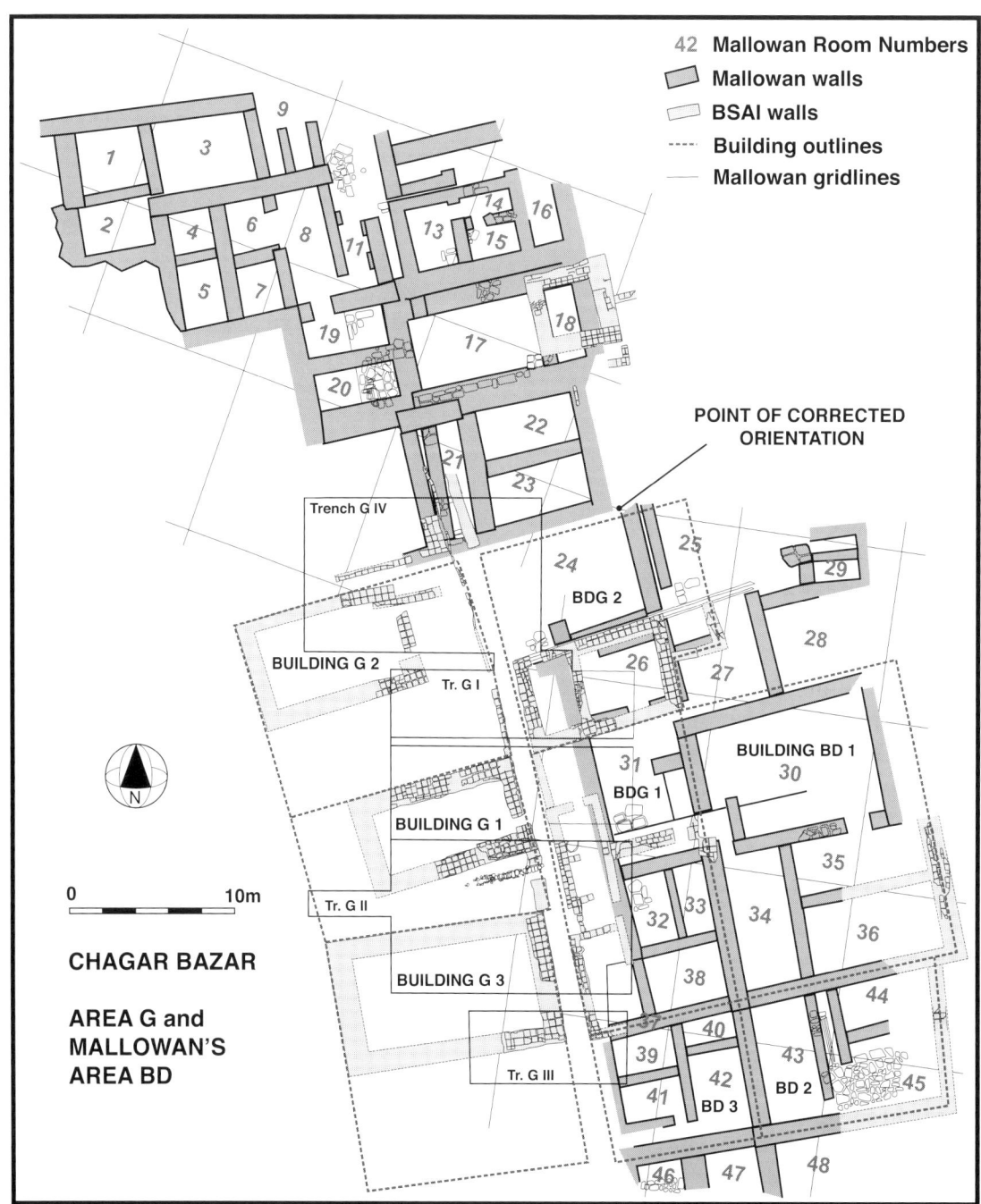

Figure 19: Combined plan of Area G (Phase II) and Mallowan's Area BD

Mallowan's reconstruction of the early 2nd millennium BC architecture downplayed variability and informality in preference for clarity or "readability" of plans. At the start of our work, it was not clear whether his published plan was an amalgamation of the five sub-phases identified in the text or represented just one of these phases. We have come to realize that the plan corresponds primarily to two of his phases, the Intermediate and Early Intermediate; very little of the Early phase was actually excavated, and the Late and Latest phases were poorly preserved. Within these two phases, Mallowan preferred to present a static and regularized plan, as appropriate to his research aims of chronology and seriation, ignoring human tendency towards irregularity and adaptation. However, once Mallowan's plans were disassembled, compared to and combined with our modern excavations, a reconstruction of the biography of a 'typical' domestic neighbourhood for the period, with clarified chronological phasing, was possible.

Area G

Area G comprised four 10 x 15 meter trenches in a north-south alignment. Four architectural phases were identified; our upper Phase (Phase I) was poorly preserved and only articulated at the northern end of Area G, while our lowest phase (Phase IV) was only reached in a sounding near the centre. All four phases belong to the early 2nd millennium BC, on the basis of the ceramic assemblages.

Axial spatial logic for this segment of the neighbourhood is provided by the central alley, which stretches almost 40 metres north-south through the area during most of the phases excavated. The soil layers that accumulated within the alley were dense in discarded animal bones and sherds, and it was the outlet for drains from the adjacent structures in at least four instances. One of its primary functions may have been refuse disposal, as well as foot traffic. Given its state, it is possible that significant foot traffic among the structures may also have been routed around what we perceive of as the "back sides" of the buildings, around their outer edges and on the upper mound slope.

Area G is located across the crest of the modern mound slope at the western edge of the site, and there is significant erosion of the western ends of some of the buildings uncovered in the upper phases. There is evidence in the southern two trenches that this area was at the edge of the ancient settlement, with a significant open and sloping area exposed in Phase III. In these two trenches, we also were able to identify an expansion of the settlement outwards to the west, occurring from Phase III to Phase II. The utilization of this rather unfavourable sloped space in Phase II, after the emptiness of Phase III, supports the idea that the entire site was expanding and houses were being placed in non-optimal locations. However, this visible expansion may be due to a small-scale, localized restructuring of this particular part of the neighbourhood.

Within our excavations, we did not identify anything that could be considered a sub-division of the settlement, larger than a house yet smaller than a neighbourhood, an aggregate of houses that might indicate a large extended family. However, when combined with Mallowan's excavations, we have been able to delineate two blocks of houses that appear to have been more closely linked, within what was already a tightly-connected neighbourhood (see below).

Synthesis of old and new excavations

Analysis of Mallowan's excavation in Area BD and reconstruction of correspondence between old and modern excavations have entailed a dissection of Mallowan's published reports, plans and schematic sections. We have achieved a reorganisation and conjoining of plans, plus a clarification of the correspondence between the BD plan and stratigraphic section as published by Mallowan (Mallowan 1937: Figs. 5, 6, respectively). As well as excavation in Area G, a comprehensive surface scraping in 2002 allowed 'fine-tuning' of the equivalent phases in Areas G and BD. It is within Mallowan's Intermediate level, corresponding to Phases II-III of the modern Area G excavations, that there is the most logical interface between the architecture recovered in Areas G and BD.

To facilitate the synthesis of the modern excavations with those of Mallowan, all rooms and built spaces have been labelled by Area and Building, *i.e.* Building G 1, Building BD 2. The labels indicate which buildings were entirely excavated by Mallowan (BD), which are a combination of Mallowan's work and the modern excavations (BDG), and which were solely exposed by the modern excavations (G).

Complementing this is the attached building number, which apart from identifying a distinct structure, is also temporal–the higher the number in the sequence, the earlier the phase of occupation to which it belongs.

Evolution in the morphology of the quarter and its buildings is visible in the variability and change across its phases and sub-phases. Phase distinctions usually entailed the re-building of structures with new walls on previous alignments and the maintenance of original ground plans, but phase changes also incorporated the relocation of doorways, superimposition of multiple occupational floors, and the new construction of stone pavements and drains that may indicate shifts in room function. Mallowan (1937: 110) reports that the structures of BD had mud-plastered walls, beaten earth floors and irregular limestone stone pavements, all features encountered in our excavations. The space in this residential area was intensely used, in both horizontal and vertical aspects.

Cultural material from Area G includes domestic artifacts for food preparation (basalt grindstones, mortars and pestles), lithics (obsidian and flint) and metal objects, tokens, jewellery and numerous animal figurines. Together with the ceramic assemblage, these items allow a general date of early 2nd millennium BC to be assigned. Unfortunately, there is no direct dating evidence (tablets or inscribed seals) from Area G. Judging from depths of deposit and generalized stratigraphy, at least three of our four phases lie above the lowest BD level in which Mallowan found the tablets dateable to Samsi-Addu. Thus, as in Area A, most of the neighborhood belongs to the post-Samsi-Addu political era.

Phasing in Areas G and BD

As mentioned above, four distinct architectural phases were identified in Area G; our Phase II was further subdivided into two sub-phases, 1 and 2^3. The phases are in each case marked by significant architectural changes, such as the razing and replacement of several walls simultaneously, or changes in building plan. But the phase changes are in a sense also somewhat arbitrary, since other walls continued in use, or one building may have retained its plan from phase to the next, while its neighbour was altered. Urban sites have long been acknowledged as loci of continuous construction and adaptation, and the same can be said for smaller "town" settlements in this region. The phase divisions identified here were the best way to allow the narrative of change and continuity to be written.

Phase I, the final phase near the surface, was preserved only at the northern end of Area G. Erosion near the centre of Area G also cut away some parts of Phase II/1. Phase IV, the earliest phase recovered, could only be explored in a limited area near the centre of Area G.

As outlined above, Mallowan's five sub-phases of Level 1 were: Early, Early Intermediate, Intermediate, Late and Latest. His "Early" corresponded to the Tablet Building at the southwest end of Area TD. Although it is unclear from the published plan, his section (and the still-visible sloped topography of the northern mound ridge) indicates that the rest of Area BD was never excavated to the same depth and level. The settlement arrangement to the north of and contemporary with the Tablet Building thus remains rather uncertain. In the large-scale schematic view of the site's stratigraphy, Mallowan's Early phase was assumed to have been the initial early 2nd millennium BC

---

[3] Part of Phase II/1 was additionally characterized by a renovation, Phase II/1A, limited to one location near the centre of Area G.

occupation[4]. Yet would a public building with an archive have been the first structure established on the site? There may yet be occupation that precedes the Tablet Building there or elsewhere.

Within TD, the "Early Intermediate" phase consisted of levelling, a platform, building foundations and graves—not particularly useful for establishing relationships with our Area G phases. More important for making the connection between Areas TD, BD and G, the "Temple Palace at the northern end of Chagar Bazar" (the north end of Area BD) was identified as built in this phase. The "Intermediate" phase is associated with the greatest occupation of the site; the "Late" phase is described as poorly preserved; while the "Latest" phase is represented only by fragmentary floors[5]. The limited amount of architecture recovered in Mallowan's final two phases and our own final phase had become more 'rustic' in both technique and ambition with thinner, flimsier walls and irregular limestone pavements. This situation complements that indicated by the thinner and more dispersed occupation of Area A in Phase I; together this evidence indicates that the site was gradually de-occupied rather than suddenly abandoned.

Table 3.1 Area BD, Area G and Area A Phase Equivalences[6]

Mallowan's Area BD	BSAI Area G	BSAI Area A
Latest	Upper material in Phase I? Surface materials?	Latest features in I?
Late	Phase I	I
Intermediate	Phase II/2 and II/1	II
Early Intermediate	Phase III-IV?	III
Early	Phase IV?	

Description of Area G
Phase IV

This is the earliest phase excavated in Area G. A single wall was exposed, at the northern edge of Trench G II (01-41; Fig. 20). The wall is on virtually the same alignment as the walls of Phases III through I, ENE-WSW. Here it must be acknowledged that this is a traditional alignment for structures across this region in many periods, because of wind and weather factors[7]. But the construction method and details are similar in this wall and in later phases; the bricks are the same standard sizes, mortar thickness is the same, brick-laying technique is the same, and so on. All these aspects speak to considerable continuity of building traditions over time. If this phase is nearly contemporary with the Mallowan's Tablet Building in Area TD, it is notable that

---

[4] His Level 2 is a mixed layer that may represent eroded 3rd millennium BC occupation but also might incorporate sparse but genuine early 2nd millennium BC reoccupation.

[5] Mallowan (1937: 114) reports that the top of Level 2 lay at 8.5 m below the benchmark (the French 1930s survey marker that sits at the site's highest point, atop the south mound). He also indicates that the levels in the southern end of Area BD were around a metre higher than their contemporaries in the north: he provides an elevation of 6 to 5m below the benchmark for his Intermediate level and 4 to 3 metres below benchmark for his Late phase. However, these elevation figures were found to be too vague to be useful for synthesizing the old and new excavations.

[6] The connections between BD and G are supported by architectural and stratigraphic evidence; direct connections with the Phases in Area A are not possible, so these connections are made on the basis of material culture and generalized site development and must remain speculative.

[7] Comparable ENE-WSW alignments appear in contemporary buildings at Tell Arbid, Tell Mozan, Tell Mohammed Diyab and Tell Hamad Agha as-Saghir, among other sites (see below).

the alignment of houses and that public building (with its north-south and east-west walls) were differentiated.

Wall 01-41 lies only slightly south of the southern wall of Building G 1 of Phase II, actually crossing under its western end on a slightly more eastern alignment. This locational consistency supports the notion of continuity of property plots. This wall appears to have been deliberately razed to the same height along most of its length, and the upper bricks were simply removed for reuse or discard elsewhere–there is no fallen brick deposit associated with the wall on either side. It is possible that the upper bricks were recycled for use in Phase III buildings. Locus 75, to its south, may have been an open space, while Locus 74, on its north, was the interior of the building.

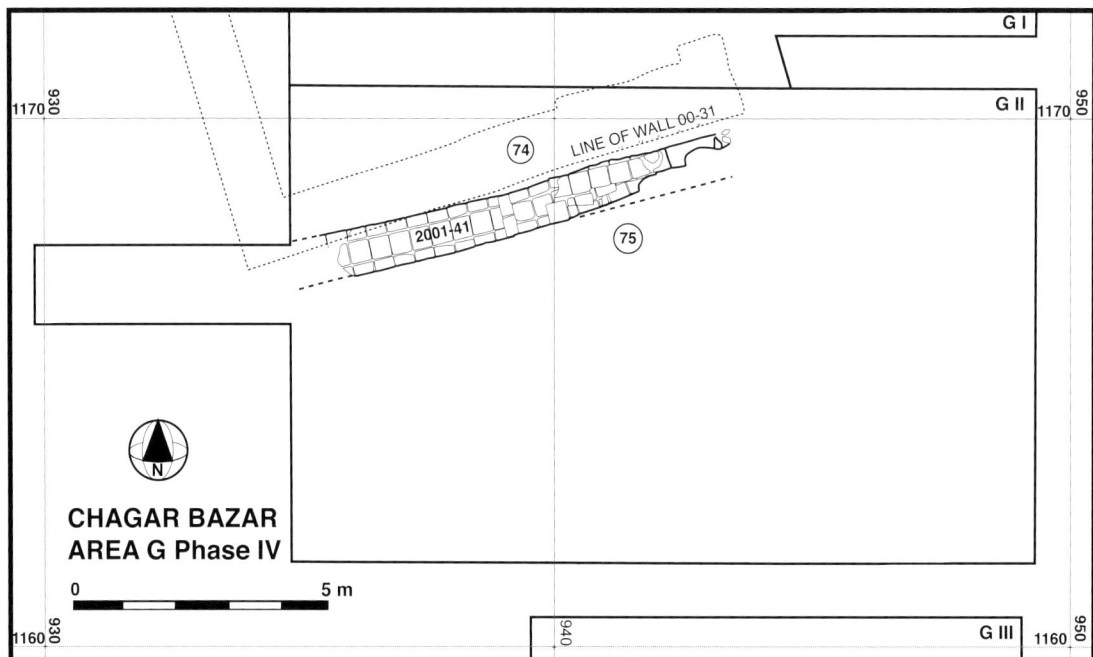

Figure 20: Plan of Area G Phase IV (Trench G II only); overlying Phase II wall shown as dashed line

Phase III

This phase was exposed in both Trenches G IV and G II. Despite no great horizontal separation, the trenches provide a notable contrast, with substantial architecture present entirely across G IV at the north, while open space at the settlement edge and more irregular architecture prevail in G II to the south (see Fig. 21). This phase probably corresponds to Mallowan's Early Intermediate, but this link is based primarily on more solid connections above this level, between our Phase II and his Intermediate Phase.

The morphology of occupation in this phase was similar to the subsequent phases, with the north-south alleyway at the northern end of our excavation (Trench G IV) forming the axis along which plots on either side were structured. In Trench G II, the eastern side of what would become the alley has been established, but the buildings open out into an un-built area to the west, presumably one means of access into this portion of the settlement, as well as a locus for rubbish disposal and small-scale activities.

Area G Architecture

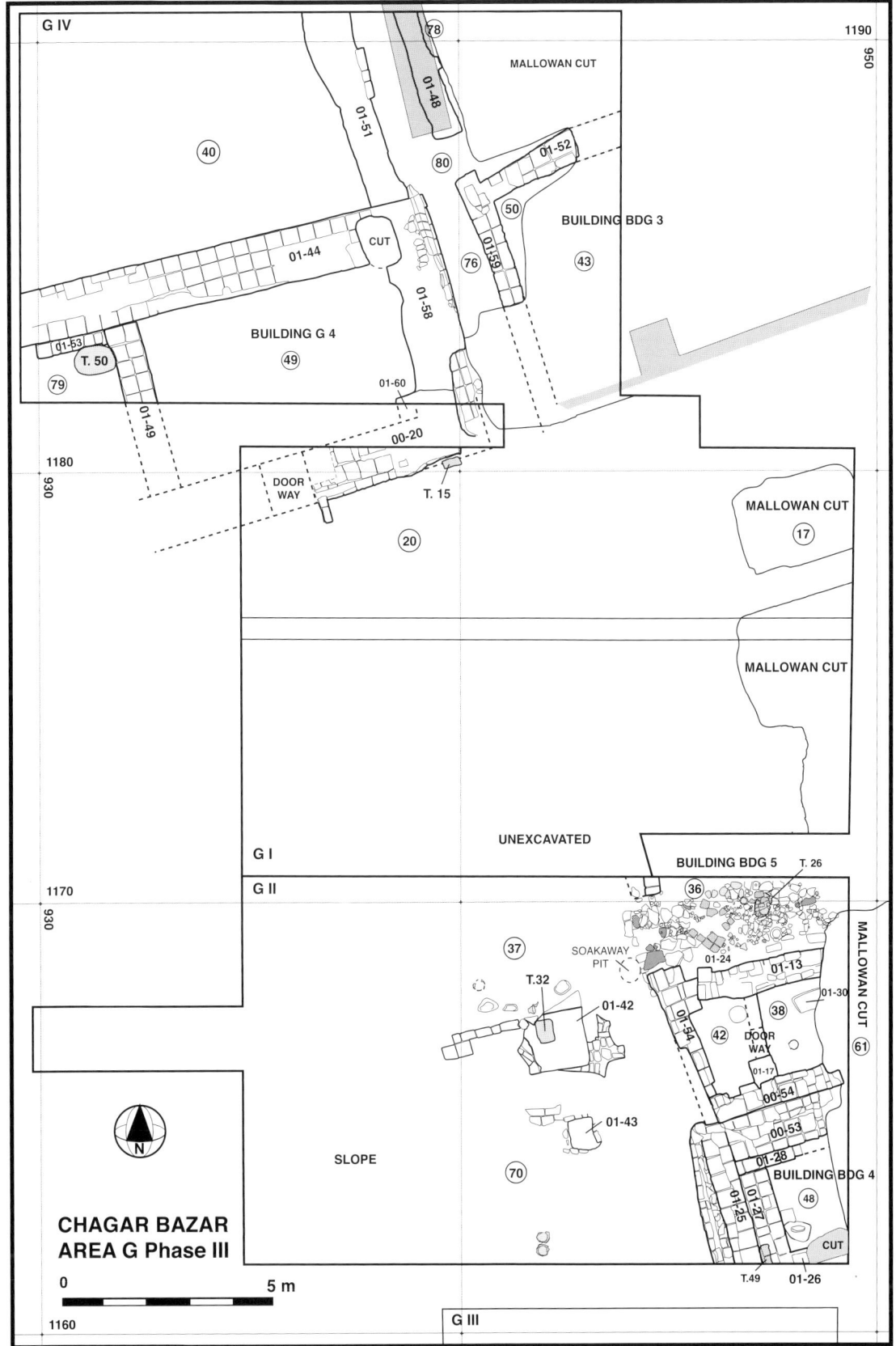

Figure 21: Plan of Area G, Phase III, including probable connecting Mallowan walls (shaded)

In Phase III, the organisation of built space on the ridge was relatively expansive, with large courtyards, open areas and under-utilised plots. The axial alley at the north

(Locus 76) separated two buildings: a large and well-constructed long rectangular house on the west (Building G 4), and a less substantial house on the east, cut by Mallowan's excavation and post-1930s erosion (Building BDG 3). The outer walls of Building G 4 are among the most massive in all phases of Area G, three bricks wide and potentially sufficient to support a second storey. A narrower 2-brick wide internal wall divides the long rectangular space into two rooms, Loci 49 and 79. The courtyard or open space (Locus 40) to the north of this building may or may not belong to it; the north wall of the building forms the southern boundary of this open area, but no doorway connected the two. The north and east walls of Building G 4 (01-44 and 01-58, respectively) are unbroken by doorways, so the means of access into this building is unclear. The southern wall (00-20) had suffered some damage due to its partial re-use and modification during the subsequent Phase II. An entrance doorway into the eastern room (Locus 49) in this southern wall seems probable, and the modifications of Phase II may have included constructing a filling wall within that doorway.

Access into the western room, Locus 79, may have been via another doorway along the southern façade or, more probably, through the internal dividing wall. This room has a narrow brick bench or storage shelf in its north corner. A poorly preserved grave with mixed bones of both an older adult and a child and without grave goods (Tomb 50) had been interred below the earliest floor in the same corner. The open area to the south of Building G 4 (L. 20) saw another burial, an infant placed against the southern face of Wall 00-20 (Tomb 15).

The courtyard to the north of Building G 4 (L. 40) was bounded to the east along the alleyway by a thick (0.75-1 metre) pisè wall. In this and the following phase, a large quantity of ash was deposited in this area, which extends to at least 10 m by 10 m. The ash did not contain slag or industrial waste but incorporated large pottery sherds and broken mud-brick fragments and was most probably derived from oven rake-out from several of the surrounding buildings; this further suggests that it was not associated exclusively with Building G 4 but was communally accessible space.

On the eastern side of the alley at the north, we exposed only the northwest corner of one room or courtyard of Building BDG 3 (Locus 50). Wall construction was less substantial than in Building G 4: one brick or two half-bricks wide. Mallowan's plan shows a bewildering variety of features located near the southeast corner of our Trench G IV which may be relevant to this eastern building: a patch of stone paving, a pipe (?) drain (apparently traced for c 15 m), and at least two phases of architecture indicated by stacked walls. The stone paving is impossible to assign to a phase, but the drain surely belongs with the upper of the two phases of architecture shown (it runs along a wall and through the doorway in a wall which clearly overlaps a lower wall). From evidence further south in Trenches G I and G II, we have surmised that most of the architecture shown in Mallowan's plan is contemporary with our Phase II, leaving the very fragmentary lower (overlapped) architecture he represents in his published plans to be associated with our Phase III. If this is the case, there is a wall approximately parallel to our wall 01-52 at the north side of Locus 50, potentially providing the room's southern limit. This wall has a perpendicular wall stub that seems to indicate the presence of an internal doorway (Mallowan's walls are shaded grey in Fig. 21).

Mallowan's plan also shows a probable Phase III NW-SE wall at the north edge of our Trench G IV; at least, one wall of the several located here on his plan is overlapped by others and is clearly the earliest element uncovered in this location. This wall is on the same alignment and in approximately same location as our wall 01-48 on the east side of the alley (also shaded grey in Fig. 21). The inaccuracies in Mallowan's plan and measurements and the difficulty in matching our plan make the slight variance acceptable.

The situation in Trench G II is very different from that in Trench G IV. The architecture is ranged along the eastern edge of our trench, facing out onto an open space to the west. This open space (Loci 37 and 70) was dotted with small features: an infant burial (T. 32), a plastered platform (01-42) and an associated small wind-break of mudbricks, and a plastered basin-like area (01-43). Ash lenses and burned areas were frequent across the space, and the sherd discard was moderately dense, including several nearly-whole vessels. Surfaces were intermittent and undulating but generally have a strong slope down to the southwest, indicating that this area was surely at the ancient settlement edge. The alley does not appear in this part of the settlement at this level, but it is significant for property lines and access that the facades of the Phase III architecture closely correspond to the eastern boundary walls of the alley in later phases. There are two buildings: BDG 5 at the north and BDG 4 at the south. Building BDG 5 has a stone- and sherd-paved courtyard (Locus 36) alongside a pair of very small rooms on its south (Loci 42 and 38). A wide doorway with a stone sill provided access between the open space Locus 37 and the courtyard, Locus 36. The paving in the courtyard was haphazardly arranged and consisted mostly of unworked limestone, with baked bricks and baked brick fragments, occasional basalt cobbles and stones and frequent sherds. The doorsill covered a drainage channel that emptied out into a vertical soakaway pit packed with sherds in Locus 37 (L. 37.5). Access from the courtyard to the two rooms on its south was unclear, but the separating wall (01-13) was not well preserved, and its apparently solid outline may conceal a mud-brick threshold and a step down allowing traffic between the courtyard and Locus 38. Both rooms (Loci 42 and 38) contained small plastered features; the thin wall that separated them was poorly preserved, but a doorway there could be traced.

Figure 22: Area G, Phase III: Building BDG 5 from northwest

This building was razed for the construction of a building in Phase II/2 (Building BDG 1), and a preparatory layer (L. 27), comprising broken mud-bricks and grey soil, was laid over its top. This layer included an infant burial (Tomb 26), possibly a stillborn or neo-nate in a very poor state of preservation.

In Trench G II's southeast corner, only the northwest corner of one room of Building BDG 4 was exposed: two sub-phases are visible, including a lower phase in which brick benches were built on at least three sides of the room (Locus 48, benches

01-26, 01-27 and 01-28), and a plaster basin was set into the floor. In the upper phase these benches and basin had been covered by built-up occupational deposit (Locus 44). The western, outer, wall of the building (01-25) had been carefully constructed on a two-course foundation of stones, including blocks of common limestone and an unusual grey-green sandstone. An additional row of mud-bricks was laid against the outer edge of this foundation. Use of stone for foundations in Area G (and across the entire site) is unique to this wall; no other wall was thus built, nor does Mallowan mention finding this technique within his excavations. It is probable that this was a protective measure, given that the wall faced an open area at the settlement edge and would have been subject to erosion from rain, traffic and water percolation. The northern wall of the room and the internal benches were built of standard bricks.

Figure 23: Area G Phase III, Building BDG 4 from west

An infant grave (Tomb 49) was cut from within the lower sub-phase of III, parallel and adjacent to wall 01-25, sealed by the corner of benches 01-26 and 01-27. Except for the disarticulated and fragmentary adult skeleton in Tomb 50, all the graves from this phase were of infants.

Phase II

This was the phase on which our work in Area G concentrated and which can be connected to architecture uncovered by Mallowan (his Intermediate Phase). This is the phase immediately visible below the surface across most of the Area BD-G excavations. We identified two sub-phases within Phase II: II/1 (upper) and II/2 (lower). The dominant features of this phase were construction of two possibly single-roomed buildings in Trenches G I and II, which persisted through both sub-phases (Buildings G 1 and G 2), along with the establishment of the north-south alley across the full extent of our excavations. There is a notable difference in the buildings on either side of the alley in both sub-phases; those on the western, outer side have more massive walls and a larger scale when contrasted to the more irregular multi-room structures on the eastern side.

Phase II/2

In Trench G IV at the north end of our excavations, the massive Building G 4 of Phase III was replaced by a slightly smaller-scale building on the same alignment (Building G 2) in Phase II/2 (see Fig. 24). Despite damage to its western end, this building is best reconstructed as a single rectangular room (Locus 73); we have placed its western end so that the building is comparable in scale to Building G 1 further south (see below). A door in the shorter eastern façade, near the southeast corner, is a feature of both Buildings G 2 and G 1. Unlike its Phase III predecessor, Building G 2 was set back from the alley and separated from it by a linked courtyard, defined by a very narrow ephemeral wall (01-19 and 00-19). The area of the courtyard immediately in front of the building's entrance may have been a covered veranda (L. 32), as it possessed clean occupational surfaces of the type normally seen in interior spaces, with a small hearth and traces of white plaster on the exterior of the building's eastern wall (01-46). The L-shaped courtyard continues around to the south of the building within Trench G I (there designated as Loci 4 and 9) and uses the north wall of Building G 1 as its southern boundary. A doorway connects the courtyard to the alley, offset from the doorway to the room for privacy. North of Building G 2, the upper layers of Locus 40 are featureless ash layers identical to the deposit in Phase III. This ash was bounded on the east by a rebuilt pisé wall which prevented it sifting into the alley; and an attempt had been made on the south edge to separate the ash from the north wall of Building G 2, by the construction of a 1-brick-wide wall (01-16). Any buildings on the opposite, eastern, side of the alley in G IV were completely removed by Mallowan's excavation; his plan in this location shows an open space with a patch of stone paving (in his Room 24) that may be a courtyard associated with a building further south (Building BDG 2, see below).

Within Trenches G I and II, Phase II/2 saw the construction of a second large and single-roomed building, better preserved than that in Trench G IV (Building G 1). Both its northern and southern walls were massive and were set into shallow foundation trenches, the only instance of this technique in Area G. The interior of the walls bore thick white plaster, and the two preserved mud floors were very clean, with minimal pottery or objects. The only preserved doorway was placed on its southeast corner and links the room directly to the street, so the building appears to be–unusually for the site and the region–unattached to a courtyard or subsidiary rooms (at least not directly). However, a courtyard lies to the south of the room (Locus 51) and on analogy with the arrangement of room and southern courtyard in Building G 2, discussed above, this southern courtyard could be linked to Building G 1. There may have been a second door in the destroyed section of the southern wall of the building that would have connected the two spaces.

Chapter 3

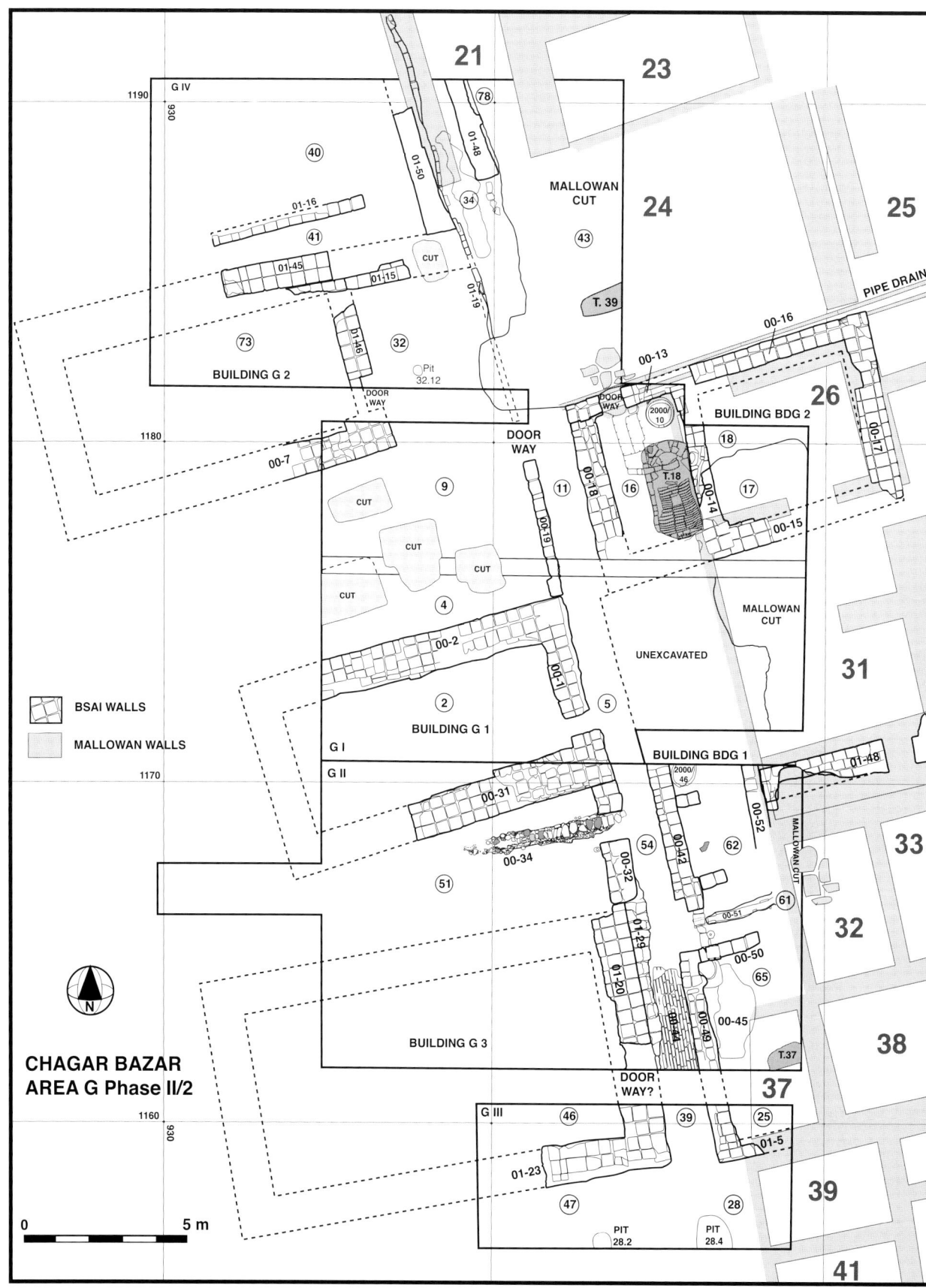

Figure 24: Plan of Area G, Phase II/2

From the walls preserved, the courtyard appears to be a massive 10 meters from north to south (extending into Trench G III) and it is bounded on the east and south by walls that are unusually heavy for courtyard walls (01-20 and 01-23), equal in scale and in care of construction to the walls of Buildings G 1 and G 2 (three neatly-laid bricks wide). Because of the erosion in the south-western quadrant of Trench G II, we cannot be certain that these walls do not in fact belong to another building, Building G 3, most of which has been lost to erosion or even was deliberately removed at some point in the past[8]. A stone-lined and stone–capped drain (00-34) leads out from the northeast corner of the courtyard, sloping down into the alley (Locus 54; Fig. 25). The built channel is roughly square-sectioned, and the area within the trench, outside the channel, is filled with a dense mixture of small sherds and kiln slag. The courtyard had layers of occupational material similar to that in the courtyard associated with Building G 2 (Loci 4 and 9), with intermittent surfaces and ashy lenses.

Figure 25: Drain 00-34 in courtyard of Building G 2, from west

The buildings on the eastern side of the alley mostly offer a contrast to the large, rectangular and probably single-room buildings on the west: smaller rooms, thinner walls and the presence of ovens, stone pavings and other small-scale and ephemeral features. The northernmost of the buildings we exposed, in the northeast corner of Trench G I, has two rooms in a rectangular plan only slightly smaller than

---

[8] This hypothetical building has been reconstructed and labeled Building G 3 on the plan (Fig. 24); however it is by no means a certainty. The orientation of the preserved walls in Trench G III (01-20 & 01/23 is not the same as those of Building G I, with the result that any courtyard between them would have narrowed significantly at its western end, creating a trapezoidal shape not seen elsewhere on the site or at other sites in the region, where most spaces at least seek to achieve the rectangular. The placement of the drain (00-34), however, would fit rather well with a significantly narrower courtyard.

Buildings G 1 and 2 (Building BDG 2)[9]. This building's western wall flanked the alley, but its entrance doorway lies at the western end of the longer northern façade, leading from an open space delineated by Mallowan (his Room 24) into a small room (Locus 16). The long pipe drain indicated by Mallowan would have run along and parallel to the northern wall, presumably just below ground, emptying into the alley on the west.[10]

The lowest floor in the entrance room of BDG 2 (Locus 16) sealed a large burial pit with a vaulted mud-brick chamber (Tomb 18). The brick chamber was roughly rectangular, with an "apsidal" northern end. The barrel vault was made of thin orange bricks. Despite the significant effort that went into construction of this tomb, it was empty (see Ch. 4). The floor that sealed the tomb was associated with a large circular oven in the northeast corner of the room (Fig. 26). As occupational layers built up there, effort was made to maintain access to the oven and to its stoke-hole at the original floor level, by a series of "steps" cut into the occupational layers and a low brick partition wall built above the grave. Since ovens do not have long life-spans, it appears that the floor build-up here was quite rapid. The small size of the room, with much of the floor area then lost to the oven and its steps, and this rapid accumulation of material, indicate that this space was probably given over to exclusive use as a kitchen (rather than being a multi-purpose room including cooking among other functions).

Figure 26: Oven 00-10 and steps in Locus 16, Building BDG 2, from south

---

[9] The eastern room of this building lies to the east of our excavations, where the walls were clearly visible on the surface after scraping; their alignments and the room size they delineate match near-perfectly with Room 26 of Mallowan's plan, although his plan shows both southern and northern doorways we did not identify.

[10] We did not recover any traces of this drain, and Mallowan does not give any details of its construction. However, his plan shows the drain as a series of short parallel segments, such as would be appropriate for a pipe drain.

The temporal conjuncture of burial place followed shortly by kitchen use is startling, but perhaps the fact of the grave being empty allowed such a sudden function shift[11]. The wall which separates this room from that on its east (L. 18) was damaged by erosion following Mallowan's emptying of that eastern room (his 26). The northern and eastern boundary walls of that room were still visible at the mound surface, but very little occupational material remained *in situ* belonging to this sub-phase. This building was abutted on the eastern end by a small square room or storage area[12]. Since it was apparently open on its northern side, this was probably a roofed 'veranda' for storage or craft activities. It continued to be used in the subsequent phase. We propose that the empty space in Mallowan's plan north of Building BDG 2 (Room 24, c 6 meters across) was a courtyard attached to it. A patch of stone paving is shown there, directly in front of the doorway in Locus 16. This is impossible to assign to a phase but could imply an enclosed but unroofed space or more specifically could be a paved doorway covering the drain. No trace of this paving is preserved at present, but Mallowan's cut was clearly definable in this area. A burial of a teenager (Tomb 39) lies just north of this paving.

A set of small rooms, possibly parts of two separate buildings, lies along the eastern side of the street in Trenches G II-III (Building BDG 1). The northern of the two is a thin rectangular room (Locus 62), further sub-divided by two wall stubs abutting its western wall. The northern segment of this space contains a small oven, while a basalt slab in the southern segment might have been used as a low seat for kitchen work. At the south end of the room, a drain leads out below a doorsill into the street, from an area or room lying further east within Mallowan's excavation (00-51). The drain existed only as a square-sectioned and almost-empty channel, but a few small stones in situ and impressions of larger stones indicate it was originally of comparable construction to the drain in Locus 51, stone-lined and stone-capped. Presumably the stones had been removed and recycled into paving or later drains. Three door-sockets, stacked in precisely the same location at the southern door-jamb, are associated with three identified floors in this space. South of this, a final room (Loci 65/25) was possibly part of a different house, although its narrow northern wall also acts as the southern wall of Locus 62. A patch of stone pebble paving against the western wall (00-45) indicates that this was an unroofed space, a small courtyard. A plaster basin was built in the north-west corner. An adult grave (Tomb 37) lies in this courtyard space, following the established pattern in the neighbourhood of courtyard intramural burials.

The precise link of these southern walls with Mallowan's plan is less clear than for Building BDG 2. His plan for this location shows a range of rectangular rooms to the east and south of our excavations, but none has a doorway and the outlines of separate buildings were not given. A Mallowan wall visible on the mound surface (01-48) abuts our wall 00-52, rather than bonding with it, but such construction technique can happen within houses as internal modifications are made, and this does not necessarily imply that these walls belong to separate buildings. The wall drawn in Mallowan's plan in this location, however, is extremely wide, probably indicating two adjacent and parallel walls; our surface scraping here did not reveal any trace of a second wall. Without an additional row of rooms associated, the rooms within Area G would have made an unusually and extremely narrow house. Thus it

---

[11] Area A Building I shows a similar *volte face* in function: burial (T. 4) in one sub-phase topped by stabling use in the next. Ideas of post-interment burial sanctity in the early 2nd millennium BC clearly were fluid.

[12] Its walls (02-8 and 02-9) were recovered by surface scraping in 2002.

seems plausible to link the set of rooms delineated by Mallowan to our rooms and to identify them as a single Building BDG 1.

The alley from north to south was dense in sherds, disarticulated animal bones and discarded broken objects, within a silty and ashy matrix comprising many discontinuous lenses and surfaces. An unusual feature was present within the alley at its southern end, in the southern quarter of Trench G II and within Trench G III. This was what appeared to be a deliberately-constructed mass of mud-bricks, laid on their edges, which filled the complete width of the alley (00-44; Fig. 27). After considering whether this might have been an attempt to block the alley, a platform, or a segment of paving designed to raise the ground level in the alley, we propose that this was simply fallen bricks which had been so well-constructed that they retained their association even when collapsed. Their regularity may indicate that their parent wall was deliberately knocked over, rather than allowed to deteriorate gradually. Ten courses are preserved in the width of the alley, representing what would have been a height of just one meter. Above these bricks and along the western side of the alley, against the east face of wall 01-20, a veneer of slanting bricks was laid, probably protecting this wall against erosion. The same wall seems to be the most likely parent wall for the fallen bricks, if that wall originally defined a building (our proposed Building G 3) that went out of use and was remodelled into a courtyard.

Figure 27: Alley in Area G, from south, with fallen mud-brick in foreground

A similar area of on-side bricks was clearly identifiable on the surface at the eastern edge of Mallowan's BD excavation. This on-side collapse phenomenon appears in contemporary levels at nearby sites. At Tell Barri, a well-arranged area of bricks on their sides has been identified as a pavement (Period 5, Pavimentazione 445; Pecorella 1998: Fig. 20). At Tell Muhammad Diyab there are many similar patches of bricks indicated on the sections and identified as fallen walls (mur écroulé; Durand 1992: Coupe CD, Coupe IJ). This raises the question of whether the composition of the bricks or mortar in this period was unusually strong, which allows walls to be so well-preserved after collapse, or whether it was the way the walls were deliberately razed that makes this peculiar pavement-like arrangement occur so frequently. Comparable areas of fallen mud-bricks with well-preserved relationships, dated to the Middle Bronze Age at Salat Tepe in the Ilusu Dam reservoir basin, have been attributed to an earthquake-caused collapse (Ökse 2007). However, comparable patches of on-side mud-bricks appear again later in the 2nd millennium BC, within deliberately razed Mitanni houses in Area HN at Tell Brak (pers. obs. 2006) and in a Mitanni level at Tell Arbid (Bielinski 2002: 310-311, Fig. 9).

The area south of the buildings and the alley, in Trench G III, may have been an open area (Loci 28, 47), to judge by the small pits and trampled surfaces. These surfaces, like those in the open area of Phase III below (L. 37) sloped down from northeast to southwest, and we may again have revealed the edge of the ancient settlement.

The houses delineated by Mallowan include Building BD 1, a 4-room large house east of Building BDG 1 that would have been one of the largest houses in this neighbourhood (see Fig. 19: Mallowan's Rooms 30, 34, 35, 36, approximately 17.5 x 14.5 metres). A 2-roomed rectangular house, Building BD 2, lay to its south (Mallowan's Rooms 43 and 44/45), and a much smaller 4-room house (Building BD 3) lay directly south of BDG 1 (Rooms 39-42). Together these four houses would have formed a discrete block within the neighbourhood, sharing a core north-south party wall. However, despite their tight co-operative clustering, this core party wall meant that the entrances would have been split between east (east edge of Mallowan's excavations: BD 1 and BD 2) and west (the Area G alley: BDG 1 and BD 3).

Beyond the north end of Area G, the 2002 surface scraping defined several walls, including those of a small square room we have tentatively linked to Mallowan's Room 18 (see Fig. 19). Together with Room 17 on its west, this may be yet another long rectangular building comparable to Buildings G 1, G 2 and BDG 2. North and west of this building lie at least two, and possibly three, multi-roomed houses (Rooms 1-11, 13-16, 19-20). This group also forms a tight, linked block with party walls and is separated from the southern group by a wide open space which may have been collectively owned, to judge by the dumping of ash at the north end of Trench G IV.

Phase II/1

This sub-phase retains earlier spatial layouts and structures, continuing to maintain the integrity of the north-south alley and of the individual plot boundaries (Fig. 28). The buildings on the eastern side of the alley remained substantially the same, and new features were created in the buildings on the west of the alley. The northern end of Area G remained in use for ash dumping, with further walls and features designed to contain this unstable material. Deposits in the alley (Loci 34, 11, 5, 54, from north to south) continued to be rich in sherds, animal bones and discarded objects, within fine water-laid layers that sloped up to the walls on either side and were trodden down in the centre.

Both single-roomed buildings on the western side of the alley (Buildings G 1 and G 2) continue in use during the upper sub-phase of II. Building G 2 had its northern wall rebuilt (01-8), and subdivisions were made within its northeast corner, creating two bins (01-31 and 01-32). Further modifications were made to the space north of G 2 (lower layers of L. 33), which still seems to be communal space for ash and rubbish disposal. An additional wall was built in the southern courtyard along the south wall of Building G 2 (00-11-12); although it is quite substantial this wall may simply be part of the brick capping of an adult grave, Tomb 13.

Chapter 3

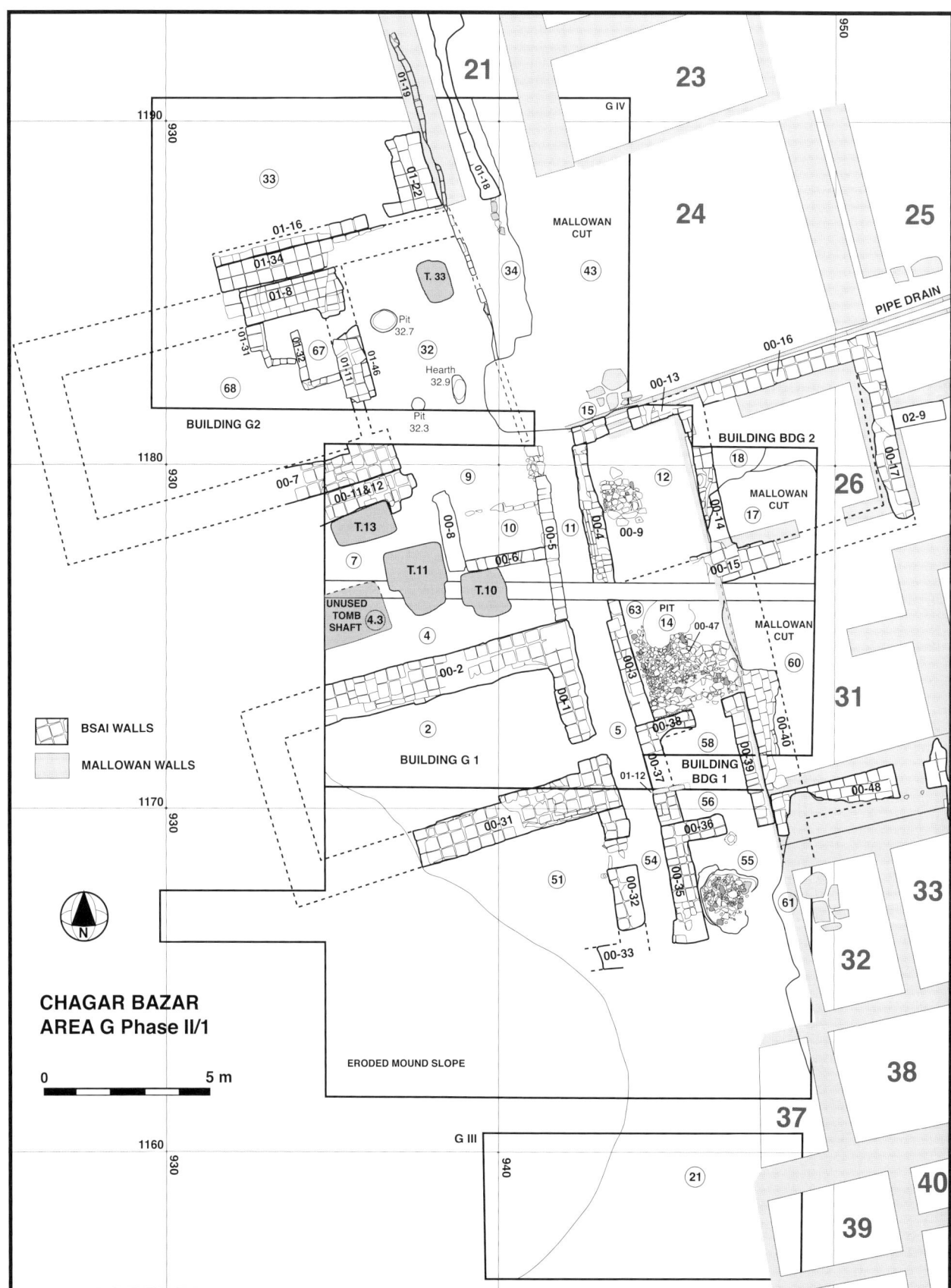

Figure 28: Plan of Area G, Phase II/1

The courtyard to east and south of Building G 2 (Locus 32 at the north, Loci 4, 7 and 9 at the south) was maintained with the same outline. However, part of the wall separating the courtyard from the street was rebuilt at this sub-phase (00-5, with a doorsill of unworked limestone blocks), and the southeast quadrant of the courtyard was further subdivided by construction of three small walls, enclosing an ash dump (L. 10), probable hearth rake-out that was notably free of sherds or other rubbish. The northeast portion of this ash deposit was stained a grey-green colour that probably indicates its use as an informal toilet. Ash–particularly from dung fuel–can be "valuable" as fertilizer, so it seems probable that this was a temporary storage bin, comparable to a modern compost heap. Its relatively small scale suggests use of the ash in garden production, rather than in larger fields. The layers within the southern portion of the courtyard (Loci 4, 7 & 9) were quite ashy, with sloping lenses and intermittent surfaces that indicate the courtyard was not regularly swept. The high number of discarded objects (figurines, stone tools and metal items; see Ch. 6) supports this theory.

The most notable feature of this courtyard was the presence of three adult burials (Tombs 10, 11 and 13) and one possible burial shaft (the rectangular pit L. 4.3), all located in the area south of the room and west of the ash bin. Tomb 13, at the north, appears to have been the first interment (in a mud-brick vaulted tomb), followed by Tombs 10 and 11, which were buried at virtually the same time. The final possible grave pit (L. 4.3) had been cut near the end of this phase[13], possibly contemporary with the Phase II/1A modification to Building BDG 1 (see below and Ch. 4 for descriptions of all graves). The clustering of graves near to each other and in this area of the courtyard is probably deliberate, to set them aside from the presumed main traffic route across the courtyard to the building's doorway (Fig. 29). The grouping also means a shift in space use and a degree of functional restriction within this location; yet the closeness of the immediately adjacent ash bin indicates that the grave area did not hold excessive sanctity. A further child's grave, Tomb 33, was cut into the courtyard near the northeast corner. The frequency of courtyard burials can be seen as the practice of an established and permanent family occupation.

To the south, Building G 1 continued in use, and there was still a courtyard lying to its south (L. 51). It remained essentially unmodified during this phase (although a mud-brick sill in the doorway to the alley belongs to this phase). Erosion was more severe at this elevation, and much of the southern end of Trench G II held no preserved architecture of this or the subsequent phase. There is some indication of a cross-wall having been built in the courtyard in this phase (00-33), which may mark a further sub-division of this space. The upper fill in the room of Building G 1 held fallen mud-brick, and its walls, although preserved to a reasonable height of c 1.5 m, were flat at the top as if they had been deliberately razed. This building may indeed have stood as a ruin for a brief time, and the brick fill was placed during Phase I, when the occupation in this area was clustered further north.

---

[13] Pit 4.3 is here identified as a grave shaft because of its size and regular rectangular shape; it also held a complete wide-mouth vessel (CB 1989); it is probable that the bell-shaped pit would have been cut to the west of the pit's base.

Chapter 3

Figure 29: Courtyard of Building G 2 at right, Building BDG 2 at left, stone paving 00-47 at rear left, from north

The smaller multi-roomed structures on the east side of the alley persist into this sub-phase from II/2, with scattered modifications. It is also possible to identify a further sub-phase within II/1 (identified as II/1A) in some rooms. At the northern end, in Building BDG 2, the large oven of Phase II/2 went out of use and that room (Locus 12) was given a partial stone paving (00-9); resting on this paving was a group of four hammerstone/ whetstones, which indicate a shift in use of this space from cooking to tool production or another small-scale manufacturing activity (CB 1944-1947; see Ch. 6). Its western wall (00-18 in II/2) had been razed and rebuilt as wall 00-4, on the same alignment but slightly further to the west, actually slightly encroaching on the alley. The new wall was thinner than the underlying wall in II/2 and this, together with the stone paving, may signal a change from roofed to unroofed space. The eastern room of this pair apparently remained unmodified, as far as it was preserved (Locus 18). The open area or courtyard to the north of this house also remained the same.

South of this, lying across Trenches G I and II, a north-south line of three rooms was present in this phase (the upper phase of Building BDG 1). The north room (Locus 63) has a wall-to-wall stone paving (Figs. 29, 30). The paving has two elements: a tightly-packed surface of relatively small cobbles, mostly limestone but with an admixture of basalt and baked brick fragments, over most of the room, plus a slightly raised area of larger limestone flags at the south end only, in front of the doorway into the central room, Locus 56/58. A second unroofed space (L. 55), with a partial stone paving of mixed baked bricks, basalt and limestone, lay to the south of the centre room. The two doorways connecting these three spaces were on the same line. This direct alignment of doorways is fairly unusual in the region and, combined with the small size of Locus 56/58, reduces this room's potential range of functions (since any activities would be directly in any flow of traffic). A pipe drain (01-12) ran below the western wall (00-37) and into the street (L. 54). The drain consisted of several interlocking segments of ceramic pipe, c 45 cm long and 10-15 cm in diameter; the pipes were placed in a channel that cut into the razed top of the Phase II/2 wall 00-42). A small pit at the western doorjamb in the southern room, Locus 55, surely once held a door-socket, which had been removed and recycled.

Area G Architecture

Figure 30: Paving 00-47 in foreground, façade of Building G1 and courtyard of Building G2 at rear, from east

In the final sub-phase of II/1 (II/1A), the central room Locus 56/58 may have become an entry room; the doorway in its northern wall (00-38) was narrowed by the addition of a mud-brick jamb on the eastern side, western wall 00-39 was extended further north by the addition of the abutting wall stub 00-41, and the paving in Locus 63 was covered by occupational layers (Locus 59). Western wall 00-3, which had previously separated the house from the alley, was also covered with occupational material (compare Fig. 31 to Fig. 28). This area was thus another open veranda no longer physically separated from the alley (Locus 3), although it may have still conceptually belonged to the inhabitants of the house.

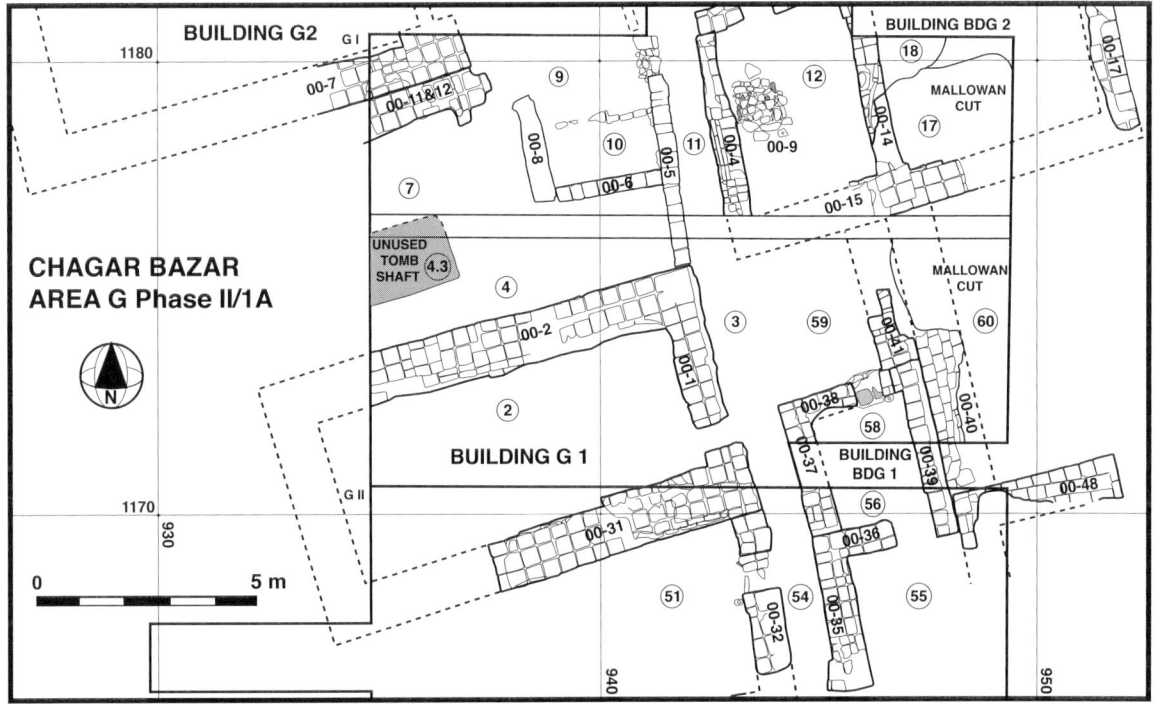

Figure 31: Plan of Area G, Trench II, Sub-phase II/1A

Chapter 3

This line of rooms seems too thin and limited to have stood on its own, so we assume that it was connected to the architecture revealed by Mallowan on its east. A solid wall was visible at the surface to the east of the central room, so the doorway connection to the eastern half of the house may have been either north or south. The block of four houses identified in Phase II/2 (BD 1, BD 2, BD 3 and BDG 1) persisted into Phase II/1.

Phase I

This phase was only preserved at the north end of Area G, in Trench IV. Elsewhere, to the south and east, the architecture immediately at or below the surface belongs to Phase II. There is a slight rise in the modern mound surface towards the north, but currently this is mostly obscured by the deeper excavation at the north end of Mallowan's BD (which reached 3rd millennium BC levels) and by the high spoil heaps which surrounded this trench. It does appear that Phase I may have been restricted to this northern area–it is not the case that it was present, but eroded, further south. This possible shrinking of the settlement and retraction to this northern high point is relevant for our reconstruction of the site's reaction to local political trends and events and mirrors the sparse occupation in Phase I of Area A. Our Phase I in Area G seems to correspond to Mallowan's Late Phase, while his final "Latest" phase may be partly contemporary with the end of our Phase I or scattered surface material.

Architecturally, Phase I structures are poorly-built with thin walls and some re-use of previous walls (see Fig. 32). There was a noticeable change within the lifespan of the phase, with an upper sub-phase rapidly succeeding a lower phase. It is plausible that our Trench G IV would have been at or near the southern edge of the remaining settlement, if our reconstruction of the settlement's retraction northwards is correct; the buildings we uncovered may not have been for human habitation but instead for storage, stables, etc. Mallowan's excavations had cut this phase on the east; spoil heaps from those excavations lay to north and southwest of Trench G IV, and it is apparent that the trench lay in the path of Mallowan's workmen, as they removed earth. This traffic also contributed to the poor preservation of the upper phase here.

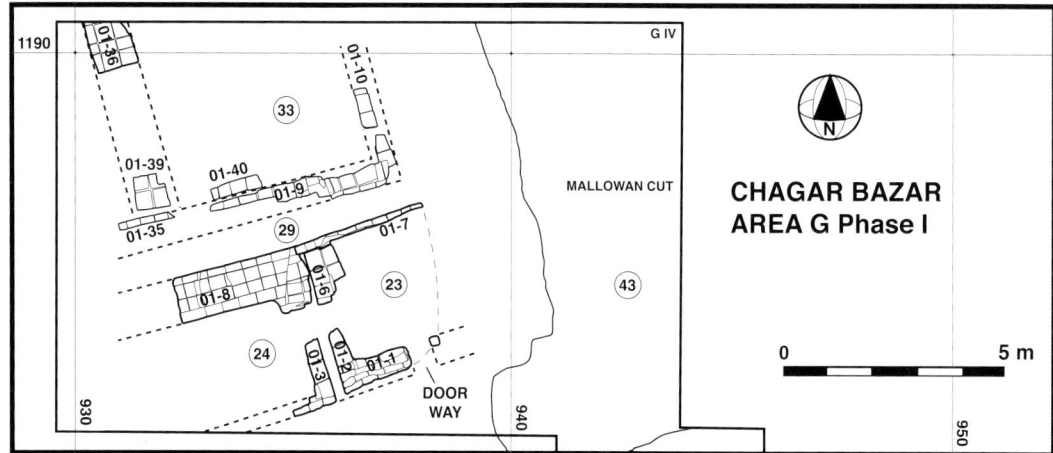

Figure 32: Plan of Area G, Phase I

Two rooms (Loci 23 and 24) lay at the south edge of the trench, and an unroofed space belonging to a separate building (Locus 33) lay to the north, reconstructed from sparse remaining wall fragments. Probable continuation of the architecture on the west was completely removed by erosion; the possible alley on the east (if it persisted into this level) was cut away by Mallowan. A narrow east-west alley (c 75 cm wide) separated the two buildings (L. 29). Locus 23 has a narrow doorway to the south, and an internal doorway connected it to Locus 24. The north wall of the latter room was reused from Phase II and was notably more substantial than the thinner walls of this phase built against it. The extreme thinness of wall 01-7, the north wall of Locus 23, only half a brick wide, suggests that this was an unroofed space with a low partition wall. The northern space (L. 33) was present only in the lower half of this phase and was later sealed by occupational deposits (Locus 26) that covered it and built up against the north faces of walls 01-7 and 01-8.

Construction methods and details

Mallowan (1936, 1937) described a difference in the construction quality and wall thickness across Area BD, with superior layout and design visible in the northern half of the excavation (his so-called 'Temple-Palace'). This was contrasted to what he considered the poor quality and more disorganised layout of the southern half, an area of domestic units. Mallowan states (1936: 110) that the private housing in the southern end of BD had walls that were poorly built and poorly bonded (often lacking the alternating headers and stretchers which mean a stronger bond). From the perspective of the modern excavations, these differences do not seem so pronounced. The general quality of construction of the units is high, in places comparable to that seen in Area A; it is primarily the courtyard boundary walls that are of a lesser, flimsier quality, while the walls of most roofed spaces are strong and well-built.

The use of space both horizontally and vertically was intense across the entire north-south stretch of Area G, and the superimposition of walls implies restriction by formal plot boundaries. There is no evidence in the area for artisan activities (kilns such as Mallowan's or workshops as described in the texts) and the function was habitation throughout.

The majority of mud-bricks used in Area G (as in Area A) are a standardized square 36-38 x 36-38 x 8-10 cm; half-bricks were also used regularly in Area G, while they were relatively rare in Area A. The bricks are quite clean, with only occasional small inclusions of sherds or bones. There is some colour variation, greyish through tan to orange, but these variations do not appear to be deliberate or consistent. Mortar is usually thin and of the same colour as the bricks. Occasionally, a thick layer of mortar was laid through wall centres, or where one wall abutted an earlier wall. The bricks thus display the variations to be expected over the span of a few generations and manufacture by assorted builders.

The brick sizes seen most often at Chagar Bazar are the same as those at Tell Mohammed Diyab and other sites in the Upper Khabur region (see also Ch. 2), understandably since they share availability of materials and economic systems. But less expected, closely similar dimensions are found in the Upper Tigris, despite the different building techniques seen there, most notably the common use of stone foundations. For instance, the excavators of Tell Rijm report brick dimensions in Middle Bronze Age houses of 34 x 34, 30 x 30 and 38 x 38 cm, as well as extended rectangular bricks of 12-14 x 40-46 cm, not seen in the Khabur (Kolinski 2000: 11).

In general, published brick sizes from sites across the region range between 32-40 x 32-40 x 8-10 cm for this period, tending to cluster around 36-38 cm square.

Chapter 3

There is no distinct size difference according to type of building (house or community building). The significance of this consistent measurement lies in mud-bricks as indicators of shared building traditions, incorporating the practice of using bricks as a means of laying-out the dimensions of a structure[14]. Specific numbers of bricks were used in the foundations to establish the desired proportions and area of units.

Doorway widths were also regularised across the site. Smaller doorways tended to be c 65-70 cm wide, while main doorways were 90 cm to 1 m in width. These standard doorways fit neatly with multiples of the brick sizes used in wall construction, and a precise number of bricks (two or two and one-half) would have been used either as doorsills or to measure constant widths for doorways when the buildings were initially laid out. Wall thicknesses range from 1.2-1.3 m in the thicker walls and 40 cm to 1 m in the narrower interior walls or courtyard walls, throughout all phases. Walls seem to have been simply laid on flattened areas, without foundation trenches (except in the case of Building G 1 in Phase II). Frequently, walls of a previous phase were deliberately flattened and used as foundations for walls of a subsequent phase (i.e., 00-4 built on top of 00-19). The narrowest walls, sometimes only one-half brick wide, were found in courtyard or alley boundary walls; these were certainly low enough to look over (in both directions) and to interact over, and their function would be to delineate owned from non-owned space, yet not to ensure privacy from sight or sound. Roofing beams would have also been relatively standardized in length and diameter, through within a larger envelope of variation and subject to the vagaries of natural timber growth. This beam standardization would have dictated the maximum width of roofed structures (as it still does today in the Upper Khabur).

The majority of house walls were at least one and one-half or two bricks wide, and up to three bricks wide, enough to support a roof, even a roof on which activities took place, but not enough for a full upper storey. In Area G (and A) there is no preserved evidence of staircases, although it is plausible that roofs were reached by non-permanent fixtures, such as ladders[15]. The thicknesses of the exterior walls of most structures[16] implies that this may have been a common utilisation of space, thus increasing the available living and storage space on a site that had tight spatial restrictions due to topography. In the single-room rectangular structures in particular, the need for storage areas for food, fodder and fuel would have necessitated either the construction of non-permanent structures in the courtyards or the utilisation of their roofs. Finally, some walls reached three bricks wide and potentially could have supported a second storey, yet there was no evidence from room fill or quantities of brick collapse that such heights were ever reached.

The generally high quality of construction and the aspects of standardization (bricks, doorways and walls) in both Area G and Area A imply the labour of skilled and experienced builders. Specific techniques such as barrel vaulting similarly

---

[14] In modern mud-brick constructions, such as at Tell Hamoukar in Syria (pers. obs., Colantoni), an initial course of mud-bricks is laid out to outline the entire desired ground plan of a building, with the walls subsequently built upon these foundations.

[15] For a discussion of the use of upper floors and roof space in Near Eastern urban environments cf. e.g. Brusasco 1999-2000: 86-87; Crawford 1977: 34-35; Crawford 1982: 25-26; Holladay 1997: 95; Stone 1997.

[16] At Chagar Bazar the widths of the walls of the rectangular buildings are wider than those for comparable rectangular single-room structures at other sites. It is worth noting that Stone (1996: 231) discusses the rental of second storeys in texts of the Old Babylonian period at Sippar and Tell ed-Der, where walls were over a metre thick. At Ur in this period, wall thicknesses of 0.82 m have been recorded in association with staircases (Brusasco 1999-2000: 87).

indicate professional or at least experienced builders. Belying this assumption, however, are ethnographic studies showing that architectural remodelling or major modifications in mud-brick are easily accomplished as family endeavours (Kamp 2000: 89).

Spatial arrangement in Areas BD-G

Although not a particularly large site in terms of area, lying on the border between traditional village and town, Chagar Bazar fulfils some criteria of an 'urban' settlement due to its spatial arrangement: a compact layout, distinction between domestic and community areas and the presence of communication arteries (the alleys). Cultural choices of scale and function, the probable existence of static building plots and the site's topographic restrictions joined to create a spatial organisation that is compact and in tune with larger urban sites.

The precise axial arrangement in Area G would also be unusual in a village.[17] The north-south alley remained a tightly bounded entity throughout several sub-phases and acted as a strong factor in the morphology and alignment of this quarter, structuring the access to and arrangement of the domestic architecture units on both sides. This central feature extended beyond our excavations northwards into Area BD and southwards towards Area TD[18]. As shared public space that was not intruded upon by private structures, it confirms not just the consistency of building plot boundaries, but also the operation of accepted codes in the use and maintenance of communal space.

From an unevenly distributed use of space in Phase III, Area BD-G became more densely occupied in Phases II/2 and II/1. The proportion of roofed indoor space actually remained fairly stable through all three phases. But the proportion of unroofed but bounded space (principally courtyards) did rise dramatically compared to open/public space, as available non-built space became increasingly utilised. Open communal space was at its most limited in Phase II/2.

Within Area G, it is possible to identify a characteristic set of features: communicative or access space; possible regularised plot lines; consistent use of similar house forms; bounded courtyards demarcating property ownership and loosely separating public from private; close proximity between houses; and an underlying sense of a communally accepted ordering of spatial use. Within these larger structures, functions of rooms embraced great variety, both synchronically and diachronically. These features define and form the distinctive patterning of north Mesopotamian urbanism.

The alignment of buildings in Areas G and BD is predominantly ENE-WSW or NNW-SSE, with only minor deviations. It is plausible that a combination of the general direction of the alleyway, available plot space and functional reasons (*e.g.* light, heat and wind avoidance or collection) resulted in the visible arrangement. For this period we see general similarities between both types and alignments of domestic units at Chagar Bazar, Tell Arbid, Tell Mohammed Diyab, and Tell Hamad Agha as-Saghir, among other sites.

---

[17] Normally small settlements should have a more dispersed arrangement with a greater amount of open space around the houses, such as at Tell Arbid (see below).
[18] The distinctive dense sherd and layered deposits of the alleyway are visible in the southern section of Trench G III and thus the alley continues in that direction.

Selected Architectural comparanda

By the early 2nd millennium BC the region saw a wide spread of the simple long-room rectangular house with external courtyard present at Chagar Bazar. The distribution of this architectural form stretches across the Upper Khabur and the Iraqi Jezirah and Upper Tigris regions, approximately matching the distribution of Khabur Ware ceramics. This consistency of architecture and ceramic assemblage implies a homogeneous culture comprising ways of both interacting and eating shared by the inhabitants of this region. The consistencies in the architectural and spatial character of many settlements suggest a shared cultural idiom, with forms and senses of space passed down and familiar across generations.

Tell Mohammed Diyab's Ville Haute presents many of the features and construction techniques present at Chagar Bazar in Area G, and its occupational history (including thriving post-Samsi-Addu levels) offers a close match. Operations 1 and 2 exposed early 2nd millennium BC houses; Operation 2 has a street 1.5-1.7 m wide and at least 20 m long, which, like the slightly narrower Area G alley, was "carpeted" with sherds. Operation 1 exhibits an Area G-like pattern of rectangular single-room or two-room houses, with smaller abutting units and external courtyards with low walls and pebble pavements (Bachelot *et al.* 1990: 16-20; Bachelot & Sauvage 1992: Plan 3). Room 706 is one example of such a plan, but it is worth noting that its doorway is on one of the long walls near a corner, rather than in a short wall (as in our Buildings G 1 and G 2). Many houses had been heavily modified with partitions and repairs over their lifespans. In addition, many of the structures were rebuilt by utilizing previous walls for the construction of subsequent walls. The resulting horizontally and vertically dense layout was symptomatic of the limited available space and constraints of plot boundaries, and it mirrors the density of Chagar Bazar.

The excavators have noted that the number of times floors were resurfaced and walls were repaired and/or modified indicates a length of occupation for each house of several generations. The neighbourhoods exposed were, like Area G, variable internally: houses with niches, fine plastering and interior installations were immediately adjacent to houses with little in the way of decorative elements; houses with built tombs were next to houses with simple pit graves (Castel 1996).

As with their comparable brick sizes, the ranges of wall widths at Mohammed Diyab and Chagar Bazar are identical, as are the stone paving styles seen at both sites, rather haphazardly arranged and containing a mixture of limestone, baked brick and basalt (Bachelot & Sauvage 1992). Even the stone-lined and –capped drain, with smaller stones along its edges, in our Area G (Phase II, 00-34) is directly paralleled in a set of drains at Mohammed Diyab (Bachelot & Sauvage 1992: Plan 1). The largest rooms we have in Area G, in Buildings G 1 and G 2, are equivalent in internal size to the largest rooms at Mohammed Diyab (i.e., their room 720 at 3.7 x 7+ m and room 706 at 3.1 x 7.8 m versus our G 1 at 3.5 x 7+m).

In Operation 4 at *Tell Leilan*, the area below the city wall was initially occupied during 'Period 1' (early 2nd millennium BC) by houses with some similarities to ours in Area G. Following the initial use, the area was temporarily abandoned (or saw the houses shift to an adjacent spot, leaving the Operation 4 area open for rubbish disposal; Weiss *et al.* 1990: 554). The city wall was subsequently built here. The shifting use and apparent availability of open space at Leilan are very different from the tightly-packed and rapidly recycled space situation at Chagar Bazar, but the multiple floors, "minor architectural modifications" and dense trash deposits reveal a close affinity in the way domestic space was utilised.

Levels of the "Khabour Ware Period" at *Tell Arbid* present similar building plans and construction techniques to those in Area G. In Areas D, SR and SS, there are both *pisé* and mud-brick walls (Bieliński 2001; Gimbel & Selz 2002). Pisé is frequently used in the construction of large retaining walls and wall foundations (*e.g.* Area SS, strata III-V; Bieliński 1999; 2000: 317-323; 2002), also a feature of the walls in Area G, particularly at the northern end in Trench G IV. Sector D has the partial remains of a single rectangular structure with a retaining wall to the north enclosing an open space (Gimbel and Selz 2002).

Unlike Chagar Bazar, the settlement at Arbid appears to have been quite scattered, with clusters of houses at a distance from each other. This dispersed "village" layout represents a different use of space between the houses, as they are still quite compact in internal arrangement. Given Arbid's more gradual lower slopes and the settlement's smaller size during the early 2nd millennium BC, the inhabitants were perhaps less restricted by the topography of the site.

At *Tell Barri*, (ancient Kahat), Period 5 is their "Period of dominance of Ashur and Mari" and dates to the 18th century BC (Pecorella 1990). The architecture in this period (Area G, A-D 3-6, Fase H strato 26) is a collection of flimsy fragments of mudbrick structures (*cf.* Pecorella 1998: *fig.* 20). Of architectural significance for Chagar Bazar is again the use of pisè for some walls (i.e., wall ST 469) and the use of narrow one-brick wide boundary walls for courtyards and two-brick wide walls for buildings. Spatially, a small courtyard bounded by a narrow single-course mud-brick wall abutting the northeast face of the only substantial building exposed provides an additional example of a domestic unit with external courtyard.

Area C at *Tell Mozan* presents the site's best-preserved and published architecture from the early 2nd millennium BC[19]. In Level 5, a collection of houses (I-VI and VIII) belonging to the Earlier Khabur period (1900-1800 BC) was defined (Dohmann-Pfälzner & Pfälzner 2000: 200-216; *cf. Abb.* 7). This neighbourhood comprised large areas of open space (*i.e.* Plaza A) and houses with external courtyards. Although the domestic units in this phase were not fully excavated, both House 1 and Room Q (with an attached exterior courtyard) display the characteristics of long, rectangular structures; House I has a doorway in one short wall, like our Buildings G 1 and 2 (and Buildings I and II in Area A). This architectural level is considered to be a continuation of the previous Ur III-Isin-Larsa level and maintained the integrity of the building plots (Dohmann-Pfälzner & Pfälzner 2001: 138).

Further east in the Upper Tigris, portable material culture similarities to the Upper Khabur assemblages (Khabur Ware, stone tools, etc) are notable. Within architectural traditions, a strong visible difference is the frequent use of roughly-worked stone blocks for wall foundations in the Upper Tigris. However in house plans, sites such as *Tell Hamad Agha as-Saghir* possess striking similarities to Area G, with practically identical rectangular single-room house forms and spatial

---

[19] Buccellati (1998: 31) mentions traces of possible domestic architecture of the early 2nd millennium BC in A3 and the heavily eroded partial remains of a house belonging to this period in A8.

arrangement. The quarter of domestic housing in Grabungsschnitt X, Phase IV includes a narrow north-south alley (Spanos 1990, 1992: Abb. 2) and at least four long rectangular buildings (I-IV) each with an external, walled courtyard (Spanos 1992: 89-91). One of these buildings has its door near the end of a long wall, but the other two have doorways at both the end of a long wall and central in a short wall. *Tepe Gawra* also offers a similar plan (with entrance in a long wall) in Level VI (room 517; Speiser 1935: Pl. VI) and similar rectangular forms appear at *Tell Taya* in Level IV (Reade 1973: *pl.* LXXIV). As with other sites in this region, the overall impression is one of restrictions, presumably long-standing building plots, dictating the spatial arrangement of the built environment.

Architecture and Socio-cultural Meanings

Common building plans in Areas G and A consist of relatively standardized single-room rectangular structures and more variable multi-room structures. These plans are found across the region, and the rectangular rooms in particular were often associated with an external courtyard to the front or side. When either type of house expanded, this was achieved by adding clusters of smaller units/rooms onto the existing core. Subdivision was rare. Alleys were narrow and were delineated by a combination of low courtyard walls and thicker house walls, that is, they were never themselves outlined by a single continuous wall but were defined by the external walls of other spaces.

The series of modifications between phases allow a very finely grained understanding of the life histories and interrelationships of the buildings excavated. These histories would have been entangled with the personal histories of their occupants and the micro-history of a society that was spatially compressed within the settlement yet stood within a sparsely settled landscape. The durability of building styles and of spatial organisation connotes stability of the inhabitants, their family structures and community.

House forms both create and are created by individuals and the larger community in which they are embedded. At variant scales, they may mirror regional socio-political systems as well as their occupants' status, they are affected by economic issues including household wealth and production activities (McClellan 1997: 43-44). Household size, which may be generally divided into nuclear and extended family units, also plays a factor in determining house proportions. But traditional forms of vernacular architecture (community "building blocks" in all senses of the term) are used to maintain community identity, and thus a particular plan may be adhered to even if household size is logistically too large or too small for such a plan. Regularities in form were created and maintained for both symbolic and functional reasons, and long-term adherence to regular forms may have involved a process of negotiation and compromise.

The space limitations of single-room structures would have meant substantial daily activities would have taken place in their linked external courtyards. Where these could be defined, the outer courtyard walls were thin and probably low, affording privacy only in conceptual, rather than practical terms. Communities using external courtyards are more open to public interaction, contrasting to inward-looking central courtyard houses where daily activities took place away from public scrutiny. Quotidian interaction would have reflected behavioural codes in communities, and the community in Areas BD-G appears to have been tightly linked and open to easy internal social interaction. However, its overall inward-looking aspect, with houses facing a central alley rather than the settlement exterior, speaks to an internally-open yet externally-limited set of relationships and interactions. The actions occurring in the courtyards, while in a sense "allowed" by the tight social network in which they took place, also served to maintain and reinforce that network. The material culture assemblage (comprising items used in both consumption and manufacture) and features (ovens and graves) imply a rich multi-facetted "life" within houses, with economic and ritual aspects. Formal "political" life within Area G, however, was probably limited, with no spaces large enough to accommodate significant groups. Gendered spaces are noticeably absent, although it must be admitted that we also struggle to find evidence of articulation of space according to age categories or economic status.

A final aspect regarding the use of space in Areas BD-G is the regularity and chronological stability in plot sizes and outlines. This suggests that there might have been an initial parcelling out of the available land suitable for construction at the summit of the mound by an overseeing authority. The inception of re-occupation at Chagar Bazar may have been the result of Samsi-Addu actively encouraging the settlement of previously nomadic peoples in the region (or equally might have been the result of the political and economic stability he brought). The maintenance of these plots in the post-Samsi-Addu era speaks to the acceptance and normalization of this spatial arrangement.

It is not always possible to determine plot sizes, but one can see regular use of large plots, averaging 72 m sq, for the rectangular houses and their courtyards. The multiple-room complexes range between 73.6 and 233.9 m^2, while the rectangular single-room structures range from 53.8 to 105.6 m sq (Table 3.3A). Evidence of the parcelling of land, rather than a purely organic arrangement, may be a characteristic deriving from a higher political authority (*e.g.* the intentionality of Haradum). But whether in the Chagar Bazar case this is organised by a higher authority or by commonalities and patterns that are due to a culturally shared sense of ordering space cannot be determined without textual evidence.

The ceramic assemblages from the three main phases in Area G showed significant continuity. When compared to Area A, there was a small but significant difference that reinforces the distinctions in architecture: overall, the frequencies of grey ware and fine ware were lower and the frequency of cooking pot ware was higher in Area G than in Area A (see Ch. 5).

The relationship between burial practices, corporate rights and identity is a long-established one (Hodder 1986; Porter 2002). At Chagar Bazar, burial practices may be linked at one level with property rights to the individual houses. The presence of burials within houses, a common occurrence across north and south Mesopotamia, additionally reaffirmed senses of identity and belonging to both settlement and landscape. The vast majority of graves in Areas BD and G that can be allocated[20] to specific phases of occupation were placed within walled courtyards, with only a few examples within inner rooms. While there were infants buried in the open space at the settlement edge in Phase III, there are no examples of adult burials from liminal or public spaces such as alleyways or open spaces (for further discussion, see Ch. 4).

---

[20] Mallowan recovered a large number of graves, *cf.* his 1937 catalogue and field notebooks archived in the British Museum, however only those that featured in the BD Section and plan could be related to our re-interpretation of the architecture.

Table 3.2 Mallowan's Rooms and New Building Labels

Building Label	Mallowan Room Numbers	BSAI Loci (where relevant)
BDG 1	31, 32, 33, 38	62, 65
BDG 2	24, 25, 26, 27	16, 18
BD 1	30, 34, 35, 36	
BD 2	43, 44, 45	
BD 3	39, 40, 41, 42	

Table 3.3 Area G Architectural Geometry

Table 3.3A External measurements of complete or nearly-complete buildings (see Figs. 19, 21)

Building	Area
G 1	60.8 m sq *reconstructed* (10.3 x 5.9 m)
G 2	66.6 m sq *reconstructed* (10.4 x 6.4 m)
G 3	105.6 m sq *reconstructed* (13.2 x 8.0 m)
G 4	77.9 m sq *reconstructed* (6.6 x 11.8 m)
BDG 1	158.2 m sq (9.2 x 17.2 m)
BDG 2	53.8 m sq (9.6 x 5.6 m)
BD 1	233.9 m sq *reconstructed* (13.6 x 17.2 m)
BD 2	97.4 m sq *reconstructed* (8.4 x 11.6 m)
BD 3	73.6 m sq (8.0 x 9.2 m)

Table 3.3B Enclosed space (rooms and internal courtyards, inner wall to inner wall)

Building	Function and Locus	Area and Dimensions
G 1	Room L. 2	26.4 m sq (8.0 x 3.3 m) *reconstructed*
G 2	Room L. 67 and 68	32.8 m sq (8.2 x 4.0 m) *reconstructed*
G 3	Room L. 51/46	58.8 m sq (5.5 x 10.7 m) *reconstructed*
G 4	Room L. 49	22.6 m sq (3.7 x 6.1 m)
	Room L. 79	10.4 m sq (2.8 x 3.7 m) *reconstructed*
BDG 1	Room L. 56 and 58	5.9 m sq (2.2 x 2.7 m)
	Courtyard L. 65/25	13.3 m sq (2.5 x 5.3 m) *reconstructed*
BDG 2	Room L. 12/16	10.5 m sq (2.5 x 4.2 m)
	Room L. 17 and 18	20.2 m sq (4.3 x 4.7 m)

Table 3.4 Area G Loci

Surface

Locus No.	Trench	Description and comments	Layers	Boundary walls
1	G I	Topsoil		
17	G I	Mallowan cut and erosion in E room of Building BDG 2 = L. 60, cuts L. 18	17.1: cut fill	
22	G IV	Ashy pile with fire-blackened lenses, at SE corner of trench. Possibly from fire lit by Mallowan's workmen. Part of L. 43.	22.1: ashy material	
35	G III	Mallowan cut infill, cuts 01-5		
43	G IV	Mallowan cut infill, cuts into L. 34		
45	G IV	Mallowan cut infill		
57	G II	Mallowan dump at W edge of trench, sloping gravelly layers		
60	G II	Mallowan cut infill along NE of trench, = L. 17 to N		
61	G II	Mallowan cut infill along SE of trench		

Phase I

Locus No.	Trench	Description and comments	Layers	Boundary walls
21	G III	Eroded brick above Phase II/2 architecture	21.1 and 21.2: mud-brick tumble at surface; 21.3: loose eroded material mixed with Mallowan dump at W	
23	G IV	Room, E of L. 24, small ephemeral walls	23.1: uppermost layer, melted orange mud-brick, 23.2: mottled layer above surface with pottery; 23.3: surface; 23.4: ashy material, surface/floor	01-1 on S, 01-2 & 01-6 on W, 01-7 on N
24	G IV	Room, W of L. 23, more substantial walls, built above Phase II/1 building	24.1: loose fine dark brown soil and ash lenses, much pottery	01-3 on E, 01-8 on N
26	G IV	Seals L. 29, surface material near top of phase at trench centre	26.1: very soft dark brown soil at east end, 26.2: same at west	01-7, 01-8 on S
29	G IV	Passage between two buildings, partly sealed by L. 26	29.1: compact layer, NE portion; 29.2:	01-7 & 01-8 to S, 01-9 to

Chapter 3

Locus No.	Trench	Description and comments	Layers	Boundary walls
			similar to 29.1, but to SW, brown soil, red mud-brick fragments, grey lenses, similar to 31.2	N
33	G IV	Ashy material north of building	33.1: soft dark brown fine soil, red-brown and ash lenses; 33.2: ashy deposit; 33.3: as 33.2 but with mud-brick fragments	01-9 & 01-35 on S, St. 01-10 on E, 01-36 & 01-39 on W

Phase II/1A

Locus No.	Trench	Description and comments	Layers	Boundary walls
3	G I	Upper layer in alley, merges with L. 59 on E	3.1: fallen mud-brick; 3.2: use surfaces, sherds and trash, trampled and water-laid layers	00-1 to W
30	G IV	Pit cutting into L.31, sealed by L.23.5	L.30.1: pit fill	
31	G IV	E portion of trench, surface on which Phase I architecture 01-1, 01-2 and 01-6 were built	L.31.1 burnt material: 31.2: mottled brown soil, small mud-brick fragments, grey clay blobs, ash lenses, some large sherds	
59	G I	Upper layer in "veranda", merges with L. 3 on W, seals L. 63	59.1-59.2: occupational layers; 59.3: cut at N section; 59.4: occupational layer	00-38 on S, 00-41 on E
67	G IV	Subdivisions of room in Building G 2, NE corner	67.1: coarse loose brown soil, grey lenses; 67.2: surface, dark, compact; 67.3: surface on which bin 01-32 was built, assoc. with tanur 01-38	01-31, 01-32, 01-8 on N, 01-11 on E
68	G IV	S portion of room in Building G 2	68.1: loose brown soil; 68.2: surface; 68.3: uneven compacted surface, as L.72.2	01-11 on E, 01-31, 01-32, 00-7 on S

Phase II/1

Locus No.	Trench	Description and comments	Layers	Boundary walls
2	G I	Room in Building G 1, originally N portion, (S excavated as L. 53 in Trench G II; on plans as Locus 2 only)	2.1: fallen mud-brick and soil, little pottery; 2.2: brown occupational material	00-1 on E, 00-2 on N
4	G I	South edge of courtyard of Building G 2, = L. 7 and L. 9	4.1-4.2, 4.4-4.5: lensing and sloping ashy	00-2 on S, 00-5 on E, 00-

Area G Architecture

5	G I	to its N, cut by Tombs 10 and 11 and by L. 4.3	layers, occasional mud-brick fragments; 4.3: probable tomb shaft	6 & 00-8 on N
7	G I	Central segment of alley, layers sealed by L. 3, = L. 11 to N, = L. 54 to S	5.1 & 5.2: use surfaces, sherds and trash, trampled and water-laid layers	00-1 on W, 00-3 & 00-37 on E
9	G I	Western area of courtyard of Building G 2, along W section, = L. 4 and L. 9, cut by Tombs 11 and 13	7.1: coarse red-brown layer, multiple lenses and intermittent surfaces	00-8 on E, 00-11 & 00-12 on N
10	G I	N end of courtyard of Building G 2, = L. 32 to its N, = L. 4 and 7 to its S	9.1 brown water-laid layers and sparse fallen mud-brick, 9.2-9.5: orange-brown and grey lensed ashy layers and intermittent surfaces	00-5 on E, 00-7, 00-11 & 00-12 on NW, 00-8 on S
11	G I	Ash pile in courtyard of Building G 2, slopes out into L. 9	10.1-10.2: deep clean ashy layers with multiple internal striations and sub-surfaces	00-5 on E, 00-6 on S, 00-8 on W
12	G I	Alley E of courtyard of Building G 2, = L. 5 to its south, = L. 34 to its N	11.1: silty water-laid layers with occasional fallen mud-brick fragments	00-4 on E. 00-5 on W
13	G I	W room in Building BDG 2, seals stone paving 00-9	12.1: ashy and brown soil layers	00-4 on W, 00-13 to N, 00-14 to E, 00-15 to S
14	G I	Shaft for T. 13, cut into Loci 7 and 9	13.1-13.3 pit fills	00-11 & 00-12
15	G I	Pit, possible Mallowan exploration, cuts paving 00-47 in Building BDG 1	14.1: hard, compact water-laid material	
18	G I	Courtyard north of Building BDG 2, partially exposed by Mallowan (his Room 24)	15.1: mottled layer of brown silt, red-brown soil and broken mud-bricks	00-13 on S
21	G III	E room in Building BDG 2, exposed by Mallowan (= his Room 26)	18.0: cut away by L. 17, Mallowan cut	00-14 on W, 00-15 on S, 00-16 on N, 00-17 on E
32	G IV	Eroded brick above Phase II/2 architecture	21.2: compact mass of melted mud-brick	
33	G IV	N part of courtyard of Building G 2, sealed by L. 31, merges with L. 9 to S	32.1: mottled brown, mud-brick fragments, grey ash; 32.2: same; 32.3: small pit with charred top and lining	01-34 on N, 01-11 & 01-46 on W, 01-19 on E
34	G IV	Ashy material north of Building G 2, lower layers of deposit which continued into Phase I	33.4: ashy deposit	01-16 on S, 01-22 on E
51	G II	N end of alley, = L. 11 to S	34.1: trashy lensed material, abundant sherds and bones, associated with laid stones in front of doorway in 01-18; 34.2-34.4: succession of lenses and layers, large quantities of sherds & bones	01-18 on E, 01-19 on W
		Courtyard S of Building G 1	51.1: eroded mud-brick and brown soil	00-31 on N, 00-32 on E, 00-33 on S

Chapter 3

53	G II	Southern part of room in Building G 1, = L. 2 to N	53.1: eroded mud-brick; 53.2: compact clean brown surface	00-31 on S
54	G II	S end of alley, = L. 5 to N	54.1: orange and grey soil layers and occasional fallen mud-brick frags, dense sherds and bone	00-37 and 00-35 on E, 00-32 on W
55	G II	Southwest room in Building BDG 1, partly seals L. 62, connected by doorway to L. 56 to N	55.1-55.3: compact occupational layers, red, brown, green; 55.2 associated with stone paving	00-35 on W, 00-36 on N, 00-39 on E
56	G II	Central western room in Building BDG 1, partly seals L. 62, has doorway to L. 55 on S, = L. 58 to N, with doorway to L. 63 on N	56.1-56.2: occupational layers	00-37 on W, 00-36 on S, 00-39 on E, drain 01-12 associated
58	G II	Central western room in Building BDG 1, = L. 56 to south, as doorway to L. 63 to N	58.1-58.5: occupational layers, grey, some flat-lying pottery	00-37 on W, 00-38 on N, 00-39 on E
63	G II	NW room in Building BDG 1, below "veranda" L. 59, seals stone paving St. 00/47	63.1: occupational layer	00-3 on W, 00-38 on S, 00-40 on E
72	G IV	NE corner of Building G 2, sealed by L. 67 and 68 and associated bins, of Phase II/1A	72.1: loose brown debris above surface; 72.2: uneven compacted surface; 72.3: pit at S face of 01-8, clean fill	01-8 on N, St. 01-11 on E

Phase II/2

Locus No.	Trench	Description and comments	Layers	Boundary walls
2	G I	N portion of room in Building G I, (excavated as L. 53 in Trench G II to S, on plans as L. 2 only)	2.3: original occupational material, clean brown layer	00-1 on E, 00-2 on N
4	G I	S edge of courtyard of Building G 2, = L. 9 to its north, cut by Phase II/1 grave pits	4.6-4.8: compact, reddish-brown, orange-brown and ashy layers, lenses	00-2 to S, 00-19 to E, 00-7 to N
5	G I	Central segment of alley, layers sealed by L. 3, = L. 11 to N and = L. 54 to S	5.1 & 5.2: dense sherds and trash, trampled and water-laid layers	00-1 to W
9	G I	NE end of courtyard of Building G 2, = L. 32 to its north, = L. 4 to S, cut by Phase II/1 grave pits	9.6-9.8: ashy occupational layers	00-19 to E, 00-7 to NW
11	G I	Alley E of courtyard of Building G 2, = L. 5 to S, = L. 34 to N	11.2-11.3: ash, trash and dense sherd layers	00-19 to W, 00-18 to E
16	G I	W room in BDG 2, layers associated with *tanur* St.	16.1-16.5: fine to coarse compact occupation	00-18 on W, 00-13 on N,

Area G Architecture

18	G I	00/10, sealed by L. 12, seals vaulted tomb T. 18	layers	00-14 on E, 00-15 on S
	G I	E room in Building BDG 2, = Mallowan's Room 26	18.1-18.3: fine striated occupation layers	00-14 on W, 00-15 on S, 00-16 on N, 00-17 on E
19	G I	Pit for vaulted grave T. 18 in L. 16	19.1: pit fill	
25	G III	SW room in Building BDG 2, = L. 65 to north	25.1: light brown loose gravelly soil with mud-brick collapse; 25.2: hard clay surface with sherd concentration against wall corner	00-49 on W, 01-5 on S
28	G III	Outdoor area S of SW corner of Building BDG 1, sealed by L. 21, merges with L. 39 in alley to N = L. 47 open area to W	28.1: melted mud-brick, sloping down E to W; 28.2: small pit with black ash at S section; 28.3: melted mud-brick, black ash; 28.4: second pit at S section	00-49 & 01-5 to NE
32	G IV	N part of courtyard of Building G 2, = L. 9 to S	32.4: surface running against 01-46; 32.5: same, to N; 32.6: N end, very hard deposit sloping down to E; 32.7: pit at face of 01-15; 32.8: band of hard deposit running E-W at centre of room; 32.9: pit, associated with surface 32.4; 32.10: same; 32.11: surface; 32.12: pit associated with 32.10, near 32.3; 32.13: layer below 32.11, with patch of limestone and basalt paving	01-46 & 01-11 on W, 01-15 on N, 01-19 on E
34	G IV	N end of alley, = L. 11 to S	34.5: grey silty water laid layers with pockets of trampled sherds and discontinuous stone pavings	01-50 & 01-19 on W, 01-48 on E
39	G III	S continuation of alley, sealed by L. 28, = L. 54 to N, merges with open area Loci 28 & 47 to S	39.1: hard brown clay and mud-brick; 39.2: hard layered surface against 01/-4 and 01-5; 39.3: packed grey soil surface with sherds; 39.4: very hard surface, weathered and packed, patches of flat-lying sherds	00-49 on E, 01-20 on W
40	G IV	Ash layers at N of trench	40.1: soft grey fine ashy layers	01-16 on S, 01-50 on E
41	G IV	Layer on which St. 01/16 and 01/15 are built, razed top of 01-44	41.1: dense light yellow-grey deposit, clean; 41.2 & 41.3: same	
46	G III	SE corner of courtyard S of Building G 1 (or room of hypothesized Building G 3)	46.1: gravelly chunky dark brown, soft and weathered	01-23 on S, 01-20 on E
47	G III	Outdoor area, = L. 39 and L. 28 to NE and E	47.1: mud-brick tumble and weathered surfaces, water-laid	01-23 on N

Chapter 3

Locus No.	Trench	Description and comments	Layers	Boundary walls
51	G II	Courtyard S of Building G 1, associated with drain 00-34	51.2: grey ashy layer; 51.3: compacted surface with ash lenses; 51.4: water-laid material and sherds above drain; 51.5: water-laid surface	00-31 on N, 00-32 & 01-20 on E and 01-23 on S
52	G II	Contents of stone-lined drain in courtyard L. 51	52.1: silty grey-green fill	Drain 00-34
53	G II	Southern portion of room in Building G 1 = L. 2 to N (on plans as L. 2 only)	53.3: compact clean brown surface	00-31 on S
54	G II	Alley, = L. 5 to N, = L.39 to S	54.2: pebbly surface; 54.3: compact green-grey layer with sherds; 54.4-54.10: trashy dark brown, orange and grey trampled sherd-rich layers, sloping up to walls at sides of alley	00-42 and 00-49 on E, 00-32 & 01-29 on W
62	G II	Room in Building BDG 1	62.1-62.5: compact occupational layers	00-42 on W, 00-50 on S, 00-52 on E
65	G II	SW room in Building BDG 1, = L. 25 to S	65.1: silty layer below paving 00-45; 65.2: ashy shallow pit; 65.3-65.5: occupational layers	00-49 on W, 00-50 on N
66	G II	Foundation trench along SE face of St. 00/31 in courtyard L. 51	66.1: cut; 66.2 loose fill in cut	
73	G IV	Room in Building G 2, sealed by L. 72	73.1: loose chunky brown soil; 73.2: surface; 73.3: pit, black ashy fill; 73.4: pit, SE, fine black ashy fill; 73.5: larger pit which 73.3 cuts into; 73.6: pitted layer, loose dark brown	01-45 on N, 01-46 on E, 00-7 on S
78	G IV	Room on E of alley, NE corner of trench	78.1: homogenous brown silt, hard at top, and weathered, softer below	01-48 on W

Phase III

Locus No.	Trench	Description and comments	Layers	Boundary walls
20	G I	Open area S of Building G 4, sealed by L. 4, 7 and 9	20.1: hard yellow silty layers	00-20 to N
27	G II	NE corner of trench, sealed by L. 62, flattened material before Phase II/2, at top of Phase III, seals L. 36, 38	27.1: tumbled mud-brick debris, trampled, orange & grey clay; 27.2: flat-lying sherds	Top of 01-54 to W

Area G Architecture

36	G II	NE corner of trench, sealed by L. 27, courtyard of Building BDG 5, associated with paving 01-24	on layer of gray, mud-brick tumble, ash lenses 36.1: compact red-brown soil, pockets of large sherds, possibly from paving 01-24, sloping down to E; 36.2: pit, red-brown fill, runs into N section	01-13 on S, 01-54 on W
37	G II	Eroded ancient mound slope and open area, sealed by L. 51, = L. 70 to the south	37.1: upper sherd-rich layer, ash lenses, pits, ephemeral features; 37.2: pit cut into 37.3, water-laid fill; 37.3: sherd-covered surface, mud-brick tumble; 37.4: same; 37.5: soakaway pit for drain 01-55	01-54 & 01-25 on E
38	G II	South central room of Building BDG 5, sealed by L. 27	38.1: mud-brick tumble, mottled orange and brown, red near walls, compact at centre; 38.2: compact light grey surface, hearth 01-30	01-13 on N, 01-17 on W, 00-54 on S
40	G IV	Lower ash layers at N of trench, N of Building G 4	40.2: south part, dark fine ash, mud-brick fragments, sherds, plaster chunks, occasional stones; 40.3: north continuation	01-44 on S, 01-51 on E
42	G II	SW room of Building BDG 5, sealed by L. 27, W of and connected by doorway to L. 38	42.1: stratified layers, red crumbly and blue-grey compact, sloping up towards surrounding walls	01-17 on E, 00-54 on S, 01-54 on W, 01-13 on N
44	G II	NW room of Building BDG 4, upper layers, cut by T. 37, seals L. 48	44.1: top layer, compact grey-yellow surfaces; 44.2: surfaces; 44.3: shallow pit with jar, cut from 44.2, SW corner	00-53 on N, 01-25 on W
48	G II	NW room of Building BDG 4, lower layers, cut by pit L. 44.3 and T. 37, sealed by L. 44	48.1: surface, sloping up to walls, plaster and charcoal flecks	01-28 on N, 01-27 on W, 01-26 on S
49	G IV	E room of Building G 4	49.1: hard light brown surface, patchy and discontinuous, mottled ash and white flecks, pockets of sherds and animal bones; 49.2: similar, patches of stones and sherds	01-49 on W, 01-44 on N, 01-58 on E, 00-20 on S
50	G IV	Open area opposite alley from Building G 4	50.1: silty soil, mud-brick and sherds	01-52 on N and 01-59 on W
69	G II	Sealed by pavement 01-24, lower levels of same room as L. 36, Building BDG 5	69.1: dense sherds, lensed medium-compact material	01-13 on S, 01-54 on W
70	G II	Outdoor area and ancient mound slope, = L. 37 to N	70.1: loose brown eroded outdoor surfaces	01-25 on E

Chapter 3

	Trench	Description and comments	Layers	Boundary walls
		assoc. with broken jars in situ and mud-brick bin 01-43; 70.2: slightly denser layer, tumbled mud-brick; 70.3: continuation of outdoor layers, associated with 01-42 and 01-43		
71	G II	SE corner of trench, sealed by L. 48, cut by T. 37, compacted surface, bottom of Phase III/ top of Phase IV	71.1: compact layer on which 00-53 was built	
76	G IV	Lower layers in N end of alley, sealed by L. 34	76.1: dense sherds, trash; 76.2: same	01-58 on W, 01-59 on E
77	G II	Compacted surface, with L. 71 an early episode in Phase III, sealed by L. 70	77.1: surface on which 01-54 and 01-25 were built, runs at sandstone foundations of 01-25; 77.2: sounding	
78	G IV	Room on E of alley, NE corner of trench	78.2: brown compact surface	01-48 on W
79	G IV	W room of Building G 4, associated with bench St. 01/53, cut by T. 50	79.1: loose chunky brown soil; 79.2: surface associated with 01-44 and 01-53	01-44 on N, 01-49 on E
80	G IV	Doorway leading E from alley, N end of excavation, = L. 76 to S	80.1: loose silty soil, some stones, above flat-lying sherds	N of 01-52

Phase IV

Locus No.	Trench	Description and comments	Layers	Boundary walls
74	G II	NW corner of trench	74.1: buff clayey layer	N of St. 01/41
75	G II	Sealed by L. 37	75.1: brown-grey silty clay surface	S of St. 01/41

* Locus Numbers L. 6, 8 and 64 were not used.

Table 3.5 Area G Structures (Walls and Features)

Phase I

Structure No.	Trench	Description and comments	Associated loci	Associated walls and features
01-1	G IV	NE-SW mud-brick wall, 2 bricks wide, doorway, 36 x 36 x 8 cm bricks	23	01-2, 01-6, 01-7
01-2	G IV	NW-SE mud-brick wall, 1 brick wide, doorway, 36 x 36 x 8 cm bricks, continued to N as 01-6	23	01-1, 01-6, 01-7
01-3	G IV	NW-SE mud-brick wall, 1 brick wide, doorway, built along 01-2 with thick mortar layer between, 36 x 36 x 8 cm bricks	24	01-2, 01-8
01-6	G IV	NW-SE mud-brick wall, 2 bricks wide, 36 x 36 x 8 cm bricks, = 01-2 to S	23	01-2, 01-1, built against corner of 01-7 & 01-8
01-7	G IV	Thin NE-SW mud-brick wall, one half-brick wide	23, 26, 29	01-6, 01-8
01-8	G IV	NE-SW mud-brick wall, 3 bricks wide, 36 x 36 x 8-10 cm bricks, still in use from Phase II/1	24, 29	01-3, 01-6, 01-7
01-9	G IV	NE-SW mud-brick wall, 1.5 bricks wide, 36 x 36 x 8-10 and 18 x 36 x 8-10 cm bricks, damaged by erosion	29, 33	Part of one construction with 01-35 and 01-40, forms corner on E with 01-10, on W with 01-39 & 01-36
01-10	G IV	NW-SE mud-brick wall, 1 brick wide, square orange bricks different from the other bricks of this phase	33	01-9
01-35	G IV	Four half-bricks in NE-SW line, W part of 01-9	33	01-9, 01-39
01-36	G IV	Small block of mud-bricks, remains of NW-SE wall, 2.5 bricks wide, probably part of 01-39 to S	33	01-39
01-39	G IV	Block of 4 bricks, probably S extension of 01-36, NW-SE wall	33	01-35, 01-36
01-40	G IV	Single course of half-bricks, along N face of 01-9	33	01-9

Phase II/1A

Structure No.	Trench	Description and comments	Associated loci	Associated walls and features
00-41	G I	N-S mud-brick wall at N end of Building BDG 1, 1.5 bricks wide, 36 x 36 x 8-10 cm bricks, some half bricks and other irregular sizes	59	Abuts N end of 00-39, against 00-40

Chapter 3

Phase II/1

Structure No.	Trench	Description and comments	Associated loci	Associated walls and features
00-1	G I	NW-SE wall, E wall of Building G 1, 2.5 bricks wide, square buff mud-bricks 35-40 x 8-10 cm and half-bricks 18 x 38-40 cm, has doorway to alley, in use from Phase II/2	2, 3, 5	00-2, 00-31
00-2	G I	NE-SW mud-brick wall, N wall of Building G 1, 3 bricks wide, square buff mud-bricks 38 x 38 x 8-10 cm, in use from Phase II/2	2, 4	00-1, 00-31
00-3	G I	NE-SW mud-brick wall, W wall of Building BDG 1, 1.5 bricks wide, 36 x 36 x 8 cm and half-bricks 16 x 36 cm	5, 63	= 00-4 to N, abuts corner of 00-37 & 00-38
00-4	G I	NW-SE mud-brick wall, W wall of Building BDG 2, 1.5 bricks wide, square and rectangular bricks and some irregular fragments, 36 x 36 x 10 cm bricks, built on top of 00-18	11, 12	= 00-3 to S, abuts 00-13 at N
00-5	G I	NW-SE mud-brick wall, W wall of courtyard of Building G 2, 1 brick wide, square bricks 36-39 x 10 cm, doorway with stone sill, built on 00-19	4, 10, 11	Abuts corner of 00-1 & 00-2, abutted by 00-6
00-6	G I	NE-SW mud-brick wall, 1 brick wide, thick plaster on N face, square bricks 36 x 33-36 cm, containing wall for ash in courtyard of Building G 2	4, 10	Abuts 00-5, associated with 00-8
00-7	G I	NE-SW mud-brick wall, S wall of Building G 2, 3.5 bricks wide, 36 x 36 x 8-10 cm bricks and half-bricks 16 x 38 cm	7, 68, 72	Makes corner with 01-11
00-8	G I	NW-SE mud-brick and pisé wall, western containing wall for ash pile in courtyard of Building G 2	7, 9, 10	00-6
00-9	G I	Pavement of limestone and basalt, set into L. 12, W room in Building BDG 2, stones range from 4 x 8 to 25 x 40 cm	12	Runs against wall 00-4
00-11	G I	NE-SW mud-brick wall, 2-3 bricks wide, built on top of 00-12 in courtyard of Building G 2, coarse orange-red square bricks 36-38 x 36-38 x 8 cm and half-bricks 16 x 36-38 cm, top of vault for grave T. 13	7, 9	Built against 00-7, above 00-12
00-12	G I	NE-SW mud-brick wall, 2 bricks wide, lower part of vault for T. 13, below 00-11, square bricks 38-40 x 38-40 x 8-10 cm	9	Sealed by 00-11
00-13	G I	NE-SW mud-brick wall, N wall of Building BDG 2, 2 bricks wide, has doorway connecting Loci 12 and 15, rectangular bricks 32 x 36 x 8-10 cm, in use from Phase II/2	12, 15	00-14, 00-15, 00-16, 00-17, abutted by 00-4
00-14	G I	NW-SE mud-brick wall, inner wall of Building BDG 2, 2 bricks wide, cut by Mallowan, square bricks 36 x 36 x 8 cm and rectangular bricks 32 x 40- and 24 x 36 cm, in use from Phase II/2	12, 18	00-13, 00-15, 00-16, 00-17

Area G Architecture

00-15	G I	NE-SW mud-brick wall, S wall of Building BDG 2, 2-2.5 bricks wide, square bricks and rectangular half bricks 36-40 and 18 x 36 cm, headers alternate faces with each course, cut by Mallowan, in use from Phase II/2	12, 18	00-13, 00-14, 00-16, 00-17
00-16	G I	NE-SE mud-brick wall, N wall of Building BDG 2, visible on surface, previously excavated by Mallowan, 1.5 bricks wide as preserved, square bricks and rectangular half bricks 36-38 and 18-20 x 36-38 cm, still in use from Phase II/2	18	= 00-13 to W, 00-14, 00-15, 00-17
00-17	G I	NW-SE mud-brick wall, E wall of Building BDG 2, visible on surface, partly excavated by Mallowan, 1.5 bricks wide as preserved, square bricks and rectangular half bricks 36-38 and 18 x 38 cm, in use from Phase II/2	18	00-14, 00-15, 00-16
00-31	G II	NE-SW mud-brick wall, S wall of Building G 1, 3 bricks wide, 36 x 36 x 8-10 cm bricks and half-bricks 18 x 38 cm, mortar between bricks 5-8 cm thick in places, in use from Phase II/2	2, 51, 53	00-1, 00-2, abutted by 00-32
00-32	G II	NW-SE mud-brick wall, E wall of courtyard S of Building G 1, 1.5 bricks wide, mostly 36 x 36 cm (some 36 x 44 cm), eroded on S end and at corner with 00-33, doorway connects L. 51 to alley L. 54	51, 54	Abuts corner of 00-1 & 00-31
00-33	G II	NE-SW mud-brick wall, within courtyard S of Building G 1, 1.5 bricks wide, very eroded at W end	51	00-32
00-35	G II	NW-SE mud-brick wall, W wall of Building BDG 1, 2 bricks wide, built on top of 00-42, 34-36 x 34-36 x 8 cm bricks and half-bricks 16 x 34 cm	54, 55	Makes corner with 00-36
00-36	G II	NE-SW mud-brick wall in Building BDG 1, 1.5 bricks wide, 36 x 36 x 8 cm square and half-bricks 21 x 42 cm, doorway connects Loci 55 & 56	55, 56	Makes corner with 00-35
00-37	G I & II	NW-SE mud-brick wall, W wall of Building BDG 1, 1.5-2 bricks wide, built on top of 00-42, 36-38 x 36-38 x 8 cm square bricks and half-bricks 18 x 34 cm	5, 54, 56, 58	Makes corner with 00-38 at N, abuts corner of 00-35 and 00-36 at S
00-38	G I	NE-SW mud-brick wall in Building BDG 1, 1.5 bricks wide, baked brick doorsill and stone door-socket belong to Phase II/1a, 36 x 38 x 8 cm and half-bricks	58, 63	Makes corners with 00-37, 00-39
00-39	G I & II	NW-SE mud-brick wall in Building BDG 1, 1 brick wide with thick plaster/ mortar slab placed between it and 00-40, cut by Mallowan and eroded on S end, 36 x 36 x 8 cm bricks and half-bricks 16 x 38 cm	55, 56, 58	Built against 00-40
00-40	G I	NW-SE mud-brick wall within Building BDG 1, 3 bricks wide, plastered W face, against parallel wall 00-39, 36 x 36 x 8-10 cm bricks and rectangular bricks 26 x 38 cm	63	00-39
00-47	G I	Stone paving in NW room of Building BDG 1, slopes up slightly towards	63	00-38, 00-3, 00-40

Chapter 3

Structure No.	Trench	Description and comments	Associated loci	Associated walls and features
		face of 00-38, stones vary from 5 to 50 cm in max dimension, mostly limestone but occasional basalt slabs and baked bricks laid in brown clay		
00-48	G II	NE-SW mud-brick wall in Building BDG 1, also visible on surface in Mallowan excavation, doorway, 34-36 x 36 x 8-10 cm mud-bricks and half bricks 18 x 36 cm		Abutted by 00-40
01-8	G IV	NE-SW mud-brick wall, N wall of Building G 2, 3 bricks wide, 36 x 36 x 8-10 cm and half-bricks 16 x 36 cm	32, 67, 68	00-7, 01-11, abutted by 01-31
01-11	G IV	NW-SE mud-brick wall, E wall of Building G 2, 2 bricks wide, built on top of 01-46, 36 x 36 x 8-10 cm bricks, doorway at S	32, 67, 68	00-7, 01-8
01-12	G II	Clay pipe drain, sloping into alley L. 54, below 00-37, cuts into Phase II/2 wall 00-42	54, 56/58	00-37
01-16	G IV	NE-SW mud-brick wall at N corner of excavation, 1 brick wide, 36 x 36 x 8-10 cm square bricks, S containing wall for ash layers L. 40, forms corner with 01-22	40	01-22, 01-34
01-18	G IV	NE-SE pisé wall, E wall of alley at N of excavation	34, 78	01-19, 01-22
01-19	G IV	NW-SE mud-brick wall, single row of half-bricks 18 x 40 cm, laid as stretchers, a face/ veneer laid against wider wall 01-22 in alley at N	34	01-22
01-22	G IV	NW-SE mud-brick wall, 3 bricks wide, forms corner with 01-16, 36-38 x 36-38 x 8-10 cm square	34, 40	01-16, 01-19
01-31	G IV	NW-SE ephemeral mud-brick wall subdividing corner of room in Building G 2, 1 brick wide, 36 x 36 cm mud-bricks and 24-44 cm rectangular bricks	67, 68	Abuts 01-8
01-32	G IV	NW-SE ephemeral mud-brick wall subdividing corner of room in Building G 2, one rectangular brick wide, 25 x 37 cm	67, 68	Abuts 01-11
01-34	G IV	"Pavement" or razed wall, 2 bricks wide, N of Building G 2	32	01-16, 01-8
01-38	G IV	*Tanur* in L. 67, near St. 01/11, Building G 2	67, 72	

Phase II/2

Structure No.	Trench	Description and comments	Associated loci	Associated walls and features
00-1	G I	NW-SE wall, E wall of Building G 1, 2.5 bricks wide, square buff mud-bricks 35-40 x 8-10 cm, doorway to alley, traces white plaster on interior	2, 5	00-2, 00-31
00-2	G I	NE-SW mud-brick wall, N wall of Building G 1, 3 bricks wide, square buff mud-bricks 38 x 38 x 8-10 cm, traces white plaster on interior	2, 4	00-1, 00-31
00-10	G I	*Tanur* in corner of L. 16, Building BDG 2, 86 cm base, stoke-hole in side.	16	In corner of 00-13 and 00-14

Area G Architecture

		later than grave T 18 in same room		
00-13	G I	NE-SW mud-brick wall, N wall of Building BDG 2, 2 bricks wide, doorway connecting Loci 15 and 16, rectangular bricks 32 x 36 x 8-10 cm	15, 16	00-14, 00-15, 00-16, 00-17, 00-18
00-14	G I	NW-SE mud-brick wall, inner wall of Building BDG 2, 2 bricks wide, cut by Mallowan, rectangular bricks 32 x 40 and 24 x 36 cm	16, 18	00-13, 00-15, 00-16, 00-17, 00-18
00-15	G I	NE-SW mud-brick wall, 2.5 bricks wide, S wall of Building BDG 2, square bricks and rectangular half bricks 36-39 and 18 x 36 cm, headers alternating faces with each course, cut by Mallowan	16, 18	00-13, 00-14, 00-16, 00-17, 00-18
00-16	G I	NE-SW mud-brick wall, N wall of Building BDG 2, visible on surface, previously excavated by Mallowan, 1.5 bricks wide as preserved, square bricks and rectangular half bricks 36-38 and 18-20 x 36 cm	18	00-13, 00-14, 00-15, 00-17, 00-18
00-17	G I	NW-SE mud-brick wall, E wall of Building BDG 2, visible on surface, previously excavated by Mallowan, 1.5 bricks wide as preserved, square bricks and rectangular half bricks 36-38 and 20x 38 cm	18	00-13, 00-14, 00-15, 00-16, 00-18
00-18	G I	NW-SE mud-brick wall, 2-3 bricks wide, W wall of Building BDG 2, square bricks and rectangular half-bricks ca 40 x 40 and 20 x 40 cm., underlies 00-4	11, 16	00-13, 00-14, 00-15, 00-16, 00-17
00-19	G I	NE-SW mud-brick wall, E wall of courtyard of Building G 2, underlies 00-5, rectangular bricks 38 x 34 cm	9, 11	Abuts corner of 00-1 and 00-2
00-31	G II	NE-SW mud-brick wall, S wall of Building G 1, 3 bricks wide, 36 x 36 x 8-10 cm bricks, mortar between bricks 5-8 cm thick in places, foundation trench L 66 on S face	2, 51, 53, 66	00-1, 00-2, abutted by 00-32
00-32	G II	NW-SE mud-brick wall, E wall of courtyard S of Building G 1, 1.5 reddish-brown bricks wide, mostly 36 x 36 cm bricks, eroded at juncture with 01-20	51, 54	Abuts corner of 00-1 & 00-31, has doorway with drain 00-34 running below
00-34	G II	Drain in courtyard L. 51 S of Building G 1, NE-SW, slopes down to E, lined with basalt and limestone, capped with smaller stones, slag, baked brick fragments and sherds	51, 54	Runs through doorway in 00-32
00-42	G II	NW-SE mud-brick wall, W wall of Building BDG 1, 1.5 bricks wide, has two projecting stubs informally subdividing L. 62, doorway at S end with wall corner 00-49 & 00-50, stack of 3 door-sockets, threshold and drain 00-51 below, 36-37 x 36-37 x 8 cm square bricks and rectangular bricks 25 x 37 cm	54, 62	St. 00-52, drain 00-51
00-44	G II	Mud-brick wall collapse which retained its organization and appears as vertically-laid pavers in the alley, S end, 36 x 36 x 8-10 cm bricks, also	54	Between 00-49 and 01-20

Chapter 3

		extends into G III		
00-45	G II	Paving of small stones, mostly 5-10 cm pebbles, in SW room of Building BDG 1, occasional larger basalt or limestone slabs up to 20 cm	65	Runs against 00-49 and 00-50, around plaster bin in corner of room
00-46	G II	*Tanur*, c 80 cm diameter, consciously sheared off after it fell into disuse, in Building BDG 1	62.3	Built against 00-42
00-49	G II	NW-SE mud-brick wall, W wall of Building BDG 1, 1.5 bricks wide, poorly built, 35-36 x 35-36 x 8-10 cm and fragments	54, 65	00-50, 00-45, makes a corner with 01-5
00-50	G II	NE-SW mud-brick wall, room in SW corner of Building BDG 1, 1 brick wide, 36-38 x 36-38 x 8-10 cm	62, 65	Makes corner with 00-49
00-51	G II	Drain, E-W, below floor of L. 62, Building BDG 1, most stones robbed-out and missing, drains into L.54 from L. 62	62	Runs below doorway in 00-42
00-52	G II	Thin mud-brick wall, NW-SE, within Building BDG 1, 1 brick wide, underlies 00-39, 36 x 36 x 8-10 cm	62	Abutted by 01-48
01-5	G III	NE-SW mud-brick wall, S corner of Building BDG 1, 1.5 bricks wide, 36 x 36 x 8 cm bricks	25, 28, 39	Makes corner with 00-49
01-15	G IV	NE-SW mud-brick wall, 1.5 bricks wide, N wall of courtyard of Building G 2, alternating rectangular headers and square bricks 38-39 x 38-39 cm, cut by T 33, partly underlies 01-8	32, 41	Abutted by 01-46, part of 01-45
01-16	G IV	NE-SW mud-brick wall 1 brick wide, 36-40 x 36-40 x 8-10 cm square bricks and half-bricks 24 x 40 cm, N of Building G 2	40, 41	01-45, 01-50
01-19	G IV	NW-SE mud-brick wall at N of trench, single row of large half-bricks 32 x 50 cm, laid as stretchers, a face/ veneer laid against wider wall 01-50 and 01-22	34	01-50
01-20	G II & III	NW-SE mud-brick wall, W wall of courtyard S of Building G 1 (or W wall of Building G 3), 3 bricks wide, 40 x 40 cm, faced by 01-29	51, 54	01-29, makes corner with 01-23
01-23	G III	NE-SW mud-brick wall, S wall of courtyard S of Building G 1 (or S wall of Building G 3), 2.5 bricks wide, 36-38 x 36-38 x 8-10 cm square	46, 47	Makes corner with 01-20
01-29	G II	Mud-brick and plaster protective packing against base of E face of wall 01-20 in alley, S end, runs over fallen brick 00-44	54	01-20
01-45	G IV	NE-SW mud-brick wall, N wall of Building G 2, 2.5-3 bricks wide, 40 x 40 cm, combined with 01-15	41, 73	01-15
01-46	G IV	NW-SE mud-brick wall, foundation for St. 01/11, E wall of Building G 2, 2 bricks wide, 36-38 x 36-38 x 8-10 cm	32, 73	01-45 & 01-15, makes corner with 00-7
01-48	G IV	NW-SE pisé wall, E side of alley, N end, same location as 01-18 of Phase II/1 but wider	34, 78	Opposite 01-50

| 01-50 | G IV | N-S mud-brick and pisé wall, N end of trench, W wall of alley, built above 01-51, below 01-22 | 34, 40 | 01-45 |

Phase III

Structure No.	Trench	Description and comments	Associated loci	Associated walls and features
00-20	G I	ENE-WSW mud-brick wall, S wall of Building G 4, underlies 00-7, square bricks 38-40 x 38-40 cm, doorway connects Loci 20 and 49	20, 49, 79	Makes corner with 01-58, abutted by internal buttress 01-60, probably abutted by 01-49
00-53	G II	NE-SW mud-brick wall, N wall of Building BDG 4, 2.5 bricks wide, 36-38 x 36-38 x 8-10 cm bricks	44, 48	Built along 00-54, abuts 01-25, abutted by 01-28
00-54	G II	NE-SW mud-brick wall, S wall of Building BDG 5, 1.5 bricks wide, 36-40 x 36-40 x 8-10 cm and half-bricks 18 x 38 cm	38, 42	00-53 built along it, makes corner with 01-54, abutted by 01-17
01-13	G II	NE-SW mud-brick wall in Building BDG 5, irregularly built, ill-defined mixture of half-bricks and pisé	36, 38, 42	Abuts 01-54, associated with paving 01-24
01-17	G II	NNW-SSE mud-brick wall, internal wall in Building BDG 5, narrow non-load-bearing division of room	38, 42	Abuts 01-13, 00-54
01-24	G II	Stone and sherd paving below L. 36, Building BDG 5, mixed stones, sherds, baked brick fragments	36	01-13, 01-54
01-25	G II	NW-SE mud-brick wall, W wall in Building BDG 4, large square mud-bricks 40-42 x 40-42 cm, with sandstone foundation	44, 48, 70	Abutted by 00-53, 01-27
01-26	G II	NE-SW mud-brick wall, internal "bench" in room of Building BDG 4, small square bricks	48	01-27, 01-28
01-27	G II	NW-SE mud-brick wall, internal "bench" in room of Building BDG 4, 2 bricks wide, small square bricks 34 x 34 cm, built against E face of 01-25	48	01-26, 01-28, abuts 01-25
01-28	G II	NE-SW mud-brick wall, internal "bench" in room of Building BDG 4, 1 brick wide, small square bricks, built against S face of 00-53	48	01-26, 01-27, abuts 00-53
01-30	G II	Plastered and fire-hardened basin in L. 38	38	
01-42	G II	Plastered platform and NE-SW narrow line of mud-bricks, half and whole bricks 39 x 39 cm, work feature	37	N of 01-43
01-43	G II	Depression outlined with bricks, bin or work feature	37	S of 01-42
01-44	G IV	NE-SW mud-brick wall, N wall of Building G 4, 3 square bricks 40 x 40 cm wide	40, 49, 79	Makes corner with 01-58, abutted by 01-51, 01-53
01-48	G IV	NW-SE pisé wall, E side of alley, N end, same location as 01-18 of Phase	76, 78, 80	Opposite 01-51

Chapter 3

	Trench	Description and comments	Associated loci	Associated walls and features
		II/1, continues into Phase II/2		
01-49	G IV	NW-SE mud-brick wall, interior wall in Building G 4, 2 bricks wide, 36-40 x 36-40 x 8-10 cm	49, 79	Abuts 01-44 (and probably 00-20), abutted by 01-53
01-51	G IV	N-S mud-brick and pisé wall, W wall of alley at N, 2 square bricks wide	40, 80	Abuts corner of 01-44 & 01-58
01-52	G IV	NE-SW mud-brick and pisé wall, c 1.5 bricks wide, 40 x 40 cm and half-bricks 18 x 40 cm	50, 80	Makes corner with 01-59
01-53	G IV	NE-SW wall stub or bench, along S face of 01-44, 1 brick wide, 37 x 37 cm		Abuts 01-44, 01-49
01-54	G II	NW-SE mud-brick wall, W wall of Building BDG 5, 1.5-2 bricks wide, runs over drain 01-55, abutted by 01-13	36, 37, 42	Makes corner with 00-54
01-55	G II	E-W drain, stone-lined and –capped, drains from L. 36 into L. 37, including sherd-filled soakaway pit L. 37.5	37	01-54
01-58	G IV	NW-SE mud-brick and pisé wall, E wall of Building G 4, has veneer of upright bricks laid against E face, in alley, to prevent or repair erosion, cut by T 33	49, 76	Makes corner with 01-44
01-59	G IV	NW-SE mud-brick wall, E wall of alley, 2 bricks wide, rectangular bricks 27 x 40 cm	50, 76	Makes corner with 01-52
01-60	G IV	Buttress or bench at inner corner of walls 00-20 and 01-58	49	00-20, 01-58

Phase IV

Structure No.	Trench	Description and comments	Associated loci	Associated walls and features
01-41	G II	NE-SW mud-brick wall, 2 bricks wide, 36 x 36 x 8-10 cm	74, 75	

* Structure numbers 00-21 through 00-30, 00-43, 01-4, 01-14, 01-21, 01-33, 01-37, 01-47, 01-56 and 01-57 were not used.

Chapter 4

Chagar Bazar Burial Practices

A. McMahon

Ideational and physical context

The relationship between the living and the dead in Mesopotamia involved substantial continuity of social connections after death. Burial in this region is not so much "disposal" as it is the marking of an individual's transition from active life to a different, far more restricted, "afterlife". Textual descriptions from the Old Babylonian Period indicate that the underworld may be a dusty, gloomy, liminal space or a more structured place beyond a river, additionally separated from the living by a long road and/or set of gates (i.e. in *Ishtar/Inanna's Descent to the Underworld* and *Nergal and Ereshkigal*). The underworld is frequently linked with or denoted by the same word as 'mountain' (KUR, also "foreign country"), not intended to specify an actual or even generic mountain but perhaps instead the natural feature which bears the greatest contrast to the flat alluvial plains which were home to the living[1].

The boundary between these lives, while not porous, was still flexible enough to allow for continued contact. *Kispu* rituals in the 2nd millennium BC retain the possibility of a direct dead-to-living link despite gates or utterly alien environments, while descriptions of the underworld (*Gilgamesh, Descent of Ur-Namma*; Katz 2003: 113 ff.) suggest a structured afterlife society including a hierarchical pantheon of deities and officials, which mirrored the urban life of the living. Literary texts imply that passage from the world of the living to that of the dead was virtually impossible and extremely dangerous for the living (*Gilgamesh* Tablet XII), but this does not rule out connectivity and especially the movement of food and drink from the world of the living to that of the dead. 'Magico-medical' texts imply that the movement of the dead "backward" to the world of the living was slightly less restricted; ghosts or spirits could plague the living, for instance (Scurlock 2006). Archaeologically, the ongoing relationship between the living and dead is presented through the presence of graves– the gateways to the underworld–within the domestic sphere, through the evidence for libations and food offerings above graves (including altars in some cases, e.g. Old Babylonian Ur), and even in the common practice of clothed whole-body interment, which suggests that the form of the body retained a conceptual value. Textual material supplements archaeological evidence through descriptions of post-burial rituals offering food and drink to the dead and rituals involving speaking the name of the dead aloud.

Mesopotamian texts focus on the negative aspects of this living-to-dead connectivity: the possibility of ghosts bringing disease or stealing children, or the inversion of normal life when the dead visit the living. Post-burial food and drink offerings are often described in a language of fear and prevention, while incantations to

---

[1] See Katz 2003 for a full analysis of textual descriptions of the underworld and discussion of the paradox of a mountain being imagined below ground.

keep away evil spirits are rife.[2] Texts that describe the obligations to the dead held by the first-born or the occupier of an inherited house do not imply that this was a particularly joyous obligation, more one which was contractual and came with penalties for omission. The positive, benevolent side to the dead-living association, that of persistence of social connections and the reassuring permanency of family, is underplayed in texts but comes through clearly in archaeological terms: burial of the dead under house floors in such close proximity should be unbearable if we use the texts alone as witnesses.

Recent theoretical views of mortuary practices hold that these practices may have as much to do with living relations as with the dead individual, burial being a chance for the living to reinforce or in fact to alter relationships or perceptions of relationships (Gamble *et al.* 2001, Parker Pearson 1999, Härke 1997, Jensen & Nielsen 1997). But the theoretical reduction of the dead to a passive role, as a mere tool for social distortion, does not hold true for Mesopotamia, because of the flexible boundary between life and the afterlife. On the negative side, if one misrepresents the dead, he or she may return to redress the problem; on the positive side, because social relations endure, an artificial or "incorrect" representation of the dead would be unsustainable. Mortuary practices in Mesopotamia thus must be seen as simultaneously representing the wishes and priorities of the living and reflecting the dead's social identity or identities, within a generalized adherence to regional cultural traditions.

In urban or town settlements in northern Mesopotamia, such as Chagar Bazar, death presented the living with a choice between two main options for burial placement: open areas such as cemeteries, off-site locations or other unoccupied areas, versus enclosed, home-based, under-floor interment. Cemeteries unfortunately are rarely recovered in this region; there is scattered supporting evidence for the use of abandoned sites or unused parts of sites for burials, but these are the first locales to suffer erosion or damage from subsequent re-occupation, and such cemeteries are not frequently recovered. The existence of cemeteries at times is proposed because of low numbers of dead or unusual age ratios found in grave samples within occupied and excavated parts of sites. We logically assume that there should have been more dead individuals during the length of time represented by a stratigraphic phase, or that there should have been more dead children in contrast to the number of dead adults or vice versa, and therefore that an additional mode and location was utilized for burial, such as conveniently-missing cemeteries[3].

The use of abandoned mounds for cemeteries fits with concepts of 'timemarks' and 'persistent places' visible in regional settlement patterns (see Chapter 7). Presence of the dead on an 'abandoned' site maintains that site as a paradoxically active locale, a landscape marker with ongoing significance. In addition, an overlooked area with potential for burials is the lower slopes or outer rings of inhabited sites, particularly in the 3rd and 2nd millennia BC with the growth of high tells and the conscious use of earlier occupational accumulations as site foundations. Burials on the outskirts of

---

[2] When such offerings appear to honour the dead (versus ensuring their continued contentment so that they do not return), these are mostly likely to be directed to kings or royal family members (i.e., *Death of Ur-Namma*). The distinction between honouring the dead (*palahu*) and taking care of the dead (*kunnu*) is subtle (van der Toorn 1996).

[3] See e.g. Schwartz 2007: 42, Kepinski-Lecomte 1996: 194. The extreme scarcity of burials from both southern and northern Mesopotamia during the 4th millennium BC may indicate that a third option was in play during that time.

settlements would add figuratively to the solidity of the site's base, adding a layer of actual ancestors to the layers of ancestral occupation, reaffirming the site as a Place in the landscape and acting as virtual anchors or foundation stakes for the settlement.[4]

The multiple modes of burial have repercussions for reconstruction of social memories. Cemeteries are single-purpose sites dedicated to memory, but burials below houses lie within multi-purpose spaces (courtyards in particular), spaces not set aside for the sole purpose of commemoration. Does that make these individuals less important, less worthy of remembrance, since their memory would be diluted by the continued weaving, cooking, sleeping, and other life activities taking place in proximity? Or does their very proximity to the living mean they are more important to the social unit and its continued operation than are those separated into cemeteries? No self-conscious rituals or scheduled visits would be necessary to maintain the past-present-future continuity with ancestral individuals in below-floor burials, since the full social unit continues to "live" together.

The issue of surface marking of burials–a virtually unknown variable in both north and south Mesopotamia–is an additional complication. Visible commemoration, a "gravestone" or marker, is more likely to be found in a cemetery, and less likely to be present within a house because of the awkward logistics and multiple-use of space. Yet visual commemoration of grave location (barrows, mounds, gravestones) is generally linked to persistence of memory and to the continued existence of the idea and identity of the dead. Under-floor burial thus would have the added aspect of negotiation between practical concerns and emotion.

There are other social aspects relevant to burial placement choice beyond the importance of memory and ancestral connections: the dead in cemeteries may have had a broader social identity and may have "belonged" to the whole community, while those below houses belonged solely to the family unit.[5] But in such a case, one would expect children to be far more consistently buried below house floors, since they are the least likely to have a corporate identity or importance beyond the family. There may be more prosaic reasons for the two modes of burial, such as seasonal—it being pragmatic to bury someone in a cemetery at a remove from habitation during hot seasons, for instance. There may be alternate valid mortuary practices (cremation, disarticulation, excarnation, mass burial) which we see represented archaeologically only occasionally and are perhaps too quick to describe as aberrant. Clearly our studies of burials in the ancient Near East have only touched the surface of a complex range of past choices.

Identity and variability

Variability and specificity of grave goods, skeletal treatments, and burial forms may reveal aspects of individuals' or families' wealth, status, profession, ethnicity, or other social categories. At Chagar Bazar in the early 2nd millennium BC, there are potential ethnic differences to be signalled, given the mixed Hurrian, Amorite and Akkadian population evidenced by personal names in texts from the site and region.

---

[4] Much the same logic has been proposed for occupation of prehistoric mounds in South East Europe: "Tell living, with its roots in the ideology of descent, is reinforced by human bone deposition in ancestral space" (Chapman 2000: 140).

[5] For the variation in numbers of below-floor burials in houses at 3rd millennium BC Abu Salabikh, and the possibility that those households with "public" identities used cemetery burial as an opportunity for public display, see Steele 1990. Similar ideas have been put forth for the Ur Royal Cemetery (Pollock 1991, 2007).

There is the possibility that graves may include representation of different professions that are recorded in texts (agricultural, herding or craft specialization). During times of political change (such as the shifting political groups and allegiances of the early 2nd millennium BC) social rituals and routines may change, including mortuary practices, to emphasize attachment to one group or another. However, there is simply not enough variability among grave goods, skeletal treatments and graves to illuminate differentials among the Chagar Bazar burials excavated, and thus among the living individuals they represent.

Northern Mesopotamia in the early 2nd millennium BC in fact seems to be a world in which there is very little social signalling for the majority of the dead. Mortuary practices are "routinised", with little variation visible inter-site or intra-site. Broadly within Mesopotamia, wealth and social status (whether of the individual or family) may be indicated by quality and quantity of grave goods, and some specific prestige items indicate authority or ownership (cylinder seals) while other objects convey the ability to host significant feasting events (large numbers of vessels). [6] Extremes of hierarchical and heterarchical variability are routinely uncovered in southern Mesopotamia dating to the 3rd millennium BC[7]. Contemporary burials with evidence of hierarchy display are fewer, but still present, in northern Mesopotamia[8]. Yet that great variety of the 3rd millennium is flattened in the early 2nd millennium BC. Most northern Mesopotamian dead in the early 2nd millennium BC are interred with either nothing or with small groups of pottery vessels and occasional tools, weapons and sparse personal ornaments. Burial pits do not vary greatly in size or elaboration[9], and burials simply do not seem to be the stage on which distinct identities were presented in the early 2nd millennium. Despite the social, economic and political complexity of early 2nd millennium BC northern Mesopotamian society, mortuary practices are not correspondingly complex, at least not complex in ways represented archaeologically.

Most of the Chagar Bazar burials (in Mallowan's and our more recent excavations) are single primary inhumations. Several of the graves are of shaft-and-pit form or are vaulted tombs of mud-brick, but most are simple oval pits that opened straight down from the associated surface (floors in rooms occasionally, or surfaces in courtyards more often). One empty vaulted grave (Tomb 18 in Area G) opens a window onto the possibility that the vaulted graves were prepared ahead of time, before a relevant death. In such a reconstruction, the tomb becomes akin to a room or courtyard and an intrinsic part of the living building.

---

[6] Anomalies such as the Early Dynastic Royal Graves at Ur have received disproportionate discussion (e.g. Cohen 2005, Dickson 2006), yet even these extremely rich graves are arguably the extreme of a continuum, rather than something unique. The human sacrifices could be viewed as very expensive grave goods and the fact of their deaths as an expression of ownership or power only a few steps beyond the possession of a seal, harp or golden bowl.

[7] As well as the Royal Graves and linked burials at Ur, Early Dynastic and Akkadian Period burials have been recovered at e.g. Abu Salabikh, Khafajah, Kish, Nippur, Umm al-Hafriyat and Uruk, showing a remarkably wide range of wealth and status. Specific objects offer the possibility of isolating social identities (i.e., warriors [Philip 1995] and priestesses [Pollock 1991]).

[8] E.g. the Umm el-Marra tombs (Schwartz 2007); Tell al-Banat tombs (Porter 1995); Til Barsip hypogeum (Thureau-Dangin & Dunand 1936).

[9] The later 2nd millennium BC tombs at Qatna seem to revive the practice of conspicuous consumption, but the early portion of this millennium is, at the moment, fairly barren.

The presence of grave goods (personal ornaments) in at least two burials of children (T. 41, Area A, Plate 3c; T. 33, Area G, Pl. 9a) indicates that children were not viewed as unimportant. Only one grave of our sample includes tools (Area A, Tomb 4): a pair of bone weaving needles and a bone spindle whorl (Plate 1). The minimal presence of working tools is similar in the larger sample of "Level 1" graves excavated by Mallowan; only a single grave (G 3) held a possible metallurgist's crucible (Mallowan 1936: 20, Fig. 4: 25). The clarity and specificity of these few tools' function is notable and may hint at a distinct approach to death and identity for these individuals, but one in a minority. For the vast majority of the dead in Mesopotamia in all time periods, work was not a factor in the afterlife: weapons relatively often accompany the dead, but tools, in the sense of industrial equipment, are extremely rare. Texts make no mention of work in the afterlife, so this lack of tools mirrors texts and indicates that at least one of the strongest identities a living individual may hold was not transported with him or her to the underworld. Pottery vessels, followed by ornaments, dominate the grave assemblages of all periods in Mesopotamia, and Chagar Bazar in the early 2nd millennium BC is no exception: seven graves included pottery vessels, and four included ornaments.

Northern versus southern Mesopotamian mortuary traditions

We must tackle the problem of whether funerary traditions and the concept of the afterlife for text-poor northern Mesopotamians were the same as those in the text-rich south. Many of the same mortuary practices are visible in both south and north across the millennia, such as the majority of burials being primary inhumations in simple pits, the comparable choice between cemetery/external burials and domestic/under-floor burials, the inclusion of pottery vessels for food and drink and the presence of personal ornaments.

Yet there is a subtle difference between northern and southern burials in the make-up of pottery sets buried with the dead. Woolley insisted that all Larsa Period graves at Ur contained a plate or bowl (1976: 36, 38), but his Analysis of Pottery Types and Tabular Analysis of Graves (*ibid.*: 178 ff and 195 ff, respectively) indicate that plates were popular, but in fact tall narrow jars and beakers were more common (his Types 45, 48, 50-53, 69-72). Similarly, tall flasks were the most common form found in Old Babylonian graves at Uruk, although plates/ bowls were close behind (Boehmer *et al.* 1995). In graves at Ur, Uruk and Tell ed-Der (de Meyer 1978), the tall beakers often came in groups, frequently four to six, with smaller numbers of small plates or bowls and large jars (frequently only one example of each of the latter). At Chagar Bazar and other northern sites, graves frequently include a single large jar (classic "Khabur Ware" jars or their unpainted cousins), but an equivalent to the tall beakers of the south are absent in the north, and shallow bowls are virtually non-existent. Instead, small fine ware cups or jars are the drinking vessel provided.

Within the overall ceramic assemblage, there is an emphasis on communal dining from large dishes in northern Mesopotamia, when contrasted to individual dining in southern Mesopotamia (see Chapter 5). Yet this difference does not come through in the burial "sets" in the north, where jars for storing liquids and small individual drinking vessels are the main types represented. The large shallow bowls or plates in the domestic assemblage are completely absent from the grave sets. Some of the Chagar Bazar jars contained bronze strainers from the ends of reed straws, which might indicate that the jar would have been a communal one (although it must be admitted that these jars only ever contained a single strainer, not multiple ones). By contrast, both domestic and grave assemblages of southern Mesopotamia emphasize an individualized "pouring" culture, in which food would have been more often consumed from separate serving bowls or cups.[10] Grave assemblages in the south also cater for consumption by large numbers of people either at the point of burial or in the afterlife: groups of small bowls, numerous examples of tall beakers. Northern grave assemblages are more oriented to the single dead individual, for instance usually containing only one drinking cup.

The shaft-and-pit grave form seen in some of the Chagar Bazar graves (i.e. Tombs 10, 11, 13, below) is not usually seen in the south, where straight-sided simple oval pits are the norm. There were a few examples of shaft-and-pit graves uncovered at Tell ed-Der, in Sondage A (de Meyer 1978: Phases III through I, Isin-Larsa through Old Babylonian), but these are fewer than 5% of the graves encountered there.[11] The Der examples are not exactly the same shape as those in the north, having a deeper shaft and more extended, lateral chamber, versus the shorter shaft and bell-shaped chamber of Chagar Bazar.

Burial of infants or children in pottery vessels within domestic spaces is relatively common in the south during the Old Babylonian Period. But the south sees a common format of infant burial in a pair of bowls, one inverted over the other (i.e., Uruk: Boehmer et al. 1995, Tell ed-Der: de Meyer 1978, 1984) or within pots with plates as lids (i.e., Haradum: Kepinski-Lecomte 1996). We have no examples of this use of bowl pairs or covered jars at Chagar Bazar; some infants are in jars (in Area A), often with the neck broken away to allow insertion of the body. In all these instances of burial in jars and bowls, the ceramic vessels have not retained any of their customary function but have been re-identified as coffins.

Area A and Area G Graves

A total of 23 burials were found in Areas A and G, twelve in Area A and eleven in Area G. Of the twelve in Area A, one is relatively recent (Tomb 7) and another was a 3rd millennium BC grave that emerged through erosion of the slope east of and below the early 2nd millennium BC levels (Tomb 30). Of the remaining ten burials in Area A, six were infants or children, three were adults and one grave contained partial skeletons of both an adult and a child; all were early 2nd millennium BC in date. In Area G, all eleven burials belonged to the early 2nd millennium BC; five of these were adults, five were children (most belonging to Phase III) and one grave contained the partial skeletons of both an adult and a child. (See Appendix to Chapter 4 for full scientific analyses.) Apart from these burials, one elaborately constructed vaulted grave (Tomb 18) was empty. The preservation of all the skeletons was poor; the bones were fragile and apt to splinter, from the water percolation and fluctuations of temperature and humidity found relatively near to the mound surface.

During the 1930s excavations, Max Mallowan excavated a significant number of burials in Areas TD and BD, adjacent to Area G. While the stratigraphic relationships of these graves to each other and their relationships to the more recent

---

[10] There is ample 3rd millennium BC southern Mesopotamian iconography of banqueting, involving drinking with straws from large communal vessels (most notably on Early Dynastic cylinder seals and reliefs). But the evidence of the overwhelming number of individual bowls/cups in grave and house contexts (i.e., Nippur WF during the ED through Old Babylonian Periods; McMahon 2006) indicates that pouring was a more common option in those theatres.

[11] No shaft and lateral chamber graves appear in Isin-Larsa and Old Babylonian levels at Nippur, Ur or Uruk. The northern Babylonian location of Tell ed-Der and connections with regions further north may explain their presence there.

phasing in this part of the site often must remain undecided, the graves provide a good general sample of approximately contemporary dead individuals within which the Area G graves in particular must be set.

Grave locations and types

The graves in Area G were dug below surfaces of open courtyards or, more rarely, below the floors of rooms; in Area A they were found in rooms of the subsidiary structures in the complex, not below the administrative building, and in an open area to the southwest, particularly in Phase I. Spatial associations between graves in either area were not particularly strong, with most graves being on their own within any particular context. The exception comprises Tombs 10, 11, 13 and 33, all in the largest courtyard exposed in Area G, associated with Building G 2, Phase II/1 (a courtyard which also held L. 4.3, a probable grave shaft; see Fig. 28 and Plate 6b). These four graves were all contained within the same architectural phase and are approximately contemporary; Tombs 10 and 11 were adjacent and aligned and so presumably quite close in time, while Tomb 13 was in a different corner of the courtyard but also in comparable alignment. Tomb 33, in yet another corner, is less closely linked. The first three graves were clearly deliberately positioned so as not to overlap, although whether this was through unaided memory or because the graves' locations were marked at the surface is unanswerable. The close proximity of graves to the numerous living activities that would have taken place in the courtyard context supports the assumption that the dead were not viewed as remote and alien. The visual accessibility of this courtyard, separated from the street by a low wall, maintains the dead as members of the wider community, as well as the family.

Energy expenditures on grave construction have been viewed in Processualist analysis as relevant to determination of the deceased's status, while in post-Processual reconstructions expenditures are deemed indicative of the resolution of statements regarding the dead, the dead's family, and the social setting. There is minimal variability represented at Chagar Bazar with regard to either of these approaches. Three grave types are present: simple pits, shafts-with-pits, and constructed brick tombs. The scale of the pits is not such that there was a great difference between shaft-with-pit and simple pit graves, although logically the smaller infant graves (all simple pits) involve less energy expenditure. The grave with the greatest expenditure, Tomb 18, with its large pit and carefully-constructed mud-brick vault, did not have an occupant or any grave goods (Plate 5a). The only other vaulted grave in Area G, T. 13 (with a poorly-constructed and collapsed vault), was moderately rich, with a range of metal ornaments and tools, as well as ceramics and a few beads (Plate 8). Similar vaulted tombs were recorded during Mallowan's excavation of the adjacent Area BD: Graves G1, G 133, G 137, G 139, G 141, G 143 and G 154 all had mud-brick vaults.[12] Of these six vaulted, relatively labour-intensive graves, at least one (G 141) was quite richly endowed with grave goods; however, G 133, for example, was not comparably rich. Thus, the expense denoted by the tomb construction was not carried on consistently in the realm of grave goods.

There is episodic evidence that vaulted graves in the region were used for sequential burials over time, with original interments occasionally being pushed to one

---

[12] Mallowan distinguished between 'domical" (G 133, G 137) and "corbel" (G 1, G 139, G 141) vaults. The distinction is a subtle one, based on shape of the roof and 'ceiling' in section: domical has a rounded form, corbel has a slightly pointed arch. The construction method appears the same in both cases. Area G Tomb 18 had a slightly pointed or corbelled roof.

side to make room for subsequent ones (e.g. at Tell Arbid; Bielinski 2005: 486-488; as in Isin-Larsa and Old Babylonian Period Ur). This aspect of long-term use, together with the fact that the Area G chamber was empty, compels a more nuanced interpretation of these vaulted tombs. They are perhaps not to be associated with one individual and related to that individual's status or proposed status; instead they are corporate tombs and may be built well before the death of any specific individual, when death was only an abstract concept or problem. We assume this is the case with the Area G Tomb 18, built in anticipation but never utilised. In such circumstances, the tomb may say more about property ownership, permanency and future planning than about the dead or burial ritual.

Age, body position and orientation

The ratio of adult to child skeletons in Areas A and G, combined, is almost equal, ten adults to thirteen children[13]. This figure conflates two distinct architectural phases in Area A and four phases in Area G. However, if the assemblage of graves is divided by architectural phase and Area, the numbers are so small as to be statistically insignificant. Area A appears to have seen slightly more child than adult burials (four adults to seven children), while the numbers are equal in Area G (six adults and six children). The Area A numbers in particular are potentially skewed by the nature of the primary structure in this area (administrative) and its lack of burials; the majority of Area A burials belong to Phase I.

Mallowan's publication of the burials from Area BD (Mallowan 1936, 1937) did not always specify whether a burial was of a child or an adult. If we tentatively infer that he identified child graves every time and that unspecified graves contained adults (as well as any graves definitely recorded as adult), his ratio of adults to children would be roughly 9:1. This ratio does not match ours nor the higher expected child mortality rate for "pre-industrial" societies. As well as the issue of unidentified graves, Mallowan probably ignored many of the less-rich infant and child burials; but even our ratio must mean that burials of infants and children are archaeologically less visible, either because of complete post-depositional decay or off-site placement.

The positioning and orientation in the Area A and G burials vary widely when viewed in aggregate, but there appears to be an underlying patterning distinguishing children and adults. Among adults, three heads were oriented to the north, and two each were oriented northeast, east and southwest. Among children, there were two each oriented to east, south, southwest and west. There are thus some areas of overlap and non-overlap: east and southwest are shared by both ages, but only children's heads are associated with south and west, while only adults' heads were associated with the opposite north and northeast. The sample from our excavations, however, was too small to be statistically significant. Unfortunately, this tentative distinction between adult and child burials cannot be isolated within Mallowan's larger sample because of his lack of age specifications.

Mallowan recorded the orientations of graves in a rather haphazard manner, although it is possible to determine orientations of many graves from their cross-shaped representation in his plan of Area BD. He noted in passing that there was "no fixed rule for the direction of the head" (Mallowan 1937), and that the graves were simply aligned with the walls of the structures below which they were buried.

---

[13] These figures count the adult and child in each of the dual graves and omit the possibly Islamic and 3rd millennium BC burials, as well as the empty tomb (see Catalogue and Table 4.1 for descriptions).

Grave goods

The grave goods with the Chagar Bazar burials correspond generally to the Mesopotamia-wide belief that the dead required food and drink in the afterlife. Pottery vessels are the most common grave goods, but these are not consistently found in all graves, implying that immediate provision for the afterlife was a strong but not crucial element of burial practice. Possible reasons for the apparent absence of vessels include extreme poverty (no "spare" vessels to donate to the dead), perishable vessels invisible in the archaeological record or family dynamics that emphasized the promise of future food offerings over the immediacy of offerings at burial. It is plausible but unfortunately un-provable that the lack of pottery could be an ethnic, religious or profession indicator (such as the tradition of a pastoral population); burials with few or no grave goods may be uncommon but are widespread in all periods across Mesopotamia.

Most of the vessels found in the graves are matched within the ceramic assemblages from the houses (i.e., the Khabur Ware jars, Narrow-Mouth Jars and Fine Ware Beakers). These vessels may have had a pre-burial use-life. Other grave vessels that are not paralleled or are infrequent in the non-grave ceramic assemblage include the burnished grey fine ware beaker with Tomb 13 in Area G (CB 2078; Pl. 8), a funnel in the same grave (CB 2079; Pl. 8), and bottles in Tomb 12 (CB 2497; Pl. 2b), Tomb 41 (CB 3114; Pl. 3c) and Tomb 39 (CB 3092; Pl. 6a). The latter bottle was so warped and off-kilter that it could not stand upright; this would have been a waster or irregular jar of low value. Some grave vessels are simply smaller versions of "normal" vessels: CB 2077 in Tomb 13 (Pl. 8) and CB 2977 in Tomb 33 (Pl. 9a) are small Khabur Ware jars, and CB 3093 in Tomb 39 (Pl. 6a) is a small Wide-Mouth Jar. These rarer types and variants thus might have had very short and non-complex lives used only in graves. The inclusion of unusual rare types in graves (and the exclusion of the wide shallow bowls so common in the domestic assemblage, as mentioned above) points to a nuanced distinction between the types of vessels used in the world and in the underworld.

While labour effort was put into the excavation of the burial pits (at least for the adults), there is not a great deal of economic expenditure evidenced in non-ceramic grave goods. Personal ornaments are few and are limited to beads, metal pins, bracelets and a ring; only sparse precious metals and semi-precious stones are included. There was a silver pin in Tomb 4 (Pl. 1), a silver ornament, three bronze pins and a bronze ring in Tomb 13 (Pl. 8), three bronze bracelets in Tomb 41 (Pl. 3c), and beads in Tombs 41, 13, and 33 (Pls. 3c, 8, 9a).

Tomb 4 in Area A was the only burial that contained real working tools: two bone weaving needles and a bone spindle whorl (Pl. 1). The weaving needles had signs of use wear (high polish) and were clearly not merely symbolic grave goods[14]. It is tempting to see the weaving needles and whorl as personal possessions of the deceased, which would have been not value-less for the living but so closely associated with the dead that their use by another was inconceivable. In this case, deposition in the grave with the dead approaches simple disposal of the items but has similar complex nuances to the post-use ritual deposition in caches of votive statues and other items of great symbolic weight. The resulting interment with the dead is a compromise

---

[14] The right arm of this individual was more developed than the left, with bony spurs, possibly from long-term and repetitive labour such as is typical of weaving. See Appendix for details.

between value and a valued association on the one hand and the cessation of usability on the other.

As was noted above, Mallowan's publications focussed on those burials that included grave goods, so an assessment of number of graves without burial offerings in his sample is impossible. However, child burials tended to include pottery as their only offering, and then single vessels only (his Graves 5, 93, 155, 157), while adults more often were buried with weapons or ornaments, as well as pottery, often more than one vessel. Within our own sample, most of the very young infants and children (Tombs 8, 15, 26, 32, 34, 35, 49) were buried with only a burial jar, while one young (Tomb 41) and one slightly older child (Tomb 33; age 11) were interred with pottery and ornaments.

Catalogue of graves[15]:

Area A Graves

Phase II (see Fig. 9 for architectural context of all Area A Phase II graves)

Tomb 4 (see Plate 1 for plan and grave goods)
Description: Below lowest floor in the northeast corner of Building I, early in Phase II. This is the only grave in this building; and the filled pit was covered almost immediately by a small storage bin, while the room use shifted from human occupation to animal stabling. The lack of grave commemoration and even insult implied here, to Western eyes, was surely not the past intention. This grave was, in fact, one of the more comprehensively equipped graves on the site.
The grave has a slightly bell-shaped pit, maximum ca. 0.85 m wide, 1.37 m long, and ca. 1.00 m deep. The skeleton was an adult, probably female, tightly flexed, lying on its left side, with the arms bent and hands in front of the face. The head was to the north, facing east; the teeth were worn and indicate an older adult.
Contents: 1 Khabur Ware jar: CB 989, 1 Narrow-mouth jar CB 990, 1 fine ware beaker CB 984 (inside jar CB 989)
2 bone weaving needles: CB 988, 991
1 bone spindle whorl: CB 986
1 silver pin: CB 992
1 bronze beer strainer CB 985 (inside jar CB 989)
The bone tools and silver pin were found near the head, while the jars had been placed at the feet.

Tomb 8 (Plate 2a)
Description: Cut from a now-eroded surface into the northwest corner of Building IV, Locus 55. This is one of two contemporary graves in the corners of this room (see Tomb 9), dated late within Phase II.
The grave is a roughly oval simple pit, maximum 0.7 m long, 0.55 m wide; its original depth is lost. It contained a young child's skeleton, flexed on its left side, with the

---

[15] The series of numbers is broken here because a single series was used for all burials on the site. Numbers missing were assigned to burials excavated by Syrian or Belgian colleagues and will be published separately. See Ch. 5 for full details of all pottery, Ch. 6 for details of objects. See Table 4.1 for tabulated summary of grave variables.

arms straight and hands between the knees. The head points to west-southwest, the face to the north. The body had been pressed into the northern side of the pit, with the head bent back slightly and the knees tight against the pit edge. No grave goods were included.

Tomb 9 (Plate 2a)
Description: Cut from a now-eroded surface into the northeast corner of Building IV, Locus 55. It is roughly contemporary with Tomb 8, datable late within Phase II. The pit was oval, maximum 1.8 m long, 1.4 m wide; its original depth is lost. It is very slightly bell-shaped on its eastern edge and had undercut the base of wall 00-12. The pit was partially outlined with mudbrick fragments on the western edge and there was an irregular scatter of half mudbricks and large sherds in the base of the pit.
The pit held an adult skeleton, lightly flexed, lying on its left side. The right arm was bent and the hand placed in front of the face; the left arm was bent under the body. The head was placed to the north, the face to the east.
No grave goods were included; the pottery from the pit comprised mostly non-diagnostic sherds from several different vessels, intended as a paving or platform for the dead. The size of the pit and location of the body at its eastern edge would have left space remaining for a second (and possibly even a third) skeleton to be added.

Phase I (see Fig. 18 for architectural context of Phase I graves)

Tomb 12 (Plate 2b)
Description: Cut from a now-eroded surface along the northern edge of Phase II's wall 99-16 (then a still-visible ruin). It was subsequently cut at its western end by the erosion gully L. 67. The pit was at maximum 1.75 m long and 0.49 m wide; its original depth is lost. It dates to the use of the northern building in Phase I.
The only preserved remains were the lower half of an articulated adult skeleton, the legs lightly flexed, lying on its back. The head would have been to the west-southwest but is missing, along with the upper body, removed by the erosion gully.
No grave goods remain, possibly due to erosion damage, but complete bottle CB 2497 was found nearby in erosion gully L. 67 and may have originated from this grave.

Tomb 34 (Plate 2c)
Description: One of four child or infant burials located in the southwest of Area A, cut from within the open space L. 76, adjacent to wall 01-14. The pit was an irregular oval, maximum 0.6 m long, 0.35 m wide, depth ca. 0.5 m.
It contained an infant's skeleton, on its back, the head to the east, the face turned to the north. The left arm was at the side, the right arm bent across the body, the right leg flexed and the left leg bent upwards. The preservation of the bones was very poor and some disturbance had occurred. No grave goods were included.

Tomb 35 (Plate 3a)
Description: Another infant grave in the southwest of Area A, cut into the open space L. 74 from a now-eroded surface, west of possibly still-visible wall 01-16 of Phase II's Building V. The burial pit was sealed by a line of mudbricks (01-6) and by a baked brick paving (01-7), perhaps intended to mark the location of the grave and to prevent erosion and exposure.

This grave had an oval pit, maximum 0.40 m long and 0.29 m wide; its original depth is lost. The pit was just large enough to contain the burial jar.

Inside the jar was an infant skeleton, on its right side, the head to the east, facing north. The legs were tightly flexed, the left arm bent and left hand between the knees, while the right arm lay under the body.

Burial jar: CB 4159, rim and neck broken in antiquity, red painted X on shoulder. This paint mark is remarkably sloppy in comparison to the other decorative effects of Khabur Ware, although the red paint colour is the same as is seen in the striped decoration on other vessels. Potters' marks are otherwise virtually absent in the early 2nd millennium BC. This sign almost seems to mark a manufacturing "second" or irregular that might still be sold and was deemed appropriate for an infant burial.

Tomb 38 (Plate 3b)

Description: A third burial in the southwest of Area A, cut into L. 73, adjacent to wall 00-6 of Building V, from a now-eroded surface. It probably belongs to Phase I and was buried in the ruins of Building V, rather than belonging to Phase II. Similar to Tomb 35, this was a small oval pit, maximum 0.25 cm long and 0.20 cm wide, just large enough for the burial jar.

The jar contained a random collection of bones from a foetus and an adult, reduced to small fragments of skull and a possible arm bone, respectively. Preservation should not have been so poor inside a jar (especially when compared with the comparatively better preservation of the skeleton inside the jar in Tomb 35); this raises the possibility that this might have been a secondary burial, as there was no sign of disturbance of the burial jar or the soil immediately above it. The orientation of the jar was north to south, with the mouth of the jar pointed towards the south.

Burial jar: base and lower body only, broken in antiquity (not registered or illustrated)

Tomb 41 (Plate 3c)

Description: Final infant/ child burial in the southwest of Area A, cut from within L. 76, at the south section, dated to early Phase I.

This grave has a sub-rectangular pit, maximum 0.7 m long and ca. 0.26 m wide. An area of baked bricks and cobbles (01-5) covered the area of the grave and extended further to its north; this may have been a grave marker and protective capping.

The skeleton was of a very young child, older than that in Tombs 34, 35 and 38, laid on its left side, the head to the west, facing south. The legs were lightly flexed, the arms were bent in front of the body.

Contents: Bottle: CB 3114, next to head
Three fragmentary bronze bracelets: CB 3104, 3105, 3106
Two beads: CB 3107 a & b

Skeleton A (not illustrated)
Description: Newborn skeleton inside disused bread oven 00-20, north end of Area A.

Skeleton B (not illustrated)
Description: Newborn skeleton in upper layer of pit Locus 9, north end of Area A.

Area G Graves

Phase III (see Fig. 21 for architectural context of Area G Phase III graves)

Tomb 15   (Plate 4a)
Description: North edge of Area G Trench I, cut into the outdoor/ unroofed space L.20 along the south face and slightly cut into wall 00-20 of Building G 4.
This grave was a simple oval pit just over 40 cm long and only 20 cm wide, partly outlined with mud-bricks, containing an infant skeleton, flexed with its head to the west, looking up, its hands crossed on the chest. No grave goods were included.

Tomb 26   (not illustrated)
Description: Northeast corner of Area G Trench II, cut from within L. 27 in Building BDG 5, at the top of Phase III.
The skeleton was placed in a small oval pit, maximum 0.64 cm long, 0.33 cm wide, and possibly only 25 cm deep (immediately sealed by wall 00-52).
The grave held a fragmentary infant skeleton in an extremely poor state of preservation, possibly lying on its left side, the head oriented to the southwest.
Sherds of two incomplete jars lay below and around the skeleton, probably as a paving since both were too fragmentary to be a burial jar (as in Area A Tomb 9); there were no grave goods.

Tomb 32   (Plate 4b)
Description: Western half of Area G Trench II, cut from L. 37.1, late in Phase III.
The pit was sub-rectangular and maximum 0.47 m long and 0.42 m wide, possibly only 25 cm deep; mud-bricks were placed along the west edge.
The pit held another infant skeleton in an extremely poor state of preservation, as in Tomb 26, flexed, lying on its left side, with the head to the south, facing west. No grave goods were included.

Tomb 49   (Plate 4c)
Description: Near the southern edge of Area G Trench II, cut into L. 77, sealed by corner of subsidiary walls 01-26 and 01-27.
The oval pit was 0.45 m long (as excavated; it is probably c 50-55 cm), 0.25 m maximum wide and runs into the south section of the excavation.
The pit held an infant skeleton on its back, with its head to the south, facing up. The legs were flexed and tilted to the left, the right arm was bent across the body, left arm at the side. No grave goods were included.

Tomb 50   (not illustrated)
Description: Western end of Area G Trench IV, cut into the western room of Building G 4 (L. 79.1) from a now-eroded surface, dated to late within Phase III.
The pit was difficult to articulate and poorly preserved because of its proximity to the mound surface and the erosion in this area, but it appeared to be roughly oval, maximum 1.28 m long, 0.84 m wide. The east end of the pit skims the west face of wall 01-49.
The contents were a disarticulated and partial mixture of the skeletons of an adult and a young child. The adult skull fragments lay at the east end of the pit but this may not have been the original position of the head. No grave goods were included.

Chapter 4

Phase II/2 (see Fig. 24 for architectural context of Phase II/2 graves)

Tomb 18   (Plate 5a)
Description: This grave is one of the very few within a roofed room, rather than open space or an unroofed courtyard, placed below a room floor, within L.16 in Area G Trench I.
The grave had a large and deep oval pit, with a barrel-vaulted mud-brick tomb constructed inside it. The pit was 2.9 m long and 1.4 m wide, and the vault was constructed tightly against its sides at the southern end; the northern end had a curved outline of mud-bricks that surrounded the access point. The bricks are an unusual orange colour and thinner than the bricks used for architecture in Area G (c. 6 cm). The arched layers of brick are sloped slightly to lean against the southern edge. The grave fits along the east wall of the room, and the pit skims the walls to south (00-15) and east (00-14).   There was no evidence of tomb robbing or other disturbance, yet this grave was empty.

Tomb 37   (Plate 5b)
Description: Southeast corner of Area G Trench II, in the southern half of courtyard of Building BDG 1. There was minor root disturbance.
The grave had an irregular sub-rectangular pit, maximum 1.05 m long, 0.66 m wide.
It contained an adult skeleton on its left side, the head to west-southwest, facing north, neck curved up against pit edge. The legs were flexed, the right arm bent, and the left arm extended. No grave goods were included.

Tomb 39   (Plate 6a)
Description: Eastern edge of Area G IV, cut into the courtyard north of Building BDG 2, from a surface removed by Mallowan's excavation. The grave runs into the east section of our excavation and was only partly revealed. It probably dates to Phase II/2, although Phase II/1 is also a possibility.
The grave had a sub-rectangular pit 1.2 m long (as excavated), maximum 0.65 m wide. The skeleton was of a adolescent, on its right side, with the head to the northeast, legs slightly flexed, one arm straight along the body (finger bones were found below the pelvis), the other slightly extended; only the lower half of the body was excavated.
Contents: 1 fine ware beaker CB 3091, and Wide-mouth jar CB 3093 near the feet
1 bottle: CB 3092 near the pelvis (the body had collapsed over the top of this jar)
Bronze beer strainer: CB 3090 (inside jar CB 3093)

Phase II/1 (see Fig. 28 for architectural context of Phase II/1 graves)

Tomb 10   (Plate 6b, c)
Description: Area G Trench I, below a courtyard surface, within L.4 (sealed by L. 4.2). Tomb 10 is contemporary with and east of Tomb 11, separated from it by ca 50 cm.
This grave had a rectangular, vertical shaft (c 1.3 m x 75 cm x 1.3 m deep), with a bell-shaped pit (1.4 m x 65 cm x 1 m deep) off its base, to the south. The pit contained an adult, flexed, lying on its back, partly covered with mud-bricks. Its right arm was bent, with the hand on the chest, the left arm lay across the body. The head points to the east, facing north.
Contents: 2 Khabur Ware jars at the feet: CB 1998, CB 1999

Tomb 11 (Plate 6b, 7a)
Description: Area G Trench I, below a courtyard surface, within L.4 (sealed by L. 4.2), approximately 50 cm west of and contemporary with Tomb 10.
Like Tomb 10, this grave had a clear rectangular shaft (1.75 m x 1.15 m x 1.3 m deep) and a bell-shaped pit (1.25m x 85 cm x 1 m deep) to its south. The pit contained an adult skeleton, flexed, lying on its right side, with the head to the northeast, facing north. Like the skeleton of Tomb 10, the body was partly covered by mud-bricks.
Contents: 2 Narrow-mouth jars: CB 2000, CB 2001 at the feet
1 fine ware beaker: CB 2093 near the head
1 copper "beer strainer" with attached reed straw: CB 2066 (inside jar CB 2000)

Locus 4.3 (Plate 6b, 7b)
Trench G I, Courtyard L. 4/7, below courtyard surface (sealed by L. 4.4). This pit is suspiciously square with vertical sides (2.1 m x 1.5 m x 80 cm deep), and it most probably is a tomb shaft, possibly unused. It lies just west of Tombs 10 and 11 but was slightly earlier within this phase.
Contents: Pottery vessel upright at shaft base: CB 1989

Tomb 13 (Plate 6b, 8)
Description: Area G Trench I, below a courtyard surface, L.7 and 9. This is the same courtyard that contained Tombs 10 and 11 (and 4.3); T. 13 lies at the northern side of this space.
This grave had a rectangular burial pit (1.8 m x 95 cm x c 1 m deep), containing an adult skeleton. The body had been placed in the pit and then covered with a loose vault of mud-bricks that filled the northern edge of the shaft to the ground surface and above. Some of the lower bricks had subsequently dropped into the pit and the vault had crumbled at the centre, but the arrangement had remained stable at each end. The skeleton was flexed, lying on its left side with its head to the east, facing south. There were several rodent burrows in the shaft fill.
Contents: 1 Narrow-mouth jar CB 2076, 1 small Khabur Ware jar CB 2077 near feet
1 fine ware beaker: CB 2078 near the shoulder
1 funnel: CB 2079 near the face
2 bronze pins: CB 2080, CB 2081 near face
1 lead ingot: CB 2083 near face
1 bronze ring: CB 2082 below the head
1 bronze tweezers: CB 2084 below the head
1 silver object: CB 2085 below the head
4 stone beads: CB 2086 below the head

Tomb 33 (Plate 9a)
Description: Area G Trench IV, cut from L. 32.2 through Locus 32 and into Phase III walls 01-15 and 01-44. This grave lies in the northeast corner of the same L-shaped courtyard as Tombs 10, 11, 13 and L. 4.3. Unlike most of the other graves, there was identifiable rodent disturbance to this grave (clear tunnels in the fill and into the surrounding pit sides).
This grave has a sub-rectangular pit, with a narrow rectangular access shaft on its west side; the pit was maximum 1.1 m long, 0.5 m wide and c 1 m deep.
It held an older child on its back, the head to the north, while it faced east. The right hand was near the face, the left arm crossed over the chest, the legs were flexed to the right and slightly raised.

Chapter 4

Contents: Bottle: CB 2977 near the feet
Bead necklace: CB 2978 on the chest

Area A, Un-phased Graves

Tomb 30 (Plate 9b)
Description: This 3rd millennium BC grave was discovered eroding from the mound slope east of and below Area A. The pit outline was severely eroded and its original context and depth are lost (unillustrated).
The adult skeleton was represented only by fragments of the skull and finger bones. The pottery group probably had been near the head and was the last part of the grave to be revealed by the erosion, while the body had completely eroded away.
4 jars: CB 2910, 2912, 2913, 2914
1 bowl: CB 2911

Tomb 7 (Plate 9c)
Description: The final grave lies in the north-centre of Area A Trench II, cut from a now-eroded surface and within the disturbed topsoil layer, possibly Ottoman/ recent.
The grave was an oval pit, maximum 1.1 m long and 0.62 m wide; its original depth has been lost but was over 60 cm. Three slabs of local limestone were placed vertically along the northern edge within the pit. The pit contained a child's skeleton, extended on its back, the right foot crossed over the left, the arms crossed on the chest. The head was pointed towards the west-southwest, and the face turned to the south.
Contents: Bronze bracelet: CB 1767

Regional perspective

North Mesopotamian sites with contemporary mortuary material include Tell Arbid, Tell Mozan, Tell Leilan and Tell Mohammed Diyab[16]. At Tell Arbid, Chagar Bazar's nearest neighbour, graves with Khabur Ware pottery and occasional bronze pins, beads or bronze weapons have been found in Areas SA, SD, SS and D (Bieliński 2000, 2001, 2002, 2004, 2005). This site also contains children's burials placed in jars (Bieliński 2004: 339) and, unusually, at least two multiple burials (Bieliński 2002: 283-4; Bieliński 2005: 486). Although the burials' contexts are often eroded or poorly preserved since they lie near the mound surface, the burials in general are associated with contemporary domestic architecture and offer close parallels in structure and contents for our Chagar Bazar graves.

Tell Mozan has Old Babylonian houses and graves in Areas AA, AP, C1 and C2 (Buccellati & Kelly-Buccellati 2001: 62). As at Chagar Bazar, the burials' context seems to be below floors within occupied houses. Further east at Tell Leilan, in Operation 4 (the city wall excavation), there was a Period 1 extramural burial with two adults (Burials 5 and 6) and a structure comparable to Chagar Bazar Tomb 13: a short mud-brick lining along the north edge of the burial pit (4 rectangular bricks), and a layer of flat-lying bricks over the top (Weiss *et al.* 1990: Fig. 25, p. 555). The

---

[16] No Old Babylonian graves have been found at the key neighbouring site of Tell Brak; soundings in 1926 at Tell Hamidi (also known as Tell Hamidiyah and Tell Ahmedi) revealed vaulted tombs with Khabur Ware although little is published (Mallowan 1947: 45). The more-distant Tell al-Rimah lacks excavated graves of this period, and the excavated contemporary levels at sites in the Upper Tigris region (i.e., Tell Billa, Tell Rijm, Tell Taya, Nineveh) also all lack burials for comparison.

skeletons were flexed, on their sides with heads to the west, and pottery vessels had been placed near the heads. Thus, despite the extramural location, interment rituals seem to be closely comparable to those represented in below-floor burials at Chagar Bazar.

Vaulted graves were found previously by Mallowan in Areas BD and TD at Chagar Bazar (Mallowan 1937: Fig. 8: 2, 3) and more recently at Tell Arbid in Areas SD and D in particular (Bieliński 2001: 326, Fig. 10; Bieliński 2004: 339; Bieliński 2005: 486-488, Fig. 10). Further east, vaulted graves in baked brick appear at Tell Mohammed Diyab and Tell Barri.[17] These vaulted tombs usually consist of a square or rectangular lining of bricks within the pit, capped by a relatively low vault. The effort is not especially great, particularly if the bricks were re-used or left over from building construction. Yet it is significantly more elaborate than even the shaft and pit graves, involving a larger pit, more intermediate steps and a wider range of materials. The vault construction technology is slightly tricky, yet it has clearly been mastered for larger rooms elsewhere at Chagar Bazar and other sites, and these burial vaults did not span large distances.

The absence of contrasts in funerary arrangements across these sites is unsurprising, since they belong within a generalized northern Mesopotamian cultural continuum. But given the growth of the Kingdom of Upper Mesopotamia under Samsi-Addu, and its subsequent collapse into city-states and "princedoms," as well as the region's ethnic heterogeneity, one might expect some site-to-site contrasts to have emerged. By the date of the excavated levels in Areas A and G at Chagar Bazar, the site potentially no longer belongs to the same kingdom as Tell Leilan or Muhammed Diyab, although it may maintain a link with Tell Barri. But the political situation in fact is irrelevant to funerary ritual, and the consistency of practice speaks to an underlying regional cultural and social unity that surely even transcends ethnic difference.

---

[17] For a baked-brick barrel-vaulted tomb at Tell Mohammed Diyab with many structural similarities to the Chagar Bazar tomb, see Bachelot 1992: Pl. IV, Dépliant I: tombe 899 & Dépliant II: Coupe EF, 899. For the Tell Barri baked brick barrel-vaulted tomb and its contents (Tomb 593, Area G), see: www.storia.unifi.it/_onr/Tell%20Barri/fototbarp5.htm. Vaulted graves constructed in baked brick also appear in contemporary southern Mesopotamia (i.e., Old Babylonian Larsa: Calvet 1996 and Isin-Larsa to Old Babylonian Ur: Woolley 1976). Tomb placement within houses in the south appears to be structured differently that that in the north, often below the largest room in the house, a main reception room, yet separated from the central courtyard.

Chapter 4

Table 4. 1 Summary of early 2nd Millennium BC Burials in Areas A and G *

Area & Grave Number	Location	Pit type	Age	Pose	Head orientation	Face orientation	Pottery	Ornaments	Tools, other
A, T. 4	Below floor, Building I; Phase II	Bell-shaped pit	Adult, possibly female	Flexed, left side	N	E	2 jars	1 silver pin	2 bone needles, 1 bone spindle whorl, 1 bronze beer strainer
A, T. 8	Below floor, Building IV, late Phase II	Oval pit	Child	Flexed, left side	W-SW	N			
A, T. 9	Below floor, Building IV, late Phase II	Oval pit	Adult	Flexed, left side	N	E			
A, T. 12	Open area, Phase I	Oval pit	Adult	Legs flexed, on back	W-SW	?	1 bottle (?)		
A, T. 34	Open area, Phase II	Oval pit	Infant/ newborn	Legs flexed, on back	E	N			
A, T. 35	Open area, Phase II	Oval pit, burial jar	Infant	Flexed on right side	E	N	Burial jar		
A, T. 38	Open area, Phase II	Oval pit, burial jar	Infant & adult, both partial	?	?	?	Burial jar		
A, T. 41	Open area, Phase II	Sub-rectangular pit	Infant/ child	Flexed, left side	W	S	1 bottle	3 bronze bracelets, 2 beads	
G, T. 10	Courtyard, Phase II/1	Shaft & pit	Older adult, possibly male	Flexed	E	N	2 jars		
G, T. 11	Courtyard, Phase II/1	Shaft & pit	Adult, probably male	Flexed	NE	N	2 jars, 1 cup		1 bronze strainer
G, T. 13	Courtyard, Phase II/1	Shaft & pit	Adult	Flexed	E	S	2 jars, 1 cup, 1 funnel	2 bronze pins, 1 bronze ring, 1 silver ornament, 1 lead ingot, 4 beads	1 bronze tweezers

Burial Practices

Area & Grave Number	Location	Pit type	Age	Pose	Head orientation	Face orientation	Pottery	Ornaments	Tools, other
G, T. 15	Open area, Phase III	Oval pit	Infant/newborn	Flexed	W	Up			
G, T. 18	Below room floor, Phase II/2	Mud-brick vault	Empty						
G, T. 26	Open area?, Phase III	Oval pit	Infant/newborn	Extended, left side	SW	W?			
G, T. 32	Open area, Phase III	Sub-rectangular pit	Infant	Flexed, left side	S	W			
G, T. 33	Courtyard, Phase II/1	Shaft & pit	Child	Legs flexed, on back	N	E	1 jar	Bead necklace	
G, T. 37	Courtyard, Phase II/2	Sub-rectangular pit	Adult, female	Flexed, left side	W-SW	N			
G, T. 39	Courtyard, Phase II/2	Sub-rectangular pit	Adolescent, possibly female	Flexed, right side	NE	?	1 jars, 1 bottle, 1 cup		1 bronze strainer
G, T. 49	Room? Phase III	Oval pit	Infant	Legs flexed, on back	S	Up			
G, T. 50	Room, Phase III	Oval pit	Infant & adult	Disarticulated					
Non-2nd mill. BC Graves									
A, T. 7	Surface, recent	Oval pit, limestone slab edging on one side	Young child	Extended	W-SW	S		1 bronze bracelet	
A, T. 30	Eroded surface, 3rd mill.	Oval pit (?)	?	?	?	?	4 jars, 1 cup		

127

* Gender and precise age determinations are courtesy of Dr. A Sołtysiak; see Appendix to Chapter 4 for greater detail.

Appendix to Chapter 4
Human bones from Chagar Bazar: scientific analyses

Arkadiusz Sołtysiak

Introduction

During the British excavations at Chagar Bazar the skeletons of 22 individuals as well as seven small deposits of human bones were found[1]. All but two individuals were dated to the Middle Bronze Age, ca. 1750–1650 BCE. One well-preserved skeleton of a child (T. 7) came from a 20th century CE burial and the smell of decomposed lipids and collagen was still present. Two skeletons of newborn children were not assigned a tomb number, and here they are referred to as A (from oven 00-20 in Area A) and B (pit Locus 9.1 in Area A). In one bag the tag was completely rotten: there were only few hand and foot bones and it is possible that they belonged to the individual T.50/1, although a complete lack of degenerative joint disease makes this attribution uncertain.

All skeletons and single bones were described and measured with use of a form based chiefly on standards developed for North American collections (Buikstra & Ubelaker 1994). Apart from standard set of metric and nonmetric measurements, the occurrence of degenerative joint disease and additional observations of bone robustness were scored on a 3-point or 4-point scale. A full database of the human remains from Chagar Bazar is presented here in 56 tables[2].

State of preservation

Most skeletons were heavily fragmented, weathered and discoloured from post-burial processes and several years of storage post-excavation. Teeth were usually broken into pieces, and in some individuals (especially T.10 and T.11) chiefly small fragments of tooth roots have been preserved. The only exception was the almost complete and well preserved skeleton of the modern child (T.7). Plant root traces were observed on bone surfaces (especially T.11, T.32, T.41), and in one case (T.11) a rodent left deep toothmarks on a strongly eroded tibia. In few cases bones were stained green by bronze or copper objects, especially clear in the right arm bones of T.41. Some bones were covered with salt crystals, most visible in T.33.

In general, the skeletons of children were much better preserved and more complete than adult skeletons (Tables 4.2-14.3, Fig. 33)[3]. The preservation difference between children and adults is highest in teeth, despite the fact that most deciduous teeth represented early stages of development and were not fully mineralised before the individual's death. Another striking feature is the general lack of difference between four defined body parts in children and better preservation of both extremities, compared to axial skeleton and skull in adults. This difference between

---

[1] From 2006 they were stored in the excavation house at Tell Brak and studied in April 2009 by the author.

[2] Statistics were calculated with a simple Pascal program for χ^2 written by the present author and a t-test calculator available online at www.usablestats.com. Tables are found at the end of this Appendix.

[3] There were two adult individuals for whom only the lower part of the body was excavated (T.12 and T.39) and these are not included in the diagramme.

children and adults may have been partially related to the climatic conditions and a high amplitude of humidity throughout the year, which caused larger and denser adult bones to be subject to tension due to rapid desiccation of a part of a bone while another parts were still damp. A similar bias in preservation towards child skeletons has been observed in a much larger sample of human remains from Tell Masaikh (Tomczyk & Sołtysiak 2007a). Female skeletons were better preserved than male skeletons, but the number of individuals with a sex diagnosis was extremely small and this difference may have been accidental.

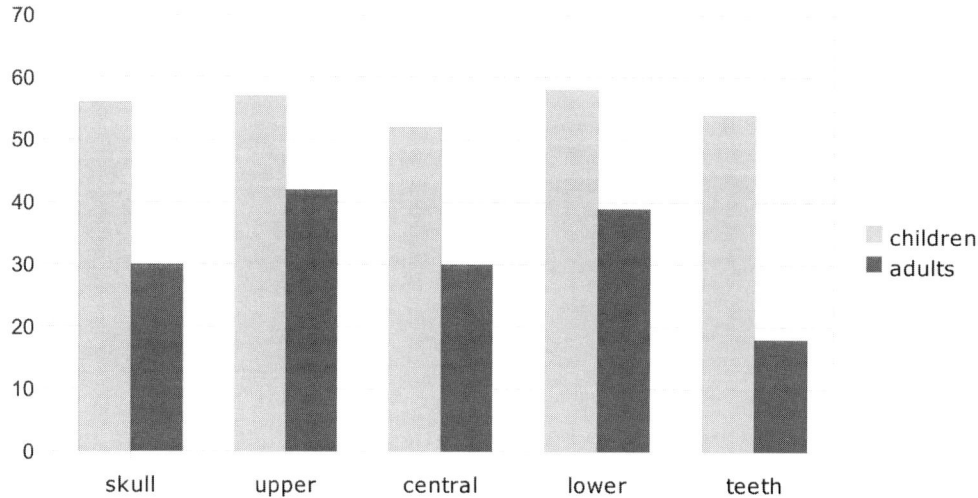

Figure 33: Average state of preservation in children and adults (see Table 4.2).

Sex and age pattern

Sex diagnosis was possible only in six individuals (Tables 4.14-4.15) and the sample is far too small to analyse pattern. The age distribution reflects the pattern expected for a cemetery in a pre-industrial society, with 42% children less than one year old, 38% adults and 20% older children and adolescents. However, there are clear differences in age distribution between the three periods of occupation represented by the skeletal sample. In the oldest Phase III there are four infants (or foetuses), one older child and one adult. In Phase II there are no infants, two children, one adolescent and as many as six adults. In Phase I again there are six infants and only two adults. Chronological sub-samples are very small, but this scarcity of adults in Phases I and III and scarcity of infants in Phase II seems not accidental ($\chi^2=12.11$, $p<0.02$, but all cells with expected frequencies less than 5). In many Near Eastern sites burials of infants were located within the settlement, beneath floors, in walls or *tannurs*, so only the high number of adults in Phase II is unexpected.

Bone measurements

Most bone metric measurements presented in Tables 4.16-4.24 are too few for comparison with other sites, although some were useful in sex assessment in adults or age assessment in children. In four cases, stature estimation was possible: 151 cm for female T.13 (tibia), 152 cm for female T.4 (radius & ulna), 161 cm for female T.37 (humerus, radius & ulna) and 166 cm for male T.10 (fibula) (Trotter & Gleser 1952, formula for American white males and females). At Tell Ashara (middle Euphrates), the average male stature in a small Bronze Age sample was c 170 cm and the average female stature was c 160 cm (Tomczyk & Sołtysiak 2007b).

Non-metric trait scores are also too few for inter-population analyses, but they may be included in future in a larger regional sample. Apart from the traits scored in Tables 4.25-4.30, two cases of absent spina bifida (T.10 and T.37), one case of double root of RP^1 (T.10) and an absent rocker mandible (T.37) were noted. In T.10 arachnoid granulations were present in the frontal bone. The only striking peculiarity of the Chagar Bazar sample is the quite high incidence of double mental foramen, especially in children, 5/23 in both sides pooled.

Tooth size and oral health

In Mesopotamia, tooth size exhibited gradual reduction from the Chalcolithic to the Iron Age, and the average size of permanent teeth from Chagar Bazar (Tables 4.46-4.49) is similar to other Middle Bronze Age dental samples from the Khabur basin (cf. Sołtysiak 2007). In deciduous teeth, the dentition of the one modern individual (T.7) is much smaller than the teeth of Middle Bronze Age children, but this difference needs comparison with a larger regional sample.

The frequency of dental caries in Chagar Bazar adults is quite high (8/42 teeth), chiefly because of two females T.4 and T.37 (Tables 4.44-4.45). Again the sample size makes statistical analysis impossible, but in general carious lesions were very few (less than 5%) in other Bronze Age sites from the Khabur basin (Sołtysiak 2006), and the individual T.37, with as many as six cariotic teeth, seems to be exceptional. In all instances the lesions developed in the cemento-enamel junction or slightly above it on medial or distal sides of a tooth. The most extreme case was the left upper premolar of T.37 with most part of the crown's medial side affected. Antemortem loss of as many as five teeth of this relatively young individual may have been the consequence of dental caries. Also in two other individuals (T.10 and T.50/1) some teeth were lost antemortem, but both died in old age and tooth loss was likely related to advanced resorption of the alveolar process (Tables 4.36-4.37).

Most teeth were worn in a regular way, and only in the older woman in T.4 the upper incisors and canines were worn flat on the right side and more lingually (with a part of their roots) on the left side; this perhaps reflects malocclusion. Dental calculus was slight in all individuals, except the central lower incisors of T.33 and especially T.37 (Fig. 34).

Figure 34: T.37, dental calculus on central lower incisor

Stress markers

The most common stress markers were scored, including various kinds of porosities (porotic hyperostosis, cribra orbitalia, femoral cribra), linear enamel hypoplasia in permanent teeth and irregular enamel hypoplasia in deciduous teeth. Porotic hyperostosis of the cranial vault is related to megaloblastic anemia caused by vitamin B_{12} deficiency in particular (and food of animal origin deficiency in general). Cribra orbitalia—porosity in the orbital roof—may be caused by megaloblastic anemia or scurvy (Walker *et al*. 2009). The etiology of femoral cribra is not clear but some scholars think it may reflect nutritional stress during childhood (Djuric *et al*. 2008).

There was no case of porotic hyperostosis in the sample, although in two individuals (T.9 and T.10) some areas of the parietal bone were thickened up to 9 mm, and especially in T.9 the expansion of diploë was evident, which may suggest that porotic hyperostosis occurred in the past but was obliterated after disappearance of the deficiency condition. Initial cribra orbitalia were observed in two children (T.7 and T.33) but are absent in all infants (T.15, T.26, T.32, T.41, A) and adults (T.4, T.10) in which the orbital roof was present. Unfortunately, the bone of T.33 with the most developed cribra orbitalia was strongly eroded and only a small part of the porotic area remained (Fig. 35). Femoral cribra were present in T.33 (Fig. 36), and some porosity in the femoral neck was observed in T.7 and T.35. Distinct porosity was present also in the palates of T.4 and T.10.

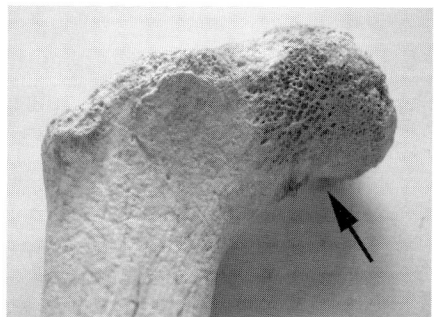

Figure 35: T.33, cribra orbitalia   *Figure 36:* T.33, femoral cribra

Another stress marker that reflects periods of nutritional deficiency during childhood is linear enamel hypoplasia in permanent teeth (Tables 4.40-4.43). Both intensity and position of hypoplastic lines were scored, as well as any occurrence of irregular hypoplasia in deciduous dentition: the latter condition occurred in the sample of Chagar Bazar only once, in the upper right canine of T.8. Linear enamel hypoplasia was present in all individuals with preserved permanent teeth, although its intensity and frequency of lines was variable. However, it may be safely stated that nutritional stress during childhood was common in the Middle Bronze population from Chagar Bazar.

Degenerative joint disease

Osteoarthritis was common in the sample of adults, which reflects the quite high frequency of mature and old individuals (Tables 4.31-4.33). However, this degenerative joint disease is correlated not only with age but also with degree of biomechanical stress, and some activities may accelerate the development of osteoarthritis and spondylosis only in involved areas (Table 4.34). In the population from Chagar Bazar, the clear prevalence of both osteoarthritis and spondylosis in cervical vertebrae over the central and lower part of the spine suggests that heavy loads were usually carried on heads (Fig. 37). A saddle-like depression in the anterior parietal bones of T.9 supports this explanation; the activity-related origin of this feature is ascertained by reduction of bone thickness in this area (6.5mm in bregma, 5mm in depression, 7mm behind it). Also related to carriage may be asymmetry in lower articular surfaces in T.37's axis and lumbar vertebral body compression in adolescent T.39 (21mm in ventral, 16mm in dorsal side).

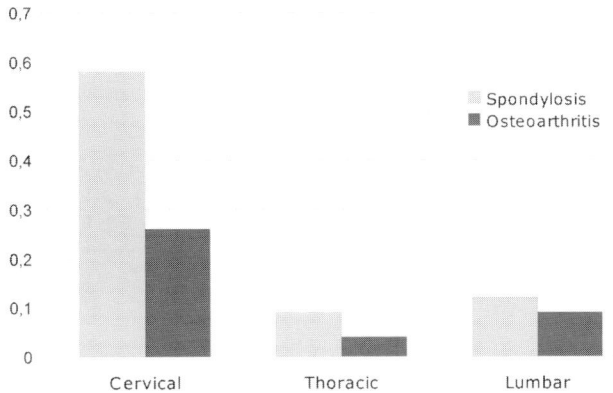

Figure 37: Frequency of degenerative joint disease in the spine (see Tables 4.31, 4.34)

Many cases of advanced degenerative joint disease were observed in the older male individual T.10, with an extreme example of eburnation in the left patella and distal femoral epiphysis (Fig. 38) and many joints with advanced osteoarthritis (Tables 4.31-33). Apart from the long bones, there were distinct osteophytes and occasionally porosity of articular surfaces also between atlas and axial dens (although the lateral articular surfaces of both vertebrae and occipital condyles were not affected), between navicular and first cuneiform, between right calcaneus and cuboid, in all joints of the first right toe (including sesamoid), in distal left 4th and right 2nd metatarsals and in the three first toe segments. No carpal bones were affected but initial osteoarthritis (osteophytes only) was present in 2/10 proximal ends of first, 1/5 proximal and 5/8 distal ends of second, and 3/5 third finger segments. All cervical vertebrae exhibited spondylosis, which was most advanced in C5-C7 (Fig. 39); only the upper surface of C3 and lower surface of C7 were not affected. Also osteoarthritis in cervical vertebrae was common in both sides. The upper surface of S1 was also heavily deformed (Fig. 40) which allows the deduction that there was also spondylosis in L5.

 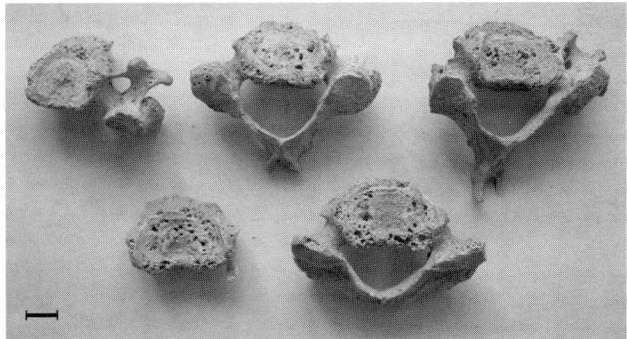

Figure 38: T.10, extreme eburnation of left patella
Figure 39: T.10, degenerative joint disease in cervical vertebrae

Other skeletons were much less affected by degenerative joint disease. In the individual T.4 there was evident osteoarthritis in a fragment of acetabulum and very initial disease in the right humerus, between atlas and axial dens and in the left mandibular condyle. Advanced osteoarthritis with eburnation was present between the left greater multangular and first metacarpal, and it is possible that this was a consequence of a traumatic event (Fig. 41). A similar pattern of osteoarthritis was noted in the individual T.11, again a fragment of an acetabulum and joint between atlas and axial dens show moderate osteoarthritis. Some osteophytes were observed in foot bones (some toe segments, both right 5th toes) and in one of the third finger segments. Initial degenerative joint disease affected acetabula of T.13 and T.50/1 (also the femoral head of the latter), as well as the left mandibular condyle of T.50/1. There is more advanced osteoarthritis in the tibial articular surface of T.37's right talus and an initial condition also in the calcaneal articular surface (Fig. 42).

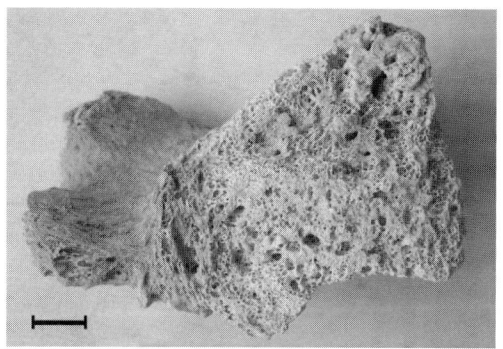 

Figure 40: T.10, degenerative joint disease in sacrum
Figure 41: T.4, eburnation in first metacarpal

 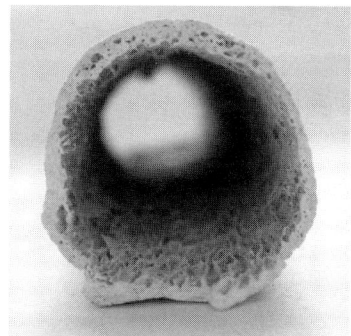

Figure 42: T.37, osteoarthritis in right talus
Figure 43: T.4, osteoporosis in femoral midshaft

Other diseases and trauma

The older woman in T.4 suffered from advanced osteoporosis and thus her long bones were more damaged than in other individuals. Cortical bone of the femur was very thin (Fig. 43) and the distal end of the fibula shows local demineralisation of its articular surface (Fig. 44). Osteochondrosis was present in both distal ends of T.39's femora (Fig. 45).

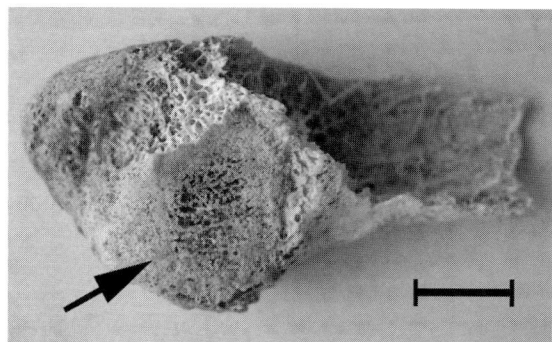 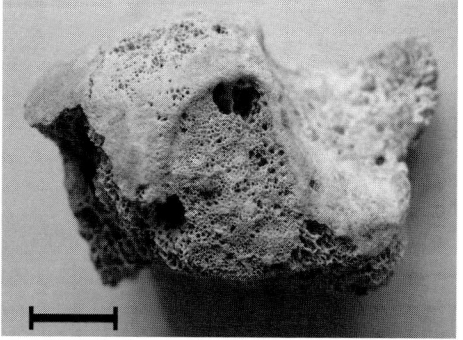

Figure 44: T.4, osteoporosis in articular surface of fibula
Figure 45: T.39, osteochondrosis in femoral condyles

In the femoral midshaft of the single bone recovered from L 54.1 there was a thickening of cortical bone ~69x15 mm, perhaps well-healed periostitis (Fig. 46). In the left occipital bone of T.34 there was a small oval, thinned, convex area (Fig. 47).

Figure 46: Local thickening of femoral cortical bone from L 54.1

Fractures or dislocations were observed in as many as four individuals. Individual T.9 had one scapular acromion broken, and it had just started to fuse (Fig. 48). At least three ribs of T.4 (the woman with advanced osteoporosis) were broken, but well healed without displacement (Fig. 49). One rib of T.11 was broken and slightly displaced before healing (Fig. 50), and some others show irregular developments of inferior margins (Fig. 51). In T.37 one of upper ribs had a clearly dislocated sternal end (Fig. 52).

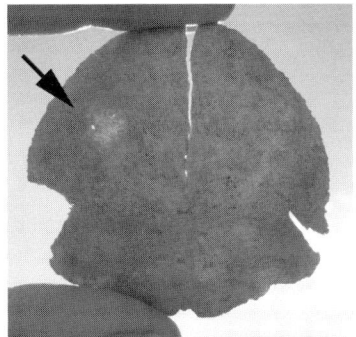 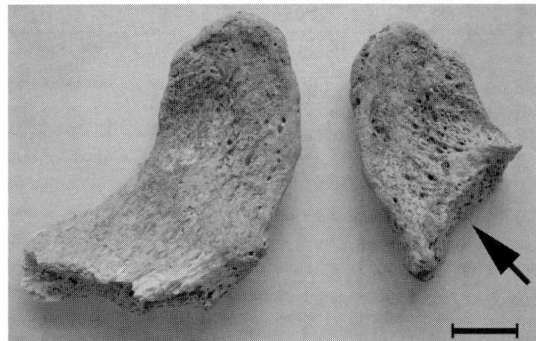

Figure 47: T.34, local thinning of parietal bone
Figure 48: T.9, fracture in scapular acromion

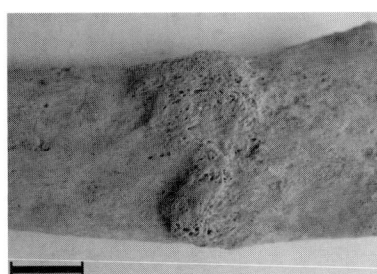 

Figure 49: T.4, broken and healed rib
Figure 50: T.11, broken and healed rib

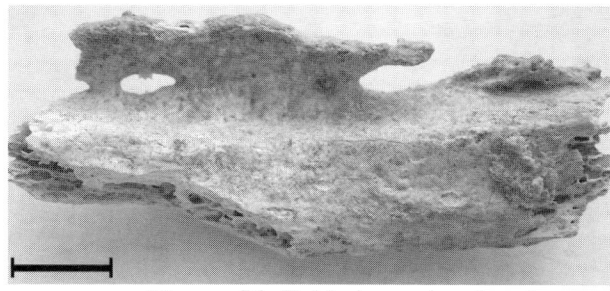 

Figure 51: T.11, irregular development of interior margin of rib
Figure 52: T.37, dislocated sternal end of rib

Physical activity

Reconstruction of physical activity patterns in ancient populations is based on observations of modified articular surfaces, bone robustness and asymmetry, musculoskeletal stress markers, atypical degenerative joint disease, unusual dental wear, and other alterations (*cf.* Molleson 2007). In the small sample from Chagar Bazar only a few activity related skeletal morphologies were scored (Table 4.35) and others noted occasionally. Squatting was the common position of rest and work in ancient populations. There are several bone modifications usually associated with squatting: squatting facets on the anterior side of tibial distal articular surface, vastus notch in patella, and side-to-side flattening of proximal shafts in femur (platymeria) and tibia (platycnemia) due to muscular tension. Only two distal ends of tibia were preserved and in both a squatting facet was present, very large in T.10 (6.5 mm) and average in T.39 (3 mm). A vastus notch was absent in T.12, T.13 and T.37, minimal in T.39 and present in T.9 (larger on left side).

Shape indices of tibial and femoral shafts have been counted for several individuals. Platymeric (shape of proximal femoral shaft), pilastric (development of linea aspera) and cnemic (shape of proximal tibial shaft) indices in Chagar Bazar were compared with those from three sites in the middle Euphrates valley (Table 4.58, Euphrates valley sample from Tomczyk & Sołtysiak 2009). In the comparative sample from Tell Ashara and other sites on the Euphrates we observed no sex differences in platymeric and pilastric indices, but significant difference in cnemic index, with male tibiae more flattened in the proximal shaft. This was interpreted as the result of difference in activity patterns: in contemporary Syria women are busy with household activities and their body positions are variable while many males (especially adolescents) spend many hours a day as pastoralists, squatting and watching sheep and goat flocks. Such an interpretation is not valid in Chagar Bazar, where the sample of male tibiae is too small, but female tibiae there are much more flattened than tibiae of both women and men from the middle Euphrates valley. In spite of a very small sample size, the difference between Chagar Bazar and Euphrates females is statistically significant (t=4.26, p=0.0008). Also proximal femoral shafts in two Chagar Bazar females are more flattened (lower platymeric index), but this difference may be accidental (t=2.44, p=0.25). There is no significant difference of any kind in the pilastric index.

Robustness of lower long bones was less than average in the Chagar Bazar population; only in one individual (T.11) linea aspera was robust, in two others (T.10 and T.50/1) lateral tuberosity occurred in the proximal part of the shaft. In T.50/1 a distinct asymmetry was observed in the subtrochanteric area. All popliteal lines were moderate, only in T.37 a shallow fossa was developed and in T.13 clear asymmetry was observed, with the right line more marked and longer. The right fibula of T.50/1 had very robust shaft, 20x15mm in the middle.

Articular surfaces of the first metatarsals of T.4, T.13, T.50/1 and L 33.2 were not extended, but in T.4 and T.13 the first toe segments were distorted laterally (probably hallux valgus, Fig. 53). A broad plantar calcaneal spur was present in the left foot of T.10 (Fig. 54). Lateral edges of both T.39's naviculars were pinched, especially the left (Fig. 55).

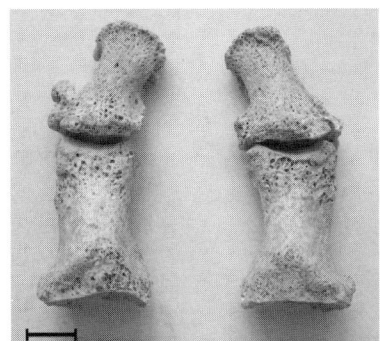
Figure 53: T.4, distorted 1st toe segments

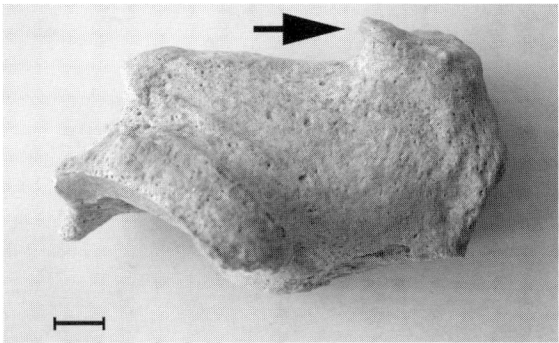
Figure 54: T.10, plantar calcaneal spur

Figure 55: T.39, pinched lateral edge of left navicular

In contrast to the legs, upper long bones were usually robust, especially radius and ulna (Table 4.35). Muscular attachments on deltoid tuberosities were most developed in males T.10 and T.11 (Fig. 56), but also in the child T.49. Radial and ulnar interosseus crests as well as radial tuberosities were usually marked and all preserved articular facets in the radial head more developed on the medial side due to pronation. There is clear asymmetry in forearm bones of T.4: bony spurs are present only on the right ulnar head and also the right radial interosseus crest is more developed (max. right 16mm vs left 15mm). Small bony spurs occurred also in both ulnar heads of T.10. Asymmetry of clavicles was noted in T.4, T.10 and T.50/1.

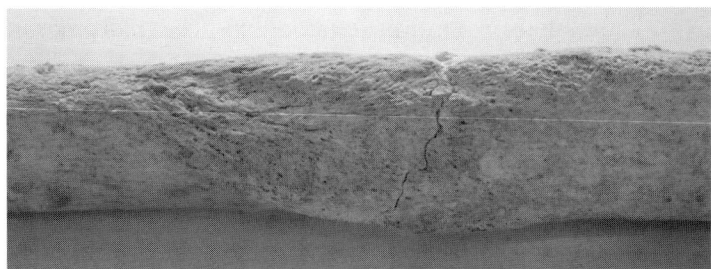
Figure 56: T.11, deltoid tuberosity

In T.9 and T.10, distal articular surfaces of the first metacarpals were enlarged (Fig. 57), and in T.50/1 the right first metacarpal was crooked (Fig. 58). Margins of finger segments were very well developed in T.4, T.9 and T.10 (Fig. 59), average in T.50/1 and NT, and gracile in T.12. All this suggests that habitual firm grasp was common.

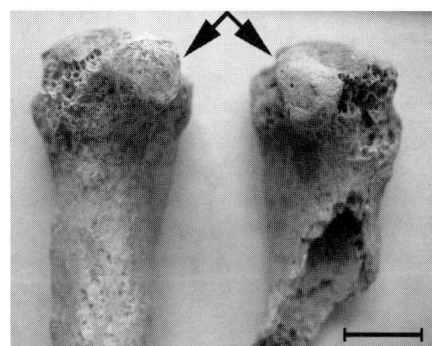
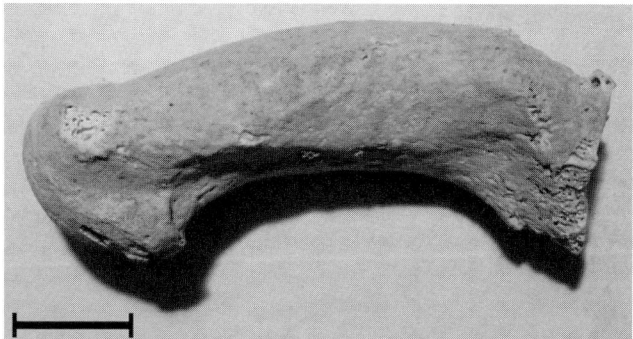

Figure 57: T.10, distal articular surfaces of first metacarpals
Figure 58: T.50/1, crooked right first metacarpal

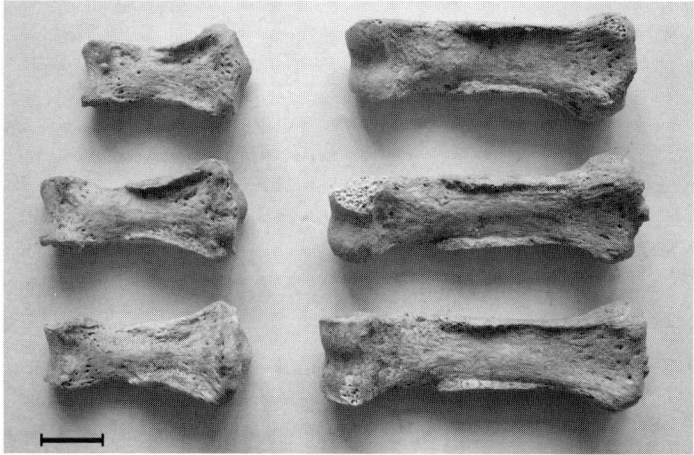

Figure 59: T.10, developed margins in finger segments

Conclusions

The sample of human remains excavated at Chagar Bazar is small, but in spite of this some preliminary characteristics of a local Middle Bronze Age population may be reconstructed. People from Chagar Bazar were physically active (especially women) and probably transported goods on their heads frequently. They were also relatively healthy, but exposed to injuries and childhood undernutrition. However, their diet was perhaps more abundant in sugars than at other sites in the Khabur basin, which may have been related to increased mobility of goods or people.

Table 4.2: Human bones from Chagar Bazar

Tomb	Area	Phase	Sex	Age	Preservation (%)				
					Skull	Upper	Central	Lower	Teeth
T.4	A	II	F??	old	45	62	26	40	50
T.7	A II	Modern	–	2	81	98	93	89	92
T.8	A II	II	–	2	67	0	39	11	63
T.9	A II	II	?	adult	10	39	33	27	0
T.10	G I	II/1	M??	old	40	62	41	50	3
T.11	G I	II/1	M?	adult	30	20	17	22	16
T.12	A I	I	?	adult	0	1	6	21	0
T.13	G I	II/1	F	30–35	0	0	8	55	0
T.15	G I	III	–	birth	74	47	82	87	58
T.26	G II	III	–	foetus	6	51	42	61	0
T.30	A II	3rd mill BC	?	adult	2	0	0	0	0
T.32	G II	III	–	0–0.25	62	93	68	57	33
T.33	G IV	II/1	–	11	23	52	61	49	84
T.34	A II	I	–	birth	77	96	49	84	13
T.35	A II	I	–	0.25	76	88	65	71	75
T.37	G II	II/2	F	25–30	47	78	55	64	50
T.38/1	A II	I	–	foetus	6	0	0	0	0
T.38/2	A II	I	?	adult	0	0	2	0	0
T.39	G IV	II/2	F??	15–18	0	1	18	43	0
T.41	A II	I	–	0.75–1	73	79	75	81	88
T.49	G II	III	–	0.75	60	67	51	42	71
T.50/1	G IV	III	?	50–60	23	13	18	32	22
T.50/2	G IV	III	–	2	17	4	5	4	21
A	A II	IA	–	birth	46	16	12	0	29
B	A	I	–	birth	71	56	28	64	75
Locus	Bones from secondary contexts								
33.2	A	III	?	adult	0	1	2	1	0
54.1	G II	II/1	–	child	0	0	0	2	0
68.2	A II	II	–	1–9	0	0	0	0	4
St. 01/7	A II	I	?	adult	0	0	0	0	3
no tag			?	adult	0	1	0	5	0

Appendix

Table 4.3: State of preservation (adults, skull); T. Tomb number, O complete, X broken, + fragment(s) only, * side not determined

T.	Frontal		Parietal		Occip-ital		Temp-oral		Sphen-oid		Zygo-mat.		Nasal		Maxilla		Palatine		Man-dible	
	R	L	R	L	R	L	R	L	R	L	R	L	R	L	R	L	R	L	R	L
4	X	X	X	X	X	X	+	O	+	+		X			+	+	+	+	X	+
9	+	+	+*		+*			X												
10	X	X	+	+	X	X	X	+			X		+	+	+	+	+	+	X	+
11	+	+	+	+	+	+	+	+			O	+			+	+	+	+	+	+
30			+*																	
33		+	X*		X*		+	+	+	+		O							+	+
37	+	+	+	+	X	X	X	X	+	+	O	O			+	+	+	+	X	X
50	+	+	+	+	+	+	+	+				+			+	+			X	+

Table 4.4: State of preservation (adults, upper limbs); P proximal end, D distal end

T.	R Humerus					R Radius					R Ulna					L Humerus					L Radius					L Ulna				
	P	¼	½	¾	D	P	¼	½	¾	D	P	¼	½	¾	D	P	¼	½	¾	D	P	¼	½	¾	D	P	¼	½	¾	D
4			+	O	O	X	O	O	X	X	X	O	O	X			+	X	O	O	O	X		+	O	O	O	X		
9		+	+	O	X	+	+			X	+	X	O	O	X	O	O	O	X				+	+		+				
10	+	X	O	X	O	X	+	+	+	X	O	X	X	+	X	+	X	O	O	X	X	+	+	+	X	O	X	X	+	X
11	+*				+*											X	O	X	+		+	X		+	X	+	+			+
33	O	X	+	X			X	X	X	O		O	X	O		O	X	+	X			X	X	X			O	O	O	
37	O	X	O	O	O	O	O	O	O	O	X	X	O	O	O	+	+	+	O	O		O	O	O		X	X	O	O	+
50	+*	X	X	+*		+	X	+				+*	+*																	

Table 4.5: State of preservation (adults, lower limbs); P proximal end, D distal end

T.	R Femur					R Tibia					R Fibula					L Femur					L Tibia					L Fibula				
	P	¼	½	¾	D	P	¼	½	¾	D	P	¼	½	¾	D	P	¼	½	¾	D	P	¼	½	¾	D	P	¼	½	¾	D
4		X	X	+	+*	+*	X	O	X	+*	+	X	+	O	+		+	+	X			+	+	+				X		X
9	+*	X	O	X	+*	+*		O			+*	X	+*			X*	X	X	+			+	+	+						
10	X	O	X	+	+	+*		+*			+	O	O	O	O		X	+		+		+	O	O		+				+
11		+*	X	+	+	+*	+*	X	+*		+*	+*	+*	X					+				+	X						
12	+	+	X	+	+	+	+	+*	+*			+*				+	X	X	X											
13	+	X	+	X	+	X	O	X	+	+	X	O	O	+		+					O	O	O	O	X		+	O	O	+
33	X	O	+		X	O	+*		+	X	X*	+*	X*			X	O	+		X	X			O	O				O	O
37	X	O	O	X	X	X	O	O	O	+			+	O	O	+	X	O	X	X	+	X	O	O		X	X			
39	X	+	O	X	X	+*	+	O	+	X			X			X	X	X	+	X	+*	+	X	+	+		+	X		
50	X*	O	X	X	+*		+	O	O	+	+	O	+			+		O	X	+		+	X				+	+	X	
nt			+*	+*													+													

Table 4.6: State of preservation (adults, central skeleton); At atlas, Ax axis, C cervical, T thoracic, L lumbar, S sacrum, Str sternum, M manubrium, B body, Clav clavicle, Scap scapula, Ilm ilium, Isch ischium, Ha Hand, Fo Foot, Calc calcaneus

T.	Vertebrae						Ribs	Str		Clav		Scap		Ilm		Isch		Pubis		Ha	Fo	Talus		Calc		Patella		Hy-oid
	At	Ax	C	T	L	S		M	B	R	L	R	L	R	L	R	L	R	L			R	L	R	L	R	L	
4	X	+			+	+		X	+	X	X	+	+	+*						O	X	O	+	X			+	+
9		X	+	+	+	+	+	+	+	X	X	+	+	+*									+			O	O	
10	+	X	X	+	+	X	+	+	+	X	X	X	X	+	X		+			X	X	O	O	X	X		O	
11	X	+			+	+				X	X	+*		+*								X	+	+				
12													+	+*								+	+	+	+	+	+	
13													+*			X		X				+	O	+	X			
33	X	X	O	O	X	X	X		X	O	O	X	+	X	+	+	X	X	X			O	O	X	+	O	O	
37	X	O	X	O	X	X	X		+	O	X	+	+	+	+	X	X			X	X	O	O	X	O	O	O	
38							+																					
39				+	X									+		X	X				+	X	+	X	X	O	+	
50		+	+	+			+			X	X	+	+	+*		+*					+			+	+			
L 33.2									+*											+	+							
nt																				+	+	+*						

Table 4.7: Vertebrae (adults); C complete vertebrae, B bodies, BF body fragments, A neural arches, AF fragments of neural arches

T.	Cervical					Thoracic					Lumbar					Coccyx
	C	B	BF	A	AF	C	B	BF	A	AF	C	B	BF	A	AF	
4			2		6		1			8			1		4	2-4
9					2			4		10	3					1
10	5							11		12					10	1
11					6			3		4			2		2	
37	3	2			1	12					4					1
39											1	2			4	
50	1									4					3	

Appendix

Table 4.8: Foot and hand bones (adults)

T.	Carpals		Metacarpals		Finger segments			Tarsals		Metatarsals		Toe segments		
	R	L	R	L	I	II	III	R	L	R	L	I	II	III
4	8	8	5	5	10	8	9	5	5	5	5	9	6	5
9	5		7*		5	8	3	2	2	1	3*	2		
10	2+4*	1	5	4	6	8	6	4	5	5	5	9	2	6
11		6	4*		8	3	3	5	5	5	5	8	6	5
12	1	2	2*		6	2	3	2+2*	2	7*		5		1
13								5	5	5	5	10	5	6
33	10*		5	5	10	8	4	5	5	9*		7		1
37	13*		7*		8	8	10	4	4	5	5	7	1	1
39					11*			3+2*	3	8*		8*		
50/1	1	1	5	5	10	5	2	1	1	1	1	1		
L 33.2	1		1								1			
nt	2	3*		3	4	1	1	2+3*	2	2		3	2	3

Table 4.9: State of preservation (children, skull); S squamous part, P petrous part, W wing, B body, L lesser, G greater wing

T.	Front		Parie		Occipital					Temporal				Sphenoid					Zyg		Max		Palat		Mand	
	R	L	R	L	SR	SL	WR	WL	B	SR	SL	PR	PL	LR	LL	B	GR	GL	R	L	R	L	R	L	R	L
7	O	+	O	X	O	O	O	O	O	O		O	O	X	X	X	O		O	X	O	X	O	O	O	X
8	+	+	X	X	X	X	O	X	O	+	X	O	O	X	X	X	+	+	X	O	X	X	X	X	X	X
15	X	X	X	X	X	X	O	O	O	+	X	O	O	X	X	O	O	O	O	O	X	X	+	+	+	X
26		+	X	X																						
32	+	+	+	+	+	+	X	O	O		O	O	O	O		O	O	O		O	X	X	+	+	X	X
34	X	X	O	O	O	O	O	O	O	O	O	O	O	O	O	O	O	O			+	X		+	X	X
35	+	O	X	O	X	X	O	O	O	X	X	O	O	X	X	O	O	O	O		+	O	+	X	X	X
38		+*	X	X																						
41	X	X	X	X	X	X	O	O	O	X	X	O	O	X	X		O	O	O	O	X	X	+	+	X	X
49	X	X	X	X	X	X	+	X	O	X	+	O	O	O	O	X	+	X	O	X					X	X
50	+	+	X	X	+*							X													X	X
A	+	+	+	+	+	+				+	+	O	O		O	O	O				X	O	X	X	X	X
B	O	+	X	X	X	X	O	O	O	O	X	O	O			O	O	O	X	O	X			+	X	X

Table 4.10: State of preservation (children, upper limbs)

T.	R Humerus				R Radius				R Ulna				L Humerus				L Radius				L Ulna			
	P	¼	½	¾	D	P	¼	½	¾	D	P	¼	½	¾	D	P	¼	½	¾	D	P	¼	½	¾	D
7		O	O	O			O	O	O			O	O	O			O	O	O			O	O	O			O	O	O	
15		O	O	O			O	O	O			O	O	O																
26							O*					X	O	O			O	O	O								O	O	O	
32		O	O	O			O	O	O			O	O	O			X	O	O			O	O	X			O	O	O	
34		O	O	O			O	O	O			O	O	X			O	O	O			O	O	O			O	O	O	
35		X	O	X			X	O	X			O	O	+			O	O	O			O	O	O			O	O	O	
41		O	O	O			O	O	X			O	O	X			O	O	O			X	X				O	X			
49		X	O	O			O	O	O			X	O	O			X	X	O				+				O	X			
50												X*																		
A																	O	O	O											
B		+	+				X	O	X			O	O	X			X	O	O			X	O	X						

Table 4.11: State of preservation (children, lower limbs); P proximal epiphysis, D distal epiphysis

T.	R Femur					R Tibia					R Fibula					L Femur					L Tibia					L Fibula				
	P	¼	½	¾	D	P	¼	½	¾	D	P	¼	½	¾	D	P	¼	½	¾	D	P	¼	½	¾	D	P	¼	½	¾	D
7		X	O	O	O	O	O	O	O	O		O	O	O			X	O	O	O		O	O	O	X	O		O	O	O
8	O*									O*							O													
15		O	O	O			O	O	O			O	O	O			O	O	O			O	O	O			O	O	O	
26		O	O	O			X	O	O								O	O	X			X	O	O			O	O	O	
32		X	O	X			X	O	X				+	X			O	O	+			X	O	X			X	O	X	
34		O	O	O			O	O	O			O	O	O			O	O	O			X	O	O			O	O	O	
35	O	X	O	O			O	O	O			O	O	O		O	O	O	O			O	O	X			O	O	O	
41		O	O	X			X	O	X			X	O	X			O	O	X			O	O	X			O	O	X	
49		+	O	+			+	O	+			X	O	X			O	X					+	X					X		
50												+	X	+																
B		X	O	X			X	O	X			X	O	X			X	O	X			X	O	X			O	O	O	
L 54.1		X																												

Appendix

Table 4.12: State of preservation (children, central skeleton)

T.	Vertebrae						Ribs	Stern		Clav		Scap		Ilium		Isch		Pubis		Ha	Foot	Talus		Calc		Hyoid
	At	Ax	C	T	L	S		M	B	R	L	R	L	R	L	R	L	R	L			R	L	R	L	
7	O	O	O	O	O	O	O		X	O	O	O	O	O	O	O	O	O	O	X	X	O	O	O	O	X
8	X	X	X	X	X		X	+	O	X				+	+	X					+					
15	O	X	X	O	O	O	X		X	O	O	+	X	O	O	O	O	O	O			O	O			
26				+	X	X	+							O	O	O	O	O	O							
32	+	O	O	O	O	X	X		+	X	O	X	X	O	O	+	X	O		+	+					
34		+					X		X	O	O	X	O	O	O		O		O	X	X	O				
35	X	O	X	X	X	X	X		+	O	O	+	X	+	X		O	O	O	X	X	O			O	
41	O	O	X	O	O	X	O		+	X	O	X	O	O	X	O	O			X	X	X	X	O		O
49	+	X	X	X	X	X	X	O	X	X	X	+	+	+*				X	X			+	+			
50							+					X														
A			X				X							O												
B							X		+	O	+	X		X			O		X							

Table 4.13: Vertebrae, foot and hand bones (children); B bodies, AC fused neural arches, AH non-fused halves of neural arches, C/T carpals/tarsals, M metatarsals, S finger/toe segments

T.	Cervical			Thoracic			Lumbar			Sacrum			Coccyx	C/T	M	S
	B	AC	AH	B	AC	AH	B	AC	AH	B	AC	AH				
7	5	5		12	12		5	5		5	5			5	15	24
8	4		7	11		18	4		5				1	2	8	2
15	4		5	12		24	5		9	4		8			15	22
26				3		4	4		10	4					4	2
32	4		10	12		24	5		10	2		1			6	13
33				12	12		4	4		3			1			
34	2		7	7		15	5		9	4		1			13	18
35	2		8	10	1	22	3		10	3		3		13	17	17
41	5		7	12		24	5		10	2		5		6	19	31
49	1		9	10	2	13	4		7	3					3	
A						19										
B	4		7	12		21	4		6	3		3			5	3

Table 4.14: Sex and age (adults, pelvis); scores after Buikstra & Ubelaker 1994

T.b	Ventral Arc		Subpubic Concavity		Ischio-pubic Ridge		Gr. Sciatic Notch		Preauric. Sulcus		Pubic S. (Todd)		Pubic S. (Suchey-Brooks)		Auricular Surface	
	L	R	L	R	L	R	L	R	L	R	L	R	L	R	L	R
10							2	3/4							3/4	
13	F		F		F						6		4			
37					F*	F*	2		3	1					2/3	2/3
50									0						7*	

Table 4.15: Sex and age (adults, skull); scores after Buikstra & Ubelaker 1994

T.	Nuchal Crest	Mastoid		Orbita		Gla-bella	Mental Emin.	External Cranial Vault				Int. Sag.
		L	R	L	R			Obel.	Sag.	Breg	Coron	
4		4	3*	2	2	1		3	2		2/3	
9		4										
10	4*		5			3	4	3	2	1	2	
11			2*	3				3	3			3
37		1	1				2					
50		2*		3*		1						

Table 4.16: Cranial and mandibular measurements (adults); MFB max. cranial breadth, OB orbital breadth, IOB interorbital breadth, CH chin ht., HMB ht. of mandibular body, BMB breadth of mandibular body, BGW bigonial width, BCB bicondylar breadth, MRB min. ramus breadth, XRB max. ramus breadth, MRH max. ramus height, ML mandibular length, MA mandibular angle, CSL condylo-symphyseal length, GGL gonion-gnathion length

T.	MFB	OB	IOB	CH	HMB	BMB	BGW	BCB	MRB	XRB	MRH	ML	MA	CSL	GGL
4					r25.5	r10.0			r28.5						
10	*92	*34.5	*24												
11										r49.0					
33									30.0	*36.0					
37				29.0	27.0	11.5	90.0	118.0	31.0	46.5	53.5	70.5	129.0	117.0	81.0
50					r31.0	r16.0									

Table 4.17: Postcranial measurements (adults, upper limbs); ML max. length, EB epicondylar breadth, VDH vertical diam. of head, XD max. diam. at midshaft, MD min. diam. at midshaft, PEB max. proximal epiphyseal breadth, DEB max. distal epiphyseal breadth, APD anterior-posterior diam. at midshaft, MLD medial-lateral diam. at midshaft, PL physiological length, MC min. circumference

T.	Humerus					Radius					Ulna				
	ML	EB	VDH	XD	MD	ML	PEB	DEB	APD	MLD	ML	APD	MLD	PL	MC
4		r53.5				204	20.0		15.0	10.0	**224	14.0	9.5		r28.5
4												r13.0	r10.5		
9												r13.5	r10.5		r35.0
10		r64.0	>46.0				21.5	31.0							
37	r294	r52.0	r37.0	r20.0	r15.0	230	19.0	28.5	13.5	11.0	r*248	14.5	11.0	r217	37.0
50			>45.0												

Table 4.18: Postcranial measurements (adults, lower limbs); EB epicondylar breadth, FH max. diam. of femur head, APS anterior-posterior subtrochanteric diam., MLS medial-lateral subtrochanteric diam., APD anterior-posterior midshaft diam., MLD medial-lateral midshaft diam., MC midshaft circumference, ML max. length, L length, PEB max. proximal epiphyseal breadth, DEB max. distal epiphyseal breadth, NF max. diam. at nutrient foramen, MN medial-lateral diam. at nutrient foramen, NC circumference at nutrient foramen, MD max. diam. at midshaft

T.	Femur							Tibia							Fibula			
	EB	FH	APS	MLS	APD	MLD	MC	ML	L	PEB	DEB	NF	MN	NC	ML	MD	PEB	DEB
4					r23.5	r23	r73					r*30	r*18.5					23
9		43	r25	r31	r*25	r*27	r*81											
10					29.5	29.5	92			52					r351	r20		r29
11					r*34	r30	r*100										27.5	28.5
12		>41			r27	r26.5	r82.5											
13	75	41	*22.5	*33.5	r27	r28	r*84.5	325	309	69.5		30	19	79				r27
13												r33.5	r19.5	r85				
37		38	23	30.5	26	26	81.5					34	21	87.5				23
39		41			r26	r23	r*76					r32	r22	r85				
50		48	28	35	32.5	*29	*96					**37.5	**26					
50			r27.5	r38	r33	r29.5	r96											

Table 4.19: Postcranial measurements (adults, others); ML max. length, AP anterior-posterior diam. at midshaft, SI superior-inferior diam. at midshaft, Sc Gl vertical diam. of scapular glenoid fossa, Sacrum max. transverse diam. of S1 base, TH total height, CH height without dens, B breadth, L length, H height, Ar upper articular surface length, Navic B navicular max. breadth

T.	Clavicle			Sc Gl	Sac-rum	Atlas L	Axis				Patella		Calcaneus		Talus		Nav-ic B
	ML	AP	SI				TH	CH	B	L	H	B	L	B	L	Ar	
4													r*66		r*49	32.5	
9											45	43					
10							36.5	21	*50.5	49	*42	*44	83	*44.5	*52	33.5	41.5
11															**53	38	
12																	36
13											37	42.5	66		50	36	r37
33					35.5		27	15		37	25	27			44	28	29
37	r133	r 11.5	r9.5	32.5	50		30	18	43	45	35.5	42.5	67	38	45	29.5	35
39											39.5	41					38
nt																	36

Table 4.20: Diaphyseal measurements (children, upper limbs); ML max. length, DM max. distal metaphyseal breadth, PM max. proximal metaphyseal breadth, XD max. midshaft diameter, MD min. midshaft diameter, APD anterior-posterior midshaft diameter, MLD medial-lateral midshaft diameter, PL physiological length, MC min. circumference

T.	Humerus					Radius					Ulna				
	ML	DM	PM	XD	MD	ML	PM	DM	APD	MLD	ML	APD	MLD	PL	MC
7	124.5	28	24	12	10	89	10	14.5	8	5.5	101	7.5	7.5	86	21.5
15	70	17	14	6	5	57	6	9.5	4.5	3.5	63	4	3.5	55	14
26	58	14	11	4	3.5						52	3	2.5	46.5	10
32	64	15.5	11.5	5.5	5	52			4	3	59.5	4	3	51.5	14
33		39	29				13	21			182	*11	*10	160	*24
34	62	15.5	11.5	4.5	4	52	5	8	3	3	59.5	4	2.5	51	12
35	73.5	18.5	14.5	6.5	6	59	7	10	4.5	4	67.5	4.5	3	57	16
41	89	20.5	17.5	7.5	6							5	4		
49	r*79	r21		r8	r7	r62.5	r7	r12	r5.5	r4.5	r68.5	r5	r5	r61	r16
A	61	15	12	5	4.5										
B	*66			5.5	5						r*58	r4	r3	r*49	r14

Appendix

Table 4.21: Diaphyseal measurements (children, lower limbs)

Tomb	Femur						Tibia						Fibula	
	ML	DM	PM	APD	MLD	MC	ML	PM	DM	NF	MN	NC	ML	MD
7	167	41.5	*20.5	12	14	41	r130	r33	r24	r15.5	r12	r44	r128	r7
15	81	20	18	6.5	6.5	22	70.5	15.5	11.5	8	7	24	67	4
26	r63	r17	r13	r5.5	r5	r17.5	55		9	6.5	6	19	53	2.5
32	r76			r6	r6	r20.5				7.5	7	23		3.5
33									33					
34	75	18.5	16	4.5	6	18	r65.5	r15	r10	r6	r6	r20	61	3
35	86	24.5	21	7	7	23	r73.5	r18.5	r13	r9.5	r8	r25.5	69	3.5
41	>96		23	7	8	24	91	20		9.5	7.5	27.5	*85	4
49			26	9	8.5	28			15	r9	r8.5	r28	>72	4.5
L 54.1				18										

Table 4.22: Skull and os coxae measurements (children); WL lesser wing length, WW lesser wing width, BL body length, BW body width, LB length of body, WA width of arc, FLH full length of half mandible, H height, B breadth, Au max. length of auricular surface, W width

T.	Sphenoid				Occipital		Mandible			Ilium			Ischium		Pubis
	WL	WW	BL	BW	BL	BW	LB	WA	FLH	H	B	Au	L	W	L
7	28	17.5			18	27				69.5	61.5		42	26	33
8					17	26						25			
15			12	20	12	16	37			37	33	14	20	14	16
26										29	26	11	16	10.5	13
32	22	12	9.5	17.5	12.5	14.5				32.5	30	13		11	16
33										r104			57		47
34	19	11.5	9	17	12	14	r36	r17	r46.5	32	29.5	11	18	12	15
35	26.5	15	12.5	20	13	17	40			*35	*36	13	22	13	18.5
41					15	19.5				r47	r43	15.5	27.5	17.5	*22
49	24	15			13	19									
50							27								
A			12	18			33.5	*15	45						
B			11	18.5	11.5	15.5	r36.5	r*18	r47	r*33			19.5	r12	r17

Table 4.23: Postcranial measurements (children); ML max. length, AP anterior-posterior diameter at midshaft, SI superior-inferior diameter at midshaft, L length, W width, LS length of the spine, B breadth, PE max. proximal epiphyseal breadth, DE max. distal epiphyseal breadth

T.	Clavicle			Scapula			Talus		Calcaneus		Femur		Tibia	
	ML	AP	SI	L	W	LS	L	B	L	B	PE	DE	PE	DE
7	74	6	4	69	48.5	57	24	17	32	19		32	23	16
8	r66	r6	r4.5								14	24		16
15	49	3.5	3.5		32	35	10	7.5						
32	45	4	3											
33	102	8	6								32	59	r52.5	37
34	44.5	3.5	2.5	33.5	29	31	9	6						
35	47	4.5	3.5				12	8	13.5	10	8			
41	56	5	3.5	49.5	37	45	14	9	19.5	11.5				
49	r53.5													
A	40	3	2.5	32	27	30								
B	r*40	r4	r3	r*35										

Table 4.24: Additional measurements

Tomb	Measurements
4	manubrium sterni B 51; acetabulum 47.5
33	radius, distal epiphysis r21.5; humerus head 29; distal fibula, epiphysis 18.5, metaphysis 18
7	hyoid body, breadth 11; parietal chord 106, occipital chord 89, frontal chord 89*, orbital breadth (maxillofrontale) 31.5; mandible, bigonial 68, bicondylar 79*, maximum ramus breadth 30, minimum ramus breadth 24, chin height 20.5, height of the mandibular body 17, breadth 9.5, condylo-symphyseal length 80, gonion-gnathion length 57.5, mandibular length 48, ramus height 32.5, mandibular angle 125°
8	gonion-gnathion length 56, chin height 23, height of the mandibular body 19.5, breadth 11, minimum ramus breadth 24
38	maximum breadth of occipital bone 51
49	manubrium sterni, height 15, breadth 17

Table 4.25: Nonmetric traits (adults, cranium I); scores after Buikstra & Ubelaker 1994. MS metopic suture, SN supraorbital notch, SF supraorbital foramen, ZFF zygomatico-facial foramina, PF parietal foramen, Bregm bregmatic sutural bone, Ast L left asterionic sutural bone, Par L left parietal notch bone, DHC divided hypoglassal canal, SSS flexure of superior sagittal sulcus

Tomb	MS	SN		SF		ZFF		PF		Bregm	Ast L	Par L	DHC		SSS
		L	R	L	R	L	R	L	R				L	R	
4	0	0	1	1	0			0	1				1	0*	
9	0														
10	0	2	2	0	0			1	1	0	1	0	0	0	
11	0	1		0			1								
33						1									
37						5	1						0	0	1
50	0		1		0*										

Appendix

Table 4.26: Nonmetric traits (adults, cranium II); scores after Buikstra & Ubelaker 1994. FOI foramen ovale incomplete, FSI foramen spinosum incomplete, PSB pterygo-spinous bridge, PAB pterygo-alar bridge, TD tympanic dihiscence, AE auditory exostosis, MFL mastoid foramen location, MFN mastoid foramen number

T.	FOI		FSI		PSB		PAB		TD		AE		MFL		MFN	
	L	R	L	R	L	R	L	R	L	R	L	R	L	R	L	R
4	0	0	0	0	0	0	0	1	0		0	0				
10															1	2
37	0	0	0	0	1	1	1	1	0	0	0	0				

Table 4.27: Nonmetric traits (adults, mandible and postcranial); scores after Buikstra & Ubelaker 1994. MF mental foramen, MT mandibular torus, MBL mylohyoid bridge location, MBD mylohyoid bridge degree, ABL atlas bridging lateral, ABP atlas bridging posterior, SA septal aperture, TAS talar articular surfaces (0 – joint, 2 – separated), TT third trochanter

T.	MF		MT		MBL		MBD		ABL		ABP		SA		TAS		TT	
	L	R	L	R	L	R	L	R	L	R	L	R	L	R	L	R	L	R
4	1	1		0		0		0							0	0		
9													0	1*				
10	1	1	0	0									2	0	0	0		
11		2													0			
13															0			
33				0		0		0	0	0	0	0	0		0	0	0	
37	1	0		2	2	2	1	0	0	0	0	2	0	0	0			
39																2		
50		1		0											2	2		

Table 4.28: Nonmetric traits (adults, accessory transverse foramina in cervical vertebrae); scores after Buikstra & Ubelaker 1994

Tomb	C3		C4		C5		C7	
	L	R	L	R	L	R	L	R
10		0	0	1	1	2		
33	0	0	0		0		0	0
37	0	0	0	0	1	0	0	

Table 4.29: Nonmetric traits (children, cranium I); scores after Buikstra & Ubelaker 1994. MS metopic suture, SN supraorbital notch, SF supraorbital foramen, IS infraorbital suture, MIF multiple infraorbital foramina, ZFF zygomatico-facial foramina, PF parietal foramen, CC condylar canal, DHC divided hypoglassal canal, SSS flexure of superior sagittal sulcus

T.	MS	SN	SF	IS		MIF		ZFF		PF		CC		DHC		SSS
		R	R	L	R	L	R	L	R	L	R	L	R	L	R	
7	0	1	0	2	2	0	0	1*	0			1	1	0	0	1
8	0			2	2	0	0	0	0*			0	1		0	
15		0	0					2	2			1	1	0	0	
32								1				1	1	0	0	
34												1	1	0	0	
35				0		0			2			1	1	0	0	
41								1	2			1	1	0	0	
49								1*	1	1	1	1		0	0	
50												1	0			
A				2		0										
B					1		0							0	0	

Table 4.30: Nonmetric traits (children, cranium II and other bones); scores after Buikstra & Ubelaker 1994. FOI foramen ovale incomplete, FSI foramen spinosum incomplete, PSB pterygo-spinous bridge, PAB pterygo-alar bridge, MF mental foramen, MT mandibular torus, MBL mylohyoid bridge location, MBD mylohyoid bridge degree, SA septal aperture, TT third trochanter

T.	FOI		FSI		PSB		PAB		MF		MT		MBL		MBD		SA		TT	
	L	R	L	R	L	R	L	R	L	R	L	R	L	R	L	R	L	R	L	R
7		0		2		2		2	2	1	0	0	0	0	0	0	0	0	1	0
8		0		1		0		0	1	1	0	0	0	0	0	0				
15																				
32	0	0	1	1	0	1	2	2	1		0		0		0					
34									2*	2	0	0								
35									1	1										
41	0	0	0	0	1	2	1	1	1	1	0	0					0	0		
49	0	1	1	2						2			0	0	0	0	0	0	2	
50									1	1			0	0	0	0				
B									1	1										

Appendix

Table 4.31: Degenerative Joint Disease (adults, vertebrae and ribs); Up upper articular surfaces, Lo lower articular surfaces, 0 no osteoarthritis, 1 osteophytes, 2 porosity and/or eburnation

T.	Atlas		Axis	Cervical			Thoracic			Lumbar			Ribs		
	Up	Lo	Up	0	1	2	0	1	2	0	1	2	0	1	2
4	0*			9	4		9			6			1		1
9				4			9			5			4		
10			1	10	2	3	4		2	6	1		3		
11	0*	0*	0*	5	1	4	2			1			3		1
37	0	0	0	13			39			10			10		
50				2	1		2		1	1		2			

Table 4.32: Degenerative Joint Disease (adults, upper limb); M medial, L lateral, A acromion, G glenoid, D distal, P proximal, 0 no osteoarthritis, 1 osteophytes, 2 initial porosity and/or eburnation, 3 advanced porosity and/or eburnation

T.	Stern		Clavicle				Scapula				Humerus				Ulna				Radius			
	L	R	LM	RM	LL	RL	LA	RA	LG	RG	LP	RP	LD	RD	LP	RP	LD	RD	LP	RP	LD	RD
4	0	0	0	0	0*					0*			0*	0/1	0					0	0*	0
9	0	0		0/1			0	0					0	0	0*		0			0*		
10			2			2	2			1*	0	0	1*	1*	0	0	0/1	0/1	0/1	0/1	0	0
11					1												0*				0/1	
37			0	0		0		0*	0	0	0	0	0	0	0	0	0	0		0		0
50										0*												

Table 4.33: Degenerative Joint Disease (adults, lower limb); M medial, L lateral, D distal, P proximal

T.	Os Coxae				Femur				Tibia				Fibula				Patella	
	LM	RM	LL	RL	LP	RP	LD	RD	LP	RP	LD	RD	LP	RP	LD	RD	L	R
9					0	0											0	0
10	0		0/1	0/1			3	2			0	0*			1	3		
11											0*		0*			0		
12								0										0
13					0	0	1	0*	0	0*	0	0*		0			0/1	0
37					0	0	0	0	0*			0*					0	0
50											0*			0				

Table 4.34: Spondylosis (adults); 0 none, 1 small/medium osteophytes and/or Schmörl nodes, 2 large osteophytes, compression

Tomb	Cervical			Thoracic			Lumbar		
	0	1	2	0	1	2	0	1	2
4		2							
9				3			3		
10			5	5		2			
37	5			12			4		

Table 4.35: Bone robustness (adults); ASP-S size of linea aspera, ASP–R morphology of linea aspera, POPLIT tibia, popliteal line, RAD–C radius, interosseus crest, RAD–T radial tuberosity, RAD–H measurements of the proximal articular surface in radius, MN minimum circumferential breadth, MX maximum circumferential breadth, HUM–D humerus, deltoid tuberosity, F-LAT femur, lateral tuberosity

T.	ASP-S		ASP-R		POPLIT		RAD-C		RAD-T		RAD-H		HUM-D		F-LAT	
	R	L	R	L	R	L	R	L	R	L	MN	MX	R	L	R	L
4	0	0	0	0			2	2	2	2	3	7.5				
9	0	0								2			0	0		
10	0		1						2	2	2	9	1	1	2	
11	2		2										2			
12	1	1	0	0	0											
13					1	0										
37	0	0	0	0	0	0	0		1		4.5	8	0			
39			0	0	0	0										
50	1	1	1	1					0				0		2	2

Table 4.36: Dental wear (permanent teeth, maxilla); scores after Buikstra & Ubelaker 1994; in molars min. and max. wear on 10-point scale. pm postmortem tooth loss, am antemortem tooth loss, + tooth fragment(s)

T.	RM³	RM²	RM¹	RP²	RP¹	RC	RI²	RI¹	LI¹	LI²	LC	LP¹	LP²	LM¹	LM²	LM³
4			9/10				7	7/8	7/8			7/8	6	9/10	4/9	
10			am	pm	pm	pm	8	am	pm							
11	4	4	pm	pm	pm				pm	pm	pm	pm	pm			
33	0	1	1	1	1		1		1		+	1		1	1	0
37		3	5	pm	pm	3/4	3	3/4	pm	5	4	6	4/7		3/4	
50							pm	pm								
01-7																1

Appendix

Table 4.37: Dental wear (permanent teeth, mandible)

T.	LM₃	LM₂	LM₁	LP₂	LP₁	LC	LI₂	LI₁	RI₁	RI₂	RC	RP₁	RP₂	RM₁	RM₂	RM₃
4						8	7/8	7/8	6	6	6		6	5/6	am	am
10			am	pm	pm	pm	pm		pm	pm	pm	pm	pm	am	pm	pm
11	4	4/5										pm	pm	pm		4
33	0	1	1	1	+	1	1		1/2	+	1	1	1	1	1	0
37	pm	am	am	pm	am	pm	3	3	3	3	4			am	am	3/4
50	8	5/7		6								5/6	5	am	4/5	4/5

Table 4.38: Germ development (permanent teeth, maxilla); scores after Buikstra & Ubelaker 1994

T.	RM³	RM²	RM¹	RP²	RP¹	RC	RI²	RI¹	LI¹	LI²	LC	LP¹	LP²	LM¹	LM²	LM³
33	4														11	4
8							5	5	5	5						
41								2								

Table 4.39: Germ development (permanent teeth, mandible)

T.	LM₃	LM₂	LM₁	LP₂	LP₁	LC	LI₂	LI₁	RI₁	RI₂	RC	RP₁	RP₂	RM₁	RM₂	RM₃
33	4		13	10		11	13					10	10		11	4
7								5								
8									6							
41						1	2/3			2/3	1					

Table 4.40: Enamel hypoplasia degree (maxilla); 0 none, 1 small to medium irregularity, 2 small to medium hypoplastic line(s), 3 more than one distinct hypoplastic line

T.	RM³	RM²	RM¹	RP²	RP¹	RC	RI²	RI¹	LI¹	LI²	LC	LP¹	LP²	LM¹	LM²	LM³
4							2						0			
11	2	0														
33		2	0	2	2			1		2	3	2		1	2	
37			0	0			2	0	1			1	1	0	0	0
8							2*	2*	2*	2*						
01-7																2

Table 4.41: Enamel hypoplasia degree (mandible)

T.	LM₃	LM₂	LM₁	LP₂	LP₁	LC	LI₂	LI₁	RI₁	RI₂	RC	RP₁	RP₂	RM₁	RM₂	RM₃
11	1	0														1
33		1	1	3		3	2		2	2	3	3	3	0	2	
37						0	0	0	0	1						0
50	0	0		2								1			0	1
8							2									

Table 4.42: Enamel hypoplasia measurements (maxilla)

T.	RM³	RM²	RM¹	RP²	RP¹	RC	RI²	RI¹	LI¹	LI²	LC	LP¹	LP²	LM¹	LM²	LM³
4							2.1, 3.6									
11	1.4, 2.6															
33		1.1, 3.0		1.8, 3.2	1.8, 2.6		2.8, 4.8, 5.6		1.4, 2.4, 4.7	2.1, 3.5, 4.7, 5.3	1.2, 3.8			3.3	1.2, 2.8	
37							1.6, 3.0, 4.8		1.8, 4.3		2.1, 3.9	1.7, 3.4				
01-7															1.4, 2.5	

Table 4.43: Enamel hypoplasia measurements (mandible)

T.	LM₃	LM₂	LM₁	LP₂	LP₁	LC	LI₂	LI₁	RI₁	RI₂	RC	RP₁	RP₂	RM₁	RM₂	RM₃
11	1.3															0.9
33		2.6, 3.4		1.6, 2.8, 4.3		2.6, 3.8, 5.0, 6.0	2.6, 3.8, 5.1		2.6, 3.6	2.9, 3.9	2.5, 3.9, 4.9, 5.9	1.4, 2.3, 3.8	1.5, 3.1, 4.1	1.5, 2.6		
50				1.3, 7.7								4.4				
8									1.2, 2.1, 3.8							

Table 4.44: Dental caries (permanent teeth, maxilla); 0 none, 1 initial lesion (< 2 mm diam), 2 medium lesion (2 to 6 mm diam), 3 large lesion (> 6 mm diam)

T.	RM³	RM²	RM¹	RP²	RP¹	RC	RI²	RI¹	LI¹	LI²	LC	LP¹	LP²	LM¹	LM²	LM³
4		0					0	0	0			0	0	0	2	
11	0															
37			1				2	0	1		0	3	0	0		1
01-7																0

Table 4.45: Dental caries (permanent teeth, mandible)

T.	LM₃	LM₂	LM₁	LP₂	LP₁	LC	LI₂	LI₁	RI₁	RI₂	RC	RP₁	RP₂	RM₁	RM₂	RM₃
4						0	0	0	0	0	0		0	1		
11	0	0														0
37							0	0	0	0	0					1
50	0	0		0									0		0	0

Appendix

Table 4.46: Mesiodistal diameters (permanent teeth, maxilla)

T.	RM³	RM²	RM¹	RP²	RP¹	RC	RI²	RI¹	LI¹	LI²	LC	LP¹	LP²	LM¹	LM²	LM³
4													6.7			
11	7.9															
33	9.1	8.9		6.3	6.6			8.4		5.7			6.7	10.5	8.8	10.0
37			10.7				6.1	8.2	7.9			7.6	*6.7	6.3	10.3	6.9
8							7.2	9.7	9.6	7.2						
01-7																9.2

Table 4.47: Buccolingual diameters (permanent teeth, maxilla)

T.	RM³	RM²	RM¹	RP²	RP¹	RC	RI²	RI¹	LI¹	LI²	LC	LP¹	LP²	LM¹	LM²	LM³
4													8.9		*10.5	
11	9.3															
33	10.3	9.6		8.8				6.7					8.9	10.6	10.3	10.2
37			11.6				6.0	7.1	7.1		8.5		8.7	11.8		11.6
01-7																9.9

Table 4.48: Mesiodistal diameters (permanent teeth, mandible)

T.	LM₃	LM₂	LM₁	LP₂	LP₁	LC	LI₂	LI₁	RI₁	RI₂	RC	RP₁	RP₂	RM₁	RM₂	RM₃
4														9.7		
11	10.5															
33	10.9	9.7	10.9	6.7		5.8	5.4		4.9		6.0	6.5	6.7	10.9	9.7	10.5
37							5.8	4.8	4.8	5.9	6.8					9.4
50	11.7	11.9		7.2								7.4	*7.6		12.4	10.8
8									5.5							

Table 4.49: Buccolingual diameters (permanent teeth, mandible)

T.	LM₃	LM₂	LM₁	LP₂	LP₁	LC	LI₂	LI₁	RI₁	RI₂	RC	RP₁	RP₂	RM₁	RM₂	RM₃
4									6.4	6.5	7.3			10.1		
11	9.1	10.2														9.0
33	9.4	9.2	9.8	7.5		6.7	5.4		5.3		6.6	7.7	8.0	10.1	9.3	9.3
37							6.2	5.1		5.8	7.6					9.8
50	12.1	11.7		*8.4								9.0			11.6	11.0

Table 4.50: Dental wear (deciduous teeth, maxilla)

Tomb	RM¹	rm²	rm¹	rc	ri²	ri¹	li¹	li²	lc	lm¹	lm²	LM¹
7			1	1	1	1/2	1/2	1	1	1		
8		1	1	1			1	1	1	1	1	
33											2	
50		1										

Table 4.51: Dental wear (deciduous teeth, mandible)

Tomb	LM₁	lm₂	lm₁	lc	li₂	li₁	ri₁	ri₂	rc	rm₁	rm₂	RM₁
7			1	1	1	1/2	1/2	1	1			
8		1	1							1	1	
33		2/3									2/3	
50		pm	1							pm	1	
L 68.2		1										

Table 4.52: Germ development (deciduous teeth, maxilla); scores after Buikstra & Ubelaker 1994

Tomb	RM¹	rm²	rm¹	rc	ri²	ri¹	li¹	li²	lc	lm¹	lm²	LM¹
7	6	11	12	11	12	13	13	12	11	12	11	6
8	6	9	12	10				12	10	12	9	6
15			4	2	5	5	5	5		4	2*	
32							5	5		4	2	
34		3/4			5							
35		3	5		6	6	6	6		5	3	
41	2/3	5	8	6			9	9	6	8	5	
49	3	5	7	5		9	9			7	5	
50	5/6	10										
A				2*	5	5	5	5			2	
B		2	4		5/6	5/6	5/6	5/6	3		2	

Table 4.53: Germ development (deciduous teeth, mandible)

Tomb	LM₁	lm₂	lm₁	lc	li₂	li₁	ri₁	ri₂	rc	rm₁	rm₂	RM₁
7		11	12	11	12	13	13	12	11	12	11	
8	6	9	12						10		9	6
15			4	2	5	5				4	2*	
32		2	4		5/6						2	
33		14									14	
34											3/4	
35		3	5	3	6	6	6	6	3	5	3	
41	3	5	8	6	9	10	10	9	6	8	5	3
49	3	5	7	5				8	5	7	5	3
50	5/6		12									5/6
A					5							
B		2	4	3	5/6	6	6	5/6	3	4	2	

Table 4.54: Mesiodistal diameters (deciduous teeth, maxilla)

Tomb	RM¹	rm²	rm¹	rc	ri²	ri¹	li¹	li²	lc	lm¹	lm²	LM¹
7	9.7	**7.1	6.5	6.2	4.6	5.7		4.5	6.4	6.4	8.0	9.8
8	12.0	10.0	8.0	6.9			7.5	5.5	7.3	8.1	9.9	11.5
35					5.0	6.7	6.6	5.0				
41		8.2	7.3	6.7			6.2	5.0	6.6	7.0	8.3	
49		8.3	6.7			6.1	6.1			6.5	7.9	
50	*10.9	9.0										

Table 4.55: Buccolingual diameters (deciduous teeth, maxilla)

Tomb	RM¹	rm²	rm¹	rc	ri²	ri¹	li¹	li²	lc	lm¹	lm²	LM¹
7	9.8	8.8	7.2	5.6	4.2	4.8	4.8	4.3	5.5	7.3	8.8	9.9
8	12.3	11.0	9.6	6.6			5.4	5.2	6.5	9.5	10.9	12.6
41		9.1	8.4				4.4	4.5		8.5	9.3	
49		8.7	7.8			4.8	4.7			7.9	8.8	
50	*11.8	10.0										

Table 4.56: Mesiodistal diameters (deciduous teeth, mandible)

Tomb	LM₁	lm₂	lm₁	lc	li₂	li₁	ri₁	ri₂	rc	rm₁	rm₂	RM₁
7		9.0		5.6	3.9	3.7	3.8	4.0	5.5	7.5	9.3	
8	12.0	11.1	8.8					6.1			11.1	11.9
33		9.3									9.3	
35					4.6	4.2	4.3	4.5				
41		9.6	8.0	5.5	4.7	4.1	4.0	4.7	5.6	8.0	9.5	
49		9.1	7.3					4.3		7.1	9.2	
50	*10.9		8.3								*10.2	*10.9
L 68.2		9.0										

Table 4.57: Buccolingual diameters (deciduous teeth, mandible)

Tomb	LM₁	lm₂	lm₁	lc	li₂	li₁	ri₁	ri₂	rc	rm₁	rm₂	RM₁
7		8.0	6.5	5.0	3.7	3.5	3.5	3.7	5.0	6.3	8.0	
8	11.3	9.3	7.5						5.7		9.5	11.1
33		8.6									8.5	
41		8.3	6.9		3.8	3.3	3.2	3.9		7.0	8.2	
49		8.0	6.7					3.8		6.8	8.1	
50	*10.2		6.7								*8.7	*10.3
L 68.2		8.3										

Table 4.58: Femoral and tibial shaft indices (adults); CB Chagar Bazar, MEV Middle Euphrates Valley (Tomczyk & Sołtysiak 2009)

Index	CB - females			CB - males			MEV - females			MEV - males		
	N	mean	SD	N	mean	SD	N	mean	SD	N	mean	SD
platymeric	2	71.3	5.83	1	80.0		21	82.3	8.30	19	82.2	8.23
pilastric	4	102.9	7.16	3	108.5	7.36	11	104.9	5.58	11	105.7	6.89
cnemic	4	63.9	3.37	1	69.3		14	76.5	9.10	12	69.9	3.85

Chapter 5

Ceramic Assemblage and Social Inference

A. McMahon & J. Frane

The ceramics of the early 2nd millennium BC in northern Mesopotamia are notably homogeneous and standardized. Although the introduction of Khabur Ware predates Samsi-Addu's reign (Mallowan 1947, Postgate *et al.* 1997: 52; Oguchi 1997), this ceramic homogeneity was perhaps encouraged by the political unity under Samsi-Addu, which would have fostered economic exchange that then survived the collapse of his kingdom. It is also likely that there was a prior regional cultural community, which weathered political variation and was expressed through similarities in material culture. The restructuring of settlement in the terminal 3rd millennium BC to very early 2nd millennium BC, after the Post-Akkadian disjunction, would have created the opportunity or even necessity for the conscious visible restatement of a regional identity, achieved through ceramic style among other aspects of material culture. Additionally, production technologies and mental templates for ceramics in northern Mesopotamia may reflect long-term household economy and consumption patterns unchanged by politics.

Khabur Ware and the larger ceramic assemblage within which it is included have been characterised extensively elsewhere[1]. This description of the Chagar Bazar assemblage of the early 2nd millennium BC aims to present its site-specific variations in forms but also to explore the assemblage and wares in a holistic way, in terms of social and economic inferences, as presented by this "bottom-up" data. Questions we asked include: How did domestic and administrative ceramic assemblages compare? Do the assemblages emphasize storage (jars) or dining (plates), and what implications do any emphases have for the consumption practices of the inhabitants of Chagar Bazar? Was storage of food and drink also an opportunity for aesthetic or symbolic expression, or was decoration limited to "publicly visible" vessels?

Aspects of Regionality and Chronology

In recent years, the division drawn between Eastern and Western Upper Khabur ceramic zones during the 3rd millennium BC has wavered between the Wadi Khanzir and the Wadi Jaghjagh to its east (Lebeau *et al.* 2000). A Central Upper Jezirah zone has been delineated for the terminal 3rd millennium BC (Early Jezirah V), but throughout the 3rd millennium BC, the zone between the parallel Jaghjagh and Khanzir wadis may have been a wide cultural frontier, technically neither eastern nor western (for instance, both Ninevite 5 and Metallic Ware occur at Chagar Bazar). By the early 2nd millennium BC, the eastern and western separation within the Upper Khabur was not as strong, and Chagar Bazar was firmly incorporated within a larger northern Mesopotamian cultural area.

---

[1] Comprehensive studies of site assemblages include: Frane 1996, Oates, Oates & McDonald 1997, Postgate, Oates & Oates 1997, Kolinski 2000 and Oguchi 2006a. Synthetic studies of Khabur Ware include: Oguchi 1997, 1998, 2000, 2001, 2006b; Stein 1984; Hamlin 1971; and Hrouda 1957.

Chapter 5

The early 2nd millennium BC ceramic assemblage from Areas A and G at Chagar Bazar has particularly close parallels at contemporary Tell Brak, Tell Leilan and Tell al-Rimah.[2] Tell al-Rimah's sequence for the early 2nd millennium BC is well dated by epigraphic material; Temple Level 3 and Area C Palace Level 6 and 6a are post-Shamshi-Addu to "Late Old Babylonian" (Postgate *et al.* 1997: 21) and are the best potential match with the Chagar Bazar levels. The comparability of assemblages occurs despite the fact that Rimah is c 145 kilometres to the east-southeast of Chagar Bazar and in a rather different steppe environment. Also, the contexts are not directly comparable: a temple and palace at Rimah versus houses and an administrative structure at Chagar Bazar.

The Khabur Ware sub-assemblage, in form and decoration, is notably consistent across a wide geographical area, with closely comparable material from Ashur, Nineveh, Tepe Gawra, Tell Billa, sites in the Saddam Dam region of the Iraqi Tigris (i.e., Tell Rijm; Kolinski 2000) and across the Upper Khabur and as far west as the Balikh Valley (e.g. Hammam et-Turkman). Similar, or related, assemblages appear to the east at Nuzi and Dinkha Tepe (Hamlin 1971), to the north in southeast Turkey (Kenan Tepe; Parker & Dodd 2003; Lidar Hüyük), to the west at Alalakh and to the south at Terqa, Haradum, 'Usiyeh and Shuweimiya (Oguchi 2006a).

While there had been substantial connections in pottery technology and style between the Post-Akkadian pottery of Chagar Bazar and the EB IV-MB I ceramics of the Syrian Euphrates and Northern Levant (McMahon & Quenet 2007), these western connections were cut back in the MB II, and "Khabur Ware" and its linked assemblage is a truly "Mesopotamian" style.

Much of Mallowan's initial discussion of Khabur Ware dealt with its absolute dates and with comparanda from then-known sites to the west (Hammam et-Turkman) and east (Tell Billa and Tepe Gawra; Mallowan 1936: 35). His subsequent publications focussed more on the possible source of the ware–influence or migration– as well as additional possible comparanda from Iran (Mallowan 1947: 23-25). He remained convinced that Khabur Ware marked a sudden break from preceding ceramic traditions and that its appearance demanded a radical explanation, such as immigration of a Hurrian population. He tied Khabur Ware approximately to Samsi-Addu and his sons but in fact was careful to link their reigns with the "extensive use" of this ware, rather than its introduction, explicitly stating that the introduction of Khabur Ware preceded them (Mallowan 1947: 82-83)[3]. Recent excavations across the region have begun to fill in the Post-Akkadian gap, and this material indicates that there remains a stark difference in the decorative schemes and fabrics of the early 2nd versus late 3rd millennium BC assemblages; however, a few elements of decoration, fabric and form of the early 2nd millennium do have post-Akkadian antecedents (see below).

Khabur Ware was divided into Older and Younger styles in the 1940s/1950s, based primarily on subjective impressions of changes in style and form presented by the then-available materials (Hrouda 1957; see also discussion in Stein 1984: 4 ff.). Rather uncomfortably, "Younger" Khabur Ware was linked in particular to an increase in fine-ware cups and small jars (beakers) relative to a decrease in larger coarse-ware

---

[2] The early 2nd millennium materials from Tell Brak and Tell al-Rimah are, non-coincidentally, the most comprehensively published at this time. There is contemporary, but mostly as-yet-unpublished, material from nearby Upper Khabur sites such as Tell Mozan, Tell Barri and Tell Arbid.

[3] This proposal is followed by Stein (1984), Oguchi (1997, 1998) and Postgate *et al.* (1997) on the basis of stratigraphic correlations at Kanesh, Tell al-Rimah and elsewhere. By contrast, Kantor (1958: 22) linked Khabur Ware to the reign of Samsi-Addu.

jars, which had been representative of "Older" Khabur Ware (Mallowan 1937, Hrouda 1957, Kantor 1958). However, in order for temporal change in an assemblage to be properly characterized, the elements identified as changing should not be elements that might vary spatially, or according to context. Frequency of beer jars versus fine ware jars is the sort of suspect variable that is likely to be heavily context-dependent. This issue of contextual comparability, as well as the characterization of Khabur Ware, is addressed extensively by Stein (1984).

Our own excavations at Chagar Bazar reveal significant continuity in frequency of "beer jars" across all phases in Areas A and G (our 'Khabur Ware Jars' and 'Narrow Neck Jars'). There is, in fact, a very slight increase in relative frequency of these two types together within Area G from Phase III to Phase II (from 26.9% to 29.1% of the total assemblage), and a stable percentage of 29.1-30.7% for the remainder of the phases. In Area A, there is more variability and a decrease in these jar types, from 26% in Phase III to 21.5% in Phase II, but an increase to 22.8% in Phase I (and finally a very low 15.7% in the mixed surface material of Phase IA). Some increase in fine-ware beakers was visible within both Areas A and G, but the relative percentages of fine ware within the assemblage are so small that even limited increases may become magnified. The percentage increase of fine ware beakers within Area G was, however, potentially significant, as it describes a slow and gradual curve: from 1% in Phase III to 3.2% in II/2, 3.4% in II/1 and 4.2% in I. However, these figures need to be used with caution; we would not expect the variations in frequency of fine ware beakers and storage jars to be particularly closely related, given their disparate functions. The percentages of Khabur Ware and Narrow-Mouth jars are more likely to have varied in relation to changes in frequency of Wide-Mouth jars, while Fine Ware jars would have varied against Cups and small bowls. Additional details, such as a tendency for the base diameters of small fine-ware jars to become smaller and approach a "button", are visible in our assemblage and transition fluidly into Nuzi Ware (the same tendency in base diameter is visible in the sequence from Tell Billa, among other sites). The genuine changes in forms and assemblage over time are backed up by stratigraphic material from other recently-excavated sites such as Tell Rijm, but the degree to which context and micro-regionality may be responsible for variation has not yet been fully addressed.

In more recent years, certain aspects of Khabur Ware have been further deconstructed (Oguchi 1997, 2000, 2001; Hrouda 2001). However, the purpose of even the most recent work has generally been analysis of internal diachronic variation: presence or absence of forms within any site's assemblage has been approached from the basis of chronological change, rather than functional variation among loci or sites.

Our excavations in Areas A and G at Chagar Bazar present us with a post-Samsi-Addu assemblage; Mallowan's lowest sub-phase was not reached. These excavations offer, from a single settlement, both domestic (Area G) and administrative (Area A) contexts and assemblages. They also offer a total site assemblage that may typify a mid-sized site of some regional political significance in a western "sub-region" at the frontier of a pastoral zone.

Approach to Ceramic Typology

The typology presented here is based on some 1100 drawn diagnostic sherds or vessels, plus a further c 4500 diagnostic sherds noted and described but not drawn. Further counts of non-diagnostic body sherds (by ware and context) provide supplemental information on ratios of common ware, cooking pot ware, fine ware and decoration[4]. Types are illustrated in Plates 10 through 68. This is primarily a sherd-based typology, since whole vessels were rarely found outside graves, and grave assemblages provide a picture of only the vessels deemed appropriate for a very specific ritual context. The grave and house assemblages correspond fairly closely; there were not many types restricted for funerary use in the early 2nd millennium BC at Chagar Bazar nor at other sites in the region. That said, there are some forms that are represented in the graves but are very rare in non-grave contexts, such as small bottles (i.e., CB 3092 from Area G Tomb 39); and the shallow bowls so common in domestic assemblages were not represented in graves.

Minimal vertical movement of material from phase to phase or level to level is indicated by the low presence of identifiably early sherds within the collection units. Certainly sherds of Halaf and 3rd millennium BC date did appear in early 2nd millennium levels, but their frequency was low in both open and roofed spaces and even in the more disturbed street and open settlement-edge contexts. The usual number of non-2nd millennium BC sherds in any collection unit was from one to six, within total numbers of sherds per collection unit customarily numbering in the hundreds. The streets in Areas A and G were the densest contexts in terms of pottery per cubic metre, and all of these sherds are presumably out of their original primary contexts. However, in terms of a generalized sequence, we do not believe that the vertical movement of sherds (or other street contents such as faunal material or objects) was great. Horizontal movement is certainly an issue, with the street and edges of the ancient site being receptacles for rubbish from nearby buildings.

The typology is intuitive and hierarchical in structure: sherds were placed into two basic classes, open or closed, with further distinctions made on the basis of carination/ angularity, shallowness or depth, vessel size and relative rim diameters. For the latter, an assessment was made whether the vessel was narrow- or wide-mouthed in relation to its size, then vessels were sub-divided into small, medium and large categories on the basis of breaks in the graphs of rim size frequencies; see below). These types were further divided into multiple specific variations dependent on rim morphology and other details. This resulted in nine primary categories, subdivided to create 30 main "functional" and size-related categories (plus Stands and a "Miscellaneous" group including types such as strainers, funnels, trays and miniature vessels; see Fig. 60). The typology was further refined by ware–e.g. common versus grey burnished–and by presence or absence of decoration or surface elements such as horizontal ridging-and-grooving. Bases were separately assessed on the basis of shape, since it was not always possible to determine whether they came from open or closed vessels.

All ceramic typologies flatten variability to a certain extent, but we hope that this typology comprises an accepted degree of variability without excessive detail. A high percentage of most types is illustrated in order to indicate the range of decoration and the degree of variability that results in the same type allocation.

---

[4] The number of non-diagnostic sherds assessed and counted was over 36,000. The relative frequencies of some ware types within the diagnostic and non-diagnostic assemblages were sometimes at variance (e.g. fine ware); in these cases, the non-diagnostic ratios may provide a more accurate assessment of the importance of the wares within the assemblage.

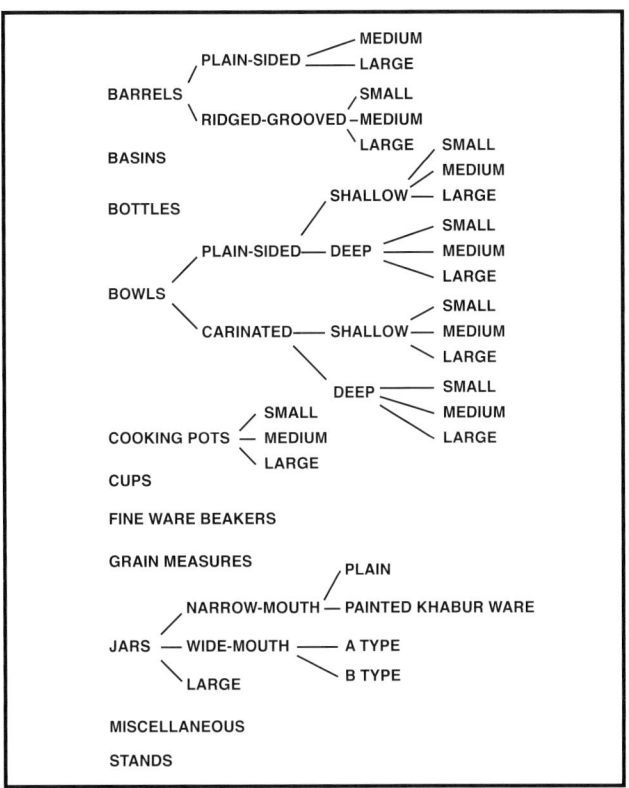

Figure 60: Ceramic typology hierarchy

Most forms identified here have a standardized morphology and, in some cases, what may be near-standard volume (within certain margins) and standard measurements (rim and maximum diameters, neck height, etc). It has been argued that standardization, particularly of measurements (rather than decorative style), is in part a factor of the experience- and routine-derived skills of individual potters (Longacre 1999).[5] But standardization is also "an expected correlate of increasing specialized production" (Longacre 1999: 44), especially linked with efficient and rapid state-controlled modes of production. Beyond issues of routinized skills and state rules, there remains an open-ended question regarding the impact of consumers' desire on standardization, and whether demand for standardized products from purchasers could drive production rules more than would potters' experience or any political agenda.

This question of consumer desire, and desire's unpredictability, may also have an impact on variation of assemblages between contemporary sites. For instance, the banded beaker was common in the Late Old Babylonian to early Mitanni levels at Tell al-Rimah (Postgate *et al.* 1997: 52) but rare in contemporary contexts at Tell Brak (only "two or three" certain examples: Oates *et al.* 1997: 63). The banded beaker does not appear at all at Chagar Bazar in Areas A and G, although our final phase in each should surely have temporally overlapped with the relevant levels at Rimah and Brak. Similarly, there is only one rough-based shallow bowl from Brak, while this form was

---

[5] In Longacre's ethnographic study, measurements were taken of "standardized" vessels. Inexperienced potters' wares varied the most in rim diameter and maximum diameter, when compared to the variability in these dimensions seen in experienced potter's vessels, while standard heights appeared easier for the inexperienced to achieve. Our proposal of a degree of standardization is based primarily on the consistency of rim diameters.

Chapter 5

extremely common at Rimah and Leilan. The Chagar Bazar assemblage contains no examples of these rough-based bowls.[6]

At the same time, other distinctive aspects of assemblages are found consistently across these three sites. The ribbed-band bowl or jar is cited as one of the most important early Khabur Ware types at Brak (Oates *et al.* 1997: 64) and is dated to the time of Shamshi-Adad at Tell al-Rimah. This form (our small and medium ridged-and-grooved pot) is indeed more common in the earliest levels at Chagar Bazar. Within Area A it is significantly more common (5.8% of the total assemblage) in Phase III than in Phases II (1.8%) and I (2.5%). In Area G, its popularity appears to drop but then increases: 6.6% of the assemblage in Phase III, 3.0% in II/2, 4.5% in II/1 and 9.1% in I. The Phase I figure may be skewed because of the limited size of excavation of this phase. The ribbed shallow bowl considered characteristic of earlier Khabur Ware at Brak (Oates *et al.* 1997: 65) also decreases with time at Chagar Bazar, although the overall percentage within the assemblage is very low throughout (our small and medium ridged bowls): in Area A, it drops from 1% in Phase III to 0.3% in Phases II and I, while in Area G, it drops from 1.7% in Phase III to 0.5% in II/2, 0.7% in II/1, and slightly back up to 1.2% in I.

The consistencies in some types and parallel absence of other types within these assemblages may in part be the consequence of different types of context at these sites, but the comparability of our Areas A (community) and G (domestic) seems to belie that conclusion. Subtle intra-regional differences and variant social demands should be in play.

Fabrics

The early 2nd millennium BC *common ware* pottery at Chagar Bazar is distinctively coarser in fabric than that dominating the 3rd millennium BC and is primarily chaff-tempered rather than mineral-tempered.[7] Firing is subtly different (lower temperature kilns or shorter firing time), since non-oxidised dark cores appear more frequently in the early 2nd than in the 3rd millennium. As a general rule, the larger the vessel, the denser and coarser the chaff temper. The chaff in most common ware vessels is supplemented by sparse white lime, fine sand- to grit-sized. The smaller common ware forms are exceptions to the chaff-temper dominance; they are sometimes tempered with fine lime only. The dominant colour is a buff to dark buff, followed by pink-red and finally greenish-buff. In most phases of both Areas A and G, common ware makes up 91.1 to 95.2% of the non-diagnostic sherds (see Table 5.1); the exception which drops below 90% is Phase III in Area A, which also involved a smaller excavated volume than did the upper phases. There are no discernible changes in fabric, vessel wall thickness, or other manufacturing aspects across the chronological phases of either Area A or Area G.

---

[6] Some of our Z-sided bowls have a raised ridge similar in concept to the band on the more vertically-sided banded beakers at Rimah (cf. Pl. 31: 8, 14), but they remain a different type. Our medium shallow bowls with incurving and flat-top rims are similar in rim, vessel morphology and scale to the rough-based shallow bowls, but this Chagar Bazar type is wheel-made and does not exhibit the rough base. Two of our examples have marks of knife-shaving near the base (CB 2839, Pl. 11: 5; CB 3218, Pl. 11: 22), and it may be that this manufacture technique mirrored the rough-based bowls elsewhere. No body sherds with the characteristic rough surface were recovered from any context.

[7] In addition, there is a generalized colour shift, with 3rd millennium northern Mesopotamian fabrics being subjectively "brighter", light buff or greenish, as contrasted to the dull buff, pink or reddish-orange of the early 2nd millennium BC.

Table 5.1 Ware Type Percentages within non-diagnostic material (absolute numbers of sherds in parentheses)

	Common Ware	*Cooking Pot Ware*	*Fine Ware*	*Grey Ware*
A, Phase I	93.7 (2983)	3.7 (118)	2.1 (68)	0.5 (16)
A, Phase II	93.7 (14233)	3.8 (461)	1.6 (187)	0.9 (103)
A, Phase III	86.2 (1221)	10.0 (141)	2.2 (31)	1.6 (23)
G, Phase I	93.8 (1621)	5.9 (102)	0.3 (5)	0.0
G, Phase II/1	95.2 (5770)	4.0 (241)	0.5 (31)	0.3 (16)
G, Phase II/2	93.1 (8198)	5.8 (514)	0.6 (57)	0.4 (40)
G, Phase III	91.1 (2750)	7.6 (229)	0.9 (28)	0.4 (12)

The common wares are supplemented by a *grey burnished ware* with chaff or grit temper, exclusively used for shallow bowls in all three sizes[8]. In terms of labour input, burnished grey ware may be the highest "value" ware produced in this period–given the sequence of production steps, the care needed during clay preparation and firing to achieve the distinctive colour, the dense surface burnishing, plus the probability that vessels which did not achieve the colour parameters would be discarded. There is precedent for the grey colour and highly burnished surfaces in the late Early Dynastic and Akkadian Periods, but the post-Akkadian assemblage does not contain anything that would have served as a technological bridge between the 3rd and 2nd millennia in this case[9]. The relative percentage of grey ware bowls within the diagnostic assemblage was very consistent between our two areas and from phase to phase, varying only between 1.6% and 2.2% (see Table 5.2 at end of chapter); the percentage of grey ware sherds within the non-diagnostic material, however, was lower, from 0.0 to 1.6% (Table 5.1) and shows a slight decrease in the popularity of this ware with time. There is an overall higher percentage of grey ware within Area A's assemblage, contrasted to that of Area G, reinforcing our reconstruction of its potential high value.

Cooking pot wares are hand-made, brown to black or occasionally dark red, horizontally burnished on the exterior, with dense white (limestone) and/or grey (basalt, chert/quartz) angular grit temper and external soot stains[10]. The walls are generally thin (c 1 cm or less), surprisingly so, especially near the base. The cooking pot fabric is far more fragile than that used for storage and eating vessels, and broken sherd edges are prone to further crumbling. This fragility may be an acquired factor derived from the frequent reheating of these vessels post-production ("thermal fatigue") or may have to do with the dense angular temper, which is a positive factor

---

[8] The grey burnished ware category includes examples in less common black and dark brown colour variants.

[9] Post-Akkadian assemblages at Chagar Bazar and Tell Brak include burnished green and pink fine wares, but their colour, wall thickness and even burnishing styles (radial or spiral, versus the horizontal of the early 2nd millennium BC) all differ.

[10] There are a few examples of forms here included with cook pots that are made in common chaff-tempered buff wares (CB 1758, Pl. 63:8, 2126, Pl. 64:1). They have been included in the cook pot group because their morphology–round shoulders, low necks–place them functionally with the other cooking pots and apart from other jars. Their function may have been storage, however.

Chapter 5

against expansion and contraction during repeated heating and cooling but is a negative factor in physical shocks.

It is important to note that despite this fragility, cooking pots do not appear disproportionately frequently in the ceramic assemblages; in fact they are relatively rare (present in most lots, but represented by fewer than ten sherds in most cases, even in lots with hundreds of sherds). Cooking pots make up a small but significant proportion of the diagnostic assemblages, at their highest percentage in Phase III in both Areas A and G. Unusually, the percentage of cooking pots in the diagnostic assemblage for Area A was higher than that in Area G, the inverse of what we would expect, given the functions of these two areas (Area A: 7.7% in Phase III, 4.8% in Phase II, 7.0% in Phase I, versus Area G: 7.0% in Phase III, 3.8% in Phase II/2, 3.9% in Phase II/1 and 3.6% in Phase I; see Table 5.2 at end of chapter). This situation is ameliorated by the percentages in the non-diagnostic assemblage (Table 5.1), which show generally higher percentages of cooking pot ware in Area G (the small-volume Area A Phase III again being the exception).

It is unlikely that the use-lives of cooking vessels were long; their frequent use and handling should lead to relatively frequent breakage. Ethnographic studies have shown that cooking pots have shorter "use lives" than most other categories of pottery (eating, storage) and should often be the most common type in any archaeological assemblage (Varien & Potter 1997: 198). The low number of cooking pot sherds recovered from Chagar Bazar thus may be due to their fragility, which means that they fragment down to a small sherd size less likely to be extracted during excavation.[11] Alternatively, this low number may imply that kitchen rubbish was consciously discarded off-site (given that the kitchen is the context in which most cooking pots would have broken).

The dark colour of the cooking pot ware would have been produced by a reducing kiln atmosphere, versus an oxidizing atmosphere needed for the majority of common and fine wares. This does not necessarily imply that different kilns were employed to produce cooking pot wares and the other wares, since the air supply into a kiln can simply be closed off or left open to produce different atmospheres. But in many other aspects–hand-made versus wheel-made, temper type, temper density and surface treatments–cooking pots are utterly distinct from common ware, which suggests different potters and production traditions. It is probable that cooking pots were household-produced, rather than manufactured by specialist potters. The early 2nd millennium cooking pot fabric and forms are the descendants of wares and forms that have been in use at least since the 3rd millennium BC. Cooking pots from the Post-Akkadian period at Chagar Bazar are nearly identical (McMahon & Quenet 2007), while those from Tell Beydar in the mid-3rd millennium have also been noted for their mixture of limestone and basalt temper, rounded forms and thin burnished walls that become notably thinner near the base (Broekmans, Adriaens & Pantos 2004).

The *fine ware* is distinguishable from common ware by very thin walls (usually 2-3 mm), "clean" fabric with fine mineral temper, little to no chaff temper and a higher frequency of painted decoration than is found among the assemblage as a whole. An occasional chaff impression appears on fine ware vessels, but this may have been

---

[11] Alternative explanations for the low frequency of cooking pot sherds include the possible use of metal vessels for cooking, as a supplement to ceramic vessels; this would mean that any ceramic cooking pot would be used less frequently and have a longer life than if it were the only option. Metal vessels would have been melted down or retained as heirlooms and do not appear in the archaeological record to the extent they were in use. However, this explanation is speculative at best.

accidental, from proximity in the manufacturing area (and a possible indictor that common and fine wares were produced by the same specialists and/ or at the same kilns). Fine ware is unsurprisingly restricted to small vessels, specifically cups and beakers (= Tell Brak's "shouldered cups"). These two forms were only produced in fine ware; the same form template was not used for common ware vessels. The limited range of shapes may imply only a few functions for fine ware vessels; the palm-filling size and vertical form are such that drinking seems the most probable function. The percentages of fine ware within non-diagnostic sherds and in the diagnostic assemblage again are slightly at variance but both show a higher percentage of fine ware in Area A compared to Area G (see Tables 5.1 and 5.2).

Like the grey ware vessels, fine ware vessels would have required significant time in various production steps (fabric preparation, particularly removal of impurities and sieving/ settling of the clay), plus investment of effort (careful shaping and decoration) and skill (stable high firing temperature) compared to a common ware vessel. Thus the production costs and labour investment are high. But these fine ware and grey ware vessels do not appear to be "elite wares" restricted to certain individuals or families and indicative of their wealth or status; there is not a strong contextual restriction in evidence in our excavations that would indicate high "exchange value" (Sahlins 1972), which would have put these wares out of reach of some households. Decorative motifs on fine wares are identical to those on common wares, overwhelmingly horizontal stripes and cross-hatched triangles (see below). Rather than restriction to certain individuals or families, both wares were possibly restricted to use at certain occasions, special use rather than elite use; this still carries with it a sense of high "social value" (Sahlins 1972). Such vessels could also have had a degree of medium-range social visibility, extending beyond the members of the family to include guests.

However, at least two fine-ware vessels (CB 2514, Pl. 46: 3 and CB 2932, Pl. 31: 13) contain blobs or smears of bitumen, as if they had been used to transport or melt this material. The quantity is small, and it may be that these were being used as "paint pots", for application of black paint bands to other vessels[12]. This mundane use for vessels we assume had high labour costs and use value is surprising and warns that our assumptions of value and function may not accurately track past ideas.

Decoration

Bluntly stated, the ceramics of early 2nd millennium northern Mesopotamia were aesthetically impoverished, with a decorative repertoire restricted to a very few motifs, overwhelmingly horizontal paint stripes in varied numbers and widths, and cross-hatched or hatched triangles, with occasional internal paint splashes and (especially in final phases) rare painted birds. The individual elements are few, and the creation of designs from these elements is inherently limited. The painted designs are supplemented by horizontal or wavy shallow grooves and incisions. The motifs are so unimaginative as to appear meaningless or habitual, but the subtle variations and the relatively high proportion of the common ware non-diagnostic assemblage that bears painted decoration (an average of just above 10% from both areas and all phases) nevertheless imply choices and design decisions by the potters.

Virtually the only zone of decoration is the rim to shoulder of jars or rim and upper part of bowls; exterior decoration rarely strays below the mid-point of any

---

[12] The same secondary use of fine-ware jars for bitumen paint is seen at Tell Brak, Old Babylonian levels in Area HH (pers. obs.)

vessel.[13] There may be a cultural explanation, or an encultured view of the "right" place for decoration. Alternatively, the upper zone of a vessel is most visible during use or storage, so the reason may be practical–why decorate a part of the vessel that is unlikely to be seen? Or the answer may be even more prosaic, that the vessels were decorated while spinning on the wheel. Vessels which are dried before decoration are more likely to be held in the hand for application of decoration, and decorative elements may then cover the lower part of the vessel and even the base; but access to the lower half of a vessel is more difficult if the vessel is decorated on the wheel immediately after forming (the vessel would be at the height of the waist or lower for the potter, and access to its lower half would be awkward). In the case of the latter explanation, this restricted zone of decoration adds support to the notion of mass production, with the decorative effects added in the most efficient and rapid way possible.

Painted and unpainted versions of the same type exist in most instances (i.e., our categories of Khabur Ware Jars and Narrow-mouth Jars). The paint used is either red-to-brown or a thick, bituminous, black. Both colours can be relatively fragile, but the black in particular frequently did not bond well with the vessels' surface and crumbled away, leaving a paler ghost of the pattern with a few adhering fragments of paint. The painting is usually commendably neat and precise, without sloppy overlaps or deviation from the horizontal. The properties of the paint were occasionally consciously manipulated, with some red-brown paint bands over-painted in different densities, in order to create a wide band with variable internal colour intensity (i.e., CB 3207, Pl. 50:4).

Decorated painted pottery makes up 11.2% of the non-diagnostic sherd assemblage from Area A and 9.4% from Area G[14]. This subtle difference adds to the slightly larger percentages in fine ware and grey ware in Area A in delineating a picture of higher value and specialized use ceramics in use in the administrative area than in the houses. Painted decoration is noticeably more varied in Area G Phase III, compared with subsequent Phases II and I. Phase III motifs more often include hatched and cross-hatched triangles with horizontal bands, while later phases see a dominance of horizontal bands alone. This is especially clear in the examples of small cups. Area G Phase III also includes the single example of unusual dense cross-hatching covering a bowl rim (CB 4016; Pl. 18: 21).

An interior paint splash pattern noted at Brak (Oates *et al.* 1997: 65) and Rimah (Postgate *et al.* 1997: 52) also appears at Chagar Bazar, exclusively on the interior of medium to large open vessels (Fig. 61).[15] This is clearly a deliberate effect, not an accidental drip but produced by a quick wrist flick of a loaded brush; some of the examples (i.e. CB 1924, Pl. 32: 14) show carefully executed spiralling designs, although it must be admitted that others (CB 4016, Pl. 18: 21) are more haphazard. At Tell Brak, this was thought to be possibly the mark of a particular workshop, which is

---

[13] Exceptions include CB 3998, Pl. 24: 12, a carinated bowl from Area G, which has a horizontal band fairly low on the body. Painted decoration never occurs on grey ware or cooking pots.

[14] The phase breakdowns show some variety within Area A: 7.5% in Phase III, 11.2% in II and 14.8% in I. The chronological variability is less within Area G, with the exception of Phase III: 20.7% in Phase III, 8.1% in II/2, 10.0% in II/1 and 10.0% in I. The Phase III figure has been omitted from the averages and appears to have been in part inflated by a large number of painted sherds used in the courtyard paving 01-24. The selection of mostly painted sherds for this paving reinforces the idea of a cultural engagement with materials and colours that is also seen in some objects (see Ch. 6).

[15] Most often seen on bowls, this decorative element also occasionally appears on the interior of barrels with wide mouths (i.e., Fig. 61 and CB 30: 1, Pl. 37: 2).

an attractive idea. Although tolerably portable, these vessels' transport would not have been easy, nor are they manufactured in technically-tricky fine ware—for both reasons, they are more likely to have been locally made than centrally produced in one workshop at Brak and exported. A guild that comprised workshops at Brak, Rimah and Chagar Bazar, or an emulation effect among these sites, are equally plausible. A further possibility of this being the mark of a group of itinerant potters is intriguing but speculative.

Figure 61: Paint splash pattern inside a medium barrel (CB 1924)

Another motif, groups of two to ten parallel short lines painted across the ledge rims of bowls and jars, is a common feature in all phases and also appears throughout Old Babylonian levels at Brak and Leilan, although it appears to be rarer at Rimah. This set of lines is not exclusive to specific volumes or vessel types (it appears on both jars and bowls) and so may also refer to a guild or set of workshops. Its lack of symmetry stands in contrast to the majority of Khabur Ware decoration and thus may separate it from the purely aesthetic and symmetrical patterns of triangles and horizontal bands, giving it a deeper but unfortunately more obscure meaning. The possibility of these line groups belonging to specific potters, so that their work could be distinguished after firing in a communal kiln, is belied by their absence on a majority of vessels. Another distinctive, relatively rare, decorative effect is the combination of painted cross-hatched triangles with dots (cup CB 4255, G Phase III, Pl. 45:8; grain measure CB 2842, A Phase II, Pl. 47: 8); this may be an early Khabur Ware element[16]. By contrast, a six- or eight-armed 'star' within a square or rectangular metope is found only in Area A surface and Phase IA material and may be a Late Khabur element (Pl. 14:1, Pl. 31:1 and a non-illustrated example next to *tannur* 00-20)[17].

The relatively deep single or double groove, sometimes horizontal, sometimes with a shallow or peaked wave, is probably a hold-over from Post-Akkadian, terminal 3rd millennium BC material (see McMahon & Quenet 2007). In the Post-Akkadian Period, the wave can be quite steep and angular; but in the early 2nd millennium BC it has been modulated to a wide shallow curve in most instances. This decoration is

---

[16] This design is a feature of Oguchi's Period 2 Khabur Ware assemblage, dated 1813-1700 BC (Oguchi 1997: Fig. 1: 11, 12).

[17] This "star design" is found in Oguchi's Period 3 (Oguchi 1997: Fig. 1: 34).

exclusive to large barrels (i.e., Pl. 34: 4, Pl. 35: 5), deep bowls (Pl. 15: 3, 4; Pl. 17: 2, 4-7) and wide-mouth jars (Pl. 57:13, 14). Another motif commonly associated with the mid/late-3rd millennium BC that appears occasionally is a raised ridge with oblique notches or finger impressions ("rope ridge"; see Pl. 43: 5; Pl. 55: 12). In the former case, this may be a transition to an early Mitanni type, a pot-stand or jar (compare Tell al-Rimah, Postgate *et al.* 1997: Pl. 95; or Tell Brak, Oates *et al.* 1997: no. 627). Other examples may be throw-backs to the 3rd millennium.

Finally, there are a few examples, mostly from upper layers, of stylized painted birds associated with Late or Younger Khabur Ware (Oguchi 2006b: Fig. 1: 1-14; his Khabur Ware Periods 3 and 4; see also Frane 1995: Fig. 55: 3, 56: 4). These include CB 1801 (Area A Phase 1; Pl. 68: 3); CB 1926 (Area A, Phase II; Pl. 68: 2); and CB 2799 (Area G Phase I; Pl. 68: 4). Two examples of birds and animals in a blobby and less elegant style from Area G Phase II/2 (Pl. 68: 6, 7) are consistent with a date in Early or Older Khabur Ware (Oguchi's Period 2: 1997: Fig. 1: 14, 15; Oguchi 2006: Fig. 1: 15-17). White over-paint appears only once, as circles with a red-brown stripe (CB 1795, Area A Phase I; Pl. 68: 1). Figural designs and white paint are characteristic of Nuzi Ware/ Mitanni Ware but are present in late Old Babylonian material from Rimah.

Overall, the value added to individual vessels by decorative effects seems low. But the effort, time and materials expended to produce the decoration were also minimal and there was a relatively good return of value for the low time and labour investment. It is easy to dismiss the horizontal paint bands as repetitious and dull, but horizontal paint on its own or especially in combination with carination or grooves provides a strong horizontal axis in contrast to the usually vertical lines of ceramic vessels. Horizontal features subtly emphasise volume and width and can make a vessel appear larger than it actually is, potentially important for both seller and buyer.

The maximum height for most decorative elements (i.e., groups of paint stripes) is about 5 cm, a size which is visible and easily legible from 6.5 meters distance at maximum (Ramsey & Sleeper 2000). The simple and high-contrast motifs (stripes, cross-hatched or hatched triangles, stepped triangles; Pl. 68: 5) may expand this distance to an extent, but as a rule, the visibility of decoration would remain less than ten meters. This distance fits well with the presumed dominance of close private or public-near interactions that took place at Chagar Bazar in both Areas A and G (see Chs. 2, 3 and 7).

Mode of Production

The consistency exhibited by the early 2nd millennium BC pottery assemblage may be linked to specialized manufacturing. The persistence of both forms and decoration across political boundaries in time and space argues that the manufacture was self-administered, not politically-administered, one factor in its survival during the post-Samsi-Addu political collapse[18]. The level of "consumption" of pottery–its use, breakage and discard without repair–in both Areas A and G was relatively high, indicating local and inexpensive production. The volume of pottery–the density of sherds per cubic meter–at Chagar Bazar, as in most contemporary settlements in the region, argues that pottery was easily accessible, easily replaced when broken, and of

---

[18] The texts recovered deal only with production of textiles, beer and food or the management of animals at or near the site and do not mention pottery.

low value and cost, all of which support the probability of economically-efficient, local, industrialized production.

Thus far, no kilns or pottery manufacturing areas have been discovered at Chagar Bazar, although small numbers of wasters and slag fragments were consistently present (concentrations of slag lumps and wasters were recovered particularly from the alley and open areas in Area G: courtyard L. 51, open settlement edge L. 37 and alley L. 54). Two fragments of kiln stilts come from Area A (L. 30.1) and Area G (L. 10.1). The Wadi Khanzir provides adequate clay and water, while the surrounding fields would have provided chaff temper; fuel may have been an issue in the increasingly deforested landscape, but animal dung fuel is a possibility and this would have been widely available. We would expect most production at the site, of ceramics and more, to have taken place outside the houses and probably "off-site", due to lack of open space on the mound.

New Archaeology's typology of production levels (van der Leeuw 1992, Peacock 1982, Arnold 1985) is still a valid framework with which to approach the ceramic assemblage of Chagar Bazar, despite its linear and evolutionary flavour. Most scholars distinguish four or more "levels" of production: 1) household production— vessels are manufactured by household members for use only in those households, and production is a "chore" (Peacock 1982: 8) performed out of need, with basic technology; 2) household industry–vessels are produced in the household but may be traded outside the household, potters are part-time and may take up this craft out of economic necessity to supplement income derived from farming; 3) workshop industry–production is geared towards market demands and is the primary income source for near-full-time specialist potters, efficient technology and investment in production items such as potter's wheels exist, but workshops are still run by and owned by families; and finally 4) large-scale industry–production is in the hands of specialized workers in clustered workshops or factories at specific resource areas, run by non-family groups.

The dominant production mode in Chagar Bazar is not simple household production, since the great quantities of pottery, plus the standardization of fabric, form and decoration, argue against such piecemeal and occasional work. Household industry is a possibility and would fit the degree of standardization seen, as well as the significant skills and practice represented by many vessels. However, investment in technology would be low in such a mode, and it is clear that high temperature kilns and the potter's wheel were present. At the other end of the spectrum, workshop industry with assembly-line, highly specialist production seems inapplicable. That kind of hyper-efficiency is more usually associated with state control of production, which the persistence of Khabur Ware beyond the reign of Samsi-Addu belies. Workshop industry seems most likely, particularly if technological factors are taken into account. The idea of a family workshop intersects well with the other family-based economic aspects we know from texts, such as agriculture, pastoralism, and other trades. The notion of full-time specialisation may need qualification for the Chagar Bazar case, but our notions of the efficiencies of "full-time" versus "part-time" labour are more nuanced than in the 1970s/1980s. Even part-time specialists may produce large quantities of technically-tricky goods in response to market demands.

Estimates for household vessel consumption in other regions vary from c 12 vessels/ household per year (Frankel and Webb 2001: MBA Cyprus) through 7-28 (Sebastian 1992: 55, citing Toll for Chaco Canyon) and 30 (Sinopoli 1999, 2003:

Chapter 5

South India) to 50-100 (Whitelaw 2001: Mycenae). We have figures for numbers of sherds per context, phase and area, but it was not possible to calculate the number of sherds into which any vessel might have broken. This is a key number for calculation of specific household breakage and discard rates. In addition, since our ceramic sample was sherd-based and included material from secondary contexts such as streets, we do not have a precise "starting assemblage" (Mills 1989) from which to work, in terms of numbers of different vessels to be found in any household at a precise moment in time.

Using a mean number of 30 replacement vessels per household per year, and an estimated 14 houses per hectare (from the density of Areas G-BD), the 7-hectare site would have demanded just under 3000 vessels per year. Sinopoli (1999: 124) estimates a production rate at Vijayanagara of 100 vessels per workshop per week or 5000 vessels per workshop per year (factoring in seasonality). Roux (2003) estimates a larger 6000 vessels per year for part-time producers, 15,000 per year for full-time specialists. Taking these figures as reasonable approximations for northern Mesopotamia, a single semi-specialist workshop would have been able to cater to the settlement's needs. These figures are very rough estimations and omit a number of potential factors of interest (funerary or ritual use, feasting and public use, storage of "spares"[19], household production of cooking pots), but they are illustrative of the ability of the local economic system to fill the needs of the site in ceramic production.

Common and fine wares appear to have been produced in workshops, probably the same workshops for both wares. But the probability remains that the cooking pots were produced within the household; their very different ware, restricted number of forms with little overlap of shapes in other wares and relative infrequency mark their manufacture as a separate mode. This may be an economically resilient strategy or may simply reflect the low profit generated by cooking pots. However, the likelihood that workshops producing common and fine wares were family-owned reduces the contrast between "industry" and "craft" this might otherwise imply.

Ceramic Assemblage and Social Inferences

Pottery may contain meaning and social rules as well as food and drink. Consumers' desires and routines have an effect on ceramic style and design. Larger community traditions of use are reflected in both physical and mental templates. Ceramic analysis should go beyond function to the meanings that functions have for cultural practices and social categories. Cups may be used for drinking; but the key questions are the quantity, frequency and visibility of that drinking. Ceramics can be the physical proxy for how we think about food, drink and their consumption.

One notable social aspect to the Chagar Bazar assemblage is the relatively large number of "medium to large" bowls (diameters greater than 20 cm), in contrast to the relatively low number of "small" bowls (diameters less than 20 cm).[20] This size differential implies that eating from a common dish may have been the dominant form of food consumption in the settlement. In contrast, there is a reasonably large number of small individual drinking vessels, cups and fine ware jars. These two type clusters allow a fairly detailed reconstruction of the eating routine, where liquids would have

---

[19] All vessels from large assemblages may not be in use at the same time (Varien & Potter 1997). The storage of "spares" against breakage has an impact on both house space usage and production mode (especially whether the latter was year-round or seasonal).

[20] Although relative rim diameter is not an exact match to relative volume, it is a good indicator of volume for bowls in particular (Mills 1999). See below for descriptions of bowl forms and methodology of size distinctions.

been presented in individual portions but the focus of the meal would be one or two shared dishes. Close household connections are thus reinforced by this face-to-face interaction.

Those small open bowls that are present are predominantly fine ware and decorated, possibly indicating a different approach to formal meals ("feasts") involving extra-family groups.[21] Feasts are often intended to reinforce group solidarity and community ties, and the individual vessels may appear paradoxical in this interpretation. But the separate individual dishes would have been filled from a communal vessel or vessels and could have been conceptually parts of a "feasting set" rather than individual items (see e.g. Borgna 2004 for Minoan parallels). Feasting in this circumstance was intended to focus on the importance of each individual within the group.

The ledge rims on many of the wide-mouthed vessels and bowls would have aided handling (lifting or sliding), supporting the idea that these are communal dishes which would have been carried into a room "ceremonially" and perhaps moved about frequently during a meal. But it should be acknowledged that there is a general trend towards ledge rims on storage jars as well; this rim type could simply be fashion.

This eating routine reconstruction is greatly reinforced (and in part has been identified) by the contrast with the ceramic assemblages of southern Mesopotamia. The southern situation is one of many individual eating vessels, with small (diameters c 10-15 cm) shallow bowls dominating assemblages of the Early Dynastic, Akkadian, Ur III, Old Babylonian and Kassite Periods[22]. Southern Mesopotamia does produce a flat-based shallow bowl or tray with a bevelled rim in the Old Babylonian Period, which could be an ideal communal eating bowl.[23] But large numbers of small shallow bowls correspond to individual portions. In the Old Babylonian Period, the relative numbers of this small bowl within site assemblages had decreased from a high point in the Early Dynastic to Akkadian Periods, but it remains an extremely common type. It may be that the flat-based tray is a preparation or serving vessel rather than a communal eating dish.

Is this size contrast in bowls entirely a question of communal eating versus individual serving? Vessel size can also have to do with family size and logistic efficiency; Mills (1999) cites the increase in number of individuals within extended family households–as well as the increased importance of "supra-household" feasting–to explain a chronological trend towards increased vessel size in the southwest United States. Further complexity is added by the fact that large households will generally own many vessels: more in use and more spares. Full understanding of this relationship between household size, vessel size and vessel numbers in northern versus southern Mesopotamia would require knowledge of total volumes in use. The same volume may have been divided into, for instance, ten individual vessels in the south versus one or two larger vessels in the north. We are not in a position to calculate this, and yet house sizes–another route to determination of household size–actually appear to have been larger in southern than in northern Mesopotamia. Another explanation

---

[21] This reconstruction ignores the possibility of metal vessels (recycled and thus largely invisible) filling gaps in the ceramic assemblage. No metal vessels have been recovered, even from graves, but the past presence of sufficient metal vessels to change this picture seems unlikely.

[22] See McMahon 2006 for diameters of bowls in the late Early Dynastic through Ur III Periods at Nippur; Franke in Gibson *et al.* 1978: p. 78, Pl. 59: 1a, 1b (Nippur) and de Meyer 1978: Pl. 18: 1-2, 4-10 (Tell ed-Der) for Old Babylonian examples; Zettler 1993: Pls. 72-77 for Kassite Nippur.

[23] See e.g. Gibson *et al.* 1978: Pl. 59: 2a, 2b, 2d (Area WB, Old Babylonian Period, Nippur).

for the difference noted in vessel diameters could be different kinds of foods–and differentials in their bulk and liquidity–in northern versus southern Mesopotamia. Vessel diameter variation could map onto the dates and onions of the south versus bread and yoghurt of the north.

Within the typology hierarchy (Fig. 60), it is notable that most of the 30 main types are open vessels (21) while closed forms are split into far fewer types (9)[24]. The significance of this larger number of open types lies in its reflection of an elaboration and emphasis on, and even demand for, variety within this vessel class. Although closed vessels are slightly more common than open in both areas and all phases (see Table 5.2), in terms of absolute numbers, the elaboration of the open types illuminates a probable greater importance for these forms within the assemblage in terms of choices and use.

The comparison of relative frequencies of open versus closed forms points up another subtle difference between Areas A and G. Closed vessels were more common than open in both areas, but the degree to which closed outnumbered open in Area A was greater than in Area G (Area A's ratio for all phases was 61.5 Closed to 36.9 Open, versus Area G's all phase ratio of 50.0 Closed to 45.8 Open). In particular, wide-mouthed jars (possible grain or water storage?) were more frequent in Area A than in Area G.

It is worth a final note in regard to a rather broad but still useful statement by Mallowan that the jars from his Level 1 were more often "large-sized" in contrast to those from previous levels (Mallowan 1936: 34). His main comparison was between the jars of Level 1 and those of Level 5 (Ninevite 5), the two levels for which there were the greatest number of examples; his view is clearly impressionistic and relies on material from graves but is no less valid. Was there a need to store larger quantities of food and drink in the early 2nd millennium than in the mid-3rd millennium (perhaps related to a change in diet or to larger household sizes)? Or was it the case that 3rd millennium households had smaller jars but in larger numbers, making the volume of stored material equivalent?

Descriptions of forms

BOWLS
Plain-sided bowls

Plain-sided bowls are relatively shallow open forms; but there is a wide range in size and degree of depth or shallowness. The shallow versus deep distinction was admittedly subjective, based on angle of the side and its distance from vertical. Divisions between small, medium and large categories have been made quantitatively on the basis of rim diameter clusters: 9-19 cm, 20-34 cm and 35-53 cm, respectively. It should be noted that even within the "small" category, 9-19 cm, the majority of vessels lies in the 14-19 cm range, and it may be useful to sub-divide this category into "very small" (9-13 cm) and "small" (14-19 cm). A difference of 5 cm in the diameter of a relatively small vessel can be significant, while a 5 cm difference in a larger vessel is less so.

---

[24] Many of those 21 open types designate the three sizes of a particular form; and the three-size division was more common among open than among closed forms. But even at the first tier of the typology division, of the nine types defined, six were open and only three closed.

The graph of diameters of common ware bowls (the white line in Fig. 62) showed no sharp breaks.[25] The designation of a category change between 19 and 20 cm coincides with a small dip in the curve, but it is the shapes of the curve segments before and after 20 cm that reinforce the separation; the curve before is relatively flat (especially if one focuses on 14-19 cm), while the curve from 20-34 cm is notably peaked. The division between medium and large sizes is again not striking, but the curve segments are indicative: following the peaked curve from 20 to 34 cm, the curve from 35 to 53 cm, while very jagged, averages to a relatively flat shape at less than 2% for each diameter unit.

The highest percentage of common ware bowls is in the 23-28 cm range (35.6% of common ware bowls are in this range). While 23 cm is acceptable for the diameter of a modern Western dinner plate, 28 cm would be notably large in the same context; these figures stand in even starker contrast to the customary diameters of southern Mesopotamian bowls, as discussed above.

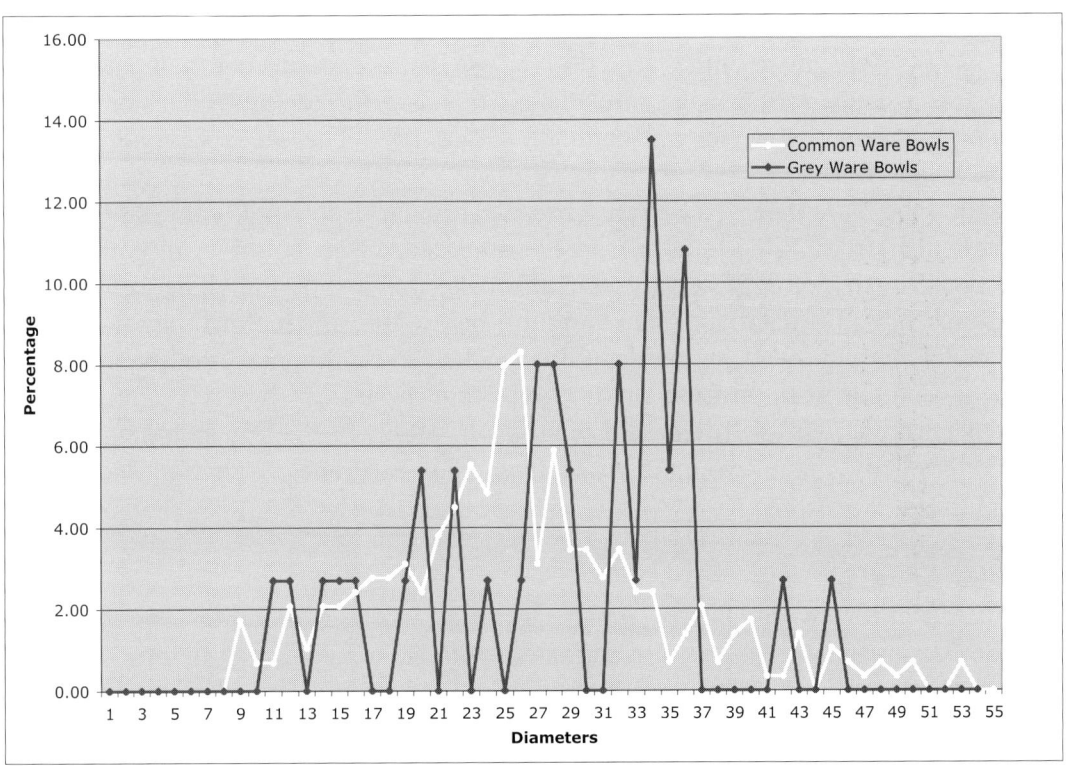

Figure 62: Rim diameters of Common Ware and Grey Ware bowls, as percentage of excavated sample of bowls of each fabric type

Although small bowls can be used for drinking, the more probable uses for all bowls are eating, serving and (inverted) as lids. The plain-sided small shallow bowls have rims that are plain, "hammer-head" or T-shaped, incurving, and rounded and externally-thickened (Plate 10: 1-8). The small deep bowls may have rounded and thickened rims and internally-angled rims like their shallow cousins (Plate 10: 9-13). The small deep bowls also include a group of finer thickened rims that would not look out of place in the 3rd millennium BC (Plate 10: 14-18; but compare Leilan: Frane

---

[25] This graph records in the white line the percentage of the total number of common ware bowls made up by examples of specific diameters, using 1 cm units. The graph groups most of the bowl forms found in common ware together (carinated and straight-sided, with ridged variants). The percents of grey ware bowl diameters are calculated in a separate curve (black line in graph; see below for interpretation).

1996: Fig. 12:1). The incurving or internally-angled rims are potentially created to be suitable for liquid or semi-liquid contents and appear on small bowls at Rimah (Postgate *et al.* 1997: Pl. 52) and Leilan (Frane 1996: Fig. 11: 3).

This range of rim forms is closely matched among medium shallow bowls: plain, "hammerhead" and especially incurving (Plate 11: 1-15); these are joined by a flat-top incurving rim which appears only on shallow medium bowls (in common and grey ware), but not on deep bowls or bowls of other sizes (Plate 11: 16-22, compare Leilan, Frane 1996: Fig. 4:1). On medium deep bowls, plain, hammerhead and rounded rims (Plate 12) are joined by triangular and squared ledge rims, while incurving rims were rare (Plate 13). The medium bowls are matched at Rimah (Postgate *et al.* 1997: Pl. 42) and Leilan (Frane 1996: Figs. 7, 8, 10). Among large shallow bowls, only "hammerhead" and incurving rims were represented (Plate 14: 1-4), while in large deep bowls, squared and triangular ledge rims are the most common (Plate 14: 5-8, Plate 15). The largest deep bowls from Area A are significantly larger than those from Area G, 40 to as much as 60 cm in rim diameter, which suggests 'feasting' was one of the activities which took place in the community building.

There is a sub-set of the large deep bowls that is even deeper than the rest, near-cylindrical, usually with a ledge rim (Plates 16, 17). Horizontal grooves or combined horizontal and wavy grooves are common (Plate 17). These deep cylindrical bowls approach the 'Barrel' type (see below) but are cylindrical or vertical at the top, as opposed to the more incurved barrels. These particular deep bowls can also be difficult to distinguish from Wide-mouthed Jars, Sub-type A (see below), since there is no sharp break in size or depth along which to make this distinction. The difference lies in the presence of a neck and the restriction below the rim seen in the jars, versus a more-or-less straight wall on the deep bowls. However, this may well be an artificial distinction unrelated to past use or function. Our large deep bowls can be compared with "deep bowls" from Rimah (Postgate *et al.* 1997: Pl. 64-65, including both Old Babylonian and Mitanni examples) and from Leilan (Frane 1996: Fig. 26, 27:2, 29, 30:1, 32).

Carinated bowls

A significant number of bowls, especially of the medium- and large-sized varieties (diameters of 20+ cm) are carinated, with an angular break in the side, usually fairly high near the rim. Both shallow and deep forms are carinated, and all three sizes are present.

Figure 63 unpacks the common ware bowl curve in Figure 62 and splits carinated from non-carinated bowls. The carinated bowl curve (black line) is more compressed than the non-carinated (white line), particularly at the beginning: the smallest carinated bowls are larger than the smallest non-carinated examples. The peaks of popularity are also at odds in several places. The non-carinated bowl curve corresponds fairly closely to the aggregate common ware curve in Fig. 62, with dips at 19 cm and 35 cm. By contrast, the percentages of carinated bowls smaller than 17 cm are low, and those that can be categorized as "small" peak at the higher end of the range, 17-19 cm. The highest peaks of both carinated and non-carinated are "medium" and virtually the same, 25 and 26 cm, respectively. But carinated bowls have additional high peaks at 28 cm and 32 cm, while the non-carinated bowls have a smaller peak at 23 cm and steadily decline beyond 26 cm to 36 cm. In effect, "medium" carinated bowls are larger than "medium" non-carinated. Among very large bowls, 40 cm or more in diameter, a larger number and percentage are carinated.

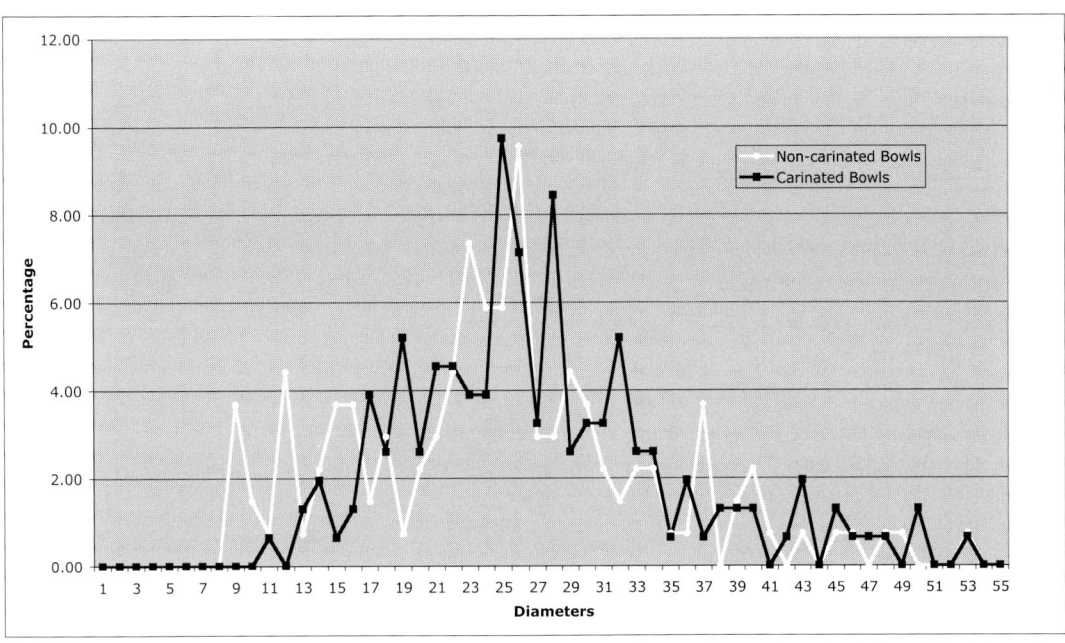

Figure 63: Relative percentages of rim diameters in carinated and plain-sided bowls

It is tempting to see both grey ware bowls (see below) and carinated bowls, with their bias towards larger diameters, as closely linked in function and use. However, a comparison graph of the percentages represented by carinated, non-carinated and grey ware bowl diameters is instructive. Despite the above differences between the diameter curves of carinated and non-carinated common ware bowls, their curves are still closer to each other than either is to grey ware. This is particularly true in the medium through large diameter ranges (see Fig. 64).

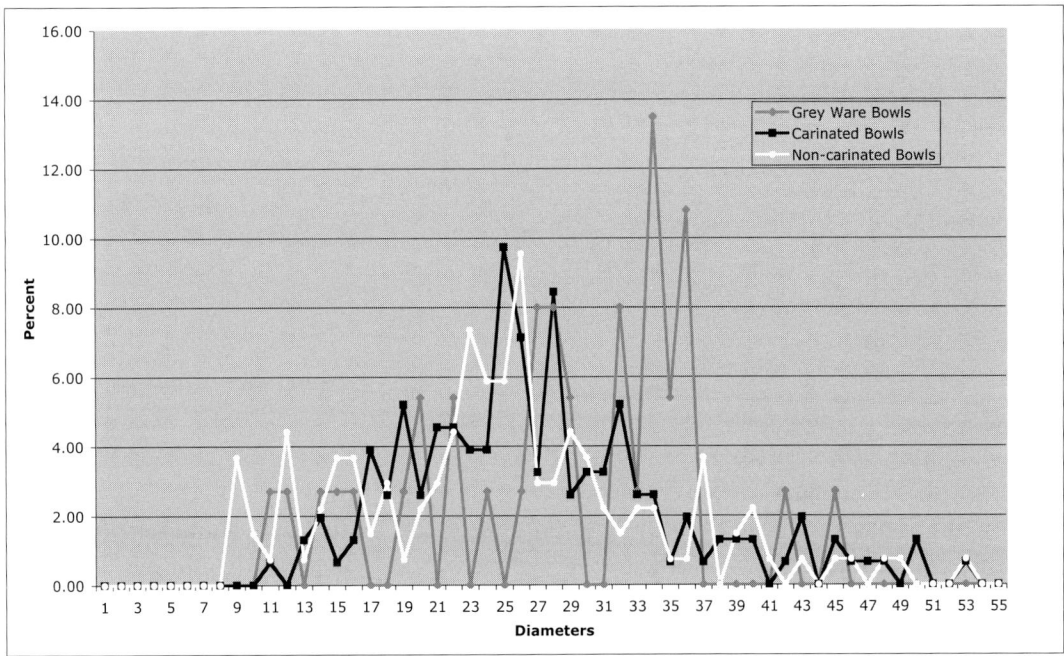

Figure 64: Relative percentages of rim diameters of plain-sided common ware, carinated common ware and grey ware bowls

The percentage of carinated vessels is higher in Area G than in Area A (see Table 5.2); their relative percentages seem to vary inversely against those of shallow bowls, which are less common in Area G. The most probable function of carinated bowls is serving vessels, since a carination makes the bowl easier to hold and carry than a straight-sided bowl. Carinated sides also allow for a slightly larger volume than is contained in straight-sided bowls of the same rim diameter, and the centre of gravity of a carinated bowl is lower than that of a straight-sided bowl, giving greater stability in use. Carinated bowls have a long life, as a form, continuing into Mitanni and Middle Assyrian Periods without exhibiting much morphological change (see e.g. Middle Assyrian carinated bowls from Rimah, Postgate *et al.* 1997: Pl. 28-30). Carinated bowls are present at Mohammed Diyab (Faivre 1992: Fig. 21) and Leilan (Frane 1996 esp. Figs. 38-42) and are the most common form at Kenan Tepe (Parker & Dodd 2003), although it is worth noting that rim diameters there are reported as usually less than 20 cm.

Both shallow and deep small carinated bowls are dominated by triangular rims; rounded rims are also common, particularly in the deeper forms (Pl. 18). Rarer subtypes include the incurving "liquid retaining" rim, a very fine triangular rim (Pl. 18: 8) and a flat-top rim with high carination, the latter on deep bowls only (Pl. 18: 22-24; similar to bowls from Leilan: Frane 1996: Fig. 19: 1-3). Medium carinated bowls can also be separated into shallow and deep variants, although the deep bowls are noticeably less common than shallow. Squared ledge rims and triangular rims (both small and extended) dominate the shallow variants (Pls. 19-22); both often have a thickening into the bowl interior, similar in idea to the incurving "liquid retaining" rims. Medium carinated bowls also exhibit occasional exaggerated morphology: an extended sharp ledge rim with a pronounced ridge (i.e., Pl. 19: 18, 19; Pl. 24: 1-4). The shallow medium bowls include smaller numbers of a flat-top rim (Pl. 22: 8, 9) and a club rim with near-vertical sides to the carination (Pl. 22: 10, 11). The deep versions are equally dominated by squared ledge rims and triangular rims (Pls. 23, 24: 1-4); but they also include a rounded rim not seen among the shallow versions (Pl. 24: 5-8) and a triangular rim with an interior extension and a very strong horizontal groove on the interior (Pl. 24: 9-15). The latter often has an S-shaped rim-to-neck profile, and it is plausible that the groove was to support a lid. Large carinated bowls can be separated into much the same categories, and again the shallow outnumber the deep. Triangular and triangular ledge rims are found on the shallow versions (Pls. 25, 26: 1-3); triangular, triangular ledge and rounded rims are the most common on the deep (Pl. 26: 4-8, Pl. 27: 1-4). The deep bowls with a triangular rim, interior lid-groove and S-profile also come in the large size (Pl. 27: 5-7).

Grey Ware Bowls

The range of bowl forms seen in grey ware is narrower than the range in common ware. Like common ware bowls, grey ware bowls come in plain sided, carinated, and ridged formats, but only in shallow, never deep forms. Three sizes are represented within grey ware, but the precise sizes do not map exactly onto the three size distinctions in common ware. The graph of grey ware bowl diameter percentages shows a more internally choppy curve than that described by common ware bowl diameters (see grey line in Fig. 64 above). Its range is also more compressed at both ends: the smallest grey ware bowls are larger than the smallest in common ware, and the largest grey ware bowls are smaller than those in common ware.[26] The curve of grey ware can be divided into small, medium and large, respectively, at: 11-16 cm, 19-

---

[26] The sample size of grey ware bowls is less than that for common ware, and this discrepancy may explain some of the differences noted.

36 cm and 42-45 cm. Like the sub-divisions of the small category in common ware, "medium" grey ware bowls should probably be divided into "small-medium" (19-24 cm) and "medium" (26-36 cm) categories. The majority of the grey ware examples are at the larger end of medium (27-36 cm) barely overlapping with and mostly larger than the most common diameter of medium common ware bowls.

Grey ware bowls are thus, generally, larger and subjectively shallower than non-grey ware bowls, the kind of vessel that would be ideal for "feasting" or presentation and consumption of communal dishes. They do not appear to imitate metal forms (there are no sharp angles or exaggerated hardness), but the silver-grey burnished surface may be an attempt to "quote" the appearance of metal. Although the relative frequencies in the diagnostic assemblage show very little difference between Areas A and G, the percentage of grey ware in the non-diagnostic sherd material shows a slightly higher frequency in Area A.

Small shallow grey ware bowls are few, with a restricted range of rims: incurving and a unique flat-top with grooves on plain-sided forms (Pl. 28: 1-5); plain, incurving or triangular on carinated examples (Pl. 28: 6-10). The plain rim, carinated small bowl is very similar to the classic carinated bowl of the Ur III Period in southern Mesopotamia and the Post-Akkadian Period of northern Mesopotamia. Medium shallow plain-sided grey ware bowls are dominated by triangular rims and incurving "liquid" rims (Pl. 28: 11-15 and 18-22 respectively[27]). In addition there are less common sharply angled rims (Pl. 28: 16, 17); these are paralleled at Late Old Babylonian Rimah (Postgate *et al*. 1997: Pl. 41: 213, Pl. 45: 269), Leilan (Frane 1996: Fig. 2: 3, 4) and a late Level 1 grave in Mallowan's Area EH at Chagar Bazar (Mallowan 1936: 29, Fig. 9: 5). A rounded-thickened rim (Pl. 28: 24, 25) and an elongated triangular rim (Pl. 28: 14, 15) may be exclusive to grey ware. The carinated medium grey ware bowls overwhelmingly have triangular and "hammerhead" rims (Pl. 29: 1-3, 5-9); the only plain rim example represented (Pl. 29: 4) is paralleled in late Old Babylonian Rimah (Postgate *et al*. 1997: Pl. 40: 205, 206). One unusually heavy and flat-based example (CB 1788; Pl. 29: 7) is almost exactly paralleled at Rimah (Postgate *et al*. 1997: Pl. 44: 262).

Ridging occurs only on the medium sized bowls in grey ware (see below for small and medium ridged bowls in common ware). The plain-sided ridged versions all have plain rims and quite narrow ridges/ grooves (Pl. 29: 10-12; compare Leilan, Frane 1996: Fig. 9: 6), while the carinated forms have plain or small triangular rims and wider grooves and sharper ridges (Pl. 29: 13-17)[28]. The latter are among the most elegant and aesthetically pleasing vessels represented; they also appear at Tell Mohammed Diyab (Faivre 1992: Fig. 23: 15) and Leilan (Frane 1996: Fig. 45: 1, 3, 5-7). The only examples of large grey ware bowls have plain sides and flattened and incurving rims (Pl. 29: 18, 19).

Ridged bowls

This is a relatively rare category, involving bowls of small and medium size. Like the grey ware examples, the common ware ridged bowls exhibit a range of ridge

---

[27] Burnished grey ware bowls at Leilan most frequently have channel or flat bases; e.g. Frane 1996: Fig. 5: 4, 5).

[28] Several examples of burnished bowls in other colours have been included here because their form and surface finish implies that they conceptually belong to the grey ware category, although the intended colour was not achieved during firing: CB 1894 in over-fired burnished green ware (Pl. 29: 9) and CB 2297 (Pl. 29: 13) in burnished brown-grey ware. Similar burnished bowls at Tell Leilan are often grey-brown or black.

shapes, from low and sharp, akin to corrugation, through low and smooth to very sharp and high. The ridges are moderately aesthetic but also can be functional, potentially aiding in the gripping and carrying of these vessels when full. Within the small versions, there are shallow plain-sided and deep carinated versions (Pl. 30: 1-7) and a single example of a vertical-sided bowl with finer ridges and grooves (Pl. 30: 8). The same shallow plain-sided, deep carinated and vertical-sided variants exist in medium versions (Pl. 30: 9-24). The vertical-sided variants in the medium size have very fine ridges/ grooves, almost like combing, which covers the full vessel side to the base; comparable examples from Leilan are found in brown-gray burnished ware (Frane 1996: Fig. 25: 1-2). Paint stripes were sometimes combined with the ridges.

Ribbed or ridged bowls appear, fairly sparsely, at Brak Area HH in late Old Babylonian levels (Oates *et al.* 1997: 236-238, 241, 242) and in contemporary levels at Leilan (e.g. Frane 1996: Figs. 45, 46), but they seem less common at Rimah (cf. the slightly different examples illustrated as Postgate *et al.* 1997: Pl. 49: 349, 350). This may reflect a functional difference between the contexts excavated at these sites, or there may be a local preference for these at Chagar Bazar. Within Chagar Bazar, ridged bowls were very slightly more frequent in Area G than in Area A, but the numbers were very low overall.

Z-sided bowls

This small sub-type has a distinctive carinated side, with a further sharp articulation of the short neck, creating an expanded Z-shaped profile. Where preserved, the bases are rounded or ring. They are only seen in the small and medium sizes. The small versions are all fine ware and come in both shallow (Pl. 31: 1-7) and deep forms (Pl. 31: 8-20). The medium versions are in common ware and are deep only (Pl. 31: 21-26). Rims are plain or slightly rounded, and painted decoration is common. There are parallels in late Old Babylonian examples from Brak Area HH and the top of Area TW (Oates *et al.* 1997: Fig. 190: 208, 240; Fig. 192: 284, 285), from Leilan (Frane 1996: Fig. 36: 2), from Rimah (Postgate *et al.* 1997: Pl. 58: 512, although quite angular, Pl. 79: 896) and another from Tell Billa Stratum 3 (Speiser 1933: Pl. LX: 4).

The frequencies of Z-sided bowls at Chagar Bazar were almost the same between Area A and Area G, and there is a slight indication of an increase in popularity with time. The function of the small deep versions may be close to that of fine ware beakers, a drinking vessel.

Barrels

Barrels are deep, with a wide mouth, no neck or a very short neck, and rounded sides often bearing horizontal shallow grooves on the shoulder or at the maximum diameter. Most barrels come in medium, large and very large (45-60 cm rim diameter) sizes (Pls. 32-36). Rims on the medium-large forms are overwhelmingly squared or triangular ledges. Paint bands and wavy grooves appear but are rare, and wide horizontal grooves and ridges appear on some of the largest examples (Pl. 36: 4). One example from Area A Phase III (Pl. 32: 15) has a pair of loop handles from shoulder to rim. Very few small versions are represented, and among these fine ware dominates (Pl. 37: 1-9). The most common diameters are 26 and 30 cm (within the medium category) and 33 and 38 cm (in the large category). This type is slightly more common in Area G than in Area A and there is a particularly notable density of barrel sherds discarded in the alley in Area G during Phase II/2.

The wide mouth and large volumes imply storage of a non-liquid, yet scoopable, commodity, such as grain. At other sites, this type is usually classified as a "deep bowl" (e.g. Tell al-Rimah, Postgate *et al.* 1997: Pl. 65).

Ridged Barrels

These open vessels are similar to the plain-sided barrels in relative width of mouth, rounded sides and minimal neck, but they additionally have a raised ridge or band on the shoulder or side, usually with horizontal grooves and often with paint stripes. Size categories (based on rim diameter frequencies) are: small at 14-19 cm (peaking at 17 cm), medium at 20-28 cm (most falling between 20 and 22 cm) and large at 30-38 cm. There are also fine ware small versions and a small number of "very large" ridged barrels with rim diameters greater than 40 cm.

Within the small fine ware group, there are both shallow (Pl. 37: 10-15) and deep (Pl. 37: 16-27) versions, and the shallow forms are close in concept to the deep Z-sided bowls. Rims in the small fine ware group are not well-articulated, most being plain or rounded. A significant number have rounded shoulders and are close in form to small cups (e.g. CB 1696, Pl. 37: 24). A very high proportion of the fine ware group bears painted decoration. The common ware versions are found only in deep format, in small, medium, large and very large sizes (Pls. 38-40). Rims in common ware are more elaborated than in fine ware: ledges, triangles and extended triangles. These ridged and grooved barrels may be slightly under-represented, and wide-mouth jars inversely over-represented—these two types can be difficult to distinguish if the ridged shoulder of the barrel is not preserved.

The fine ware and small ridged and grooved barrels find parallels at Brak HH (Oates *et al.* 1997: Fig. 191: 243-249; Fig. 193: 293-302), as do the medium (*ibid*. Fig. 192: 289) and large examples (*ibid*. Fig. 192: 290). Medium and large examples are represented at Tell Mohammed Diyab ("cratères", Faivre 1992: Fig. 11), along with fine ware versions ("gobelets", *ibid*. Fig. 25: 3-17). At Chagar Bazar, they are more common in Area G than in Area A.

Basins

This type is a wide (22-35 cm in diameter), substantial vessel with thick vertical, slightly concave or rounded walls and a heavy flat base (Pls. 41, 42: 1-9). Horizontal grooves at the middle of the vessel (e.g. Pl. 41: 4, 12) and/ or near the base (e.g. Pl. 42: 4, 9) are common; ledge rims dominate, occasionally with grooves in the upper surface. The only close example represented at Rimah is slightly smaller and comes from a Mitanni level (C 5; Postgate *et al.* 1997: Pl. 66: 642), although the Old Babylonian fenestrated stands are similar (*ibid*. Pl. 96). A basin is illustrated from Tell Mohammed Diyab (Faivre 1992: Fig. 15). There is an unusually high number of large sherds of these basins (bases plus walls, rims, etc) from Area G in the open area of Phase III and the alley of Phase II/2, and a domestic use, perhaps in food preparation, seems possible. A less common basin form has a channel rim and rounded body (Pl. 42: 1-3), also seen at Tell al-Rimah in the Mitanni Period (Postgate *et al.* 1997: 612, although the diameter is larger than our examples).

One base from Area G Phase II/2 bears an incised decoration that may be a schematic date palm, in a similar style to Post-Akkadian decorative elements (CB 3797; Pl. 42: 6).

Stands

The Stands category is quite mixed, incorporating both cylindrical short stands not dissimilar from the basins, as well as larger concave stands with a variety of rim morphologies. Corrugated rims are rare but distinctive (Pl. 42: 10-13). Many flaring rim (or base) sherds have been included in the "stand" category, especially if they have ridges (Pl. 43: 8, 9, 13-15) and/ or paint stripes (Pl. 43: 10-12). A small group with internally-angled rim and steeply angled sides has been included here (despite some similarities to small and medium bowls with similar rim morphology) because of the straight conical sides which do not match the more rounded appearance of bowls (Pl. 43: 16-18). The same holds for the equally small group of ledge-rim, steeply angled vessels (Pl. 44: 8, 9); these very angled forms presumably came from short stands with concave sides such as are represented at Rimah (Postgate *et al*. 1997: Pl. 95: 1135 ff) and Tell Brak (Oates *et al*. 1997: Fig. 217). Also included in "Stands" is a larger group of ledge rim cylindrical vessels (Pl. 44: 1-7). Some of these might be better categorized as wide-mouthed jars or deep bowls, but their cylindrical forms suggest stands.

Three decorated stand fragments came from the upper layers in Area G (Pl. 43: 1-3); these are the distinctive angular tops to tall conical stands such as are found in late Old Babylonian and Mitanni levels at Tell al-Rimah (Postgate *et al*. 1997: Pl. 98). A flared stand with notched "rope" ridge (Pl. 43: 5) hints at decorative elements which will become more common in the Mitanni Period, while a ridge-sided form has the organized internal paint spatter seen on some bowls (Pl. 43: 7). A final group of flared-rim cylindrical forms may be from segments of drainage pipe (Pl. 44: 14-16).

Cups

"Cup" is something of a catch-all term, since the examples may have quite straight sides (e.g. Pl. 45: 1-10), angled sides (e.g. Pl. 45: 11-14) or be near-spherical with a short neck (e.g. Pl. 45: 15-32). Where preserved, bases are flat or a small ring. Overall, the form and size (fine ware or near-fine ware, diameters mostly less than 10 cm, small volume, easily held in one hand) indicates a drinking use, and it is this function that unites the morphological variants within this type. A high percentage bears painted decoration, located from the rim to the maximum diameter. Within the spherical group, some have a low rounded rim and no neck, but there is a continuum through to a short flared neck, which in turn links to the slightly taller neck of the Fine Ware Beakers (below).

At Rimah, these vessels are termed "small shouldered beakers"; spherical and angular sub-types are present (Oates *et al*. 1997: Pl. 79: 882 ff.). They seem to be less common at Brak (but see Oates et al. 1997: Fig. 190: 206) and at Tell Mohammed Diyab (Faivre 1992: Fig. 25: 1).

Cups are more frequent in Phase III of both Areas A and G than in later phases; there is a particular concentration of cups and fine-ware small ridged-grooved barrels in the northern stretch of the alley in Area G during Phase II/1 (L. 34.4).

Fine ware beakers

The small fine ware beakers are similar in scale to small cups but are distinguished by having a genuine neck–taller than those seen on the spherical cups– and a distinct shoulder (Pl. 46). In addition, beakers are usually taller and have a smaller maximum body diameter than "cups". Three variations are identifiable: very narrow with rim diameters c 5-6 cm (Pl. 46: 1-6), slightly wider with rim diameters c 8-9 cm and a short neck (Pl. 46: 7-16) and slightly larger with a tall neck (Pl. 46: 17-

24). Bases are usually a low ring, sometimes flat or concave. The small rings are clearly separately added, and the pointed base of the initial form may protrude below the ring base (Pl. 46: 13). This would have meant the beaker would not have been able to stand upright and would have needed to be held in the hand while full.

These fine ware beakers are called "shouldered beakers" elsewhere, such as Tell Brak (especially the narrowest versions; compare Oates *et al.* 1997: Pl. 73: 766-772 for undecorated, Pl. 75 for painted versions). They have been dated late within the Khabur Ware sequence (Hrouda 1957, Oguchi 2000). Like the small cups, fine ware beakers represent drinking vessels and are notable for their frequency of decoration, usually two or three thin paint stripes on the shoulder or, more rarely, a stripe at the rim.

Grain measures

This type has a cylindrical or concave-sided body, plain or small ledge rim, low body carination and frequent painted decoration, usually rows of bands and hatched or cross-hatched triangles which may cover the entire vessel to near the base. Mallowan is responsible for the "grain measure" label assigned to these vessels (Mallowan 1937: 148) but he backtracked and acknowledged that they could be for holding liquids, after he recovered an example from a Chagar Bazar grave containing a conical copper strainer from a drinking straw (Mallowan 1947: 250-251). The decoration and rarity of these vessels certainly point to a less prosaic function than the name denotes.

Complete examples were not preserved, and some rims included here may belong to wide-mouthed jars. The samples can be divided into thinner-walled (Pl. 47: 1-5) and thicker-walled (Pl. 47: 6-13) varieties. Grain measures were very slightly more common in Area A than in Area G. Although they are in some ways iconic of the early-mid 2nd millennium BC, grain measures are widespread but not particularly numerous at any site (for Tell Mohammed Diyab, see Faivre 1992: Fig. 14: 10; for Tell Brak, see Oates *et al.* 1997: 262, 265, 270-277; for Tell al-Rimah, see Postgate *et al.* 1997: Pl. 78).

JARS
Narrow-mouth and Khabur Ware storage jars

"Khabur Ware" is exemplified by the tall ovoid jar with a narrow neck and a ledge or triangular rim, with painted stripes on the neck and/or shoulder. Khabur Ware jars are a very common form within the assemblage at Chagar Bazar, but in fact unpainted Narrow-mouth jars of similar size and shape outnumber the painted versions in all phases of both areas. There is great variety in rim morphology of the painted jars: a rounded projecting triangle (Pl. 48), flattened triangle (Pl. 49: 1-4), squared ledges (Pl. 49: 5-20) and rounded (Pl. 50: 1-4). An uncommon sub-type has a narrow sloped shoulder and smaller rim diameter than the "normal" Khabur Ware jars. (Pl. 50: 10-13). The necks of the regular Khabur Ware jars are a near-standardized 4-5 cm high (which may have more to do with average adult hand size and manufacturing technique than any conscious or desired standard height); the necks are markedly concave, while the rim diameters cluster around 12 to 14 cm. This near-standard rim dimension has also been noted at Tell Mohammed Diyab (Faivre 1992: 59, Figs. 8-10) and appears at Brak (Oates *et al.* 1997: Fig. 193: 303, 310, 312) and Rimah (Postgate *et al.* 1997: Pl. 90, diameters from 12-13.5 cm).

The unpainted Narrow-mouth jars exhibit a similar range of rim variations (rounded, projecting or flattened triangular and squared ledge; Pls. 51, 52) and comparable dimensions. Both Khabur Ware jars and Narrow-mouth jars have a comparable dimensions that may have been designed to support a lid set inside the jar mouth, but a few examples of both unpainted and painted jars have a slightly thickened rim with an internal ledge or groove to support a lid (Pl. 50: 5-9; Pl. 53: 10-15). Sometimes this internal groove is so deeply articulated as to make the rim appear to have an "S" shape. A similar small number of the Narrow-mouth jars bear an external decorative ridge on the neck or at the neck-shoulder join (Pl. 53: 1-9); this decorative ridge is less common, but occasionally present, on painted Khabur Ware jars (i.e., Pl. 48: 8). These ridges are present in Mallowan's Level 1 assemblage on painted and unpainted forms (Mallowan 1936: Fig. 14: 5, 10, Fig. 16: 1).

The relative frequencies of Khabur Ware and Narrow-mouth jars in the diagnostic assemblage vary somewhat erratically from phase to phase in both Areas A and G, although Khabur Ware is at its most common in Phase III in both. Together, these two types were more common in Area G than in Area A, while the inverse was true of Wide-mouth jars (see below).

Wide-mouth Jars

As well as the Narrow-mouth jars and Khabur Ware jars, there is an important jar form that is larger, deeper and wider-mouthed. These Wide-mouth Jars have been divided into A and B sub-types here. While similar in their proportions and their rounded bodies with low sloped shoulders, sub-type B is distinguished from sub-type A by a less distinct or even an absent neck and different proportions: the maximum diameter and rim diameter are closer to each other in the B sub-type than in the A sub-type. The A sub-type has a clear constricted neck. Both the A and B sub-types of these wide-mouthed jars are elsewhere described as a "large jar" (Brak: Oates *et al.* 1997: Fig. 214: 639-641 for our A sub-type, Fig. 214: 642-648 for our B sub-type; Rimah: Postgate *et al.* 1997: Pl. 88: 1013-1025 for our A sub-type).

The smallest examples in each case have rim diameters of c 13 cm, although these are relatively rare. The A sub-type clusters around 18-20 cm in rim diameter; the majority lie between 18 and 24 cm (with maximum diameter c 32 cm). The A sub-type has been divided into medium and large sizes: Medium comprising 13 through 26 cm in rim diameter, the less common Large being 27 through 40 cm. The Medium-to-Large split was assigned to 27 cm in part because of an observed dip in the relative frequency of diameters at 26 cm and in part because of a generalized larger scale (thicker walls, heavier rims) observable in vessels with 27+ cm rim diameters. The most typical Medium forms are shown in Plates 54-56, and some thinner-walled examples (1-6) and smaller versions (7-13) on Plate 57; rim and neck morphologies in the Large category are more varied (Pl. 57: 14, Pl. 58).

The Medium-to-Large split within the B sub-type is made at 30 cm, rather than 27 cm, again because of a dip in the relative frequency of rim diameters at 29-30 cm and a generalized larger scale of vessels with rims greater than 30 cm. The majority of the B sub-type (Pls. 59-61) has rims from 20 to 27 cm in diameter (overlapping with but larger than the A sub-type), and the largest examples of the B sub-type also reach 50 cm or more, significantly larger than the largest versions of the A sub-type (Pl. 61: 6, 8, 9). Rim forms encompass squared and rounded ledges, extended triangles, and rarer rounded forms on both A and B sub-types. Within the Medium vessels, there are a few examples with an internally-thickened rim with a lid-groove in both the A sub-type (Pl. 58: 2, 10, 15) and B sub-type (Pl. 60: 1-10).

The largest examples of the Wide-mouth jars, particularly the B sub-type, are very close to "deep bowls" in our own assemblage and that at Rimah (Postgate *et al.*

1997: Pl. 65) and "barrels" at Tell Rijm (Kolinski 2000); ultimately, it may be that functionally these different types should have been grouped together. Our A sub-type is more common than the B type in most phases of both areas. Wide-mouth jars are significantly more common in Area A than in Area G and are more common than Narrow-mouth jars there, while Area G shows the inverse frequency, more Narrow-mouth jars than Wide-mouth jars.

The larger examples of these Wide-mouth jars can be so large that, when filled, they would have been prohibitively heavy to lift for serving or pouring, so it is probable that they remained stationary for use. The wide mouth would have made the contents easily accessible by scooping yet at the same time would make long-term storage use unlikely. A healthy number of both sub-types have painted or grooved decoration, indicating that visibility was an aspect to their use. The larger examples often have horizontal grooves, or horizontal grooves framing a wavy groove just at and above the maximum diameter. Medium examples are more often decorated with horizontal paint bands on the shoulder and near the rim.

In reconstruction of past vessel functions and probable contents, one staple resource is often overlooked: water. Within the household, water was probably the single most important material stored, and any specific jar used for water storage was most likely to be a jar without multiple uses, because of both avoidance of contamination and the probability that such a jar was never entirely empty for use transfer. Water arguably may have been stored in this wide-mouth jar form; examples are very common in our assemblage and of a scale and form compatible with a good volume of storage and with easy access (ladling with a smaller vessel from the mouth). This is not to say that every vessel of this type was used for water storage; some may have held grain and other goods, especially those with a slightly more constricted neck. This Wide-mouth jar provides a further contrast between cultural practices of north and south. Southern Mesopotamia across the 3rd millennium BC has a plethora of spouted jars; and while the frequency of spouts drops in the early 2nd millennium, the south can still be characterized as a "pouring" culture. (In the absence of spouts, vertical non-complex rims with small diameters are well-adapted to pouring.) By contrast, spouted vessels are rare during most periods in the north, making this a "ladling" culture.

Cooking pots

Cooking pots are primarily defined by their distinctive dark-coloured, densely grit-tempered fabric, external horizontal burnishing and soot staining or burn marks. However, the rim morphologies, size, volume and vessel shapes–overwhelmingly round-based and near-spherical–are also very consistent across this type. The forms and ware are very similar to Post-Akkadian cooking pots and even to Late Chalcolithic examples.

Rims of cooking pots tend to be slightly thickened and rounded and between 15 and 23 cm in diameter, and necks are usually virtually non-existent (Pl. 62) or extremely low, less than 2 cm (Pl. 63).[29] There are a few examples of a slightly taller neck, c 3 cm high, with a plain rim, but these are rare (Pl. 64: 4-6); and there are some uncommon quite angular rims on a low neck (Pl. 64: 1-3). The rim diameters can be divided into small (10-17 cm), medium (18-21 cm) and large (22-31 cm). Small

---

[29] Sherds of several true "hole-mouth" cooking pots were recovered Pl. 62: 3), but these may be prehistoric or 3rd millennium BC in origin, the similarity of wares across the millennia makes temporal determination difficult.

cooking pots were infrequent, large are only slightly more common; the majority are medium, especially clustering at 19 cm in rim diameter. Even 19 cm is quite a small rim diameter, making access to the vessel difficult for stirring while cooking or for cleaning. The relatively small rim diameter may be designed to maintain interior temperatures, a precisely balanced compromise between access to contents and heat retention.

Their handmade manufacture places cooking pots in a different production category than the rest of the assemblage. It is probable that cooking pots were the only vessel to be produced with the household. As kitchen vessels, their social visibility would have been low, complementing the idea of non-specialist occasional manufacture. This does not mean, however, that they lacked standardization or a mental template. The persistence of the distinctive ware from the 3rd millennium speaks to an extremely strong regional tradition. And closely similar forms appear at Tell Mohammed Diyab (Faivre 1992: Fig. 13) and Tell al-Rimah (Postgate *et al.* 1997: Pl. 63: 595, 596). As was mentioned above, the frequency of cooking pots within the diagnostic assemblage was higher in Area A than in Area G, which does not fit well with our proposal of an administrative function for the primary building in Area A; however, there were houses in association with the community structure Building III. And the percentage of cooking pot sherds in the non-diagnostic assemblage does indicate a higher frequency in Area G in most phases.

Bottles

There is a very low number of small jar forms, with small rim diameters, rounded bodies and very constricted necks, here labelled "bottles" (Pl. 64: 7-16). This type is most strongly represented in graves (Area A, T. 12 and T. 41; Area G, T. 39 and T. 33), but the numbers are so small overall that this may not be a significant association. Several examples in this group (Pl. 64: 12, 15, 16) may be miniaturized versions of Khabur Ware jars.

Miscellaneous

This category includes a few hand-made miniature vessels (Pl. 65: 1-5, perhaps children's experiments), and two miniature painted stands (Pl. 65: 6, 7). Small tubular (Pl. 65: 8) and cup-like (Pl. 65: 9) funnels are represented, the latter from a grave (Area G, T. 13). A range of perforated strainer bowls appears, mostly small hemispherical or carinated bowls with very regular circular perforations (Pl. 65: 12); two miniature handmade strainers came from Area G (Pl. 65: 10-11). Very similar strainers appear in the Post-Akkadian Period at Chagar Bazar and Tell Brak. There are two unusual painted conical cups, with pointed bases, sides decorated with combined ridges and paint bands (Pl. 65: 14, 15). One example of the best-preserved jar stopper has been illustrated here (Pl. 65: 13); its convex upper surface and short "stem" are typical. Fragments of stoppers and possible lids appeared relatively frequently but were mostly of unbaked clay and were poorly preserved. A boat-like object with punctate decoration (Pl. 65: 16) may be a lamp.

A unique tray-like vessel from Area G Phase III is included in this category, a large flat disc with (two or four?) raised semi-circular handles (Pl. 66: 11). Its base was partially pierced numerous times (none of the holes are visible on the interior/ upper side) and the fabric is a dense grit-tempered buff-orange, with interior burnishing (close to the ware used for cooking pots). Comparison examples come from Tell al-Rimah (Postgate *et al.* 1997: Pl. 46: 283; late Old Babylonian and Mitanni dates), Tell Leilan (Frane 1996: Fig. 1: 3; Old Babylonian) and Tell Brak (Oates *et al.* 1997: 653;

Mitanni). Their function is probably not that of a modern tray (transport of other vessels), but cooking or serving food (bread or other "dry" foods).

A selection of jar forms that betray a possible 3rd millennium BC origin has been included (Pl. 66: 1-10). Most of these types bear strong Post-Akkadian traits, especially grooved rims (Pl. 66: 1-5, 9, 10) and double-ridged rims (Pl. 66: 6); see McMahon & Quenet 2007 for comparanda). Given the lack of Post-Akkadian occupation on the northern mound, the usual explanation for the presence of earlier types in any context–percolation from lower levels–is not adequate. These examples might have been transported from the south mound within bricks or as deliberate fill material, but they may in fact be in situ early 2nd millennium BC items with "heirloom" traits that connect them to a late 3rd millennium BC tradition.

Bases

The most "typical" and common bases represented in the early 2nd millennium BC are low ring bases and "channel bases". The ring bases are frequent on bowls and jars and are not distinctively different in the early 2nd millennium BC than in prior or subsequent periods (Pl. 67: 25, 26). The channel base is essentially a flat base with a groove near its outer edge that may slightly raise that edge (Pl. 67: 22-24); it is found on jars and medium-large bowls in particular.

Fine ware and small vessels tend to have low disk (Pl. 67: 1-7) or small ring bases (Pl. 67: 9-21), although some have quite high ring bases (e.g. CB 2900), approaching a pedestal foot. Button bases (Pl. 67: 8) appear in upper phases of both Areas A and G and provide a link with the succeeding Mitanni assemblage. There are also a few examples of unusual bases found, such as a tripod formed by the addition of three loops to a "normal" disc base (Pl. 67: 31). Parallels for this type are found in the Mitanni level at Tell Brak Area HH (Oates *et al.* 1997: Fig. 205: 535, 536). Broken bases were frequent in every pottery lot. It is probable that many bases, once broken from their original vessel, found a secondary use as jar lids.

Design and Style

Khabur Ware is, for most Near Eastern archaeologists, an instantly-recognisable 'style', not confused with any product of a different era. This recognisability rests mainly in decoration and forms, and to a lesser extent in fabric. The repetition and limited range of motifs, together with the patterned symmetry of decoration, combine to make this one of the most visible and distinctive styles for us, as well as one of the simplest to learn.

Beyond morphological types and decorative styles, it is also possible to assess the Chagar Bazar ceramic assemblage in terms of macro-style or "design" (Carr 1995a: 157ff.). "Design" in this case goes beyond surface decoration (although this is included), to refer to complexity of fabric production, elaboration of the morphologies of discrete vessel parts–such as addition of ridges or carinations, plus non-decorative surface treatments. It comprises the effort and the decision-making put into manufacturing each vessel, as well as its visual effect[30].

Design has been articulated as the "mental map" that affects the physical appearance of objects, including complexity of form and mode of production.

---

[30] I will not here engage with ideas of the hierarchy of choices and message transmission which artifact style theory encourages (e.g. Wobst 1977, Carr 1995b). The Chagar Bazar assemblage is not internally variable enough to allow for identification of artisans' individual choices in technology or decoration.

Chapter 5

Conceptualizations of shape (symmetrical or asymmetrical, continuous or angular) speak to "topology", "partonomy" and "sequence" (van der Leeuw 1992: 256-259). *Topology*, the geometric shapes that underlie vessels' forms, varies moderately within the Chagar Bazar assemblage. Most of the bowls are shallow, less than a full hemisphere. The shapes underlying both narrow-mouth and wide-mouth jars and barrels are less distinct from each other than the varied typology of their rims indicates, most being based upon a vertically-extended ovoid. Cylinders were avoided; jar necks, basins, grain measures and other near-vertical-walled vessels or vessel elements are persistently slightly concave. Wheel manufacture almost certainly means that the *sequence* of manufacture and conceptualization was bottom-up, the inverse of archaeologists' illustration-based top-down approach to vessel deconstruction. *Partonomy*, the concept of how many 'things' are put together to create a vessel, is perhaps the most revealing of design. Most of the Chagar Bazar assemblage, both open and closed vessels, has smooth profile curves with incremental transitions from convex to concave. Even the carinated bowls, with their sharp exterior angle that implies a concept of lower and upper vessel as separate geometric entities, do not always have a sharp angle on the interior corresponding to the exterior ridge and angle. This surely means the bowl profile had a single unified form as mental template and was not thought of as a set of divisible elements such as base, body, shoulder and rim.

Expectations of use-life are also part of design decisions. Those forms with the greatest complexity of design would only be "economical" to both make and use if their lives were also relatively extended. This highly variable use-life factor makes it difficult to generate a single constant value for the number of vessels consumed per household per year (see above), however tempting such a value is for comparative analyses and assessments of ceramic production specialisation.

The plain shallow bowls (Pls. 10, 11) are our best examples of simple design, a single geometric shape with no decoration or surface elaboration. Shallow carinated bowls (Pl. 18) and Narrow-mouth jars (Pls. 51-53) have moderately complex designs, because they stitch together several distinct geometric shapes. Perhaps slightly oddly, cooking pots fall into this moderately complex design category, despite having very simple vessel shapes and non-elaborated rims. Here the relative complexity is derived from the specialised and relatively rare temper, which would have affected speed and resource range at the fabric-production and throwing stage. The burnished surfaces, although visually not dramatic, were arguably more time-intensive than addition of the more visible paint bands on other forms.

The carinated, ridged and painted bowl (e.g. CB 4268, Pl. 30: 19) is an example of the most complex design achieved, involving elaboration at the throwing and decorating stage. The carinated and ridged grey ware bowls (Pl. 29:13-17) and fine ware cups with ridged and painted decoration (e.g. CB 4255, Pl. 45: 8) are similarly complex in design, given that their fabric would have required time and effort to process (selection, settling), with additional complexity inserted at throwing and decorating stages (painting, burnishing) and even possibly in firing and post-production handling. The overall time investment is high, and this corresponds to their probable contextually-specific use. Vessels with the most complex designs are implicated in complex social interactions; they are more likely to be seen, both within and outside the immediate family: serving and eating open forms, not storage jars.

Ceramic Assemblage

Table 5.2 Relative Percentages of Types by Area and Phase (absolute numbers in parentheses)

Area & Phase	Shallow Bowls	Deep Bowls	Carinated Bowls	Grey ware bowls	Ridged Bowls	Z-sided Bowls	Bowls, uncertain type	Barrels	Ridged Barrels	Cups	Fine-Ware beakers
A IA	12.9 (69)	5.2 (28)	7.8 (42)	2.1 (11)	0.4 (2)	0.8 (4)	0.2 (1) All Bowls 29.4	2.1 (11)	3.0 (16) All Barrels 5.1	2.4 (13)	3.9 (21) All drinking vessels 6.3
A I	7.0 (42)	3.4 (20)	7.4 (44)	2.2 (13)	0.3 (2)	0.8 (5)	0.2 (1) All Bowls 21.3	1.7 (10)	2.5 (15) All Barrels 4.2	2.2 (13)	4.5 (27) All drinking vessels 6.7
A II	9.3 (167)	5.0 (90)	8.3 (150)	1.7 (30)	0.3 (6)	0.7 (12)	0.1 (1) All Bowls 25.4	1.2 (22)	1.8 (32) All Barrels 3.0	3.0 (54)	4.0 (72) All drinking vessels 7.0
A III	9.6 (10)	1.9 (2)	6.7 (7)	1.9 (2)	1.0 (1)	0	0 All Bowls 21.1	2.9 (3)	5.8 (6) All Barrels 8.7	8.6 (9)	1.9 (2) All drinking vessels 10.5
G I	6.7 (11)	3.6 (6)	12.7 (21)	1.8 (3)	1.2 (2)	1.2 (2)	0 All Bowls 27.2	3.0 (5)	9.1 (15) All Barrels 12.1	3.6 (6)	4.2 (7) All drinking vessels 7.8
G II/1	8.4 (60)	2.7 (19)	14.1 (101)	2.5 (18)	0.7 (5)	0.8 (6)	0.8 (6) All Bowls 30.0	3.2 (23)	4.5 (32) All Barrels 7.7	3.1 (22)	3.4 (24) All drinking vessels 6.5
G II/2	6.6 (67)	4.6 (47)	16.7 (169)	2.0 (21)	0.5 (5)	0.5 (5)	0.4 (4) All Bowls 31.3	4.5 (46)	3.0 (30) All Barrels 7.5	1.7 (17)	3.2 (32) All drinking vessels 4.9
G III	2.1 (12)	2.8 (16)	12.8 (73)	1.6 (9)	1.7 (10)	0.3 (2)	0 All Bowls 21.3	1.0 (6)	6.6 (38) All Barrels 7.6	8.7 (50)	1.0 (6) All drinking vessels 9.7

Chapter 5

Table 5.2, continued, Relative Percentages of Types by Area and Phase (absolute numbers in parentheses)

Area & Phase	Grain Measures	Narrow-neck jars	Khabur Ware jars	Wide-mouth jars A	Wide-mouth jars B	Wide-mouth jars uncertain	Cook pots	Bottles	Stands	Basins	Misc
A IA	1.3 (7)	10.1 (54)	5.6 (30)	6.5 (35)	3.7 (20)	24.4 (131)	4.7 (25)	0.2 (1)	0	0	2.8 (15)
			All narrow-neck jars 15.7			All wide-mouth jars 34.6					
A I	0.8 (5)	16.9 (101)	5.9 (35)	4.9 (29)	3.4 (20)	25.5 (152)	7.0 (42)	0	0.3 (2)	0.2 (1)	2.8 (17)
			All narrow-neck jars			All wide-mouth jars					
A II	0.7 (12)	16.7 (301)	4.8 (87)	5.0 (91)	6.1 (110)	24.4 (440)	4.8 (87)	0.1 (1)	0.3 (6)	0.2 (4)	1.5 (27)
			All narrow-neck jars 21.5			All wide-mouth jars 35.5					
A III	1.0 (1)	13.5 (14)	12.5 (13)	5.8 (6)	4.8 (5)	13.5 (14)	7.7 (8)	0	0	0	1.0 (1)
			All narrow-neck jars 26.0			All wide-mouth jars 24.1					
G I	0	23.0 (38)	7.3 (12)	6.7 (11)	2.4 (4)	5.5 (9)	3.6 (6)	0	1.2 (2)	0.6 (1)	2.4 (4)
			All narrow-neck jars 30.3			All wide-mouth jars 14.6					
G II/1	0.4 (3)	21.8 (156)	8.9 (64)	7.1 (51)	4.3 (31)	4.9 (35)	3.9 (28)	0.4 (3)	1.3 (9)	0.8 (6)	1.9 (14)
			All narrow-neck jars 30.7			All wide-mouth jars 16.3					
G II/2	1.0 (10)	23.3 (236)	5.8 (59)	7.5 (76)	4.1 (41)	6.8 (69)	3.8 (38)	0.2 (2)	1.1 (11)	0.4 (4)	2.3 (23)
			All narrow-neck jars 29.1			All wide-mouth jars 18.4					
G III	0.2 (1)	16.4 (94)	10.5 (60)	9.8 (56)	4.5 (26)	3.3 (19)	7.0 (40)	0	1.2 (7)	6.1 (35)	2.1 (12)
			All narrow-neck jars 26.9			All wide-mouth jars 17.6					

Chapter 6

The Material World: Objects from Areas A and G

A. McMahon

Objects from Area A and G comprise the usual range of materials and artifact types found at northern Mesopotamian sites in early 2nd millennium BC contexts. Baked clay figurines were the most common object class, but ornaments, metal objects, grinding stones and other stone tools were also frequent. Less common were weaving tools, clay sealings and other administrative items.

The objects offer general support to the early 2nd millennium BC chronological attributions in these two excavation areas but are, for the most part, not precisely dateable. The number of earlier (prehistoric or 3rd millennium BC) objects was very few; and these were mostly "precious" or interesting pieces (a polished celt, a broken stamp seal), which may have been consciously collected in the past (perhaps even from another site), rather than moved into secondary context through pit cutting or surface percolation. This is reassuring for our analysis of all the objects and especially the ceramic assemblage, since there does not appear to have been much mixing with earlier material.

Contextual Associations

Many of the discrete contexts or loci in both Areas A and G contained object clusters or groups. In most cases where clusters of objects were found, there is a wide range of items, indicating that most rooms or spaces were not limited to one type of function or activity. The richest collections of objects came from alleys, where the objects would have been out of their original use context; yet, as for the ceramics, we do not believe that there was much vertical or horizontal movement of materials, and the alley objects surely derived from the immediately adjacent buildings.

Area A:

The distribution of objects in Phase II of Area A complements the evidence of the architectural plans[1]. In Phase II (see Fig. 65), the northern stretch of the eastern alley (Loci 14, 16) was dense in sherds and animal bones and also collected significant numbers of discarded objects: three animal figurines (CB 951, 952, 954), a wagon model (CB 788), a basalt pestle (CB 789), a bronze ring (CB 725) and an incised clay disk (CB 2211). This discard pattern continued into the doorway into Building I (L. 21), where a schematic human figurine (CB 2596) and a stone disk (CB 917) were found. The northern alley deposit was similar (Loci 19, 30, 47, 49); baked clay objects dominated, comprising animal figurines (CB 2589, 2591, 2592), a human figurine (CB 384), and a wagon model (CB 2590), with a single bead (CB 2593) and a bronze pin fragment (CB 2416).

---

[1] The sample of objects from Phase III is small and their distribution is uninformative, given the limited excavation; but the range of objects recovered was comparable to that of the upper phases.

Chapter 6

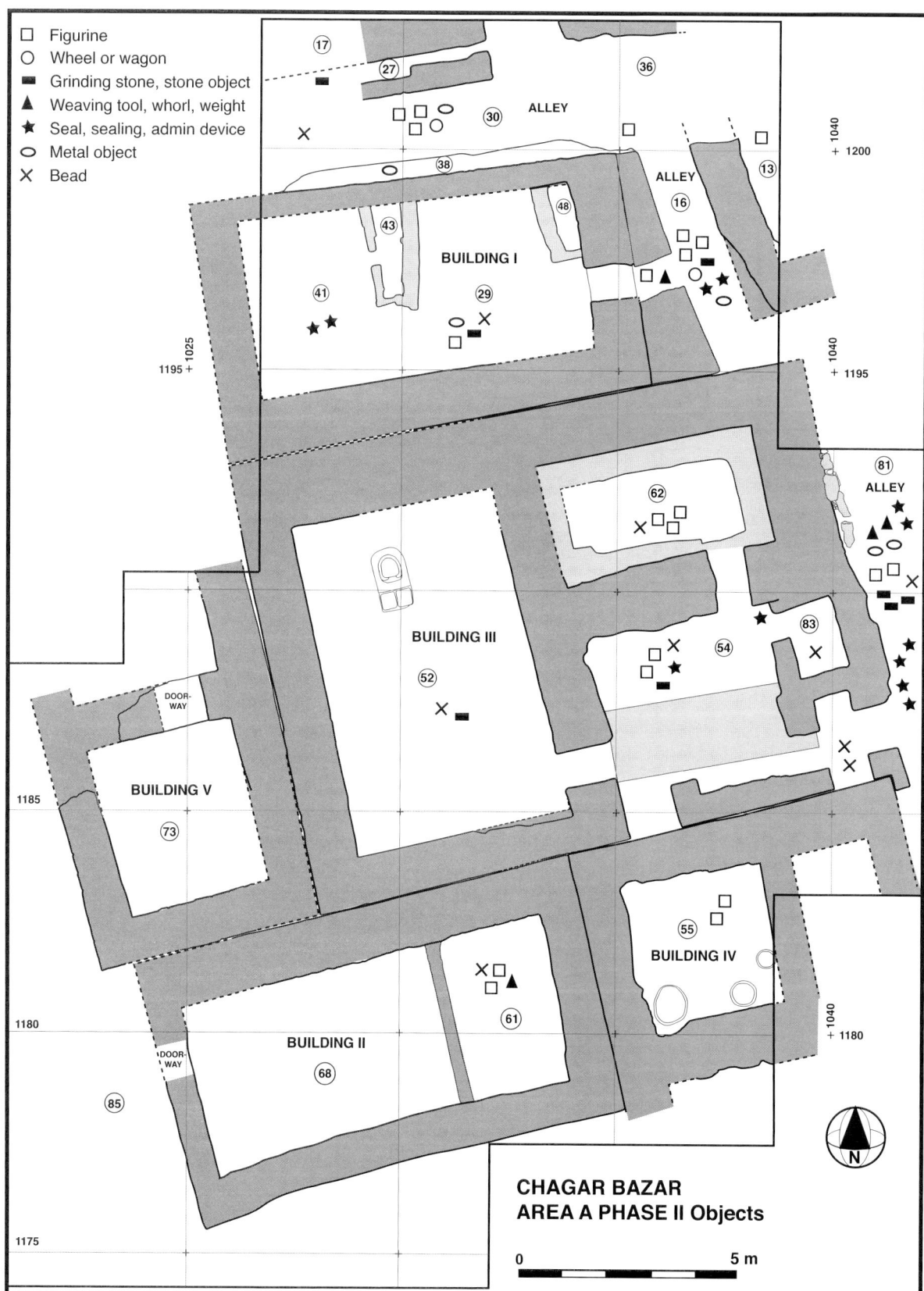

Figure 65: Distribution of objects, Area A, Phase II

The southeast extension of the alley into A II, in front of Building III (Loci 75, 81) received a slightly expanded range of items, including animal figurines (CB 2956, 2958), a bone tool (CB 2981), a whetstone (CB 2957), two hammer-stones (CB 2790,

2984) and a weight (CB 2909). Discarded metal objects from this part of the alley included a piece of lead wire (CB 2982) and a bronze pin (CB 2980). Finally, six clay sealings from the alley and drain (CB 2802, 2908, 3032, 3765, 3766, 3767) surely relate to administrative activities in Building III. These may have been swept out the door after original deposition within the building or have been dropped directly in the alley by someone departing the building.

Within Building I, the upper material in the eastern end (L. 29) contained a horse figurine (CB 775), cuboid hammer-stone (CB 747), a loose bead (CB 772) and a lead ingot (CB 751). These domestic items are contrasted to two administrative objects that came from the initial occupational layers in the building's western end (L. 41.1): a conical clay stamp seal (CB 1806) and an incised clay oblong "tally" or administrative device (CB 2414). These support the reconstruction of an initial close relationship between Buildings I and III, before the façade shift on Building I. Building II (L. 61.1 and 61.2) had a more domestic collection of an animal figurine (CB 1916), a human figurine (CB 2417), a loose bead (CB 2420) and a cobble hammer-stone or weight (CB 2047)[2].

The very small number of objects from the main assembly room in Building III (L. 52) bears out its non-domestic function: a stone bowl sherd (CB 1876), a pierced basalt slab (CB 2046, possibly a door-socket) and a loose bead (CB 2421) were the only objects found there, despite its large volume. The courtyard deposits (Loci 54, 56) include a few more items, such as two animal figurine fragments (CB 1804, 2050), a pendant (CB 1805), and a basalt pestle (CB 2051), but this space also contained a second conical clay stamp seal (CB 2791) and a numerical tally (CB 1879). The side storage room (L. 62) also has three animal figurines (CB 1897, 2539, 2789) and one loose bead (CB 2540). A similar range of objects, including animal figurines, grinding stones and metal objects was found in the courtyard of the Palace of Qarni-Lim at Tell Leilan (Pulhan 2000); such 'domestic' items clearly do not contradict a primarily administrative function.

The very few objects from Chagar Bazar that have strong southern Mesopotamian associations (clay sealing CB 2801 with an introduction scene and date-shaped haematite weight CB 1779[3]) both come from Area A. This reinforces the distinctions drawn between Areas A and G on the basis of architectural forms and arrangement and is suggestive of an underlying thread of "elite-elite interaction" and southern Mesopotamian emulation within the administrative sphere. The seal in particular may have been part of a conscious or sub-conscious strategy of using imported symbols to reinforce political status. Such a strategy does not contradict the proposed informal, consensus-leading format of administration (Ch. 2); both objects were small in scale and would have been visible only in small-audience face-to-face interactions.

In Phase I and IA, the pits contained the largest number and densest concentrations of objects; for instance, Pit L. 32 in Phase IA contains three animal figurines (CB 797, 913, 977), a female figurine (CB 1777), spindle whorl and loom weight (CB 911, 912), bronze pin (CB 907) and a single bead (CB 796). By contrast, the late erosion channel (L. 67) had a relatively low number of objects, despite its

---

[2] Two figurines came from the northwest room in Building IV; the apparent lack of objects from the western room in Building II and from Building V reflects their poor state of preservation.

[3] This weight was found at the northern wall of Building II and may have come from a pit in Phase I. Its heirloom status in that phase, however, is possible though cannot be ascertained.

length and high density of sherds: only two animal figurines (CB 1949, 2415), a model wheel (CB 2419) and a loose bead (CB 2422). The open southwest area in Phase I, like the alleys of Phase II, had a large number and wide range of discarded objects: pieces of two bronze objects (CB 2927, 2928), two animal figurines (CB 2801, 3048), a whetstone (CB 2818), biconical weight (CB 2816), bone awl (CB 2824), stone burnisher (CB 3046) and a pin fragment (CB 2970). The most common objects in all types of context were figurines, but metal items and tools were close behind.

Area G:

The range of figurines, beads and tools across the phases of Area G matches the range seen in non-assembly-room contexts of Area A. In Phase III, the areas excavated do not present an informative distribution, but in particular the open area and mound slope at the southwest of Area G (L. 37), like the alleys in Area A and later phases in Area G, received a good number of discarded objects: a model wheel (CB 3880), model wagon (CB 4233), stone bowl rim sherd (CB 3769), pottery stand fragment (CB 4218), sling bullet (CB 4219) and a loose bead (CB 3780). The northern area of hearth ash accumulation (L. 40) was rich in sherds but held comparatively few objects, despite its significant depth and horizontal extent: only a polished stone celt (CB 3094) and hammer-stone (CB 3427). The rooms of the buildings excavated contained relatively low frequencies of objects, with no particular clusters.

In Phase II/2 (Fig. 66), the alley held a large number of objects: an animal figurine (CB 3938) and bottle stopper (CB 4192) from its northern end (L. 34), supplemented by five animal figurines (CB 2114, 2865, 2919, 2921, 2999), three human figurines (CB 2974, 2975, 2976), a model wheel (CB 3779), a basalt pestle (CB 2538), two bone tools (CB 2866, 2920), a loom weight (CB 3770), a ceramic stand fragment (CB 2922), a sling bullet (CB 3099), two tokens (CB 2201, 2918), two bronze pin fragments (CB 2199, 2205), a lead ingot (CB 2200) and three loose beads or pendants (CB 2917, 2973, 3877) from Locus 54 to the south. The open area at the south end of the street (L. 28) held two additional clay tokens (CB 2944, 2945) and a fragment of bronze wire (CB 3097). These objects cover practically the full range of object classes found in the early 2nd millennium levels on the site and speak to the usefulness of streets and alleys for assessing material culture assemblages, despite the fact that materials there are invariably mixed, fragmentary and in secondary or tertiary contexts. The greater density of objects at the southern end of the alley (L. 54) in contrast to the north (L. 34) may in part be derived from the greater depth of deposit excavated. But the direct connection of several houses to the alley at that point (contrasted to the separation from alley by courtyards at the north in G2 and BDG 2) may also be a factor.

The courtyard of Building G2 (Loci 4, 9) held a similar but more restricted range of objects to that in the alley: two loose beads (CB 2619, 2628) and a piece of lead wire (CB 2622) from Locus 4 at the south; plus a model wheel (CB 2632), a biconical spindle whorl (CB 2615) and a second lead ingot (CB 2424) from its northern part (L. 9). By contrast to Building G 2's courtyard, the courtyard south of Building G 1 (L. 51) was very clean, containing only a single loose bead (CB 1824). This contrast in courtyard cleanliness continued in the next sub-phase of Phase II (II/1) and is unexpected, although the access routes in these two buildings were different and may offer an explanation. The G 2 room was directly linked to its courtyard, and burials and an ash pile indicate frequent ritual and practical uses. The G 1 room was possibly not directly linked to its courtyard, and a drain was its only feature.

Objects

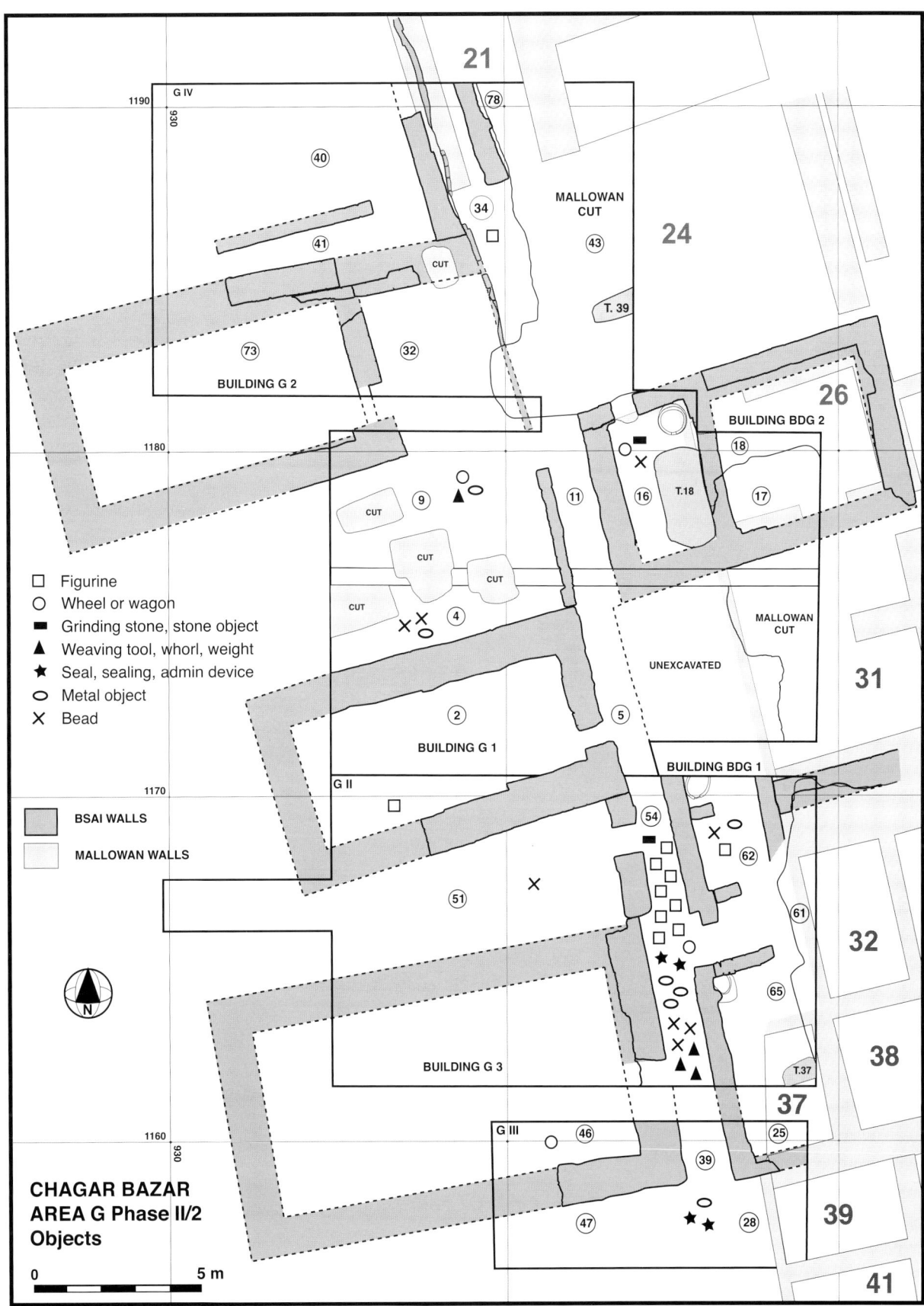

Figure 66: Distribution of objects, Area G, Phase II/2

As in the following sub-phase, the rooms of both Buildings G 1 and 2 in Phase II/2 were swept or kept clean of objects and sherds, with only a hedgehog figurine or rattle (CB 2212) coming from Building G 1 (L. 53). In Building BDG 2 on the east side of the alley, Locus 16's large oven indicates use as a kitchen; a mortar (CB 2630) is entirely at home, while a model wheel (CB 2624) may have belonged to a child (not unexpected in a kitchen). A loose bead (CB 2617) from this room is typical of the random scatter of beads across the site. There was a similar restricted set of items from rooms in Building BDG 1, further south: an animal figurine (CB 2625), bronze fragment (CB 2623) and loose bead (CB 2541) from L. 62.

In Phases II/1 and II/1A, the alley continued to contain a healthy number of discarded objects, as well as a high density of sherds and animal bone refuse (Fig. 67). Objects include a human figurine (CB 3000) and two whetstones (CB 3001, 3002) from the northern end of the alley (L. 34); an animal figurine (CB 1942) from the centre (L. 11); a cuboid grindstone and pestle found together (CB 1839 and 1840, respectively), plus a clay disk/ tally (CB 1829), all from near the centre in Locus 3 (above L. 5); and a bone tool tip (CB 2202) and clay token (CB 2057) from its southern end (L. 54). This is a smaller number of objects than was seen in this context in Phase II/2, probably explainable through a smaller excavated volume.

The courtyard of Building G 2 was also rich in objects: four animal figurines (CB 1826, 1827, 2106, 2629) and one loose bead (CB 1939) come from the southern portion (Locus 4), while an additional animal figurine (CB 2112), a model wheel (CB 2107), a whetstone (CB 2109), a stone disk (CB 2620) and a lead ingot (CB 2196 and) come from its northern area (L. 9). The "veranda" directly in front of the entrance into the main room (L. 32) was kept cleaner, with a clay sealing (CB 2873), and lead wire fragment (CB 2872) from this area, plus a basalt pestle (CB 2826) and bone needle (CB 2827) from a capping layer and pit (L. 30, 31). The relatively frequent presence of metal here and elsewhere, carelessly lost within courtyard or street debris, supports the assumption of a generally economically thriving settlement which could afford occasional loss. No doubt many metal objects were curated and refashioned at the end of their use lives, but the rate of loss indicates this was not an absolute necessity. The ash pile within the courtyard (L. 10) was relatively clean of sherds but contained two enigmatic clay objects, a lightly baked cylinder (CB 2058) and a small trough or mould (CB 2209). By contrast, the courtyard south of Building G 1 (L. 51) was cleaner (as in Phase II/2), and the only object associated with the Phase II/1 levels was an heirloom Late Chalcolithic stamp seal (CB 1828). The roofed rooms of Buildings G 1 and 2 were kept extremely clean, with only a conical schematic human figurine (CB 2061), lead wire loop (CB 1880) and beer strainer (CB 2626) from L. 2 in Building G 1.

On the opposite side of the alley, the western room of Building BDG 2 (L. 12) was a work space which held a cluster of four stone hammerstone/ whetstones (CB 1944, 1945, 1946 and 1947) resting on the stone paving. To its south, Building BDG 1 has a particularly diverse collection of objects, especially in its southwestern room (L. 55): a miniature stone plate (CB 2060), two clay tokens (CB 2056, 2059), a bone token (CB 1941) and an olive shell pendant (CB 2049)—this concentration of small but wide-ranging items suggests a child's collection of "interesting things" rather than a functional group. Also in this locus were a whetstone (CB 2542) and two animal figurines (CB 1940 and 2048). The room/veranda at the north east corner of BDG 1 had a single bead in the lower level (L. 63, CB 2618) and several objects in the upper layers (L. 59; Phase II/1A): an animal figurine (CB 2115), a loose bead (CB 2197) and a copper pin (CB 2198).

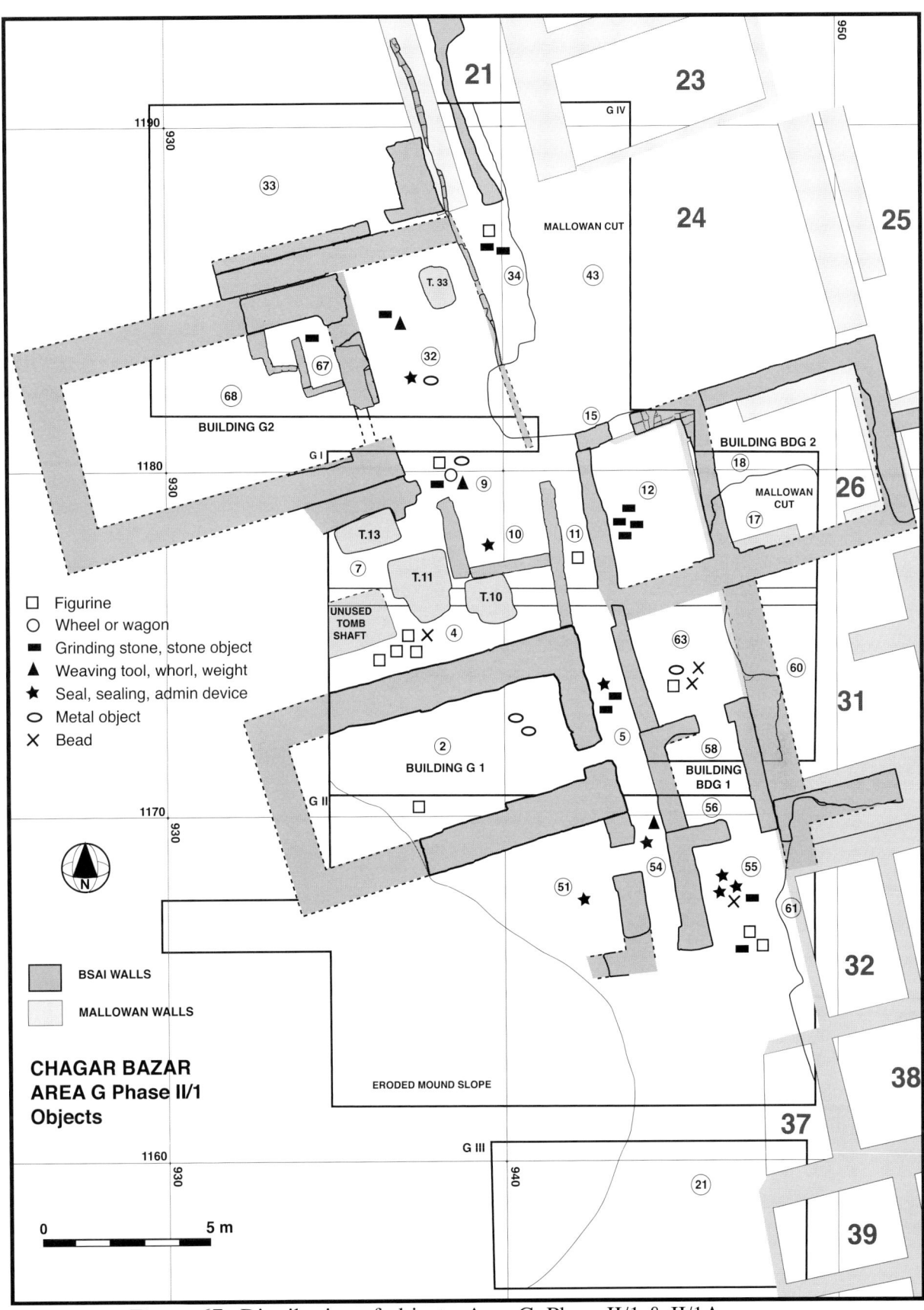

Figure 67: Distribution of objects, Area G, Phase II/1 & II/1A

Chapter 6

Object Categories and Materials

Beyond contextual associations, the Chagar Bazar objects, as categories, have cultural implications. Some objects (i.e., the figurines) are images or icons whose meanings may be more or less easily read. Questions are almost instinctive: what do they show? how were they used? Other objects, such as grinding stones, may have an apparently obvious function, no hidden sub-text, and significance only for our reconstruction of past technology and food processing. But even manufacturing tools (e.g. stone burnishers, bone weaving tools) have themselves been manufactured and are the end result of a series of design and material choices and transformations. Both fine-grained and coarse-grained basalt were found at the site and would have been selected and sought for their particular abilities. Some whetstones and other small stone objects, in particular, have aesthetic qualities unrelated to any strictly functional use (e.g. the dark, very smooth stones of CB 917, 2052 and 2109, the shiny veined red and brown stone of CB 2825, the smooth green stone of CB 3094). The makers of these objects consciously or unconsciously engaged with these materials, as well as thinking about the functional use of the objects they created. The use of haematite for weights and foundation deposits in Southern Mesopotamia may begin from its objective heaviness, but its link with concepts of stability, permanence and justice and its high value (i.e., the *Lugal-e* myth of Ninurta) may derive from its smoothness, low reflective shine and subjective assessments of density. The tactile qualities, density and smoothness, as well as the deep colours, of these Chagar Bazar stones are in the same multi-sensory range as haematite. Some things are "good to think" (Levi-Strauss 1963), but these objects would have been "good to hold" and "good to see", their aesthetic complexity invoking a emotional reaction (Gosden 2004).

A. Clay Figurines, Model Wheels and Wagons

Clay figurines were the most numerous object in both Areas A and G: there are 54 in total, 31 from Area A and 23 from Area G[4]. The ubiquity of clay as a resource, together with its inter-penetration with all aspects of Mesopotamian life, makes this frequency unsurprising. The majority of the figurines are hand-made animals, with far fewer human figurines.[5] Generally in northern Mesopotamia, human figurines are common through the Early Bronze Age, declining in the Middle Bronze Age. The early 2nd millennium BC dominance of animals is contrasted to the situation in southern Mesopotamia, where human figurines (especially naked females) vastly outnumber animal figurines in most periods from the late 3rd through 1st millennium BC. As with the differences noted in size of eating vessels between south and north Mesopotamia (see Ch. 5), this subtle difference in the ratio of human to animal figurines during the early 2nd millennium BC may have larger implications for economies, ethnicity and both human-animal and human-human relationships in these related regions.

Toy wheels were also fairly common, fragments of wagons or chariots were found occasionally, and both are potentially linked to the animal figurines. The contexts for most figurines found are not primary (for instance, the largest number of figurines comes from discard in the alleys in Areas A and G). The lack of primary

---

[4] The numbers of figurines per phase are too small to allow identification of any chronological changes. We assume that the relative scarcity of figurines from lower levels (e.g. Area G Phase III) is due to the restricted volume of excavations in that phase.

[5] This contrast in numbers of human versus animal figurines has also been noted for the sequence at Tepe Gawra (Speiser 1935: 66).

contextual information means we are best able to assess the objects' aesthetic and production aspects; the functional gap these objects filled is more elusive.

Interpretations of animal figurines from the historical periods of the Near East have, as in other regions, covered the spectrum from toys (McDonald 1997) through "receipts" for donations of sacrificial animals (Liebowitz 1988) to cultic or magical talismans (Downey 2003, Liebowitz 1988) and religious equipment (Matthews 2003b, McAdam 1993). By contrast, most scholars propose a solely ritual/religious aspect for historical period human figurines, either "mother goddesses" or fertility symbols. This assumption of ritual function for the human figurines may depend ultimately on the fact that such a large percentage of them in both northern and southern Mesopotamia are naked females. By contrast to assessments of historical period figurines, interpretations of both human and animal figurines in the prehistoric Near East have been more wide-ranging and imaginative, comprising the above range of toys, talismans and ritual objects but adding teaching aids, sympathetic magic, articulation of desires, representation of "femaleness" and images of ancestors (Broman Morales 1983, Lesure 2002, Ucko 1968, Voigt 2000). Analysts of figurines from other regions have even proposed "representation of individuals" (e.g. Bailey 1994).

The functions of human and animal figurines are unlikely to have been the same, despite their close similarities of scale, medium, production steps and ultimate disposal. It is not even necessarily the case that the functions of all animal figurines were the same; representations of wild versus domestic animals, or common domesticated versus rare domesticated animals, may have been created for very different purposes. The possibility of multiple functions for a single object must also be acknowledged (Moorey 2003). With their breakage and discard, we can read the final chapter in these objects' biography, but however short those biographies were destined to be, we are still missing vital chapters on use.

Animal Figurines:

All the animal figurines are at least slightly broken and many are fragmentary, with legs and heads missing, as one might expect equally from use as toys or use in ritual magic incorporating symbolic breakage. Bodies appear far more often than do separated heads or legs and this raises the question of the fate of those elements.[6] When separated, the heads and legs (already smaller and more fragile than the bodies) may have been comprehensively shattered into tiny fragments, too small or not visually distinctive enough to be easily retrieved during excavation. Alternatively, a different mode of disposal for these elements may have been used, particularly if the breakage was ritualistic. Most of the figurines, while broken, have only minimal surface wear or abrasion. There are only a few that are badly abraded, and most of these were lightly baked, the abrasion thus possibly being due to post-depositional destruction rather than use. It is safe to conclude that these are objects with intentionally short life-spans and that their use left little traces.

In every case, the animals are presented as stationary on all four legs, a static icon rather than a moving figure. The legs are extremely schematic and conical–in part reflecting the limits of the clay matrix but also evidence of a choice during production. The figurines needed to be able to stand, and the legs needed to be indicated as four separate units. Beyond that, however, details were unimportant. The heads and torsos were the foci of attention, and in most cases there was a reasonable attempt to present

---

[6] A similar situation of a large number of bodies and few heads has been noted in the assemblage of (mostly Early Bronze Age) animal figurines from Selenkahiye (Liebowitz 1988: 15).

appropriate proportions and to make the species identifiable. Genitalia, however, were almost never indicated (with one exception: CB 1940; Pl. 71: 14), thus species rather than gender was the key concept presented.

All the animals were hand-made, and the clay used is close to that used for the ceramic assemblage, a buff-pink-brown with lime, grit and occasional chaff inclusions. All the figurines had been fired, and most appear to be fired to a hardness comparable to the ceramics, but there is a significant minority of low-fired examples. Most are plain, but a few have painted details in red or black. Within the assemblage there was a small group of three from Area A (Phases I and IA) that stand out because of their distinctive medium and "design": dark well-fired clay, small scale and finely-executed incised details. It is entirely plausible that these are the work of one artisan with greater skills or more free time than other individuals producing these items. The group includes one equid, CB 308 (Pl. 69: 17), and two zebu, CB 373 and CB 797 (Pl. 69: 2, 3); all are from Area A Trench I. The rest of the assemblage is much more varied, and no particular cluster stands out; they are generally larger, less carefully detailed, and made from light-coloured, less well-fired clay.

In size, those figurines that are well enough preserved to determine overall scale fall into two categories. The smaller figurines (the above group and i.e., Pl. 71: 7-10) are so small that they can and should be moved about by gripping only one or two fingers and the thumb (pincer grasp), while the large, chunkier animals (i.e., Pl. 69: 16, Pl. 70: 1) are better suited to grasping with the whole hand, including contact with the palm. If these are indeed toys, the different sizes could cater to two different age groups of children; motor coordination skills typically are developed enough for the pincer grasp by one year old, and small objects are of greater interest in general to 1.5-3-year olds; the larger animals could be toys for children younger than one year.

Animal figurines were found in both domestic (Area G) and "community" (Area A) areas, a spread of contexts also noted for Area HH at Tell Brak (Oates *et al.* 1997: 131) where there are a few from public buildings but most derive from houses.

There is a limited range of animals represented, overwhelmingly of domesticated species: especially equid, zebu (*Bos taurus indicus*, easily identifiable by its distinctive 'hump' and dewlap), sheep, dogs and cattle. Some figurines were recognizable as animals but are too broken to determine species–this includes single legs and body segments (Pl. 71: 11-15). The numbers of equids and zebu are almost equal: sixteen definite or probable zebu, and fifteen definite or probable equids. There are an additional four cattle or bulls (these may also be zebu), two possible sheep and three possible dogs, two hedgehogs, one lion, one possible owl, and ten figurine fragments whose species is indeterminate. The majority of figurines that are well enough preserved for definite species identification are thus equids and zebu[7]. These two animals would paradoxically have been the least common live species present on the site or in the region. The faunal assemblage includes many pigs, especially in the Area G alley, and significant numbers of sheep and goat (K. Dobney, pers. comm.). Pigs are not represented at all in the clay figurine assemblage.[8] No figurines are definitively identifiable as sheep or goat, despite how common these would have been

---

[7] It must be admitted that zebu figurines have very distinctive characteristics—several identifications of very fragmentary figurines as zebu were made on the basis of the preserved hump (in one case the hump was all that remained (CB 2983; Pl. 69: 8).

[8] Pigs are also usually absent from texts, since they tend to be part of the "unofficial" household-managed diet, unrecorded by state administration. The faunal assemblage will be presented in a future publication.

in the immediate area of the site and how important these species were to the economy, according to both textual material and faunal remains. Zebu were probably a relatively new introduction into northern Mesopotamia in the early 2nd millennium BC, and equids, while familiar since at least the early 3rd millennium BC, are likely to have remained rare, given their limited functions and association with elites. There is thus a mismatch between the most common live animals and those most often represented among the figurines. Neither toys nor religious/magical items are economically rational, however. Indeed, the creation of figurines as the materialization of desire or aspiration is the best match with this economic irrationality of the species represented.

Zebu figurines make a quite sudden appearance at many northern Mesopotamian sites in the early 2nd millennium BC (i.e., Brak, Oates *et al.* 1997: Fig. 239: 20-23), and at least one zebu vertebra has been collected from an early 2nd millennium BC level at Tell Brak (Matthews 2003a, 2003b). Zebu tolerate arid climatic conditions well; and evidence is increasingly pointing to an aridity trend in northern Mesopotamia and beyond in the terminal 3rd-early 2nd millennium BC (although the severity and speed of the shift to aridity continues to be a subject of debate). Zebu were domesticated in Baluchistan or India from ca 8000-6000 BC and appear occasionally on objects in southern Mesopotamia during the 3rd millennium BC, such as imported chlorite "Intercultural Style" vessels. But they are not a common image in the indigenous Mesopotamian artistic tradition until the early 2nd millennium BC and then only in northern Mesopotamia, not in the south.[9] Genetic evidence points to their having successfully interbred with local *Bos Taurus* cattle after introduction into the Near East (Loftus *et al.* 1999).

Among *equid* figurines, a few are painted (Pl. 70: 3, 6) while one each were incised (Pl. 70: 1) and perforated (for a harness, Pl. 70: 7). The last quarter of the 3rd millennium BC sees an increase in equid figurines and wagons all over northern Mesopotamia (Moorey 2001). By contrast, equids rarely feature among figurines in southern Mesopotamia before the Persian Period. Equids do appear there in more formal "elite" artworks from the 3rd millennium BC (i.e., the Ur Standard and rein rings from the Ur Royal Cemetery), and actual animals appear in late Early Dynastic through Akkadian burials at the Ur Royal Cemetery, Kish (Moorey 1978), Nippur (McMahon 2006) and Tell Razuk (Gibson 1981). The animals themselves are similarly associated with elite burials in the north (i.e., the Umm el-Marra Early Bronze Age tombs; Schwartz *et al.* 2006). However, the images in southern Mesopotamia did not trickle down to non-elite society, not even as the materialization of desire.

Cattle are rare, if indeed there are any represented. The three heads and single horn of long-horned animals (Pl. 70: 11-14) may be either zebu or cattle and may have in fact been attached to vessels rather than to figurine bodies. The *sheep* and *dogs* have been identified as such because of drooping ears (Pl. 71: 3; sheep) or a raised shoulder (Pl. 71: 2; dog), but this identification is not clear in any case. The complete *hedgehog* figurine (Pl. 71: 18) is a hollow, near-spherical form with pinched and applied features

---

[9] See Matthews 2003a for full discussion of archaeological and artistic evidence for zebu. Zebu figurines appear in variable numbers in early-late 2nd millennium BC contexts at Alalakh, Umm el-Marra, Emar, Munbaqa, Sabi Abyadh, Tepe Gawra, Tall Hamad Aga and Haradum, as well as Brak and Chagar Bazar. At Tell Hamida, in the Iraqi Jezirah, among the animal figurines there were twice as many zebu as other species in the Late Khabur/ early Nuzi Ware Period (1650-1550 BC) (Nashef 1990: 272). Zebu also appear at about the same time, or slightly later, in Egypt and Jordan (Clason 1978). While the artistic evidence indicates that these animals were no longer an exotic import but an accepted part of the economic world of the 2nd millennium BC, the faunal evidence is still ambiguous.

Chapter 6

and painted stripes along the body; similar figurines appear in southern Mesopotamia, with pebbles inside for use as a rattle (i.e., McMahon 2006: Pl. 163: 12). An additional hollow fragment, CB 4335 (not illustrated), although narrower, is a second example of hedgehog rattle. The lion (Pl. 71: 16) is identified as such because of the distinctive short curved foreleg, traces of incision of the mane and the elongated narrow body. The "owl" (Pl. 71: 17) has a peculiar flaring head and emphasised eyes; it is possibly a very schematic human figurine.

Table 6. 1 Animal Figurines

Species	Plate	CB Numbers
Zebu	69: 1-16	CB 373, 797, 951, 954, 977, 1827, 2112, 2532, 2539, 2589, 2629, 2789, 2865, 2919, 2983, 3048
Horse	69: 17-21; 70: 1-10	CB 308, 775, 952, 1826, 1942, 2048, 2114, 2206, 2368, 2591, 2614, 2625, 2921, 2956, 2999
Cow	70: 11-14	CB 780, 1949, 2050, 2958
Dog	71: 2, 8, 9	CB 1807, 1823, 2415
Sheep	71: 3, 6	CB 2801, 4216
Hedgehog	71: 18	CB 2212, 4335 (not illustr.)
Lion	71: 16	CB 2592
Indeterminate	71: 1, 4, 5, 7, 10-15, 17	CB 913, 1804, 1897, 1916, 1940, 1943, 2106, 2115 (owl?), 2289, 2418, 3938

Model Wheels:

The wagons and wheels were not simply models to look at—the wheels are pierced for wooden axles in appropriate places to allow them to move or be dragged, and they bear traces of use—badly chipped edges in particular. Wheels and wagons are possibly to be associated with the equid figurines, at least one of which was perforated for an attached harness. However, given that any chariot would have two wheels and any wagon four, we should expect to find relatively more wheels than equids if there is a strong association. But the animals far out-number the wheels and wagons/ chariots were rare. The possibility exists that, as at Kurban Huyuk, what we call 'wheels' may have been spindle whorls (Wattenmaker 1998: 147).

All the wheels are hand-made, hard-fired and of similar fabric to that of the animal figurines and ceramics. All were originally circular with projecting hubs on both sides. There is a wide variation in degree of care and effort put in to the wheels and chariots. There is also a wide range of wheel sizes (diameters range from 3.9 to 10.3 cm, but most fall around 4.5-7 cm). Painted examples are rare (only two: Pl. 72: 2, 5) and one wheel has a serrated or cog-like edge (Pl. 72: 4). Fragments of carts or chariots number only four examples; usually the base is the element preserved, occasionally with incised or punctate decoration. Again, the numbers were so small that identification of changes from phase to phase and any contrast between Area A and G were not possible.

Table 6. 2 Model Wheels and wagons

Type	Plate	CB Numbers
Wheels	72: 1-12	CB 68, 721, 1849, 1948, 2107, 2419, 2613, 2621, 2624, 3779, 3880, 3946
Wagons	73: 1-4	CB 788, 2590, 3954, 4233

Human Figurines:

Human figurines were rare in comparison to animal figurines, only thirteen from Areas A and G. Only two human figurines were mould-made, both from Area A: CB 384, a plaque showing a frontal female torso (Pl. 73: 6), and CB 1777, a female head with a tall headdress (Pl. 73: 5). The manufacturing technique in these two, when contrasted to the hand-made animal figurines, further emphasizes their probable different functions. The other human figurines are hand-made and schematic. Some are barely identifiable as human, again a contrast to the animal figurines where effort was usually made to present correct proportions and details, making the animal's species identifiable. Three conical figurines (Pl. 73: 9-11), plus a cylindrical figure of similar scale (Pl. 73: 12), have been identified here as human since they are relatively similar in lack of detail to some of the other, slightly more articulated, human figures (i.e., Pl. 73: 8, 13, 16). Like the animal figurines, those human figurines with articulated anatomy were presented in static poses, and facial features are the elements chosen for what little degree of detail exists. But the extremely schematic nature of the human figurines makes it unlikely that they shared a purpose with the animal figurines, despite their contextual connections at discard.

The moulded torso fragment (Pl. 73: 6) bears strong similarities to a complete example recovered by Mallowan (1947: Pl. XLII: 5, Pl. LV: 8); both are rough-surfaced and schematic, depicting a slender naked female with hands clasped in front of her body. A hand-made body of a female with hands on her chest (CB 4214, Pl. 73: 17) is a version of a south Mesopotamian figurine type common in the Ur III and Isin-Larsa Periods. Here the breasts are strangely applied at the sides of the hands and near the shoulders, as if the artist had not really grasped the idea that the figurine has her hands over her breasts. This awkward anatomy is a strong indication that this figurine is an attempt to emulate a southern figurine type but that the southern iconography was imperfectly embraced. The applied bracelets on the wrists and rows of impressed circles on the back are comparable to the decoration of South Mesopotamian figurines, where applied necklaces are common and the backs of the figures may have an incised necklace counterweight. Naked female figurines are unlikely to have been toys; sympathetic magic (fertility, childbirth, love incantations) is the most probable use.

The three cones (Pl. 73: 9-11) have flat bases and pinched features and might be argued to be prehistoric. Heads and arms of Halaf figurines appear occasionally in later levels, as is to be expected given the site's history (see, for instance, Pl. 73: 15, included for comparison). But Halaf figurine heads are usually flattened and rounded or rectangular forms, rather than the genuine cones here. These conical figurines are very close in size and two are complete, with a flat base, rather than snapped from a larger figure. All are too large to be tokens. The human figurine collection is completed by torsos with the remains of outstretched arms (Pl. 73: 7, 8, 13, 16). CB 2974 (Pl. 73: 14) may have had a conical head and certainly had vestigial arms, with a flat base and no legs. Although broken now, its breasts were originally a prominent feature, but this is one of only two indications of sex in the hand-made group.

Table 6. 3 Human Figurines

Type	Plate	CB Numbers
Female, mould-made	73: 6, 5	CB 384, 1777
Female, hand-made	73: 14, 17	CB 2974, 4214
Cone	73: 9-11	CB 1933, 2061, 2062
Torso	73: 7, 8, 13, 16	CB 2417, 2596, 2976, 3000
Halaf Period head	73: 15	CB 2975

B. Grinding stones and whetstones

The grinding stones at Chagar Bazar are overwhelmingly of a medium-grained grey basalt; but a few are made from a coarser and more porous dark grey basalt, and others from fine denser basalt. Hammer-stones and whetstones are of fine-grained limestone, slate or varieties of sandstone. The range of shapes and materials has been usefully tabulated for Tell Brak's 2nd millennium BC levels (Oates *et al.* 1997: Table 8), and although the Chagar Bazar material is mostly slightly earlier, a similar table is below, for comparison.

Table 6. 4 Stone tools

Shape	*Material*	*No. of objects*	*Areas & Phases*	*CB Numbers*	*Plate*
Cuboid	Brown stone	1	G Phase II/1	CB 1947	75: 4
Cuboid	Limestone	1	A, Phase II	CB 747	74: 3
Cuboid	Basalt	1	G Phase II/1A	CB 1839	74: 5
Facetted pear-shaped pestle	Basalt	2	A Phase II; G Phase II/1A	CB 327, 1840	74: 2, 6
Pear-shaped pestle	Basalt	3	A Phases IA, II; G Phase II/2	CB 43, 789, 2538	74: 1, 4, 8
Conical/cylindrical pestle	Basalt	2	A Phase II; G Phase II/1A	CB 2051, 2826	74: 11, 7
Cylindrical pestle	Gray stone	1	A Phase II	CB 2790	74: 9
Oblong pestle/hammer-stone	Basalt	2	A Phase II; G Phase II/1	CB 1946, 2984	75: 3; 74: 10
Mortar or Bowl	Basalt	6	Area A Phase II; Area G Phases II/2, III	CB 1778, 1876, 2116, 2630, 2863, 4217	76: 1-5, 8
Small bowl	Steatite? and marble	2	G, Phases II/1, III	CB 2060, 3769	77: 11; 76: 9
Disk	Basalt	1	A Phase IA	CB 16	75: 5
Slab	Basalt	2	G Phases II/1A, III	CB 3899, 4220	76: 6, 7
Irregular	Basalt	1	G Phase III	CB 2864	75: 6
Hammer-stone	Sandstone? Dense stone	3	G Phases II/1, III	CB 1944, 1945, 3427	75: 1, 2; 77: 12
Whetstone	Slate? other fine dark stone	6	A Phases II, III; G Phase II/1	CB 2052, 2109, 2542, 2957, 3001, 3002	77: 3, 4, 6-9
Whetstone	Sandstone	1	A Phase I	CB 2818	77: 1
Burnisher	Red & black stone (breccia?) Other fine stone	2	A Phase I; G Phase I	CB 2825, 3046	77: 2, 5
Celt	Green stone	1	G Phase III	CB 3094	77: 10

Grinding Stones:

The basalt and limestone cuboids are reminiscent of weights but are more likely to be small grinding stones, which had been used on all sides in such a way as to create facets and a cubic shape. Their similar scale and occasional association with pear-shaped pestles (e.g. CB 1839 and 1840, found together) imply that the pear-shape may be the first step in the developing morphology of this object, which ultimately became a cube as all sides and both ends were utilized. Several of the pear-shaped pestles (Pl. 74: 2, 6) have two sides flattened or facetted from horizontal rubbing rather than vertical rotational grinding and may have been on their way to becoming cuboid. Pear-shaped and cuboid basalt grinders come from contemporary levels at Tepe Gawra (III through V: Speiser 1935: Pl. XLb 2, 4, 5).

We might ask what was being ground or abraded in such small quantities that these small cubes and pestles, which fit in the palm of a hand, were appropriate. The presence of these small grinders in Area A as well as G may indicate "special food" preparation (spices?) that would have been consumed normally in households and in Building III as part of its assembly function. Alternatively, the small grinders are never found in association with mortars, which may imply a different use than for food production; the cuboid versions in particular are akin to a modern sanding block. There is no direct evidence for manufacture of inlay or beads at the site, but an activity such as these, or furniture production, might be plausible. There are larger, "two-handed" pestles (Pl. 74: 11), and oblong hammer stones that may have also been used for grinding (Pl. 74: 9, 10, Pl. 77: 12). A disk-shaped grindstone (Pl. 75: 5) would have fit in one hand; the tapered cross-section may be simply an irregularity but was plausibly intentional and "ergonomic". More irregular single-handed grindstones include CB 2864 (Pl. 75: 6).

Mortars are infrequent and usually fragmentary. CB 1778 and 2116 are relatively small mortars with three low feet (Pl. 76: 1, 2), CB 2863 and 4217 are larger mortars with flat bases (Pl. 76: 3, 4). There is a complete, unusual "bathtub" shaped mortar from Area G (CB 2630; Pl. 76: 5). But there are only two large flat grindstones (CB 3899, 4220; Pl. 76: 6, 7), which raises the possibility that a communal grinding facility existed elsewhere on site or that significant recycling of larger basalt implements took place. CB 1876 is a plain small bowl fragment in basalt (Pl. 76: 8); in other stones, there is only one bowl rim (CB 3769; Pl. 76: 9) and one small cut-down plate (CB 2060; Pl. 77: 11). Stone vessel production was apparently not a thriving industry at Chagar Bazar—these few examples may well have originated in prehistory or the 3rd millennium BC and survived as heirlooms.

While most of the tools appear singly, there was one cluster of stone tools lying on the stone paving in Area G, Building BDG 2, Phase II/1: CB 1944, 1945, 1946 and 1947 (Pl. 75: 1-4). The cluster included two very heavy 2-handed sandstone cylinder halves (CB 1944 and 1945, two pieces that fit together but had been used separately), both multi-purpose tools used as pestles, hammer-stones, and whetstones. The other two objects were an oblong basalt grinding and pounding stone (CB 1946) and a cuboid pestle (CB 1947).

Whetstones and celt:
There is a single beautiful celt from the northern ash discard area in Area G Phase III (CB 3094; Pl. 77: 10), a trapezoid in fine-grained dark green veined marble. Celts have been found at Tell Brak in contemporary levels (Oates *et al.* 1997, Fig. 231: 141, HH level 2), but generally this object type is more distinctive of the Late Chalcolithic Period (Tell Brak Area TW, pers. obs.). Further examples derive from Tepe Gawra (Speiser 1935: Pl. XXXIXa), but these are from Strata VIII through VI and are therefore substantially earlier than the early 2nd millennium BC. It is probable that this celt was a Late Chalcolithic artifact discarded in prehistory and re-encountered in the early 2nd millennium (on the surface or while digging a pit for bricks or burial). The smoothness of the celt is such that it can feel wet even when dry, the marble density means it can feel surprisingly cool to the touch, and the deep green colour and shine are visually arresting. Such a synaesthetic object compels an emotional response (Gosden 2004), and its retention in the early 2nd millennium BC is explainable in terms

of the reaction mentioned above: it is "good to hold" and "good to see". The biography of this object transcends its initial user(s) and incorporates at least two different meanings, as well as comprising a period of potential intermission some millennia long. As an "ancient object" it was still part of the material culture assemblage of the early 2nd millennium BC, in equal measure to the rapidly-produced and equally rapidly discarded baked clay figurines.

Whetstones exhibit some variety, from elegant smooth oblongs in dense dark gray stone, pierced for suspension (Pl. 77: 4, 6), through more irregular shapes (Pl. 77: 1, 3, 7, 8), and fragments with grooves near one end perhaps for suspension (CB 3002; Pl. 77: 9—see Brak Oates *et al.* 1997: Fig. 231: 144). Alongside these are two burnishing tools: a tapered and smoothed conglomerate object (Pl. 77: 5) and an ovoid with flattened ends (Pl. 77: 2). Less formally-worked whetstones, near-natural elongated ovals pierced at one end, were recovered at Tepe Gawra (Speiser 1935: Pl. XLI: a: 1-3; Levels IV and V).

C. Spindle Whorls, Loom Weights and Bone Weaving Tools

There are only four probable spindle whorls, in baked clay or stone, with the plano-convex or bi-conical profile associated with aerodynamic spinning (Pl. 78: 1-4). There is some question whether even these should be spindle whorls or fishing net weights, as none seems heavy enough to achieve the necessary spin inertia a spindle whorl requires. The plano-convex or biconical shape is adapted to spinning, however, and would be an overly elaborate shape for a net weight. These objects are invariably too light to have been loom weights. There are several stone pierced disks made from natural river pebbles, or pierced disks cut from sherds, which could be either spindle whorls or net weights (Pl. 78: 5-8). Their durable material, as well as flat cross-section, makes net weights a possibility. The Wadi Khanzir does not currently have sufficient and large enough fish at any season of the year to make fishing viable, but the past situation may have been very different.

The low number of spindle whorls is disturbing, given the importance of textile production in the economy–known from texts–and the close physical link with a nomadic pastoralist population producing quantities of wool and goat hair. There may have been whorls in organic materials. Or it may be the case that yarn spinning was performed by pastoralist nomads outside the site, and prepared yarn was brought to the site for weaving.

In this light, there is a set of enigmatic pierced objects, usually basalt, roughly rounded with a quite large central hole (Pl. 78: 9-11) and two even larger examples (Pl. 78: 12, 13). They are too heavy and large to be net-weights, too small and too uneven to be mill-stones, and too irregular to be balance weights or door-sockets. However, they could be loom weights, especially for a type of textile with hefty warp threads—i.e., carpets or blankets.

There is a group of three bone weaving tools from an adult (probably female) grave, Tomb 4, in Area A. The plano-convex bone "whorl" (CB 986; Pl. 79: 3) does not seem to have been used, as no wear traces were visible, and it is very light and thus may be a "model" rather than a functional tool, particularly given its burial context. The two bone "weaving needles" (CB 988, 991; Pl. 79: 1, 2) are polished from use and are matched almost exactly by a further example from Area G IV (CB 2827, Pl. 79: 4). Each is carved and polished from a long bone, with a triangular section at the head tapering to a round-sectioned point. They are too long and heavy to be simple sewing needles, although this is a customary identification for this type of object. They look plausibly like cloak pins, and the location of the two in Tomb 4–on the body, near the neck–is appropriate for such a use. But their placement, with the points towards the neck rather than along the body, is more compatible with a relationship to the right hand–raised before the face– than to the body, and the need for two cloak pins is not clear. Cloak pins in the Near East are usually metal; and the silver pin CB 992 from Tomb 4 is a more obvious candidate for a cloak pin. These bone tools are identical in form to modern "weaving needles", used to draw weft threads across a loom. Bichrome or tapestry weaving in particular is facilitated by the use of two weaving needles. A comparable matched pair, though shorter at ca. 10-11 cm long, was found in a well at Tepe Gawra (Speiser 1935: Pl. LIIb: 1, 5, well in J7 dug in Stratum VI but probably not filled until Stratum IV: *ibid*.: 19).

The remaining bone tools are all fragmentary; these include bone points with circular cross-sections, which may come from weaving needles (Pl. 79: 5-7). Two tools with extremely narrow points and flat cross-sections (CB 2866, CB 2981; Pl. 79: 8, 9) seem small in scale to be weaving tools; perhaps they are analogous to modern "stitch pickers" or detail tools.

Table 6. 5 Weaving Tools

Type	Plate	CB Numbers
Spindle whorls	78: 1-4; 79: 3	CB 911, 986, 2615, 2816, 2909
Net weights	78: 5-8	CB 917, 2620, 2792, 3878
Loom weights	78: 9-13	CB 370, 912, 997, 2047, 3770
Weaving needles	79: 1, 2, 4	CB 988, 991, 2827
"Stitch pickers"	79: 8, 9	CB 2866, 2981
Broken tool tips, probably from weaving needles	79: 5-7	CB 2202, 2824, 2920

D. Tokens, tallies, seals and sealings

A baked clay cylinder seal from Phase I in Area A (CB 1836; Pl. 80: 1) is the only cylinder seal to be recovered from Areas A and G. It has a very schematic scene in gouged style showing two figures, standing and facing left with their right arms raised, each with an altar or vertical object in front of them.[10] The single cylinder seal impression from the drain in the street in Area A II, in front of Building III (CB 2802; Pl. 80: 2) has a clearly southern Mesopotamian style scene of introduction, with three standing figures facing right, hands raised and approaching a seated figure facing left with its hand raised. Unfortunately, the seal appears to have been very worn at the time the impression was made, and the sealing was abraded after discard, thus the details are not very clear. The reverse is slightly concave, from a jar shoulder, and shows impressions of three strands of string and a knot.

There are two conical clay stamp seals from Area A with engraved concentric circles on their bases: CB 1806 and CB 2791 (Pl. 81: 1, 2). If there had been only one of these simple stamps, it might be assumed to be earlier in date, but with two from good contexts a date in the early 2nd millennium BC seems plausible. A nearly-identical seal came from Tell Brak (Oates *et al.* 1997, Fig. 180: 23, from the surface of Area HH). The excavators cite 3rd-2nd millennium BC Anatolian parallels, including

---

[10] Mallowan's assemblage of recovered seals was also notably sparse, despite the greater horizontal exposure he achieved. A southern Mesopotamian-style introduction scene in schematic gouged style came from Area TD (Mallowan 1936: 29, Pl. I: 4).

Alishar Huyuk (von der Osten 1937, II, fig. 258); another example comes from the Asvan/ Keban region (Sagona 1994: Fig. 135: 1, 2). Closer to Chagar Bazar, here is an example from Tell Mozan (Buccellati & Kelly-Buccellati 1988: 151, pl. 41), and further east, a slightly squared seal of the same size was found in a dump at Tepe Gawra (Tobler 1950: Pl. CLVII: 70).

These seals and sealing are supplemented by four baked clay "tallies" (Pl. 81: 3-6). Each is unique and relatively elaborate. They come from Area A in Phase II (CB 2211, a disc with incised circle and X; CB 2414, an oblong with incised lines; CB 1879, a circular dome with punctates) and Area G Phase II/1A (CB 1829, a roughly hemispherical dome with incised central line and random punctates on each side). Thus they appear often enough in early 2nd millennium BC levels that these are unlikely to be earlier re-deposited objects but are surely in their correct temporal context. Related to these but not baked or incised is CB 2908, an oblong with a pinched "tail", and CB 3767, a piece of deliberately squeezed clay, both from Area A Phase II (Pl. 81: 7, 8). Similar objects have been found at Tepe Gawra (Tobler 1950: Pl. CLVII: 71; an oblong with lateral incisions, Level XIII). Two similar clay objects with rows of shallow circular depressions were recovered from Ninevite 5 levels at Brak (Matthews 1995: Figs. 3, 7), where they have been suggested to be numerical tallies.

Finally, there are several "unsealed sealings", including two covers for small containers (CB 40, 3766; Pl. 82: 1, 2); an ovoid lump of clay bearing a cloth impression, which appears to have been accidentally made but nonetheless was lightly fired (CB 72; Pl. 80: 3); a basket sealing (CB 3765; Pl. 80: 5); and two possible jar sealings bearing only fingerprints on the obverses (CB 2873 (not illustrated) and CB 3032; Pl. 80: 4 a and b).

The object assemblage includes one true date-shaped haematite weight, similar to those from Ur III and Old Babylonian Period South Mesopotamia (CB 1779; Pl. 82: 3). It is tempting to say this may be an heirloom from the southern-influenced Samsi-Addu occupation of the site, retained in the post-Samsi-Addu era because of its symbolic value. Haematite objects are rare in northern Mesopotamia in any period, in contrast to its use for weights and seals in the south, particularly in the late 3rd and early 2nd millennia BC. Paradoxically, the Anatolian sources for haematite were closer to the north than the south, which raises the question of haematite's lack of value or even a taboo against use in this region.

All of the small geometric tokens recovered come from Area G. The conical tokens (Pl. 82: 4-6) are matched at Brak (Oates *et al.* 1997: Fig. 239: 34, also conical with a perforation near the top, from Trench C 5). A slightly larger cylinder (Pl. 82: 7) may be similar in function. The broken clay cone CB 2201 (Pl. 82: 8) may be one of the schematic human figures (see Pl. 73: 9-11, above); the top of the cone is missing through damage and may be plain (token) or have a pinched face and eyes (figurine). A bone bi-lobed object (CB 1941; Pl. 82: 9) could be a token or a small pendant. The three perfect clay spheres (CB 2056, 2057, 2059; Pl. 82:10-12) are the sort of object we would expect in Late Chalcolithic contexts, rather than early 2nd millennium BC. All these come from Area G II (the bone object CB 1941 and tokens CB 2056 and 2059 are in fact all from L. 55, which also includes other small-scale objects, such as the stone plate CB 2060 and which has been suggested as a child's collection). Like the Late Chalcolithic celt, small prehistoric tokens recovered from the surface or in pit excavation might have invoked an emotional response and been retained as curiosities, but since they are relatively non-complex plain clay objects, that response should have been relatively weak. Again it is likely that these items are in the correct context in the early 2nd millennium BC. Whether the clay spherical tokens have the same meaning and function in the early 2nd millennium BC as such objects did in the Late Chalcolithic is a question. A more certain Late Chalcolithic object is half of a single square stamp seal with an incised and excised geometric design (CB 1828; Pl. 82: 13).

Table 6. 6 Administrative objects

Type	Plate	CB Numbers
Seals	80: 1; 81: 1, 2; 82: 13	CB 1836, 1806, 2791, 1828
Sealings	80: 2, 4, 5; 82: 1, 2	CB 40, 2802, 3032, 3765, 3766, 2873
Tallies	81: 3-6	CB 1829, 1879, 2211, 2414
Tokens	82: 4-12	CB 1941, 2056, 2057, 2058, 2059, 2201, 2918, 2944, 2945
Squeezed clay	80: 3; 81: 7, 8	CB 72, 2908, 3767
Weight	82: 3	CB 1779

E. Metal objects

Most of the complete metal objects found were preserved in burials, but fragmentary and whole metal objects appeared in occupational contexts, presumably lost rather than deliberately discarded. Most of the metal objects are fragments of pins, rings or pieces of wire. There are no obvious weapons; although two blade fragments (CB 2927, 2928; Pl. 84: 12, 13) may be from knives, they may be equally from tools or weapons. Bronze and lead are the most common materials, silver is rare, and gold is non-existent. Evidence for metallurgy taking place on the site is limited to a few fragments of a mould from Area A II, L. 79.1. Although too fragmentary to illustrate, it was clearly rectangular in plan, with a U-shaped cross-section, made of thick green chaffy ware. The interior surface of the mould was heavily vitrified.

The numbers of bronze objects from Areas A and G are almost the same (16 from A and 15 from G), and there is one silver object each from both Areas A and G (from burial contexts in both cases), but lead was slightly more common in Area G than in Area A: eight objects versus four, respectively.

The most distinctive of the metal objects are the lead "pins" with looped heads (CB 751, CB 2203, CB 2200, CB 2424 and CB 4154; Pl. 83: 1, 2, 9, 10, 12).[11] There are two further examples of the same blunt straight "pin" without the looped head preserved (CB 2083, CB 2196; Pl. 83: 6, 7). At least two identical lead objects with looped heads come from Middle Bronze Age Kenan Tepe, on the upper Tigris in Turkey just north of the Upper Khabur plain[12]. Other blunt lead objects similar in shape and size, although without a looped head, come from Tell Brak (Oates *et al.* 1997 Fig. 234: 60, HH Level 4, Mitanni rather than Old Babylonian but from fill). There are five additional fragments of fine lead wire from both Areas A and G at Chagar Bazar (CB 1880, 2597, 2622, 2872, 2982; Pl. 83: 3-5, 8, 11). A lead "pin"

---

[11] CB 751, from L. 29 in Area A Phase II, has damage from rodent teeth along its entire length. The sweet taste of lead explains this oddity.

[12] See http://arcserver.usc.edu/reports/kt2003.html: Figure 25; Parker & Dodd 2003: 66-67 & Fig. 14 D, with some western Syrian and Anatolian parallels listed.

would be useless for piercing or holding together any material, and given that some of these objects have one end drawn into a thin wire and looped around the stem, these lead "pins" are probably ingots or, in fact, akin to spools of wire—the lead is stored in an oblong shape, and when wire is needed it can easily be "drawn out" from one end through simple spot-heating. The coiling of the thin end around the shaft would have kept it from snapping off between uses.

Only two silver items were found, both in graves: a short pin from Tomb 4 in Area A (CB 992; Pl. 83: 13) and an ornament made of a flat sheet and a separate wire from Tomb 13 in Area G (CB 2085; Pl. 83: 15). The latter tomb also held a pair of bronze tweezers (CB 2084, Pl. 83: 14, cf. Mallowan 1936: 28, Fig. 8: 19). A very corroded flat bronze pendant (CB 2623; Pl. 83: 16) came from Area G.

Bronze straight pins and pin segments (CB 907, 2198, 2199, 2205, 2423, 2970, 2980, 3047: Pl. 84: 1-3, 5-7 10, 11) or more elaborate pins with spherical or flattened heads (CB 2080, 2081, 2416; Pl. 84: 4, 8, 9) were almost as common as the lead ingots. One pin (CB 2970; Pl. 84: 2) bears an engraved herringbone pattern near the top, and another has a fluted spherical head (CB 2080; Pl. 84: 8), but most pins are plain with a square cross-section near the head and circular cross-section near the tip. The bronze pin with flat circular head (CB 2416; Pl. 84: 4) is paralleled in Mallowan's excavation (Mallowan 1947: Pl. XLI: 2-4). The only items that can be classed as tools rather than ornaments are two knife fragments (CB 2927, 2928; Pl. 84: 12, 13) and a possible tool handle segment (CB 3098; Pl. 84: 14). Other metal ornaments include simple looped bronze rings, ring segments and small bracelets (CB 725, 1831, 2082, 2204, 2788, 3097, 3104, 3105, 3106; Pl. 85: 1-9).

Bronze beer strainers were found inside jars in graves T. 4 (CB 985; Pl. 85:10), T. 11 (CB 2066; Pl. 85: 11), T. 13 (CB 2092; Pl. 85: 12) and T. 39 (CB 3090; Pl. 85: 13). Two additional examples come from non-grave contexts: CB 2626 (L. 2 in Area G; Pl. 85: 14) and CB 4215 (Area G, L. 79, Pl. 85: 15). Mallowan frequently noted strainers in the burials he excavated in Area BD. They are hollow bronze tapered cylinders formed from a flat sheet of metal wrapped around the end of a straw or reed, with vertical rows of perforations of ca. 1-2 mm diameter. Some of our examples (CB 985, 2066 and 2092) retained preserved reeds in the open end—these were clearly tips for drinking straws. De Feyter (1988) dates them to 2000-1200 BC, but a nearly identical strainer–slightly smaller than the northern Mesopotamian ones–comes from inside a jar in a late Akkadian grave at Nippur, firmly dated by two classic late Akkadian cylinder seals (Gibson & McMahon 1998; McMahon 2006)[13].

Mallowan called the jars in which these strainers were found "wine jars", and most scholars refer to these objects as "beer *or* wine strainers". Beer and wine in the early 2nd millennium BC were equally likely to have had significant suspended particulate materials and to have required straining before drinking. The predominant drink produced across the region was probably barley beer; however, as all the examples of these strainers are from burial contexts, it may be that the jar contents were unusual and that wine, imported from Anatolia or Assyria, was involved. At least two strainers that Mallowan recovered (from his Graves G2 and G3) were found in jars with centrally-pierced bases (Mallowan 1936: 28; "copper nail": Fig. 8: 18; jars: Fig. 28: 1, Fig. 16:2). Such jars are used for beer production (settling and clarifying) in both south and north Mesopotamia.

---

[13] See Oates *et al.* 1997: 116 for a full list of references to sites in Syria and Iraq in which these strainers appear.

Table 6.7 Metal Objects

Type	Plate	CB Numbers
Lead ingots	83: 1, 2, 6, 7, 9, 10, 12	CB 751, 2083, 2196, 2200, 2203, 2424, 4154
Lead rings and wire fragments	83: 3-5, 8, 11	CB 1880, 2597, 2622, 2872, 2982
Bronze beer strainers	85: 10-14	CB 985, 2066, 2092, 2626, 3090
Bronze hollow cone	85: 15	CB 4215
Bronze pins	84: 1-11, 14	CB 907, 2080, 2081, 2198, 2199, 2205, 2416, 2423, 2970, 2980, 3047, 3098
Bronze rings and wire fragments	85: 1-9	CB 725, 1831, 2082, 2204, 2788, 3097, 3104, 3105, 3106
Bronze tweezers	83: 14	CB 2084
Bronze ornament	83: 16	CB 2623
Bronze knives	84: 12, 13	CB 2927, 2928
Silver pin	83: 13	CB 992
Silver ornament	83: 15	CB 2085

F. Beads/ jewellery

All the groups of beads found were burial goods, although single lost beads appeared frequently, scattered randomly throughout both Areas A and G. Frit/ faience is the most common medium, with 151 examples; but most of these frit beads (143) come from a single string in grave T. 33 (CB 2978; Pl. 87: 2o) (see Table 6. 8). The faience colour in most cases has faded to grey or white, but there are trace indications that the colour range originally included green and blue. There are relatively many shell beads and pendants–twenty in all, but again fourteen of these come from the same string in grave T. 33. Stone (marble and variants) in various shades from white through grey to black is the next most common medium, with sixteen examples, followed by six rock-crystal, four baked clay, three carnelian, and smaller numbers of agate, haematite and steatite.

The most common bead form is a simple ring (144), but this number includes 134 ring-shaped beads from T. 33 (Pl. 87: 2o; see Table 6. 9). There are an additional ten ring-shaped beads from other contexts, and eleven cylindrical beads (e.g. Pl. 86: 1, 2). There are six each of ball-shaped/spherical (e.g. Pl. 86: 32) and bi-conical (e.g. Pl. 86: 10), three hemispherical or plano-convex (e.g. Pl. 86: 6), four disk-shaped (Pl. 86: 11) and smaller numbers of rounded rectangles (Pl. 86: 18), barrel-shaped (Pl. 86: 7), date-shaped (Pl. 86: 29), fluted (Pl. 86: 3) and irregular forms or pendants. The bead collection is supplemented by a small number of unworked pieces of inlay, or un-pierced beads or pendants (CB 2803, CB 2959, CB 2997; Pl. 86: 13, 15, 20).

The clay bi-conical beads (CB 2421 and CB 2960 from A Phase II, CB 3879 and CB 3955 from G Phase III; Pl. 86: 10, 16, 35, 36) are few in number but form an interesting set since they are made from a cheap and ubiquitous medium and may have been a by-product of either figurine or pottery production. By contrast, the carnelian beads, the most exotic material in the assemblage, may be heirlooms from as early as the 3rd millennium BC, when they were far more common in the region. All the shells are un-worked and retain their natural outlines. The olive shell (CB 2049; Pl. 86: 23) is a marine species (*Olividae*); the mother-of-pearl inlay pieces (CB 2804, 2959; Pl 86: 14, 15) are probably from local river molluscs. The unworked inlays and un-pierced beads indicate that bead and inlay manufacture must have taken place on the site, although no loci for this production have been identified through tool groups or debitage. The materials and techniques were fairly common and unsophisticated, and such production may have taken place in households.

Table 6. 8 Ornaments, by Medium

Medium	*CB Numbers*	*Plate*	*Areas where represented*
Frit/ faience	CB 4?, 1802, 1877, 2086 (2), 2541, 2616, 2978 (143), 3107	86: 1, 3, 5, 6, 19, 26; 87: 1b, c, 2b, f, g, I-k, m, o	A Phases IA, I; G Surface, Phases II/1, II/2
Glass	CB 1825	86: 18	G Surface
Shell	CB 2049, 2086 (1), 2617, 2804, 2917, 2959, 2978 (14)	86: 14, 15, 23, 27, 31; 87: 1, 2n	A Phase II; G Phases II/1, II/2
Stone	CB 772, 796, 1805, 1824, 1939, 2086 (2), 2540, 2618, 2619, 2978 (5), 2997	86: 2, 7, 8, 11, 20, 22, 24, 25, 28; 87: 1a, 1d, 2a, e, h, l	A Phases IA, II; G Surface, Phases II/1, II/2
Rock crystal	CB 2197, 2422, 2593, 2628, 2803, 2978 (1)	86: 4, 12, 13, 21, 30; 87: 2d	A Phases IA, II; G Phases II/1A, II/1 II/2
Agate	CB 2288, 2978 (1)	86: 17; 87: 2c	A Phase III; G Phase II/1
Dark green stone (steatite?)	CB 2420	86: 9	A Phase II
Baked clay	CB 2421, 2960, 3879, 3955	86: 10, 16, 35, 36	A Phase II; G Phase III
Haematite	CB 2627	86: 29	G Phase II/2
Carnelian	CB 2973, 3780, 3877	86: 32-34	G Phase II/2, III

Table 6. 9 Ornaments, by shape

Shape	CB Numbers	Plate	Areas where represented
Ring-shaped	CB 2086 (1), 2197, 2420, 2422, 2593, 2616, 2618, 2619, 2978 (134), 3780, 3877	86: 4, 9, 12, 19, 21, 24, 28, 33, 34; 87: 1a, 2l, o	A Phases IA, II; G Surface, Phases II/1A, II/1, II/2, III
Fluted ring-shaped	CB 1802	86: 3	A Phase IA
Disk-shaped	CB 2540, 2617, 2628, 2978 (1)	86: 11, 27, 30; 87: 2a	A Phase II; G Phases II/1 II/2
Ball-shaped/spherical	CB 2973, 2978 (5)	86: 32; 87: 2m	G Phases II/1, II/2
Cylindrical	CB 4, 796, 1877, 1939, 2086 (2), 2288, 2541, 2978 (3)	86: 1, 2, 5, 17, 22, 26; 87: 1b, c, 2d, h, j	A Phases IA, I, III; G Phases II/1, II/2
Cylinder with hubs	CB 2978 (1)	87: 2g	G Phase II/1
Barrel-shaped	CB 772	86: 7	A Phase II
Date-shaped	CB 2627	86: 29	G Phase II/2
Rectangular	CB 1825, CB 2086 (1)	86: 18; 87: 1d	G Surface, Phase II/1
Bi-conical	CB 2421, 2960, 2978 (2), 3879, 3955	86: 10, 16, 35, 36; 87: 2c, i	A Phase II; G Phases II/1, III
Curved pendant	CB 1805	86: 8	A Phase II
Plano-convex/hemispherical	CB 1824, 2978 (1), 3107	86: 6, 25; 87: 2f	A Phase I; G Phases II/1 II/2
Natural shell	CB 2049, 2086, 2917, 2978 (14)	86: 23, 31; 87: 1, 2n	G Phases II/1, II/2
Disk-shaped inlay	CB 2803, 2959	86: 13, 15	A Phase II
Large ring-shaped inlay	CB 2804	86: 14	A Phase II
Lion-shaped	CB 2978 (1)	87: 2b	G Phase II/1
Triangular	CB 2978 (1), 2997	86: 20; 87: 2e	G Surface, Phase II/1
Trapezoid	CB 2978 (1)	87: 2k	G Phase II/1

G. Miscellaneous stone and clay objects

The "Miscellaneous" object category includes a squat cylinder in over-fired clay (CB 2817; Pl. 88: 1). A small slag blob on its surface and vitrification point to possible repeated firings, thus its function may have been separation of vessels in a kiln during firing. A rather larger cylinder with flared foot may be a "firedog" or vessel support (CB 987; Pl. 88: 2). Also included with these is the leg of fenestrated stand or house model (CB 2922; not illustrated), paralleled at Tell Brak (Oates *et al.* 1997: Fig. 239, no. 14, Trench D) and the stem of a small stand (CB 4218; Pl. 88: 3).

Two unbaked clay "sling bullets" (CB 3099, 4219; Pl. 88: 4, 5) come from Area G; this object type is far more common in the region during the Late Chalcolithic, and there is a possibility that these derived from the Late Chalcolithic part of the site, in Area C. An unbaked clay miniature trough (CB 2209, Pl. 88: 6), unbaked clay bottle stopper (CB 4192; Pl. 88: 7) and baked clay "model brick" (CB 3947; Pl. 88: 8) complete the collection. Door-sockets are rare, presumably because they were usually recycled when buildings were renovated or rebuilt; a few examples are illustrated here (CB 34, 42, 2046; Pl. 88: 9-11).

H. Roman and Recent Objects

A single worn and corroded Roman bronze coin was found near the surface in Area A (CB 76; Pl. 87: 4). The obverse shows a head facing right; the reverse has a standard flanked by two standing figures holding additional standards or spears. The inscriptions are not clearly legible.

Tomb 7, a child burial cut into Area A II from a now-eroded surface, was relatively recent and contained a small penannular bronze bracelet with ovoid cross-section (CB 1767; Pl. 87: 4).

Chapter 7

Chagar Bazar as a Place in a Landscape

A. McMahon

The settlement archaeology approach to landscape combines acknowledgment of environmental potentials and limits with the exploration of social factors, traditions and ideas (Anschuetz *et al.* 2001: 177 ff.). Most mounded sites in the Near East were, through their continuity of occupation, "meaningful places" of significant time depth. The vertical physicality of mounds, viewed across the generally flat surrounding plains, makes these sites landmarks, while their temporal persistence makes them 'time-marks'. But a cross-plain perspective on its own reduces each site to an internally-featureless point. A comprehensive settlement archaeology approach also looks at internal structures, to determine how the settlement would have been experienced by its inhabitants and users. Finally, there is a not-often utilised mid-scale viewpoint: what do the internal structures and divisions of settlements look like and mean from a close-range vantage point immediately outside the site's boundaries?

Internal Settlement Landscape

Use of space within Chagar Bazar during the 2nd millennium BC was addressed in our excavations, supplemented by the information from Mallowan's project. The dense occupation of the north mound is a configuration usually associated with urban rather than with town or village sites, the categories which the size of Chagar Bazar (maximum seven hectares at this date) indicates.[1] The different arrangements of Areas A and G provide complementary data for a reconstruction of how the settlement functioned internally.

The physical distances within Area G were short; some party walls meant that discrete houses were nonetheless closely associated, the integrating alley was narrow, and courtyard walls were presumably low and did not block lines of sight. These short physical and visual distances mean there would have been very little social distance among this neighbourhood's occupants, although the lack of texts means we must stop short of reconstructing kinship relations among households. Material culture assemblages in Area G indicate very little variation among houses and in general suggest that a tightly-networked and easily accessible economic system existed within the settlement. The stratigraphic excavation achieved in Area G shows that the tight arrangement of houses was consistent across the chronological phases, although there was some evidence for horizontal movement and possible settlement expansion over time. The diachronic length of this neighbourhood arrangement (persisting across at least several generations) also speaks to the strength of the close social affinity.

---

[1] Many large-scale regional analyses still place sites into functional hierarchies on the basis of size alone (often the only data available), yet it is recognized that sites of similar size often have variable internal morphologies and arrangements, plus variable functions or roles within a regional system.

The domestic occupation in Area G is contrasted by an administrative function in the main building of Area A (as well as in the south of Area TD)[2]. It is notable that all the known administrative areas were located at the edges of the early 2nd millennium settlement: Area A on the northeast spur and Area TD/I on the southern end. It is distinctive, and slightly unusual, to locate large public structures on the outer edges of a town. We are more accustomed to seeing this kind of building form the core of a community and to be more or less central to any urban site, whether multiple-mounded sites in southern Mesopotamia or the citadel-centred sites of northern Mesopotamia. At Ur and Uruk, for instance, the temple and palace complexes are central to the urban sprawl. Nippur offers a slightly different option, with temples near (but not at) the settlement edges (North Temple, Enlil Temple/Ekur) as well as near its centre (the Gula-Ninurta Temple in Area WA). Mashkan-Shapir offers a counterpoint, with the temple and palace at the extremities of the settlement to the northeast and southwest (Stone 2007). In northern Mesopotamia, Tell Leilan and Tell Brak offer Ur- or Uruk-like central clusters of public buildings on an acropolis or high ridge, while Chagar Bazar comes closer to the arrangement at Mashkan-shapir.

This edge location might indicate that the public buildings–and their administrative functions–were not an original part of the settlement but were late developments, added when the edges of the site were the only locations remaining empty for new structures. But alternatively and more promisingly, this exterior location may have been consciously selected, and this selection could be linked to the re-use of an ancient site and to the very reason that the entire settlement of Chagar Bazar in the early 2nd millennium BC was clustered tightly on the top of such a high mound.

The conscious creation of an interior settlement landscape, in which both domestic and public space and the inhabitants' movement around and between them are highly structured and regulated, is generally associated with urban sites that are seats of government or state religion. But a lower order townscape might have been similarly consciously ordered. Buildings are the primary fabric of any settlement, and how they are woven together or held apart will affect the social cohesion of their inhabitants. Inversely, social order and social relations will also have an effect on the templates deemed available and appropriate for space use.

"As the spaces of the city take on a visible form, they also give a kind of form to the lives led within them. In turn, those "social forms" inevitably imprint themselves onto the urban landscape." (Sandweiss 1996: 320)

It is our conjecture that the "tight" physical structure of the Chagar Bazar neighbourhood in the later sub-phases of the early 2nd millennium BC was inherited from an original idea conceived at the site's reoccupation during the reign of Samsi-Addu. It is plausible that a non-occupied site with a horizontally-restricted inhabitable area was a conscious and sought-out template, because such a space would necessitate a tightly structured built environment. The initial inhabitants of the site in the early 2nd millennium BC are likely to have been very heterogenous or socially "loose": we know from personal names in the texts from Area TD that at least

---

[2] The foundation of the Tablet Building of Mallowan's Area TD (Liège Area I) pre-dates the administrative building of Area A Phase II and the house phases we articulated in Area G, and any upper phases in TD that might be contemporary with our phases are unclear. However, the substantial building in TD may have had an extended use that overlapped with some of our phases in Area G.

three different ethnicities were represented (Akkadian, Hurrian, Amorite). There was also likely to have been an economic mixture of newly-settled nomads, craftsmen, farmers, administrators whose original home was Shubat Enlil or elsewhere, and still others, all unrelated, and potentially reluctant, occupants. The consciously "tight" physical building arrangement is a Pascalian approach to generating a social tightness in this disparate group.[3] Through an imposed structure that physically binds people closely together and directs intra-site movement and frequent person-person interactions, the inhabitants should come to believe in both the idea and the ideology of a unified community. And indeed, by the time of the later levels, after the collapse of Samsi-Addu's political system that had conceived of the initial tight townscape, the tight physical structure remained. The inhabitants of the site stayed together in the same townscape because this approach, together with the passage of time and the inertia this brings, had genuinely worked. Multiple layers of interaction over time meant that they had become a tight social community by the post-Samsi-Addu era.

The placement of public buildings at the edges of the space, inscribing this social community, injects a physical and conceptual distance between administration and domestic occupation, but not so much distance that there was an alienation effect. In Area A, the use of a house plan for the community building (although on a larger scale) signified the informality of administration. And the proximity of houses to the administration buildings implies the intent to maintain and to visually present connections. The placement of these buildings additionally may have aimed to take into account the effect on an outsider gaze (see below) as well as internal access.

Regional Landscapes: Modern views

The Upper Khabur is one of the most intensively surveyed regions in the Near East. Mallowan's survey in late 1934 (Mallowan 1936) closely tracked the river valley along the Lower Khabur. In the Upper Khabur, his approach was less river- and wadi-based but focused on prominent and visible tells, with the result that multiple-period sites along wadis were over-represented. The eastern boundary of his survey zone, probably because of logistics, was the Wadi Jaghjagh. In an intriguing presentation of one scholar's mental image of the region, his map (Mallowan 1934: Fig. 1) is literally blank east of the Jaghjagh. Although he was refreshingly open to the opportunity for research represented by the region, Mallowan's insistence that the region was "provincial" is unsettling, given current knowledge of the rich and dynamic nature of settlement here. He subjectively assessed the material culture of the Upper Khabur as inferior to that produced in Assyria, bemoaned the near-lack of inscribed material, and subscribed to the view that the area was merely a not-particularly-interesting space between the two key transport routes of the Tigris and Euphrates. On the positive side, he acknowledged the agricultural promise of the region and (slightly perversely) states: "precisely because the area is provincial it has a special scientific interest, for provinces are generally backward and slow to receive, and hence likely to exhibit ancient forms side by side with innovations, and, being a prey to the rapacity of their stronger neighbours, they afford us side-lights on contemporary civilizations." (Mallowan 1934: 5).

---

[3] Pascal's *Pensees*, IV, 250: usefully summarised as "Kneel and you will believe." By performing an act, one's belief in the ideology behind that act is reinforced or even created (see also Bourdieu's concept of *habitus* and Giddens' structuration theory). Use of the terms "tight" and "loose" here owes inspiration to Sandweiss 1996: 333-336.

More recent extensive surveys of Lyonnet (1996, 2000) and Meier (1986) added significantly to our large-scale picture of early 2nd millennium BC occupation across the Upper Khabur. The eastern Khabur was densely occupied, particularly along and between the Jaghjagh and Jarrah wadis (Meier 1986: Fig. 10, Fig. 34). But some empty sub-areas in the central and western Khabur indicate a patchy occupation overall (Lyonnet 2000); settlement blanks are seen most notably around Tell Beydar but also in less-often discussed areas lying both north and south of Chagar Bazar. The northern swathe of Lyonnet's survey area, along and within 15 km of the Turkish border, was reasonably densely occupied, as was the southern limit (the lower reaches of the Wadis Jaghjagh and Khanzir) (Lyonnet 2000: Fig. 9). However, the east-west band between these zones saw fewer sites at greater distances from their nearest neighbours (an average of over 9 km between identified sites, versus the average c 6 km spacing between the sites near the Turkish border). Chagar Bazar's two nearest neighbors are Tell Arbid (some 12 km to the east) and (possibly) Lyonnet's Tell 60, an equivalent distance to the east-southeast. This general picture of variability and of substantial "empty" space has been further addressed by various site-centred intensive surveys and is particularly relevant for the "outsider" view of Chagar Bazar.

Intensive surveys around Tell Leilan (Weiss 1986, Ristvet 2005, Stein & Wattenmaker 1990) present a clear picture of the landscape use associated with the region's major political centre. The density of early 2nd millennium BC occupation and range of site sizes is impressive (Weiss *et al.* 2002: fig. 13; Ristvet & Weiss 2005), although not all the sites were necessarily contemporary and Leilan itself may have been largely given over to public buildings, with a relatively low population. By contrast, the Tell Beydar-centred survey (Wilkinson 1998, 2000b, 2002) is eloquent proof of the difference in primary economies from grain agriculture in the eastern Upper Khabur to pastoralism in the west. The area around Tell Beydar has been described as "largely abandoned" during the early 2nd millennium BC (Wilkinson 2000: 235), a desolate-sounding situation with which the inhabitants of Chagar Bazar, on the opposite northeast "edge" of this empty space, would also have grappled. Two sites with Khabur Ware at the northern edge of the Beydar survey have been called "strongholds" within this de-settled landscape (Wilkinson 1998); Chagar Bazar's dense arrangement of structures, mixture of houses and administrative buildings, and mounded physicality provide a good model for the type of "stronghold" settlement one could expect there.

Texts from Mari and Chagar Bazar refer to a substantial nomadic population in the area, and this de-settled landscape would not have been empty. Grazing land may have built features and "domesticated" places, such as temporary corrals and shelters, trails, watering places and wells; and at some times of year it may be quite densely occupied, in terms of human and animal load.

A powerful contrast is thus presented in the early 2nd millennium BC between the eastern and central-western Upper Khabur sub-regions. The eastern Khabur presents us with massive sites (i.e., Tell Mohammed Diyab at 43 hectares, Tell Leilan at 90 hectares[4]) surrounded by a complex hierarchy of towns and villages. Settlement numbers and total settled hectares had increased from late 3rd millennium BC levels.

---

[4] Tell Leilan has been characterized as a "hollow city" (Ristvet & Weiss 2005); substantial parts of the Lower Town were utilized for widely separated and expansive public buildings, such as the Northern and Eastern Lower Town Palaces. The density of domestic occupation there remains an open question. The difference between hollow or sparsely occupied sites and densely occupied ones has been noted (Ristvet & Weiss 2005), but the elevation and mound-top orientation was not specified there.

The situation in the central-western Khabur is one of smaller, densely occupied sites, often located on high mounds (e.g. Chagar Bazar, Tell Arbid) (Ristvet & Weiss 2005), within a sparsely populated landscape. The boundary between these two modes of settlement pattern appears to be roughly the Wadi Jaghjagh. The contemporary situation at Tell Brak in this boundary zone is gradually becoming clearer and presents a blended pattern. Excavations in the 1980s (Oates *et al.* 1997), from 1994 to 1996 (Matthews 2003) and in 2006-9 (McMahon *et al.* 2007) indicate that the Old Babylonian occupation there is comparable to the settlement at Chagar Bazar: dense, occupying the highest ridge of the site, and (perhaps) featuring public buildings at key and highly visible locations (albeit central to the settlement). The occupied area of Brak was reduced in size from its 3rd millennium BC extent, although texts indicate that it retained religious and political importance. The Brak-centred surveys (Eidem & Warburton 1996; Wright *et al.* forthcoming) present an image of reasonably dense occupation of the outlying region during the site's decrease in size. The Eidem and Warburton survey (1996) recorded 19 sites with 2nd millennium BC pottery; most are located along the Wadi Jaghjagh or Wadi Radd, and the area around Brak itself is significantly empty. In size, only one site was ca. 5 hectares, and none of the rest is over 3.2 hectares. The larger Brak survey of 2001 through 2005 greatly expanded these findings across a wider area; sites of the early 2nd millennium BC increased in number compared to the 3rd millennium BC (J. Oates, pers. comm. 2007). Reconstruction of a simple two-tier site hierarchy would over-simplify the situation, but this pattern may be a crossover between the emptier landscapes of the west and the site hierarchies of the east[5]. This subtle variation indicates a shading of intensity of land use, a continuum rather than a frontier between two types of settlement pattern.

Although the temptation exists to categorize the variant settlement patterns into wadi-based strips moving from east to west, the greater density of early 2nd millennium BC sites along the northern and southern "edges" of the Upper Khabur, near the Taurus foothills and the Wadi Radd, respectively, indicates that there are subtle north to south variations which must also be acknowledged. These different arrangements should be related to rainfall and water availability differentials. Marshes along the Radd may be a factor in the increased carrying capacity of the land in the south, while higher rainfall at the north is a simple explanation for the denser settlement pattern there. Meanwhile Chagar Bazar lies roughly in the middle of the band defined by the 300-350 mm isohyets, with significantly more rainfall (at least 50 mm more on average) than Tell Brak or Tell Barri, but substantially less (up to ca. 100 mm less) than that received by Tell Leilan. This specific micro-environment surely had an effect on the local economy and the site's placement.

Chagar Bazar as a Place in the Landscape

"Place" here denotes a human creation and idea. "Place is space objectified" (Chapman 2000: 183). Places are structured spaces; places encapsulate investment and both economic and social uses, and they thus have economic and social values, plus practical and symbolic meanings. Places are at the same time both abstract

---

[5] The east-west variation in settlement pattern corresponds to an extent with a distinction between lower town sites versus ridge-top sites. Among the latter are Tell Brak at c 35 m (?) above plain level; Tell Barri, at a less-notable c 8-9 m above plain level. Chagar Bazar at c. 17-19 m (?) above the plain falls roughly between the two.

concepts and physical loci (Feld & Basso 1996); they exist and can be studied at several different scales (Bowser 2004). The clearest 'places' in the ancient Near East are mounds or tells, loci of repeated structuring and definition of space and of both horizontally and vertically dense activities[6]; they are the physical signifiers of long-term settlement traditions. "Space and time come together in place" (Casey 1996: 36).

Despite intensive survey data informing us that high mounds are not the most common settlements in many periods, many Mesopotamian archaeologists still tend to think of tell living as inevitable, as traditional, as the most visible settlement option in Mesopotamia and therefore as an unconscious habit. But it may equally be that tell living was a conscious part of Mesopotamian identity, a positive choice from among many options of equal or unequal value. The dominance of low-mound or plain-level living in some periods of northern Mesopotamian history (such as the Late Bronze Age and Iron Age) indicates that the non-tell alternative choice was often being made and that particular historical or climatic circumstances may have made tell-living the dominant choice at other times. For prehistoric south-eastern Europe, the choice of tell-living has been identified as an aspect of "vertical dominance" or "vertical competition", with higher tells expressing stronger ownership of valuable ancestral traditions and offering a link to cosmological ideas implicated in social or political control (Chapman 2000). Such competition is an oversimplification in the Mesopotamian setting, given the diversity of settlements and their myriad cultural and economic connections, the absence of apparent rivalry (and utter lack of derogatory textual references to non-tell dwellers) and the absence of conformity between site size/height and wealth/functional role. Values may have existed, but value contrasts, *per se*, were not explicitly made.

Places also have diachronic meanings, and this is especially visible in tells, although we need to emphasise that precise meanings or ideas of particular sites–like settlement functions–were not unchanged over time. "Places created by people at a past point in time are continually engaged in the negotiation of meaning at a later point in time;…places are charged with past events and personalities that are integral to current practices" (Kantner 2008: 58-59). In the Mesopotamian past, excavation of brick pits, burials and wells were all opportunities for the living to interact with previous occupants of their settlements. Knowledge of 'older things' under the ground would have been taken for granted and learned at an early age. Similarities of previous and current building materials, burial practice and material culture would also have been learned and absorbed. That knowledge of earlier places would have been woven into the story of the current place, and the piling-up of earlier chapters in the story meant the meaning of any place would continuously evolve.

The concept of landscape used here is the "constructed landscape" (Knapp & Ashmore 1999), a natural underlay deeply entangled with meaningful human constructions that serve as guides and markers. Occupational mounds are both monuments to past lives and indicators of current activities (Alcock 2002:30-31) and they define Mesopotamian landscapes even when they are not the dominant settlement location. Landscape as used here is *contra* Chapman's (1988, 2000) Foucauldian idea of landscape as a locus of social power accrued to a few via control

---

[6] Fields, canals and resource clusters, all loci of intermittent or less intensive activities, may equally be significant places with extended biographies, but their visibility tends to be lower than that of settlements.

of space or control of specific activities in that space. Such landscapes of power do exist within Mesopotamia. Chagar Bazar might even be argued–at the historical moment of Samsi-Addu's reign–to have been the core of a micro-landscape that sent a message to an associated nomadic population regarding state power and control. But less hierarchical views of the landscape can also be expressed, and it is the longer-term post-state view of the landscape on which I wish to focus.

The landscape of southern Mesopotamia offers a stark example of artificial constructions inextricably interwoven with a natural underlay: man-made mounds and canals within the otherwise-featureless alluvial plain. These mounds and canals were structuring features that expressed pronounced oppositions: vertical points and down-cut linear features. Northern Mesopotamia's rolling plains mean that the vertical prominences of mounds are less striking and that the down-cutting natural *wadi* channels are less visible. Yet both features are still strong elements that would have structured movement, land use and value perception. Viewed from a structuralist perspective, the human construction versus natural feature opposition expressed by mounds versus *wadis* would have resonated as the equal long-term and stable presence of both elements, thus naturalizing human occupation.[7] Certainly the occupants of the Upper Khabur in the early 2nd millennium BC would never have lived in a landscape that was not marked by earlier mounds and steeped in history (as do its modern occupants). They would have known the lifespan of objects and houses as well as they knew those of people, yet mounded settlements–abandoned or occupied–would have taken on the air of permanent phenomena beyond the power of humans to alter.[8]

Those few ancient texts that refer to landscapes primarily describe sites' distance from each other and on which bank of the relevant river or *wadi* they lie. Old Assyrian and Old Babylonian itineraries utilised named towns as markers of journey stages (and these are invariably mounded sites, wherever these ancient names have been identifiable), and they only very rarely mention natural features. Middle Assyrian and Neo-Assyrian accounts of military campaigns did the same (i.e., the annals of Tukulti-Ninurta I and Assurnasirpal). The result is a "synoptic" landscape, horizon-based and visually long-range.

The place that was Chagar Bazar in the early 2nd millennium BC was created by its cumulative physical and social situations established since prehistory. The earlier occupations at the site affected the location and nature of subsequent use of the space and the full biography of the site. The early 2nd millennium BC buildings were, in the best tradition of "organic" buildings, "married to the ground" (in Frank Lloyd Wright's famous phrase). Memory–social, collective and individual– intersects dynamically with internal and external landscapes.

---

[7] It should be stressed that the inverse of this, the "domestication" of nature, is a possibility but does not fit Mesopotamian religious belief as well as does the naturalization of human activity. The generalized belief that such man-made things as canals, cities and tools were divine responsibilities, as were rivers, mountains and agricultural fertility, effectively links these human things to the natural world rather than vice versa.

[8] Settlement pattern maps in publications of regional or site-based surveys inevitably offer a sequence of maps, with the sites occupied during the period as the only sites indicated on the map of that period. But for a truer picture of the human landscape, such maps should show both currently-occupied sites plus any earlier sites (identified by alternative symbols?) which, even unoccupied, would have still been markers of human settlement. Only through such mapping can the palimpsest of regional occupation be read (cf. Barrett 1999: 258 for discussion of this issue for Iron Age Britain).

That the ancient mound below the early 2nd millennium BC site was selectively chosen for reoccupation, for reasons related to its precise location, relationship to other sites or resources, height and size and past history. The close *wadi*-side location was certainly advantageous, yet (as mentioned in Ch. 1) there are other nearby mounds to north and south comparably close to the watercourse (i.e., Tell Khanzir to the south). While the higher southern mound may have been attractive for its elevation, the extremely limited space at its peak rendered it unusable. Indeed the southern mound only bears traces of pits and ephemeral installations low on the southern slopes and some re-working and minimal architectural features on its eastern mid-slope (our Area B). But the slightly lower and longer northern mound apparently offered an ideal location for re-settlement. The restricted space at its top may have even been an advantage for the ideology of settlement (as discussed above). From the point-of-view of an external observer, the selection of the mound does not seem to have been made with defense in mind. Area A, with its important structures, was "out on a limb" to the northeast, separated from the mass of other structures and potentially vulnerable in conflict. Symbolic defense– an appearance of strength–may have been a factor, and it is plausible that the mound was selected as a foundation which would be incorporated into the living settlement as a continuous solid base.

Particularly in a changing landscape being resettled and redefined in the wake of an occupational hiatus and gradual climate change, the selection of a high mound (rather than open space or a low mound) would be an acknowledgment of a link across that hiatus to a deep past occupation, a quotation of past lives, a reaffirmation of past values and meaning and power. In this way, Chagar Bazar is one of Chapman's "timemarks" (2000: 188; 1997), a significant monument in what might be termed a "timescape", as well as a landmark in a landscape. The site and its landscape may have begun in this era as an imposed power landmark or political landscape, but in the post-Samsi-Adad era, both had been transformed by use into a place and a landscape which are more "vernacular" than political (Jackson 1984). Ancestors were buried, houses were built and rebuilt in persistent locations, traffic patterns among structures and activity areas had become habitual, and the ideology of a community had been internalized. The timescape and timemark include this subtle change from the imposed to the real. And it may be the relative emptiness and low slopes of the landscape around Chagar Bazar in the early 2nd millennium BC that made the site into the specific place it became. The contrast between the tightly-packed town and the empty surrounding land dovetailed to create the symbolism of the Place.

Chagar Bazar's landscape status lends itself to two distinct scales of observation: as a man-made feature from a distance of kilometers–the view of a traveler or non-resident–, and as an internally-variable settlement viewed from close range–the gaze of a local resident. These two patterns of observation map onto two common modes of wider landscape use that would have been dominant in the past: texts referring to settlements are written from the viewpoint of the traveler or external administrator, while the agricultural basis for the economy implies that many of the site's residents would have been accustomed to looking at their town from neighbouring fields. And if one thinks of the settlement not as a static picture but one viewed by an active moving agent, there are dynamics of concealing/revealing within the settlement landscape, dependant upon angle of view and arrival. It is indicative that when Mesopotamian texts (until the 1st millennium BC) refer to landscape, they do so in the context of moving across it, usually for economic reasons (long distance trade or taxation). An alternative "moving" landscape interaction, un-represented in texts, is that of the farmer or pastoralist who travels within a restricted range yet, like the long-distance trader, would have had a distinct sense of local landscape and landmarks. The trading landscape and the agro-pastoral landscape have differing scales, variant depths of knowledge and ownership, and different value assignments for features (i.e., a *wadi* as barrier versus a water source or transport route). An agricultural viewpoint might not see sharp boundaries between "site" and fields, since both would be equally familiar and lived-in; a travel or administration viewpoint would focus upon "sites" as opportunities and ignore fields as less relevant areas; a pastoralist viewpoint might be very heavily temporally coloured, with access restricted to certain seasons. But all viewpoints may have been unconscious factors in the arrangement of settlement at Chagar Bazar and presentation of its outer face.

Area A reaches out towards the Wadi Khanzir and would have presented its substantial buildings for inspection particularly to anyone traveling southwards along the water-course, from the direction of Turkey or northern sites such as Tell Mozan. These substantial buildings projecting towards the *wadi* would have had a higher back-drop of more irregularly-outlined private houses (Areas G-BD) on the main part of the mound. This view emphasizes the "architecture of power" aspect of the site. By contrast, the view from the "land" side, to anyone in a field or coming overland from the west (i.e., from Girmayir), would have been one of closely-packed architecture on that solid base of ancient occupation, not an image of political power, but perhaps more one of settlement strength and integrity, a different framing mechanism. Viewers arriving along the watercourse from the south (from the direction of Tell Brak) would have been presented with a still different picture, with the high unoccupied peak of the south mound filling the foreground, and the substantial buildings of Area A projecting outward to the east, just beyond. Intriguingly, the buildings at the mound centre would have been only gradually revealed as one came closer and circumnavigated the south mound. The unoccupied south mound would be an obstacle that would direct anyone approaching it to move around to either side. Finally, anyone approaching overland from the east (i.e., directly from Tell Leilan) or working in a field on the east bank of the wadi would have seen the central cluster of houses in Area G, bracketed by the unoccupied peak of the south mound and by the large buildings of Area A on left and right, respectively. Each of these approaches is presented with a different, but strong, visual statement.[9] However, the dominant element of each statement is generally not that of a powerful administrative authority, but instead of a vibrant and variable, yet permanent and tightly-woven, settlement.

---

[9] The degree to which these pictures may have been affected by a surrounding low "industrial" zone of pottery manufacture, brick production or metallurgy remains unknown. Pottery and mud-bricks were surely produced near the site, albeit seasonally.

References Cited

Anschuetz, K. F., R. H. Wilshusen & C. L. Scheick 2001. An Archaeology of Landscapes: Perspectives and Directions. *Journal of Archaeological Research* 9: 157–211.

Arnold, D. 1985. *Ceramic Theory and Culture Process.* Cambridge: Cambridge University Press.

Bachelot, L. 1992. Une tombe construite du deuxième millénaire av. J.-C., à Mohammed Diyab. Pp. 31-38 in J.-M. Durand, ed. *Recherches en Haute Mesopotamie, Tell Mohammed Diyab, Campagnes 1990 et 1991.* Paris: Mémoires de NABU 2.

Bachelot, L., C. Castel, D. Charpin, and M. Sauvage. 1990. Les Fouilles de Tell Mohammed Diyab (1987-1988). Pp. 9-46 in Durand, J.-M., ed. *Tell Mohammed Diyab. Campagnes 1987 et 1988.* vol. 1. *N.A.B.U.* Paris: SEPOA.

Bachelot, L. & M. Sauvage. 1992. Les campagnes de 1990-1991 dans le secteur de la ville haute de Mohammed Diyab. Pp. 9-22 in J.-M. Durand, ed. *Recherches en Haute Mesopotamie, Tell Mohammed Diyab, Campagnes 1990 et 1991.* Paris: Mémoires de NABU 2.

Barrett, J. 1999. The Mythical Landscapes of the British Iron Age. Pp. 253-265 in Ashmore, W., and Knapp, A. B. (eds.), *Archaeologies of Landscape: Contemporary Perspectives.* Oxford: Blackwell.

Bieliński, P. 2005. Tell Arbid, The Ninth Season of Syrian-Polish Excavations, Preliminary Report. *Polish Archaeology in the Mediterranean* 16: 475-489.

Bieliński, P. 2004. Tell Arbid, The 2003 Campaign of Polish-Syrian Excavations, Preliminary Report. *Polish Archaeology in the Mediterranean* 15: 335-353.

Bieliński, P. 2002. Tell Arbid, The Sixth Campaign of Excavations, Preliminary Report. *Polish Archaeology in the Mediterranean* 13: 279-294.

Bieliński, P. 2001. Tell Arbid, Interim Report of the Fifth Season. *Polish Archaeology in the Mediterranean* 12: 315-326.

Bieliński, P. 2000. Tell Arbid, The Fourth Season. *Polish Archaeology in the Mediterranean* 11: 273-284.

Boehmer, R.M., F. Pedde, & B. Salje. 1995. *Uruk: Die Gräber.* Mainz: Philipp von Zabern.

Borgna, E. 2004. Aegean feasting: a Minoan perspective. Pp. 127-159 in J. C. Wright, ed. *The Mycenaean Feast. Hesperia* 73:2. Princeton: American School of Classical Studies at Athens.

Broekmans, T., A. Adriaens & E. Pantos 2004. Analytical investigations of cooking pottery from Tell Beydar (NE-Syria). *Nuclear Instruments and Methods in Physics Research Section B: Beam Interactions with Materials and Atoms* 226/1-2: 92-97.

Broman Morales, V. 1983. Jarmo Figurines and Other Clay Objects. Pp. 369-423 in L. Braidwood, R. Braidwood, B. Howe, C. Reed & P.J. Watson, eds. *Prehistoric Archaeology along the Zagros Flanks.* Chicago: Oriental Institute Publications 105.

Buikstra J.E. & Ubelaker D.H., ed. 1994. *Standards of Data Collection from Human Skeletal Remains.* Fayetteville: Arkansas Archeological Survey Research Series.

Brusasco, P. 1999-2000. Family Archives and the Social Use of Space in Old Babylonian Houses at Ur. *Mesopotamia* 34-35: 3-174.

Buccellati, G. & M. Kelly-Buccellati 2001. Uberlegungen zur funktionellen und historischen Bestimmung des Konigspalastes AP in Urkesh, Bericht uber die 13. Kampagne in Tall Mozan/Urkesh, Ausgrabungen im Gebiet AA, Juni-August 2000. *Mitteilungen Deutschen Orient-Gesellschaft* 133: 59-96.

Buccellati, G. 1998. Urkesh as Tell Mozan: Profiles of the Ancient City. Pp. 11-34 in Buccellati, G. and Kelly-Buccellati, M., eds. *Urkesh and the Hurrians. Studies in honour of Lloyd Cotsen.* Urkesh/Mozan Studies 3: Bibliotheca Mesopotamica 26. Malibu: Undena Publications.

Calvet, Y. 1996. Maisons privées paleo-babyloniennes à Larsa, Remarques d'architecture. Pp. 197-209 in K. Veenhof, ed., *Houses and Households in Ancient Mesopotamia.* Leiden: Nederlands Historisch-Archaeologisch Institut.

Carr, C. 1995a. Building a Unified Middle-Range Theory of Artifact Design, Historical Perspectives and tactics. Pp. 151-170 in C. Carr & J. Neitzel, eds. *Style, Society and Person, Archaeological and Ethnological Perspectives.* New York: Plenum Press.

Carr, C. 1995b. A Unified Middle-Range Theory of Artifact Design. Pp. 171-258 in in C. Carr & J. Neitzel, eds. *Style, Society and Person, Archaeological and Ethnological Perspectives.* New York: Plenum Press.

Castel, C. 1996. Un quartier du maisons urbaines du bronze moyen à Tell Mohammed Diyab (Djezireh Syrienne). Pp. 273-283 in K. R. Veenhof. (ed.). *Houses and Households in Ancient Mesopotamia.* Leiden: Nederlands Historisch-Archaeologisch Institut.

Casey, E. S. 1996. How to Get From Space to Place in a Fairly Short Stretch of Time. Pp. 13-52 in S. Feld & K. Basso. *Senses of Place.* Santa Fe: School of American Research Press.

Chang, K.C. 1958. Study of the Neolithic Social Grouping: Examples from the New World. *American Anthropologist* 60/2: 298-334.

Chang, K.C. 1968. Toward a Science of Prehistoric Society. Pp. 1-9 in K.C. Chang, ed. *Settlement Archaeology*. Palo Alto: National Press Books.

Chapman, J. 2000. *Fragmentation in Archaeology, People, Places and Broken Objects in the Prehistory of South Eastern Europe*. London: Routledge.

Charpin, D. 2004. Histoire politique du Proche-Orient amorrite (2002-1595). Pp. 25-640 in D. Charpin, D.O. Edzard & M. Stol. *Mesopotamien, Die altbabylonische Zeit*. Orbis Biblicus et Orientalis 160/4. Fribourg: Academic Press.

Charpin, D. 1993. Un souveraine éphémère en Ida-Maras: Ishme-Addu d'Ashnakkum. *Mari Annales de Recherches Interdisciplinaires* 7: 165-191.

Charpin, D. & N. Zeigler. 2003. *Florilegium marianum V, Mari et le Proche Orient à l'époque amorrite, assai d'histoire politique*. Paris: SEPOA.

Christie, A. 1946. *Come, Tell Me How You Live*. London: W. Collins & Sons.

Clason, A.T. 1978. Late Bronze Age–Iron Age Zebu in Jordan? *Journal of Archaeological Science* 5: 91–93.

Cohen, A.C. 2005. *Death Rituals, Ideology, and the Development of Early Mesopotamian Kingship*. Leiden: Brill.

Crawford, H. E. 1977. *The Architecture of Iraq in the Third Millennium B.C.* Vol. 5. *Mesopotamia*. Copenhagen: Akademisk Forlag.

Crawford, H. E. 1982. Architecture, Archaeology and Analogy. *Sumer* 38: 23-28.

de Meyer, L., ed. 1984. *Tell ed-Der IV: Progress Reports*. Leuven: Peeters.

de Meyer, L., ed. 1978. *Tell ed-Der II: Progress Reports*. Leuven: Peeters.

Dickson, B.D. 2006. Pubic Transcripts Expressed in Theaters of Cruelty: the Royal Graves at Ur in Mesopotamia. *Cambridge Archaeological Journal* 16 (2): 123-144.

Djuric M., Milovanovic P., Janovic A., Draskovic M., Djukic K., & Milenkovic P. 2008. Porotic Lesions in Immature Skeletons from Stara Torina, Late Medieval Serbia. *International Journal of Osteoarchaeology* 18: 458-475.

Dohmann-Pfälzner, H. and P. Pfälzner. 2001. Ausgrabungen der Deutschen Orient-Gesellschaft in der zentralen Oberstadt von Tall Mozan/Urkeš. Bereicht über die in Kooperation mit dem IIMAS durchgeführte Kampagne 2000. *Mitteilungen der Deutschen Orient-Gesellschaft zu Berlin* 133: 97-139.

Dohmann-Pfälzner, H. and P. Pfälzner. 2000. Ausgrabungen der Deutschen Orient-Gesellschaft in der zentralen Oberstadt von Tall Mozan/Urkesh: Bericht über die in Kooperation mit dem IIMAAS durchgeführte Kampagne 1999. *Mitteilungen der Deutschen Orient-Gesellschaft* 132: 185-228.

Downey, S.B. 2003. *Terracotta Figurines and Plaques from Dura-Europos*. Ann Arbor: University of Michigan Press.

Durand, J-M. 1992: *Recherches en Haute Mesopotamie: Tell Mohammed Diyab: campagnes 1990 et 1991*. (Memoires de NABU, 2). Paris: SEPOA.

Durand, J-M. & C. Nicolle. 1999. Tell Mohammed Diyab, L'acropole d'un centre regional du IIe millenaire. *Archéologia* 353: 18-27.

Eidem, J. 1993. From the Zagros to Aleppo - and Back. Chronological Notes on the Empire of Šamši-Adad. *Akkadica* 81: 23-28.

Eidem, J. 2000. Northern Jezira in the 18th Century BC. Aspects of Geo-Political Patterns. Pp. 255-264 in O. Rouault and M. Wäfler. (eds.). *La Djéziré et l'Euphrate Syriens: De La Protohistoire à la fin du IIe Millénaire av. J.-C. Tendances dans l'interprétation historique des données nouvelles.* Subartu VIII. Turnhout.

Eidem, J., and Warburton, D. 1996. In the land of Nagar: A survey around Tell Brak. *Iraq* 58: 51–64.

Faivre, X. 1992. La céramique de Mohammed Diyab, 1990-1991. Pp. 55- 89 in: J.-M. Durand. (ed.), *Tell Mohammed Diyab, Campagnes 1990 et 1991*. Mémoires de NABU, 2, Paris.

Fleming, D. 2004. *Democracy's Ancient Ancestors, Mari and Early Collective Governance.* Cambridge: Cambridge University Press.

Frane, J. 1996. *The Tell Leilān period I Hābūr Ware assemblage.* Unpublished Ph.D. Dissertation, University of North Carolina at Chapel Hill.

Frankel, D. and J. M. Webb. 2001. Population, Households, and Ceramic Consumption in a Prehistoric Cypriot Village. *Journal of Field Archaeology* 28, No. 1/2: 115-129.

Gadd, C.J. 1937. Tablets from Chagar Bazar. *Iraq* 4: 178-183.

Gadd, C.J. 1940. Tablets from Chagar Bazar and Tall Brak, 1937-38. *Iraq* 7: 22-66.

Gamble, L., P. Walker & G. Russell. 2001. An Integrative Approach to Mortuary Analysis: Social and Symbolic Dimensions of Chumash Burial Practices. *American Antiquity* 66: 185–212.

Gibson, M., ed. 1981. *Uch Tepe I, Tell Razuk, Tell Ahmed al-Mughir, Tell Ajamat.* Chicago: Oriental Institute.

Gibson, M., J. Franke, M. Civil, M. Bates, J. Boessneck, K. Butzer, T. Rathbun, E. Frick Mallin. 1978. *Excavations at Nippur, Twelfth Season.* Oriental Institute Communications 23. Chicago: Oriental Institute.

Gimbel, D.N. and Selz, G. 2002. *Preliminary Site Report of the Oriental Institute of the University of Vienna and Archaeos Excavation Project at Tell Arbid, Sector D.* http:www.archaeos.org/html/reports.htm.

Gosden, C. 2004. Aesthetics, Intelligence and Emotions: Implications for Archaeology. Pp. 33-40 in E. DeMarrais, C. Gosden & C. Renfrew, eds. *Rethinking Materiality, The engagement of mind with the material word.* Cambridge: McDonald Institute Monographs.

Hamlin, C. 1971. *The Habur Ware Ceramic Assemblage of Northern Mesopotamia: An Analysis of Its Distribution.* Unpublished PhD dissertation, University of Pennsylvania.

Härke, H. 1997. The Nature of Burial Data. Pp. 19-27 in C.K. Jensen & K.H. Nielsen, *Burial and Society, The Chronological and Social Analysis of Archaeological Burial Data.* Aarhus: Aarhus University Press.

Holladay, J. S. 1997. Syro-Palestinian Houses. Pp. 94-113 in Meyers, E. M., ed. *Oxford Encyclopaedia of the Ancient Near East,* vol. 3. Oxford: Oxford University Press.

Hodder, I. 1986. *Reading the past; current approaches to interpretation in archaeology.* Cambridge: Cambridge University Press.

Hrouda, B. 2001. About Habur-Ware, Hopefully for the Last Time. *Al-Rafidan* 22: 89-92.

Hrouda, B. 1957. *Die bemalte Keramik des zweiten Jahrtausends in Nordmesopotamien und Nordsyrien. Istanbuler Forschungen* 19. Berlin: Gebr. Mann.

Jackson, J.B. 1984. *Discovering the Vernacular Landscape.* New Haven: Yale University Press.

Jensen, C.J. & K.H. Nielsen 1997. Burial Data and Correspondence Analysis. Pp. 29-61 in C.K. Jensen & K.H. Nielsen, *Burial and Society, The Chronological and Social Analysis of Archaeological Burial Data.* Aarhus: Aarhus University Press.

Kamp, K. 2000. From Village to Tell. Household Ethnoarchaeology in Syria. *Near Eastern Archaeology* 63:2: 84-93.

Kantner, J. 2008. The Archaeology of Regions: From Discrete Analytical Toolkit to Ubiquitous Spatial Perspective. *Journal of Archaeological Research* 16: 37-81.

Kantor, H. 1958. The Pottery. Pp. 21-41 in C. McEwan, L. Braidwood, H. Frankfort, H. Guterbock, R.C. Haines, H.J. Kantor & C.H. Kraeling. *Soundings at Tell Fakhariyah.* Oriental Institute Publications 79. Chicago.

Katz, D. 2003. *The Image of the Netherworld in Sumerian Sources.* Bethesda: CDL Press.

Kepinski-Lecomte, C. 1992. *Haradum I: Une Ville Nouvelle Sur Le Moyen-Euphrate (XVIIIe-XVIIe Siecles Av. J.-C.).* Paris: Editions Recherche sur les Civilisations.

Kepinski-Lecomte, C. 1996. Spatial Occupation of a New Town, Haradum (Iraqi Middle Euphrates, 18th-17th centuries B.C.). Pp. 191-196 in K. Veenhof, ed. *Houses and Households in Ancient Mesopotamia.* Leiden: Nederlands Historisch-Archaeologisch Institut.

Kolinski, R. 2000. *Tell Rijim, Iraq. The Middle Bronze Age Layers. Eski Mosul Dam Salvage Project Excavations of the Polish Center of Archaeology, University of Warsaw.* British Archaeological Reports, International Series. Archaeopress.

Knapp, A. B. and W. Ashmore 1999. Archaeological landscapes: Constructed, Conceptualized, Ideational. Pp. 1-31 in Ashmore, W., and Knapp, A. B. (eds.), *Archaeologies of Landscape: Contemporary Perspectives.* Oxford: Blackwell.

Kupper, J.-R. 1999. Un episode de l'histoire du royaume d'Ashnakkum. *Revue d'Assyriologie* 93: 79-90.

Kupper, J.-R. 1957. *Les Nomades en Mésopotamie au temps des rois de Mari.* Liège.

Lebeau, M., A. Pruß, M. Roaf & E. Rova. 2000. Stratified Archaeological Evidence and Compared Periodizations in the Syrian Jezirah during the Third Millennium BC. Pp. 167-192 in C. Marro & H. Hauptmann, eds. *Chronologies des Pays du Caucase et de l'Euphrate aux IVe-IIIe millenaires.* Paris: Institut Français d'Etudes Anatoliennes d'Istanbul.

Lesure, R.G. 2002. The Goddess Diffracted, Thinking about the Figurines of Early Villages. *Current Anthropology* 43/ 4: 587-610.

Liebowitz, H. 1988. *Terra-cotta Figurines and Model Vehicles.* The Oriental Institute Excavations at Selenkahiye, Syria. Bibliotheca Mesopotamica 22. Malibu: Undena.

Loftus, R. T., Ertugrul, O., Harba, A. H., El-Barody, M. A. A., MacHugh, D. E., Park, S. D. E. & Bradley, D. G. 1999. A microsatellite survey of cattle from a centre of origin: the Near East. *Molecular Ecology* 8 (12), 2015-2022.

Longacre, W.A. 1999. Standardization and Specialization: What's the Link? Pp. 44-58 in J.M. Skibo & G.M. Feinman, *Pottery and People, A Dynamic Interaction.* Salt Lake City: University of Utah Press.

Loretz, O. 1969. *Texte aus Chagar Bazar und Tell Brak, Teil 1.* Alter Orient und Altes Testament 3. Neukirchen-Vluyn: Butzon & Bercker.

Lyonnet, B. 1996. La prospection archéologique de la partie occidentale du Haut-Khabur (Syrie du Nord-est): méthodes, résultats et questions autour de l'occupation aux IIIe et IIe millénaires av. N. E. *Amurru* 1: 363–376.

Lyonnet, B. 2000. Méthodes et resultants préliminaires d'une prospection archéologique dans la partie occidentale du Haut-Hābūr, depuis le Néolithique jusqu'à la fin du IIe millénaire av. n.è. Pp. 241-253 in O. Rouault and M. Wäfler. (eds.). *La Djéziré et l'Euphrate Syriens de la protohistoire à la fin du IIe millénaire av. J.-C.: Tendances dans l'interprétation historique des données nouvelles.* Subartu VII, Turnhout.

Mackay, E. 1931. *Report on the Excavation of the "A" Cemetery at Kish, Mesopotamia, Pt. 1, A Sumerian Palace and the "A" Cemetery.* Chicago: Field Museum of Natural History Memoirs I, 1-2.

Mallowan, M.E.L. 1936. The Excavations at Tall Chagar Bazar and an Archaeological Survey of the Habur Region. *Iraq* 3/1: 1-59.

Mallowan, M.E.L. 1937. Excavations at Tall Chagar Bazar and an Archaeological Survey of the Habur Region, Second Campaign, 1936. *Iraq* 4: 91-177.

Mallowan, M.E.L. 1947. Excavations at Brak and Chagar Bazar. *Iraq* 9/1 & 2: 1-258.

Matthews, R. 2003a. Zebu: Harbingers of doom in Bronze Age Western Asia? *Antiquity* 76: 438-446.

Matthews, R., ed. 2003b. *Excavations at Tell Brak. Vol. 4: Exploring a Regional Centre in Upper Mesopotamia, 1994-1996.* Cambridge: British School of Archaeology in Iraq and McDonald Institute for Archaeological Research.

Matthews, R. 1995. Excavations at Tell Brak, 1995. *Iraq* 57: 87-111.

McAdam, E. 1993. Clay Figurines. Pp. 83-109 in Green, A. ed. *Abu Salabikh Excavations Volume 4, The 6G Ash Tip and its contents: cultic and administrative discard from the temple?* London: British School of Archaeology in Iraq.

McCown, D.E. and R. Haines. 1967. *Nippur I: Temple of Enlil, Scribal Quarter, and Soundings.* Oriental Institute Publications 78. Chicago: The University of Chicago Press.

McDonald, H. 1997. The Clay Objects. Pp. 131-134 in Oates, Oates & McDonald, *Excavations at Tell Brak, Volume I: The Mitanni and Old Babylonian Periods.* Cambridge: British School of Archaeology in Iraq and McDonald Institute for Archaeological Research.

McClellan, T. L. 1997. Houses and Households in North Syria during the Late Bronze Age. Pp. 29-59 in Castel C., Al-Maqdissi M. and Villeneuve, F., eds. *Les Maisons dans le Syrie Antique du IIIe Millénaire aux débuts de l'Islam. Practiques et Representations de l'Espace Domestique.* Beirut: IFAPO.

McMahon, A. in prep. The Late Chalcolithic Settlement at Chagar Bazar. Chapter in *Excavations at Tell Brak, Volume 6.*

McMahon, A. 2006. *Nippur V: The Early Dynastic to Akkadian Transition, The Area WF Sounding*. Chicago: Oriental Institute Publications 129.

McMahon, A., C. Colantoni & M. Semple. 2005. British Excavations at Chagar Bazar 2001-2002. *Iraq* 67/2: 1-16.

McMahon, A., J. Oates, S. al-Quntar, M. Charles, C. Colantoni, M. M. Hald, P. Karsgaard, L. Khalidi, A. Soltysiak, A. Stone, J. Weber. 2007. Excavations at Tell Brak, 2006-2007. *Iraq* 69: 1-27.

McMahon, A. & P. Quenet. 2007. A Late Third Millennium BC Pottery Assemblage from Chagar Bazar (Area D, Phase II). Pp. 69-242 in Ö. Tunca, A. McMahon & A. Baghdo, eds., *Chagar Bazar (Syrie) II: Les vestiges «post-akkadiens» du chantier D et études diverses*. Leuven: Peeters.

McMahon, A., Ö. Tunca & A Bagdo. 2001. New Excavations at Chagar Bazar, 1999-2000. *Iraq* 63: 201-221.

Meijer, D. 1986. *A Survey in Northeastern Syria*, Netherlands Historical-Archaeological Institute, Istanbul.

Meier, D.J.W. 2000. State and Trade, Toward a Case Study for Northern Mesopotamia. Pp. 219-240 in O. Rouault and M. Wäfler, eds. *La Djéziré et l'Euphrate Syriens de la protohistoire à la fin du IIe millénaire av. J.-C.: Tendances dans l'interprétation historique des données nouvelles*. Subartu VII, Turnhout.

Meyer, J.-W. 1989. Die Grabungen im Planquadrat Q. Pp. 19-61 in W. Orthmann. *Halawa 1980 bis 1986. Vorläufiger Bericht über die 4. bis 9. Grabungskampagne*. Bonn: R. Habelt.

Mills, B.J. 1999. Ceramics and the Social Contexts of Food Consumption in the Northern Southwest. Pp. 99-114 in J.M. Skibo and G.M. Feinman, eds. *Pottery and People, A Dynamic Interaction*. Salt Lake City: University of Utah Press.

Mills, B.J. 1989. Integrating Functional Analyses of Vessels and Sherds through Models of Ceramic Assemblage Formation. *World Archaeology* 21: 133-14.

Molleson T. 2007. A Method for the Study of Activity Related Skeletal Morphologies. *Bioarchaeology of the Near East* 1: 5-33.

Moorey, P.R.S. 2003. *Idols of the People, Miniature Images of Clay in the Ancient Near East*. The Schweich Lectures, British Academy. Oxford: Oxford University Press.

Moorey, P.R.S. 2001. Clay Models and Overland Mobility in Syria, c 2350-1800 BC. Pp. 344-347 in J.-W. Meyer, M. Novak & A. Pruß, eds. *Beiträge zur Vorderasiatischen Archäologie, Winfried Orthmann gewidmet*. Frankfurt.

Moorey, P.R.S. 1978. *Kish Excavations 1923-1933*. Oxford: Oxford University Press.

Nashef, K. 1990. Archaeology in Iraq. *American Journal of Archaeology* 94: 259-289.

Oates, J. 1985. Tell Brak: Uruk Pottery from the 1984 Season. *Iraq* 47: 175-186.

Oates, D. & J, Oates. 1993. Excavations at Tell Brak 1992-93. *Iraq* 55: 155-199.

Oates, D., J. Oates & H. McDonald. 1997. *Excavations at Tell Brak, Volume I: The Mitanni and Old Babylonian Periods*. Cambridge: British School of Archaeology in Iraq and McDonald Institute for Archaeological Research.

Oguchi, H. 2006a. Notes on Khabur Ware from the Haditha Dam Area. Pp. 203-216 in C. Kepinski, O. Lecomte & A. Tenu. *Studia Euphratica: Le moyen Euphrate iraquien révéle par les fouilles preventives de Haditha*. Paris: de Boccard.

Oguchi, H. 2006b. The Date of the Beginning of the Khabur Ware Period 3: Evidence from the Palace of Qarni-Lim at Tell Leilan. *Al-Rafidan* 27: 45-58.

Oguchi, H. 2001. The Origins of Khabur Ware: A Tentative Note. *Al-Rafidan* 22: 71-87.

Oguchi, H. 2000. The "Late" Khabur Ware Problem Once Again. *Al-Rafidan* 21: 103- 126.

Oguchi, H. 1998. Notes on Khabur Ware from Sites Outside its Main Distribution Zone. *Al-Rafidan* 19: 119-133.

Oguchi, H. 1997. A Reassessment of the Distribution of Khabur Ware: An approach from an aspect of its main phase. *Al-Rafidan* 18: 195-224.

Ökse, A. T. 2007. Archaeological evidence for a sixteenth-century BC earthquake on the Southeastern Anatolian Faultline. *Antiquity* Vol 81, No. 312.

Parker, B. & L. Dodd. 2003. The Early Second Millennium Ceramic Assemblage from Kenan Tepe, Southeastern Turkey. A Preliminary Assessment. *Anatolian Studies* 53: 33-69.

Parker Pearson, M. 1999. *The Archaeology of Death and Burial*. Sutton Publishing.

Pearce, J. 2000. The Late Chalcolithic Sequence at Hacinebi Tepe, Turkey. Pp. 115-143 in C. Marro & H. Hauptmann, eds. *Chronologies des Pays du Caucase et de l'Euphrate aux IVe-IIIe millenaires*. Paris: Institut Français d'Etudes Anatoliennes d'Istanbul.

Peacock, D.P.S. 1982. *Pottery in the Roman World: an ethnoarchaeological approach*. London: Longman.

Pecorella, P. E. 1998. L'area G di Tell Barri/Kahat: 1983-1993. Pp. 66-134 in P. E. Pecorella, ed. *Tell Barri/Kahat 2: Relazione sulle campagne 1980-1993 a Tell Barri/*

Kahat, nel bacino del Hābūr (Siria). Rome: Instituto per gli studi Micenei ed Egeo-Anatolici del consiglio nazionale delle ricerche.

Pecorella, P. E. 1990. The Italian Excavations at Tell Barri (Kahat) 1980-1985. Pp. 47-66 in Eichler, S., Wäfler, M., and Warburton, D., eds. *Tall al-Hamidiya 2*. Freiburg: Universitätsverlag.

Philip, G. 1995. Warrior burials in the Ancient Near Eastern Bronze Age: the evidence from Mesopotamia, western Iran and Syria-Palestine. Pp. 140–155 in A.C. Green & S. Campbell, eds. *The Archaeology of Death in the Ancient Near East*. Oxbow Monographs in Archaeology 51.

Pollock, S. 1991. Of Priestesses, Princes and Poor Relations: The Dead in the Royal Cemetery of Ur. *Cambridge Archaeological Journal* 1: 171-89.

Pollock, S. 2007. Death of a Household. Pp. 208-220 in N. Laneri, ed. *Performing Death. Social Analyses of Funerary Traditions in the Ancient Near East and Mediterranean*. Chicago: Oriental Institute Seminars 3.

Pollock, S. & C. Coursey. 1995. Ceramics from Hacinebi Tepe: Chronology and Connections. *Anatolica* 12: 101-141.

Porter, A. 2002. The Dynamics of Death: Ancestors, Pastoralism, and the Origins of a Third-Millennium City in Syria. *Bulletin of the American Schools of Oriental Research* 325: 1-36.

Porter, A. 1995. Tell Banat: Tomb 1. *Damaszener Mitteilungen* 8: 1–50.

Postgate, C. D. Oates & J. Oates. 1997. *The Excavations at Tell al-Rimah: The Pottery*. London: British School of Archaeology in Iraq.

Pulhan, G. 2000. *On the Eve of the Dark Age: Qarni-Lim's Palace at Tell Leilan*. Unpublished Ph.D. Dissertation, Yale University. Ann Arbor: UMI Dissertation Services.

Ramsey, C. & H. Sleeper. 2000. *Architectural Graphic Standards* (10th ed.). New York: Wiley.

Reade, J. 1973. Tell Taya (1972-73). *Iraq* 35: 155-187.

Ristvet, L. 2005. *Settlement, economy and society in the Tell Leilan region, Syria, 3000-1000 BC*. Unpublished PhD dissertation. University of Cambridge.

Ristvet, L. and H. Weiss. 2005. The Habur Region in the Late Third and Early Second Millennium B.C. In W. Orthmann, ed., *The History and Archaeology of Syria*. Vol. 1. Saarbrucken: Saarbrucken Verlag.

Robson, E. 1999. *Mesopotamian Mathematics, 2100-1600 BC. Technical Constants in Bureaucracy and Education*. Oxford: Clarendon Press.

Rothman, M. 2002. *Tepe Gawra, The Evolution of a Small Prehistoric Centre in Northern Iraq*. Philadelphia: University Museum Monograph 112.

Roux, V. 2003. Ceramic Standardization and Intensity of Production: Quantifying Degrees of Specialization. *American Antiquity* 68/4: 768-782.

Sagona, A. 1994. *The Asvan Sites 3, Keban Rescue Excavations, Eastern Anatolia, The Early Bronze Age*. British Institute of Archaeology at Ankara, Monograph 18.

Sahlins, M. 1972. *Stone Age Economics*. New York: Aldine.

Sandweiss, E. 1996. Mind Reading the Urban Landscape, An Approach to the History of American Cities. Pp. 319-357 in L.A. de Cunzo and B.L. Herman, eds. *Historical Archaeology and the Study of American Culture*. Knoxville: University of Tennessee Press.

Sauvage, M. 1992. L'utilisation de la voûte dans l'habitat à Mohammed Diyab. Pp. 23-30 in J.-M. Durand, ed. *Recherches en Haute Mesopotamie, Tell Mohammed Diyab, Campagnes 1990 et 1991*. Paris: Mémoires de NABU 2.

Schwartz, G. 2007. Status, Ideology and Memory in Third-Millennium Syria: "Royal" Tombs at Umm el-Marra. Pp. 39-68 in N. Laneri, ed. *Performing Death. Social Analyses of Funerary Traditions in the Ancient Near East and Mediterranean*. Chicago: Oriental Institute Seminars 3.

Schwartz, G., H. Curvers, S. Dunham, B. Stuart, and J. Weber. 2006. A Third-Millennium B.C. Elite Mortuary Complex at Umm el-Marra, Syria : 2002 and 2004 Excavations. *American Journal of Archaeology* 110: 603-41.

Scurlock, J. 2006. *Magico-Medical Means of Treating Ghost-Induced Illness in Ancient Mesopotamia*. Ancient Magic and Divination III. Brill.

Sebastian, L. 1992. *The Chaco Anasazi: Sociopolitical Evolution in the Prehistoric Southwest*. Cambridge: Cambridge University Press.

Semple, M. in prep. *Pursuing Identity: Constructing Northern Mesopotamian Households, 4th to 2nd Millennium BC*. PhD dissertation, University of Cambridge.

Sinopoli, C. 2003. *The Political Economy of Craft Production: Crafting Empire in South India, C. 1350-1650.* Cambridge: Cambridge University Press.

Sinopoli, C. 1999. Levels of Complexity: Ceramic Variability at Vijayanagara. Pp. 115-136 in J.M. Skibo and G.M. Feinman, eds. *Pottery and People, A Dynamic Interaction*. Salt Lake City: University of Utah Press.

Snell, D. 1983. The Old Babylonian Cuneiform Texts from Chagar Bazar in the Aleppo Museum. *Annales archéologiques arabes syriennes* 33:2: 217-241.

Sołtysiak A. 2006. Frequency of Dental Caries as a Proxy Indicator of Mobility: A Case of the Khabur Basin Human populations. Paper presented at the Study of Food Practices in the Ancient Near East Conference, Venice (Italy), 15-17.06.2006.

Sołtysiak A. 2007. Reduction of Tooth Size in the Khabur Basin (Northern Mesopotamia). Pp. 87-99 in E.B. Bodzár & A. Zsákai, eds., *New Perspectives and Problems in Anthropology*. Newcastle: Cambridge Scholars Publishing.

Spanos, P.Z. 1992. Die Ausgrabungen in Tell Hamad Aga As-Sagir 1990. *Baghdader Mitteilungen* 23: 87-118.

Spanos, P. Z. 1990. Hamad Aga as-Sagir. Pp. 268-270 in Nashef, K., Archaeology in Iraq. *American Journal of Archaeology* 94: 259-289.

Speiser, E.A. 1935. *Excavations at Tepe Gawra, Vol. I, Levels I-VIII*. Philadelphia: ASOR and University of Pennsylvania Press.

Speiser, E. A. 1933. The Pottery of Tell Billa. *Museum Journal* 23: 249-308.

Steele, C. 1990. *Living with the Dead: House Burial at Abu Salabikh, Iraq*. Unpublished Ph.D. dissertation, State University of New York, Binghamton.

Stein, D. 1984. *Khabur Ware and Nuzi Ware: Their Origin, Relationship, and Significance*. Assur 4/1. Undena.

Stein, G. J., and Wattenmaker, P. 1990. The 1987 Tell Leilan regional survey: Preliminary report. Pp. 8-18 in Miller, N. (ed.), *Economy and Settlement in the Near East, MASCA Research Papers in Science and Archaeology*, Supplement to Vol. 7: 5–18. Philadelphia: University of Pennsylvania.

Stol, M. 1976. *Studies in Old Babylonian History*. Leiden: Nederlands Historisch-Archaeologisch Instituut te Istanbul.

Stone, E.C. 2007. The Mesopotamian Urban Experience. Pp. 213-234 in E.C. Stone, ed. *Settlement and Society, Essays dedicated to Robert McCormick Adams*. Los Angeles: Cotsen Institute of Archaeology.

Stone, E.C. 1997. Mesopotamian Houses. Pp. 91-94 in Meyers, E. M., ed. *Oxford Encyclopaedia of the Ancient Near East*. vol. 3. Oxford: Oxford University Press.

Stone, E.C. 1996. Houses, Households and Neighborhoods in the Old Babylonian Period: The Role of Extended Families. Pp. 229-235 in Veenhof, K. R. , ed. *House and Households*. PIHANS 78. Leiden & Istanbul.

Talon, P. (with H. Hammade). 1997. *Old Babylonian Texts from Chagar Bazar*. Akkadica Supplementum 10. Brussels: Fondation Assyriologique Georges-Dossin.

Thureau-Dangin, F. & M. Dunand. 1936. *Til Barsip*. Bibliothèque Archéologique et Historique 23. Paris: Paul Geuthner.

Tobler, A. 1950. *Excavations at Tepe Gawra, Vol. 2*. Philadelphia: University of Pennsylvania Press.

Tomczyk J., Sołtysiak A. 2007a. Preliminary Report on Human Remains from Tell Masaikh, Season 2005. *Athenaeum. Studi di Letteratura e Storia dell'Antichità* 95(1): 442-445.

Tomczyk J., Sołtysiak A. 2007b. Preliminary Report on Human Remains from Tell Ashara/Terqa, Season 2005. *Athenaeum. Studi di Letteratura e Storia dell'Antichità* 95(1): 439-442.

Tomczyk J., Sołtysiak A. 2009. Zmienność wskaźników platyknemii, platymerii i pilastrii w populacjach środkowej doliny Eufratu (Syria). Pp. 273–277 in W. Dzieduszycki & J. Wrzesiński, eds. *Metody. Źródła. Dokumentacja. Funeralia Lednickie. Spotkanie 11*. Poznań: SNAP.

Trotter M. & G.C. Gleser. 1952. Estimation of Stature from Long Bones of American Whites and Negroes. *American Journal of Physical Anthropology* 10: 463-514.

Trigger, B. 1967. Settlement Archaeology, Its Goals and Promise. *American Antiquity* 32/2: 149-160.

Tunca, Ö. & A. Baghdo (eds.), 2008. *Chagar Bazar III (Syrie). Les trouvailles épigraphiques et sigillographiques du chantier I (2000-2002)*. Leuven: Publications de la Mission archéologique de l'Université de Liège en Syrie.

Tunca, Ö., A. Baghdo & W. Cruells. 2006. *Chagar Bazar (Syrie) I: Les sondages préhistoriques (1999-2001)*. Leuven: Peeters.

Tunca, Ö. and D. Lacambre 2002. Note préliminaire sur les nouvelles découvertes épigraphiques de Šaġir Bāzār. Pp. 545-546 in: D. Charpin and J.-M. Durand. (eds.). *Florilegium marianum VI. Mémoires de NABU, 7*, Paris.

Tunca, Ö., A. McMahon & A. Baghdo, eds. 2007. *Chagar Bazar (Syrie) II: Les vestiges «post-akkadiens» du chantier D et études diverses*. Leuven: Peeters.

Ucko, P. 1968. *Anthropomorphic Figurines of Predynastic Egypt and Neolithic Crete*. London: Royal Anthropological Institute.

Ur, J., P. Karsgaard & J. Oates. 2007. Early Urban Development in the Near East. *Science* 317 (5842): 1188.

van der Leeuw, S. 1992. Giving the Potter a Choice: Conceptual aspects of pottery techniques. Pp. 238-288 in P. Lemonnier, ed., *Technological Choices, Transformations in Material Cultures since the Neolithic*. London: Routledge.

van de Mieroop, M. 2004. *A History of the Ancient Near East*. Oxford: Blackwells.

van der Toorn, K. 1996. Domestic Religion in Ancient Mesopotamia. Pp. 69-78 in K. Veenhof, ed. *Houses and Households in Ancient Mesopotamia.* Leiden: Nederlands Historisch-Archaeologisch Instituut.

van Koppen, F. 1999/2000. Review of P. Talon, Old Babylonian Texts from Chagar Bazar. *Archiv für Orientforschung* 46/47: 336-341.

Varien, M.D. & J. Potter. 1997. Unpacking the Discard Equation: Simulating the Accumulation of Artifacts in the Archaeological Record. *American Antiquity* 62(2): 194-213.

Voigt, M. 2000. Çatal Höyük in context: ritual at Early Neolithic sites in Central and Eastern Turkey. Pp. 163-190 in I. Kuijt, ed. *Life in Neolithic Farming Communities: Social Organization, Identity and Differentiation.* London.

Walker P.L., Bathurst R.R., Richman R., Gjerdrum T., & Andrushko V.A. 2009. The Causes of Porotic Hyperostosis and Cribra Orbitalia: A Reappraisal of the Iron-deficiency-anemia Hypothesis. *American Journal of Physical Anthropology* 139(2): 109-125.

Wattenmaker, P. 1998. *Household and State in Upper Mesopotamia, Specialized Economy and the Social Uses of Goods in an Early Complex Society.* Washington DC: Smithsonian Institution Press.

Weiss, H. 1986. The origins of Tell Leilan and the conquest of space in 3rd millennium Mesopotamia. Pp. 71–108 in H. Weiss, ed., *The Origins of Cities in Dry-Farming Syria*, Four Quarters Press, Guilford.

Weiss, H., P. Akkermans, G. Stein, D. Parayre & R. Whiting. 1990. 1985 Excavations at Tell Leilan, Syria. *American Journal of Archaeology* 94: 529-581.

Weiss, H. and R. Bradley. 2001. What Drives Societal Collapse? *Science* 291: 609-610.

Weiss, H., and Courty, M.-A. 1993. The genesis and collapse of the Akkadian empire: The accidental refraction of historical law. Pp. 131–155 in M. Liverani, ed., *Akkad: The First World Empire*, Sargon SRL, Padua, Italy.

Weiss, H., Courty, M.-A., Wetterstrom, W., Guichard, F., Senior, L., Meadow, R., and Curnow, A. 1993. The genesis and collapse of third millennium north Mesopotamian civilization. *Science* 261: 995–1004.

Weiss, H., F. de Lillis, D. de Moulins, J. Eidem, T. Guilderson, U. Kasten, T. Larsen, L. Mori, L. Ristvet, E. Rova, W. Wetterstrom. 2002. Revising the Contours of History at Tell Leilan. *Annales archéologiques arabes syriennes, Cinquantenaire.*

Whitelaw, T. M. 2001. Reading between the Tablets: Assessing Mycenaean Palatial Involvement in Ceramic Production and Consumption. Pp. 51-79 in S. Voutsaki and J. Killen, eds. *Economy and Politics in the Mycenaean Palace States.* Cambridge Philological Society Supplement 27.

Wilkinson T. J. 1994. The Structure and Dynamics of Dry-Farming States in Upper Mesopotamia. *Current Anthropology* 35/5: 483-505.

Wilkinson, T. J. 1998. Tell Beydar survey. Pp. 19-28 in *The Oriental Institute 1997–1998 Annual Report,* Oriental Institute, University of Chicago, Chicago.

Wilkinson, T. J. 2000a. Regional Approaches to Mesopotamian Archaeology: The Contribution of Archaeological Surveys. *Journal of Archaeological Research*, Vol. 8, No. 3: 219-267.

Wilkinson, T. J. 2000b. Archaeological survey of the Tell Baidar region, Syria, 1997: A preliminary report. Pp. 1-37 in K. Van Lerberghe and G. Voet., eds. *Tell Baidar: Environmental and Technical Studies.* Subartu VI, Turnhout.

Wilkinson, T. J. 2002. The Settlement Transition of the Second Millennium BC in the Western Khabur. Pp. 361-372 in: L. al-Gailani Werr, J. Curtis, H. Martin, A. McMahon, J. Oates & J. Reade, eds. *Of Pots and Plans*, London.

Wilkinson, T.J. 2003. *Archaeological Landscapes of the Near East.* Tucson: University of Arizona Press.

Willey, G. 1953. *Prehistoric Settlement Patterns in the Virú Valley, Peru.* Smithsonian Institution Bureau of American Ethnology Bulletin 155. Washington DC: Smithsonian.

Willey, G. 1968. Settlement Archaeology: An Appraisal. Pp. 208-226 in K.C. Chang, ed. *Settlement Archaeology.* Palo Alto: National Press Books.

Wobst, M. 1977. Stylistic Behavior and Information Exchange. Pp. 317-342 in C. E. Cleland, ed. *Papers for the Director: Research Essays in Honor of James B. Griffin.* Papers of the Museum of Anthropology 61. Ann Arbor: University of Michigan.

Woolley, L. 1976. *Ur Excavations VII: The Old Babylonian Period.* London: British Museum and University Museum.

Wright, H.T., J. Oates *et al.* (forthcoming) *The Tell Brak Regional Survey.* McDonald Institute Monographs.

Yuhong,W. 1994. Mebbidum of Hab(b)a'um in the tablets of Yahdun-Lim and Hab(b)a'um (not Hashshum!) of Membida in ARM 1 37. *NABU* 1994 (3): 58-59.

Zeigler, N. 2000. Aspects économiques des guerres de Samsi-Addu. Pp. 13-33 in J. Andreau, P. Briant & R. Descat, eds. *Économie antique: La guerre dans les economies antiques.* Paris: St. Bertrand de Comminges.

Zettler, R.L. 1993. *Nippur III: Kassite Buildings in Area WC-1.* Oriental Institute Publications 111. Chicago: Oriental Institute.

Plates

Plates 1-9   Burials: detailed plans and grave good groups   244-261

Plates 10-68   Pottery, by Type   262-379

Abbreviations used:
R: Rim diameter at greatest extent
M: Maximum vessel diameter
B: Base diameter
H: Vessel height

In cases of sherds or incomplete vessels, the diameters given are approximated to the nearest centimeter or half-centimeter.
Ware: subjective colours for core and exterior surface are given; if only one colour is listed, the core and surface are the same colour.

Plates 69-88   Objects, by Type   380-421

Burial Plates

Plate 1 Area A, Tomb 4

Plan and grave goods

PLATE 1

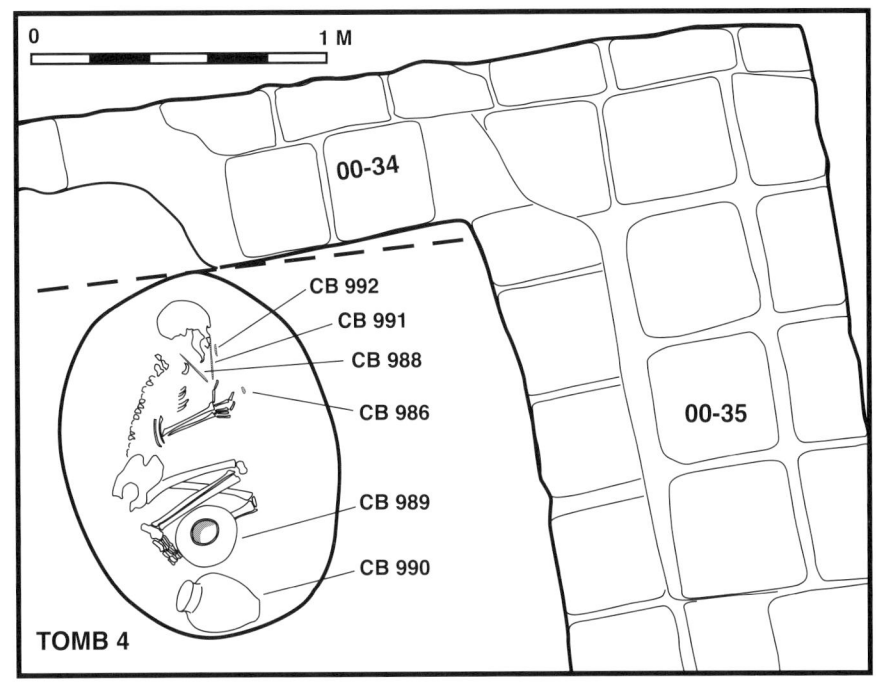

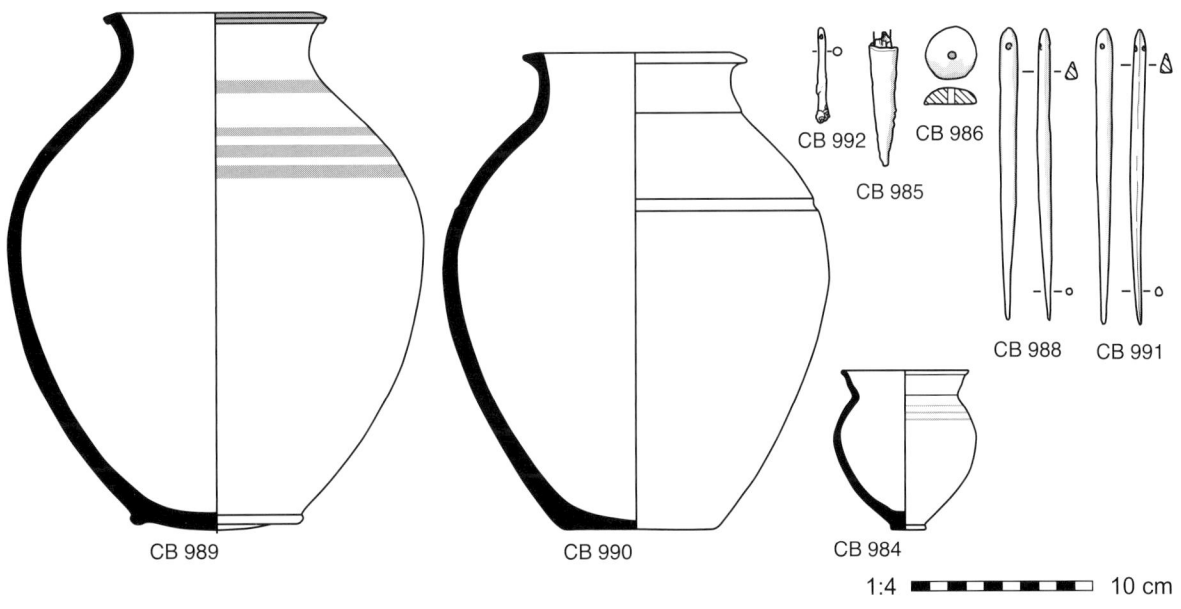

Plate 2 a) Area A, Tombs 8 and 9, plan

b) Area A, Tomb 12, plan and possible grave vessel

c) Area A, Tomb 34, plan

PLATE 2

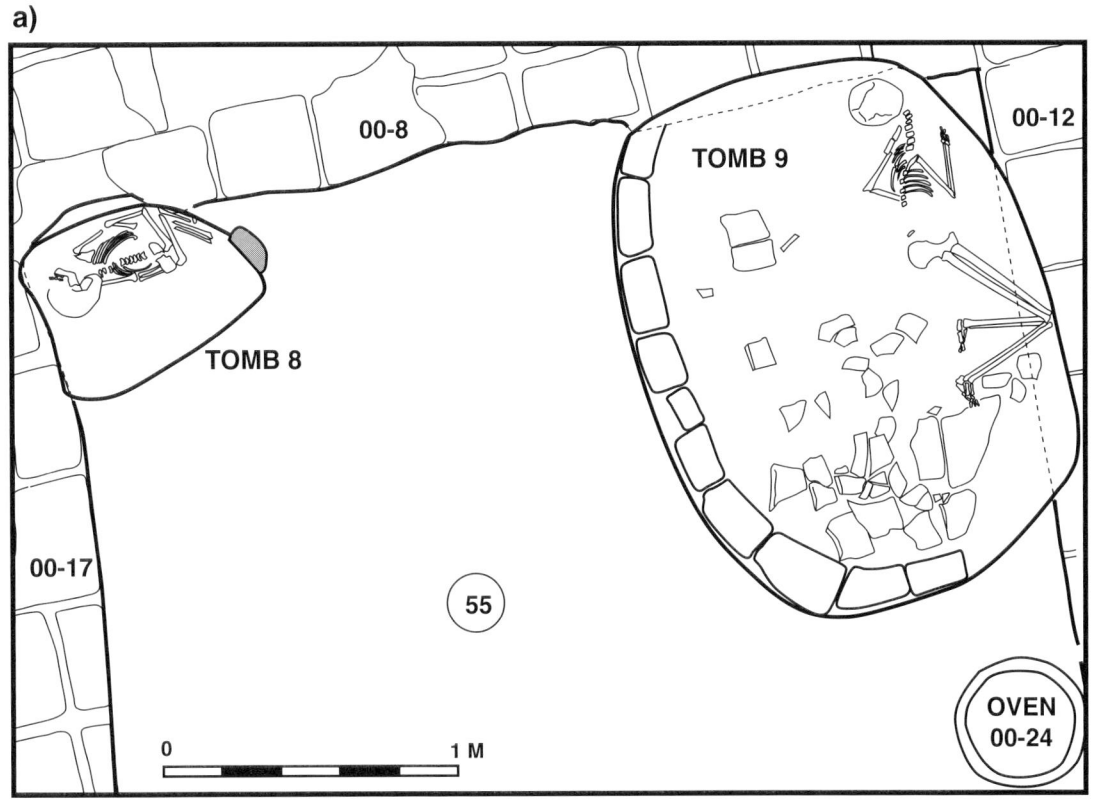
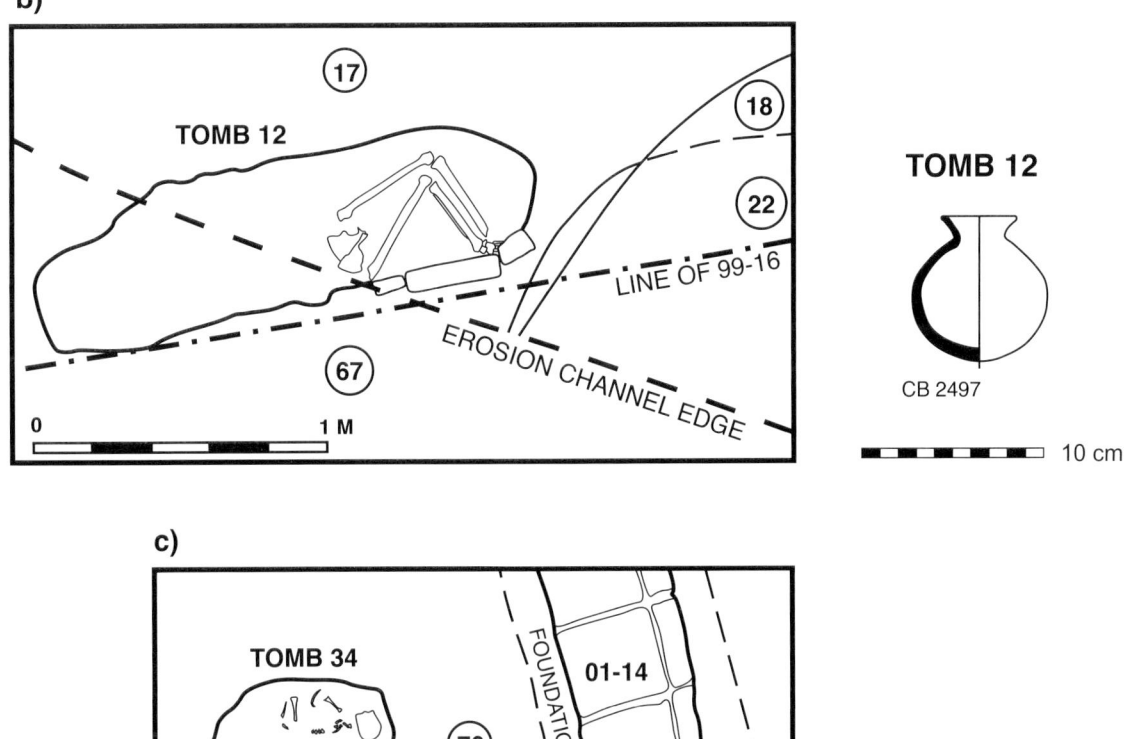

Plate 3 a) Area A, Tomb 35, plan and burial jar

b) Area A, Tomb 38, plan

c) Area A, Tomb 41, grave goods and plan

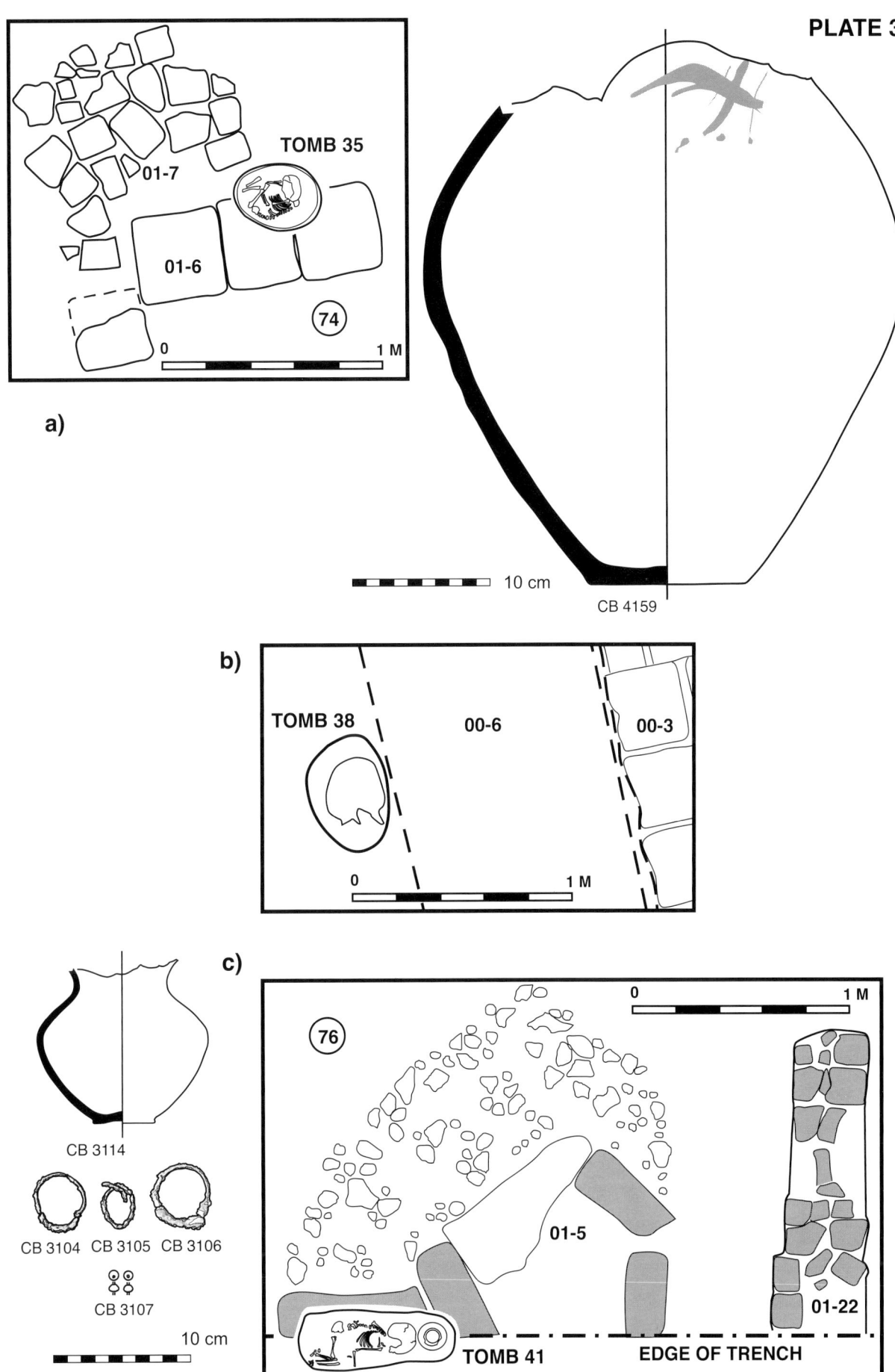

PLATE 3

Plate 4 a) Area G, Tomb 15, plan

b) Area G, Tomb 32, plan

c) Area G, Tomb 49, plan

PLATE 4

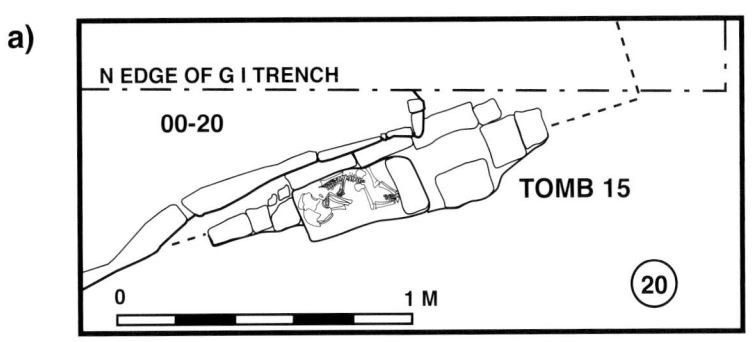

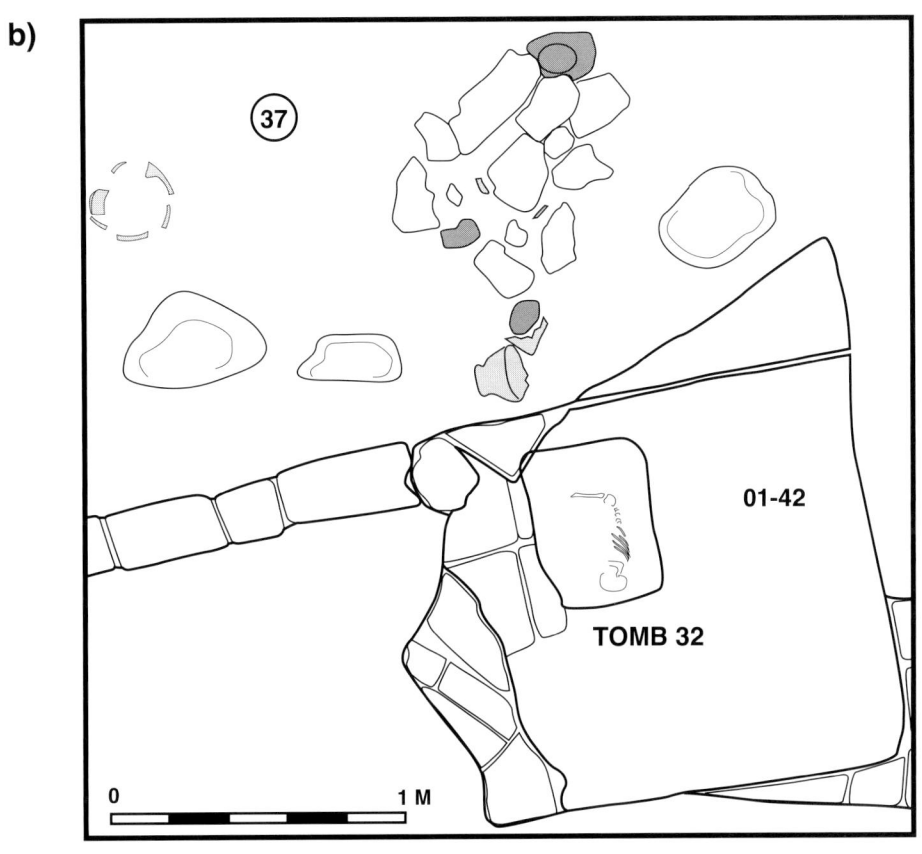

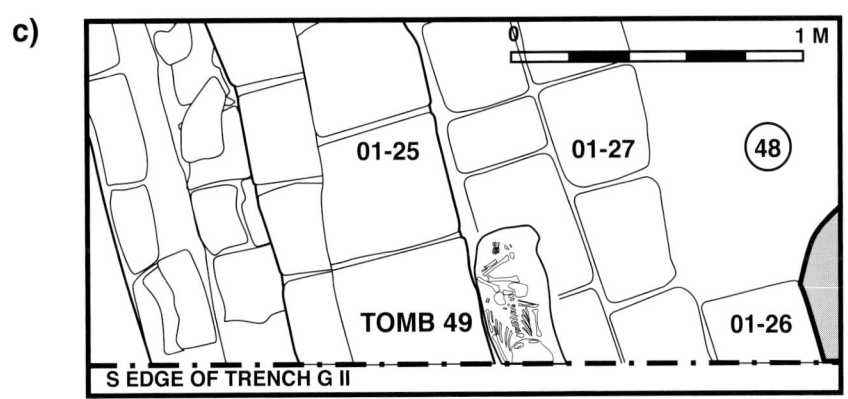

Plate 5 a) Area G, Tomb 18, plan, section, overview

b) Area G, Tomb 37, plan

PLATE 5

a)

b)
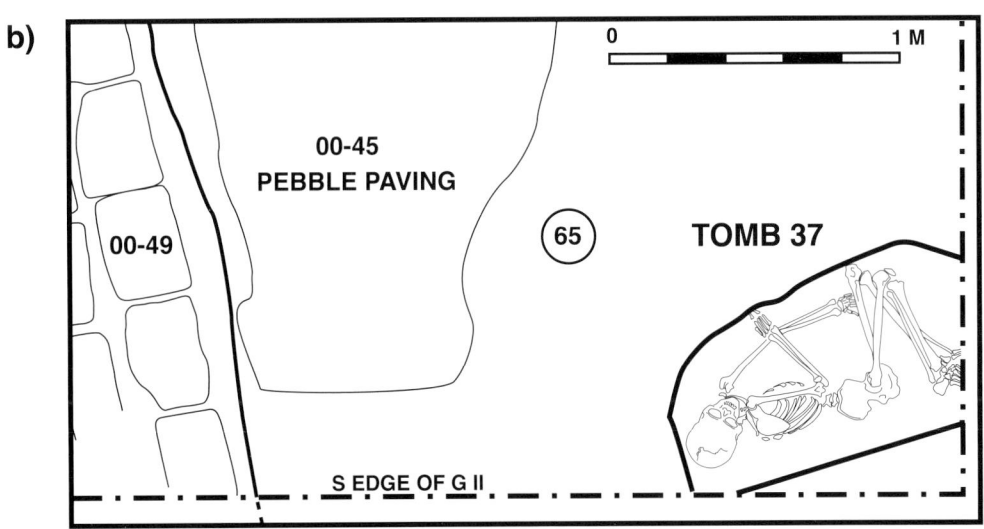

253

Plate 6 a) Area G, Tomb 39, grave goods, plan

b) Area G, plan of Building G 2 courtyard with Tombs 10, 11, 13 & 4.3

c) Area G, Tomb 10, plan and grave goods

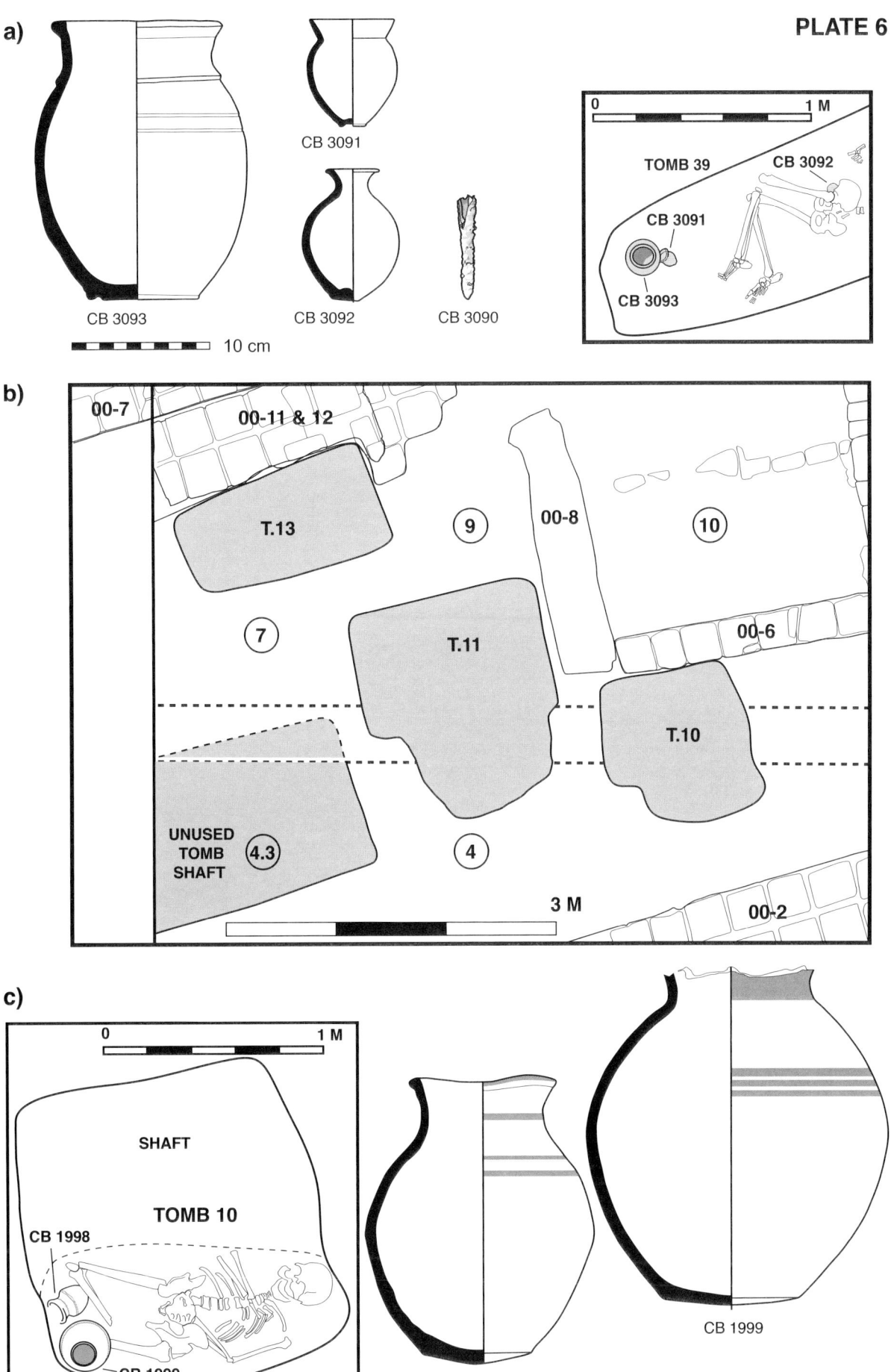

PLATE 6

255

Plate 7 a) Area G, Tomb 11, plan and grave goods

b) Area G, L. 4.3, vessel from possible grave shaft

a) TOMB 11

CB 2001

CB 2066

CB 2093

CB 2000

1:4 10 cm

b) POSSIBLE GRAVE SHAFT, L. 4.3

CB 1989

1:4 10 cm

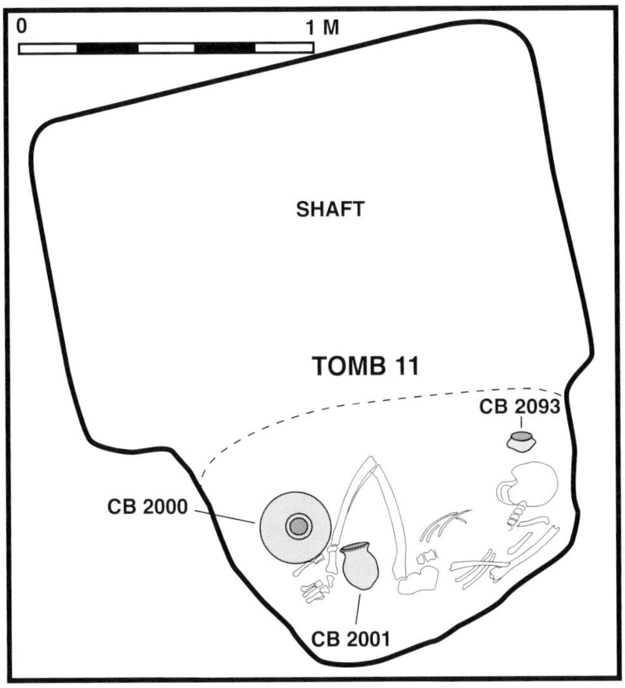

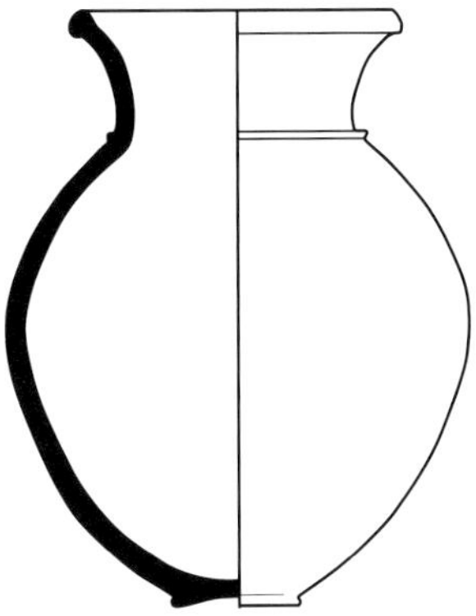

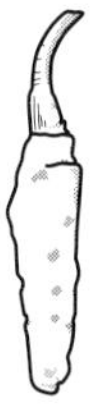

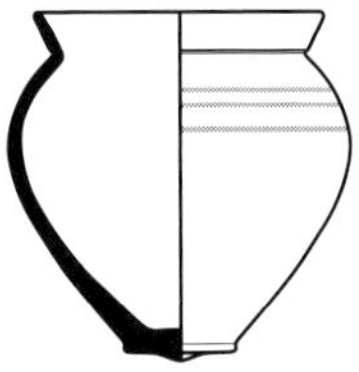

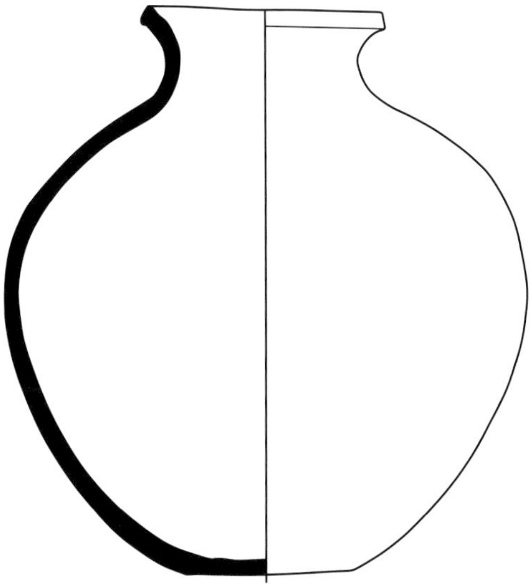

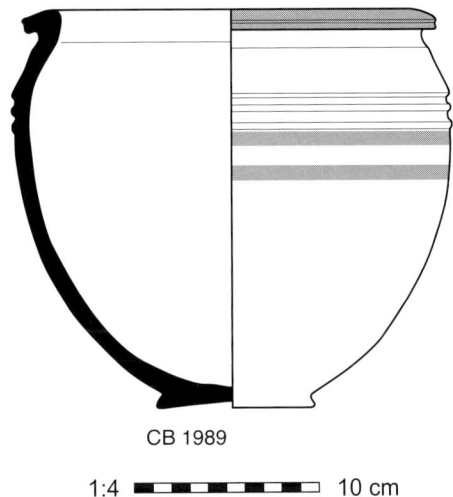

Plate 8 Area G, Tomb 13, grave goods and plan

TOMB 13 **PLATE 8**

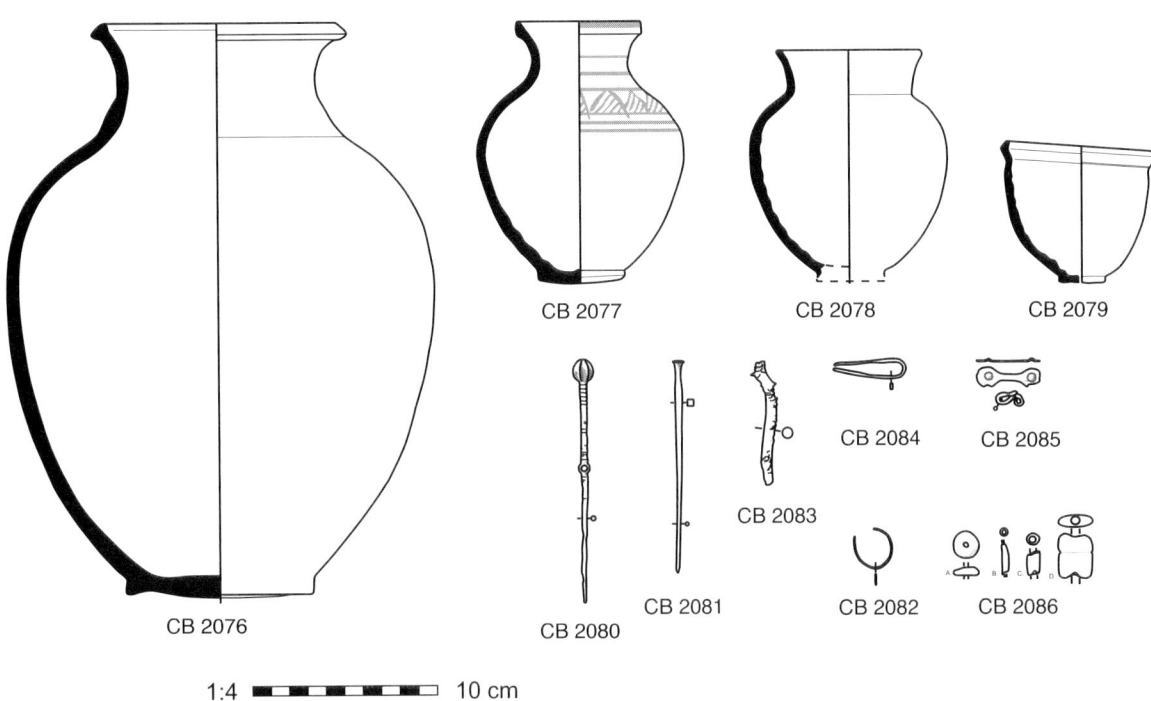

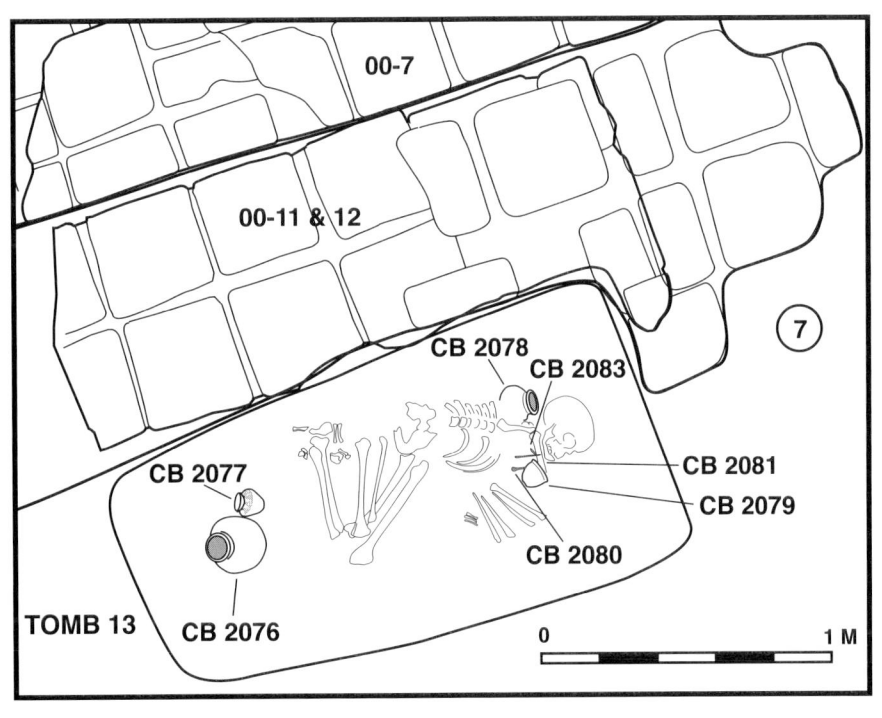

Plate 9 a) Area G, Tomb 33, grave goods and plan

b) Area A, Tomb 30, grave goods

c) Area A, Tomb 7, plan, bracelet

a) TOMB 33

PLATE 9

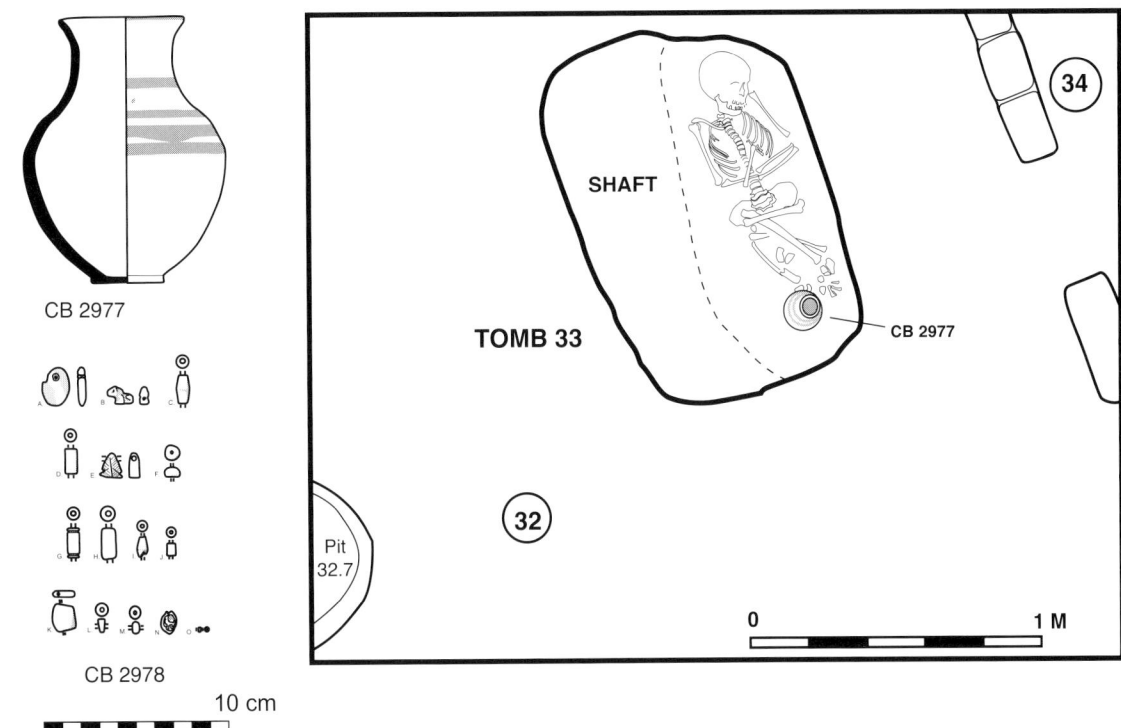

b) TOMB 30

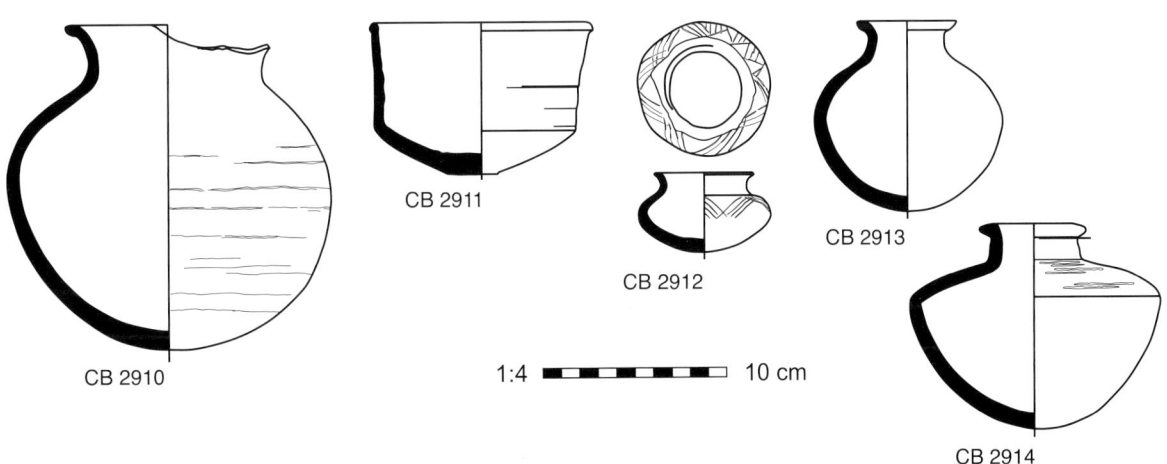

c) TOMB 7

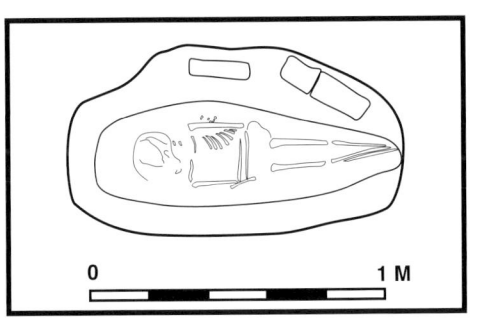
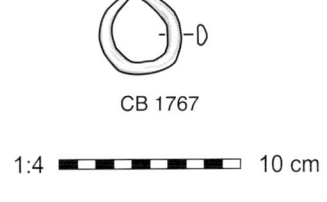

Plate 10: *Small Bowls*

	CB number	Area	Phase	Locus and Lot number	Dimensions	Ware, comments
1	CB 2169	A II	IA	L. 67.2 E 188.3	R: 12 cm	Ware: orange-brown. Temper: common fine chaff. Red paint "drip" on interior, four red paint slashes on rim.
2	CB 3205	G II	III	L. 36.1 F 207.4	R: 16 cm	Ware: buff. Temper: sparse fine lime.
3	CB 364:3	A I	I	L. 20.1 D 73	R: 10 cm	Ware: buff. Temper: sparse chaff, lime. Groups of three red paint slashes on rim.
4	CB 2034	A II	IA	L. 67.1 E 29.3	R: 17 cm	Ware: orange. Temper: sparse fine sand.
5	CB 3108	G III	II/2	L. 28.3 F 80.1	R: 9 cm	Ware: buff. Temper: sparse fine lime. Brown paint band on rim.
6	CB 1814	G II	II/2	L. 51.2 E 91.4	R: 13 cm	Ware: grey core, orange-buff surface. Temper: medium chaff. Possibly Late Chalcolithic?
7	CB 958:1	A I	II	L. 16.3 D 386	R: 18 cm	Ware: buff. Temper: common chaff, lime. Four black paint slashes across rim.
8	CB 2833	A II	I	L. 76.3 F 5.2	R: 18 cm	Ware: orange-grey core, orange surface. Temper: sparse chaff and sand, mica inclusions. Orange-brown paint bands.
9	CB 706:3	A I	II	L. 14.1 D 333	R: 10 cm	Ware: grey core, buff surface. Temper: common chaff, lime.
10	CB 3219	G IV	III	L. 40.3 F 69.2	R: 18 cm	Ware: pale orange core, pale buff surface. Temper: common fine sand.
11	CB 1793	A I	II	L. 41.1 E 37.1	R: 9 cm	Ware: grey-buff core, buff surface. Temper: sparse sand.
12	CB 1735	A I	II	L. 30.1 D 373	R: 15 cm	Ware: buff core, greenish surface. Temper: occasional lime, sand. Brown-black paint band on rim.
13	CB 1884	G I	II/1	L. 2.1 E 61.5	R: 15 cm	Ware: buff. Temper: sparse fine chaff. Internal and external red-orange paint bands.
14	CB 2798	G IV	I	L. 23.1 F 51.1	R: 17 cm	Ware: buff core, greenish-buff surface. Temper: none.
15	CB 1928	G I	II/1	L. 11.1 E 74.1	R: 12 cm	Ware: dark buff. Temper: fine lime.
16	CB 2128	G II	II/2	L. 51.5 E 93.3	R: 12 cm	Ware: buff. Temper: none.
17	CB 2166	G II	II/2	L. 54.3 E 105.2	R: 12 cm	Ware: buff. Temper: sparse lime.
18	CB 3220	G IV	III	L. 40.3 F 69.2	R: 14 cm	Ware: brown core, buff surface. Temper: common fine lime.

SMALL SHALLOW BOWLS

PLATE 10

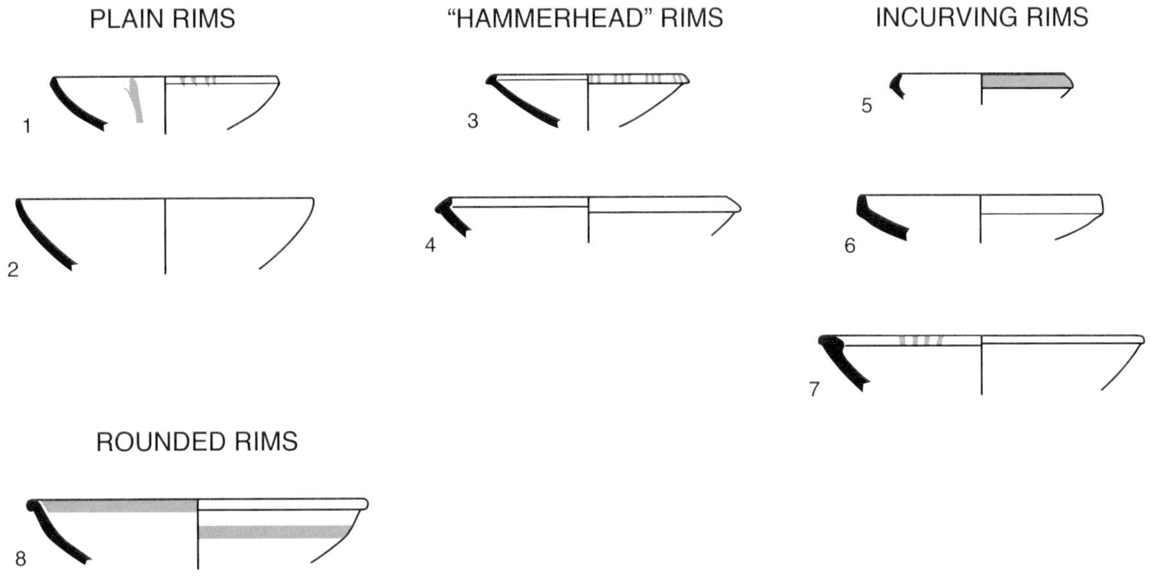

PLAIN RIMS
"HAMMERHEAD" RIMS
INCURVING RIMS
1
2
3
4
5
6
7
ROUNDED RIMS
8

SMALL DEEP BOWLS

ROUNDED RIMS
INCURVING RIMS
FINE THICKENED RIMS
9
10
11
12
13
14
15
16
17
18
1:4
10 cm

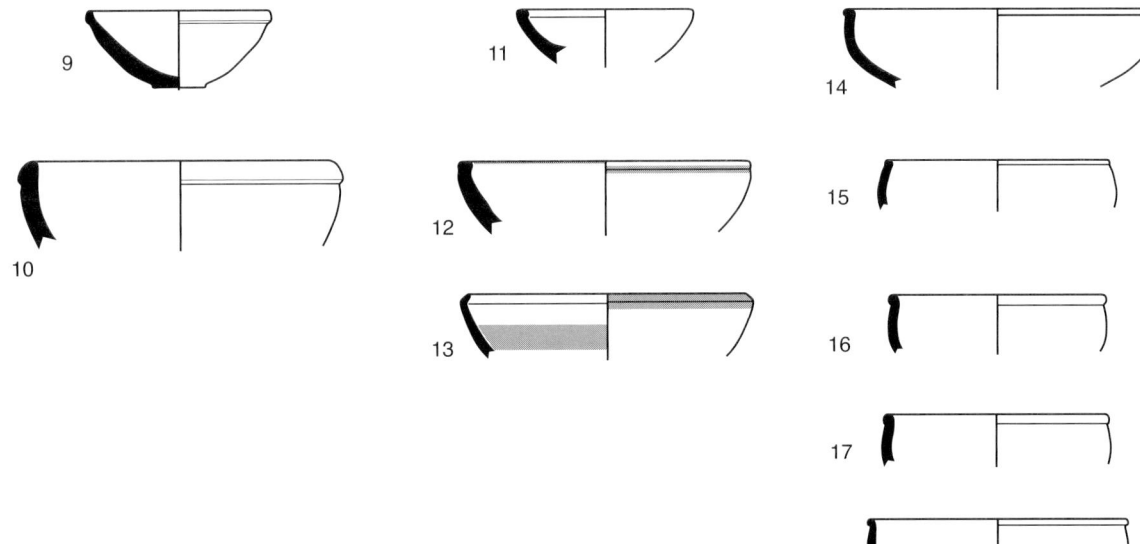

Plate 11: *Medium shallow bowls*

	CB number	Area	Phase	Locus and Lot number	Dimensions	Ware, comments
1	CB 1959	A II	II	L. 61.3 E 25.1	R: 20 cm	Ware: orange-buff core, buff surface. Temper: fine lime.
2	CB 1731	A I	II	L. 26.1 D 353	R: 21 cm	Ware: buff. Temper: occasional chaff, lime.
3	CB 1737	A I	II	L. 30.1 D 373	R: 21 cm	Ware: green-buff core, pale buff surface. Temper: sand. Red-brown paint slashes across rim.
4	CB 3255	G II	II/2	L. 54.10 F 210.1	R: 29 cm	Ware: black core, orange-buff surface. Temper: common medium chaff.
5	CB 2839	A II	I	L. 74.1 F 3.2	R: 31 cm	Ware: dark buff core, greenish-buff surface. Temper: common chaff, sparse medium lime. Knife-shaving near base.
6	CB 3040	A II	II	L. 81.2 F 35.3	R: 25 cm	Ware: grey core, buff surface. Temper: common medium chaff.
7	CB 44:1	A I	S	L. 1.2 D 17	R: 25 cm	Ware: grey core, buff surface. Temper: common chaff, lime.
8	CB 2413	G I	II/1	L. 2.1 E 68.1	R: 23 cm	Ware: pale buff. Temper: abundant chaff, occasional lime, mica inclusions.
9	CB 1909	G I	II/1	L. 2.1 E 61.6	R: 23 cm	Ware: buff. Temper: fine sand, lime.
10	CB 3944	G III	II/2	L. 39.2 F 81.2	R: 22 cm	Ware: grey core, buff surface. Temper: common medium chaff. Red paint slashes on rim.
11	CB 2550	G II	II/2	L. 62.5 E 334.1	R: 23 cm	Medium shallow bowl. Ware: buff. Temper: common medium chaff, sparse fine lime.
12	CB 3809	G II	II/2	L. 54.10 F 210.5	R: 24 cm	Ware: black core, buff surface. Temper: common chaff and medium lime.
13	CB 3891	G II	II/2	L. 54.10 F 210.6	R: 26 cm	Ware: orange core, yellow-buff surface. Temper: common medium-large chaff, sparse medium lime.
14	CB 2127	G II	II/2	L. 51.5 E 93.3	R: 29 cm	Ware: pale brown. Temper: occasional chaff.
15	CB 3030	G II	III	L. 37.1 F 208.2	R: 26 cm	Ware: buff core, green surface. Temper: common medium chaff, sparse medium lime.
16	CB 1988	A II	I	L. 58.1 E 13.4	R: 26 cm	Ware: buff core, orange-buff surface. Temper: common chaff, sparse large grey grit.
17	CB 1717	A I	II	L. 16.1 D 376	R: 28 cm	Ware: grey core, pale buff surface. Temper: common medium chaff, lime.
18	CB 1901	A II	II	L. 54.2 E 11.1	R: 23.5 cm	Ware: grey-brown core, pale buff surface. Temper: occasional medium chaff, mica inclusions.
19	CB 962:1	A I	III	L. 33.2 D 388	R: 24 cm	Ware: green. Temper: common chaff, lime.
20	CB 2457	G I	II/2	L. 4.6 E 84.2	R: 25 cm	Ware: grey-buff. Temper: common medium chaff, mica inclusions.
21	CB 2452	G I	II/2	L. 9.6 E 241.1	R: 29 cm	Ware: buff. Temper: common medium chaff, fine lime.
22	CB 3218	G IV	III	L. 40.3 F 69.2	R: 30 cm	Ware: buff core, orange-buff surface. Temper: common coarse chaff. Knife scraped near base.

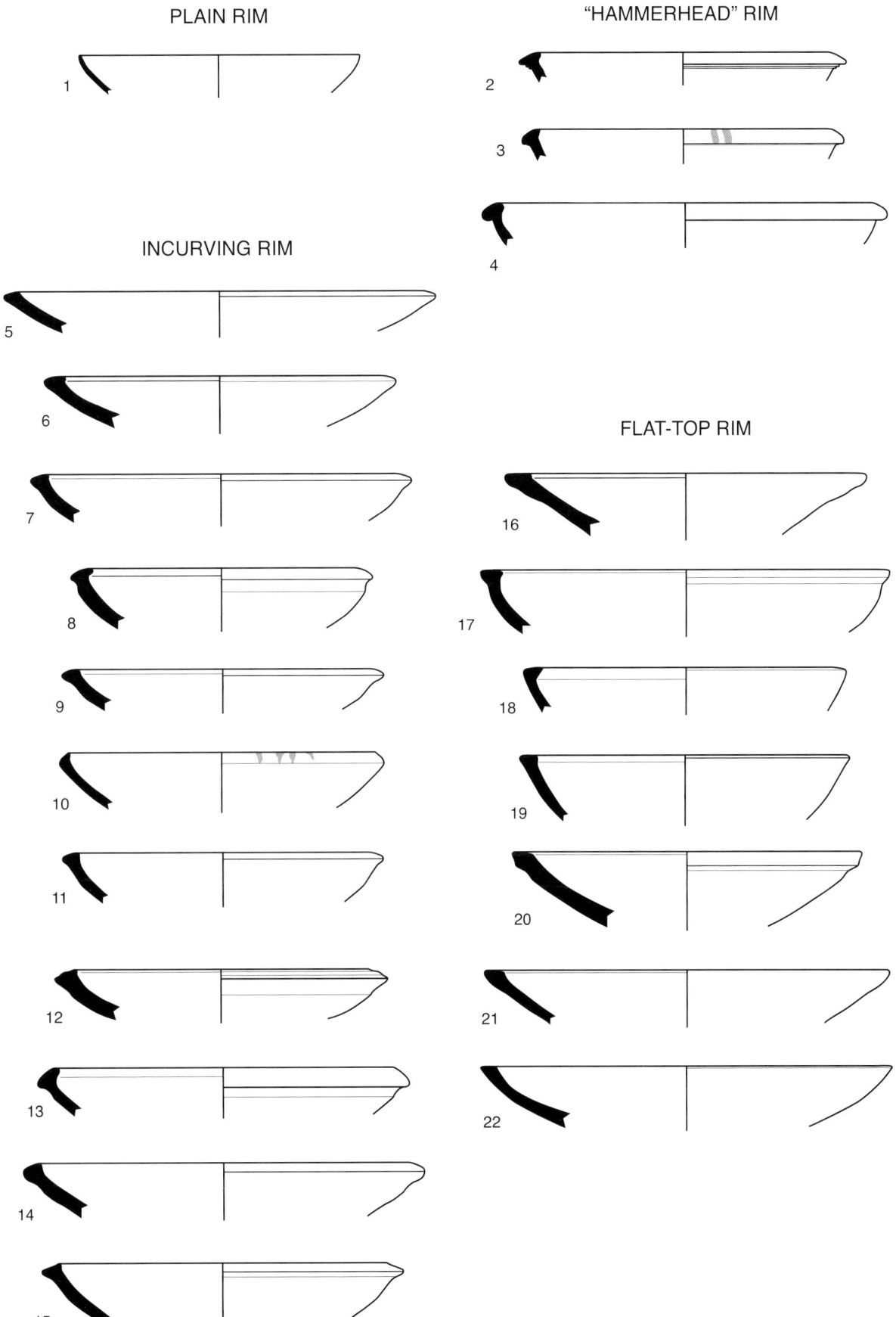

Plate 12: *Medium Deep Bowls*

	CB number	Area	Phase	Locus and Lot number	Dimensions	Ware, comments
1	CB 719:1	A I	I	L. 17.2 D 340	R: 22 cm	Ware: red. Temper: common chaff, lime. Red painted bands and cross-hatched triangles.
2	CB 4195	G II	IV	L. 74.1 F 228.1	R: 19 cm	Ware: buff core, buff-orange surface. Temper: common medium chaff, common fine-medium lime.
3	CB 1859	G I	II/1	L. 5.1 E 63.4	R: 31 cm	Ware: red-orange. Temper: abundant lime.
4	CB 4210	G II	III	01-24 F 217.1	R: 23 cm	Ware: buff. Temper: occasional medium chaff, fine lime.
5	CB 1785	A II	S	L. 50.1 E 1.1	R: 29 cm	Ware: grey core, buff surface. Temper: fine chaff. Three red-brown paint slashes across rim.
6	CB 2099	A II	IA	L. 67.2 E 188.1	R: 28 cm	Ware: pink core, buff surface. Temper: chaff and lime.
7	CB 2168	A II	IA	L. 67.2 E 188.3	R: 26.5 cm	Ware: buff core, pink-buff surface. Temper: common medium chaff, mica inclusions.
8	CB 1990	A II	II	L. 61.3 E 25.3	R: 32 cm	Ware: buff core, pale buff surface. Temper: abundant chaff, lime. Scattered horizontal burnishing on exterior.
9	CB 2152	G II	II/2	L. 54.2 E 96.3	R: 23 cm	Ware: buff-yellow. Temper: common chaff.
10	CB 2011	G I	II/2	L. 4.6 E 66.6	R: 20 cm	Ware: grey. Temper: occasional fine chaff, sparse lime.
11	CB 2836	G II	III	L. 27.1 F 202.1	R: 28 cm	Ware: orange core, buff surface. Temper: common medium chaff.
12	CB 4241	G II	III	L. 77.2 F 229.1	R: 34 cm	Ware: pink-buff core, buff surface. Temper: sparse medium chaff, common fine lime.

MEDIUM DEEP BOWLS

PLATE 12

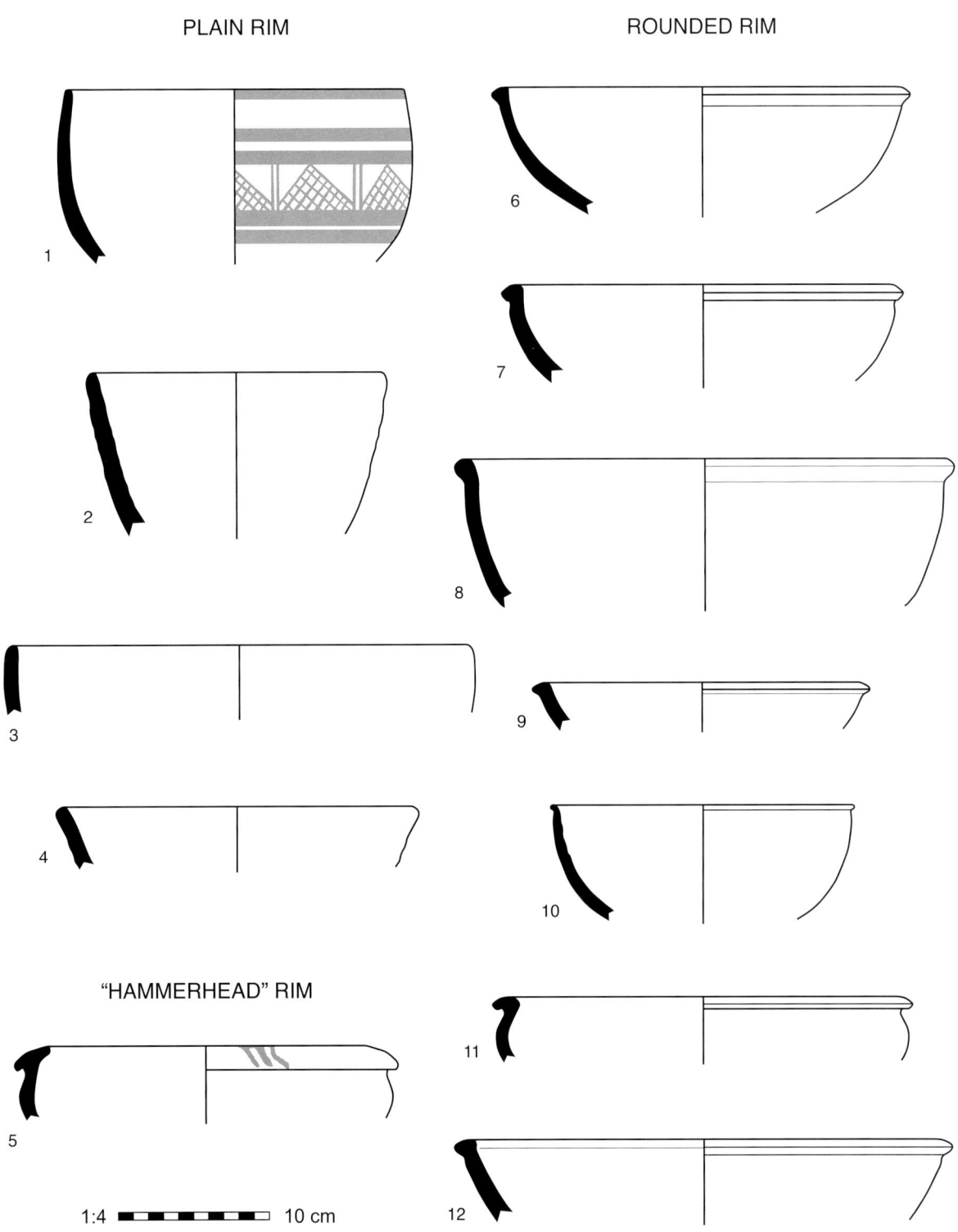

Plate 13: *Medium Deep Bowls*

	CB number	Area	Phase	Locus and Lot number	Dimensions	Ware, comments
1	CB 1834	A II	II	L. 54.1 E 7.1	R: 26 cm	Ware: grey temper, red surface. Temper: chaff and fine lime. Two red-brown paint slashes across rim.
2	CB 2595	G II	II/2	L. 65.1 E 118.1	R: 22.5 cm	Ware: buff. Temper: common medium chaff, fine lime.
3	CB 2010	G I	II/2	L. 4.6 E 66.6	R: 22 cm	Ware: pink-buff core, pale buff surface. Temper: occasional chaff.
4	CB 2024	G II	II/1	L. 55.1 E 97.1	R: 25 cm	Ware: grey core, orange-buff surface. Temper: abundant chaff.
5	CB 1974	G I	II/1	L. 10.1 E 73.1	R: 25 cm	Ware: grey core, orange surface. Temper: abundant chaff, lime.
6	CB 1966	G II	II/1	L. 56.1 E 98.1	R: 33 cm	Ware: grey core, buff-green surface. Temper: abundant chaff, lime.
7	CB 3023	G II	II/2	L. 54.10 F 210.2	R: 26 cm	Ware: black core, buff surface. Temper: common medium chaff. Smoothed surfaces.
8	CB 3801	G II	II/2	L. 54.10 F 210.5	R: 24 cm	Ware: black core, buff surface. Temper: common medium chaff.
9	CB 3181	G IV	II/1	L. 34.4 F 70.1	R: 26 cm	Ware: green. Temper: common medium chaff and lime. Black paint slashes on rim.
10	CB 3248	G II	II/2	L. 54.10 F 210.1	R: 23 cm	Ware: buff core, orange surface. Temper: common fine-medium chaff and fine lime. Smoothed surface.
11	CB 2100	A II	IA	L. 67.2 E 188.1	R: 31 cm	Ware: red-pink core, green-buff surface. Temper: fine chaff. Sharp horizontal grooves.
12	CB 2141	G II	II/1A	L. 59.1 E 101.1	R: 33 cm	Ware: grey core, orange surface. Temper: common chaff, fine lime. Shallow horizontal grooves.
13	CB 2515	G I	II/2	L. 11.3 E 248.1	R: 25 cm	Ware: buff core and surface. Temper: common medium chaff, fine lime. Horizontal grooves.
14	CB 1900	A II	II	L. 54.2 E 11.1	R: 26 cm	Ware: orange core, pale buff surface. Temper: fine sand.
15	CB 2103	A I	II	L. 41.1 E 60.1	R: 30 cm	Ware: grey core, orange surface. Temper: common chaff, fine lime.
16	CB 1987	A II	II	L. 64.1 (T. 9) E 24.3	R: 24 cm	Ware: buff core, pale buff surface. Temper: sparse chaff, lime.
17	CB 2221	G II	II/2	L. 51.5 E 93.4	R: 25 cm	Ware: buff. Temper: common medium chaff, fine lime, mica inclusions. Occasional blobs of dark red paint on rim and interior.
18	CB 3800	G II	II/2	L. 54.10 F 210.5	R: 27 cm	Ware: yellow-green. Temper: common medium chaff. Traces of black paint slashes on rim.
19	CB 2902	G II	II/2	L. 54.9 F 206.1	R: 24 cm	Ware: black core, orange surface. Temper: common medium chaff and fine lime.
20	CB 4006	G II	III	L. 70.1 F 220.3	R: 26 cm B: 12.5 cm H: 8.3 cm	Ware: pink core, buff surface. Temper: common medium chaff, fine-medium lime.

MEDIUM DEEP BOWLS

PLATE 13

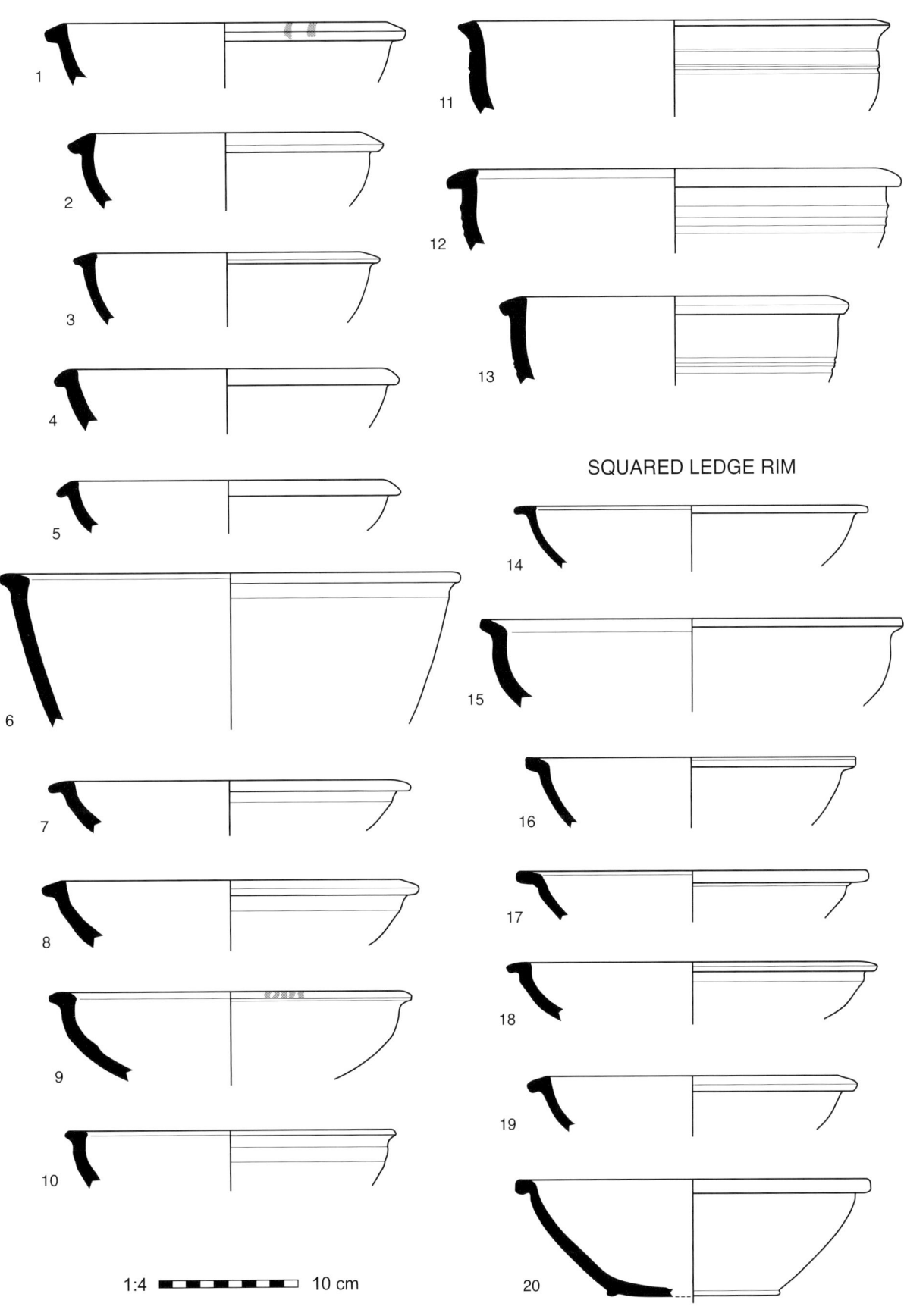

TRIANGULAR LEDGE RIM

SQUARED LEDGE RIM

1:4 ■━━■━━■ 10 cm

Plate 14: *Large Shallow and Deep Bowls*

	CB number	Area	Phase	Locus and Lot number	Dimensions	Ware, comments
1	CB 55:2	A I	S	L. 1.2 D 22	R: 30 cm	Ware: grey core, reddish surface. Temper: common chaff. Red painted star-in-metope decoration on rim.
2	CB 1798	A I	II	L. 40.4 E 36.1	R: 35 cm	Ware: grey core, reddish surface. Temper: fine chaff. Two red-brown paint slashes across rim.
3	CB 2176	G II	II/1a	L. 59.3 E 103.2	R: 40 cm	Ware: orange-buff core, buff surface. Temper: common chaff, sparse lime.
4	CB 3188	G IV	III	L. 40.3 F 69.3	R: 43 cm	Ware: pale orange core, green surface. Temper: common medium chaff. Traces of orange paint on rim.
5	CB 1833	A II	II	L. 54.1 E 7.1	R: c 40 cm	Ware: orange core, pale buff surface. Temper: medium chaff.
6	CB 2033	A II	IA	L. 67.1 E 29.3	R: c 54 cm	Ware: pink core, red-orange surface. Temper: common chaff, fine lime. Red paint band.
7	CB 2533	A I	II	L. 38.1 E 224.1	R: 39 cm	Ware: pale grey core, orange surface. Temper: common chaff, fine lime.
8	CB 2935	G IV	II/2	L. 32.6 F 60.3	R: 37 cm	Ware: orange core, buff surface. Temper: common medium chaff, rare medium lime.

LARGE SHALLOW BOWLS

PLATE 14

"HAMMERHEAD" RIM

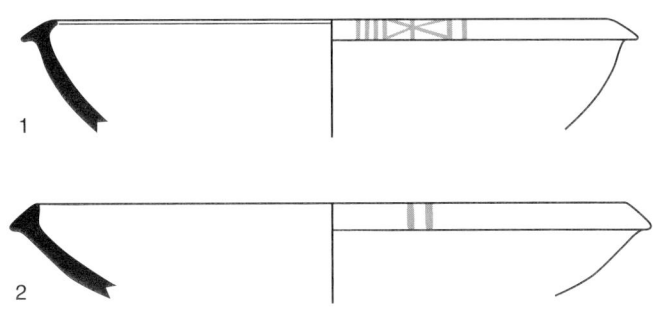

INCURVING RIM

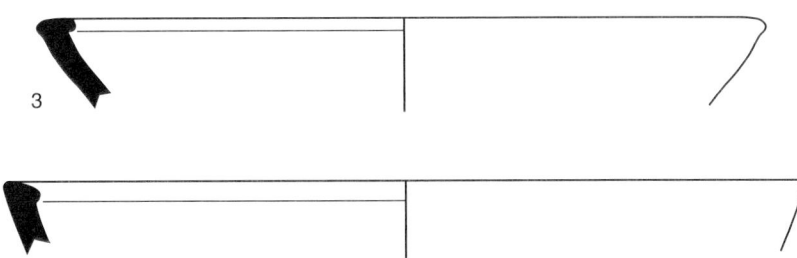

LARGE DEEP BOWLS

SQUARED LEDGE RIM

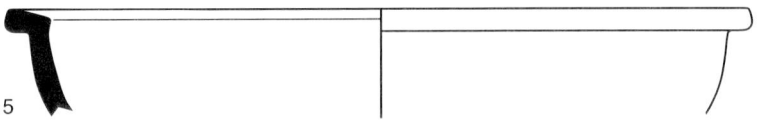

TRIANGULAR LEDGE RIM

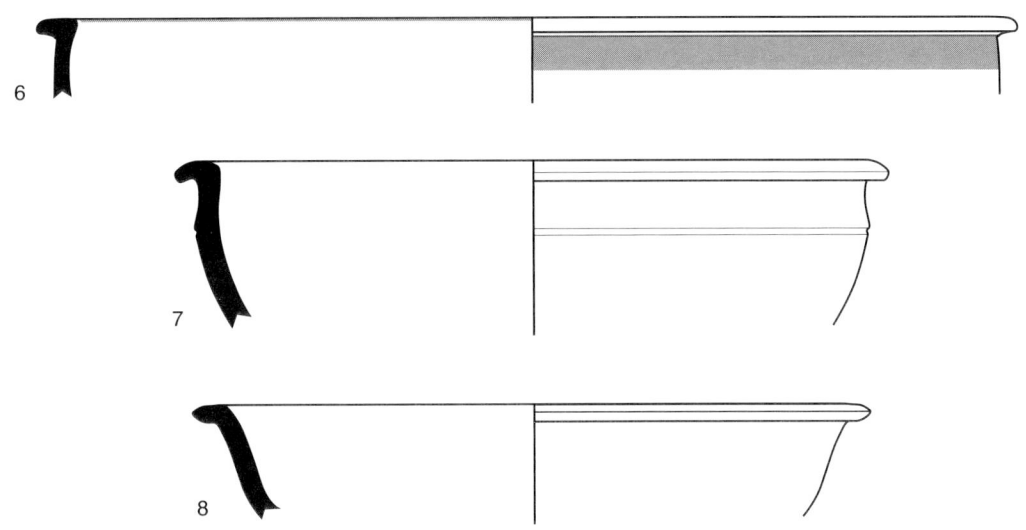

1:4 10 cm

Plate 15: *Large Deep Bowls*

	CB number	Area	Phase	Locus and Lot number	Dimensions	Ware, comments
1	CB 3042	A II	II	L. 81.2 F 35.3	R: 46 cm	Ware: black core, buff surface. Temper: common medium chaff. Two shallow grooves at maximum diameter.
2	CB 2986	A II	II	L. 81.2 F 35.2	R: 48 cm	Ware: buff. Temper: common medium-large chaff, sparse medium lime.
3	CB 2934	A II	II	L. 81.2 F 35.1	R: 48.5 cm	Ware: pink core, buff surface. Temper: common medium-large chaff, sparse fine-medium lime. Two horizontal grooves and wavy groove on lower body.
4	CB 1986	A II	II	L. 64.1 (T. 9) E 24.3	R: c 60 cm	Ware: greenish-buff core, pale buff surface. Temper: common chaff, lime. Wavy and horizontal grooves.
5	CB 2183	G I	II/1	L. 10.2 E 73.6	R: 35 cm	Ware: dark orange core, buff-orange surface. Temper: common medium chaff.
6	CB 3251	G II	II/2	L. 54.10 F 210.1	R: 36 cm	Ware: orange core, buff surface. Temper: common medium chaff, rare fine lime.
7	CB 2893	G II	II/2	L. 54.8 F 204.3	R: 45 cm	Ware: brown core, buff surface. Common medium chaff, rare fine lime. Soot staining on exterior.

LARGE DEEP BOWLS   **PLATE 15**

TRIANGULAR LEDGE RIM

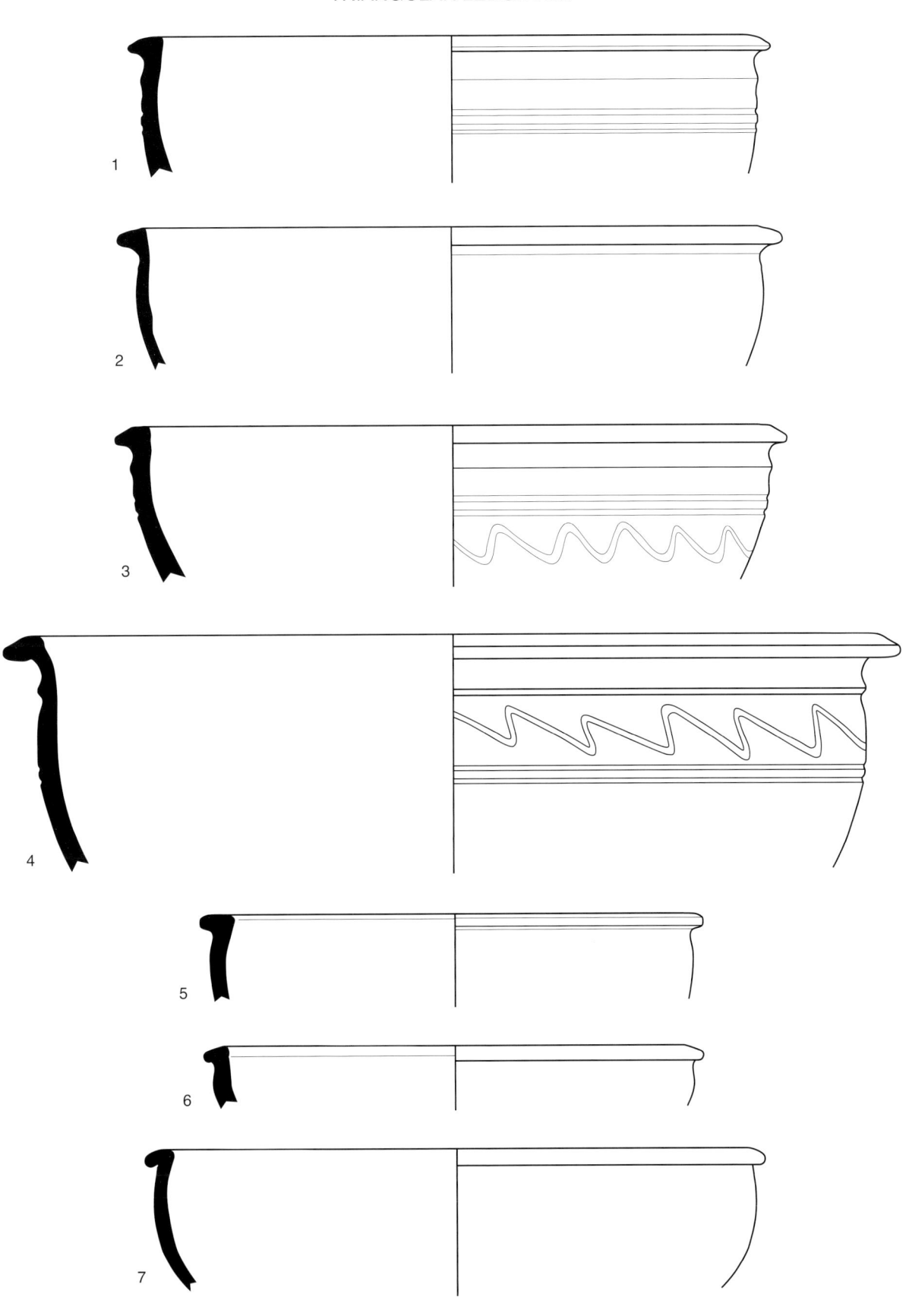

Plate 16: *Large Deep Cylindrical Bowls*

	CB number	Area	Phase	Locus and Lot number	Dimensions	Ware, comments
1	CB 3057	A II	II	L. 81.2 F 35.4	R: 37.5 cm	Ware: black core, orange-buff surface. Temper: common medium-large chaff.
2	CB 1846	G I	II/1	L. 4.4 E 66.1	R: 36.5 cm	Ware: buff. Temper: sparse chaff, lime.
3	CB 2451	G I	II/1	L. 15.1 E 89.1	R: 32.5 cm	Ware: dark grey core, orange-buff surface. Temper: common medium chaff, fine lime.
4	CB 1964	G I	II/1	L. 12.1 E 71.1	R: 37 cm	Ware: buff-green. Temper: abundant chaff.
5	CB 2151	G II	II/2	L. 54.2 E 96.3	R: 35 cm	Ware: buff core, pale buff surface. Temper: common chaff, sparse lime.
6	CB 2375	G I	II/2	L. 11.2 E 80.1	R: 37 cm	Ware: green. Temper: common chaff, fine lime. Deep horizontal grooves on body.
7	CB 3403	G II	II/2	L. 54.10 F 210.2	R: 39 cm	Ware: black core, orange surface. Temper: common medium chaff, fine sand and lime.
8	CB 1856	G II	II/2	L. 51.4 E 93.1	R: c 40 cm	Ware: buff core, pale buff surface. Temper: abundant coarse chaff, sparse lime.
9	CB 2373	G I	II/2	L. 5.2 E 69.4	R: 41 cm	Ware: buff core, pale buff surface. Temper: common medium chaff, fine lime, occasional large lime. Horizontal grooves on body.
10	CB 3117	G IV	S	L. 43.1 F 66.1	R: 36 cm	Ware: buff core, pale buff surface. Temper: rare medium chaff, common sand and fine lime.

LARGE DEEP CYLINDRICAL BOWLS   PLATE 16

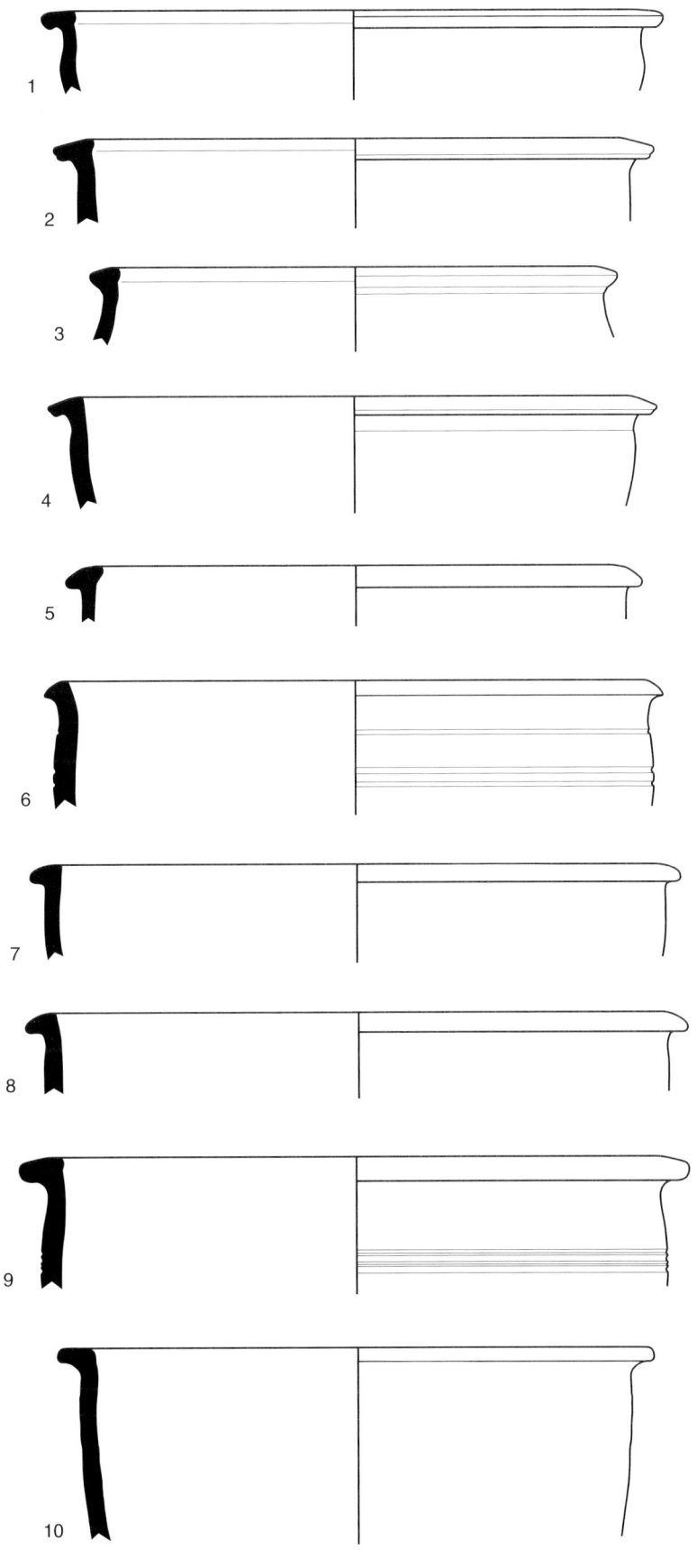

1:4 ▬▬▬▬▬ 10 cm

Plate 17: *Medium & Large Deep Cylindrical Bowls*

	CB number	Area	Phase	Locus and Lot number	Dimensions	Ware, comments
1	CB 386:1	A I	I	L. 17.1 D 322	R: 33 cm	Ware: buff. Temper: common chaff, lime. Ridges and groove below rim.
2	CB 2534	A I	II	L. 48.1 E 226.1	R: c 45 cm	Ware: orange-buff core, buff surface. Temper: sparse medium chaff, fine lime. Two sets of three horizontal grooves framing a wavy groove.
3	CB 2797	G IV	I	L. 23.1 F 51.1	R: 34.5 cm	Ware: greenish-buff. Temper: common chaff, sparse lime. Ridge below rim.
4	CB 2841	G IV	II/1A	L. 31.2 F 57.1	R: 33 cm M: 34 cm	Ware: pink core, buff surface. Temper: common fine-medium chaff. Groups of horizontal grooves framing an irregular wavy shallow groove.
5	CB 2889	G IV	II/1	L. 32.2 F 59.3	R: 33.5 cm M: 33 cm	Ware: buff core, green surface. Temper: common medium chaff, fine-medium lime. Groups of horizontal grooves framing an irregular wavy shallow groove. Ancient repair with bitumen.
6	CB 1811	G I	II/1A	L. 3.1 E 63.2	R: 37 cm	Ware: over-fired green. Temper: medium chaff, rare lime. Shallow wavy groove.
7	CB 3126	G IV	II/1A	L. 31.2 F 57.3	R: 40 cm	Ware: buff core, green surface. Temper: common chaff, sparse lime. Group of horizontal grooves and wavy groove.
8	CB 2599	G II	II/2	L. 54.5 E 108.3	R: 35 cm	Ware: buff core, greenish-buff surface. Temper: common medium chaff, fine lime.
9	CB 2016	G II	S	L. 57.2 E 99.2	R: 34 cm	Ware: buff core, pale buff surface. Temper: common chaff, sparse fine lime. Horizontal grooves.

MEDIUM & LARGE DEEP CYLINDRICAL BOWLS PLATE 17

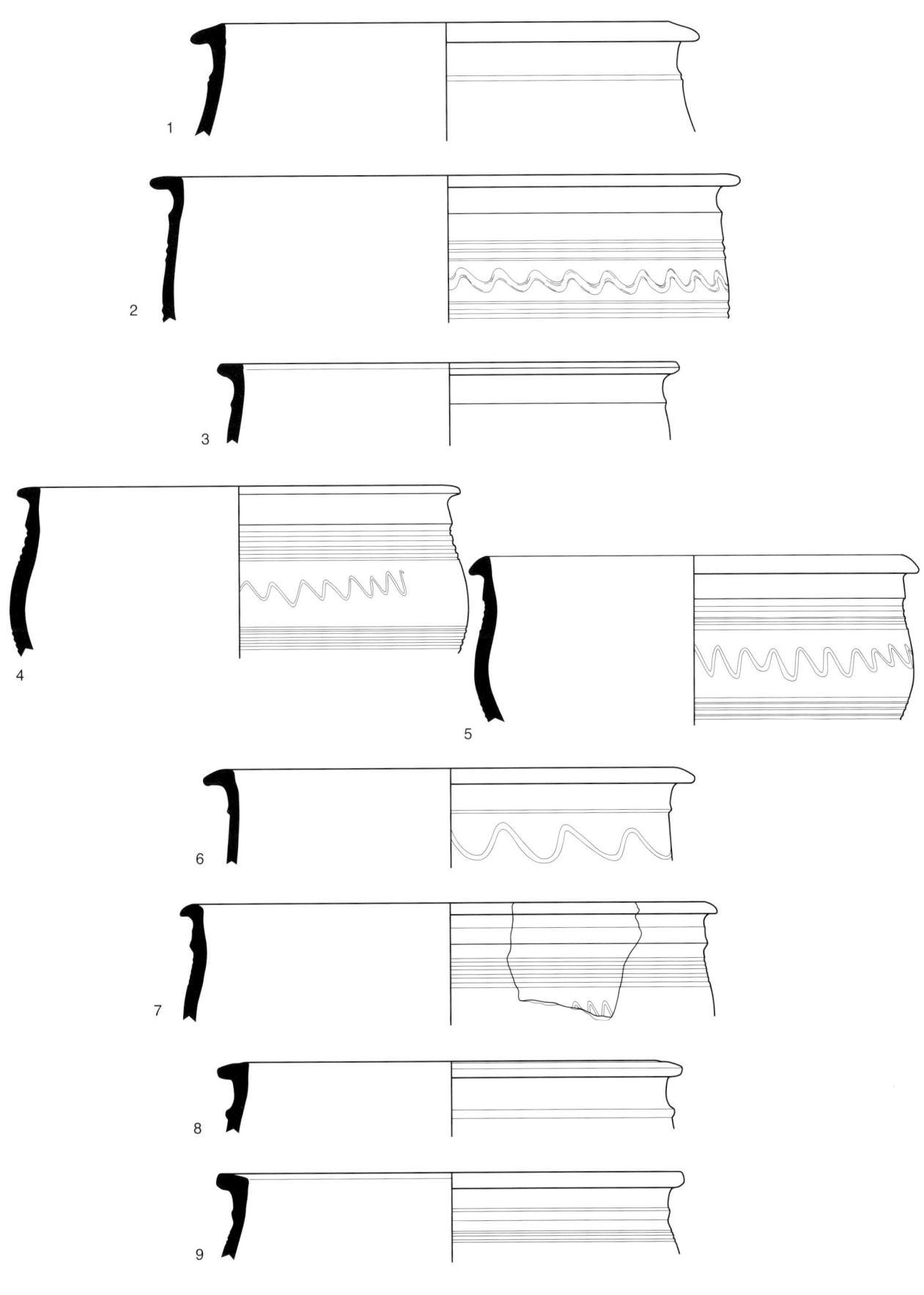

Plate 18: *Small Shallow and Deep Carinated bowls*

	CB number	Area	Phase	Locus & Lot no.	Dimensions	Ware, comments
1	CB 2161	G II	II/1A	L. 59.2 E 107.1	R: 18 cm	Ware: brown core, pale brown surface. Temper: sparse chaff and lime. Red-brown paint slashes across rim.
2	CB 2832	A II	I	L. 76.3 F 5.2	R: 18.5 cm	Ware: light green. Temper: common chaff. Fugitive brown paint slashes on rim.
3	CB 2806	G IV	I	L. 24.1 F 52.2	R: 17 cm	Ware: dark buff core, buff surface. Temper: common chaff, common fine-medium lime. Soot stain on exterior rim.
4	CB 2828	G IV	I	L. 29.1 F 55.1	R: 19 cm	Ware: pink-buff core, green surface. Temper: common medium chaff, sparse fine lime. Black paint slash on rim.
5	CB 1860	G I	II/1	L. 5.1 E 63.4	R: 19 cm	Ware: grey core, orange-buff surface. Temper: medium chaff.
6	CB 3175	G II	II/2	L. 54.10 F 210.4	R: 14 cm	Ware: green. Temper: common fine sand and lime.
7	CB 3974	G II	III	L. 37.3 F 213.6	R: 18 cm	Ware: green. Temper: occasional medium lime, common fine lime and sand. Brown paint slashes on rim.
8	CB 1759	A I	II	L. 16.2 D 361	R: 16 cm	Ware: orange core, buff surface. Temper: common lime, rare chaff. Orange-brown paint bands, interior drip and spot.
9	CB 1726	A I	I	L. 17.2 D 350	R: 13 cm	Ware: buff. Temper: fine sand, mica inclusions.
10	CB 962:2	A I	III	L. 33.2 D 388	R: 17 cm	Ware: green. Temper: common chaff, lime. Black paint band.
11	CB 1853	G I	II/1	L. 4.3 E 62.5	R: 14 cm	Ware: buff. Temper: fine sand.
12	CB 1786	G II	II/1	L. 51.1 E 91.2	R: 17 cm	Ware: grey core, red-orange surface. Temper: medium-fine chaff, sparse lime.
13	CB 1896	G II	II/2	L. 51.4 E 93.2	R: 18.5 cm	Ware: grey core, orange surface. Temper: common chaff, lime. Horizontal burnishing on interior.
14	CB 3138	G IV	II/1	L. 34.2 F 65.1	R: 16 cm	Ware: buff. Temper: common sand and fine lime. Red paint slashes on rim.
15	CB 3971A	G II	III	L. 37.3 F 213.4	R: 14 cm	Ware: buff. Temper: common fine sand, sparse medium lime.
16	CB 1960	A II	III	L. 61.3 E 25.1	R: 16 cm	Ware: orange-buff. Temper: common fine chaff, sparse lime.
17	CB 2150	G II	II/1	L. 54.1 E 96.2	R: 17 cm	Ware: orange-buff core and surface. Temper: sparse lime.
18	CB 2185	G I	II/1	L. 10.2 E 73.6	R: 17.5 cm	Ware: grey core, buff surface. Temper: common medium chaff, sparse fine lime.
19	CB 3011	G II	II/2	L. 54.10 F 210.2	R: 18 cm	Ware: orange core, buff surface. Temper: common medium chaff.
20	CB 1818	G II	II/2	L. 51.2 E 91.4	R: 19 cm	Ware: buff core, orange-buff surface. Temper: abundant chaff, sparse lime.
21	CB 4016	G II	III	L. 69.1 F 219.2	R: 19 cm	Ware: orange core, buff surface. Temper: rare medium chaff, common fine lime. Dark red paint on rim and splatter on interior.
22	CB 706:6	A I	II	L. 14.1 D 333	R: 9 cm	Ware: buff. Temper: sparse lime. Red paint band on rim.
23	CB 1716	A I	II	L. 16.1 D 376	R: 16 cm	Ware: grey core, buff-reddish surface. Temper: common chaff, fine lime.
24	CB 2946	G III	II/1	L. 21.2 F 76.5	R: 19 cm	Ware: orange core, buff surface. Temper: common medium chaff, sparse lime. Black paint slashes on rim.

SMALL SHALLOW CARINATED BOWLS

PLATE 18

ROUNDED RIM   TRIANGULAR RIMS   FINE TRIANGULAR

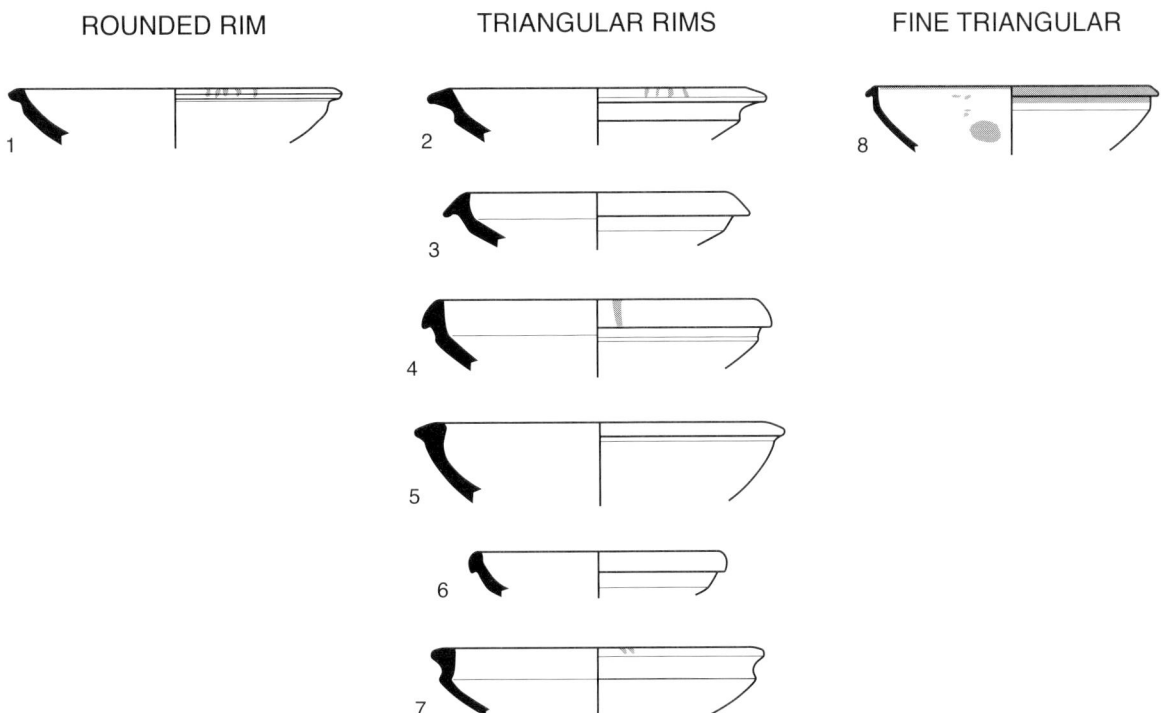

SMALL DEEP CARINATED BOWLS

ROUNDED RIM   TRIANGULAR RIMS   FLAT-TOP RIM

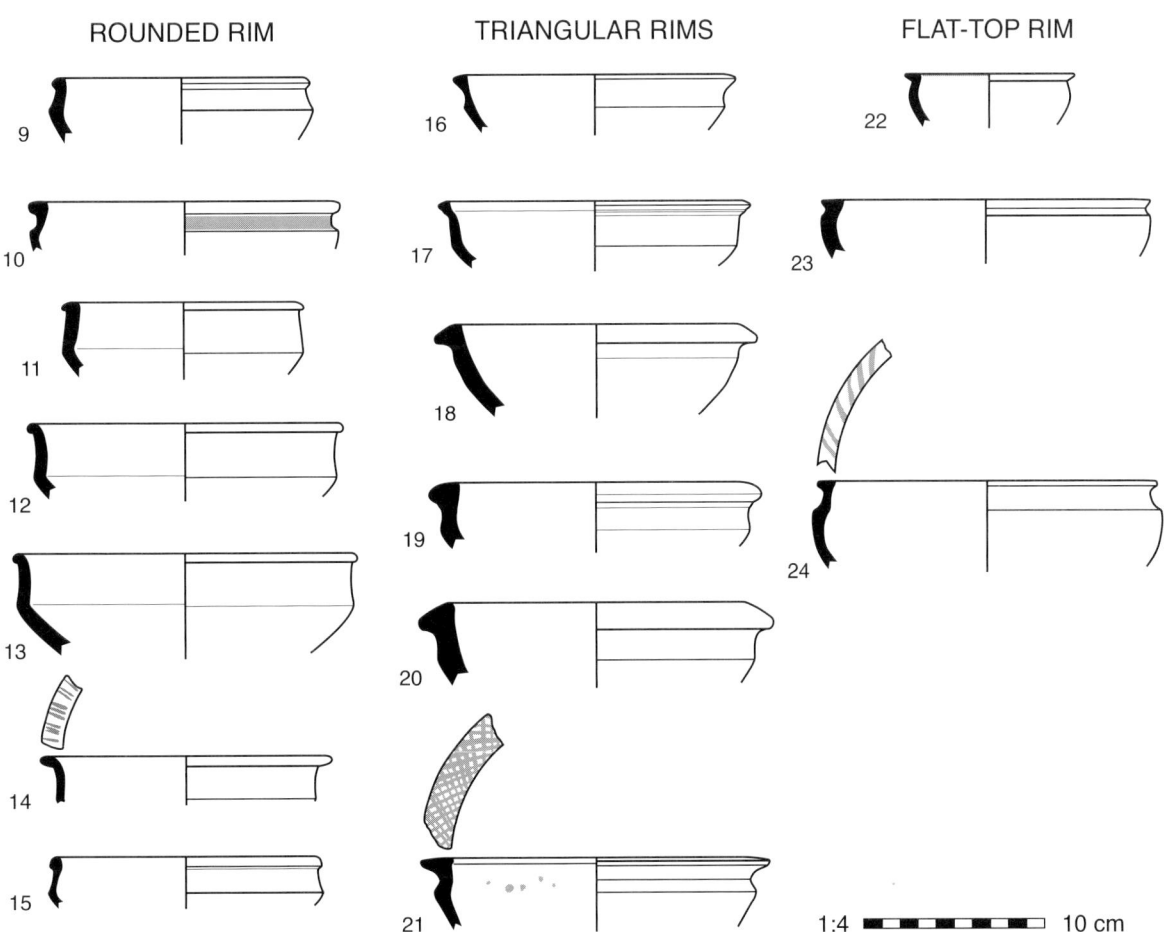

1:4   10 cm

Plate 19: *Medium Carinated Shallow Bowls*

	CB number	Area	Phase	Locus and Lot number	Dimensions	Ware, comments
1	CB 2007	A II	IA	L. 67.1 E 29.1	R: 23 cm	Ware: buff. Temper: medium chaff, fine lime. Two dark red paint slashes across rim.
2	CB 1694	A I	II	L. 30.1 D 387	R: 21 cm	Ware: buff core, orange-buff surface. Temper: sparse chaff, lime, mica inclusions.
3	CB 1700	A I	II	L. 16.1 D 376	R: 20 cm	Ware: grey core, buff surface. Temper: common chaff, mica inclusions.
4	CB 1699	A I	II	L. 16.1 D 376	R: 27 cm	Ware: grey core, reddish surface. Temper: common medium chaff, lime.
5	CB 2795	G IV	I	L. 23.1 F 51.1	R: 27.5 cm	Ware: grey core, buff surface. Temper: common chaff.
6	CB 2793	G IV	I	L. 23.1 F 51.1	R: 30 cm	Ware: buff. Temper: sparse chaff, common fine sand.
7	CB 1844	G I	II/1	L. 4.4 E 66.1	R: 28 cm	Ware: green-buff. Temper: sparse large chaff, fine sand.
8	CB 2509	G II	II/1	L. 63.1 E 111.2	R: 25 cm	Ware: greenish buff core and surface. Temper: common fine lime, fine-medium chaff. Black paint slashes across rim.
9	CB 2149	G II	II/1	L. 54.1 E 96.2	R: 26 cm	Ware: orange-buff core, pale orange-buff surface. Temper: common chaff, sparse lime.
10	CB 3112	G II	II/2	L. 54.10 F 210.3	R: 23.5 cm	Ware: brown core, buff surface. Temper: common medium chaff, rare fine lime. Red paint slashes on rim.
11	CB 4190	G IV	II/2	L. 34.5 F 454.2	R: 30 cm	Ware: grey core, buff surface. Temper: sparse medium chaff, fine-medium lime. Three red-brown paint slashes on rim.
12	CB 2602	G II	II/2	L. 54.5 E 108.3	R: 26 cm	Ware: buff core, pale buff surface. Temper: common medium chaff, sparse fine lime.
13	CB 2145	G II	II/2	L. 54.3 E 105.1	R: 25 cm	Ware: grey core, buff surface. Temper: common chaff.
14	CB 2167	G II	II/2	L. 54.3 E 105.2	R: 25 cm	Ware: buff. Temper: common fine chaff, sparse lime.
15	CB 3781	G IV	II/2	L. 41.2 F 72.1	R: 26 cm	Ware: buff core, pale buff surface. Temper: common medium chaff. Seven red-brown paint slashes on rim.
16	CB 1889	G II	II/2	L. 51.2 E 91.1	R: 30 cm	Ware: grey core, pale orange surface. Temper: common chaff, mica inclusions.
17	CB 4015	G II	III	L. 69.1 F 219.2	R: 32 cm	Ware: black core, buff surface. Temper: common medium-coarse chaff and fine lime.
18	CB 2853	G III	II/1	L. 21.2 F 76.5	R: 28 cm	Ware: dark grey core, orange surface. Temper: common medium chaff, sparse fine-medium lime. Red paint band.
19	CB 3400	G II	II/2	L. 54.10 F 210.2	R: 28 cm	Ware: orange core, buff surface. Temper: common medium-large chaff, rare fine lime. Red paint on rim.

MEDIUM CARINATED SHALLOW BOWLS   PLATE 19

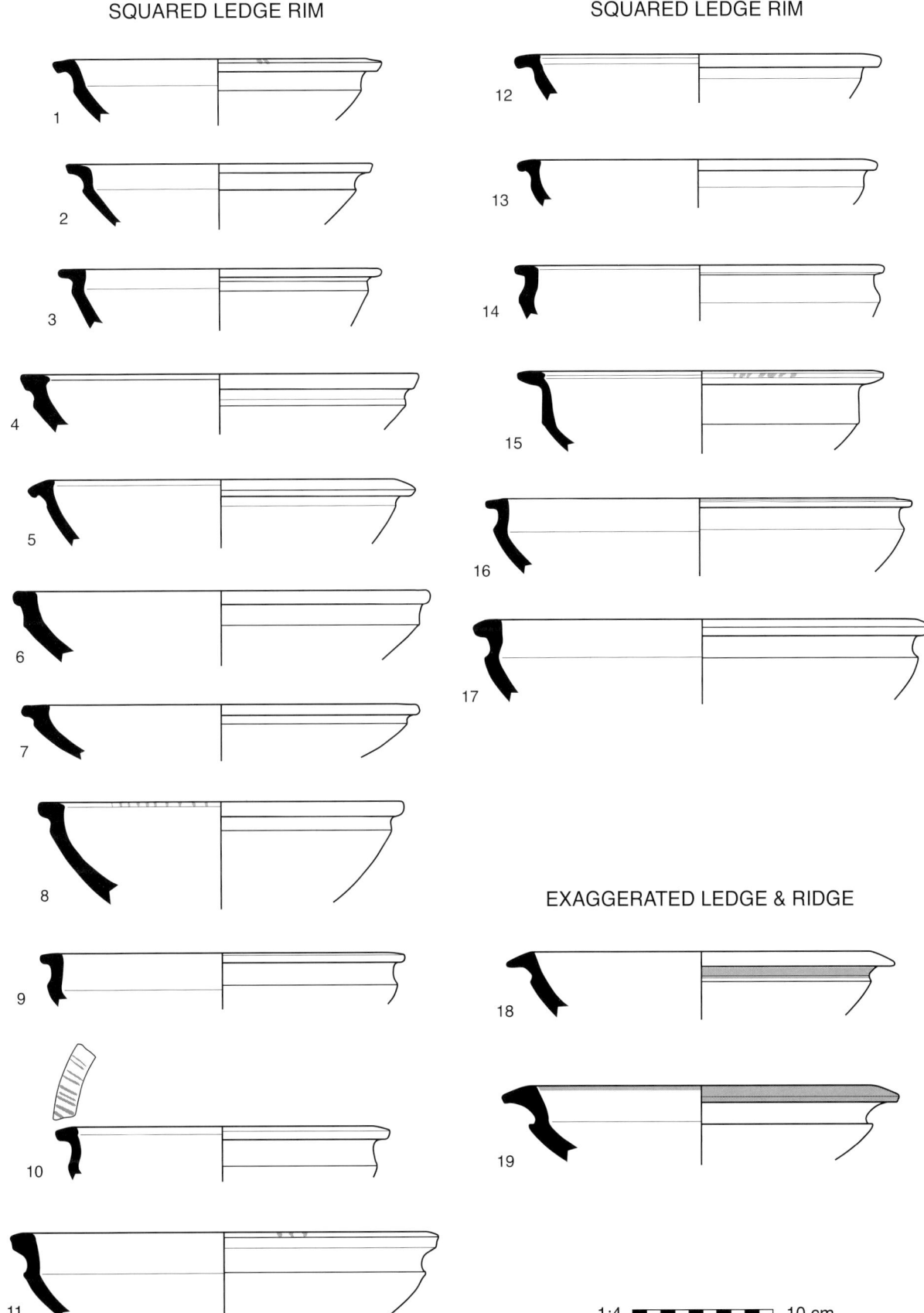

Plate 20: *Medium Carinated Shallow Bowls*

	CB number	Area	Phase	Locus and Lot number	Dimensions	Ware, comments
1	CB 3202	A II	I	L. 76.9 F 20.2	R: 31 cm	Ware: over-fired green. Temper: common medium chaff.
2	CB 1868	A II	II	L. 52.2 E 6.2	R: 25 cm	Ware: orange-buff core, buff surface. Temper: common chaff, lime. Three fugitive black paint slashes across rim.
3	CB 1874	A II	II	L. 54.1 E 7.2	R: 28 cm	Ware: grey core, orange surface. Temper: common medium chaff, lime.
4	CB 3196	A II	II	L. 81.2 F 35.6	R: 29.5 cm	Ware: black core, orange surface. Temper: common medium chaff.
5	CB 1858	G I	II/1	L. 5.1 E 63.4	R: 23 cm	Ware: buff-green. Temper: abundant chaff.
6	CB 2187	G I	II/1	L. 10.2 E 73.6	R: 22 cm	Ware: buff-grey core, buff surface. Temper: common medium chaff, occasional fine lime. Four red paint slashes across rim.
7	CB 2120	G I	II/1	L. 9.2 E 77.1	R: 23 cm	Ware: buff core, orange surface. Temper: common chaff, sparse lime.
8	CB 2121	G I	II/1	L. 9.2 E 77.1	R: 25 cm	Ware: pale green. Temper: common chaff, sparse lime.
9	CB 1843	G I	II/1	L. 4.4 E 66.1	R: 27 cm	Ware: buff. Temper: abundant medium chaff. Four red-brown paint slashes across rim.
10	CB 2118	G II	II/1	L. 58.1 E 100.2	R: 25 cm	Ware: green. Temper: common medium chaff.
11	CB 1936	G I	II/1	T.11 shaft E 67.2	R: 27 cm	Ware: grey core, buff surface. Temper: medium chaff, common fine lime. Five red paint slashes across rim.
12	CB 2037	G I	II/1	L. 13.1 E 75.1	R: 34 cm	Ware: grey core, orange surface. Temper: common chaff, mica inclusions.
13	CB 2547	G II	II/2	L. 65.3 E 120.1	R: 20 cm	Ware: buff. Temper: sparse medium chaff, fine lime.
14	CB 3136	G IV	II/1	L. 34.2 F 65.1	R: 21 cm	Ware: grey core, green surface. Temper: common medium chaff.
15	CB 1905	G II	II/2	L. 51.2 E 91.3	R: 20 cm	Ware: grey-brown core, buff surface. Temper: sparse large chaff, mica inclusions.
16	CB 2901	G II	II/2	L. 54.9 F 206.1	R: 25.5 cm	Ware: brown-orange core, buff surface. Temper: common medium chaff, rare fine-medium lime. Carefully smoothed surfaces.
17	CB 3016	G II	II/2	L. 54.10 F 210.2	R: 34 cm	Ware: orange core, buff surface. Temper: common medium lime, rare medium chaff. Red paint slashes on rim.
18	CB 4366:3	G II	II/2	L. 65.4 E 332.2	R: 33.5 cm	Ware: red-brown core, dark buff surface. Temper: common fine chaff, fine lime.

MEDIUM CARINATED SHALLOW BOWLS

PLATE 20

SMALL TRIANGULAR RIM

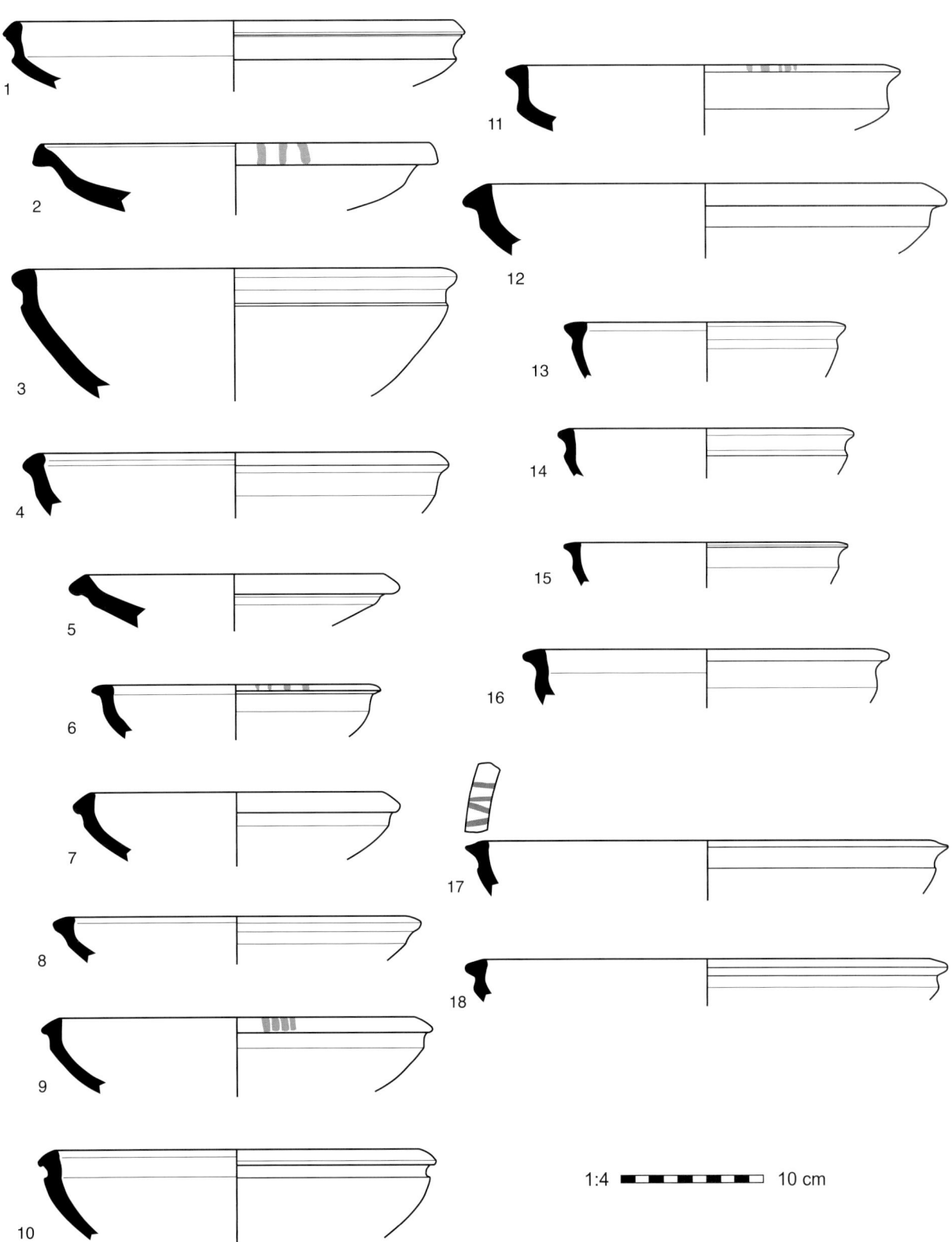

Plate 21: *Medium Carinated Shallow Bowls*

	CB number	Area	Phase	Locus and Lot number	Dimensions	Ware, comments
1	CB 1775	A I	IA	L. 32.1 D 366	R: 25 cm	Ware: pink core, pale buff surface. Temper: common chaff.
2	CB 2113	A II	II	L. 52.4 E 186.3	R: 25 cm B: 9.8 cm H: 7.4 cm	Ware: buff. Temper: common chaff, occasional large lime.
3	CB 1760	A I	II	L. 16.2 D 361	R: 25.5 cm	Ware: grey core, orange surface. Temper: medium chaff, occasional lime.
4	CB 2536	A II	II	00-13 E 282.1	R: 13 cm B: 9.7 cm H: 6.9 cm	Ware: buff core, pale buff surface. Temper: common medium chaff, occasional large lime.
5	CB 786:2	A I	II	L. 26.1 D 363	R: 22 cm	Ware: dark grey core, reddish surface. Temper: common chaff, lime. Red painted slashes across rim.
6	CB 2101	A II	II	L. 52.4 E 186.1	R: 32 cm	Ware: dark buff core, buff surface. Temper: sparse large chaff.
7	CB 2008	A I	II	L. 43.2 E 46.1	R: 32.5 cm	Ware: orange-buff core, pale buff surface. Temper: occasional chaff, lime, sand.
8	CB 2794	G IV	I	L. 23.1 F 51.1	R: 28.5 cm	Ware: dark grey core, orange surface. Temper: common chaff, sparse fine lime.
9	CB 2607	G I	II/1	L. 9.4 E 77.3	R: 21 cm	Ware: orange-buff. Temper: common medium chaff, mica inclusions. Three red-brown paint slashes across rim.
10	CB 1976	G I	II/1	L. 10.1 E 73.1	R: 24 cm	Ware: buff core, pale buff surface. Temper: medium chaff, sparse sand.
11	CB 2023	G II	II/1	L. 55.1 E 97.1	R: 26 cm. B: 12 cm H: 7.8 cm	Ware: greenish-buff. Temper: abundant chaff and lime. Black paint slashes across rim and red paint band below rim.
12	CB 1970	G II	II/1	L. 54.1 E 96.1	R: 32 cm	Ware: grey core, buff-orange surface. Temper: medium chaff.
13	CB 2449	G I	II/1	L. 15.1 E 89.1	R: 32 cm	Ware: buff core, pale buff surface. Temper: common medium chaff, fine lime.
14	CB 1968	G II	II/1	L. 54.1 E 96.1	R: 32 cm	Ware: grey core, buff-orange surface. Temper: abundant chaff, medium lime.
15	CB 2147	G II	II/1	L. 54.1 E 96.2	R: 31 cm	Ware: dark buff core, buff-grey surface. Temper: common chaff. Seven black paint slashes across rim.
16	CB 2521	G II	II/1	L. 63.1 E 111.3	R: 25 cm	Ware: buff. Temper: sparse fine-medium chaff, mica inclusions.
17	CB 2894	G II	II/2	L. 54.8 F 204.3	R: 21.5 cm	Ware: orange core, buff surface. Temper: common medium chaff and fine-medium lime.
18	CB 2378	G I	II/1	L. 12.1 E 81.2	R: 23.5 cm	Ware: pink core, green-buff surface. Temper: medium chaff. Four paint slashes across rim.
19	CB 3952	G II	II/2	L. 54.10 F 210.7	R: 24.5 cm	Ware: orange. Temper: sparse medium chaff and fine lime. Red paint slashes on rim.
21	CB 2123	G II	II/2	L. 51.5 E 93.3	R: 28 cm	Ware: grey-buff core, buff surface. Temper: common chaff, lime.
21	CB 3012	G II	II/2	L. 54.10 F 210.2	R: 25.5 cm	Ware: orange core, buff surface. Temper: common medium chaff.

MEDIUM CARINATED SHALLOW BOWLS
EXTENDED TRIANGULAR RIM

PLATE 21

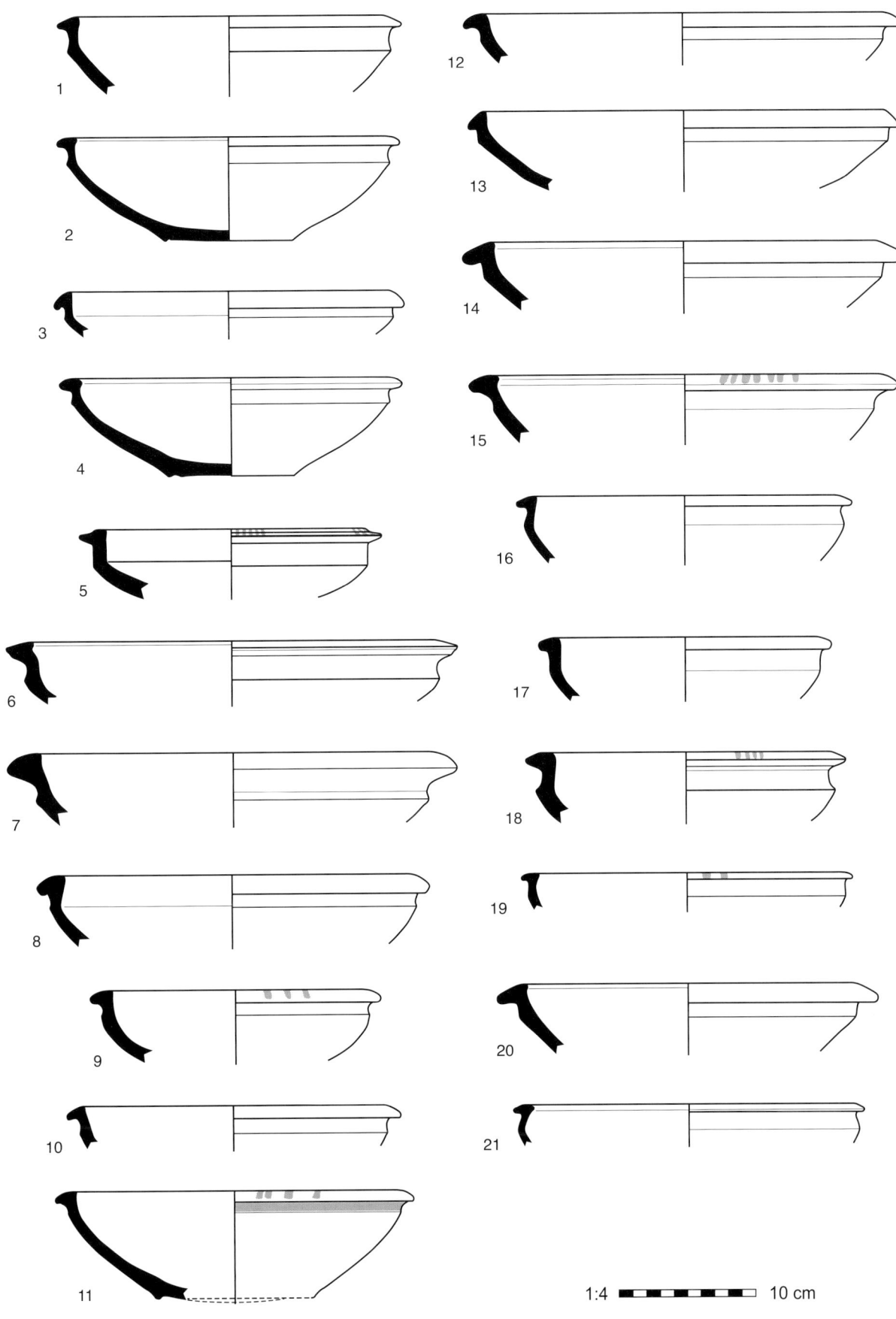

Plate 22: *Medium Carinated Shallow Bowls*

	CB number	Area	Phase	Locus and Lot number	Dimensions	Ware, comments
1	CB 3134	G IV	II/1	L. 34.2 F 65.1	R: 27 cm	Ware: pink core, buff surface. Temper: common medium chaff and fine lime.
2	CB 2383	G I	II/1	L. 12.1 E 81.2	R: 33 cm	Ware: buff core, pale buff surface. Temper: common medium chaff.
3	CB 4168	G IV	III	L. 49.2 F 455.2	R: 21 cm	Ware: buff. Temper: common medium chaff.
4	CB 4204	G II	III	01-24 F 217.2	R: 23 cm B: 7.5 cm H: 8.2 cm	Ware: orange-buff core, pale buff surface. Temper: common fine sand and lime, occasional large chaff, mica inclusions. Red paint slashes on rim.
5	CB 3226	G II	III	L. 36.1 F 207.3	R: 25 cm	Ware: orange core buff surface. Temper: common medium chaff, sand and fine lime. Dark red paint slashes on rim.
6	CB 3227	G II	III	L. 36.1 F 207.3	R: 24.5 cm	Ware: orange core, buff surface. Temper: common sand and fine lime. Red paint slashes on rim.
7	CB 4023	G II	IV	L. 75.1 F 224.1	R: 26 cm	Ware: grey core, orange-buff surface. Temper: common medium chaff.
8	CB 3022	G II	II/2	L. 54.10 F 210.2	R: 33 cm	Ware: buff core, yellow surface. Temper: common large chaff, rare medium lime.
9	CB 3802	G II	II/2	L. 54.10 F 210.5	R: 31 cm	Ware: black core, orange surface. Temper: common medium chaff.
10	CB 3130	G IV	II/1A	L. 31.2 F 57.3	R: 28 cm	Ware: grey core, green surface. Temper: common medium chaff.
11	CB 4165	G IV	II/2	L. 34.5 F 454.3	R: 25.5 cm	Ware: grey core, buff surface. Temper: common medium chaff, sparse fine lime.

MEDIUM CARINATED SHALLOW BOWLS — PLATE 22

EXTENDED TRIANGULAR RIM

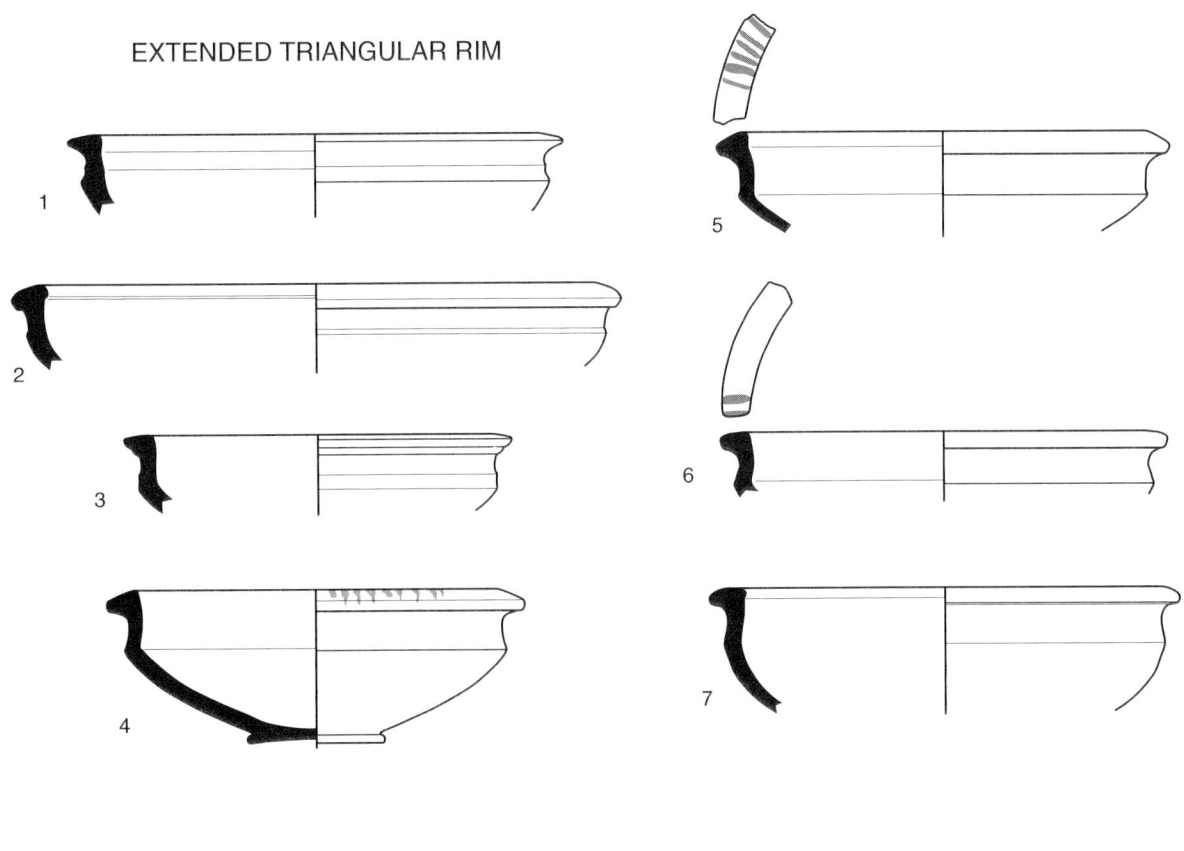

FLAT-TOP RIM   CLUB RIM

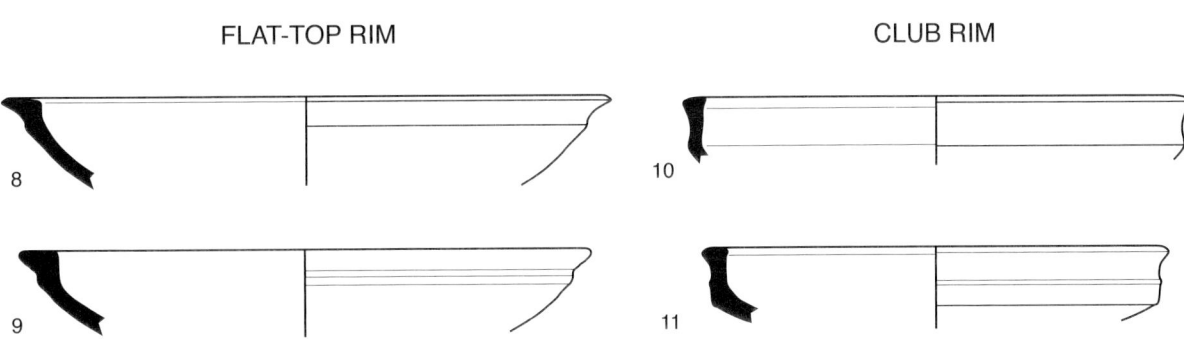

1:4   10 cm

Plate 23: *Medium Carinated Deep Bowls*

	CB number	Area	Phase	Locus and Lot number	Dimensions	Ware, comments
1	CB 1707	A I	II	L. 16.1 D 376	R: 29 cm	Ware: buff-grey core, buff-green surface. Temper: medium chaff, lime.
2	CB 318:3	A I	II	L. 15.1 D 51	R: 33 cm	Ware: grey core, reddish surface. Temper: common chaff, lime. Notched ridge.
3	CB 3951	G II	II/2	L. 54.10 F 210.7	R: 34 cm	Ware: buff core, pale buff surface. Temper: common medium chaff and fine lime.
4	CB 2526	G I	II/2	L. 4.6 E 84.3	R: 28 cm	Ware: pale grey core, orange-buff surface. Temper: common medium chaff, fine lime. Red-brown paint slashes across rim.
5	CB 3789	G IV	II/1	L. 34.4 F 70.3	R: 28 cm	Ware: grey core, orange-buff surface. Temper: common medium chaff and fine lime. Soot staining on rim.
6	CB 4164	G IV	III	L. 76.1 F 466.1	R: 27.5 cm	Ware: grey core, buff surface. Temper: sparse large chaff. Two orange paint slashes on rim.
7	CB 3221	G IV	III	L. 40.3 F 69.2	R: 30 cm	Ware: brown core, green-buff surface. Temper: common coarse chaff. Three brown paint slashes on rim.
8	CB 2171	G I	II/2	L. 4.6 E 84.1	R: 22 cm	Ware: grey core, green-buff surface. Temper: sparse medium lime, common medium chaff. Four red paint slashes across rim.
9	CB 3213	G II	III	L. 37.3 F 213.2	R: 24 cm	Ware: orange core, buff surface. Temper: common medium chaff, occasional lime. Three red paint slashes on rim.
10	CB 1878	A II	II	L. 52.1 E 4.3	R: 27 cm	Ware: buff core, pale buff surface. Temper: medium chaff, lime.
11	CB 2962	G IV	II/2	L. 32.6 F 59.6	R: 29.5 cm	Ware: buff-pink core, yellow-buff surface. Temper: common medium chaff. Red paint slashes on rim.
12	CB 2165	G II	II/2	L. 54.3 E 105.2	R: 21 cm	Ware: buff. Temper: common medium chaff, sparse lime.
13	CB 3135	G IV	II/1	L. 34.2 F 65.1	R: 26 cm	Ware: black core, buff surface. Temper: common medium chaff.
14	CB 2961	G IV	II/2	L. 32.6 F 59.6	R: 25 cm	Ware: grey core, buff surface. Temper: common medium chaff. Red paint slashes on rim.
15	CB 3401	G II	II/2	L. 54.10 F 210.2	R: 22 cm	Ware: black core, orange surface. Temper: common medium chaff, rare medium lime. Smoothed surface.
16	CB 4013	G II	III	L. 69.1 F 219.2	R: 26 cm	Ware: black core, orange surface. Temper: common medium chaff. Thick white "plaster" on exterior surface beneath carination.
17	CB 2182	G I	II/1	L. 10.2 E 73.6	R: 31.5 cm	Ware: pink core, pale buff surface. Temper: common medium chaff, occasional lime.
18	CB 2829	G III	II/1	L. 21.2 F 76.2	R: 24 cm	Ware: orange-grey core, orange surface. Temper: common medium chaff, sparse medium lime.
19	CB 3139	G IV	II/1	L. 34.2 F 65.1	R: 24.5 cm	Ware: brown core, orange surface. Temper: common medium chaff, sparse fine lime.

MEDIUM CARINATED DEEP BOWLS

PLATE 23

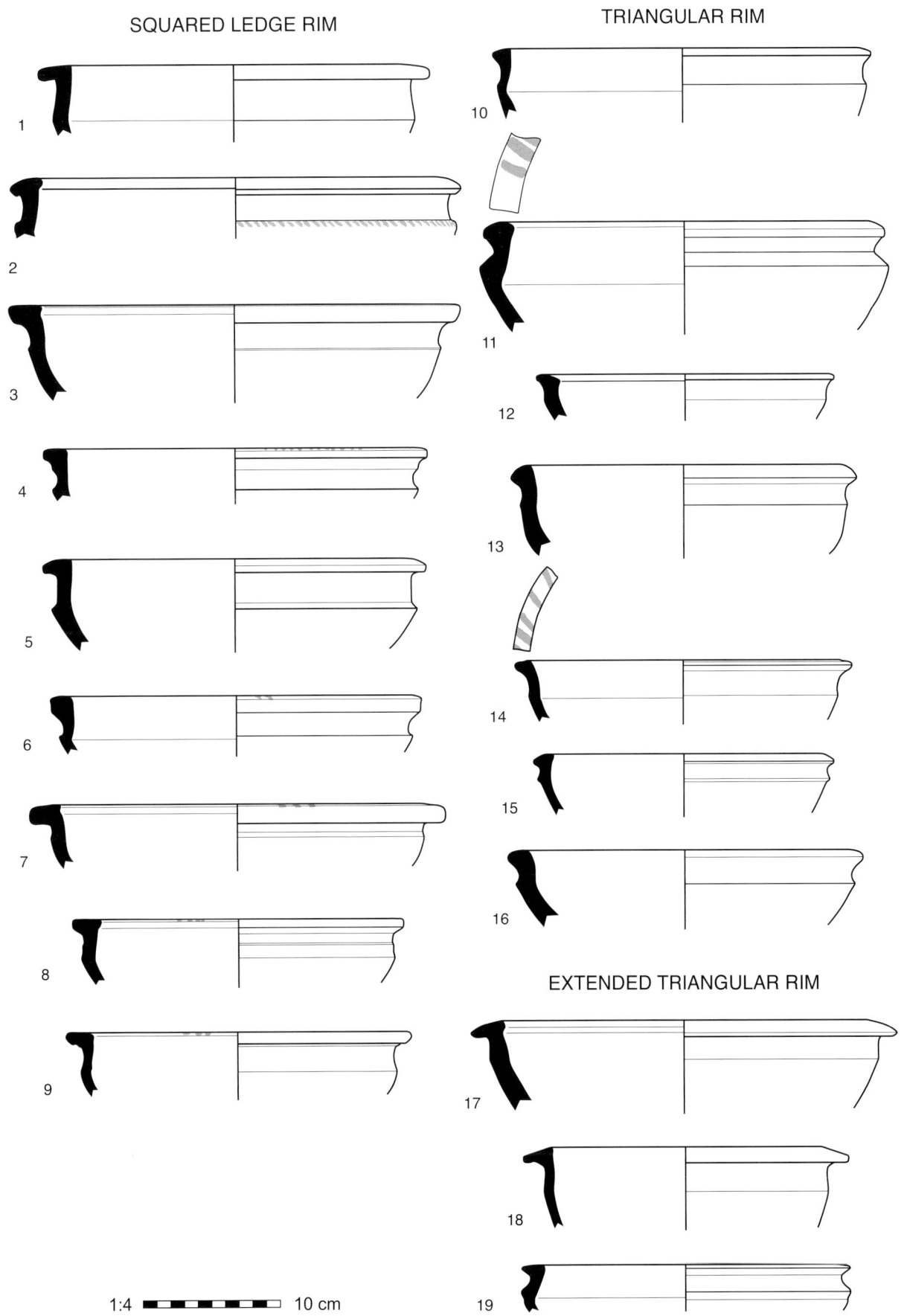

Plate 24: *Medium Carinated Deep Bowls*

	CB number	Area	Phase	Locus and Lot number	Dimensions	Ware, comments
1	CB 1698	A I	II	L. 29.1 D 368	R: 31 cm	Ware: grey core, orange surface. Temper: occasional chaff, lime.
2	CB 2157	G I	II/2	L. 4.6 E 66.5	R: 25 cm	Ware: grey core, orange surface. Temper: common chaff, occasional lime, mica inclusions.
3	CB 3177	G IV	III	L. 40.2 F 68.2	R: 23 cm	Ware: buff. Temper: common medium chaff.
4	CB 3116	G IV	S	L. 43.1 F 66.1	R: 28 cm	Ware: black core, orange-buff surface. Temper: common medium chaff and fine lime.
5	CB 3035	G IV	II/1	L. 34.1 F 64.1	R: 22 cm	Ware: pink core, buff surface. Temper: common medium chaff, rare fine lime.
6	CB 1792	A I	II	L. 41.1 E 37.1	R: 29 cm	Ware: grey core, orange surface. Temper: common chaff, sparse fine lime.
7	CB 3129	G IV	II/1A	L. 31.2 F 57.3	R: 28.5 cm	Ware: brown core, buff surface. Temper: common chaff, fine lime.
8	CB 3128	G IV	II/1A	L. 31.2 F 57.3	R: 31 cm	Ware: black core, buff surface. Temper: common medium chaff, occasional lime. Red paint band on rim.
9	CB 3115	G IV	S	L. 43.1 F 66.1	R: 32 cm	Ware: black core, buff surface. Temper: common medium-coarse chaff, rare grit. Red paint slashes on rim.
10	CB 1845	G I	II/1	L. 4.4 E 66.1	R: 23 cm	Ware: grey core, red-buff surface. Temper: abundant chaff.
11	CB 3026	G II	II/2	L. 54.8 F 204.4	R: 20.5 cm	Ware: green. Temper: common medium chaff and fine lime.
12	CB 3998	G II	II/2	L. 54.10 F 210.1	R: 23.5 cm	Ware: buff. Temper: common medium chaff. Dark red paint bands.
13	CB 2897	G II	III	L. 37.1 F 208.1	R: 28 cm	Ware: grey core, orange-buff surface. Temper: common coarse chaff. Red paint band.
14	CB 2862	G II	III	L. 27.1 F 202.2	R: 29 cm	Ware: brown core, orange-red surface. Temper: common medium chaff. Traces of red paint on rim.
15	CB 2938	G IV	I	L. 33.1 F 58.1	R: 28 cm	Ware: pale orange core, pale buff surface. Temper: common coarse chaff. Black-brown paint bands over rim.

MEDIUM CARINATED DEEP BOWLS PLATE 24

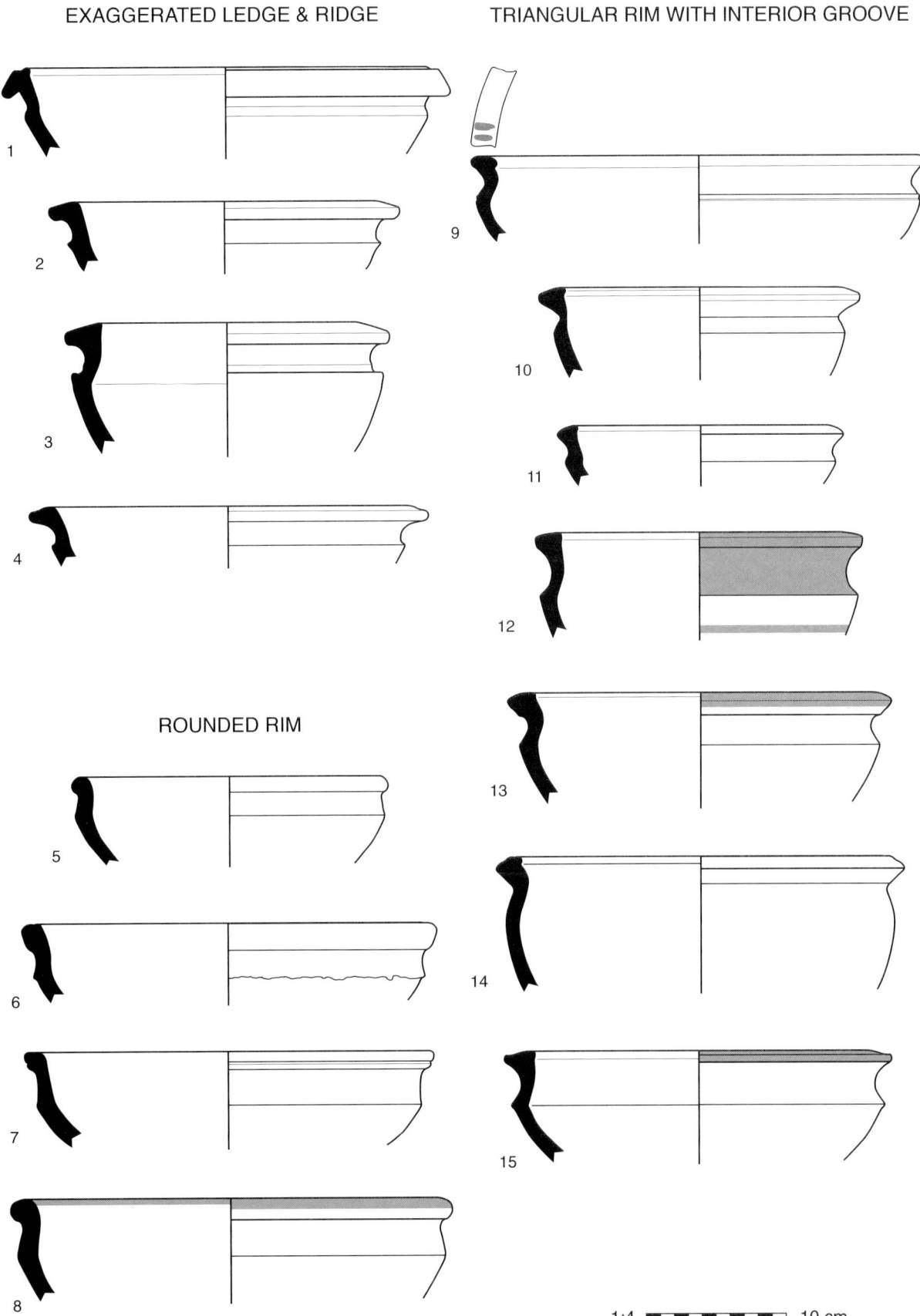

Plate 25: *Large Carinated Shallow Bowls*

	CB number	Area	Phase	Locus and Lot number	Dimensions	Ware, comments
1	CB 3109	G II	II/2	L. 54.10 F 210.3	R: 35 cm	Ware: brown core, buff surface. Temper: common large chaff, rare fine lime.
2	CB 3195	A II	II	L. 81.2 F 35.6	R: 37 cm	Ware: black core, orange surface. Temper: common chaff.
3	CB 3232	G III	II/2	L. 39.3 F 81.4	R: 36.5 cm	Same ware as cooking pots: black core, brown surface. Temper: abundant grey and white grit. Horizontal burnishing interior and exterior.
4	CB 2598	G II	II/2	L. 54.5 E 108.3	R: c 45 cm	Ware: grey core, red-orange surface. Temper: common medium-large lime, sparse chaff.
5	CB 2215	A II	IA	L 67.2 E 193.1	R: 38 cm	Ware: orange core, buff surface. Temper: common medium chaff, fine lime, mica inclusions. Orange-red paint slashes across rim.
6	CB 3197	A II	II	L. 81.2 F 35.6	R: c 53 cm	Ware: brown core, buff surface. Temper: common medium chaff, sparse fine lime.
7	CB 3834	G IV	I	L. 29.2 F 55.3	R: 35 cm	Ware: orange core, buff surface. Temper: common medium chaff.
8	CB 1863	G I	II/1	L. 5.1 E 63.4	R: 39 cm	Ware: dark grey core, buff surface. Temper: abundant chaff, medium lime.
9	CB 2227	G I	II/1	L. 9.1 E 72.6	R: 36 cm	Ware: buff. Temper: common fine chaff. Red-brown paint slashes across rim.
10	CB 1973	G I	II/1	L. 10.1 E 73.1	R: 40 cm	Ware: grey core, buff surface. Temper: medium chaff, occasional lime.
11	CB 3010	G II	II/2	L. 54.10 F 210.2	R: 39 cm	Ware: grey core, orange surface. Temper: common medium chaff.
12	CB 3110	G II	II/2	L. 54.10 F 210.3	R: 43 cm	Ware: grey core, orange-buff surface. Temper: common medium chaff, rare fine lime. Smoothed surfaces.

LARGE CARINATED SHALLOW BOWLS

PLATE 25

TRIANGULAR RIM

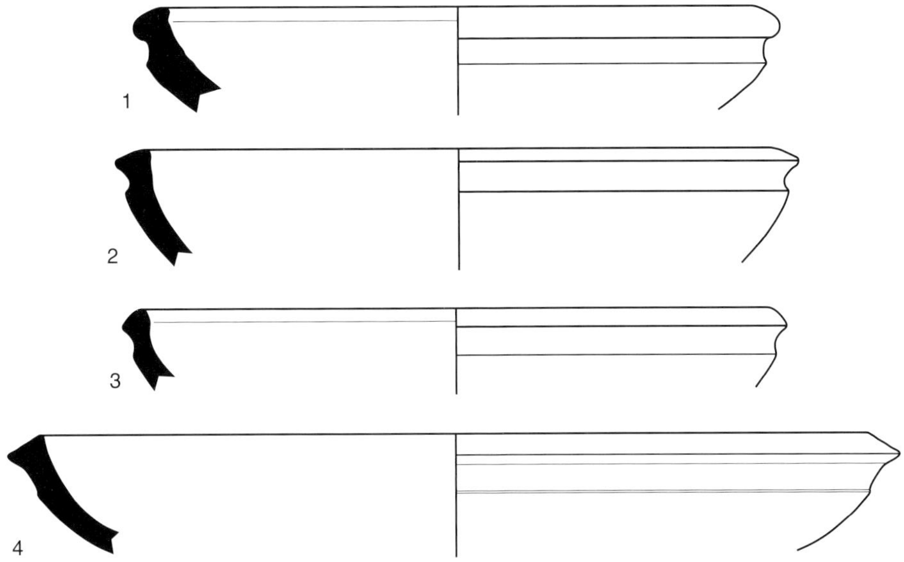

TRIANGULAR LEDGE RIM

1:4 10 cm

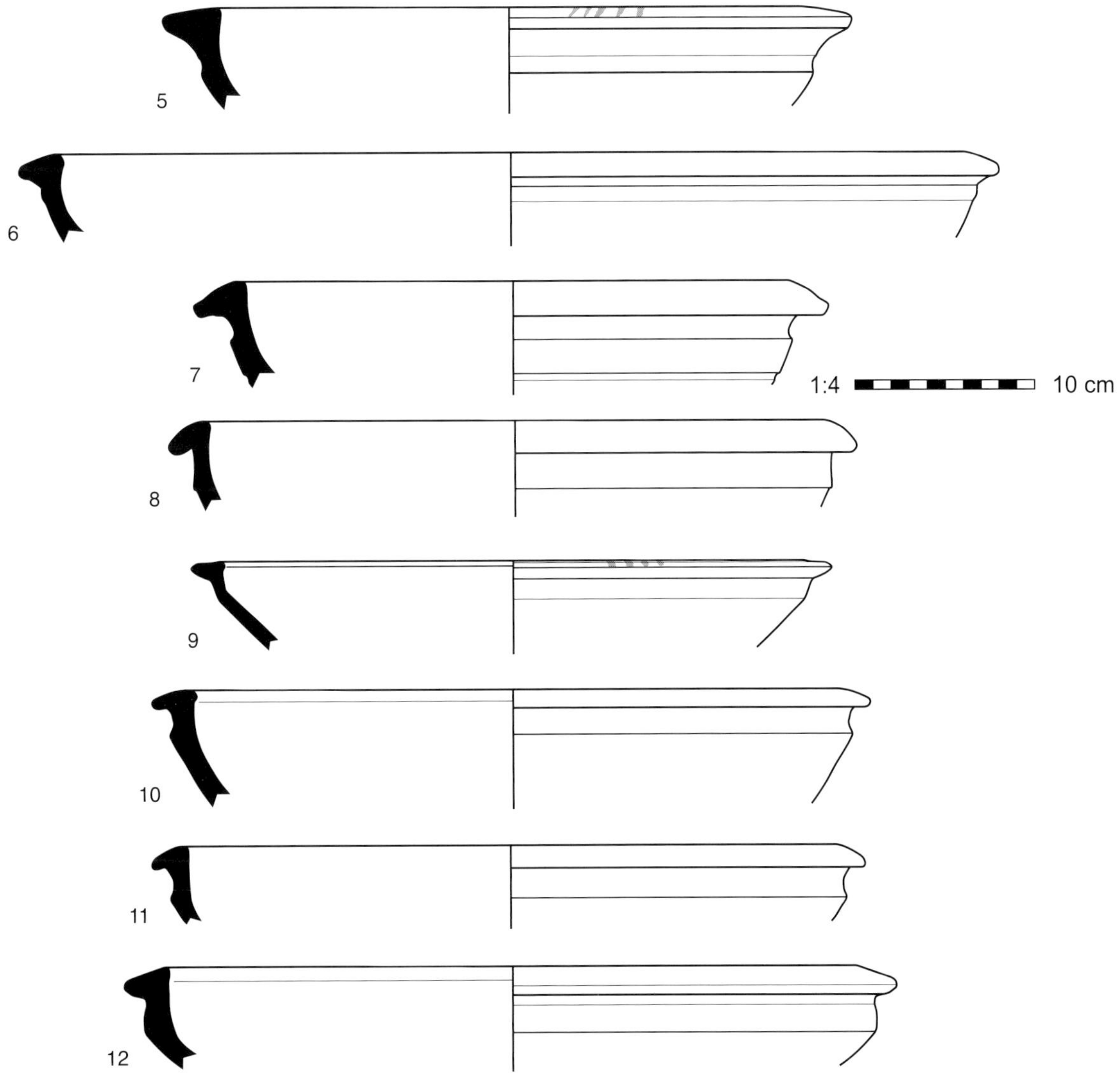

Plate 26: *Large Carinated Shallow and Deep Bowls*

	CB number	Area	Phase	Locus and Lot number	Dimensions	Ware, comments
1	CB 3212	G II	III	L. 37.3 F 213.2	R: 42 cm	Ware: black core, buff surface. Temper: common medium chaff. Red paint bands.
2	CB 3249	G II	II/2	L. 54.10 F 210.1	R: 53 cm	Ware: buff core, green surface. Temper: common medium chaff, rare fine lime.
3	CB 4252	G II	III	L. 37.5 F 226.4	R: 48 cm	Ware: grey core, buff surface. Temper: common medium chaff.
4	CB 3292	G IV	II/1	L. 34.1 F 64.1	R: 40 cm	Ware: grey core, buff-orange surface. Temper: common medium chaff. Smoothed surface.
5	CB 3250	G II	II/2	L. 54.10 F 210.1	R: 36 cm	Ware: green. Temper: common medium chaff and fine lime.
6	CB 3799	G II	II/2	L. 54.10 F 210.5	R: c 50 cm	Ware: brown core, buff surface. Temper: common medium chaff.
7	CB 3020	G II	II/2	L. 54.10 F 210.2	R: c 50 cm	Ware: black core, brown surface. Temper: common medium chaff, rare medium lime. Smoothed exterior.
8	CB 2299	G I	II/1	L. 9.4 E 85.1	R: 35 cm	Ware: grey core, buff surface. Temper: chaff.

LARGE CARINATED SHALLOW BOWLS

PLATE 26

EXTENDED TRIANGULAR RIM

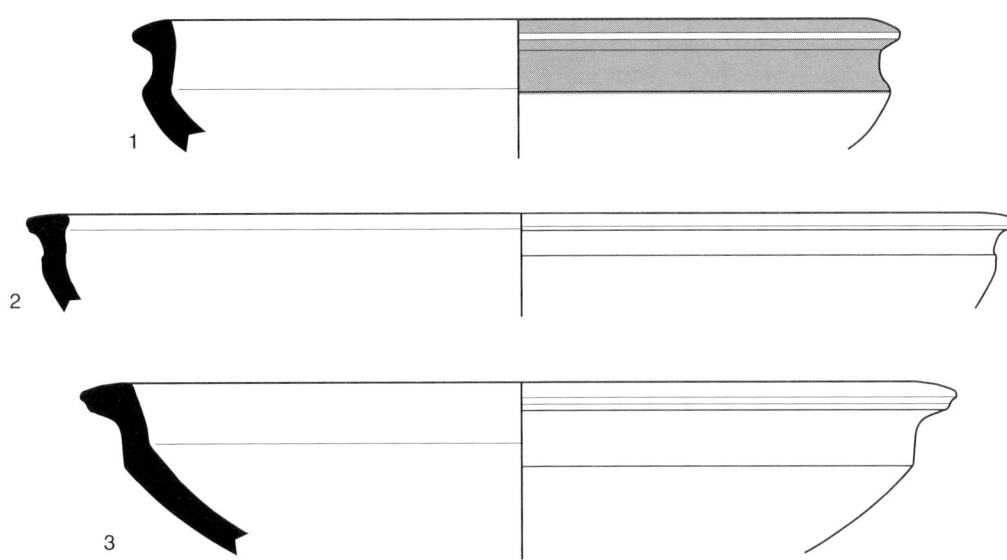

LARGE CARINATED DEEP BOWLS

LEDGE RIM

ROUNDED RIM

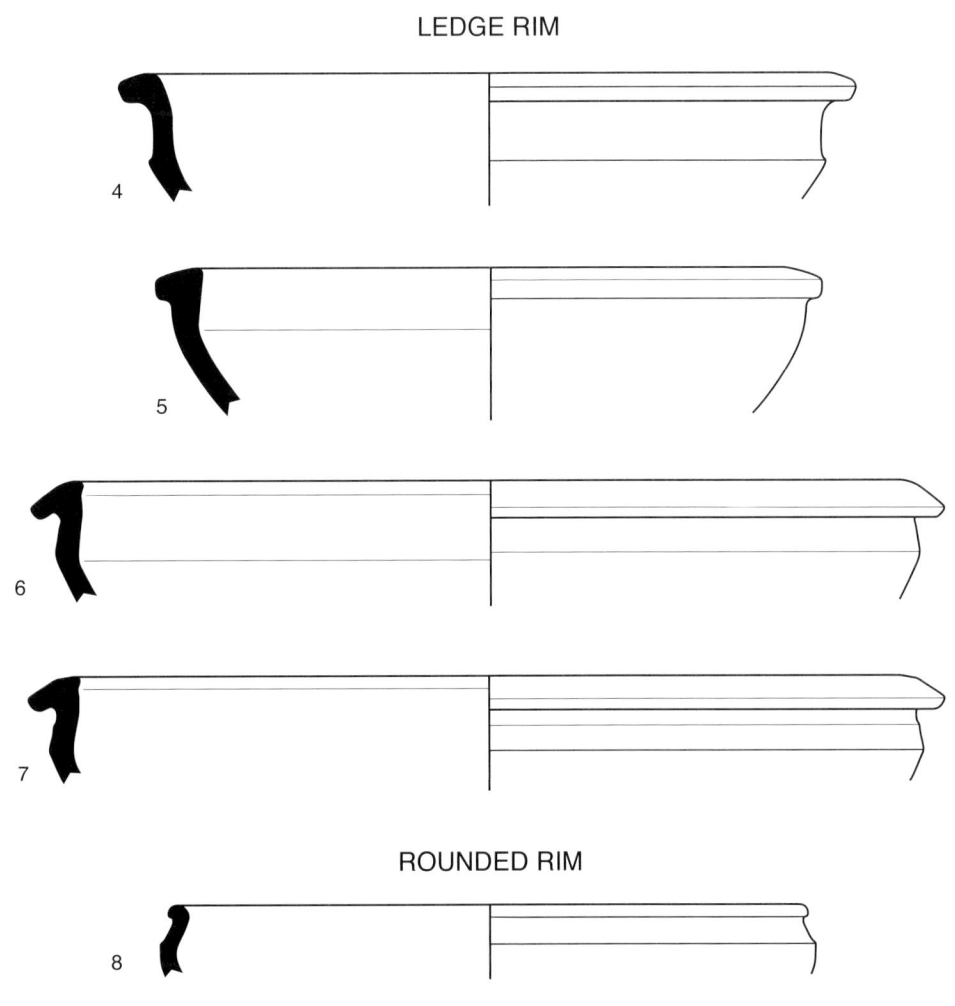

1:4 ▬▭▬▭ 10 cm

Plate 27: *Large Carinated Deep Bowls*

	CB number	Area	Phase	Locus and Lot number	Dimensions	Ware, comments
1	CB 4014	G II	III	L. 69.1 F 219.2	R: 42.5 cm	Ware: black core, orange surface. Temper: common medium chaff and fine lime.
2	CB 4004	G II	III	L. 70.1 F 220.3	R: 46 cm	Ware: black core, orange surface. Temper: common medium chaff, common fine-medium lime. Red paint band on rim.
3	CB 3191	G IV	III	L. 40.3 F 69.3	R: 40 cm	Ware: black core, orange surface. Temper: common medium chaff. Red paint bands.
4	CB 3192	G IV	III	L. 40.3 F 69.3	R: 36 cm	Ware: brown core, orange surface. Temper: common medium chaff.
5	CB 1695	A I	II	L. 30.1 D 358	R: 36 cm	Ware: grey core, reddish surface. Temper: common chaff, lime.
6	CB 4251	G II	III	L. 37.5 F 226.4	R: 47 cm	Ware: dark grey core, orange surface. Temper: sparse medium chaff.
7	CB 2528	G I	II/2	L. 9.8 E 250.1	R: c 43 cm	Ware: grey-brown core, orange surface. Temper: common medium chaff.

LARGE CARINATED DEEP BOWLS

PLATE 27

TRIANGULAR RIM

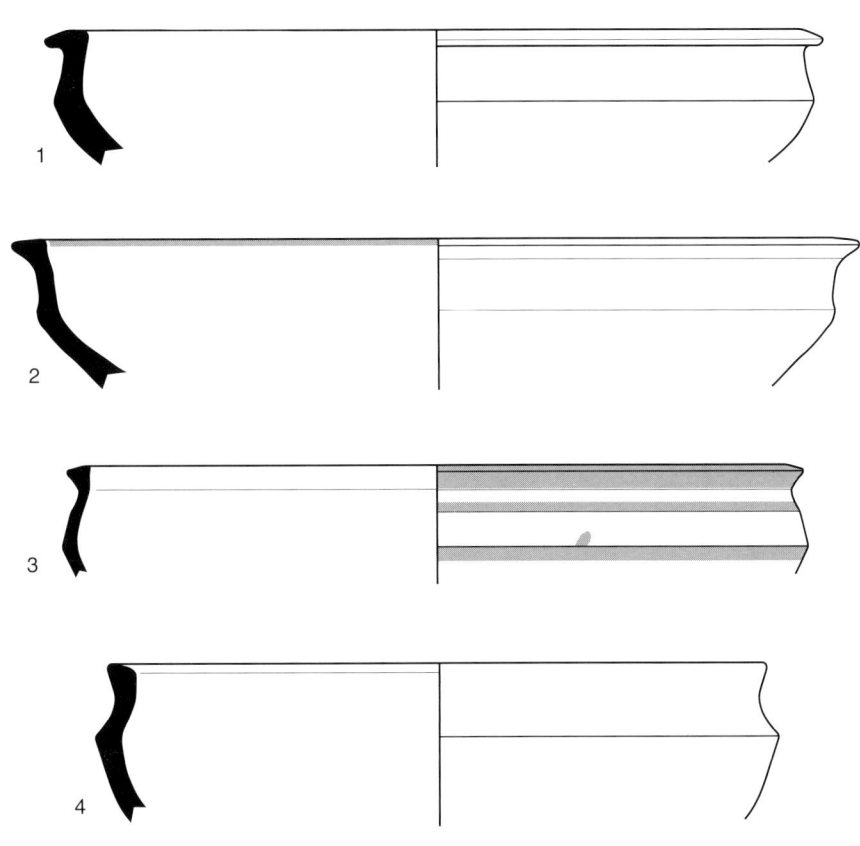

TRIANGULAR RIM WITH INTERIOR GROOVE

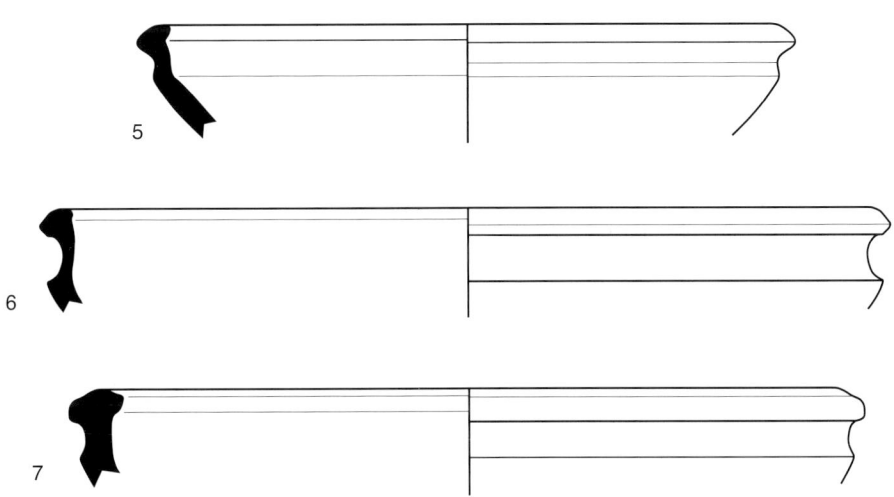

1:4   10 cm

Plate 28: *Small and Medium Grey Ware Bowls*

	CB number	Area	Phase	Locus & Lot number	Dimensions	Ware, comments
1	CB 1:4	A I	S	L. 1.1 D 1	R: 12 cm	Ware: grey. Temper: none.
2	CB 2987	A II	II	L. 81.2 F 35.2	R: 14 cm	Ware: grey. Temper: common fine-medium chaff. Burnished interior and exterior.
3	CB 1733	A I	II	L. 30.1 D 373	R: 16 cm	Ware: grey. Temper: mica inclusions. Dense horizontal burnishing on interior and exterior.
4	CB 2026	G II	II/1	L. 55.1 E 97.1	R: 19 cm	Ware: brown core, grey-brown surface. Temper: none. Horizontal burnishing interior and exterior.
5	CB 1764	A I	II	L. 16.2 D 361	R: 20 cm	Ware: grey. Temper: sparse chaff. Horizontal burnishing interior and exterior. Corrugated rim.
6	CB 4261	G II	III	L. 37.4 F 222.1	R: 15 cm	Ware: grey. Temper: sparse fine lime. Burnished interior and exterior.
7	CB 1772	A I	IA	L. 32.1 D 366	R: 19 cm	Ware: grey. Temper: common medium-large chaff. Horizontal burnishing interior and exterior.
8	CB 1771	A I	IA	L. 32.1 D 366	R: 12 cm	Ware: grey. Temper: medium chaff. Horizontal burnishing interior and exterior.
9	CB 1774	A I	IA	L. 32.1 D 366	R: 19 cm	Ware: grey. Temper: medium chaff. Horizontal burnishing interior and exterior.
10	CB 38:2	A I	I	L. 5.1 D 16	R: 11 cm	Ware: dark grey. Temper: common chaff.
11	CB 2025	G II	II/1	L. 55.1 E 97.1	R: 22 cm	Ware: grey. Temper: sparse chaff. Horizontal burnishing interior and exterior.
12	CB 1762	A I	II	L. 16.2 D 361	R: 34 cm	Ware: grey. Temper: medium chaff, lime. Horizontal burnishing interior and exterior.
13	CB 2903	G II	II/2	L. 54.9 F 206.1	R: 31.5 cm	Ware: dark grey core, light grey surface. Temper: common medium chaff, rare fine lime, occasional dark grit. Burnished surfaces.
14	CB 2892	G II	II/2	L. 54.8 F 204.3	R: 34 cm	Ware: grey. Temper: common medium chaff, rare fine lime. Horiz. burnishing on interior and exterior.
15	CB 2446	G I	II/2	L. 16.1 E 243.1	R: 36 cm	Ware: dark grey core, grey surface. Temper: common medium chaff. Horiz. burnishing on exterior.
16	CB 3201	A II	I	L. 76.9 F 20.2	R: 32 cm	Ware: grey. Temper: common large chaff. Horizontal burnishing interior and exterior.
17	CB 3056	A II	II	L. 81.2 F 35.4	R: 34 cm	Ware: grey. Temper: common medium chaff. Burnished interior and exterior.
18	CB 1870	A II	II	L. 52.2 E 6.2	R: 34 cm	Ware: grey. Temper: medium chaff. Sparse horizontal burnishing on interior and exterior.
19	CB 786:3	A I	II	L. 26.1 D 363	R: 27 cm B: 17 cm H: 3.9 cm	Ware: grey. Temper: chaff, lime.
20	CB 2447	G I	II/1	L. 9.5 E 90.1	R: 33 cm	Ware: pale brown core, grey surface. Temper: common medium chaff. Burnishing interior and exterior.
21	CB 2856	G III	II/2	L. 28.1 F 77.2	R: 34.5 cm	Ware: grey core and surfaces. Temper: common large chaff, sparse fine lime. Burnished interior and exterior.
22	CB 3888	G II	III	L. 70.2 F 221.1	R: 33.5 cm	Ware: grey. Temper: common medium chaff. Horizontal burnishing interior and exterior.
23	CB 2139	G II	II/1A	L. 59.1 E 101.1	R: 21 cm	Ware: grey-buff core and surface, burnished. Temper: common chaff, occasional fine lime.
24	CB 3021	G II	II/2	L. 54.10 F 210.2	R: 34.5 cm	Ware: grey. Temper: common medium chaff and fine-medium lime. Horiz. burnishing interior and exterior.
25	CB 3009	G II	II/2	L. 54.10 F 210.2	R: 36 cm	Ware: grey. Temper: common medium grit, rare medium chaff. Horizontal burnishing.

GREY WARE BOWLS

PLATE 28

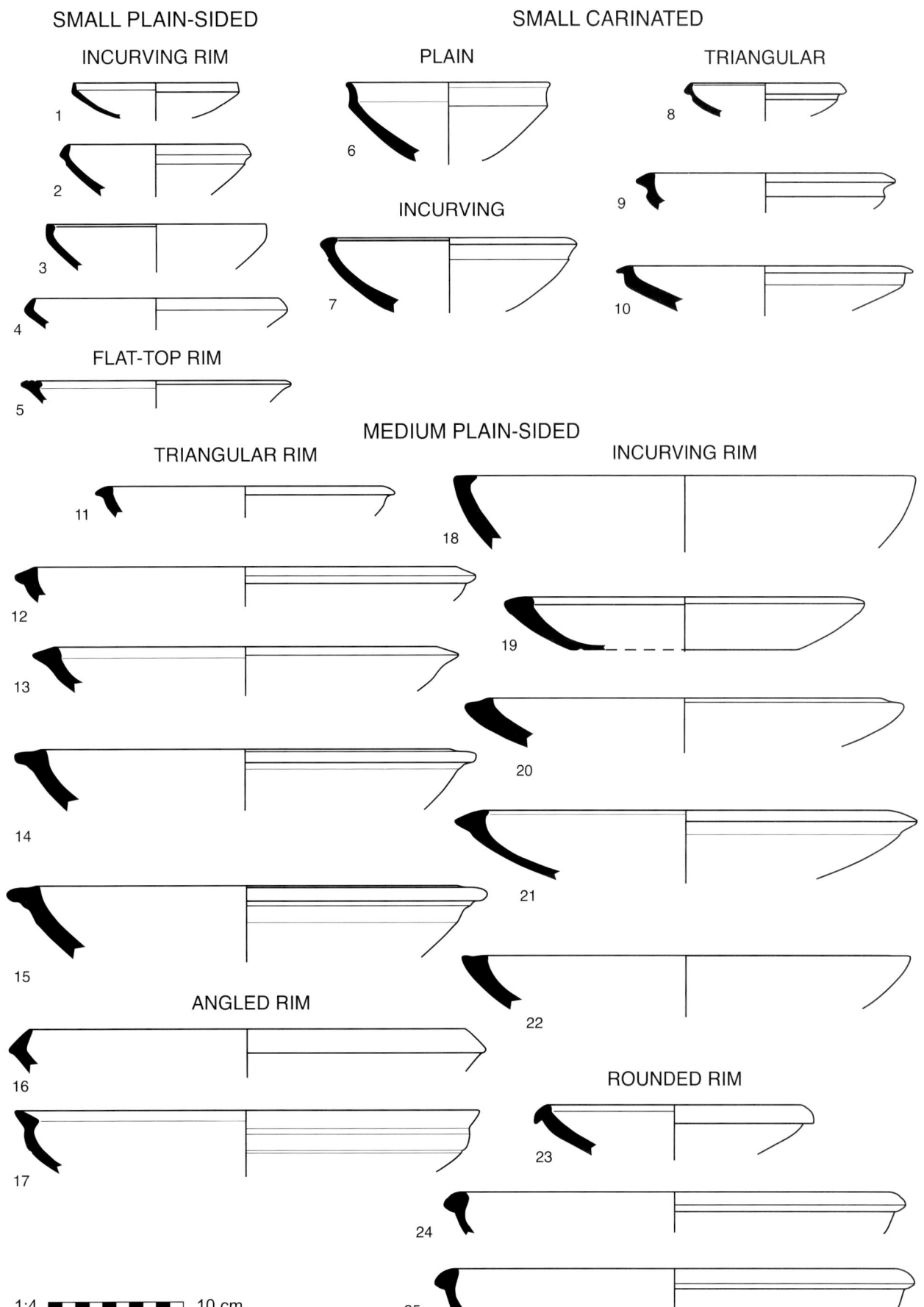

1:4 ▬▬▬▬ 10 cm

Plate 29: *Medium and Large Grey Ware Bowls*

	CB number	Area	Phase	Locus & Lot number	Dimensions	Ware, comments
1	CB 2138	G II	II/1A	L. 59.1 E 101.1	R: 28	Ware: grey core, pale grey surface, burnished. Temper: common chaff, occasional fine lime.
2	CB 1763	A I	II	L. 16.2 D 361	R: 24 cm	Ware: grey. Temper: occasional fine lime, common chaff. Horizontal burnishing interior and exterior.
3	CB 2379	G I	II/1	L. 12.1 E 81.2	R: 29 cm	Ware: grey. Temper: common chaff, sparse lime. Burnished exterior.
4	CB 1782	A II	S	L. 50.1 E 1.1	R: 35 cm	Ware: grey. Temper: common medium chaff. Sparse horizontal burnishing on interior and exterior.
5	CB 3996	G II	II/2	L. 54.10 F 210.1	R: 28 cm	Ware: grey core and surface. Temper: common fine sand and lime. Burnished interior and exterior.
6	CB 2220	G II	II/1A	L. 59.2 E 107.3	R: 28 cm	Ware: grey core, grey-green surface. Temper: common chaff, sparse lime. Horizontal burnishing interior and exterior.
7	CB 1788	G I	II/1	L. 4.1 E 62.1	R: 27 cm	Ware: grey. Temper: sparse chaff, mica inclusions. Horizontal burnishing on exterior.
8	CB 2851	G II	II/2	L. 54.8 F 204.1	R: 27.5 cm	Ware: grey. Temper: common large chaff, sparse fine lime. Burnished interior and exterior.
9	CB 1894	G II	II/2	L. 51.2 E 91.1	R: 23 cm	Ware: over-fired green. Temper: medium chaff. Horizontal burnishing interior and exterior.
10	CB 1:5	A I	S	L. 1.1 D 1	R: 32 cm B: 27 cm H: 5.2 cm	Ware: dark grey. Temper: lime, occasional chaff. Deep horizontal grooved sides.
11	CB 3965	G II	III	L. 37.3 F 213.7	R: 26 cm	Ware: grey. Temper: sparse fine lime and sand. Burnished interior and exterior.
12	CB 4249	G II	III	L. 37.5 F 226.4	R: 20 cm	Ware: grey. Temper: common fine lime and sand.
13	CB 2297	A II	III	L. 61.4 E 198.2	R: 22 cm	Ware: brown core, grey-brown surface. Temper: sparse medium chaff. Horizontal burnishing interior and exterior.
14	CB 3293	G IV	II/1	L. 34.1 F 64.1	R: 27 cm	Ware: grey. Temper: rare fine chaff, common sand. Horizontal burnishing interior and exterior.
15	CB 4236	G II	III	L. 37.5 F 226.2	R: 22 cm	Ware: grey core, dark grey surface. Temper: sparse fine sand. Horizontal burnishing interior and exterior.
16	CB 3225	G II	III	L. 36.1 F 207.3	R: 29 cm	Ware: buff. Temper: common medium chaff and fine lime. Horizontally burnished exterior.
17	CB 3224	G II	III	L. 36.1 F 207.3	R: 36 cm	Ware: buff. Temper: common medium chaff and fine lime. Horizontally burnished exterior.
18	CB 3997	G II	II/2	L. 54.10 F 210.1	R: 44.5 cm	Ware: grey. Temper: common medium chaff. Abraded surface.
19	CB 2301	G I	II/1	L. 9.4 E 85.1	R: 42 cm	Ware: grey. Temper: fine grit. Burnished interior and exterior.

GREY WARE BOWLS

PLATE 29

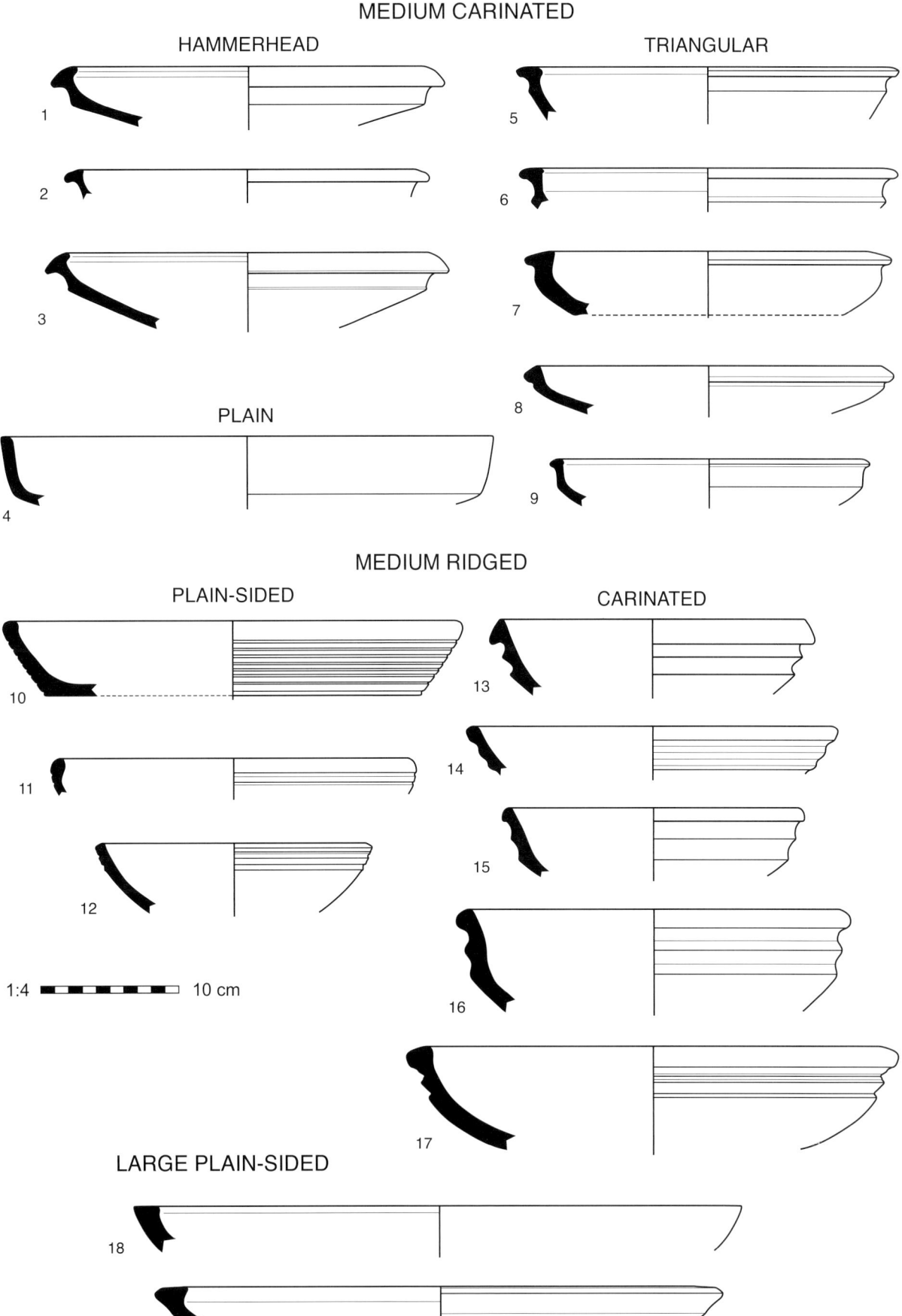

Plate 30: *Ridged Bowls*

	CB number	Area	Phase	Loc. & Lot no.	Dimensions	Ware, comments
1	CB 2290	A II	IA	L. 67.5 E 199.1	R: 18 cm	Ware: buff. Temper: sparse medium chaff, fine-medium lime. Red paint slashes across rim.
2	CB 1850	G I	II/1A	L. 3.1 E 63.3	R: 16 cm	Ware: buff core, pale buff surface. Temper: fine sparse sand.
3	CB 3291	G IV	II/1	L. 34.1 F 64.1	R: 11 cm	Ware: brown core, orange surface. Temper: common sand. Red paint slashes, horiz. grooves.
4	CB 3942	G IV	I	L. 33.1 F 58.5	R: 11 cm	Ware: buff surface. Temper: common medium chaff. Five red paint slashes on rim.
5	CB 1886	G I	II/1	L. 2.1 E 61.5	R: 16.5 cm	Ware: orange-buff. Temper: sparse fine sand, lime.
6	CB 4003	G II	III	L. 70.1 F 220.3	R: 17 cm	Ware: pink core, buff surface. Temper: abundant fine-medium lime (and surface blow-outs). Traces of red paint slashes on rim.
7	CB 4240	G II	IV	L. 74.1 F 228.2	R: 15 cm	Ware: buff core, pale buff surface. Temper: common fine lime. Brown paint slashes on rim.
8	CB 3013	G II	II/2	L.54.10 F 210.2	R: 15 cm	Ware: green. Temper: rare medium chaff. Horizontal shallow grooves.
9	CB 2035	A II	IA	L. 67.1 E 29.3	R: 23 cm	Ware: orange core, pale orange surface. Temper: fine lime.
10	CB 1835	A II	II	L. 54.1 E 7.1	R: 27 cm	Ware: grey-buff core, orange surface. Temper: common medium chaff, mica inclusions.
11	CB 4263	G II	III	L. 37.5 F 226.3	R: 21 cm	Ware: buff. Temper: sparse large chaff and medium lime. Burnished exterior, red paint slashes on rim, deep horizontal grooves.
12	CB 4235	G II	III	L. 37.5 F 226.2	R: 22.5 cm	Ware: green-buff. Temper: common fine sand and lime. Sharp horizontal grooves.
13	CB 3055	G II	III	L. 36.1 F 207.2	R: 21.5 cm	Ware: buff core, green surface. Temper: common medium chaff. Traces of black paint slashes on rim, deep horizontal grooves.
14	CB 2991	A II	II	L. 79.2 F 8.2	R: 22 cm	Ware: buff. Temper: common fine-medium chaff, rare lime.
15	CB 1953	A I	II	L. 41.1 E 48.1	R: 22 cm	Ware: buff. Temper: sparse medium chaff, fine lime.
16	CB 3881	G II	III	L. 69.1 F 219.1	R: 30 cm	Ware: grey core, buff surface. Temper: common medium chaff. Red paint band on rim.
17	CB 2964	G IV	I	L. 33.1 F 58.3	R: 19.5 cm	Ware: green. Temper: sparse medium chaff. Fugitive paint slashes on rim.
18	CB 3402	G II	II/2	L.54.10 F 210.2	R: 20.5 cm	Ware: buff. Temper: common fine-medium lime.
19	CB 4268	G II	III	L. 37.5 F 226.3	R: 24.5 cm	Ware: orange-buff. Temper: common fine sand, occasional medium chaff. Red paint bands and slashes, horizontal grooves and raised ridge.
20	CB 2600	G II	II/2	L. 54.5 E 108.3	R: 33 cm	Ware: buff. Temper: common chaff, fine lime.
21	CB 4209	G II	III	01-24 F 217.2	R: 30.5 cm	Ware: buff core, pale buff surface. Temper: common medium chaff, occasional medium lime. Brown paint band and raised grooved ridge.
22	CB 4237	G II	III	L. 37.3 F 213.5	R: 34 cm	Ware: buff core, orange-buff surface. Temper: common medium chaff and fine lime. Red paint and raised ridges.
23	CB 1992	A II	II	L. 61.3 E 25.3	R: 25.5 cm	Ware: buff core, brown surface. Temper: common chaff.
24	CB 1854	G I	II/1	L. 4.3 E 62.5	R: 26 cm	Ware: brown core, black surface. Temper: sparse fine chaff. Deep horizontal combing on exterior, horizontal burnishing on interior.

RIDGED BOWLS PLATE 30

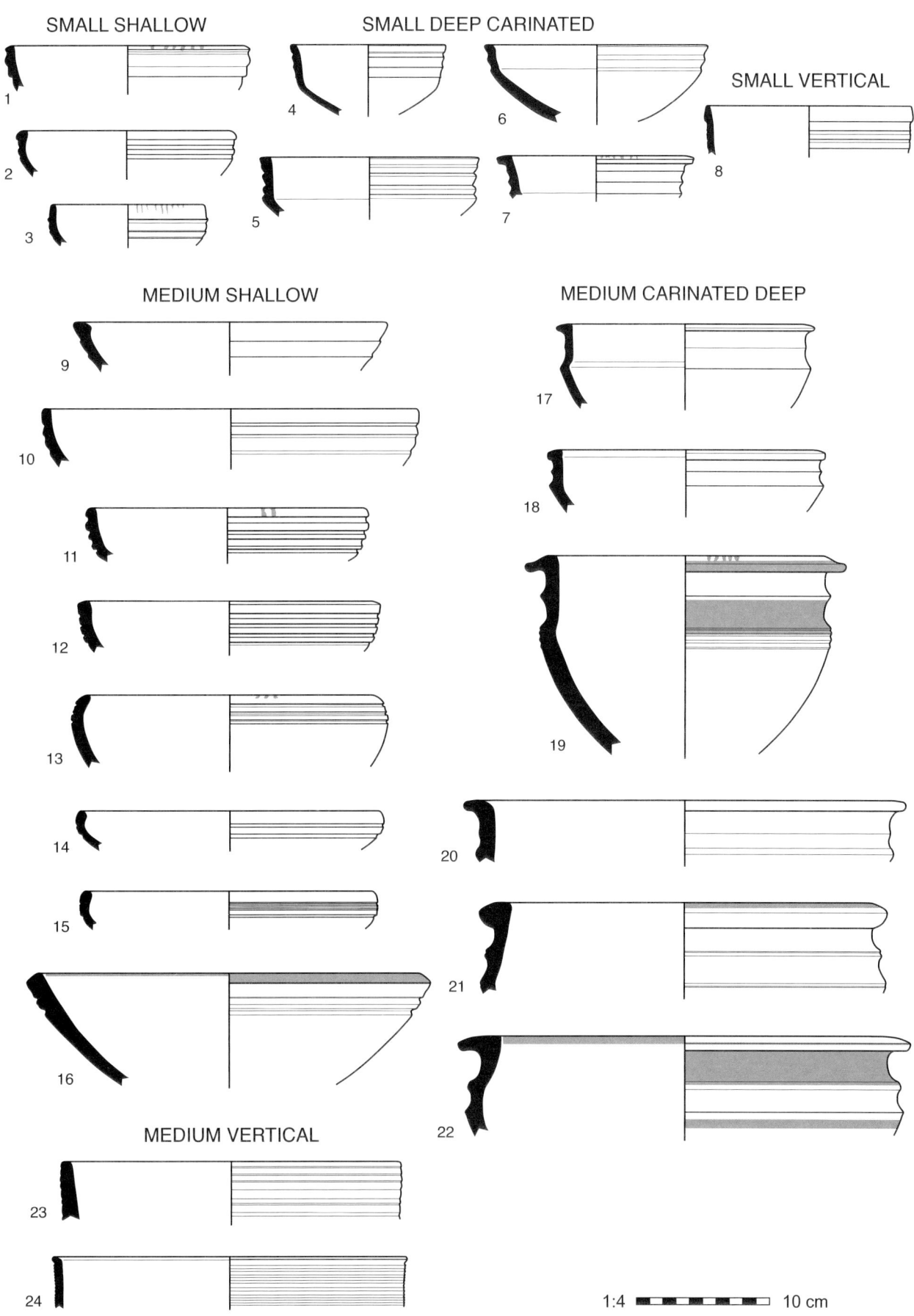

Plate 31: *Z-Sided Bowls*

	CB number	Area	Phse.	Loc. & Lot no.	Dimensions	Ware, comments
1	CB 14:1	A I	S	L. 1.2 D 5	R: 12.8 cm H: 6.8	Ware: red core, buff surface. Temper: sparse chaff, lime. Red paint.
2	CB 2371	A II	IA	L. 67.7 E 271.1	R: 14 cm	Ware: orange. Temper: sparse medium chaff.
3	CB 2388	A II	IA	L. 67.6 E 201.3	R: 16 cm	Ware: pale green. Temper: sparse fine chaff, lime. Fugitive brown-black paint bands.
4	CB 48:1	A I	S	L. 1.2 D 19	R: 10 cm	Ware: buff. Temper: sparse lime. Red paint bands.
5	CB 2993	A II	II	L. 79.2 F 8.2	R: 12 cm	Ware: green core, buff surface. Temper: rare fine lime. Black paint bands.
6	CB 2158	G I	II/2	L. 4.6 E 66.5	R: 14 cm	Ware: pale buff core and surface. Temper: common fine lime.
7	CB 1821	G II	II/2	L. 51.2 E 91.4	R: 16 cm	Ware: red core, buff surface. Temper: sparse chaff, lime. Brown-black paint bands.
8	CB 347:1	A I	I	L. 20.1 D 65	R: 15 cm	Ware: red core, green surface. Temper: sparse chaff.
9	CB 374:1	A I	II	L. 19.1 D 76	R: 16 cm	Ware: buff. Temper: sparse lime. Red paint bands.
10	CB 318:2	A I	II	L. 15.1 D 51	R: 16 cm	Ware: red core, buff surface. Temper: common chaff, lime.
11	CB 1832	A II	II	L. 54.1 E 7.1	R: 12 cm	Ware: orange-buff core, pale buff surface. Temper: none. Red paint bands.
12	CB 386:2	A I	I	L. 17.1 D 322	R: 13 cm	Ware: buff. Temper: sparse lime, chaff. Red painted bands, lines and cross-hatched triangles.
13	CB 2932	A II	II	L. 81.1 F 34.1	R: 11 cm B: 5 cm H: 10 cm	Ware: green core, buff surface. Temper: sparse medium chaff, common fine-medium lime. Black paint band. Bitumen smeared in interior.
14	CB 2915	A II	II	L. 54.6 F 33.1	R: 12 cm	Ware: green. Temper: sparse fine lime.
15	CB 2110	A II	II	L. 52.2 E 185.3	R: c 12 cm	Ware: buff core, pale buff surface. Temper: sparse fine lime. Fugitive red paint bands.
16	CB 3976	G IV	I	L. 24.1 F 52.3	R: 11 cm	Ware: green. Temper: sparse fine chaff. Black-brown paint bands.
17	CB 1911	G I	II/1	L. 2.1 E 61.6	R: 12 cm	Ware: orange. Temper: none visible.
18	CB 3194	G IV	II/1	L. 34.4 F 70.2	R: 12 cm	Ware: brown core, buff surface. Temper: common fine lime. Red paint bands.
19	CB 3934	G IV	II/2	L. 73.2 F 457.1	R: 15 cm	Ware: pale orange core, buff surface. Temper: common medium chaff.
20	CB 3783	G IV	III	L. 40.2 F 68.3	R: 12 cm	Ware: buff core, pale buff surface. Temper: sparse medium chaff and lime. Red paint bands.
21	CB 2130	G II	II/1 A	L. 59.1 E 101.2	R: 18 cm	Ware: buff-orange. Temper: common chaff sparse fine lime Red paint cross-hatched triangles and bands.
22	CB 2177	G II	II/1 A	L. 59.3 E 103.2	R: 30.5 cm	Ware: orange core, pale orange-buff surface. Temper: common chaff, lime, mica inclusions. Red paint cross-hatched triangles and horizontal bands.
23	CB 2179	G II	II/1 A	L. 59.3 E 103.2	R: 23 cm	Ware: grey core, buff surface. Temper: common chaff, fine lime, mica inclusions.
24	CB 2308	G I	II/1	L. 4.1 E 86.1	R: 23 cm	Ware: buff core, pale buff surface. Temper: common fine lime, sparse chaff. Red-brown paint over rim.
25	CB 2506	G II	II/1	L. 58.2 E 106.3	R: 22 cm	Ware: green-buff core and surface. Temper: common medium chaff. Fugitive black paint bands and hatched triangles.
26	CB 3972	G II	III	L. 37.3 F 213.4	R: 28 cm	Ware: buff. Temper: common medium chaff and lime. Brown paint.

Z-SIDED BOWLS

PLATE 31

SMALL SHALLOW

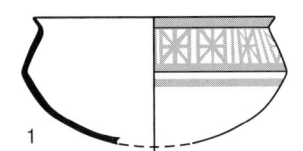
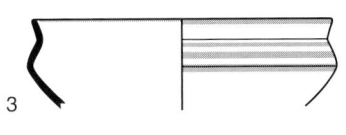
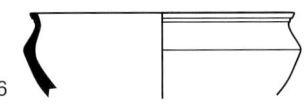
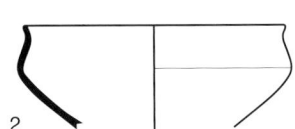

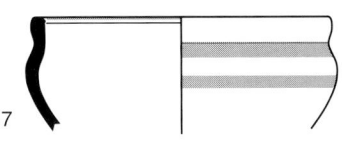

SMALL DEEP

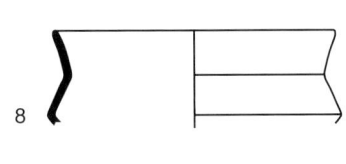
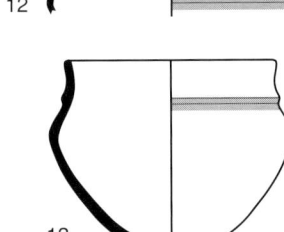
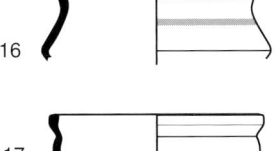
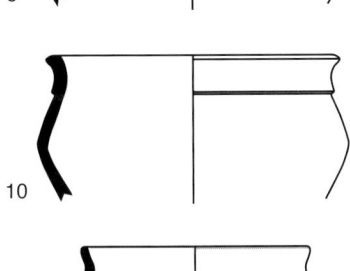
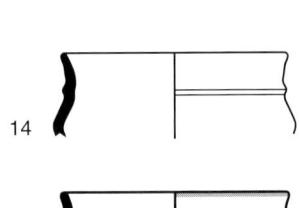

1:4 ⬛▬▬▬▬▬▬ 10 cm

MEDIUM DEEP

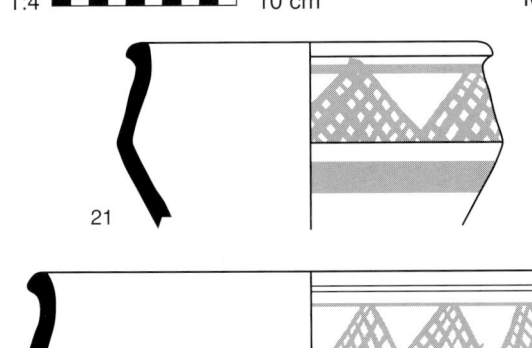
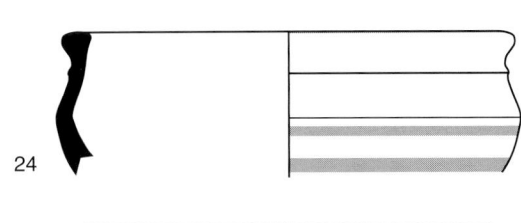
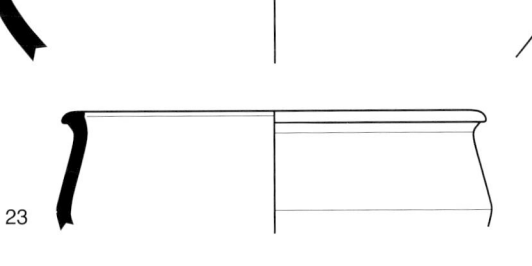
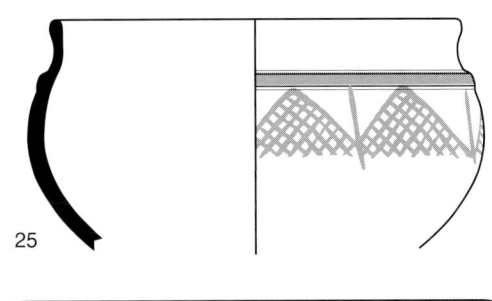

305

Plate 32: *Medium Barrels*

	CB number	Area	Phase	Locus and Lot number	Dimensions	Ware, comments
1	CB 1697	A I	II	L. 29.1 D 368	R: 25 cm	Ware: buff-brown core, pale buff surface. Temper: occasional chaff, rare large lime. Horizontal grooves.
2	CB 719:2	A I	I	L. 17.2 D 340	R: 26 cm	Ware: buff. Temper: common chaff, sparse lime.
3	CB 1869	A II	II	L. 52.2 E 6.2	R: 30 cm	Ware: buff-pink core, pale buff surface. Temper: common chaff, fine lime.
4	CB 3044	A II	II	L. 81.2 F 35.3	R: 29.5 cm	Ware: black core, dark buff surface. Temper: common medium chaff, rare medium grit. Three horizontal grooves at maximum diameter.
5	CB 1730	A I	I	L. 17.2 D 350	R: 28 cm	Ware: buff core, pale buff surface. Temper: common medium chaff, occasional lime. Horizontal grooves at maximum diameter.
6	CB 2017	G I	II/2	L. 5.1 E 69.2	R: 30 cm	Ware: grey core, buff surface. Temper: abundant chaff, occasional lime.
7	CB 2455	G I	II/1	L. 10.1 E 73.4	R: 28 cm	Ware: buff-pink core, buff-green surface. Temper: common medium chaff, fine lime. Three horizontal grooves.
8	CB 2125	G II	II/2	L. 51.5 E 93.3	R: 30 cm	Ware: orange-buff core, buff surface. Temper: common chaff, lime. Horizontal grooves on shoulder.
9	CB 3176	G II	II/2	L. 54.10 F 210.4	R: 26 cm	Ware: buff. Temper: common medium chaff, occasional fine lime.
10	CB 3252	G II	II/2	L. 54.10 F 210.1	R: 23.5 cm	Ware: buff core, green surface. Temper: common medium chaff, rare fine-medium lime.
11	CB 3050	G III	II/2	L. 39.2 F 81.1	R: 30 cm	Ware: orange core, buff surface. Temper: common coarse chaff. Soot staining on exterior.
12	CB 2387	G II	II/1	L. 58.2 E 106.2	R: 27 cm	Ware: green-buff core and surface. temper: common chaff, sparse fine lime.
13	CB 1808	A II	II	L. 52.1 E 4.1	R: 27 cm	Medium barrel. Ware: buff core, pale buff surface. Temper: common chaff, sparse lime.
14	CB 1924	A I	II	L. 43.2 E 46.1	R: 24.2 cm M: 24.4 cm B: 10.7 cm H: 18 cm	Medium barrel. Ware: pale buff. Temper: common chaff, medium lime. Red-brown paint bands on exterior and splashes in spirals on interior.
15	CB 2207	A I	III	L. 44.2 E 213.1	R: 22 cm	Medium barrel. Unusual rim-shoulder strap handle(s). Ware: buff core, pale green-buff surface. Temper: common medium chaff, fine lime, occasional large lime.

MEDIUM BARRELS PLATE 32

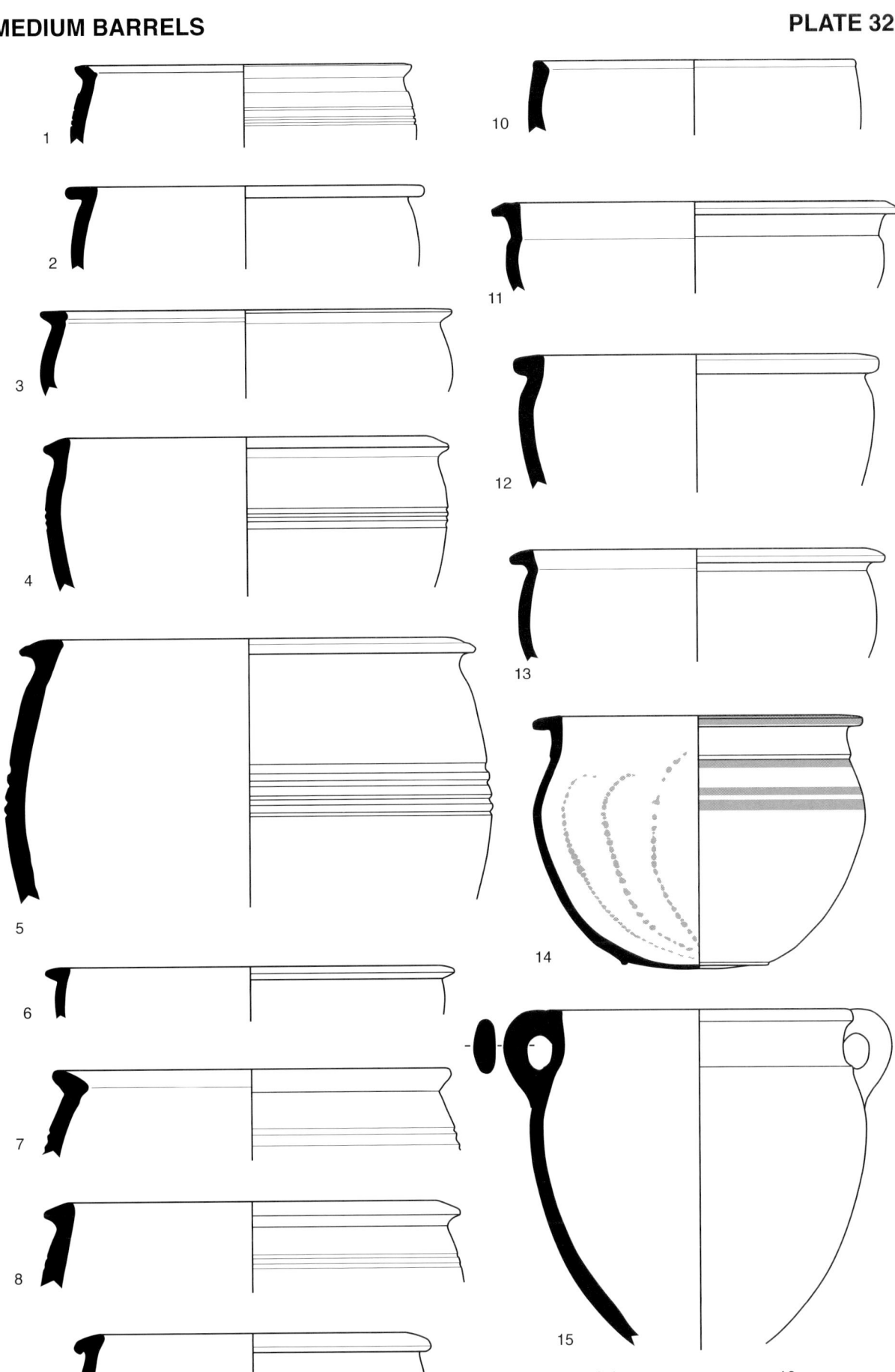

Plate 33: *Medium and Large Barrels*

	CB number	Area	Phase	Locus and Lot number	Dimensions	Ware, comments
1	CB 2131	G II	II/1A	L. 59.1 E 101.2	R: 26 cm	Ware: grey core, orange surface. Temper: common fine chaff.
2	CB 3812	G II	II/2	L. 54.10 F 210.5	R: 24 cm	Ware: green. Temper: common medium chaff and fine-medium lime.
3	CB 3247	G II	II/2	L. 54.10 F 210.1	R: 29.5 cm	Ware: orange core, yellow surface. Temper: common medium chaff and medium grit. Horizontal shallow grooves.
4	CB 2226	A II	IA	L. 67.5 E 197.1	R: 34 cm	Ware: green. Temper: common medium chaff, occasional fine lime. Horizontal grooves.
5	CB 2796	G IV	I	L. 23.1 F 51.1	R: 35 cm	Ware: buff. Temper: common chaff. Fugitive brown paint bands.
6	CB 2456	G I	II/1	L. 10.1 E 73.4	R: 33.5 cm	Ware: buff. Temper: common medium chaff, fine lime.
7	CB 1789	G I	II/1	L. 4.1 E 62.1	R: 37.5 cm	Ware: orange core, pale orange surface. Temper: common chaff, sparse lime. Red paint stripe at maximum diameter.
8	CB 2148	G II	II/1	L. 54.1 E 96.2	R: 39 cm	Ware: grey core, dark buff surface. Temper: common chaff, mica inclusions. Horizontal groove at maximum diameter.
9	CB 2940	G IV	II/1	L. 32.2 F 59.2	R: 40 cm	Ware: pink core, green surface. Temper: common medium chaff and fine lime and sand. Horizontal grooves on shoulder.
10	CB 3254	G II	II/2	L. 54.10 F 210.1	R: 32.5 cm	Ware: buff. Temper: common medium chaff.
11	CB 2013	G I	II/2	L. 4.6 E 66.6	R: 34.5 cm	Ware: pink-buff core, buff surface. Temper: sparse chaff and lime. Four dark red-brown paint slashes across rim.
12	CB 3890	G II	II/2	L. 54.10 F 210.6	R: 33 cm	Ware: black core, orange-yellow surface. Temper: abundant medium chaff and fine lime.
13	CB 3257	G II	II/2	L. 54.10 F 210.1	R: 38 cm	Ware: black core, orange surface. Temper: common medium chaff, rare fine lime. Smoothed surface.
14	CB 3253	G II	II/2	L. 54.10 F 210.1	R: 41 cm	Ware: buff. Temper: common medium chaff.

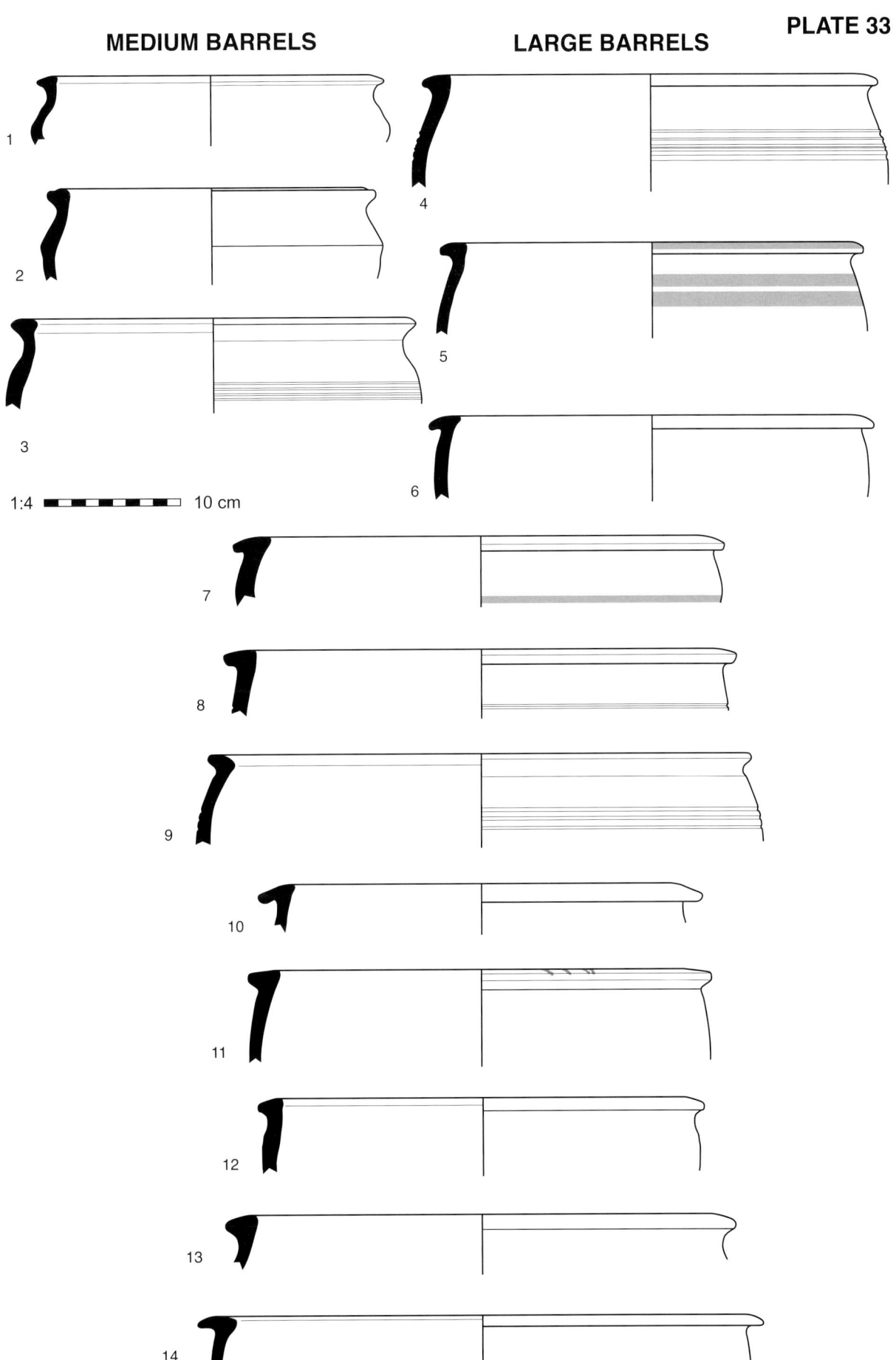

PLATE 33

Plate 34: *Large Barrels*

	CB number	Area	Phase	Locus and Lot number	Dimensions	Ware, comments
1	CB 4008	G II	III	L. 70.1 F 220.3	R: 38 cm	Ware: orange core, yellow-buff surface. Temper: common medium chaff, common sand and fine lime. Horizontal grooves at maximum diameter.
2	CB 2532	A II	IA	L. 70.1 E 205.2	R: c 45 cm	Ware: buff. Temper: common large chaff, sparse medium lime.
3	CB 2503/4	G II	II/1	L. 58.2 E 106.3	R: 32.5 cm	Ware: buff core, pale buff surface. Temper: common medium chaff, sparse fine lime. Red paint band on top of rim, with groups of slashes across rim.
4	CB 2214	A II	II	L. 52.2 E 185.2	R: 44.5 cm	Ware: green. Temper: common medium chaff, occasional large lime. Horizontal and wavy grooves just above maximum diameter.
5	CB 2068	A II	II	L. 54.4 E 28.2	R: 32.2 cm M: 33.7 cm B: 11.5 cm H: 23.7 cm	Ware: greenish-buff. Temper: common medium chaff, sparse medium-large lime.

LARGE BARRELS PLATE 34

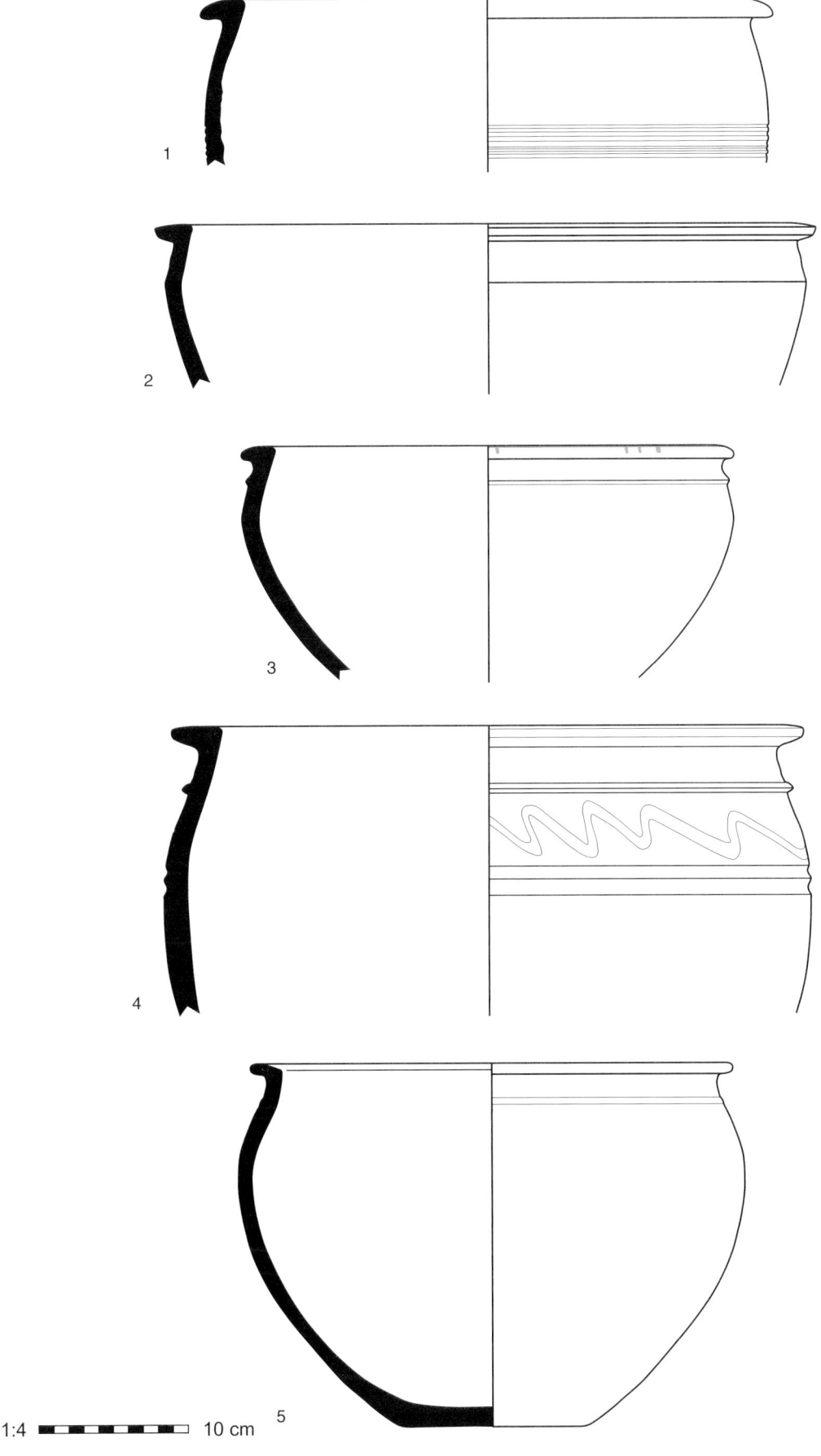

Plate 35: *Large Barrels*

	CB number	Area	Phase	Locus and Lot number	Dimensions	Ware, comments
1	CB 30:3	A I	I	L. 1.2 D 12	R: 33.5 cm	Ware: pink-buff. Temper: common medium chaff.
2	CB 1728	A I	I	L. 17.2 D 350	R: 33 cm	Ware: dark buff core, buff-green surface. Temper: common chaff, mica inclusions.
3	CB 753:2	A I	II	L. 29.1 D 351	R: 38 cm	Ware: buff. Temper: common chaff, lime.
4	CB 2502	G II	II/1	L. 58.2 E 106.3	R: 40 cm	Ware: grey core, buff-pink surface. Temper: common medium-large chaff. Low ridge on neck, three horizontal grooves at maximum diameter.
5	CB 3999	G II	II/2	L. 54.10 F 210.1	R: 32.5 cm	Ware: buff. Temper: common medium chaff and fine lime. Horizontal and wavy shallow grooves.
6	CB 2146	G II	II/2	L. 54.3 E 105.1	R: 34 cm	Ware: grey core, orange surface. Temper: common chaff, sparse lime.
7	CB 3019	G II	II/2	L. 54.10 F 210.2	R: 37.5 cm	Ware: orange-black core, yellow surface. Temper: common medium chaff, rare fine lime. Horizontal shallow groove.
8	CB 2513	G I	II/2	L. 16.4 E 247.1	R: 32.5 cm	Ware: buff. Temper: common medium chaff, fine lime.
9	CB 2160	G II	II/2	L. 52.1 E 94.1	R: 32 cm	Ware: grey-buff core, green-grey surface. Temper: common chaff.

LARGE BARRELS PLATE 35

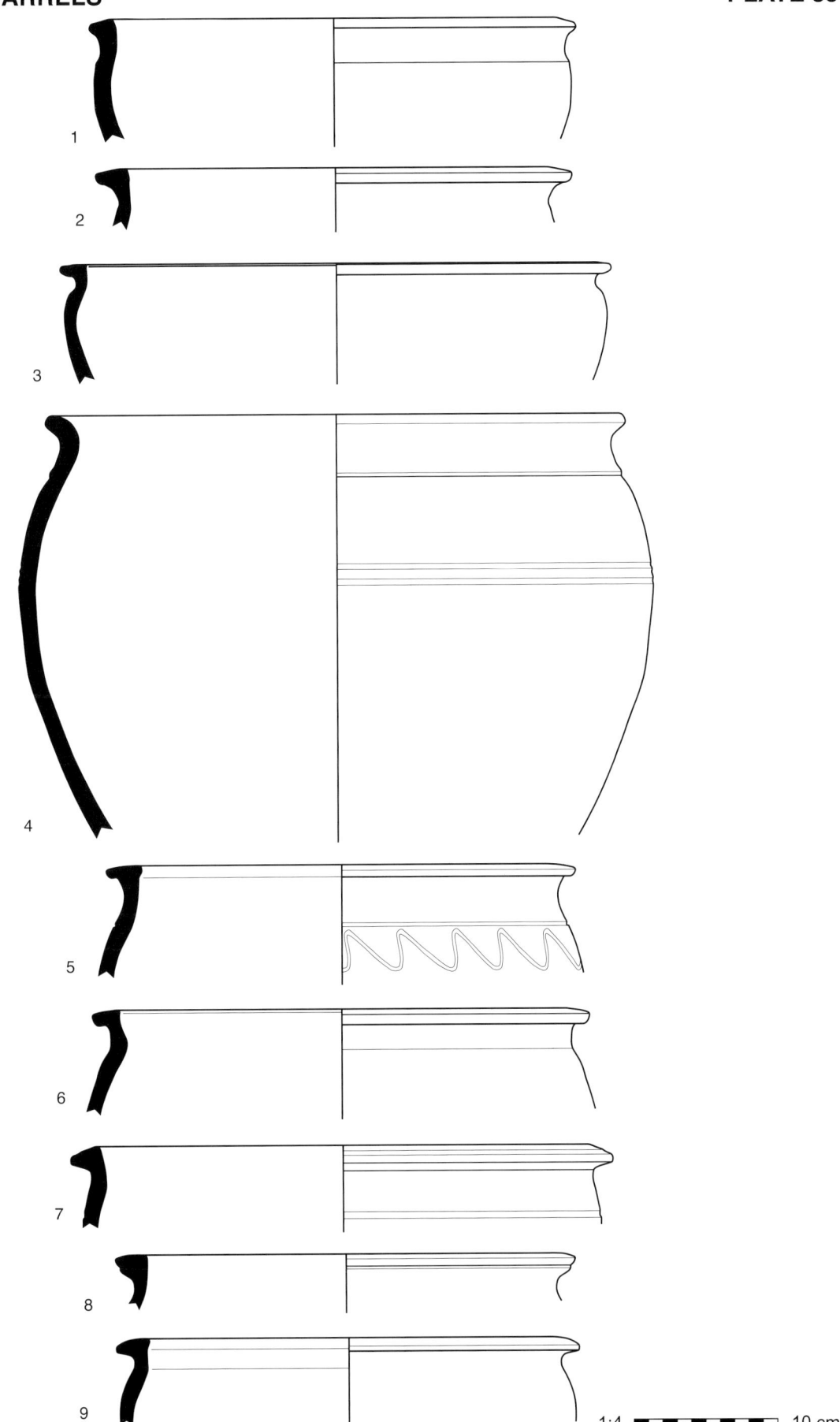

Plate 36: *Large and Very Large Barrels*

	CB number	Area	Phase	Locus and Lot number	Dimensions	Ware, comments
1	CB 2517	G I	II/2	L. 11.3 E 248.1	R: 43 cm	Ware: pink-buff core and surface. Temper: common medium chaff, medium-fine lime. Single horizontal groove on shoulder.
2	CB 4226	G IV	III	L. 76.2 F 466.2	R: 35 cm	Ware: buff core, orange surface. Temper: common fine lime and medium chaff. Red paint bands on rim and shoulder.
3	CB 2137	G II	II/1A	L. 59.1 E 101.1	R: 48 cm	Ware: grey core, buff surface. Temper: common chaff, fine lime.
4	CB 2463	G I	II/1	L. 9.4 E 85.3	R: c 50 cm	Ware: dark grey core, buff surface. Temper: common medium chaff, occasional large lime. Deep wide horizontal grooves on body.
5	CB 1971	G I	II/1	L. 11.1 E. 74.2	R: c 60 cm	Ware: buff core, pale buff surface. Temper: common chaff, occasional large grit. Single horizontal groove on shoulder.
6	CB 2510	G II	II/1	L. 63.1 E 111.2	R: c 50-60 cm	Ware: dark grey core, buff surface. Temper: common chaff, fine lime. Deep wide horizontal grooves on shoulder.

LARGE BARRELS

1

2

VERY LARGE BARRELS

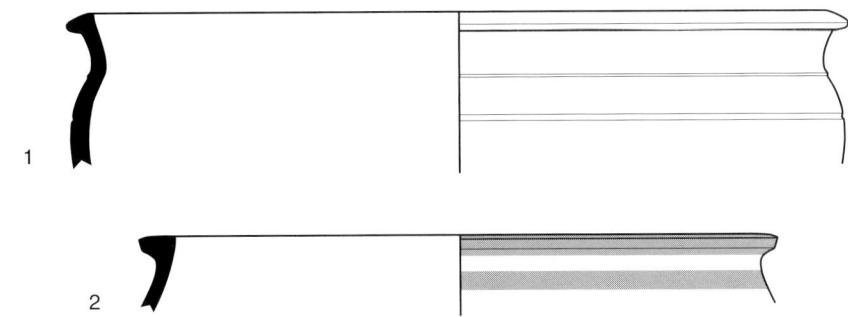

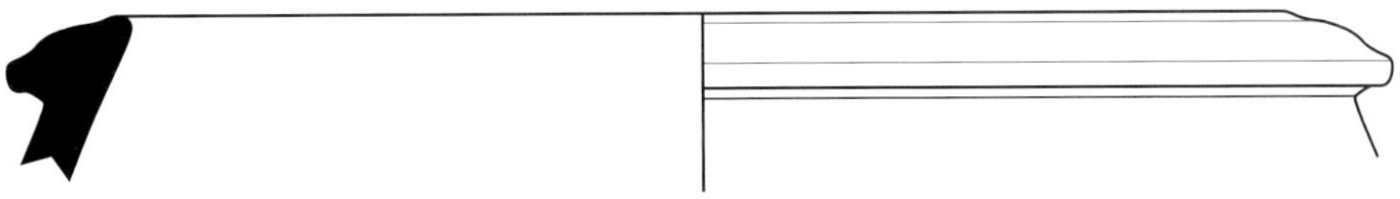

3

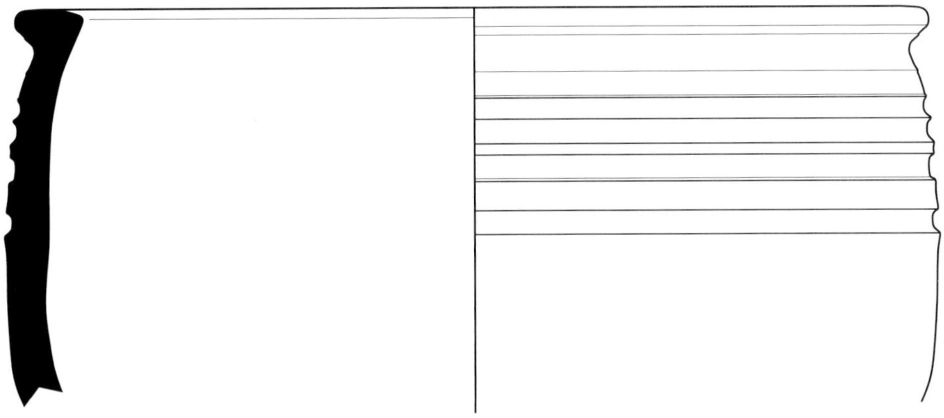

4

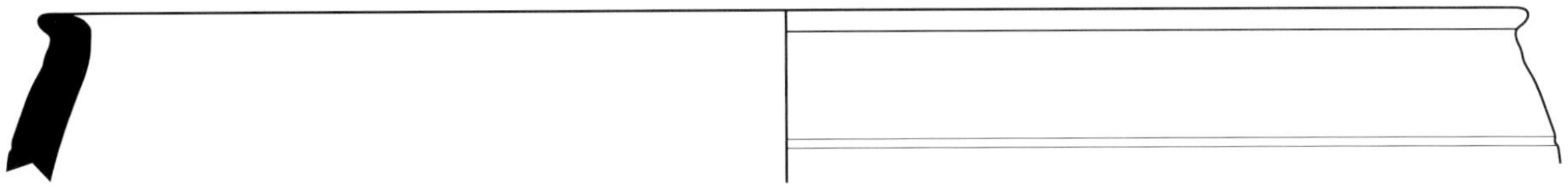

5

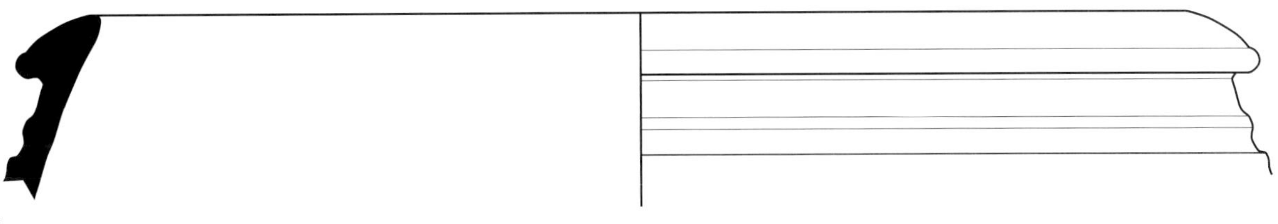

6

1:4 10 cm

Plate 37: *Small Plain-Sided and Small Fine Ware Ridged Barrels*

	CB no.	Area	Phase	Loc. & Lot no.	Dimensions	Ware, comments
1	CB 2391	A II	IA	L. 67.6 E 201.3	R: 20 cm	Ware: pale buff. Temper: common fine chaff. Fugitive brown paint bands.
2	CB 30:1	A I	S	L. 1.2 D 12	R: 12.6 cm	Ware: red-buff core, buff surface. Temper: sparse fine lime. Red paint bands and splashes.
3	CB 364:4	A I	I	L. 20.1 D 73	R: 15 cm	Ware: buff. Temper: sparse chaff, lime. Red paint band
4	CB 2213	A II	II	L. 52.2 E 185.2	R: 16 cm	Ware: orange-buff core, pale buff surface. Temper: sparse fine lime. Fugitive brown paint bands.
5	CB 3933	G IV	I	L. 29.1 F 55.4	R: 14 cm	Ware: green-grey. Temper: sparse fine chaff. Black paint band.
6	CB 2038	G I	II/1	L. 13.1 E 75.1	R: 17.5 cm	Ware: greenish core, pale buff surface. Temper: sparse chaff and large lime. Fugitive red paint band.
7	CB 2039	G I	II/1	L. 13.1 E 75.1	R: 14 cm	Ware: buff core, green-buff surface. Temper: common chaff, sparse lime. Narrow and wide brown paint slashes
8	CB 2854	G III	II/2	L. 28.1 F 77.2	R: 11.5 cm	Ware: buff. Temper: sparse fine chaff, sparse fine sand. Red paint bands.
9	CB 3970	G II	III	L. 37.3 F 213.7	R: 10.5 cm	Ware: yellow-buff. Temper: common sand. Dark red painted bands.
10	CB 4012	G II	III	L. 70.1 F 220.3	R: 8 cm	Ware: buff core and surface. Temper: rare fine lime. Dark red paint bands, raised grooved ridge.
11	CB 3190	G IV	III	L. 40.3 F 69.3	R: 9.5 cm	Ware: orange. Temper: sparse fine chaff. Red paint bands and sharp raised ridge.
12	CB 4243	G IV	II/2	L. 78.1 F 462.1	R: 11 cm	Ware: orange core, buff surface. Temper: sparse lime & fine chaff. Dark red paint bands & raised grooved ridge.
13	CB 2549	G II	II/2	L. 62.5 E 334.1	R: 14 cm	Ware: buff. Temper: sparse fine chaff, fine lime.
14	CB 3791	G IV	II/1	L. 34.4 F 70.3	R: 14 cm	Ware: green-buff. Temper: none visible. Black paint bands and raised grooved ridge.
15	CB 4227	G IV	III	L. 76.2 F 466.2	R: 16.5 cm	Ware: buff orange. Temper: sparse medium lime and medium chaff. Red-orange paint bands and grooves.
16	CB 1822	G I	II/1	L. 4.3 E 62.4	R: 11 cm	Ware: greenish. Temper: sparse fine lime. Raised grooved ridge.
17	CB 3121	G IV	II/1	L. 34.3 F 67.1	R: 10 cm	Ware: buff. Temper: sparse fine sand. Red paint bands and raised ridge.
18	CB 4011	G II	III	L. 70.1 F 220.3	R: 10 cm	Ware: grey core, green surface. Temper: common fine lime. Dark red paint bands, raised ridge.
19	CB 1776	A I	IA	L. 32.1 D 366	R: 9.5 cm	Ware: orange-buff. Temper: none. Red-brown paint band and raised grooved ridge.
20	CB 1961	A I	II	L. 41.2 E 49.1	R: 16 cm	Ware: orange core, pale buff surface. Temper: sparse fine lime, rare fine chaff. Dark red paint slashes across rim, hatched triangles on shoulder.
21	CB 2053	A I	III	L. 34.3 E 55.1	R: 10 cm	Ware: orange-buff. Temper: fine lime. Red paint bands.
22	CB 2041	G I	II/1	L. 13.1 E 75.1	R: 11 cm	Ware: orange core, pale buff surface. Temper: sparse fine lime. Red-brown paint bands and triangles.
23	CB 2843	A II	II	L. 73.1 F 1.4	R: 8 cm	Ware: greenish-buff. Temper: sparse fine lime. Dark brown paint bands.
24	CB 1696	A I	II	L. 29.1 D 368	R: 10 cm	Ware: orange. Temper: fine lime. Red paint bands, ridges.
25	CB 2012	G I	II/2	L. 4.6 E 66.6	R: 11.5 cm	Ware: buff. Temper: none. Two horizontal grooves on shoulder.
26	CB 3795	G IV	II/1	L. 34.4 F 70.3	R: 10 cm	Ware: green. Temper: none visible. Brown paint bands and raised grooved ridge.
27	CB 3784	G IV	III	L. 40.2 F 68.3	R: 10 cm	Ware: grey-buff core, green surface. Temper: sparse fine lime. Brown paint bands and grooved ridge.

SMALL PLAIN-SIDED BARRELS

PLATE 37

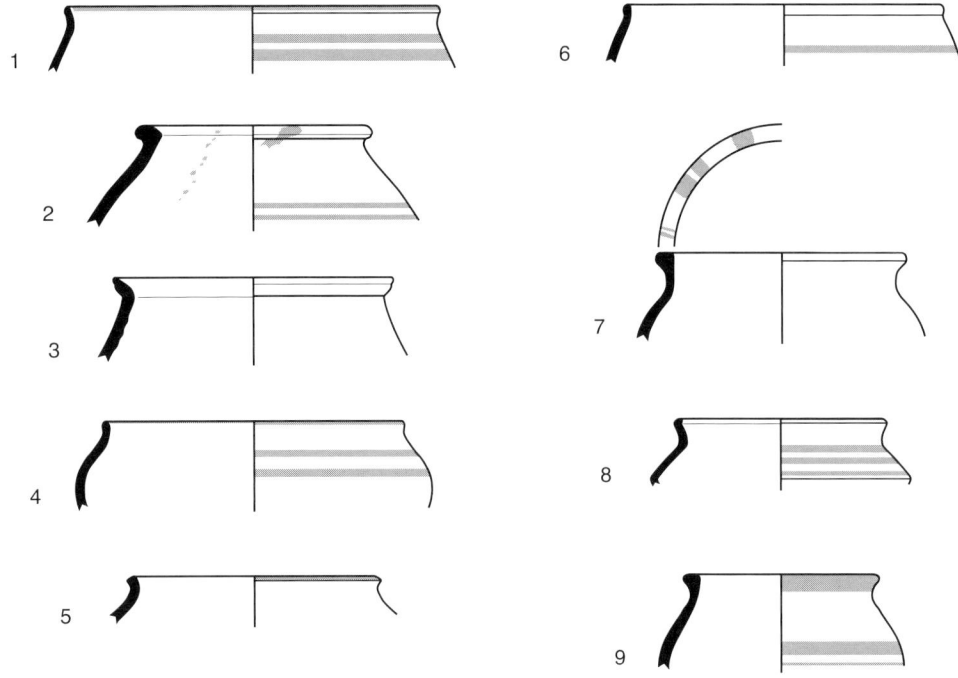

SMALL FINE WARE RIDGED BARRELS

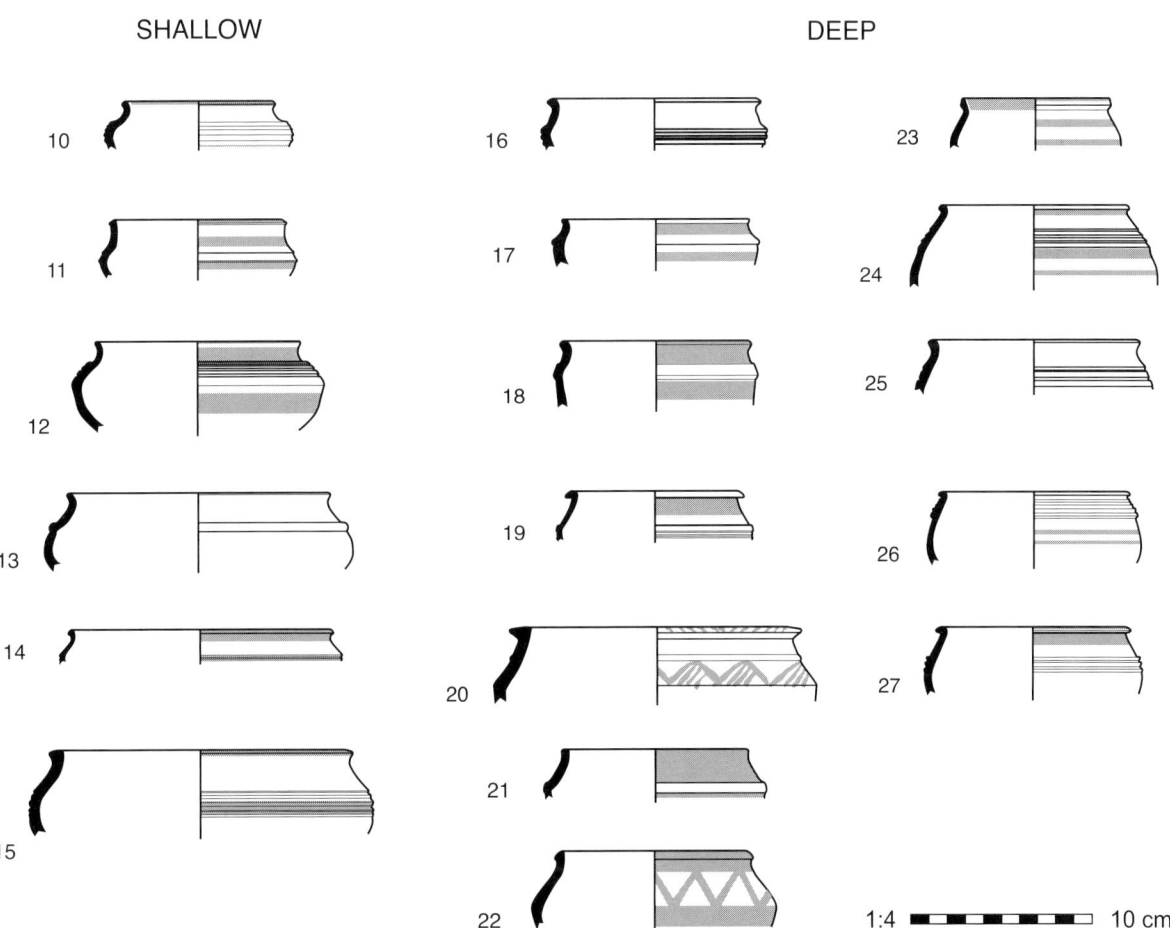

Plate 38: *Small and Medium Ridged Barrels*

	CB number	Area	Phase	Loc. & Lot no.	Dimensions	Ware, comments
1	CB 1734	A I	II	L. 30.1 D 373	R: 16 cm	Ware: buff core, pale buff surface. Temper: occasional chaff, lime. Red-brown paint slashes across rim, horizontal grooves.
2	CB 1958	A II	II	L. 61.3 E 25.1	R: 18 cm	Ware: buff-pink. Temper: common fine lime. Raised grooved band.
3	CB 2810	G IV	II/1	L. 4.2 F 54.1	R: 18 cm	Ware: dark buff core, buff surface. Temper: common chaff, sparse lime.
4	CB 3290	G IV	II/1	L. 34.1 F 64.1	R; 16.5 cm	Ware: pink core, buff surface. Temper: common fine lime. Red paint bands and horizontal grooves.
5	CB 2522	G II	II/1	L. 63.1 E 111.3	R: 15.5 cm	Ware: pale buff core and surface. Temper: common fine lime, occasional chaff. Fugitive black paint band on rim.
6	CB 1895	G II	II/2	L. 51.2 E 91.1	R: 16.5 cm	Ware: dark buff core, pale buff surface. Temper: medium chaff. Red paint bands.
7	CB 3120	G IV	II/1	L. 34.3 F 67.1	R: 17 cm	Ware: green. Temper: common medium chaff. Horizontal grooves.
8	CB 4205	G II	III	01-24 F 217.1	R: 14 cm	Ware: buff. Temper: abundant fine lime, fine sand, sparse mica inclusions. Red paint bands.
9	CB 2971	G II	III	L. 27.1 F 202.4	R: 15 cm	Ware: orange core, orange-buff surface. Temper: common medium chaff. Orange paint bands and slashes on rim, grooved raised ridge.
10	CB 4250	G II	III	L. 37.5 F 226.4	R: 18.5 cm	Ware: green. Temper: common fine-medium chaff. Fugitive black paint bands.
11	CB 3203	A II	I	L. 76.9 F 20.2	R: 21 cm	Ware: orange core, greenish surface. Temper: common chaff.
12	CB 2043	A II	IA	L. 67.1 E 29.3	R: 24.5 cm	Ware: buff core, pale buff. Temper: common chaff, occasional lime. Horizontal grooves.
13	CB 726:4	A I	II	L. 26.1 D 342	R: 24 cm	Ware: grey core, reddish surface. Temper: common chaff, lime.
14	CB 2389	A II	IA	L. 67.6 E 201.3	R: 26 cm	Ware: pale brown core, grey surface. Temper: common fine chaff.
15	CB 1739	A I	II	L. 30.1 D 373	R: 28 cm	Ware: green-grey. Temper: common chaff, lime.
16	CB 2216	A I	II	L. 30.1 E 217.1	R: 22 cm	Ware: buff core, pale green-buff surface. Temper: common fine chaff, fine lime. Fugitive black-brown paint bands.
17	CB 3943	G IV	I	L. 33.1 F 58.5	R: 20.5 cm	Ware: buff. Temper: common medium chaff. Red paint bands.
18	CB 2808	G IV	I	L. 26.2 F 53.1	R: 28 cm	Ware: buff. Temper: common chaff.
19	CB 1887	G I	II/1	L. 2.1 E 61.5	R: 21.5 cm	Ware: buff. Temper: abundant chaff. Red-brown paint bands.
20	CB 1912	G I	II/1	L. 2.1 E 61.6	R: 20 cm	Ware: buff core, pale buff surface. Temper: sparse chaff, lime.
21	CB 4392	G IV	II/2	L. 34.5 F 454.1	R: 26.5 cm	Ware: buff. Temper: common fine-medium chaff, fine lime. Red-brown paint bands.
22	CB 3289	G IV	II/1	L. 34.1 F 64.1	R: 26 cm	Ware: brown core, buff surface. Temper: common medium chaff and lime. Red paint bands, grooved raised ridge.
23	CB 1989	G I	II/1	L. 4.3 E 62.4	R: 22.5 cm M: 24 cm B: 8.5 cm H: 21.2 cm	Ware: orange-buff core, pale buff surface. Temper: common chaff, occasional large lime, mica inclusions. Red paint bands.

RIDGED BARRELS

SMALL

MEDIUM

PLATE 38

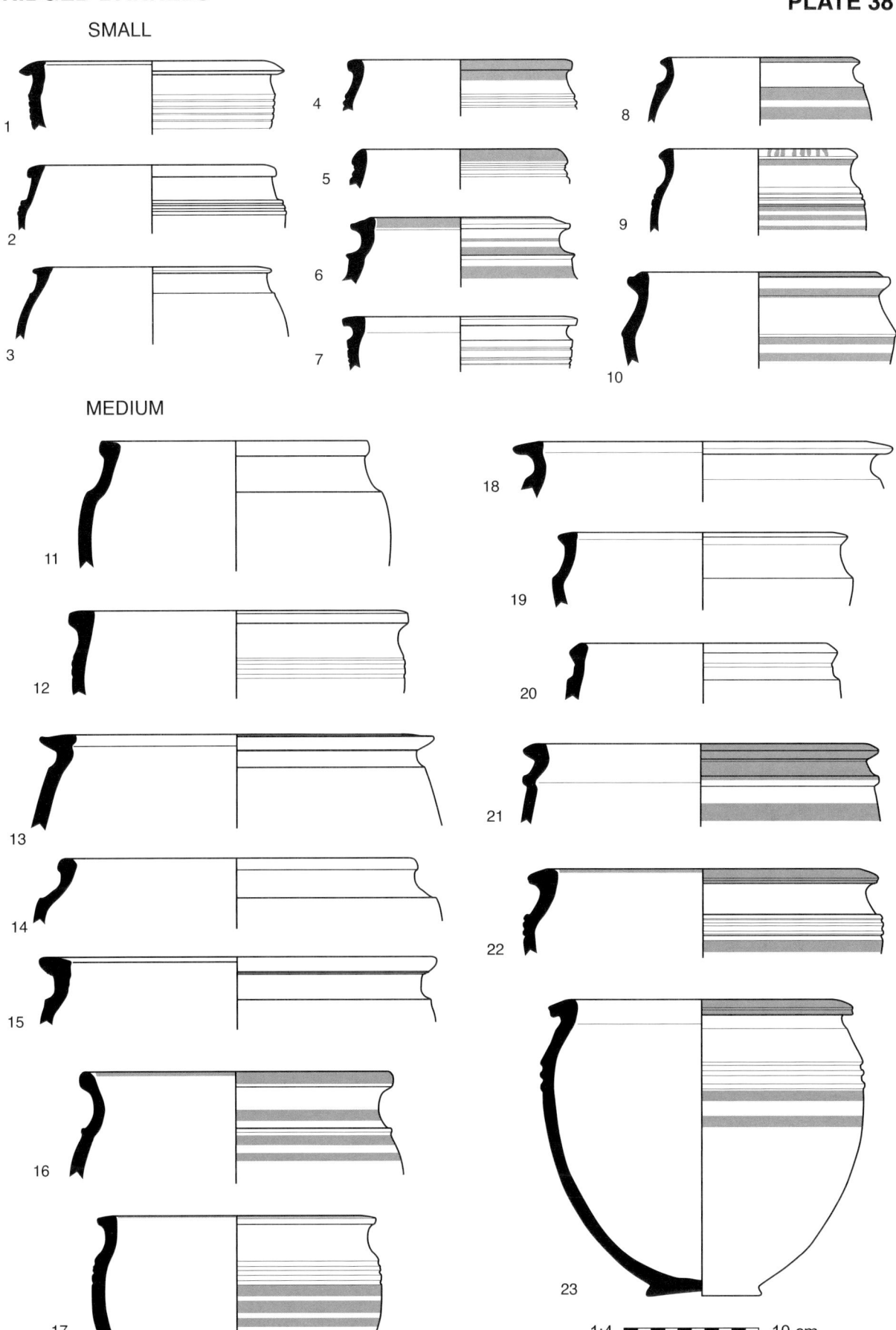

1:4 ▬▬▬ 10 cm

Plate 39: *Medium and Large Ridged Barrels*

	CB number	Area	Phase	Loc. & Lot no.	Dimensions	Ware, comments
1	CB 2905	G II	II/2	L. 54.9 F 206.1	R: 19.5 cm	Ware: dark buff core, buff surface. Temper: common fine-medium chaff, rare medium lime. Dark red paint band over rim and neck.
2	CB 2545	G II	II/2	L. 65.3 E 120.1	R: 21 cm	Ware: buff core, dark grey surface. Temper: sparse fine sand and chaff. Raised grooved ridge.
3	CB 3786	G IV	II/1	L. 34.4 F 70.3	R: 22 cm	Ware: grey core, orange surface. Temper: common medium chaff. Red paint band and raised grooved ridge.
4	CB 3399	G II	II/2	L. 54.10 F 210.2	R: 21 cm	Ware: pink core, buff-yellow surface. Temper: common medium chaff, rare fine lime. Red paint bands.
5	CB 2849	G II	III	L. 27.2 F 205.1	R: 19.5 cm	Ware: buff-grey. Temper: common chaff. Brown paint band.
6	CB 4007	G II	III	L. 70.1 F 220.3	R: 21 cm	Ware: grey core, orange surface. Temper: common medium chaff. Two bands of horizontal grooves.
7	CB 2846	G II	III	L. 27.2 F 205.1	R: 23 cm	Ware: greenish buff. Temper: common chaff. Black-brown paint bands and slashes across rim.
8	CB 3028	G II	II/2	L. 54.8 F 204.4	R: 27 cm	Ware: grey core, green-buff surface. Temper: common medium chaff, rare fine lime. Red paint bands and X-hatched triangles.
9	CB 3037	A II	II	L. 81.2 F 35.3	R: 30.5 cm	Ware: dark buff core, buff surface. Temper: common medium chaff, common fine lime. Red paint bands.
10	CB 2524	A I	III	L. 44.2 E 213.3	R: 30 cm	Ware: buff. Temper: common medium-fine chaff, sparse lime. Deep horizontal groove.
11	CB 2525	A I	III	L. 44.2 E 213.3	R: 31 cm	Ware: buff core, pale buff surface. Temper: common medium chaff, fine lime.
12	CB 3978	G IV	I	L. 24.1 F 52.3	R: 29.5 cm	Ware: orange-grey core, buff-pink surface. Temper: common large chaff. Two horizontal grooves.
13	CB 3936	G IV	I	L. 33.1 F 58.6	R: 30 cm	Ware: grey core, orange surface. Temper: common medium chaff, sparse fine lime. Red paint bands and raised grooved ridge.
14	CB 2135/6	G II	II/1A	L. 59.1 E 101.1	R: 34 cm	Ware: grey core, buff surface. Temper: common chaff, fine lime. Red paint bands and five slashes across rim.
15	CB 4242B	G IV	II/2	L. 78.1 F 462.1	R: 36 cm	Ware: buff. Temper: common medium chaff. Soot staining on rim exterior. Brown paint bands.
16	CB 1819	G II	II/2	L. 51.2 E 91.4	R: 34 cm	Ware: buff core, pale buff surface. Temper: medium chaff, lime.
17	CB 2529	G I	II/2	L. 9.8 E 250.1	R: 35 cm	Ware: buff core, dark buff surface. Temper: common medium chaff. Red-brown paint bands.
18	CB 4260	G II	III	L. 37.4 F 222.1	R: 32 cm	Ware: buff. Temper: abundant medium chaff. Red paint and raised ridge.
19	CB 4160	G IV	II/2	L. 73.2 F 457.2	R: 32 cm	Ware: buff core, green surface. Temper: common medium chaff. Fugitive black paint band and slashes on rim, horizontal grooves in raised ridge.

RIDGED BARRELS

PLATE 39

MEDIUM

LARGE

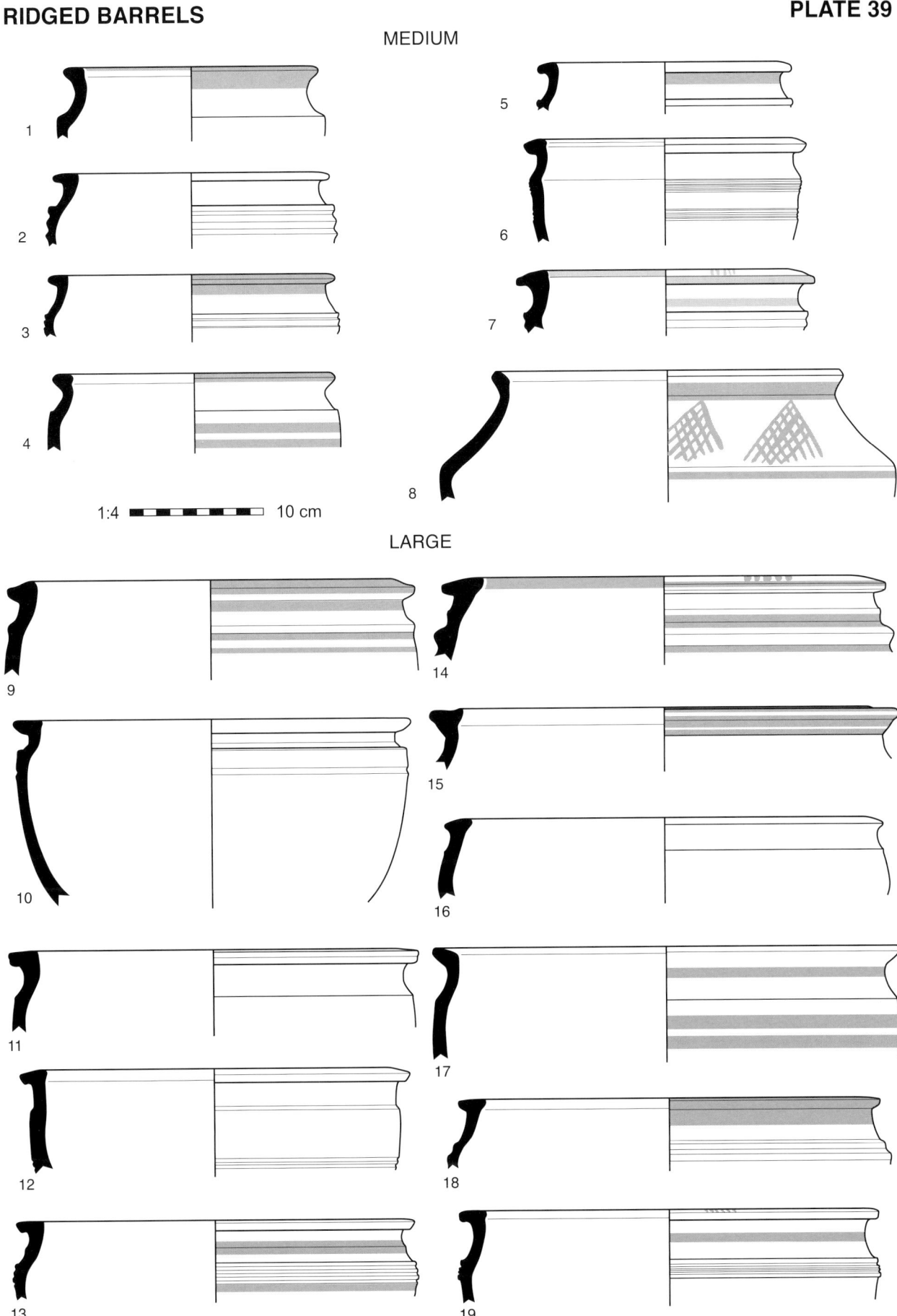

Table 40: *Large and Very Large Ridged Barrels*

	CB number	Area	Phase	Loc. & Lot no.	Dimensions	Ware, comments
1	CB 4166	G IV	II/2	L. 34.5 F 454.3	R: 38 cm	Ware: green. Temper: abundant medium chaff. Horizontal grooves on wide raised ridge.
2	CB 4221	G IV	III	L. 49.1 F 464.2	R: 34 cm	Ware: buff core, pale green surface. Temper: common medium chaff, occasional fine lime.
3	CB 4009	G II	III	L. 70.1 F 220.3	R: 33 cm M: 34.5 m	Ware: black core, orange surface. Temper: common medium chaff, rare fine lime. Grooved raised band.
4	CB 1773	A I	IA	L. 32.1 D 366	R: c 40 cm	Ware: dark buff core, buff surface. Temper: common large chaff.
5	CB 1864	G I	II/1	L. 5.1 E 63.4	R: c 46 cm	Ware: dark grey core, buff-orange surface. Temper: abundant chaff.
6	CB 2218	G II	II/1A	L. 59.2 E 107.3	R: 38 cm	Ware: orange-buff core, buff surface. Temper: common chaff, sparse lime, mica inclusions. Horizontal grooves near maximum diameter.
7	CB 3043	A II	II	L. 81.2 F 35.3	R: c 50 cm	Ware: brown core, buff surface. Temper: common medium chaff, sparse fine lime. Three horizontal grooves, traces of possible wavy groove below.
8	CB 3811	G II	II/2	L. 54.10 F 210.5	R: 56 cm	Ware: brown core, buff surface. Temper: common medium chaff, sparse fine lime. Horizontal grooves on shoulder.
9	CB 4223	G IV	III	L. 49.1 F 464.1	R: 52.5 cm	Ware: grey core, buff surface. Temper: common medium chaff. Red paint bands.

LARGE RIDGED & GROOVED BARRELS

PLATE 40

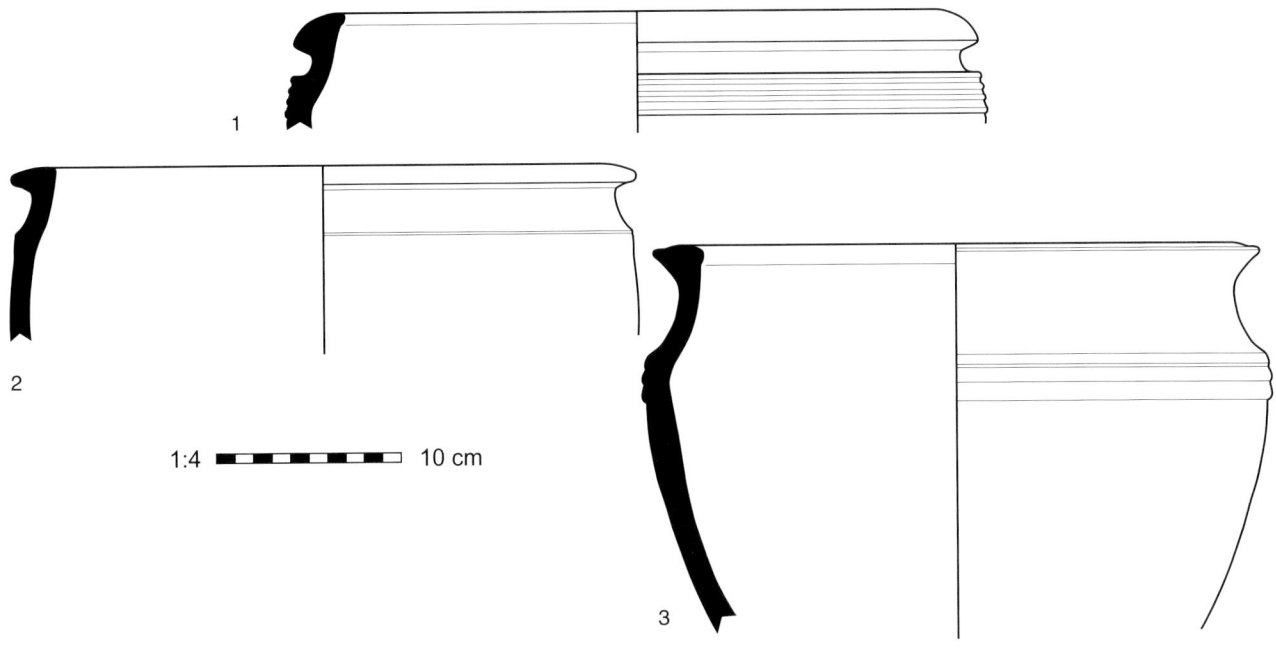

VERY LARGE RIDGED & GROOVED BARRELS

Plate 41: *Basins*

	CB number	Area	Phase	Locus and Lot number	Dimensions	Ware, comments
1	CB 374:2	A I	II	L. 19.1 D 76	R: 33 cm	Ware: grey core, reddish surface. Temper: common chaff, lime. Corrugated rim.
2	CB 3288	G IV	II/1	L. 34.1 F 64.1	R: 27 cm	Ware: green core, green-buff surface. Temper: abundant medium-coarse chaff. Corrugated rim.
3	CB 2800	G IV	I	L. 23.1 F 51.1	R: 33 cm	Ware: pale grey core, buff surface. Temper: common chaff, common fine lime. Corrugated rim.
4	CB 4244	G IV	II/2	L. 78.1 F 462.1	R: 38 cm B: 33 cm H: c 15 cm	Ware: dark grey core, orange surface. Temper: abundant medium chaff, sparse medium lime. Corrugated rim, wide horizontal grooves on side.
5	CB 4017	G II	III	L. 69.1 F 219.2	R: 28 cm	Ware: pink core yellow surface. Temper: common medium chaff, rare fine lime. Shallow horizontal grooves on side, corrugated rim.
6	CB 4206	G II	III	01-24 F 217.2	R: 29.5 cm B: 25 cm H: 12 cm	Ware: pink core, buff surface. Temper: common medium chaff, occasional medium lime.
7	CB 4239	G II	III	L. 37.3 F 213.5	R: 32 cm B: 26 cm H: 12.7 cm	Ware: grey core, orange surface. Temper: common medium chaff and fine lime. Slightly concave base.
8	CB 4238	G II	III	L. 37.3 F 213.5	R: 15 cm B: 13 cm H: 8 cm	Ware: buff. Temper: common medium-large chaff and fine-medium lime.
9	CB 3234	G II	III	L. 37.3 F 213.1	R: 24 cm B: 19 cm H: 12 cm	Ware: black core, orange-buff surface. Temper: common medium chaff, common small-medium lime.
10	CB 4254	G II	III	L. 37.5 F 226.4	R: 28 cm	Ware: grey core, buff surface. Temper: common medium-large chaff.
11	CB 4208	G II	III	01-24 F 217.2	R: 32 cm	Ware: grey core, orange-buff interior surface, pink exterior surface. Temper: common large chaff, occasional medium lime.
12	CB 4207	G II	III	01-24 F 217.2	R: 31 cm B: 25 cm H: 17 cm	Ware: grey core, orange surface. Temper: common medium chaff and fine lime. Horizontal grooves on side.
13	CB 4025	G II	IV	L. 75.1 F 224.1	R: 26 cm	Ware: buff. Temper: sparse medium chaff. Corrugated rim.

BASINS
PLATE 41

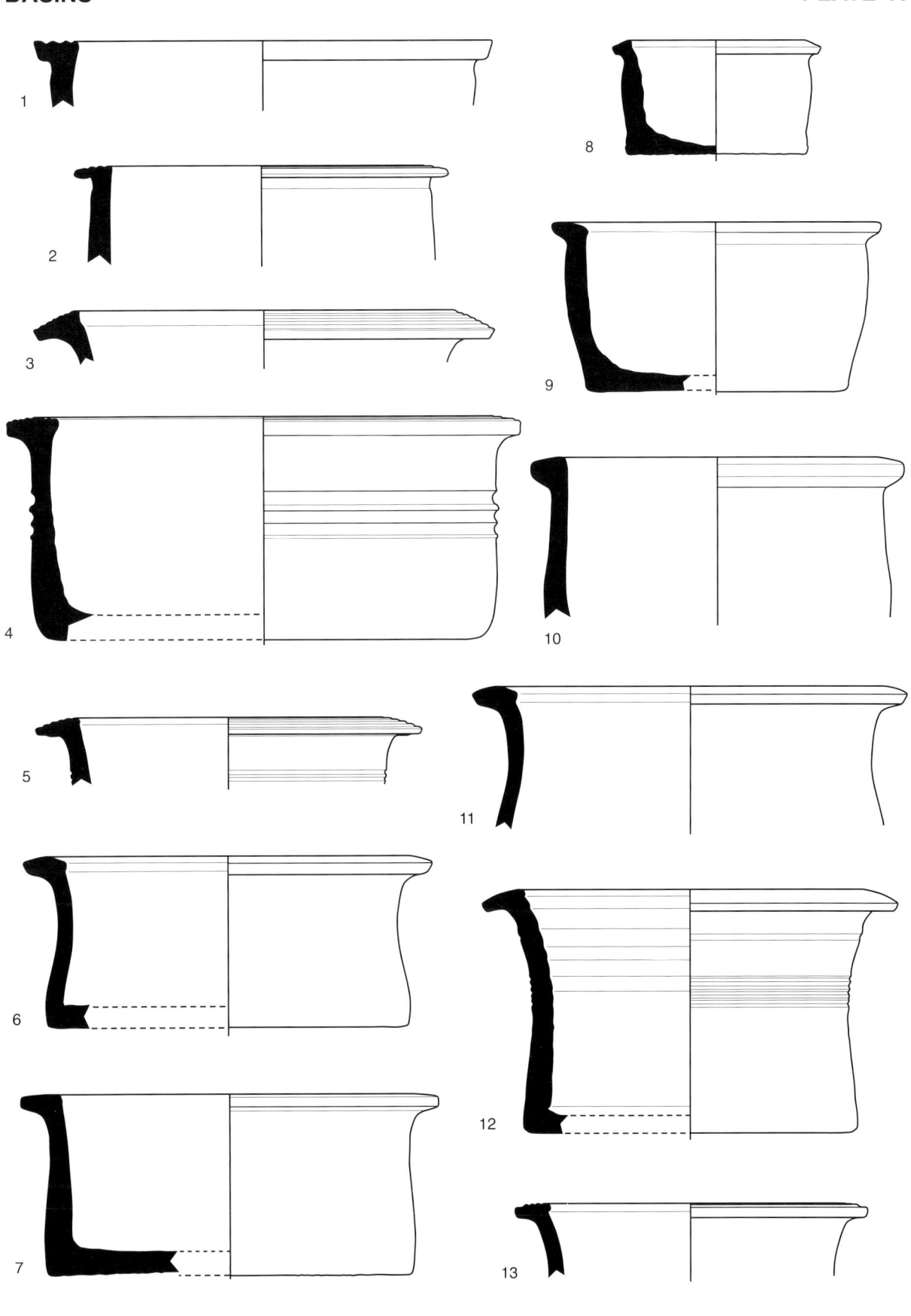

Plate 42: *Basins and Stands*

	CB number	Area	Phase	Locus and Lot number	Dimensions	Ware, comments
1	CB 2844	A II	I	L. 76.5 F 5.6	R: 24.5 cm	Ware: black core, orange surface. Temper: common medium chaff, fine lime.
2	CB 2377	G I	II/1	L. 12.1 E 81.2	R: 31 cm	Ware: grey core, brown-buff surface. Temper: common medium chaff, occasional grit. Internal spout.
3	CB 2895	G II	II/2	L. 54.8 F 204.3	R: 34 cm	Ware: orange core, buff surface. Temper: common medium chaff and fine-medium lime.
4	CB 3039	A II	II	L. 81.2 F 35.3	B: 23 cm	Ware: black core, buff surface. Temper: common large chaff, fine lime. Deep grooves and ridges.
5	CB 3409	G II	II/2	L. 54.10 F 210.2	B: 24 cm	Ware: brown core, buff surface. Temper: common medium-large chaff and medium-large lime.
6	CB 3797	G IV	II/1	L. 34.4 F 70.3	B: 28 cm	Ware: buff core, pale buff surface. Temper: common fine lime and sand, medium chaff. Incised palm tree (?) decoration.
7	CB 4021	G II	III	L. 69.1 F 219.2	B: 21 cm	Ware: black core, orange-buff surface. Temper: common medium chaff, rare coarse lime.
8	CB 4022	G II	III	L. 69.1 F 219.2	B: 25 cm	Ware: black core, brown surface. Temper: abundant medium-coarse chaff. Deep groove.
9	CB 4245	G II	III	L. 37.5 F 226.4	B: 21 cm	Ware: dark grey core, orange surface. Temper: common fine-medium chaff. Three deep horizontal grooves.
10	CB 3054	A II	II	L. 83.1 F 37.2	R: 26 cm	Ware: dark grey core, orange surface. Temper: common medium chaff.
11	CB 3930	G IV	II/2	L. 32.13 F 74.1	R: 23 cm	Ware: orange. Temper: sparse large chaff, common fine lime.
12	CB 4248	G II	III	L. 37.5 F 226.4	R: 30 cm	Ware: dark grey core, orange surface. Temper: common medium chaff.
13	CB 3968	G II	III	L. 37.3 F 213.7	R: 29 cm	Ware: brown core, pink surface. Temper: common medium chaff, abundant coarse lime. Single deep crescent notch in rim.

BASINS

PLATE 42

CHANNEL RIM

BASES

STANDS

CORRUGATED RIM

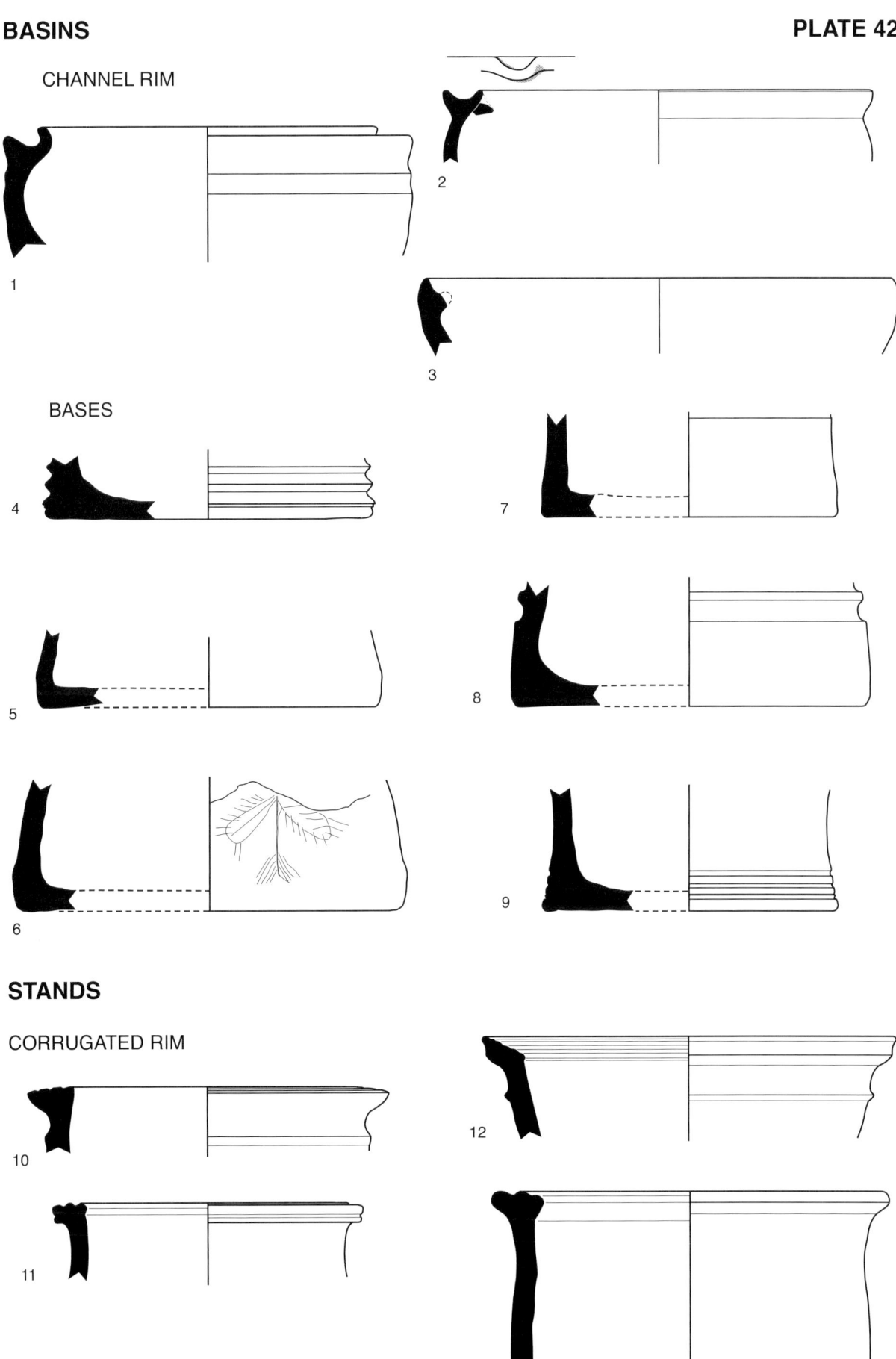

Plate 43: *Stands*

	CB number	Area	Phase	Locus and Lot number	Dimensions	Ware, comments
1	CB 1934	G II	II/1	L. 2.1 E 95.2	R: 12 cm	Ware: orange-buff core, orange surface. Temper: common chaff, fine lime. Red paint bands.
2	CB 1848	G I	S	L. 1 E 64.3	R: 9 cm	Ware: grey core, buff surface. Temper: common chaff, fine lime. Red paint on sides, black paint on top.
3	CB 1855	G I	II/1	L. 4.3 E 62.5	R: 22 cm	Ware: grey core, green-buff surface. Temper: abundant chaff. Thick black paint double-triangles and band on rim, two horizontal bands on exterior.
4	CB 3945	G III	II/2	L. 39.2 F 81.2	B: 15 cm	Stand base or top? Ware: orange core, buff surface. Temper: common large chaff. Black paint bands with white slip inverted triangles over-painted.
5	CB 1791	A I	II	L. 41.1 E 37.1	R: 21 cm	Ware: over-fired green. Temper: abundant medium chaff. Obliquely notched ridge.
6	CB 4272	G II	II/2	L. 65.4 E 332.2	Interior diam. c 20 cm	Stand segment. Ware: grey core, reddish-buff surface. Temper: common fine chaff, fine lime.
7	CB 2636	G II	II/2	L. 54.5 E 335.2	R: 17 cm	Ware: grey core, buff surface. Temper: common medium chaff, fine sand. Red paint splash on interior, horizontal grooves on exterior.
8	CB 1952	A I	II	L. 41.1 E 48.1	R: 34.5 cm	Ware: orange-pink core, pale buff surface. Temper: common medium chaff, sparse fine lime.
9	CB 2372	A I	II	L. 41.1 E 37.11	R: 33 cm	Ware; buff. Temper: common medium chaff, fine lime.
10	CB 4264	G II	III	L. 37.5 F 226.3	R: 32	Ware: orange-buff. Temper: common medium chaff. Red paint band.
11	CB 1842	G I	II/1	L. 4.4 E 66.1	R: 26 cm	Ware: buff. Temper: abundant chaff. Brown-black paint band interior and exterior.
12	CB 4247	G II	III	L. 37.5 F 226.4	R: 22 cm	Ware: buff. Temper: common medium chaff. Red paint bands.
13	CB 3788	G IV	II/1	L. 34.4 F 70.3	R: 36 cm	Ware: black core, orange surface. Temper: common medium chaff.
14	CB 3792	G IV	II/1	L. 34.4 F 70.3	R: 40 cm	Ware: grey core, orange surface. Temper: common medium chaff, fine lime. Horizontal ridge and groove.
15	CB 4366:1	GII	II/2	L. 65.4 E 332.2	R: 36 cm	Ware: grey core, red-buff surface. Temper: common medium chaff, occasional lime.
16	CB 3111	G II	II/2	L. 54.10 F 210.3	R: 17.5 cm	Ware: green (slightly vitrified). Temper: common medium chaff, rare fine lime.
17	CB 2861	G II	III	L. 27.1 F 202.2	R: 21 cm	Ware: orange-buff. Temper: common medium chaff.
18	CB 4391	G IV	II/2	L. 34.5 F 454.1	R: 19.5 cm	Ware: grey core, orange-buff surface. Temper: common chaff, fine grit.

STANDS

PLATE 43

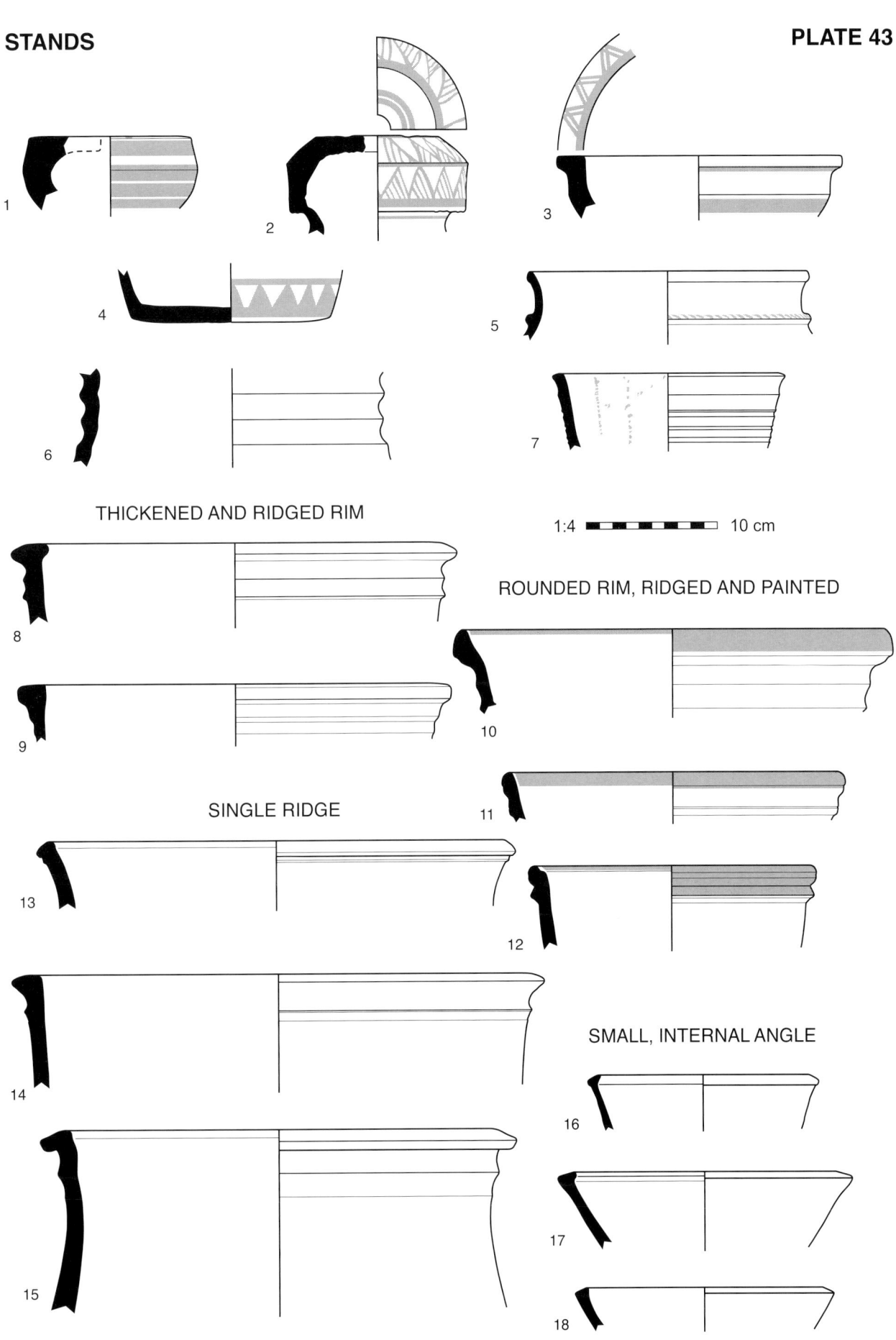

THICKENED AND RIDGED RIM

1:4 ▬▬▬ 10 cm

ROUNDED RIM, RIDGED AND PAINTED

SINGLE RIDGE

SMALL, INTERNAL ANGLE

329

Plate 44: *Stands*

	CB number	Area	Phase	Locus and Lot number	Dimensions	Ware, comments
1	CB 1766	A I	II	L. 16.2 D 361	R: 23 cm	Ware: pink-buff core, pale buff surface. Temper: common large chaff, occasional lime.
2	CB 1715	A I	II	L. 16.1 D 376	R: 27 cm	Ware: grey core, reddish surface. Temper: common chaff, occasional fine lime. Red paint slashes across rim, horizontal groove.
3	CB 1875	A II	II	L. 41.2 E 41.1	R: 32 cm	Ware: orange-buff core, buff surface. Temper: common chaff, lime. Brown-black paint slashes across rim.
4	CB 1729	A I	I	L. 17.2 D 350	R: 31 cm	Ware: buff. Temper: occasional chaff, mica inclusions.
5	CB 1965	G II	II/1	L. 56.1 E 98.1	R: 34 cm	Ware: buff core, pale buff surface. Temper: abundant chaff, common lime. Three fine incisions on rim.
6	CB 2224	G II	II/2	L. 54.4 E 108.1	R: 25 cm	Ware: orange-buff. Temper: common chaff, sparse lime.
7	CB 3189	G IV	III	L. 40.3 F 69.3	R: 26 cm	Ware: orange core, buff surface. Temper: common medium chaff. Brown paint bands.
8	CB 2518	G II	II/2	L. 62.2 E 116.1	R: 30 cm	Ware: grey core, orange surface. Temper: common fine-medium chaff, mica inclusions.
9	CB 1852	G I	II/1A	L. 3.1 E 63.3	R: 34 cm	Ware: pale grey core, pale pink-buff surface. Temper: medium chaff. Orange-brown paint on rim.
10	CB 2180	G II	II/1A	L. 59.3 E 103.2	R: 31 cm	Ware: grey core, buff surface. Temper: common chaff, fine sand, mica inclusions.
11	CB 3182	G IV	II/1	L. 34.4 F 70.1	R: 32 cm	Stand bowl or base. Ware: buff. Temper: common sand.
12	CB 4005	G II	III	L. 70.1 F 220.3	R: 26.5 cm	Possible basin. Ware: black core, orange surface. Temper: common coarse chaff, common medium dark grit. Grooved rim.
13	CB 4259	G II	III	L. 37.4 F 222.1	R: 32 cm	Possible basin. Ware: buff core, orange surface. Temper: common medium chaff, fine lime.
14	CB 2153	G II	II/2	L. 2.3 E 102.1	R: 29 cm	Ware: buff core, buff-green surface. Temper: common chaff, sparse lime.
15	CB 2896	G II	II/2	L. 54.8 F 204.3	R: 31 cm	Ware: orange core, buff surface. Temper: common medium chaff, rare fine lime.
16	CB 4242A	G II	III	L. 77.1 F 227.2	R: 34.5 cm	Ware: buff core, light buff surface. Temper: sparse large chaff, common fine lime.

STANDS

PLATE 44

LEDGE RIM, CYLINDRICAL

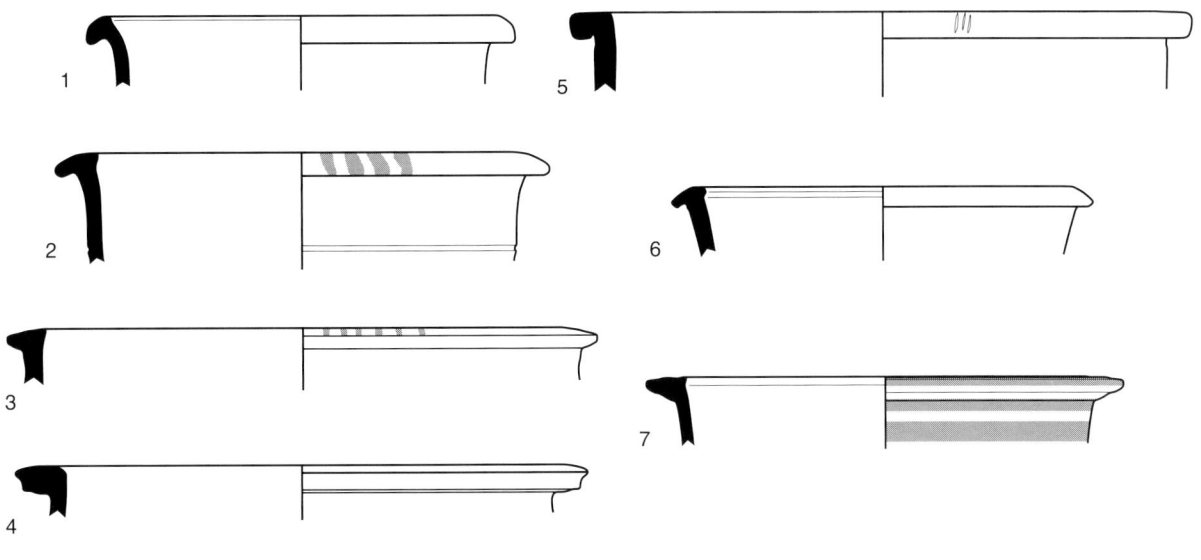

LEDGE RIM, CONCAVE SIDES

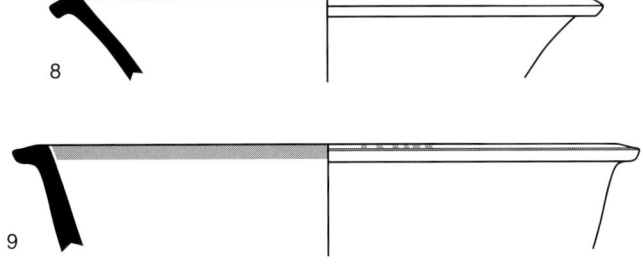

MISCELLANEOUS

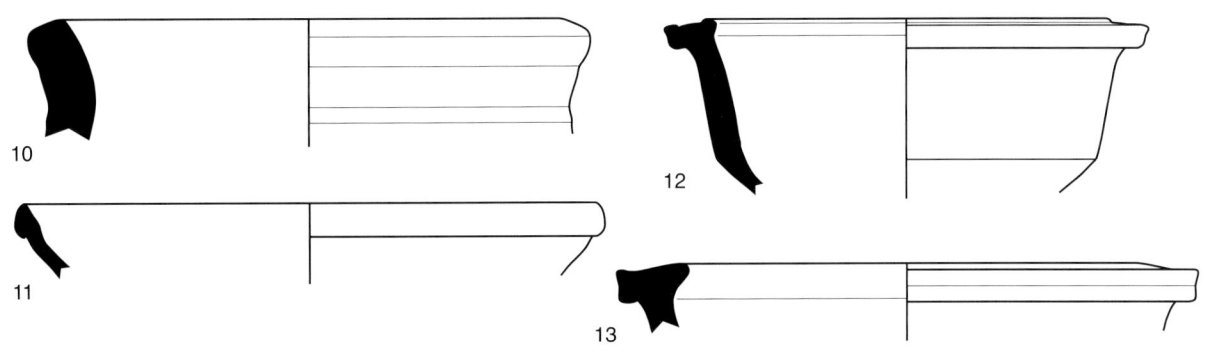

POSSIBLE DRAIN SEGMENTS

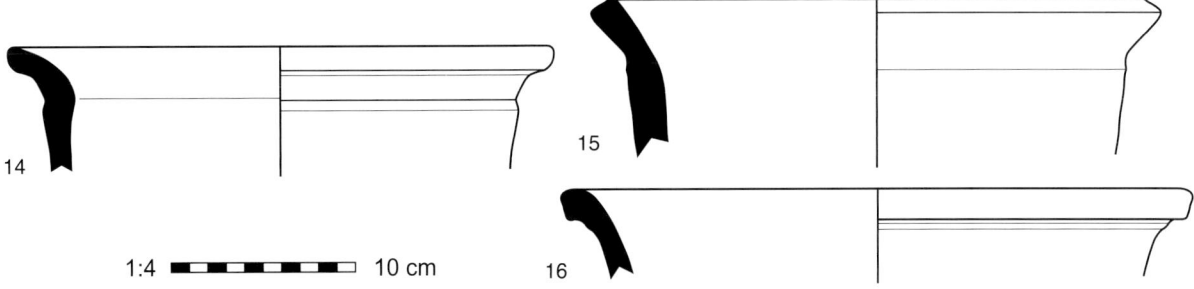

1:4 ▬▬▬ 10 cm

Plate 45: *Cups*

	CB no.	Area	Phse	Loc. & Lot no	Dimensions	Ware, comments
1	CB 2811	G IV	I	L. 23.2 F 51.3	R: 9 cm	Ware: pink-buff core, buff-range surface. Temper: common fine lime, sparse medium chaff. Red paint bands.
2	CB 3940	G IV	I	L. 33.1 F 58.5	R: 9 cm	Ware: Temper:
3	CB 1888	G I	II/1	L. 2.1 E 61.5	R: 7.5 cm	Ware: greenish-buff. Temper: fine chaff. Fugitive brown paint bands.
4	CB 1910	G I	II/1	L. 2.1 E 61.6	R: 9 cm	Ware: buff core, pale buff surface. Temper: fine lime. Red paint bands.
5	CB 2174	G I	II/2	L. 4.6 E 84.1	R: 8.5 cm	Ware: buff. Temper: fine lime.
6	CB 4010	G II	III	L. 70.1 F 220.3	R: 7 cm	Ware: brown core, orange surface. Temper: rare sand.
7	CB 2845	G II	III	L. 27.2 F 205.1	R: 9 cm	Ware: pink-buff core, pale buff surface. Temper: common fine lime. Red paint band and cross-hatching.
8	CB 4255	G II	III	L. 37.5 F 226.4	R: 10 cm	Ware: buff. Temper: common fine lime and sand. Brown paint and 5-point comb incision.
9	CB 2840	A II	I	L. 74.1 F 3.2	R: 11 cm	Ware: buff. Temper: sparse chaff, sparse lime. Red paint X-hatched triangles.
10	CB 3794	G IV	II/1	L. 34.4 F 70.3	R: 14 cm	Ware: buff. Temper: common fine chaff and lime. Red paint bands.
11	CB 4200	G II	III	01-24 F 217.1	R: 7 cm	Ware: buff core, pale buff surface. Temper: common fine lime. Red-brown paint bands.
12	CB 4203	G II	III	01-24 F 217.1	R: 8 cm	Ware: orange core, pale orange surface. Temper: common fine lime.
13	CB 4202	G II	III	01-24 F 217.1	R: 8 cm	Ware: buff. Temper: common fine lime, mica inclusions. Red paint.
14	CB 2943	G III	II/2	L. 39.1 F 78.2	R: 8 cm	Ware: grey. Temper: none visible. Horizontal burnishing interior and exterior.
15	CB 3059	A II	II	L. 86.1 F 17.1	R: 7 cm	Ware: green. Temper: rare fine lime.
16	CB 1794	A I	II	L. 41.1 E 37.1	R: 9.5 cm	Ware: buff-green core, pale buff surface. Temper: occasional fine chaff, lime. Brown-black paint band.
17	CB 2005	A I	II	L. 41.2 E 50.1	R: 9 cm	Ware: orange core, orange-buff surface. Temper: sparse fine lime. Red paint band.
18	CB 1871	A II	II	L. 52.2 E 6.2	R: 9 cm	Ware: pale buff. Temper: none.
19	CB 962:3	A I	III	L. 33.2 D 388	R: 10 cm	Ware: buff. Temper: sparse lime. Black paint bands.
20	CB 2222	G II	II/2	L. 51.5 E 93.4	R: 7 cm	Ware: buff core, pale green surface. Temper: sparse medium chaff, fine lime.
21	CB 1993	G I	II/2	L. 4.6 E 66.5	R: 8.2 cm B: 3 cm H: 7.9 cm	Ware: pale buff. Temper: sparse fine lime, occasional large chaff. Wheel-turning grooves near base.
22	CB 3932	G IV	II/2	L. 32.13 F 74.1	R: 8 cm	Ware: orange core, buff surface. Temper: common medium lime. Brown paint bands.
23	CB 3141	G IV	II/1	L. 34.2 F 65.1	R: 8 cm	Ware: buff. Temper: common sand and fine lime. Red paint bands.
24	CB 3187	G IV	II/1	L. 34.4 F 70.1	R: 9 cm	Ware: buff. Temper: sand and common fine lime. Dark red paint bands.
25	CB 3793	G IV	II/1	L. 34.4 F 70.3	R: 8 cm	Ware: pale buff. Temper: common fine sand. Dark brown paint bands.
26	CB 2855	G III	II/2	L. 28.1 F 77.2	R: 8 cm	Ware: greenish-buff. Temper: sparse fine chaff, common fine sand, sparse fine lime. Dark brown paint bands.
27	CB 3142	G IV	II/1	L. 34.2 F 65.1	R: 8.5 cm	Ware: buff. Temper: sparse sand. Red paint bands
28	CB 4201	G II	III	01-24 F 217.1	R: 8 cm	Ware: buff. Temper: common fine lime, occasional medium lime. Red-brown paint bands.
29	CB 4267	G II	III	L. 37.5 F 226.3	R: 8 cm	Ware: green-buff. Temper: common fine lime, sparse sand. Brown paint bands.
30	CB 3883	G II	III	L. 69.1 F 219.1	R: 8 cm	Ware: pink-buff core, buff surface. Temper: sparse fine sand and lime. Brown paint bands.
31	CB 3882	G II	III	L. 69.1 F 219.1	R: 7 cm	Ware: pink core, pale buff surface. Temper: common fine lime. Red paint bands.
32	CB 2898	G II	III	L. 37.1 F 208.1	R: 9.5 cm	Ware: brown core, buff surface. Temper: occasional fine chaff. Orange paint bands.

CUPS

PLATE 45

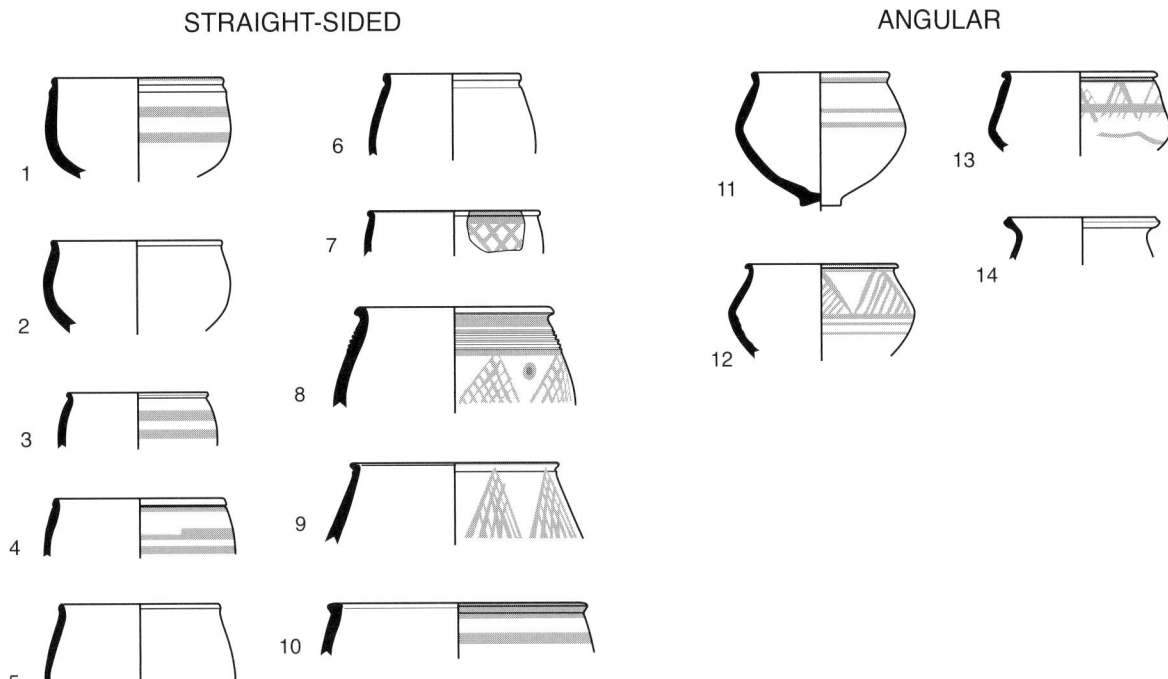

STRAIGHT-SIDED

ANGULAR

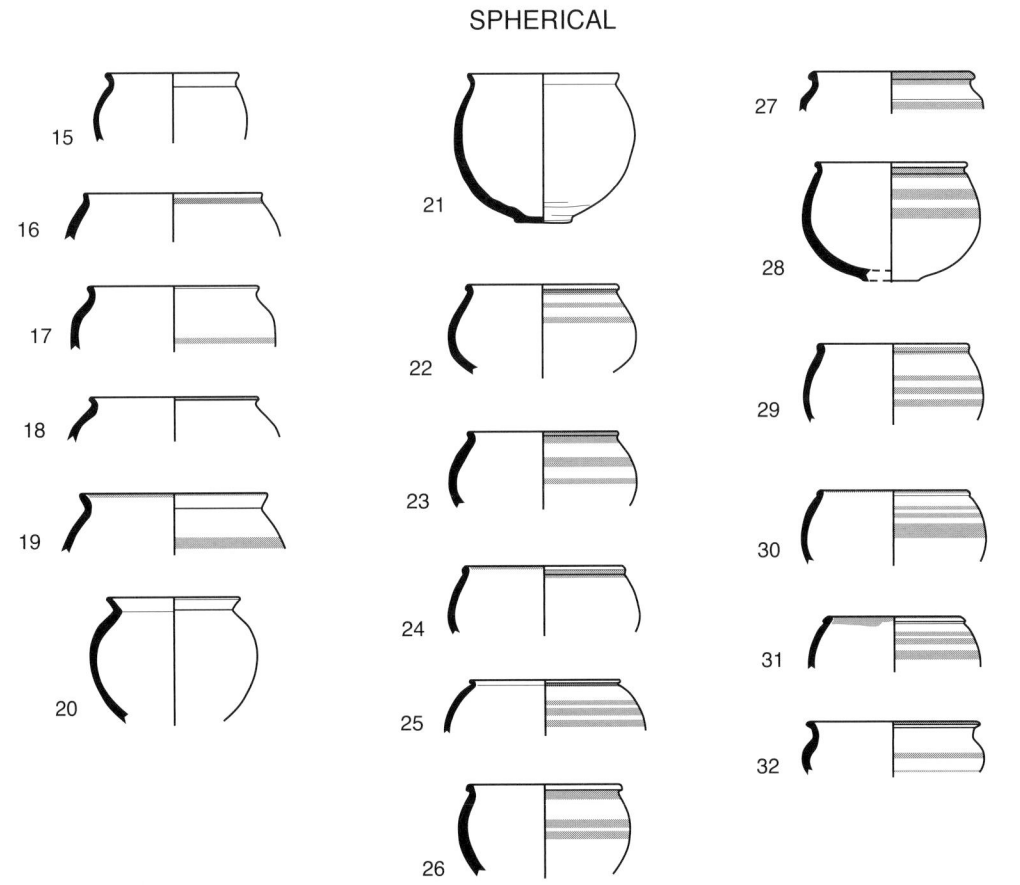

SPHERICAL

1:4   10 cm

Plate 46: *Fine Ware Beakers*

	CB number	Area	Phase	Locus & Lot number	Dimensions	Ware, comments
1	CB 1732	A I	II	L. 30.1 D 373	R: 7 cm	Ware: over-fired green. Temper: none. Brown-black paint bands.
2	CB 984	A I	II	T. 4 D 397	R: 7 cm M: 7.8 cm B: 2 cm H: 8.4 cm	Ware: pale buff. Temper: fine sparse chaff and lime. Red-brown paint bands.
3	CB 2514	G II	II/1	L. 58.4 E 114.1	R: 5.7 cm M: 7.1 cm B: 1.8 cm H: 8.8 cm	Ware: greenish-buff core and surface. Temper: common fine lime. Fugitive black paint bands. Blob of bitumen in base.
4	CB 2551	G II	II/2	L. 51.4 E 93.2	R: 6 cm	Ware: orange-pink core, orange-buff surface. Temper: common fine lime. Red paint bands.
5	CB 3124	G IV	II/1A	L. 31.2 F 57.3	R: 7.5 cm	Ware: red core, orange-buff surface. Temper: rare fine lime.
6	CB 3091	G IV	II/2	T. 39 F 71.1	R: 6.1 cm M: 6.5 cm B: 1.9 cm H: 7.5 cm	Ware: buff. Temper: occasional medium chaff, rare medium lime.
7	CB 2994	A II	II	L. 79.2 F 8.2	R: 8.5 cm	Ware: pink core, buff surface. Temper: rare fine chaff, fine lime. Red paint bands.
8	CB 3038	A II	II	L. 81.2 F 35.3	R: 9 cm	Ware: buff. Temper: rare fine lime. Red paint bands.
9	CB 1757	A I	II	L. 16.2 D 361	R: 6.5 cm	Ware: pale green-buff. Temper: none. Fugitive brown paint bands.
10	CB 1691	A I	II	L. 16.1 D 376	R: 9 cm	Ware: pink core, pale buff surface. Temper: common lime. Red-brown paint bands.
11	CB 2552	G II	II/2	L. 51.4 E 93.2	R: 7.5 cm	Ware: buff. Temper: common very fine lime. Red-brown paint bands.
12	CB 3935	G IV	II/2	L. 73.2 F 457.1	R: 8 cm	Ware: orange. Temper: sparse fine lime.
13	CB 2093	G I	II/1	T 11 E 79.2	R: 8 cm M: 9.2 cm B: 3 cm H: 9.3 cm	Ware: orange-buff. Temper: sparse large chaff, common fine lime. Faint red paint bands.
14	CB 2535	G II	II/2	St 00/46 E 331.1	R: 9 cm	Ware: buff core, pale buff surface. Temper: none visible. Thin brown paint bands.
15	CB 2904	G II	II/2	L. 54.9 F 206.1	R: 9 cm	Ware: buff. Temper: none visible. Dark red paint bands.
16	CB 3051	G III	II/2	L. 39.2 F 81.1	R: 9 cm	Ware: red core, buff-orange surface. Temper: non visible.
17	CB 1962	A I	II	L. 41.2 E 49.1	R: 9 cm	Ware: pale buff. Temper: sparse fine chaff.
18	CB 1727	A I	I	L. 17.2 D 350	R: 9 cm	Ware: buff core, pale buff surface. Temper: occasional large chaff. Brown-black paint bands.
19	CB 742:2	A I	II	L. 29.1 D 349	R: 10 cm	Ware: green. Temper: sparse lime, fine chaff.
20	CB 2078	G I	II/1	T 13 E 82.1	R: 8.0 cm M: 10.8 cm B: 3.7 cm H: 12.2 cm	Ware: grey core, dark grey surface. Temper: common large chaff. Friable and splintery fabric.
21	CB 1932	A II	II	L. 61.1 E 22.1	R: 15 cm	Ware: buff. Temper: fine lime.
22	CB 2933	A II	II	L. 81.1 F 34.1	R: 16.5 cm	Ware: pink core, buff surface. Temper: common fine chaff, rare fine lime. Red-brown paint bands.
23	CB 1963	G I	II/1	L. 4.5 E 66.3	R: 11 cm	Ware: pale buff-green. Temper: medium lime.
24	CB 3123	G IV	II/1A	L. 31.2 F 57.3	R: 13.5 cm	Ware: brown. Temper: occasional fine lime. Black paint bands.

FINE WARE BEAKERS PLATE 46

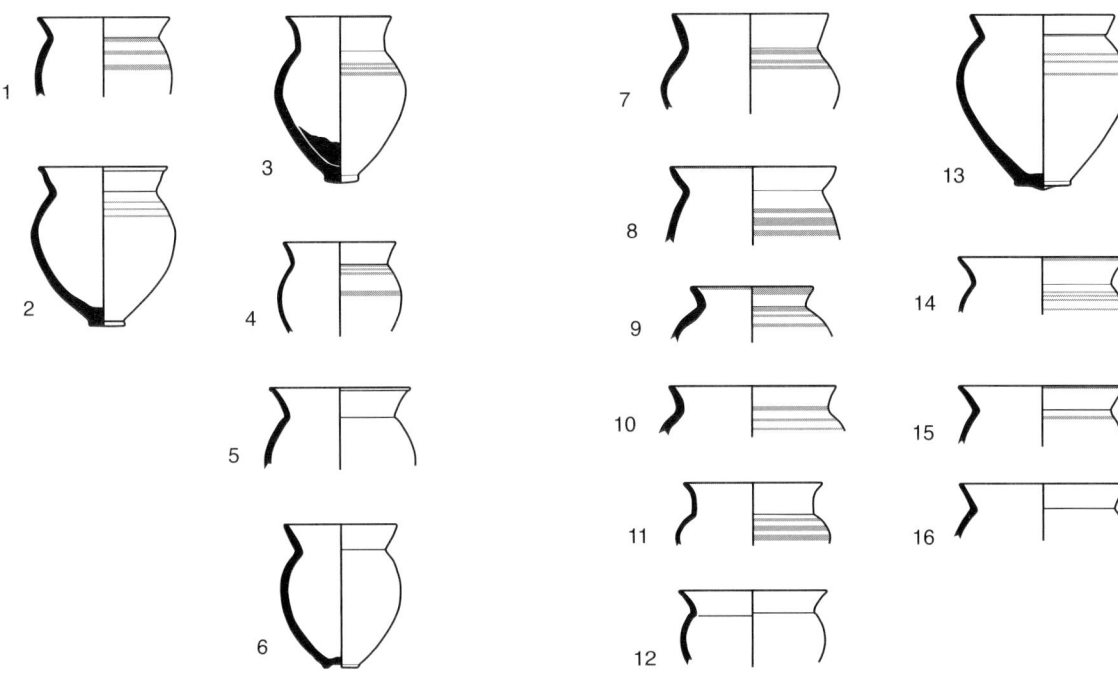
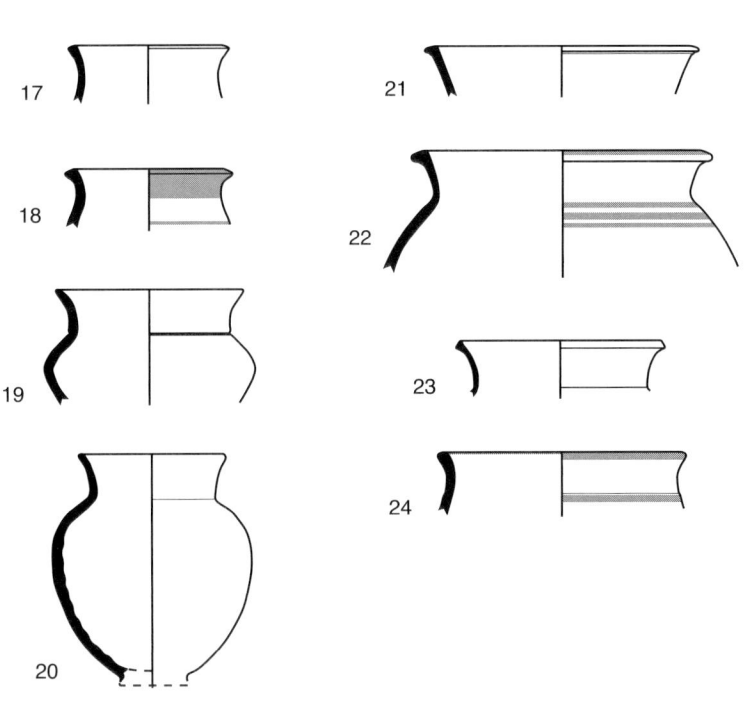

1:4　　　　10 cm

Plate 47: *Grain measures*

	CB number	Area	Phase	Locus and Lot number	Dimensions	Ware, comments
1	CB 2170	A II	IA	L. 67.2 E 188.3	R: 13 cm	Ware: buff core, pale buff surface. Temper: none. Fugitive black paint bands.
2	CB 2225	A II	IA	L. 67.5 E 197.1	R: 14 cm	Ware: pale buff. Temper: sparse fine chaff. Red paint bands.
3	CB 2042	A II	IA	L. 67.1 E 29.3	R: 15 cm	Ware: orange-buff core, pale buff surface. Temper: sparse fine chaff, rare lime. Dark red paint bands and cross-hatched lozenges., slashes across rim.
4	CB 1761	A I	II	L. 16.2 D 361	R: 13 cm	Ware: orange. Temper: sparse lime, fine chaff. Red-orange paint bands.
5	CB 1873	A II	I	L. 3.1 E 9.1	R: 14 cm	Ware: buff core, pale buff surface. Temper: sparse fine chaff. Fugitive red-brown paint.
6	CB 351:3	A I	II	L. 19.1 D 66	R: 18 cm	Ware: buff. Temper: common chaff, lime. Red painted bands.
7	CB 1979	A II	II	L. 55.1 E 12.2	R: 15 cm	Ware: grey core, orange surface. Temper: common chaff, occasional fine lime.
8	CB 2842	A II	II	L. 73.1 F 1.4	R: 14-15 cm	Ware: grey-buff core, buff surface. Temper: common chaff. Dark brown paint bands and cross-hatched triangles. Some secondary charring on interior and exterior.
9	CB 3041	A II	II	L. 81.2 F 35.3	R: 16.5 cm	Ware: buff. Temper: sparse sand and fine lime. Dark red paint bands.
10	CB 1736	A I	II	L. 30.1 D 373	R: 16 cm	Ware: grey core, buff surface. Temper: common chaff, lime. Red paint bands and triangles.
11	CB 1765	A I	II	L. 16.2 D 361	R: 18 cm	Ware: grey core, orange surface. Temper: common fine-medium chaff.
12	CB 1917	A II	II	L. 54.2 E 11.2	Max: 15 cm	Ware: red-grey core, grey surface. Temper: fine chaff, lime.
13	CB 2189	G II	II/2	L. 51.3 E 92.4	R: 16 cm	Ware: dark buff core, buff surface. Temper: common chaff, mica inclusions.

GRAIN MEASURES

PLATE 47

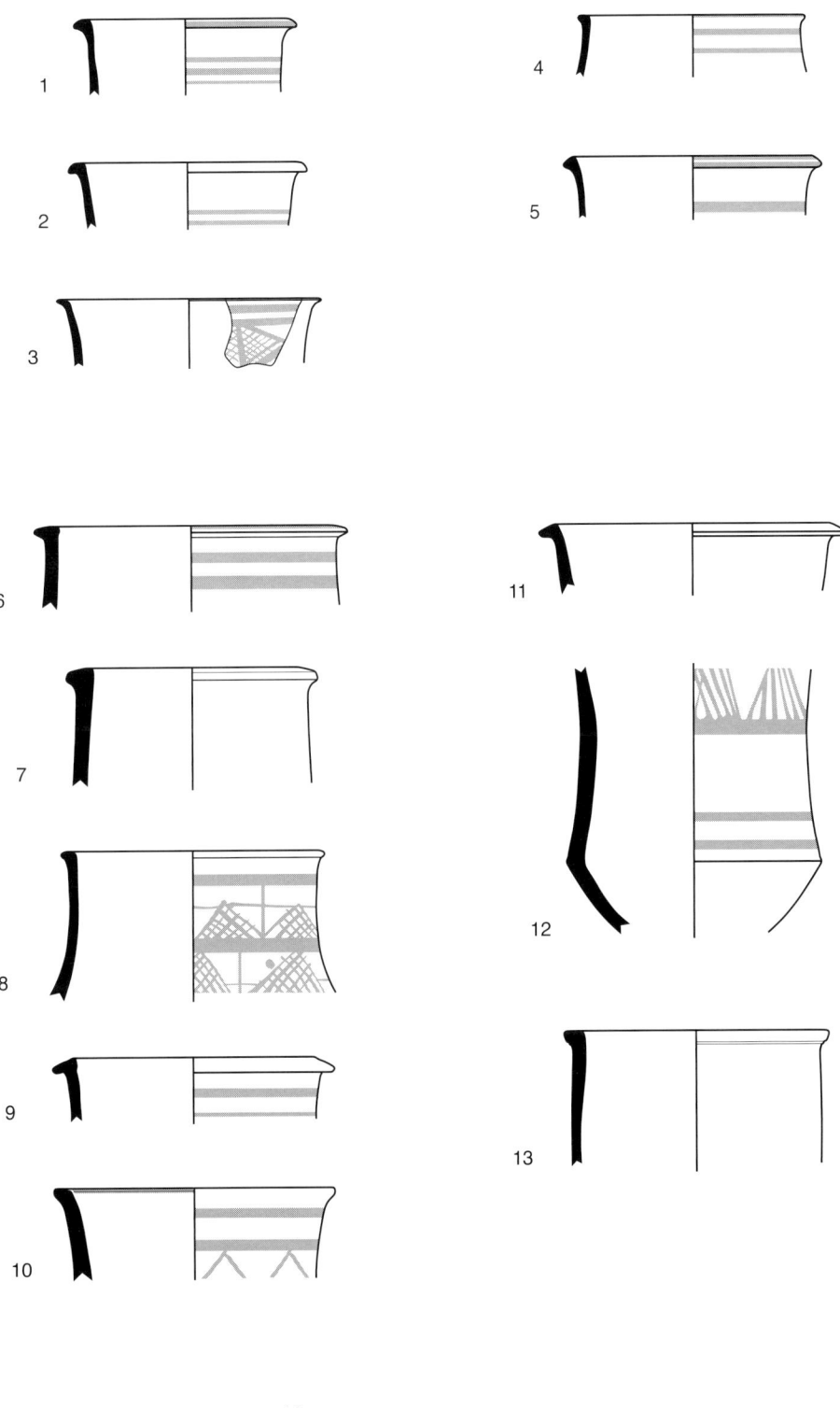

Plate 48: *Khabur Ware Jars*

	CB number	Area	Phase	Locus and Lot number	Dimensions	Ware, comments
1	CB 2108	A II	IA	L. 67.3 E 191.1	R: 14 cm	Ware: orange-buff core, pale buff surface. common medium chaff, sparse lime. Red paint band.
2	CB 2805	A II	II	L. 75.2 F 28.1	R: 14 cm	Ware: orange core, pink-buff surface. Temper: common chaff and fine lime. Brown paint bands.
3	CB 1755	A I	II	L. 16.2 D 361	R: 15 cm	Ware: buff core, pale buff surface. Temper: common lime, rare chaff. Brown-black paint bands.
4	CB 742:3	A I	II	L. 29.1 D 349	R: 16 cm	Ware: buff. Temper: common chaff, lime. Red painted bands.
5	CB 2054	A I	III	L. 34.3 E 55.1	R: 15.5 cm	Ware: buff core, pale buff surface. Temper: medium fine lime, mica inclusions. Fugitive black paint bands.
6	CB 3118	G IV	S	L. 43.1 F 66.1	R: 15.5 cm	Temper: common medium chaff, rare fine lime. Dark red paint band.
7	CB 2458	G I	II/1	L. 10.1 E 73.4	R: 11.7 cm	Ware: green. Temper: common medium chaff, fine lime. Fugitive black paint bands.
8	CB 2505	G II	II/1	L. 58.2 E 106.3	R; 14 cm	Ware: pink-buff core and surface. Temper: common medium chaff, fine lime. Red paint bands.
9	CB 3024	G II	II/2	L. 54.10 F 210.2	R: 16.5 cm	Ware: orange core, buff surface. Temper: common fine-medium chaff and fine lime. Red paint bands.
10	CB 989	A I	II	T. 4 D 397	R: 11.8 cm M: 22.7 cm B: 8.7 cm H: 27.4 cm	Ware: buff core, pale buff surface. Temper: sparse chaff. Red-brown paint bands.
11	CB 1998	G I	II/1	T. 10 E 78.1	R: c 10.7 cm M: 16.7 cm B: 7.8 cm H: 20.4 cm	Irregular rim slightly broken in antiquity, convex base. Ware: greenish-buff. Temper: common medium chaff, occasional fine lime. Fugitive brown paint bands on rim, neck and shoulder.
12	CB 2530	G I	II/2	L. 4.6 E 84.3	R: 12.5 cm M: 19.2 cm B: 8 cm H: 20 cm	Ware: grey core, orange surface. Temper: common medium chaff, sparse fine lime. Red paint bands and metopes, groups of three slashes across rim.
13	CB 3229	G II	III	L. 36.1 F 207.3	R: 13.5 cm	Ware: brown core, orange-buff surface. Temper: common coarse chaff and fine lime. Red paint bands.
14	CB 3208	G II	III	L. 36.1 F 207.4	R: 15 cm	Ware: orange core, buff-orange surface. Temper: common coarse chaff. Red paint bands.

KHABUR WARE JARS

PLATE 48

PROJECTING ROUNDED TRIANGLE RIM

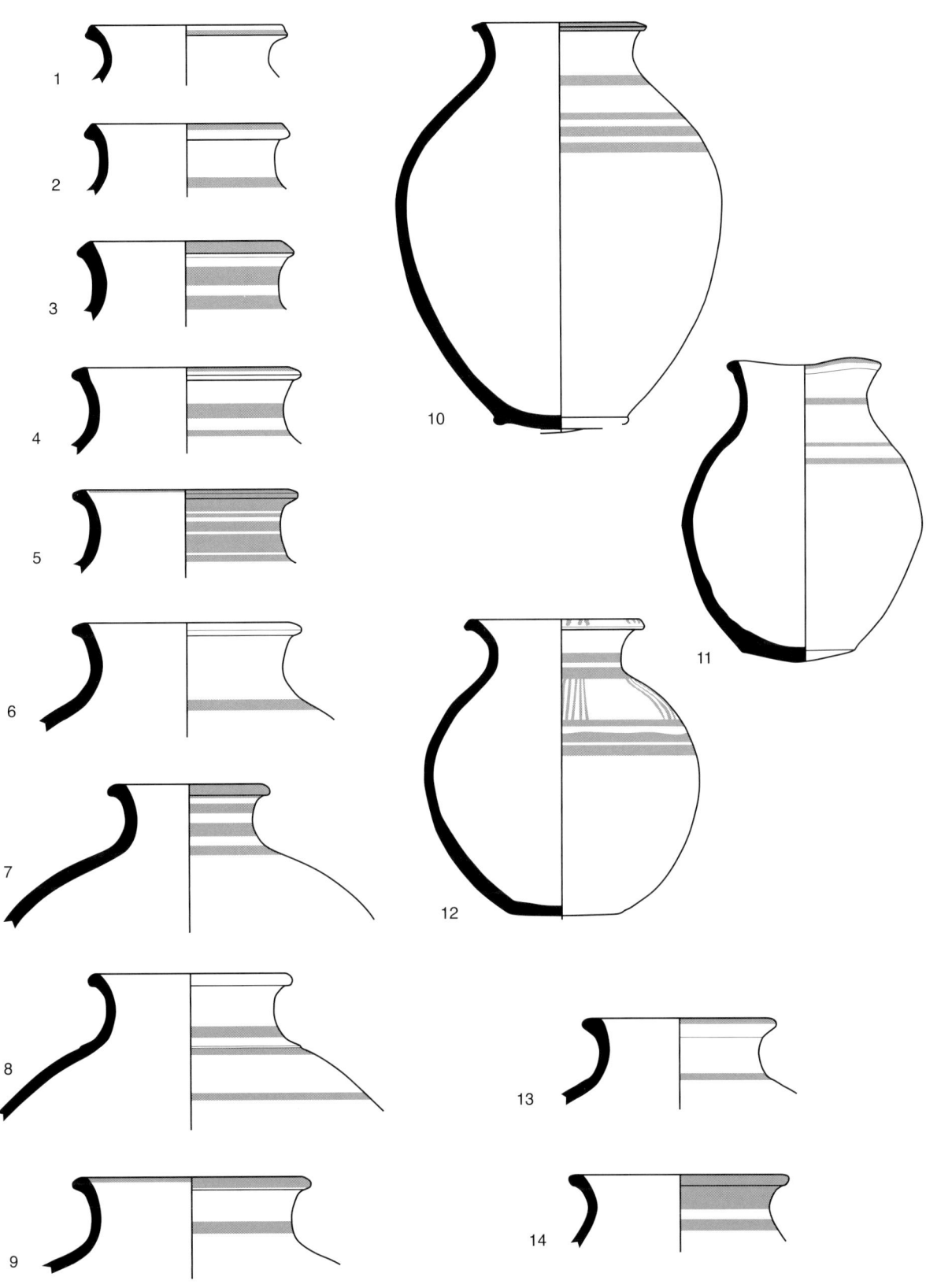

1:4 ▬▬▬▬ 10 cm

Plate 49: *Khabur Ware Jars*

	CB number	Area	Phase	Locus and Lot number	Dimensions	Ware, comments
1	CB 36:1	A I	I	L. 3.1 D 15	R: 13.5 cm	Ware: buff. Temper: common chaff. Red paint bands.
2	CB 786:5	A I	II	L. 26.1 D 363	R: 15 cm	Ware: buff. Temper: common chaff, lime. Brown paint bands.
3	CB 2382	G I	II/1	L. 12.1 E 81.2	R: 15 cm	Ware: buff. Temper: sparse medium chaff, occasional fine lime. Red paint bands.
4	CB 2077	G I	II/1	T 13 E 82.1	R: 6.8 cm. M: 11.2 cm B: 4.7 cm H: 13.9 cm	Ware: buff core, greenish-buff surface. Temper: common fine-medium lime, occasional fine chaff. Horizontal black paint bands on rim, neck and shoulder, hatched triangles on shoulder.
5	CB 2067	A II	II	L. 54.4 E 28.2	R: 14 cm M: 20.2 cm B: 9.5 cm H: 27.1 cm	Ware: pale grey core, buff surface. Temper: common medium chaff, occasional medium-large lime. Red-brown paint bands.
6	CB 980:2	A I	II	L. 36.1 D 396	R: 15 cm	Ware: buff. Temper: chaff, lime. Red painted rim and neck.
7	CB 1769	A I	IA	L. 32.1 D 366	R: 13 cm	Ware: buff core, pale buff surface. Temper: medium chaff, occasional lime. Fugitive brown-black paint bands.
8	CB 1723	A I	II	L. 16.1 D 376	R: 19 cm	Ware: buff core, orange-buff surface. Temper: medium chaff, sparse lime. Thick red paint over rim.
9	CB 1841	A II	II	L. 52.2 E 6.1	R: 15 cm	Ware: buff core, pale buff surface. Temper: medium chaff. Brown-black paint bands.
10	CB 2939	G IV	I	L. 33.1 F 58.1	R: 23 cm	Unusually high flared neck. Ware: brown-grey core, red-buff surface. Temper: common medium chaff. Orange-red paint bands.
11	CB 2040	G I	II/1	L. 13.1 E 75.1	R: 12.5 cm	Ware: orange core, orange-red surface. Temper: common chaff, sparse lime. Red paint.
12	CB 1787	G II	II/1	L. 51.1 E 91.2	R: 18 cm	Unusually high neck. Ware: buff. Temper: abundant chaff, sparse lime. Red-brown paint bands.
13	CB 2014	G I	II/2	L. 4.6 E 66.6	R: 14 cm	Ware: buff. Temper: abundant fine lime. Red paint bands.
14	CB 3149	G II	III	L. 38.2 F 212.1	R: 13.2 cm M: 21.4 cm B: 7.5 cm H: 22.4 cm	Ware: pale buff. Temper: common medium chaff. Red-black paint bands.
15	CB 3406	G II	II/2	L. 54.10 F 210.2	R: 14.5 cm	Ware: yellow-green. Temper: common medium chaff, fine lime. Dark red painted bands.
16	CB 2453	G I	II/2	L. 9.6 E 241.1	R: 15 cm	Ware: grey-buff. Temper: common medium chaff. Black-brown paint bands.
17	CB 3887	G II	III	L. 69.1 F 219.1	R: 14 cm	Ware: buff. Temper: sparse medium chaff and fine lime. Red-brown paint.
18	CB 4018	G II	III	L. 69.1 F 219.2	R: 15.5 cm	Ware: orange core, buff surface. Temper: common fine chaff and lime and dark grit. Red paint.
19	CB 3967	G II	III	L. 37.3 F 213.7	R: 15 cm	Ware: yellow-buff. Temper: common medium chaff, rare fine lime. Red paint bands.
20	CB 3179	G IV	III	L. 40.2 F 68.2	R: 16.5 cm	Ware: grey core, buff-grey surface. Temper: common fine chaff. Brown-black paint bands.

KHABUR WARE JARS

PLATE 49

FLATTENED TRIANGLE RIM   LEDGE RIM

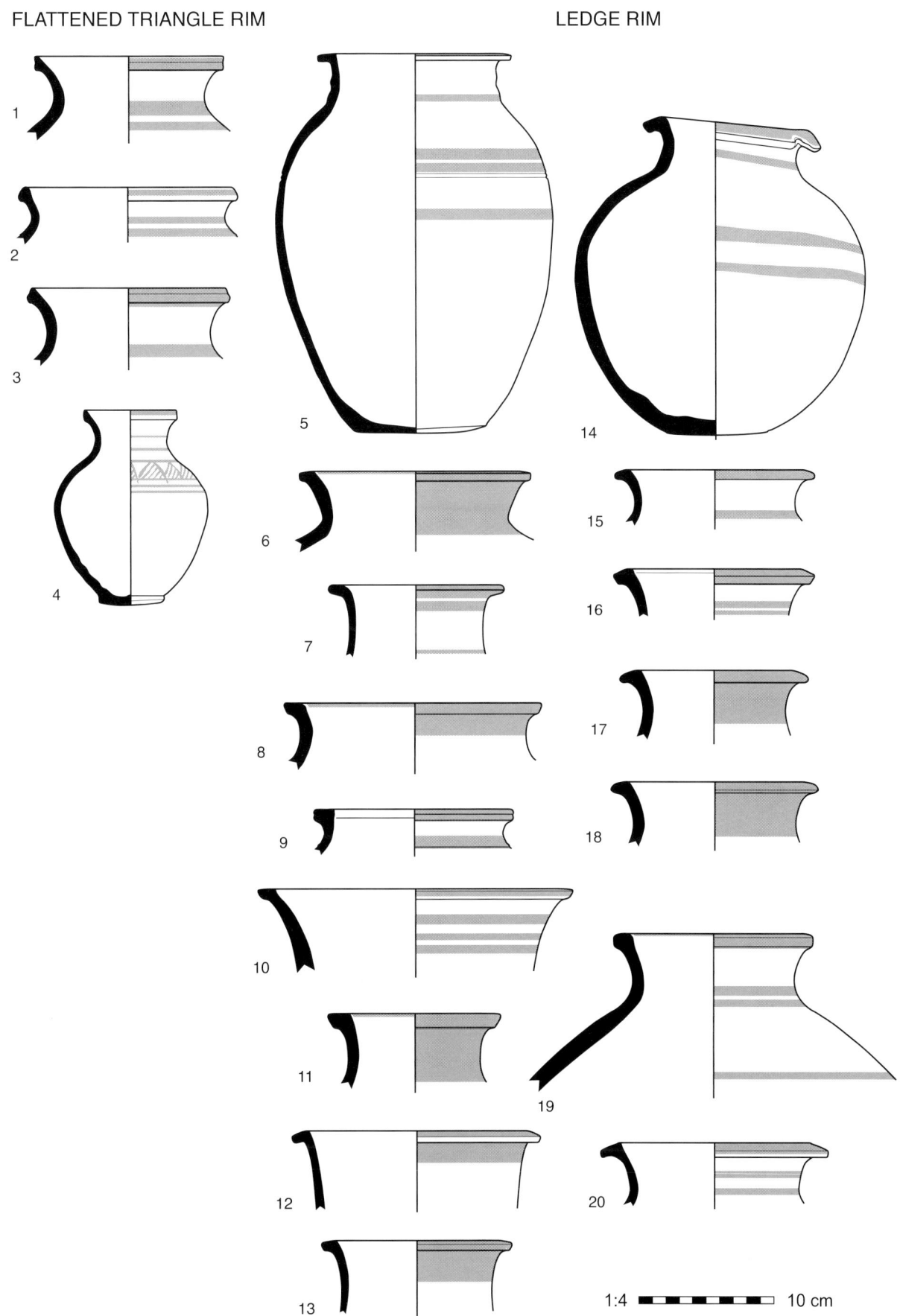

Plate 50: *Khabur Ware Jars*

	CB number	Area	Phase	Locus and Lot number	Dimensions	Ware, comments
1	CB 1915	A II	II	L. 52.2 E 6.4	R: 15 cm	Ware: buff core, dark buff surface. Temper: abundant chaff. Red paint bands.
2	CB 1995	A II	II	L. 52.5 E 30.1	R: 15 cm	Ware: orange-buff core, buff surface. Temper: common chaff, mica inclusions. Brown paint band and blob.
3	CB 2186	G I	II/1	L. 10.2 E 73.6	R: 12 cm	Ware: orange-buff core, pale buff surface. Temper: common medium chaff, occasional fine lime. Red paint triangles on rim.
4	CB 3207	G II	III	L. 36.1 F 207.4	R: 14 cm	Ware: green. Temper: common medium lime. Red-black paint bands
5	CB 1935	G I	II/1	T. 11 shaft E 67.2	R: 15 cm	Ware: greenish core, pale buff surface. Temper: medium chaff, occasional fine lime. Black-brown paint bands.
6	CB 4188	G IV	II/2	L. 34.5 F 454.2	R: 17 cm	Ware: buff core, buff-green surface. Temper: common medium chaff, fine lime. Brown paint band.
7	CB 3209	G II	III	L. 36.1 F 207.4	R: 15 cm	Ware: orange. Temper: sparse medium chaff and lime. Red paint.
8	CB 2860	G II	III	L. 27.1 F 202.2	R: 17 cm	Ware: pale orange core, buff surface. Temper: common medium chaff. Brown-black paint bands.
9	CB 4213	G II	III	01-24 F 217.2	R: 14 cm	Ware: orange core, buff surface. Temper: common fine lime, occasional large chaff. Red paint band.
10	CB 1938	G I	II/1	L. 2.1 E 68.1	R: 10 cm	Ware: buff-green. Temper: sparse fine chaff, fine sand, mica inclusions. Fugitive black paint bands.
11	CB 3941	G IV	I	L. 33.1 F 58.5	R: 12 cm	Ware: buff. Temper: common medium chaff. Red paint bands.
12	CB 2015	G I	II/2	L. 4.6 E 66.6	R: 10 cm	Ware: buff. Temper: sparse fine sand. Dark red paint bands.
13	CB 4187	G IV	II/2	L. 34.5 F 454.2	R: 13.5 cm	Ware: buff core, buff-orange exterior surface. Temper: common fine lime. Red paint bands.
14	CB 1999	G I	II/1	T. 10 E 78.1	M: 22.2 cm B: 10 cm H: 24 cm	Rim broken in antiquity. Ware: green buff core and surface. Temper: occasional chaff, fine sand. Three fugitive black paint bands on shoulder, black paint on neck.

KHABUR WARE JARS

PLATE 50

ROUNDED RIM

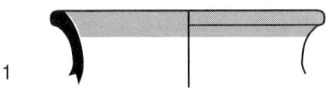
1

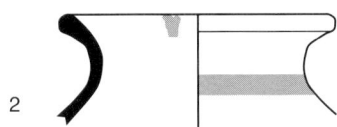
2

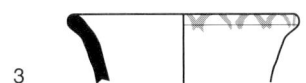
3

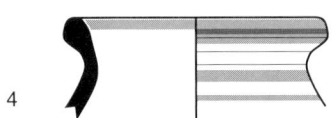
4

LID GROOVE

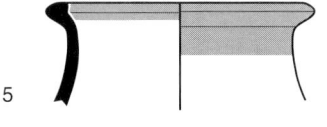
5

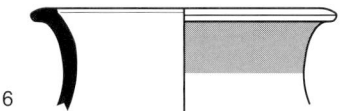
6

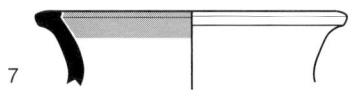
7

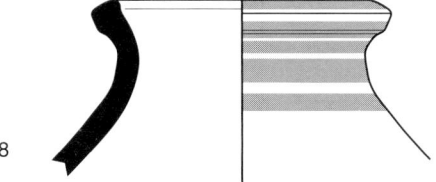
8

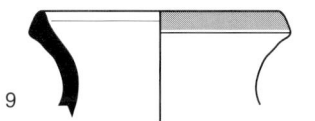
9

NARROW, SLOPED SHOULDER

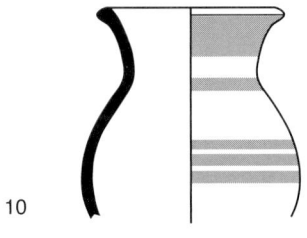
10

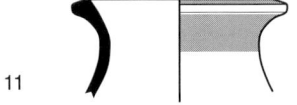
11

12

13

UNCERTAIN

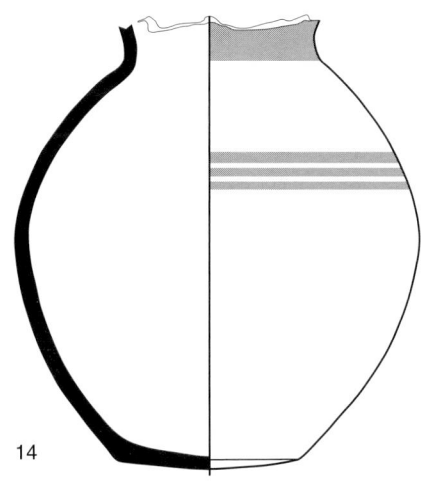
14

1:4 ■■■■□ 10 cm

Plate 51: *Narrow-Mouth Jars*

	CB number	Area	Phase	Locus and Lot number	Dimensions	Ware, comments
1	CB 2815	A II	II	L. 75.1 F 27.1	R: 11.5 cm	Ware: greenish buff. Temper: common chaff, common fine lime.
2	CB 2835	A II	I	L. 76.3 F 5.2	R: 12.5 cm	Ware: dark buff core, buff surface. Temper: common chaff, sparse fine lime.
3	CB 358:2	A I	II	L. 19.1 D 69	R: 13 cm	Ware: grey core, reddish surface. Temper: common chaff, lime.
4	CB 36:3	A I	I	L. 3.1 D 15	R: 13 cm	Ware: green. Temper: common chaff, sparse lime.
5	CB 1780	A I	II	L. 39.1 E 31.1	R: 14 cm	Ware: pink-buff. Temper: common chaff, mica inclusions.
6	CB 1872	A II	II	L. 52.2 E 6.2	R: 15 cm	Ware: buff. Temper: medium chaff, common lime.
7	CB 706:5	A I	II	L. 14.1 D 333	R: 14 cm	Ware: grey core, buff surface. Temper: common chaff, lime.
8	CB 786:4	A I	II	L. 26.1 D 363	R: 14 cm	Ware: buff. Temper: common chaff, lime.
9	CB 1720	A I	II	L. 16.1 D 376	R: 15 cm	Ware: buff core, pale buff surface. Temper: common chaff, lime.
10	CB 1756	A I	II	L. 16.2 D 361	R: 17.5 cm	Ware: grey core, red-orange surface. Temper: common chaff.
11	CB 1881	A II	III	L. 53.1 E 5.3	R: 15 cm	Ware: buff core, buff-orange surface. Temper: medium chaff, lime, mica inclusions.
12	CB 2831	G IV	I	L. 24.1 F 52.1	R: 12.5 cm	Ware: light brown core, grey exterior. Temper: sparse chaff, sparse sand. Burnished exterior.
13	CB 2029	G II	II/1	L. 55.1 E 97.1	R: 14 cm	Narrow-neck jar. Ware: buff-orange core, pale buff surface. Temper: sparse chaff.
14	CB 3404	G II	II/2	L. 54.10 F 210.2	R: 10.5 cm	Ware: brown-orange core, buff surface. Temper: common fine-medium chaff and sand.
15	CB 3405	G II	II/2	L. 54.10 F 210.2	R: 13.5 cm	Ware: grey core, buff surface. Temper: common medium chaff, rare fine lime.
16	CB 2156	G I	II/2	L. 4.6 E 66.5	R: 12 cm	Ware: buff core, pale buff surface. Temper: sparse medium chaff, common fine lime.
17	CB 2144	G II	II/2	L. 54.3 E 105.1	R: 14 cm	Ware: buff core, pale buff surface. Temper: common medium chaff, sparse large lime.
18	CB 3806	G II	II/2	L. 54.10 F 210.5	R: 15.5 cm	Ware: pink core, yellow-buff surface. Temper: common medium chaff.
19	CB 2000	G I	II/1	T. 11 E 79.1	R: 12.1 cm M: 26 cm B: 8.5 cm H: 27 cm	Ware: grey core, buff surface. Temper: common medium chaff, occasional fine lime.

NARROW-NECK JARS
PLATE 51
PROJECTING TRIANGLE RIM

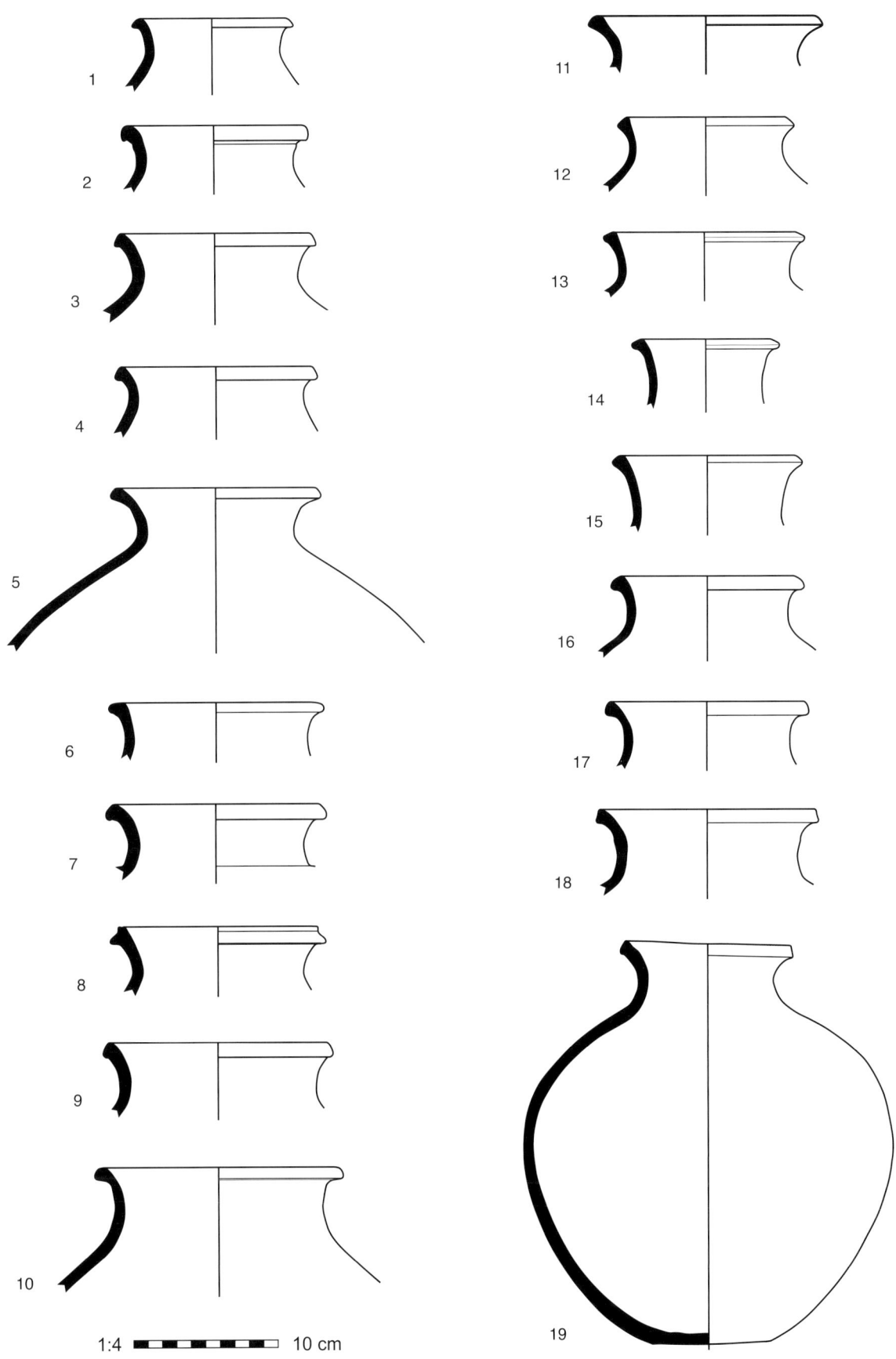

Plate 52: *Narrow-Mouth Jars*

	CB number	Area	Phase	Locus and Lot number	Dimensions	Ware, comments
1	CB 2834	A II	I	L. 76.3 F 5.2	R: 14 cm	Ware: pink core, pink-buff surface. Temper: common chaff, common sand, sparse fine lime.
2	CB 1722	A I	II	L. 16.1 D 376	R: 13 cm	Ware: orange core, buff surface. Temper: rare chaff.
3	CB 726:3	A I	II	L. 26.1 D 342	R: 15 cm	Ware: buff. Temper: common chaff, lime.
4	CB 2830	G IV	II/1A	L. 31.1 F 57.2	R: 17 cm	Ware: pink-buff. Temper: common chaff, sparse sand.
5	CB 2516	G I	II/2	L. 11.3 E 248.1	R: 13 cm	Ware: grey core, orange surface. Temper: common medium chaff, fine lime.
6	CB 3895	G II	II/2	L. 54.10 F 210.6	R: 15 cm	Ware: orange core, yellow-buff surface. Temper: common medium chaff.
7	CB 3808	G II	II/2	L. 54.10 F 210.5	R: 15 cm	Ware: grey core, buff surface. Temper: common medium chaff and fine lime.
8	CB 1891	G II	II/2	L. 51.2 E 91.1	R: 16 cm	Ware: over-fired green. Temper: medium chaff, lime.
9	CB 1693	A I	II	L. 30.1 D 387	R: 16 cm	Ware: orange core, buff surface. Temper: common chaff, lime.
10	CB 990	A I	II	T. 4 D 397	R: 12 cm M: 21 cm B: 8.5 cm H: 25.3 cm	Ware: grey core, pale grey surface. Temper: sparse fine chaff.
11	CB 2105	A I	II	L. 41.1 E 60.1	R: 12 cm	Ware: buff core, pale buff surface. Temper: common chaff.
12	CB 358:3	A I	II	L. 19.1 D 69	R: 11 cm	Ware: green. Temper: common chaff.
13	CB 1902	A II	S	L. 50.1 E 1.1	R: 14.5 cm	Ware: orange core, pale orange-buff surface. Temper: common coarse chaff, sparse lime. Red paint band.
14	CB 36:2	A I	I	L. 3.1 D 15	R: 16 cm	Ware: green. Temper: common chaff, sparse lime.
15	CB 2036	A II	IA	L. 67.1 E 29.3	R: 14 cm	Ware: pink core, buff surface. Temper: abundant chaff.
16	CB 1982	A II	II	L. 64.1 T. 9 E 24.3	R: 13 cm	Ware: buff core, pale buff surface. Temper: common chaff, lime.
17	CB 2142	G II	II/2	L. 54.3 E 105.1	R: 12 cm	Ware: pale green-buff core and surface. Temper: sparse lime.
18	CB 2527	G I	II/2	L. 9.6 E 241.3	R: 14 cm	Ware: grey-buff. Temper: common medium chaff.
19	CB 3807	G II	II/2	L. 54.10 F 210.5	R: 16 cm	Ware: grey core, buff surface. Temper: common medium chaff and fine lime.

NARROW-NECK JARS

PLATE 52

LEDGE RIM

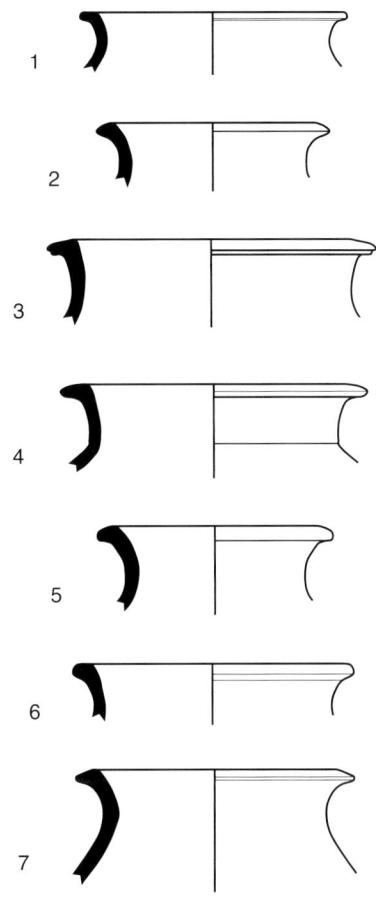

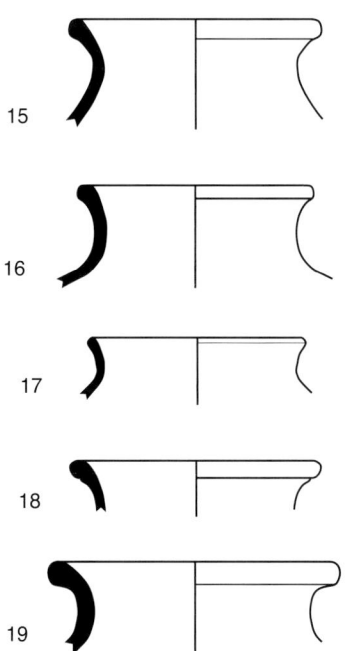

FLATTENED TRIANGLE RIM

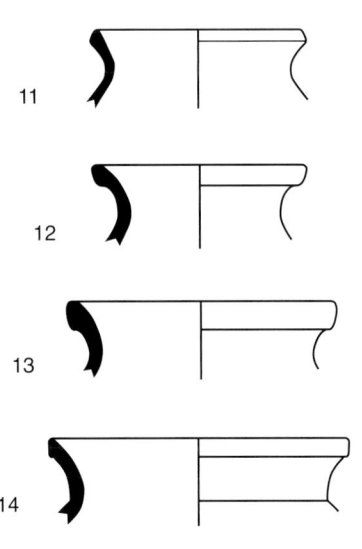

1:4 10 cm

ROUNDED RIM

Plate 53: *Narrow-Mouth Jars*

	CB number	Area	Phase	Locus and Lot number	Dimensions	Ware, comments
1	CB 1803	A II	S	L. 50.1 E 1.2	R: 13.5 cm	Ware: buff core, pale buff surface. Temper: common chaff, occasional lime.
2	CB 3199	A II	II	L. 81.2 F 35.6	R: 12.5 cm	Ware: brown core, orange surface. Temper: common medium chaff, fine lime.
3	CB 706:2	A I	II	L. 14.1 D 333	R: 15 cm	Ware: grey core, buff surface. Temper: common chaff, lime.
4	CB 706:1	A I	II	L. 14.1 D 333	R: 17 cm	Ware: buff. Temper: common chaff, lime.
5	CB 1991	A II	II	L. 61.3 E 25.3	R: 13 cm	Ware: buff core, pale buff surface. Temper: abundant chaff, sparse lime.
6	CB 1768	A I	IA	L. 32.1 D 366	R: 13 cm	Ware: buff core, pale buff surface. Temper: medium chaff.
7	CB 2807	G IV	I	L. 26.2 F 53.1	R: 15 cm	Ware: pink-buff core, buff surface. Temper: common chaff, sparse lime.
8	CB 2001	G I	II/1	T. 11 E 79.1	R: 11.1 cm M: 15.4 cm B: 4.3 cm H: 19.3 cm	Ware: buff core, greenish-buff surface. Temper: sparse medium chaff, fine lime. Ridge at neck-shoulder connection.
9	CB 2809	G IV	II/1	L. 4.2 F 54.1	R: 14.5 cm	Ware: Buff core, orange surface. Temper: common chaff and sparse lime.
10	CB 374:7	A I	II	L. 19.1 D 76	R: 18 cm	Ware: grey core, buff surface. Temper: common chaff. Internal lid ledge.
11	CB 1996	A II	II	L. 52.5 E 30.1	R: 14 cm	Ware: buff. Temper: common chaff.
12	CB 706:4	A I	II	L. 14.1 D 333	R: 17 cm	Ware: green. Temper: common chaff, lime. Interior rim groove.
13	CB 2181	G II	II/1A	L. 59.3 E 103.2	R: 14 cm	Ware: pale buff. Temper: common chaff, sparse lime.
14	CB 2076	G I	II/1	T 13 E 82.1	R: 13.8 cm M: 23.1 cm B: 10.2 cm H: 30.5 cm	Ware: buff core, pale buff surface. Temper: common medium-large chaff, occasional lime.
15	CB 2122	G I	II/1	L. 9.2 E 77.1	R: 17 cm	Ware: pale greenish-buff. Temper: common chaff, sparse lime.

NARROW-NECK JARS

PLATE 53

NECK RIDGE

LID GROOVE

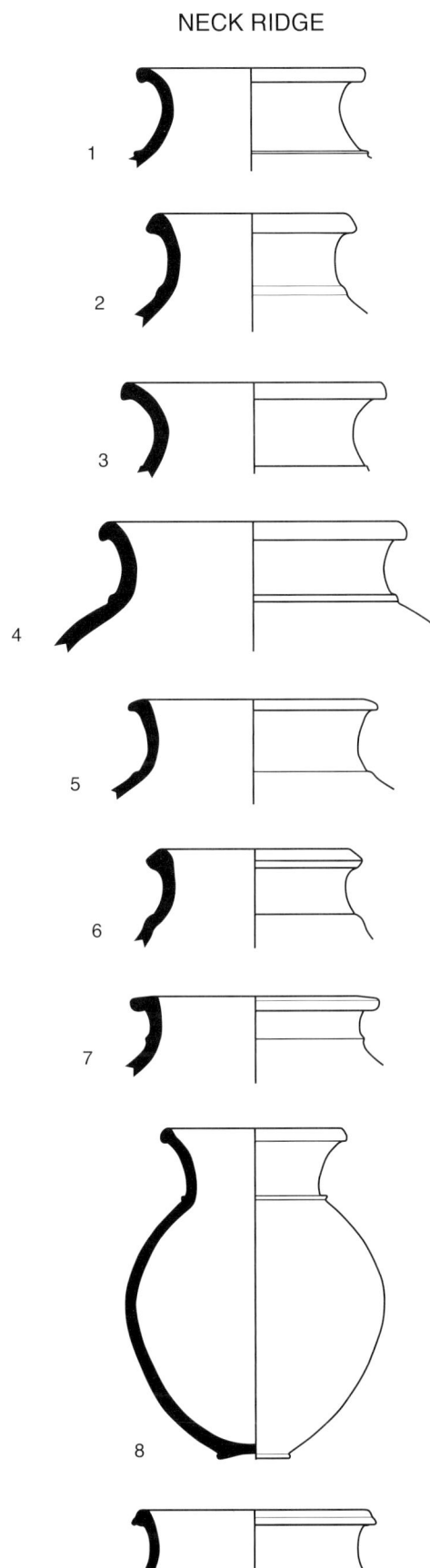

1:4 ▬▬▬ 10 cm

Plate 54: *Wide-mouth Jars, A Sub-Type, Medium*

	CB number	Area	Phase	Locus and Lot number	Dimensions	Ware, comments
1	CB 57:1	A I	I	L. 6.1 D 23	R: 20 cm	Ware: greenish-buff. Temper: common chaff.
2	CB 2812	A II	I	L. 74.1 F 3.1	R: 23.5 cm	Ware: pink-buff core, green-buff surface. Temper: common chaff and fine lime.
3	CB 1738	A I	II	L. 30.1 D 373	R: 17 cm	Ware: over-fired green. Temper: occasional chaff.
4	CB 1983	A II	II	L. 64.1 T. 9 E 24.3	R: 21 cm	Ware: buff core, pale buff surface. Temper: common chaff, lime. Horizontal grooves on shoulder.
5	CB 2916	A II	II	L. 54.6 F 33.1	R: 20 cm	Ware: yellow-green. Temper: common medium chaff. Ridges on neck, set of horizontal grooves just above maximum diameter.
6	CB 2111	A II	II	L. 52.2 E 185.3	R: 16 cm	Ware: orange-buff core, buff surface. Temper: common medium chaff, mica inclusions.
7	CB 2045	A II	II	L 64.2 (T 9) E 181.2	R: 15 cm	Ware: greenish-buff. Temper: common chaff, sparse large lime.
8	CB 1718	A I	II	L. 16.1 D 376	R: 23 cm	Ware: buff. Temper: common chaff, medium lime.
9	CB 726:2	A I	II	L. 26.1 D 342	R: 16 cm	Ware: buff. Temper: common chaff, lime. Horizontal grooves.
10	CB 2472	A II	II	L. 71.1 E 209.2	R: 18 cm M: 27.2 cm B: 11.2 cm H: 36 cm	Ware: pink-buff. Temper: common medium chaff.
11	CB 1981	A II	II	L. 64.1 T. 9 E 24.3	R: 19.5 cm	Ware: orange-buff core, buff surface. Temper: common chaff, lime. Horizontal grooves on shoulder.
12	CB 742:1	A I	II	L. 29.1 D 349	R: 22 cm	Ware: grey core, buff surface. Temper: common chaff, lime.
13	CB 962:4	A I	III	L. 33.2 D 388	R: 18 cm	Ware: buff. Temper: common chaff, lime.
14	CB 2324	A II	III	L. 61.4 E 198.1	R: 18.5 cm	Ware: buff core, buff-grey surface. Temper: common medium-large chaff, occasional medium lime. Fugitive black paint bands.

WIDE-MOUTH JARS, A, MEDIUM

PLATE 54

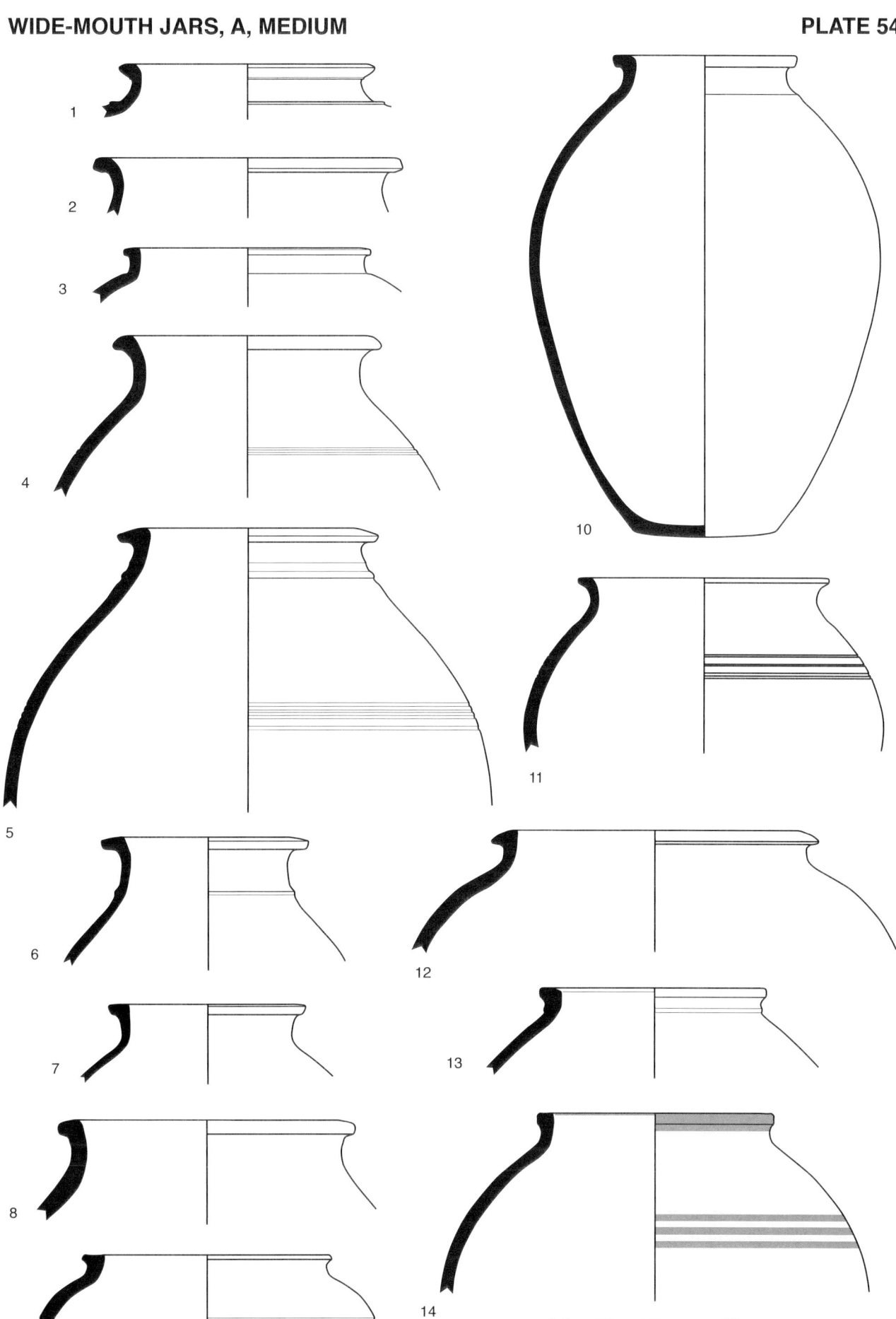

Plate 55: *Wide-mouth Jars, A Sub-Type, Medium*

	CB number	Area	Phase	Locus and Lot number	Dimensions	Ware, comments
1	CB 2134	G II	II/1A	L. 59.1 E 101.2	R: 20 cm	Ware: green-buff core and surface. Temper: common medium chaff. Fugitive black paint on rim and exterior.
2	CB 1810	G I	II/1A	L. 3.1 E 63.2	R: 20 cm	Ware: over-fired green. Temper: medium chaff, sparse lime.
3	CB 1861	G I	II/1	L. 5.1 E 63.4	R: 19 cm	Ware: buff core, pale buff surface. Temper: medium chaff, lime.
4	CB 1862	G I	II/1	L. 5.1 E 63.4	R: 20 cm	Ware: buff-orange core, buff surface. Temper: medium chaff. Three shallow horizontal grooves on shoulder.
5	CB 2178	G II	II/1A	L. 59.3 E 103.2	R: 20 cm	Ware: buff core, buff-green surface. Temper: common chaff, fine lime.
6	CB 1969	G II	II/1	L. 54.1 E 96.1	R: 18 cm	Ware: buff core, buff-green surface. Temper: abundant chaff, occasional lime.
7	CB 3127	G IV	II/1A	L. 31.2 F 57.3	R: 17.5 cm	Ware: black core, orange-buff surface. Temper: common medium chaff. occasional fine lime.
8	CB 2019	G I	II/1	L. 5.1 E 69.2	R: 21 cm	Ware: buff core, pale buff surface. Temper: common chaff, sparse lime.
9	CB 2942	G IV	II/1	L. 32.2 F 59.2	R: 19.5 cm	Ware: grey core, buff surface. Temper: common medium chaff, occasional fine-medium lime.
10	CB 2022	G II	II/1	L. 55.1 E 97.1	R: 22 cm	Ware: buff core, orange surface. Temper: abundant chaff, sparse large lime.
11	CB 2155	G II	II/1	L. 2.1 E 95.1	R: 21.5 cm	Ware: pink-orange core, pale green surface. Temper: common chaff, fine lime, mica inclusions. Three horizontal grooves at maximum diameter.
12	CB 2184	G I	II/1	L. 10.2 E 73.6	R: 24 cm	Ware: orange-buff core, buff surface. Temper: common medium chaff, occasional medium-large lime. Finger-impressed ridge.
13	CB 3805	G II	II/2	L. 54.10 F 210.5	R: 17.5 cm	Ware: grey core, brown surface. Temper: abundant medium lime and grit. Burnished surface.
14	CB 1820	G II	II/2	L. 51.2 E 91.4	R: 18 cm	Ware: grey core, orange surface. Temper: abundant medium chaff, lime.
15	CB 2143	G II	II/2	L. 54.3 E 105.1	R: 19 cm	Ware: grey core, orange surface. Temper: common large chaff, sparse lime.
16	CB 2937	G III	II/2	L. 28.3 F 78.1	R: 20 cm	Ware: grey core, buff surface. Temper: common medium chaff, sparse medium-large lime.
17	CB 2850	G II	II/2	L. 54.8 F 204.1	R: 21.5 cm	Ware: pink-grey core, greenish buff surface. Temper: common chaff, common lime.
18	CB 3931	G IV	II/2	L. 32.13 F 74.1	R: 26 cm	Ware: grey core, buff-grey surface. Temper: common medium chaff.

WIDE-MOUTH JARS, A, MEDIUM

PLATE 55

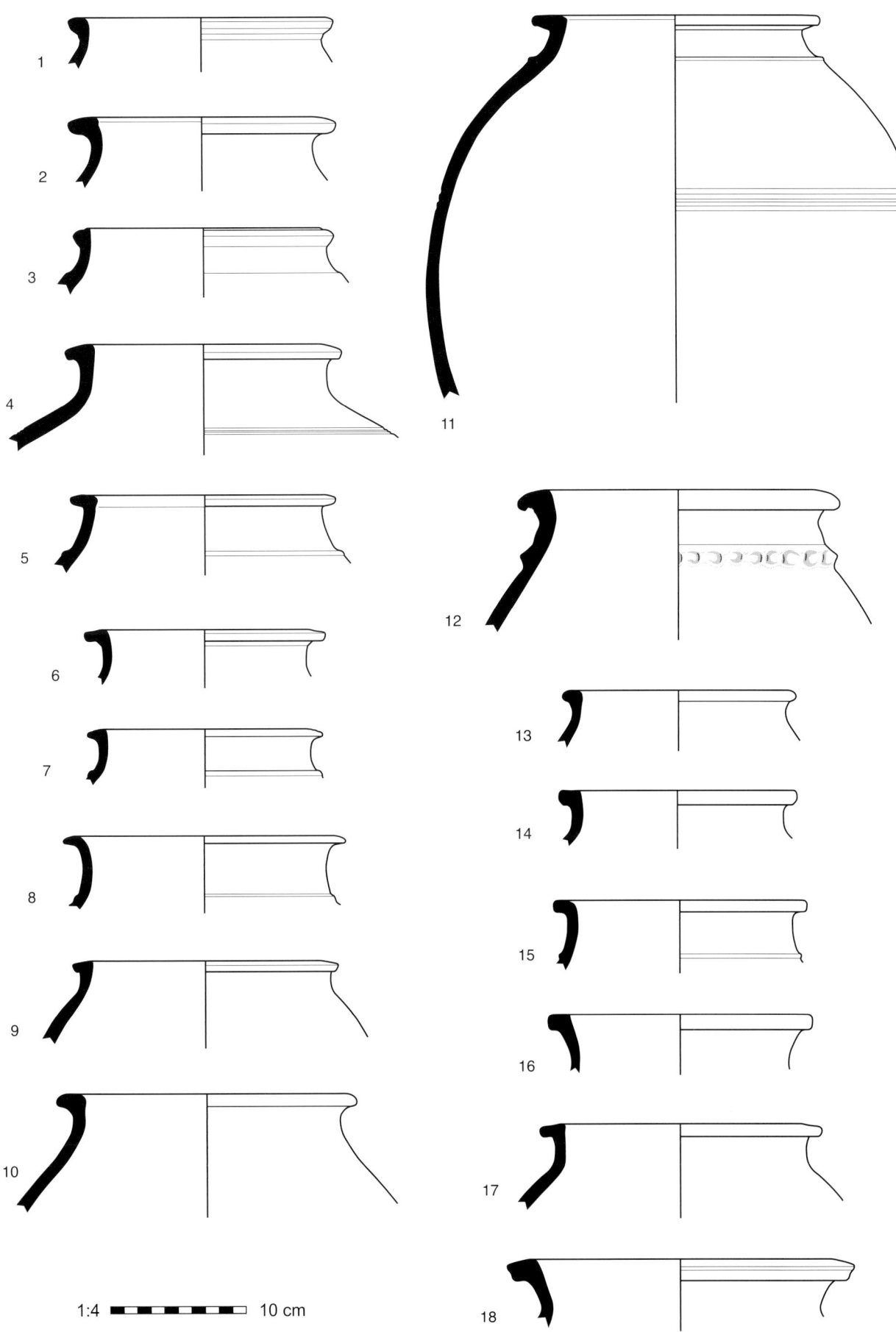

1:4 ▬▬▬ 10 cm

Plate 56: *Wide-mouth Jars, A Sub-Type, Medium*

	CB number	Area	Phase	Locus and Lot number	Dimensions	Ware, comments
1	CB 2546	G II	II/2	L. 65.3 E 120.1	R: 18 cm	Ware: buff. Temper: common medium chaff, fine-medium lime. Two deep incisions across rim.
2	CB 3803	G II	II/2	L. 54.10 F 210.5	R: 24 cm	Ware: orange core, buff surface. Temper: common medium chaff and fine lime.
3	CB 3027	G II	II/2	L. 54.8 F 204.4	R: 23 cm	Ware: grey core, orange-buff surface. Temper: common medium chaff, common fine lime, rare large lime.
4	CB 2548	G II	II/2	L. 62.5 E 334.1	R: 24.5 cm	Ware: orange-buff. Temper: common medium chaff, sparse grey grit. Red paint bands on rim.
5	CB 3787	G IV	II/1	L. 34.4 F 70.3	R: 20.5 cm	Ware: grey core, orange surface. Temper: common medium chaff. Red paint band over rim.
6	CB 2173	G I	II/2	L. 4.6 E 84.1	R: 21 cm	Ware: red core, green surface. Temper: common medium lime, chaff. Red paint bands on rim and neck.
7	CB 4189	G IV	II/2	L. 34.5 F 454.2	R: 18 cm	Ware: grey core, grey-buff surface. Temper: common medium chaff, fine lime.
8	CB 3184	G IV	II/1	L. 34.4 F 70.1	R: 25 cm	Ware: brown core, orange surface. Temper: abundant medium-coarse chaff, occasional lime.
9	CB 3256	G II	II/2	L. 54.10 F 210.1	R: 25 cm	Ware: brown core, orange surface. Temper: common medium chaff and fine lime.
10	CB 4212	G II	III	01-24 F 217.2	R: 16 cm	Ware: buff core, pale buff surface. Temper: common medium chaff, occasional medium lime. Brown paint bands and horizontal grooves on shoulder.
11	CB 3230	G II	III	L. 36.1 F 207.3	R: 20 cm M: 32.5 cm	Ware: orange core, buff surface. Temper: common medium chaff and fine-medium lime. Dark red paint bands and shallow horizontal grooves.
12	CB 3210	G II	III	L. 36.1 F 207.4	R: 19 cm	Ware: green. Temper: abundant fine-medium chaff.
13	CB 3216	G II	III	L. 37.3 F 213.2	R: 22 cm	Ware: grey core, buff surface. Temper: common medium-coarse chaff, occasional medium lime.
14	CB 2837	G II	III	L. 27.1 F 202.1	R: 26 cm	Ware: brown core, buff-orange surface. Temper: common coarse chaff.
15	CB 4163	G IV	III	L. 76.1 F 466.1	R: 23 cm	Ware: light orange core, buff surface. Temper: common medium chaff, sparse lime.
16	CB 2848	G II	III	L. 27.2 F 205.1	R: 19 cm	Ware: pink-grey core, buff surface. Temper: common chaff, sparse lime. Red-orange paint.
17	CB 3228	G II	III	L. 36.1 F 207.3	R: 22 cm	Ware: pink core, yellow-buff surface. Temper: common sand and fine lime. Dark red paint bands on shoulder and rim.

WIDE-MOUTH JARS, A, MEDIUM PLATE 56

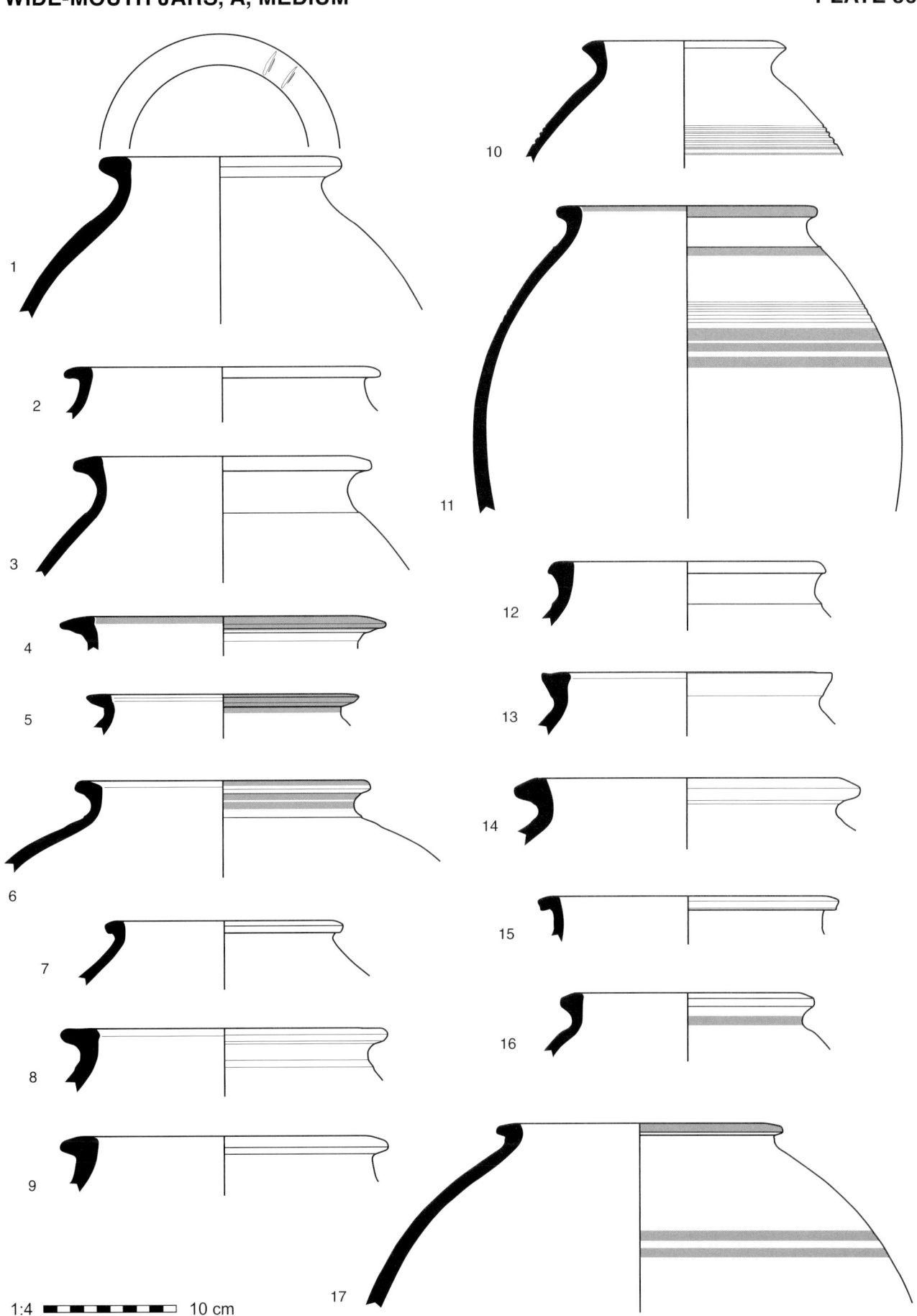

1:4 ▬▬▬▬ 10 cm

Plate 57: *Wide mouth Jars, A Sub-Type, Medium and Large*

	CB number	Area	Phase	Locus and Lot number	Dimensions	Ware, comments
1	CB 2926	G III	II/1	L. 21.2 F 76.5	R: 18 cm	Ware: green-buff. Temper: common medium chaff, rare fine lime.
2	CB 4167	G IV	II/2	L. 34.5 F 454.3	R: 20 cm	Ware: brown core, grey-brown surface. Temper: sparse fine lime. Horizontal burnishing interior and exterior.
3	CB 2298	G I	II/1	L. 9.4 E 85.1	R: 25 cm	Ware: dark buff core, buff surface. Temper: fine chaff, occasional lime.
4	CB 1866	G II	II/2	L. 51.3 E 92.2	R: 29 cm	Ware: grey core, buff surface. Temper: abundant chaff.
5	CB 1816	G II	II/2	L. 51.2 E 91.4	R: 28.5 cm	Ware: buff core, green-buff surface. Temper: medium chaff.
6	CB 2380	G I	II/2	L. 12.1 E 81.2	R: 30 cm	Ware: green. Temper: common chaff, fine lime.
7	CB 3093	G IV	II/2	T. 39 F 71.1	R: 12.4 cm M: 15.4 cm B: 8.0 cm H: 19.6 cm	Ware: pink-buff core, buff surface. Temper: common fine-medium chaff, rare fine lime. Horizontal grooves on shoulder.
8	CB 376:2	A I	II	L. 14.1 D 77	R: 22 cm	Ware: grey core, buff surface. Temper: common chaff, lime. Red paint bands.
9	CB 2140	G II	II/1A	L. 59.1 E 101.1	R: 23 cm	Ware: buff core and surface. Temper: common chaff, occasional fine lime.
10	CB 4000	G II	II/2	L. 54.10 F 210.1	R: 19.5 cm	Ware: buff. Temper: common medium chaff. Horizontal grooves.
11	CB 4001	G II	II/2	L. 54.10 F 210.1	R: 21 cm	Ware: buff core, pale buff surface. Temper: common medium chaff and medium lime. Horizontal groove.
12	CB 2601	G II	II/2	L. 54.5 E 108.3	R: 22 cm	Ware: pink-buff core, buff surface. Temper: common chaff, fine lime. Horizontal grooves on shoulder.
13	CB 2163	G I	II/2	L. 11.2 E 80.2	R: 24 cm	Ware: grey core, buff surface. Temper: common chaff. Two horizontal grooves framing wavy groove.
14	CB 2098	A II	IA	L. 67.1 E 29.4	R: 37 cm	Ware: buff core, pale buff surface. Temper: common chaff, occasional lime. Horizontal and wavy grooves on shoulder.

WIDE-MOUTH JARS, A, MEDIUM PLATE 57

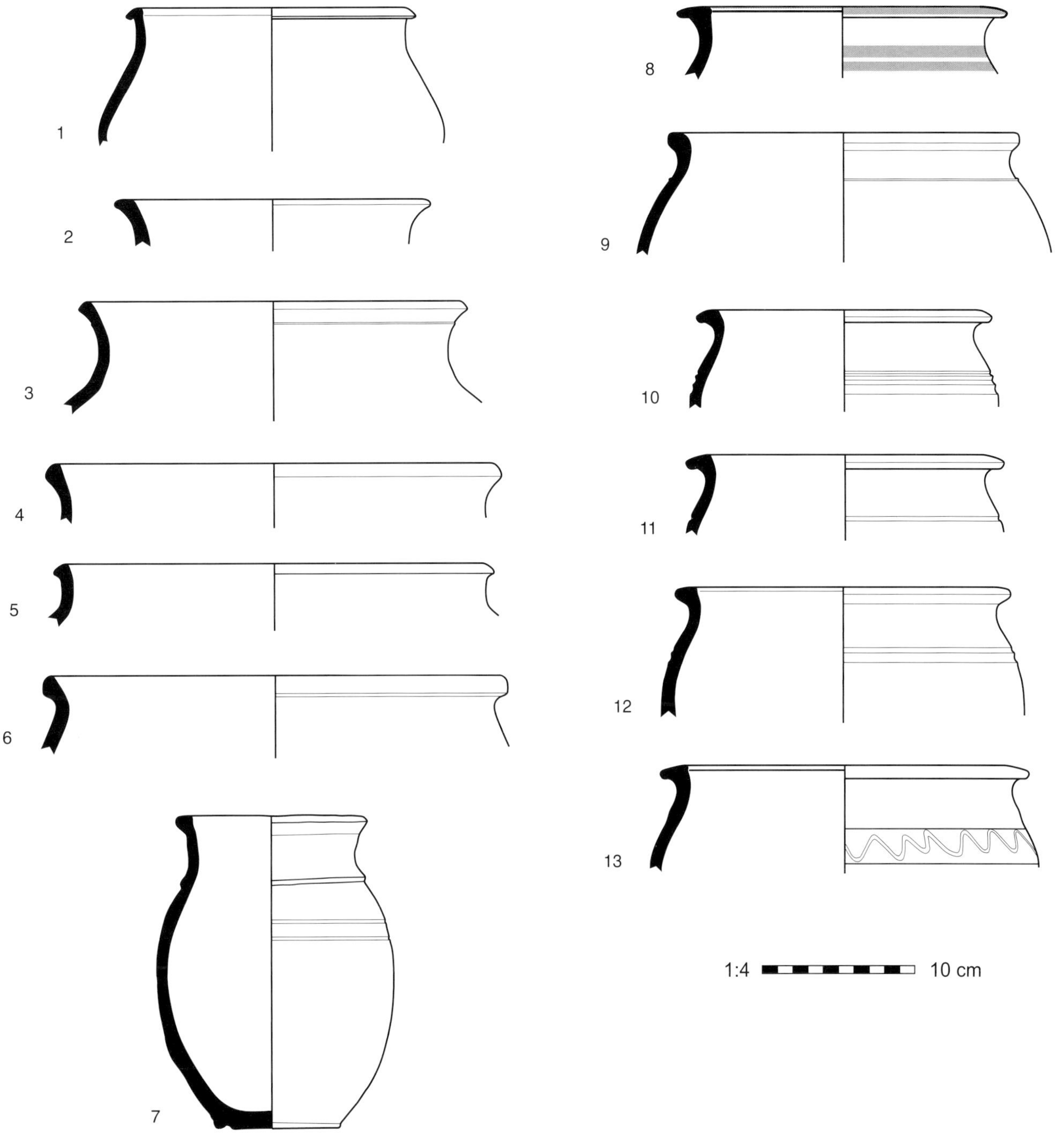

WIDE-MOUTH JARS, A, LARGE

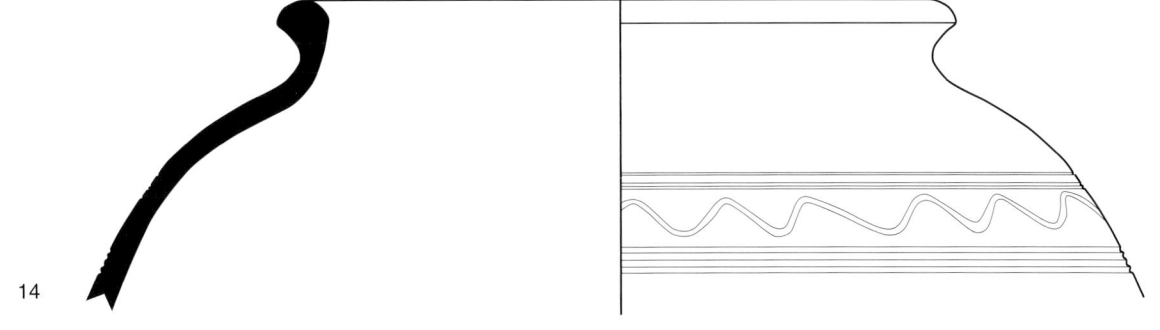

Plate 58: *Wide mouth Jars, A Sub-Type, Large*

	CB number	Area	Phase	Locus and Lot number	Dimensions	Ware, comments
1	CB 1692	A I	II	L. 30.1 D 371	R: 28 cm	Ware: buff core, pale buff surface. Temper: medium chaff, lime, mica inclusions.
2	CB 1719	A I	II	L. 16.1 D 376	R: 33 cm	Internal rim groove. Ware: buff. Temper: common chaff, sparse lime.
3	CB 2852	G IV	I	L. 29.2 F 55.2	R: 27 cm (slightly warped)	Ware: green-buff core, green surface. Temper: common coarse chaff, sparse large lime.
4	CB 1937	G I	II/1	T.11 shaft E 67.2	R: 27 cm	Ware: grey core, orange surface. Temper: abundant chaff, mica inclusions.
5	CB 2028	G II	II/1	L. 55.1 E 97.1	R: 26.5 cm	Ware: orange-buff core, buff surface. Temper: sparse chaff. Soot staining on rim.
6	CB 2027	G II	II/1	L. 55.1 E 97.1	R: 27 cm	Ware: grey core, buff surface. Temper: common chaff, sparse lime.
7	CB 2450	G I	II/1	L. 15.1 E 89.1	R: 29 cm	Ware: buff core, pale buff surface. Temper: common medium chaff, fine lime.
8	CB 4393	G IV	II/2	L. 34.5 F 454.1	R: 33 cm	Ware: pink-buff core, pale buff surface. Temper: common chaff, fine lime.
9	CB 1972	G I	II/1	L. 11.1 E. 74.2	R: 29 cm	Ware: buff. Temper: common chaff, sparse lime.
10	CB 3407	G II	II/2	L. 54.10 F 210.2	R: 31 cm	Ware: yellow-green. Temper: common medium chaff.
11	CB 3953	G IV	II/2	L. 73.1 F 456.1	R: 28 cm	Ware: green core, buff surface. Temper: common medium chaff. Black paint slashes on rim.
12	CB 3798	G II	II/2	L. 54.10 F 210.5	R: 33.5 cm	Ware: pink core, yellow-green surface. Temper: common medium chaff and lime.
13	CB 2604	G II	II/2	L. 54.5 E 108.3	R: c 38 cm	Ware: pale buff. Temper: common fine-medium lime, medium chaff.
14	CB 2374	G I	II/2	L. 11.2 E 80.1	R: 33 cm	Ware: pink-grey core, buff surface. Temper: chaff and lime.
15	CB 3893	G II	II/2	L. 54.10 F 210.6	R: 39.5 cm	Ware: black core, buff surface. Temper: common medium chaff and fine lime.

WIDE-MOUTH JARS, A, LARGE

PLATE 58

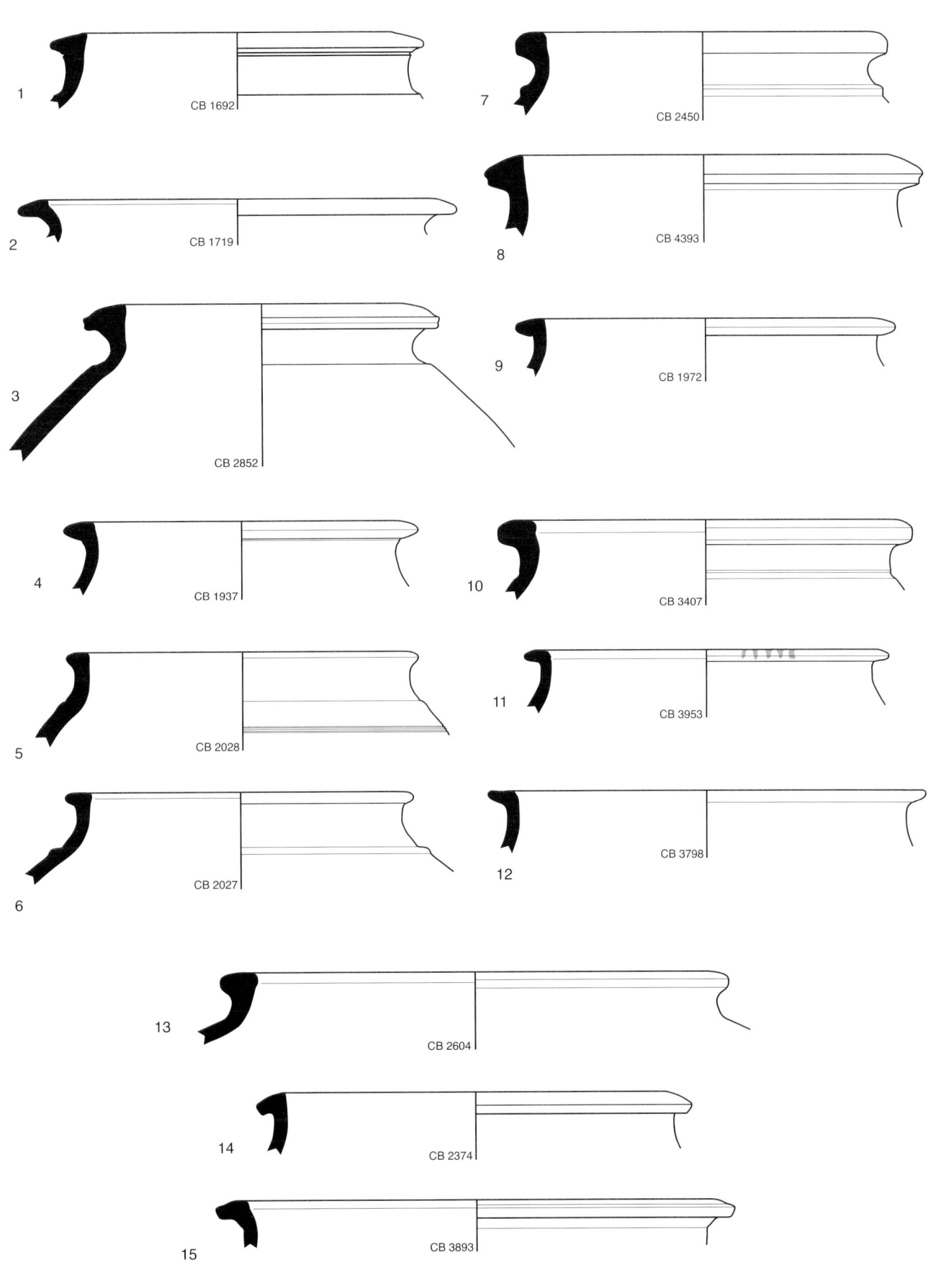

1:4 ▬▬▬▬ 10 cm

Plate 59: *Wide-mouth Jars, B Sub-type, Medium*

	CB number	Area	Phase	Locus and Lot number	Dimensions	Ware, comments
1	CB 351:2	A I	II	L. 19.1 D 66	R: 23 cm	Ware: green. Temper: common chaff, lime.
2	CB 2390	A II	IA	L. 67.6 E 201.3	R: 25 cm	Ware: orange-buff core, pale buff surface. Temper: common fine lime. Orange-red paint slashes across rim, band, hatched triangles.
3	CB 2988	A II	II	L. 81.2 F 35.2	R: 21 cm	Ware: pink core, buff surface. Temper: common medium chaff, sparse fine lime.
4	CB 1914	A II	II	L. 52.2 E 6.4	R: 26 cm	Ware: pale buff. Temper: common chaff, sparse lime. Black paint bands and cross-hatched triangles.
5	CB 3058	A II	II	L. 81.2 F 35.4	R: 28 cm	Ware: greenish-buff. Temper: common medium-large chaff, sparse lime.
6	CB 3198	A II	II	L. 81.2 F 35.6	R: 28 cm	Ware: brown core, grey-buff surface. Temper: common chaff, sparse dark grit.
7	CB 1724	A I	II	L. 16.1 D 376	R: 27 cm	Ware: grey core, reddish surface. Temper: occasional chaff, medium lime.
8	CB 4366:4	G II	II/2	L. 65.4 E 332.2	R: 18 cm	Ware: grey core, reddish surface. Temper: common fine-medium chaff, sparse fine lime.
9	CB 1809	G I	II/1A	L. 3.1 E 63.2	R: 19 cm	Ware: grey core, buff surface. Temper: abundant large chaff, sparse lime.
10	CB 3186	G IV	II/1	L. 34.4 F 70.1	R: 13 cm	Ware: red core, buff surface. Temper: common medium-coarse chaff, common fine lime.
11	CB 3133	G IV	II/1	L. 34.2 F 65.1	R: 20 cm	Ware: buff. Temper: common medium chaff and fine lime. Red paint band.
12	CB 4253	G II	III	L. 37.5 F 226.4	R: 20.5 cm	Ware: buff. Temper: common medium chaff.
13	CB 2847	G II	III	L. 27.2 F 205.1	R: 19 cm	Ware: pink core, greenish surface. Temper: common chaff, sparse lime. Fugitive brown paint band.
14	CB 4225	G IV	III	L. 76.2 F 466.2	R: 20 cm	Ware: grey core, buff surface. Temper: common medium chaff. Red paint band over rim.
15	CB 3977	G IV	I	L. 24.1 F 52.3	R: 27 cm	Ware: orange core, buff-green surface. Temper: common large chaff. Three horizontal grooves on shoulder.
16	CB 1967	G II	II/1	L. 56.1 E 98.1	R: 27 cm	Ware: buff core, pale buff surface. Temper: abundant chaff, mica inclusions. Horizontal and wavy grooves on shoulder.
17	CB 358:1	A I	II	L. 19.1 D 69	R: 29 cm	Ware: grey core, buff surface. Temper: common chaff, lime.
18	CB 3939	G IV	I	L. 33.1 F 58.5	R: 28 cm	
19	CB 1815	G II	II/2	L. 51.2 E 91.4	R: 27 cm	Ware: buff-orange core, buff surface. Temper: abundant chaff, sparse lime. Two sets of horizontal grooves and ridges on shoulder.

WIDE MOUTH JARS, B, MEDIUM

PLATE 59

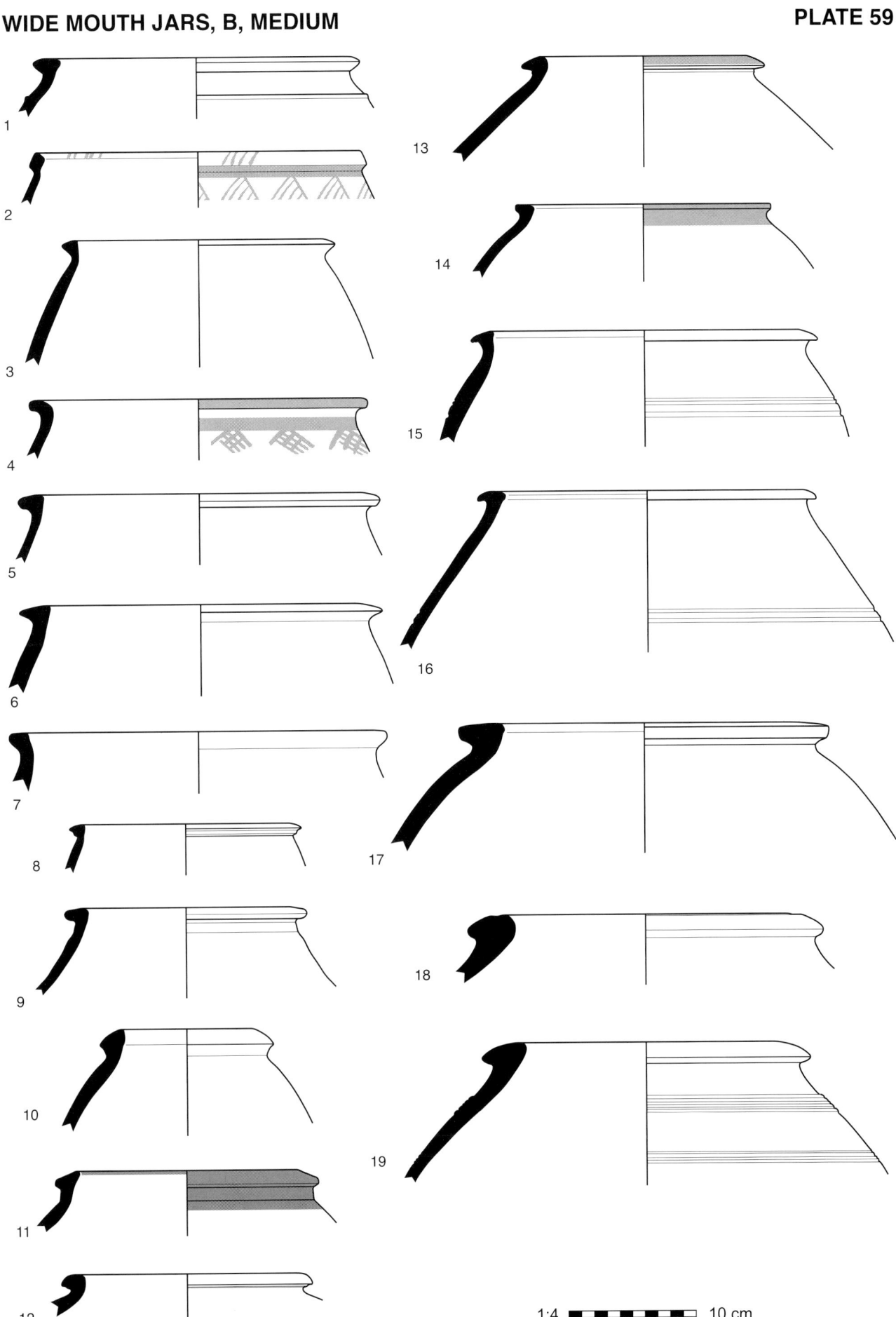

Plate 60: *Wide-mouth Jars, B Sub-type, Medium and Large*

	CB number	Area	Phase	Locus and Lot number	Dimensions	Ware, comments
1	CB 1721	A I	II	L. 16.1 D 376	R: 22.5 cm	Ware: buff. Temper: occasional chaff, lime.
2	CB 2814	A II	II	L. 75.1 F 27.1	R: 19 cm	Ware: light grey core, buff surface. Temper: common chaff, sparse lime.
3	CB 374:6	A I	II	L. 19.1 D 76	R: 19.5 cm	Ware: buff. Temper: common chaff, lime. Red paint bands.
4	CB 4366:2	G II	II/2	L. 65.4 E 332.2	R: 22.5 cm	Ware: grey core, buff surface. Temper: common fine-medium chaff, fine lime.
5	CB 3185	G IV	II/1	L. 34.4 F 70.1	R: 21 cm	Ware: brown core, red surface. Temper: common medium chaff. Red paint bands and triangles.
6	CB 3782	G IV	II/2	L. 41.2 F 72.1	R: 20 cm	Ware: grey core, orange surface. Temper: sparse medium chaff. Red paint hatched triangles and horizontal bands.
7	CB 1865	G II	II/2	L. 51.3 E 92.2	R: 18 cm	Ware: buff core, pale buff surface. Temper: abundant chaff. Three red paint slashes across rim, hatched triangles on shoulder.
8	CB 3790	G IV	II/1	L. 34.4 F 70.3	R: 24 cm	Ware: grey core, orange surface. Temper: sparse medium chaff, common fine lime. Red paint band.
9	CB 4224	G IV	III	L. 76.2 F 466.2	R: 22 cm	Ware: buff. Temper: common medium chaff. Brown paint band on neck and over rim.
10	CB 4162	G IV	III	L. 76.1 F 466.1	R: 26 cm	Ware: orange core, buff surface. Temper: common large chaff. Brown paint bands on rim and neck.
11	CB 57:2	A I	I	L. 6.1 D 23	R: 31 cm	Ware: green. Temper: common chaff, sparse lime.
12	CB 331:1	A I	II	L. 13.1 D 57	R: 35 cm	Ware: buff core, green surface. Temper: common chaff, lime.
13	CB 1783	A II	S	L. 50.1 E 1.1	R: 38 cm	Ware: orange core, pale buff surface. Temper: common chaff, sparse lime.
14	CB 958:2	A I	II	L. 16.3 D 386	R: 33 cm	Ware: reddish. Temper: common chaff, lime.

WIDE MOUTH JARS, B, MEDIUM

PLATE 60

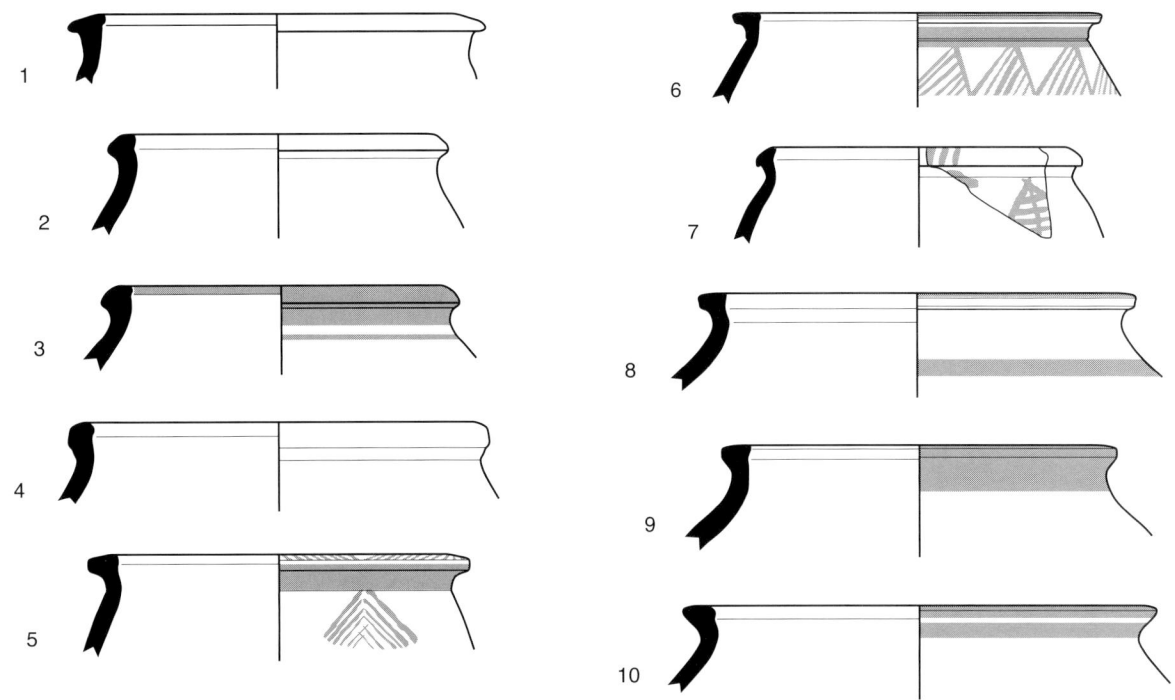

WIDE MOUTH JARS, B, LARGE

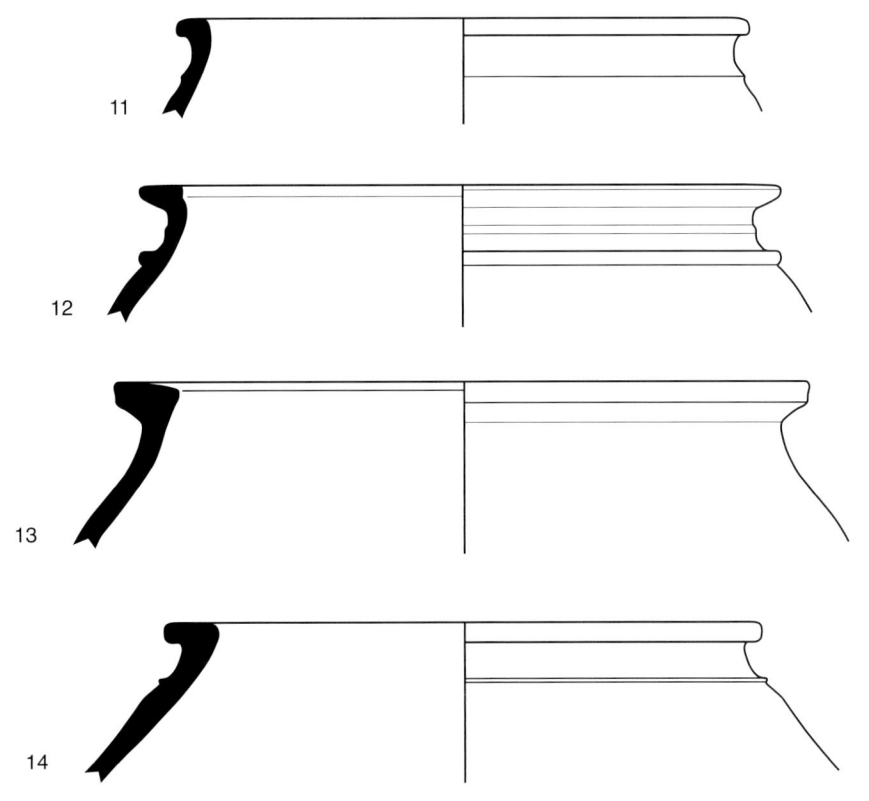

1:4 10 cm

Plate 61: *Wide-mouth Jars, B Sub-type, Large*

1	CB 791:2	A I	IA	L. 32.1 D 364	R: 37 cm	Ware: grey core, reddish surface. Temper: common chaff, lime. Horizontal grooves on shoulder.
2	CB 1931	G I	II/1	L. 11.1 E 74.1	R: 34 cm	Ware: buff. Temper: sparse chaff.
3	CB 2381	G I	II/1	L. 12.1 E 81.2	R: 35 cm	Ware: green. Temper: common medium chaff.
4	CB 1906	G II	II/2	L. 51.2 E 91.3	R: 35 cm	Ware: buff core, pale buff surface. Temper: common chaff. Fugitive black paint on rim.
5	CB 2907	G II	II/2	L. 54.9 F 206.1	R: 39.5 cm	Ware: black core, orange-yellow surface. Temper: common medium-large chaff, rare fine-medium lime.
6	CB 2603	G II	II/2	L. 54.5 E 108.3	R: c 50 cm	Ware: greenish-buff. Temper: common medium chaff, sparse fine lime.
7	CB 3222	G IV	III	L. 40.3 F 69.2	R: 32 cm	Ware: black core, orange surface. Temper: common coarse chaff. Orange paint bands.
8	CB 1994	A II	II	L. 61.3 E 25.2	R: c 53 cm	Ware: grey core, orange-buff surface. Temper: common medium chaff, sparse large lime. Horizontal grooves on shoulder.
9	CB 2992	A II	II	L. 79.2 F 8.2	R: c 62 cm	Ware: pink core, buff surface. Temper: common fine-medium chaff, sparse fine lime. Four horizontal grooves on shoulder.

WIDE MOUTH JARS, B, LARGE

PLATE 61

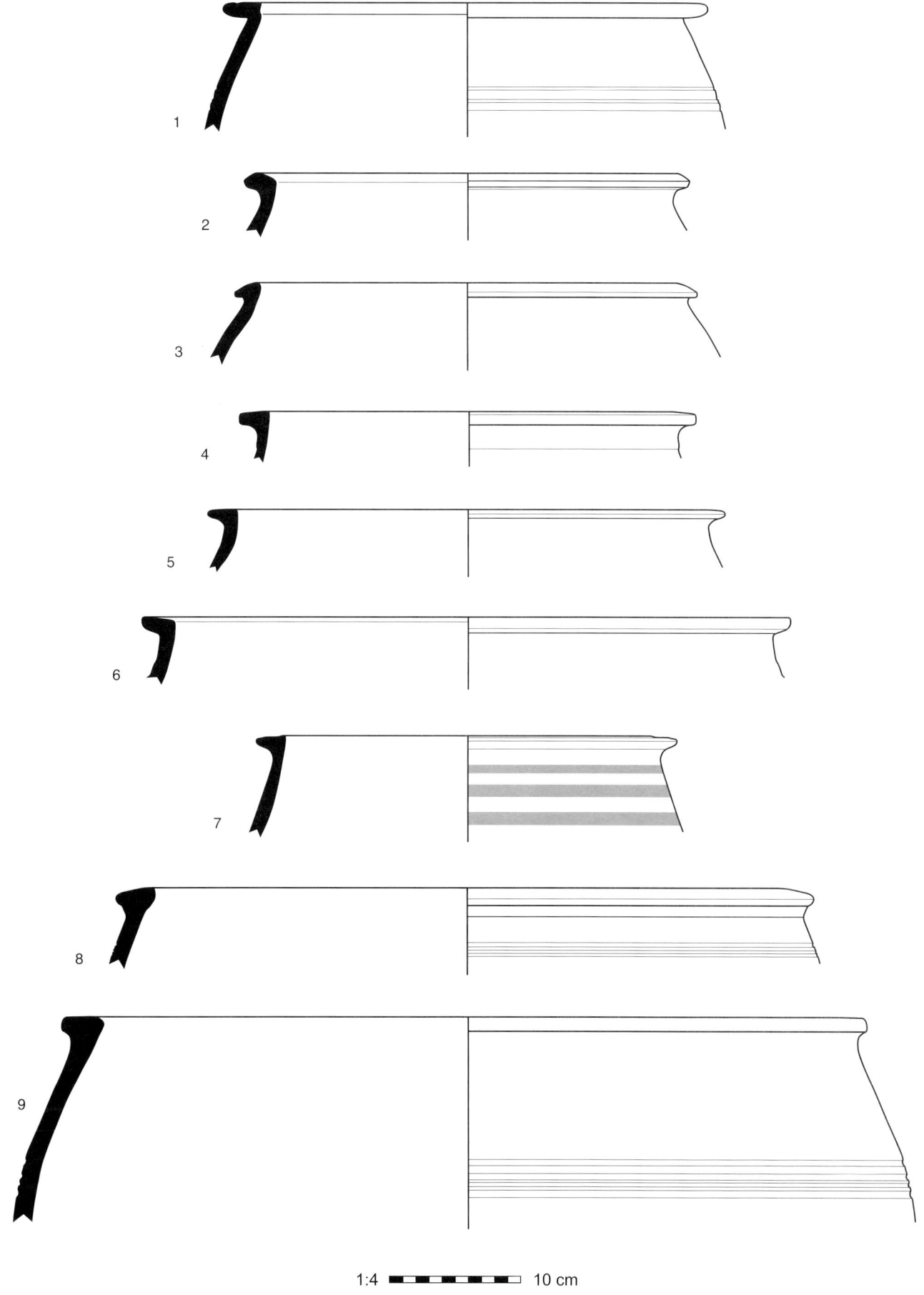

1:4 ▬▬▬▬ 10 cm

Plate 62: *Cooking Pots*

	CB number	Area	Phase	Locus and Lot number	Dimensions	Ware, comments
1	CB 1857	G II	II/2	L. 51.4 E 93.1	R: 16 cm	Ware: grey core, buff-brown-tan surface. Temper: abundant white and grey grit. Horizontal burnishing on exterior and inside rim, soot stain on rim.
2	CB 1817	G II	II/2	L. 51.2 E 91.4	R: 17 cm	Ware: black core, brown surface. Temper: abundant white grit. Horizontal burnishing on exterior.
3	CB 3017	G II	II/2	L. 54.9 F 206.2	R: 20 cm	Ware: orange core, grey-brown-buff surface. Temper: abundant medium grit. Horizontal burnishing interior and exterior.
4	CB 2386	G I	II/2	L. 4.6 E 84.4	R: 21 cm	Ware: grey core, black-brown surface. Temper: abundant sand and large grit. Horizontal burnishing on shoulder and over rim.
5	CB 3137	G IV	II/1	L. 34.2 F 65.1	R: 21.5 cm	Ware: black core, brown-orange surface. Temper: abundant angular grit. Burnished exterior.
6	CB 3031	G II	III	L. 37.1 F 208.2	R: 18 cm	Ware: orange-brown core, brown surface. Temper: common medium-large grit. Horizontal burnishing interior and exterior.
7	CB 3885	G II	III	L. 69.1 F 219.1	R: 19.5 cm	Ware: grey core, brown surface. Temper: abundant sand and grit. Burnished exterior.
8	CB 3966	G II	III	L. 37.3 F 213.7	R: 20 cm	Ware: black core, brown surface. Temper: abundant sand and grit. Horizontal burnishing exterior.
9	CB 4211	G II	III	01-24 F 217.2	R: 20 cm	Ware: grey core, brown surface. Temper: abundant sand and grit. Horizontal burnishing.
10	CB 2966	G IV	I	L. 33.1 F 58.3	R: 28.5 cm	Ware: black core, brown-black surface. Temper: abundant large grit. Horizontal burnishing exterior.
11	CB 2965	G IV	I	L. 33.1 F 58.3	R: 29 cm	Ware: brown core, red surface. Temper: abundant large grit. Horizontal burnishing exterior.
12	CB 2448	G I	II/1	L. 9.5 E 90.1	R: 24.5 cm	Ware: brown core, pale orange surface. Temper: abundant white angular grit. Horizontal burnishing exterior.
13	CB 4265	G II	III	L. 37.5 F 226.3	R: 25 cm	Ware: brown. Temper: abundant sand and grit. Burnished exterior.
14	CB 3214	G II	III	L. 37.3 F 213.2	R: 28 cm	Ware: black core, buff-brown surface. Temper: abundant grit.
15	CB 3884	G II	III	L. 69.1 F 219.1	R: 23 cm	Ware: brown core, dark brown surface. Temper: abundant sand and grit temper. Burnished exterior.
16	CB 4024	G II	IV	L. 75.1 F 224.1	R: 26 cm	Ware: grey core, brown surface. Temper: abundant medium sand and grit. Horizontal burnishing on exterior.

COOKING POTS

PLATE 62

HOLEMOUTH WITH THICKENED RIM

SMALL

MEDIUM

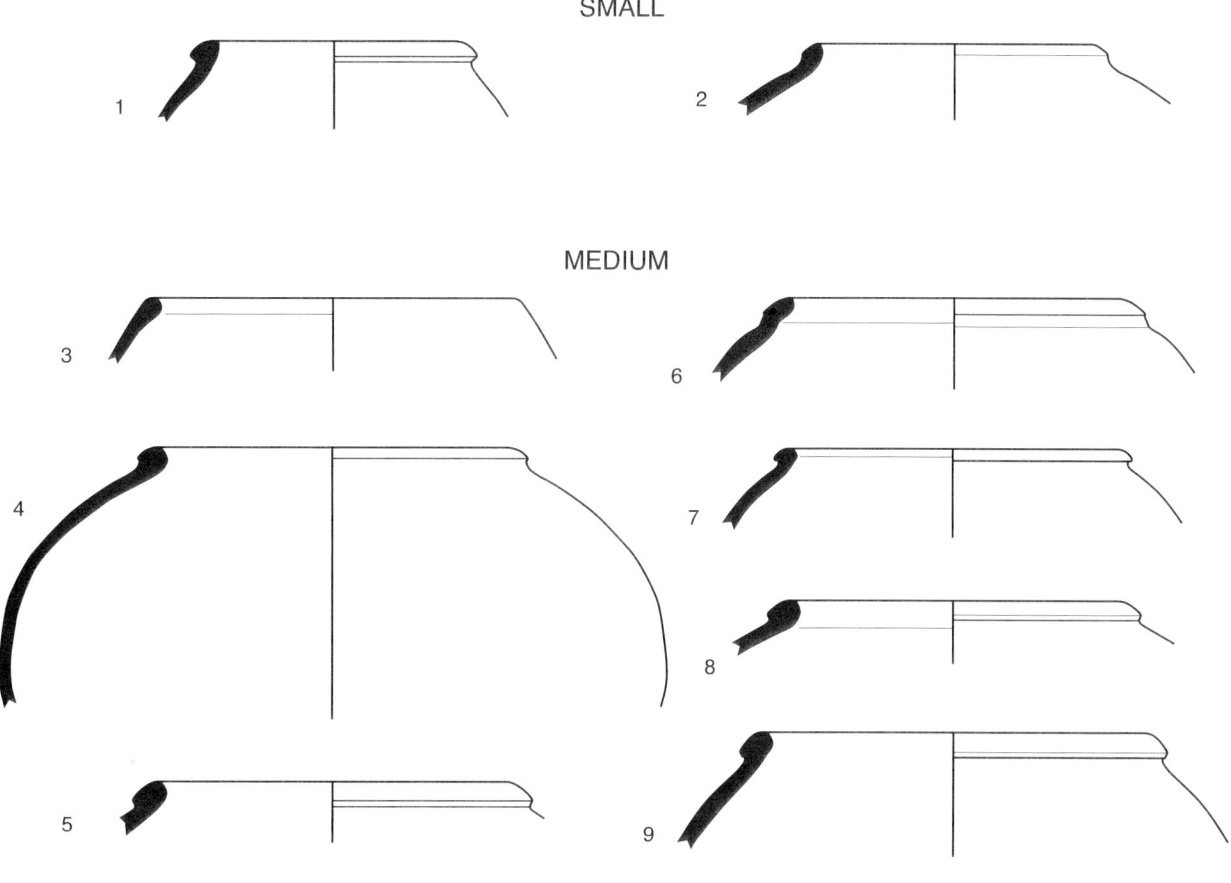

LARGE

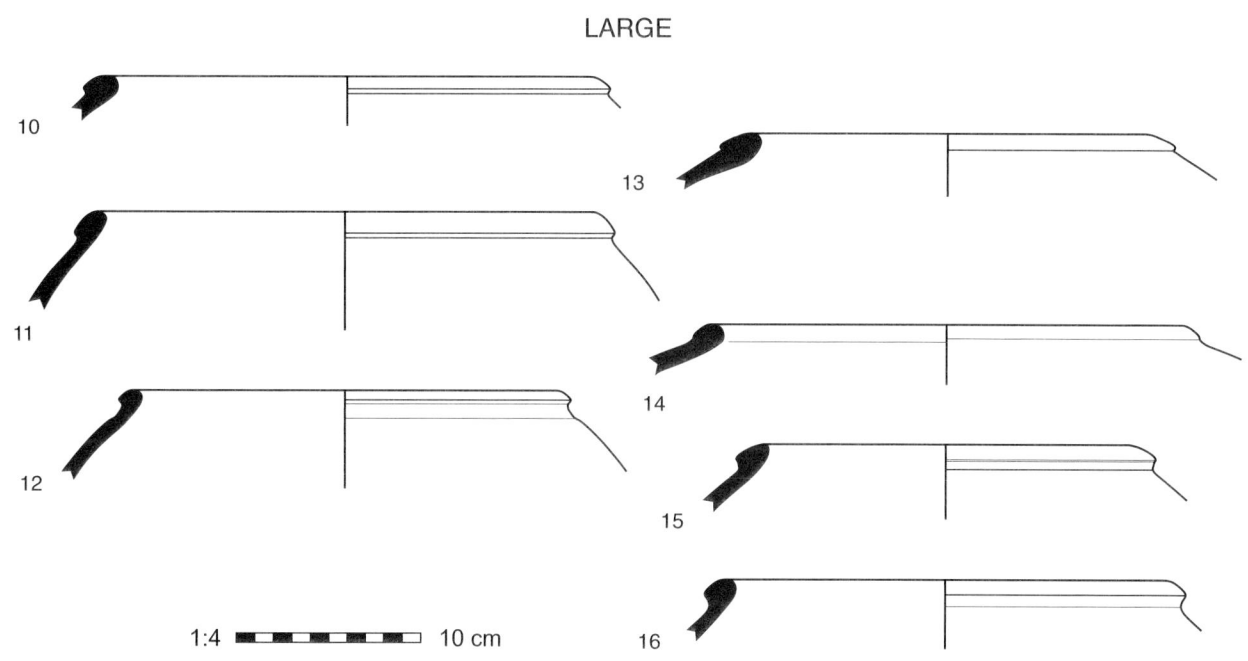

1:4 10 cm

Plate 63: *Cooking Pots*

	CB number	Area	Phase	Locus and Lot number	Dimensions	Ware, comments
1	CB 2588	A II	II	L. 59.1 E 14.3	R: 11 cm	Ware: pale brown core, dark brown surface. Temper: abundant sand, grit.
2	CB 3125	G IV	II/1A	L. 31.2 F 57.3	R: 14.5 cm	Ware: black core, orange-brown surface. Temper: abundant black and grey grit, sand. Traces of burnishing on exterior.
3	CB 1975	G I	II/1	L. 10.1 E 73.1	R: 17 cm	Ware: grey core, pale brown surface. Temper: abundant sand and grit. Horizontal burnishing on exterior.
4	CB 374:5	A I	II	L. 19.1 D 76	R: 20 cm	Ware: brown. Temper: black grit, lime. Burnishing on exterior.
5	CB 347:2	A I	I	L. 20.1 D 65	R: 20 cm	Grey core, dark red-brown surface. Temper: common grit, sand.
6	CB 1903	A II	II	L. 59.1 E 14.1	R: 20 cm	Ware: black-brown core, brown surface. Temper: abundant grey and white grit. Horizontal burnishing on exterior, soot stain at rim.
7	CB 2519	A I	II	L. 46.1 E 223.1	R: 20 cm	Ware: pale brown core, orange-brown surface. Temper: abundant sand, grit.
8	CB 1758	A I	II	L. 16.2 D 361	R: 18 cm	Ware: buff core, buff-orange surface. Temper: occasional chaff.
9	CB 2030	G II	II/1	L. 55.1 E 97.1	R: 19 cm	Ware: brown core, orange-brown surface. Temper: abundant grey grit. Horizontal burnishing on exterior.
10	CB 3029	G II	III	L. 37.1 F 208.2	R: 20 cm	Ware: brown-orange core, brown surface. Temper: common medium-large grit. Horizontal burnishing interior and exterior.
11	CB 38:1	A I	I	L. 5.1 D 16	R: 21.5 cm	Ware: grey core, buff surface. Temper: common chaff, lime.
12	CB 55:5	A I	S	L. 1.2 D 22	R: 24 cm	Black core, red-brown surface. Temper: common grit, lime. Burnishing on exterior.
13	CB 1898	A II	II	L. 55.1 E 12.1	R: 21.5 cm	Ware: dark brown-black core, dark grey surface. Ware: abundant sand, grit. Horizontal burnishing on exterior.
14	CB 1754	A I	II	L. 16.2 D 361	R: 29.5 cm	Ware: dark grey core, brown-grey surface. Temper: common sand, grit.
15	CB 2104	A I	II	L. 41.1 E 60.1	R: 23 cm	Ware: grey core, brown surface. Temper: abundant sand and grit. Horizontal burnishing on exterior.
16	CB 2972	G II	III	L. 27.1 F 202.4	R: 21.5 cm	Ware: black core, orange-buff surface. Temper: abundant large grit. Horizontal burnishing interior and exterior.
17	CB 3231	G IV	S	L. 43.1 F 66.2	R: 31 cm	Ware: black core, dark buff surface. Temper: abundant medium grit. Horizontal burnishing interior and exterior.
18	CB 3193	G IV	III	L. 40.3 F 69.3	R: 24 cm	Ware: dark brown core, buff surface. Temper: abundant large grit. Horizontal burnishing exterior.

COOKING POTS

PLATE 63

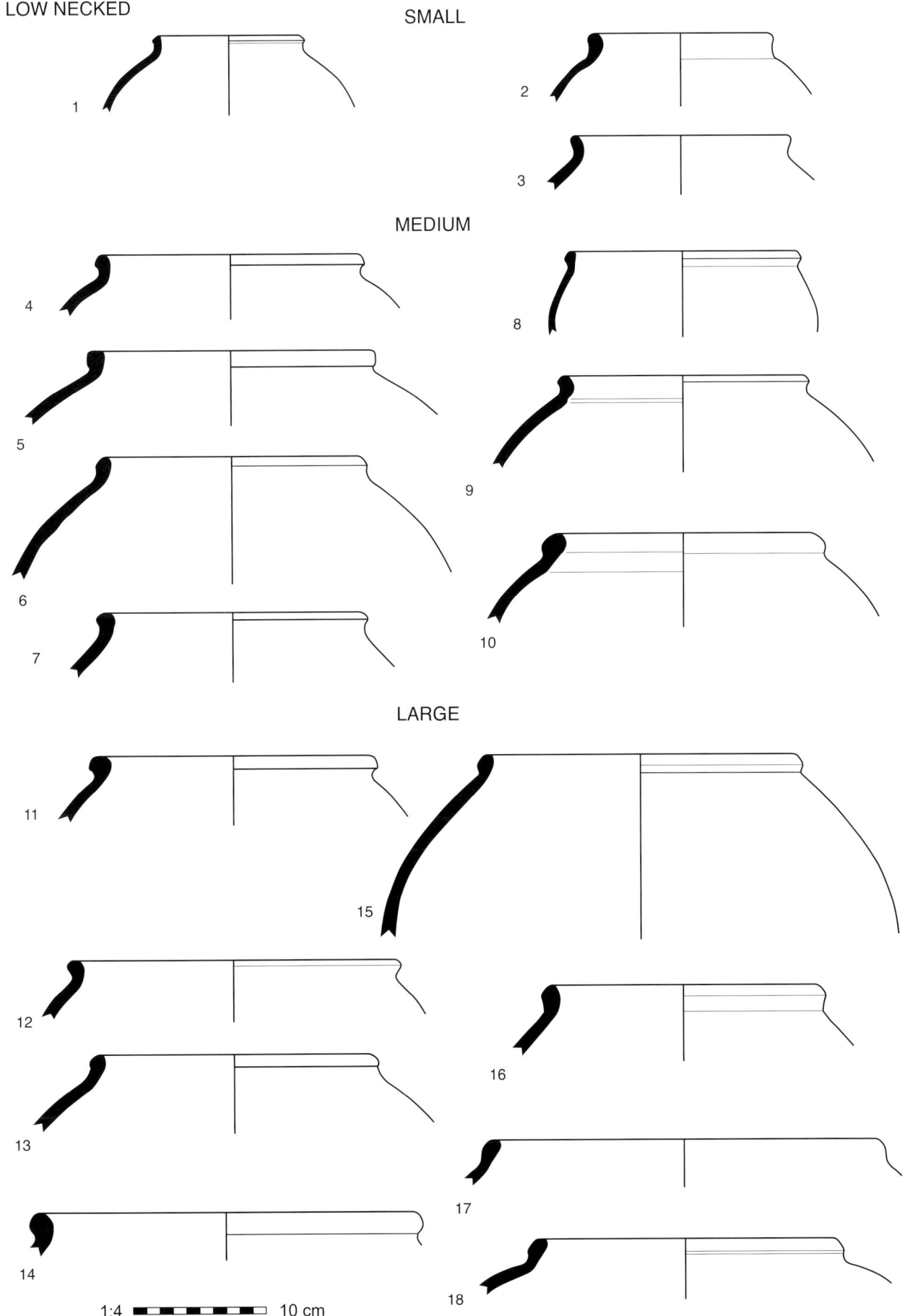

Plate 64: *Cooking Pots and Bottles*

1	CB 2126	G II	II/2	L. 51.5 E 93.3	R: 16 cm	Ware: greenish-buff. Ware: common chaff, sparse lime.
2	CB 3258	G II	II/2	L. 54.10 F 210.1	R: 20 cm	Ware: black core, brown surface. Temper: abundant medium angular grit. Burnished exterior.
3	CB 2172	G I	II/2	L. 4.6 E 84.1	R: 22 cm	Ware: red core, buff surface. Temper: common medium grit, sparse fine chaff.
4	CB 3804	G II	II/2	L. 54.10 F 210.5	R: 20.5 cm	Ware: grey core, brown surface. Temper: abundant medium lime and grit. Burnished surface.
5	CB 2608	G I	II/1	L. 9.4 E 77.3	R: 22 cm	Ware: grey core, pale brown surface. Temper: abundant sand and grit.
6	CB 2520	A I	II	L. 46.1 E 223.1	R: 26 cm	Ware: black core, orange-brown surface. Temper: common sand, grit.
7	CB 2977	G IV	II/1	T. 33 F 63.1	R: 6.8 cm M: 11 cm B: 4 cm H: 14 cm	Ware: pink core, orange-buff surface. Temper: sparse medium chaff, common fine lime. Horizontal red paint bands and occasional splashes on rim, neck and shoulder.
8	CB 3092	G IV	II/2	T. 39 F 71.1	R: 3.9 cm M: 7 cm B: 2.0 cm H: 9.3 cm	Ware: orange-buff. Temper: common medium chaff, occasional fine lime. Quite off-kilter and incapable of standing up on base.
9	CB 2497	A II	II	L. 62.3 E 279.2	R: 4.1 cm M: 7.5 cm H: 7.7 cm	Ware: buff core and surface. Temper: sparse fine lime.
10	CB 3114	A	I	T. 41 F 21.2	M: 12.5 cm B: 4.5 cm H: 11.6 cm	Ware: reddish yellow (7.5 YR 6/6). Temper: sparse fine sand, lime, mica inclusions. Ancient break in rim.
11	CB 19:1	A I	IA	L. 4.1 D 7	R: 6.4 cm	Ware: buff. Temper: sparse chaff, lime.
12	CB 2175	A I	III	L. 44.1 E 51.1	R: 11 cm	Ware: orange-buff core, pale buff surface. Temper: common sand. Red-brown paint slashes across rim.
13	CB 3295	G IV	II/1	L. 34.1 F 64.1	R: 2.5 cm	Ware: buff. Temper: common fine lime. Dark red paint bands.
14	CB 2159	G I	II/2	L. 4.6 E 66.5	R: 10 cm	Ware: dark grey core and surface. Temper: common fine lime. Horizontally-burnished rim and neck.
15	CB 2936	G IV	II/2	L. 32.6 F 60.3	R: 4 cm	Ware: orange core, buff surface. Temper: rare fine lime. Red paint bands.
16	CB 1929	G I	II/1	L. 11.1 E 74.1	R: 8 cm	Ware: buff core, pale buff surface. Temper: fine chaff. Red-brown paint bands.

COOKING POTS

PLATE 64

ANGULAR RIM

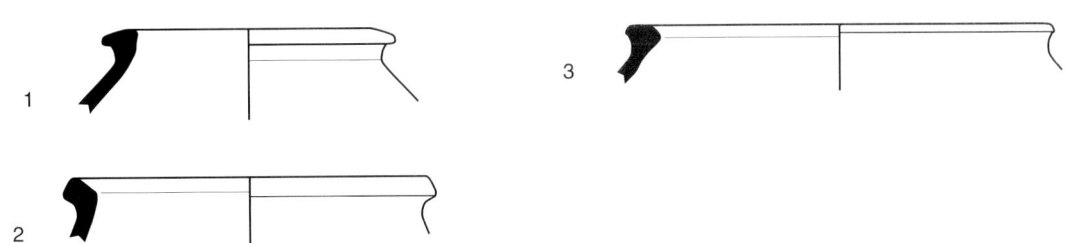

MEDIUM NECKED

MEDIUM   LARGE

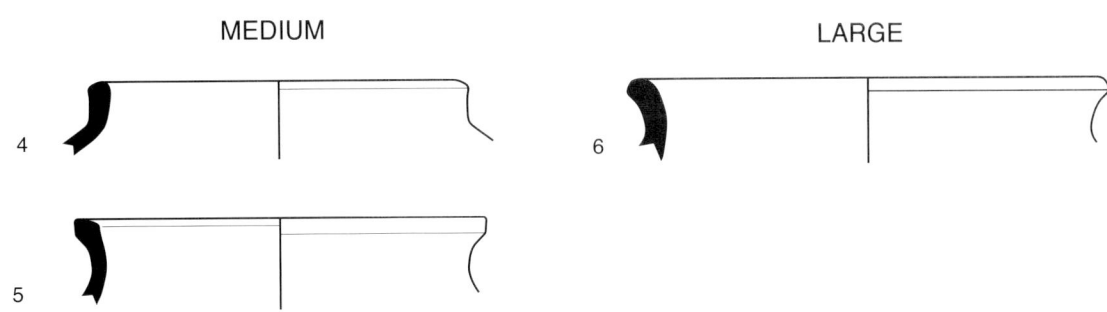

BOTTLES

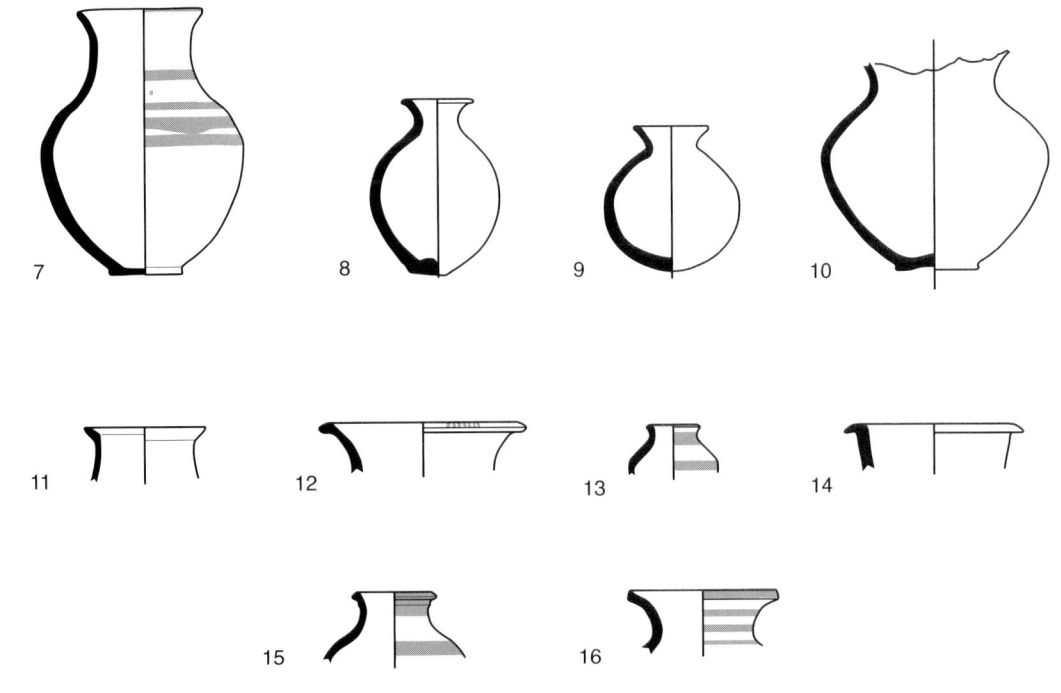

1:4   10 cm

Plate 65: *Miscellaneous*

	CB number	Area	Phase	Locus and Lot number	Dimensions	Ware, comments
1	CB 719:3	A I	I	L. 17.2 D 340	R: 5 cm B: 5 cm	Ware: brown. Temper: none.
2	CB 2129	G II	II/1A	L. 59.1 E 101.2	R: 5.5 cm B: 2.2 cm H: 2.3 cm	Ware: buff. Temper: fine chaff.
3	CB 2594	G II	II/2	L. 65.1 E 118.1	R: 8 cm B: c 4 cm H: 3.5 cm	Ware: greenish-buff. Temper: common fine chaff, lime.
4	CB 2190	G II	II/2	L. 51.3 E 92.4	R: 7 cm	Ware: orange-buff core, pale buff surface. Temper: abundant medium lime.
5	CB 3785	G IV	II/1	L. 34.4 F 70.3	R: 6.5 cm	Ware: dark buff. Temper: common medium chaff, occasional fine lime.
6	CB 4002	G II	II/2	L. 54.10 F 210.1	R: 3.3 cm	Ware: buff core, pale buff surface. Temper: common fine lime, occasional medium chaff. Brown paint bands.
7	CB 1908	G I	II/1	L. 4.3 E 65.1	R: 4 cm	Ware: buff. Temper: none. Brown-black paint bands.
8	CB 3180	G IV	III	L. 40.2 F 68.2	R: 5 cm	Ware: buff core, pale buff surface. Sparse fine lime and sand.
9	CB 2079	G I	II/1	T 13 E 82.1	R: 7.5-8.0 cm B: 2.5 cm H: 7.3 cm	Ware: buff core, pale buff surface. Temper: common fine sand, occasional large lime, chaff. Warped.
10	CB 4191	G IV	II/2	L. 34.5 F 454.2	R: 5 cm	Ware: grey core, buff-grey surface. Temper: sparse fine sand. Irregular holes.
11	CB 1921	G I	II/1	T.11 shaft E 67.1	R: 7 cm	Ware: buff core, red-buff surface. Temper: sparse chaff, fine lime. Hand-made.
12	CB 1885	G I	II/1	L. 2.1 E 61.5	R: 12 cm	Ware: orange. Temper: none.
13	CB 2055	A I	III	L. 34.3 E 55.1	M: 7.8 cm Stem dm 5 cm H: 4.2 cm	Ware: grey core, orange-brown surface. Temper: sparse large chaff, large grey grit. Use wear (polish) on upper surface.
14	CB 3233	G II	III	L. 37.3 F 213.1	R: 8 cm H: 9 cm	Ware: buff core, red-buff surface. Temper: common fine lime and sand. Red-brown paint bands and horizontal ribbing/grooving.
15	CB 3971B	G II	III	L. 37.3 F 213.4	R: 8.5 cm	Ware: orange. Temper: common fine sand. Red paint and horizontal grooves.
16	CB 2985	A II	II	L. 81.2 F 35.2	M: 10 cm	Ware: grey. Temper: common fine chaff, occasional lime. Burnished upper exterior, punctate decoration below spout.

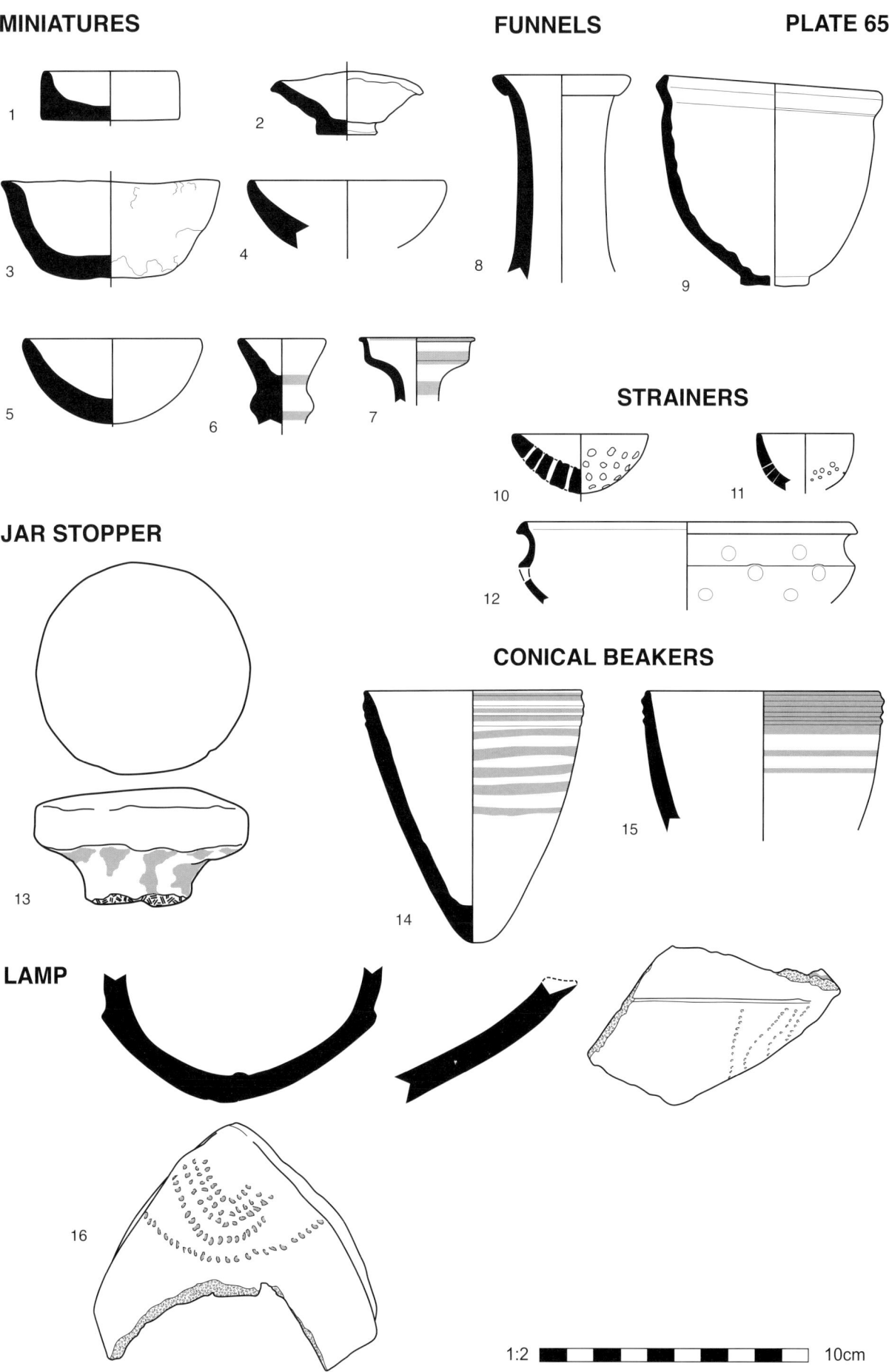

Plate 66: *Possible Late 3rd Millennium BC Forms and Tray*

	CB number	Area	Phase	Locus and Lot number	Dimensions	Ware, comments
1	CB 3045	A II	II	L. 81.2 F 35.3	R: 13.5 cm	Grooved rim. Ware: buff. Temper: common medium chaff, fine lime.
2	CB 1899	A II	II	L. 55.1 E 12.1	R: 16.5 cm	Grooved band rim. Ware: orange core, pale orange surface. Temper: occasional fine chaff, large lime, sand.
3	CB 1984	A II	II	L. 64.1 T. 9 E 24.3	R: 15 cm	Grooved band rim. Ware: orange-buff core, pale buff surface. Temper: common chaff, lime.
4	CB 2941	G IV	II/1	L. 32.2 F 59.2	R: 16 cm	Grooved squared rim. Ware: yellow-green. Temper: common fine-medium chaff, rare fine lime.
5	CB 2124	G II	II/2	L. 51.5 E 93.3	R: 14 cm	Grooved band rim. Ware: orange-buff. Temper: common chaff.
6	CB 1812	G I	II/1A	L. 3.1 E 63.2	R: 21 cm	Double-ridged rim. Ware: buff core, orange surface. Temper: abundant lime, sparse chaff.
7	CB 3215	G II	III	L. 37.3 F 213.2	R: 23.5 cm	Triangular rim and horizontal and wavy shallow grooves. Ware: buff core, buff-green surface. Temper: sand.
8	CB 3217	G II	III	L. 37.3 F 213.2	R: 21 cm	Angled neck, triangular rim. Ware: buff. Temper: common medium lime and sand.
9	CB 4194	G II	III	L. 77.1 F 227.1	R: 31 cm	Grooved band rim. Ware: green. Temper: common medium chaff.
10	CB 3206	G II	III	L. 36.1 F 207.4	R: 34.5 cm	Grooved band rim. Ware: pale buff. Temper: common sand.
11	CB 4262	G II	III	L. 37.5 F 226.3	R: 28 cm	Tray. Ware: buff core, orange surface. Temper: abundant white grit. Burnished interior. Narrow holes run partially through base.

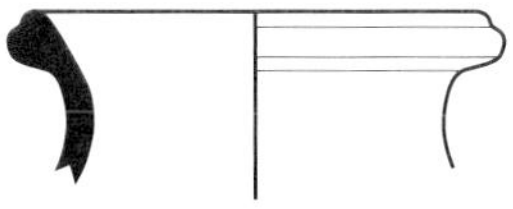

POSSIBLE LATE 3RD MILLENNIUM BC FORMS   PLATE 66

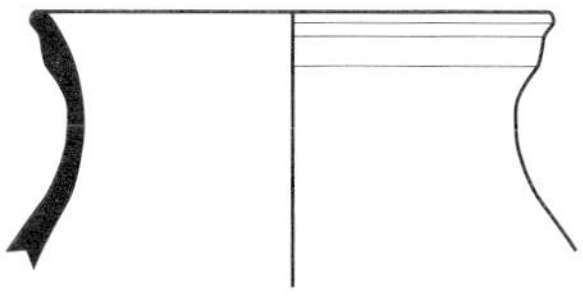

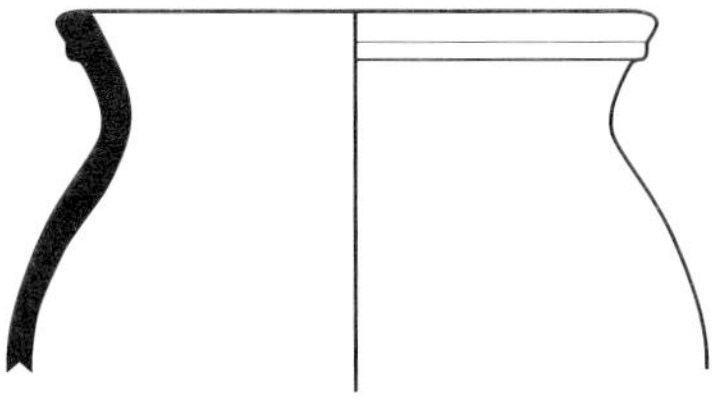

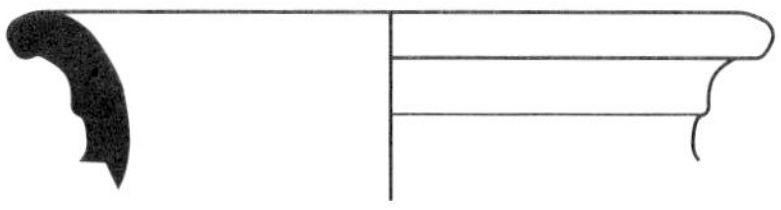

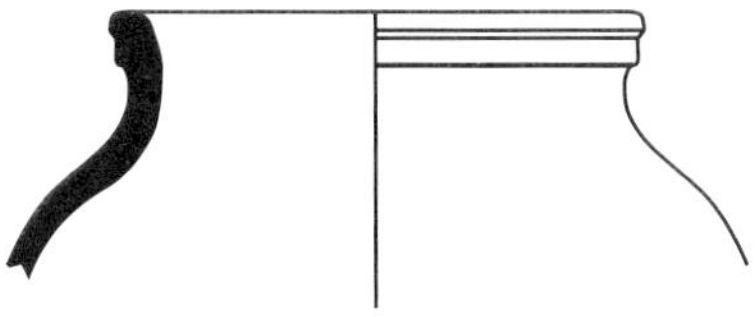

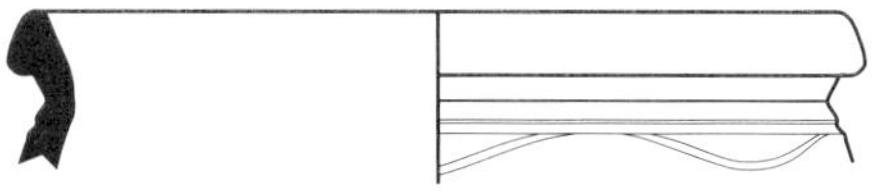

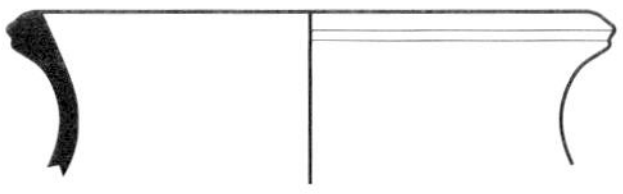

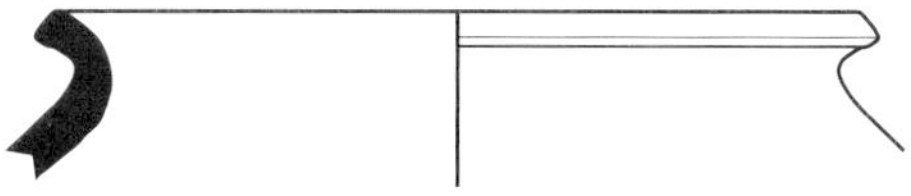

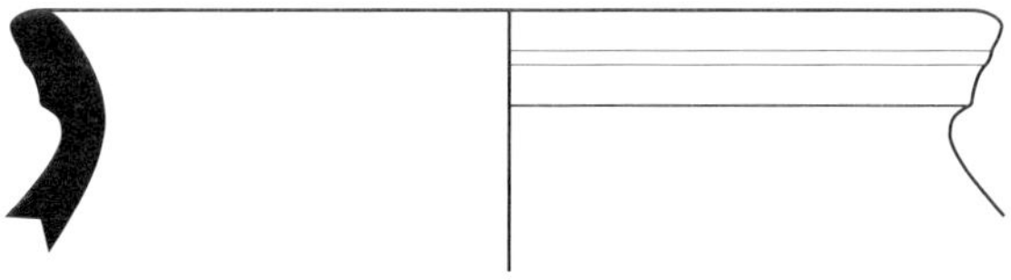

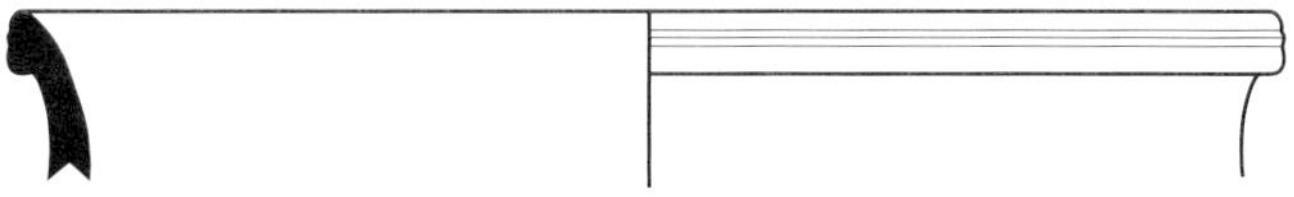

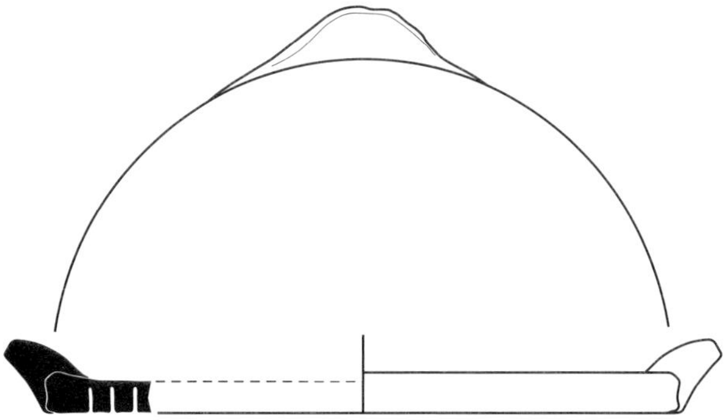

TRAY

1:4 ▬▬▬ 10 cm

Plate 67: *Bases*

	CB number	Area	Phse	Loc. & Lot No.	Dimensions	Ware, comments
1	CB 2963	G IV	II/1	L. 32.3 F 59.4	B: 8 cm	Ware: grey core, orange-buff surface. Temper: common medium chaff. Smoothed surface.
2	CB 2021	G II	II/1	L. 55.1 E 97.1	B: 5 cm	Ware: dark buff. Temper: sparse lime and chaff. Bitumen staining on interior.
3	CB 2838	G II	III	L. 27.1 F 202.1	B: 2.9 cm	Ware: green. Temper: common fine lime.
4	CB 2813	A II	I	L. 74.1 F 3.1	B: 2.1 cm	Ware: buff. Temper: sparse chaff and lime.
5	CB 358:4	A I	II	L. 19.1 D 69	B: 3.9 cm	Ware: reddish core, buff surface. Temper: common chaff, lime.
6	CB 2223	G II	II/2	L. 51.5 E 93.4	B: 4 cm	Ware: orange-buff core, pale buff surface. Temper: sparse fine lime.
7	CB 3223	G IV	III	L. 40.3 F 69.2	B: 8 cm	Ware: grey. Temper: common medium grit. Horizontal burnishing exterior.
8	CB 753:1	A I	II	L. 29.1 D 351	B: 2.2 cm	Ware: buff. Temper: sparse lime, fine chaff. Red paint bands on exterior.
9	CB 2900	G II	III	L. 37.1 F 208.1	B: 4 cm	Ware: grey. Temper: common medium grit.
10	CB 1725	A I	I	L. 17.2 D 350	B: 2 cm	Ware: grey-buff core, orange-buff surface. Temper: sparse chaff, lime. Red paint drips on exterior.
11	CB 4020	G II	III	L. 69.1 F 219.2	B: 3.3 cm	Ware: yellow-green. Temper: common fine-medium lime.
12	CB 3200	A II	II	L. 81.2 F 35.6	B: 1.5 cm	Ware: buff. Temper: none.
13	CB 1980	A II	II	L. 55.1 E 12.4	B: 1.8 cm	Ware: pale greenish-buff. Temper: sparse fine lime.
14	CB 1851	G I	II/1A	L. 3.1 E 63.3	B: 2.4 cm	Ware: pale buff-green. Temper: occasional fine chaff.
15	CB 3294	G IV	II/1	L. 34.1 F 64.1	B: 4 cm	Ware: pale grey. Temper: none visible. Smoothed surface.
16	CB 1907	G II	II/2	L. 51.2 E 91.3	B: 2.2 cm	Ware: buff core, pale buff surface. Temper: none.
17	CB 2906	G II	II/2	L. 54.9 F 206.1	B: 2.4 cm	Ware: grey core, buff surface. Temper: rare medium chaff, common fine-medium lime.
18	CB 3796	G IV	II/1	L. 34.4 F 70.3	B: 3.1 cm	Ware: green. Temper: sparse fine chaff and fine lime. Red wash interior.
19	CB 4161	G IV	II/2	L. 73.2 F 457.2	B: 3.6 cm	Ware: dark grey. Temper: sparse fine sand and lime.
20	CB 4246	G II	III	L. 37.5 F 226.4	B: 3 cm	Ware: over-fired green. Temper: sparse lime and sand. Black paint band on exterior.
21	CB 3973	G II	III	L. 37.3 F 213.4	B: 3.2 cm	Ware: pale buff. Temper: common fine lime.
22	CB 1796	A I	II	L. 40.4 E 36.1	B: 11 cm	Ware: buff. Temper: chaff, lime.
23	CB 1913	G I	II/1	L. 2.1 E 61.6	B: 5 cm	Ware: buff. Temper: fine sand, lime.
24	CB 3897	G II	II/2	L. 54.10 F 210.6	B: 9.0 cm	Ware: orange. Temper: common fine-medium chaff and fine lime.
25	CB 1847	G I	II/1	L. 4.4 E 66.1	B: 8 cm	Ware: brown core, buff surface. Temper: abundant chaff, mica inclusions.
26	CB 2119	G II	II/1	L. 58.1 E 100.2	B: 13 cm	Ware: grey core, buff surface. Temper: common medium chaff, lime.
27	CB 1985	A II	II	T. 9 E 24.3	B: 7.8 cm	Ware: orange-buff core, buff surface. Temper: common fine chaff.
28	CB 3122	G IV	II/1	L. 34.3 F 67.1	B: 17 cm	Ware: green. Temper: common medium chaff.
29	CB 3889	G II	II/2	L. 54.10 F 210.6	B: 3.8 cm	Ware: grey. Temper: rare sand.
30	CB 3204	G III	II/2	L. 47.1 F 83.3	B: 2.3 cm	Ware: orange core, buff surface. Temper: sparse fine chaff.
31	CB 1:2	A I	S	L. 1.1 D 1	B: 4.7 cm	Ware: buff core, pale buff surface. Temper: none.
32	CB 4234	G II	III	L. 37.5 F 226.2	B: 12 cm	Ware: buff core, pale buff surface. Temper: common fine lime.

BASES **PLATE 67**

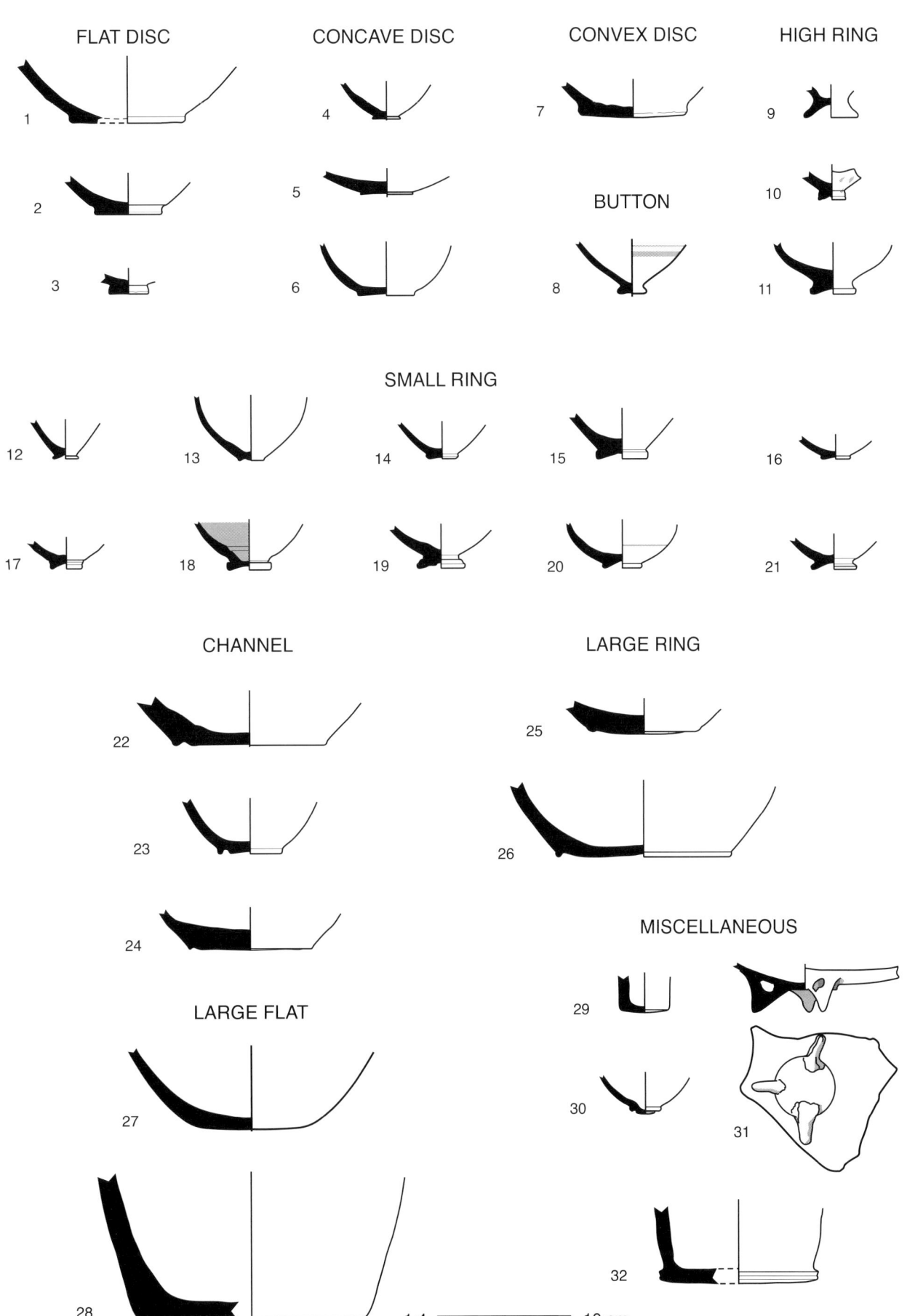

377

Plate 68: *Painted sherds*

	CB number	Area	Phase	Locus and Lot number	Dimensions	Ware, comments
1	CB 1795	A I	II	L. 40.4 E 36.1		Ware: pale buff. Temper: common chaff, occasional lime. Red-brown horizontal stripes with over-painted white circles.
2	CB 1926	A II	II	L. 55.1 E 12.1		Ware: pink core, buff surface. Temper: abundant chaff. Black painted schematic bird between horizontal stripes, cross-hatching above.
3	CB 1801	A II	S	L. 50.1 E 1.2	R: 25 cm	Ware: grey core, buff surface. Temper: common chaff, lime. Red painted upright bird and band on rim.
4	CB 2799	G IV	I	L. 23.1 F 51.1		Ware: grey-green. Temper: sparse large chaff, sparse large lime. Black paint bands, swags, hatching and row of birds.
5	CB 2899	G II	III	L. 37.1 F 208.1	N/A	Ware: orange core, buff surface. Temper: common medium lime. Reddish-orange paint and horizontal ridges and grooves.
6	CB 3018	G II	II/2	L. 54.10 F 210.2	N/A	Ware: grey core, buff surface. Temper: common medium chaff, rare medium lime. Red paint bird and possible animal above two horizontal stripes.
7	CB 3898	G II	II/2	L. 54.10 F 210.6	N/A	Ware: black core, buff surface. Temper: common medium chaff, rare medium lime. Red paint.

PAINTED SHERDS

PLATE 68

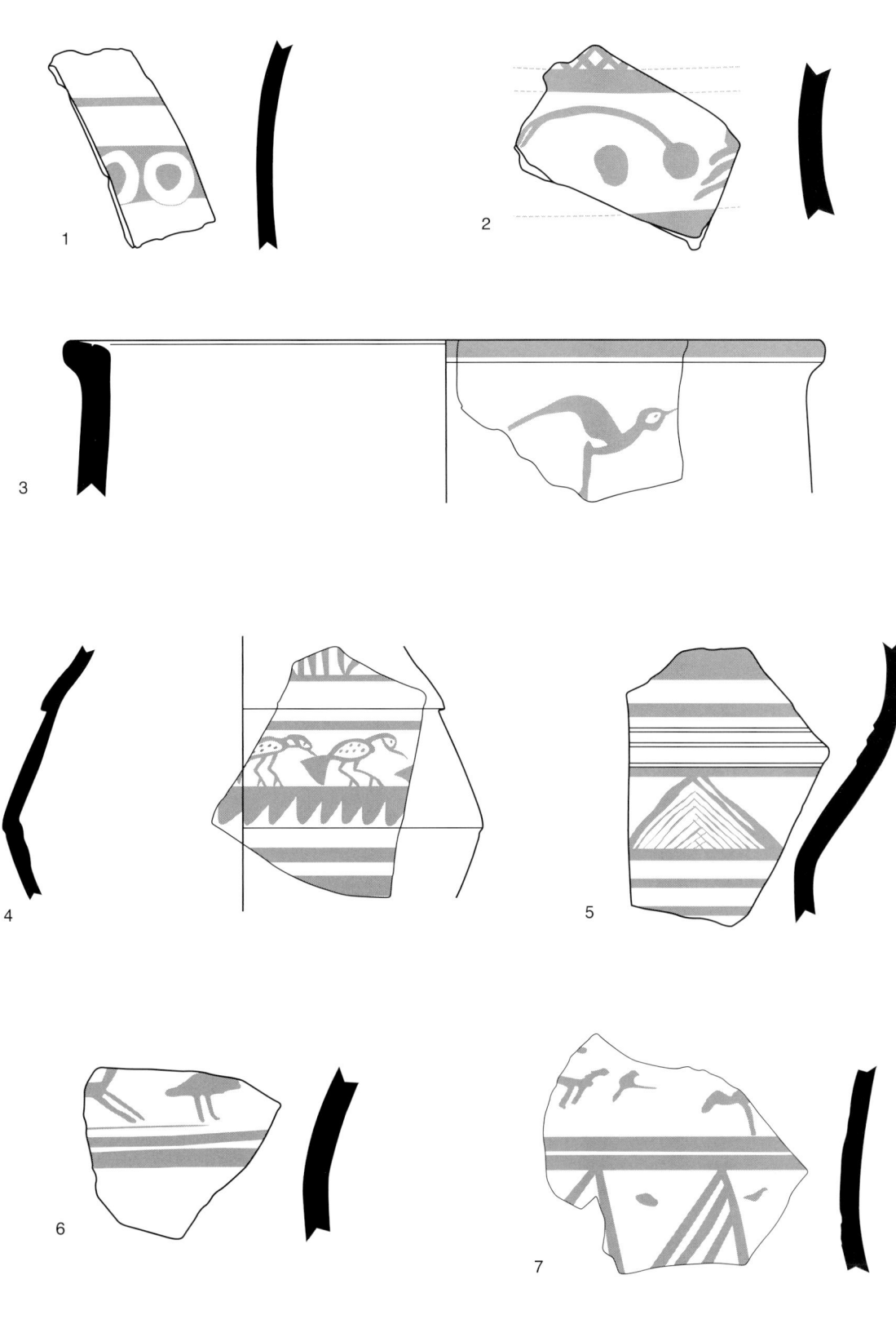

Plate 69: *Animal Figurines–Zebu and Equids*

	CB number	Area and Phase	Loc & Lot No.	Description, dimensions
1	CB 977	A, Phase IA	L. 32.1 D 395	Head and legs missing. Buff clay, fine-medium chaff and sparse grit temper. 7.2 cm long, 3.7 cm high, 2.8 cm wide.
2	CB 797	A, Phase IA	L. 32.1 D 364	Head and legs missing. Well-baked dark grey-brown un-tempered clay. 3.7 cm long, 2.2 cm high, 1.4 cm wide.
3	CB 373	A, Phase I	L. 20.1 D 73	Feet, ends of horns missing. Well-baked dark brown-black un-tempered clay, finely-made. 6.2 cm long, 4.1 cm high, 2.0 cm wide.
4	CB 3048	A, Phase I	L. 76.5 F 5.6	Torso and one leg only. Pale buff clay, light chaff temper. 6.8 cm long, 4.9 cm high, 2.6 cm wide.
5	CB 951	A, Phase II	L. 16.3 D 384	Head and legs missing, surface worn. Buff clay, light chaff temper. 4.6 cm long, 2.0 cm high, 1.9 cm wide.
6	CB 954	A, Phase II	L. 16.3 D 384	Front end and one leg only. Buff-green clay, light chaff temper, traces of red paint. 3.5 cm long, 6.1 cm high, 2.3 cm wide.
7	CB 2539	A, Phase II	L. 62.2 E 206.1	Torso only. Greenish clay, common fine chaff temper, sparse lime temper. 6.8 cm long, 3.8 cm high, 3.5 cm wide.
8	CB 2983	A, Phase II	L. 81.2 F 35.3	Hump only. Brown clay, no temper. 2.9 cm long, 2.2 cm high, 2.3 cm wide.
9	CB 2589	A, Phase II	L. 47.2 E 229.2	Head and legs missing. Pale buff clay, common fine lime temper. 7.8 cm long, 4.1 cm high, 3.1 cm wide.
10	CB 2789	A, Phase II	L. 62.3 E 279.1	Head and hump only, horns broken, eyes incised. Very dark grey clay, 2.5Y 3/1, no visible temper. 3.7 cm high, 3.8 cm long, 2.0 cm wide.
11	CB 2532	A, Phase III	L. 61.5 E 207.2	Head and legs missing. Pale brown clay, brown surface. 4.2 cm long, 4.2 cm high, 2.4 cm wide.
12	CB 1827	G, Phase II/1	L. 4.4 E 66.1	Torso only, species indeterminate but probable zebu since traces of hanging dewlap are preserved. Dark brown-black clay, fine sand temper. 6.0 cm long, 3.0 cm high, 3.2 cm wide.
13	CB 2112	G, Phase II/1	L. 9.2 E 77.1	Head and legs missing. Pale buff clay with burned patches, sparse fine chaff temper. 5.1 cm long, 3.3 cm high, 2.4 cm wide.
14	CB 2629	G, Phase II/1	L. 4.1 E 86.2	Head, legs and rear half missing, identifiable as zebu from dewlap and remaining part of hump. Dark grey core, brown surface, medium chaff temper. 6.0 cm long, 4.5 cm high, 3.5 cm wide.
15	CB 2865	G, Phase II/2	L. 54.9 F 206.1	Part of torso only, zebu (hump and dewlap). Reddish yellow clay (5YR 6/6) clay with medium chaff and lime temper, trace of red paint stripe along left side. 7.5 cm long, 4.0 cm high, 3.25 cm wide.
16	CB 2919	G, Phase II/2	L. 54.10 F 210.1	Torso only. Buff clay, fine chaff temper. 7.6 cm long, 6.0 cm high, 3.2 cm wide.
17	CB 308	A, Phase I	L. 2.2 D 45	Legs and tail missing. Well-baked dark brown (10YR 4/2) un-tempered clay, lightly-polished surface, incised details on mane. 5.9 cm long, 3.0 cm high, 1.8 cm wide.
18	CB 2206	A, Phase I	00-20 E 195.1	Head and three legs missing, probable equid. Dark brown-grey clay, sparse fine sand temper. 4.3 cm long, 3.1 cm high, 2.2 cm wide.
19	CB 775	A, Phase II	L. 29.1 D 357	Head, legs and tail missing. Dark brown (7.5YR 7/4) clay, sparse fine chaff temper. 4.3 cm long, 2.8 cm high, 1.7 cm wide
20	CB 952	A, Phase II	L. 16.3 D 384	Species indeterminate but probably equid, front end and legs missing. Orange core and buff surface, fine sand and chaff temper. 6.1 cm long, 3.5 cm high, 3.5 cm wide.
21	CB 2591	A, Phase II	L. 47.2 E 229.2	Probable equid, head and legs missing. Buff clay, light chaff temper. 7.3 cm long, 3.0 cm high, 3.1 cm wide.

ANIMAL FIGURINES–ZEBU

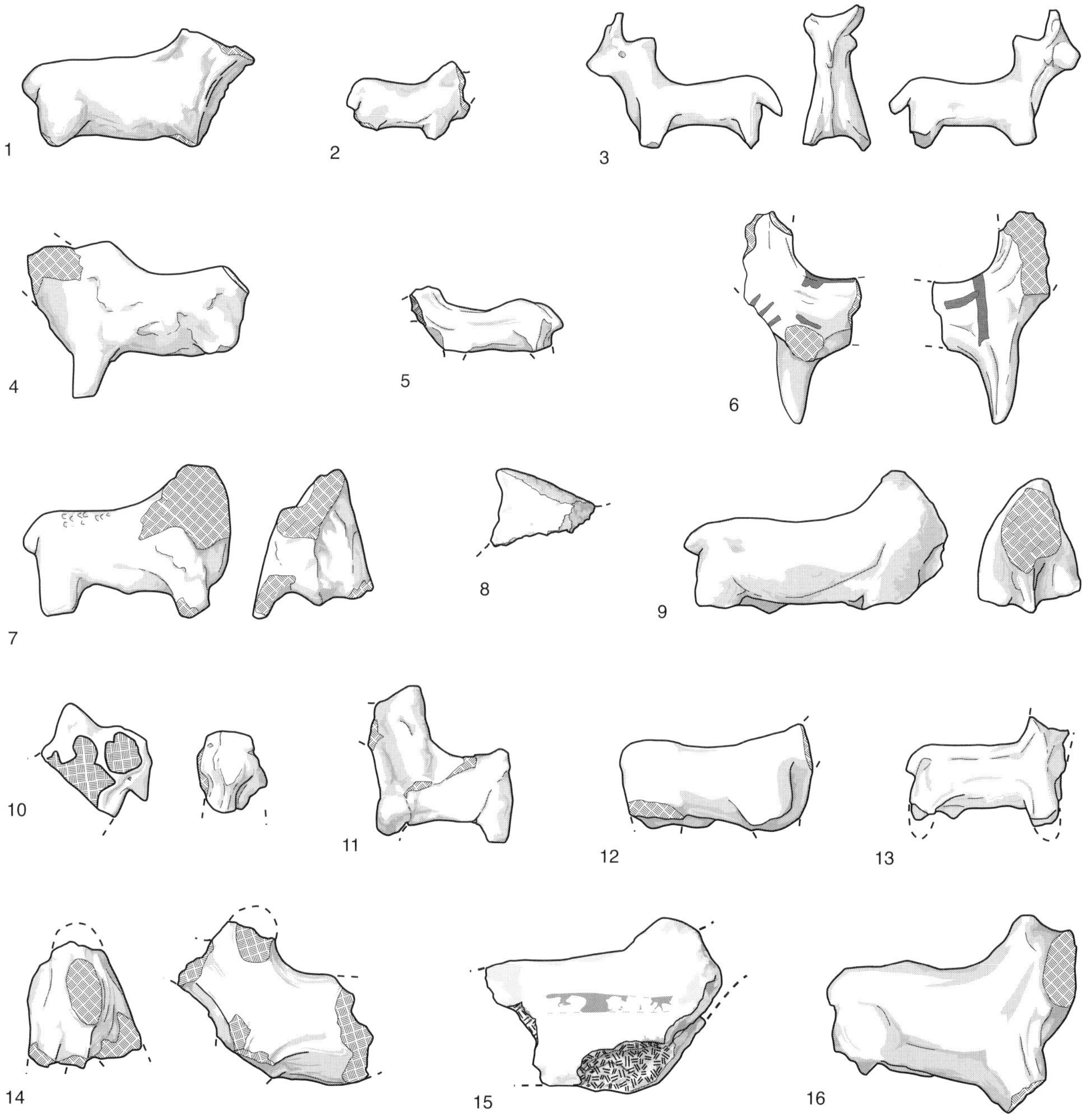

PLATE 69

ANIMAL FIGURINES–EQUIDS

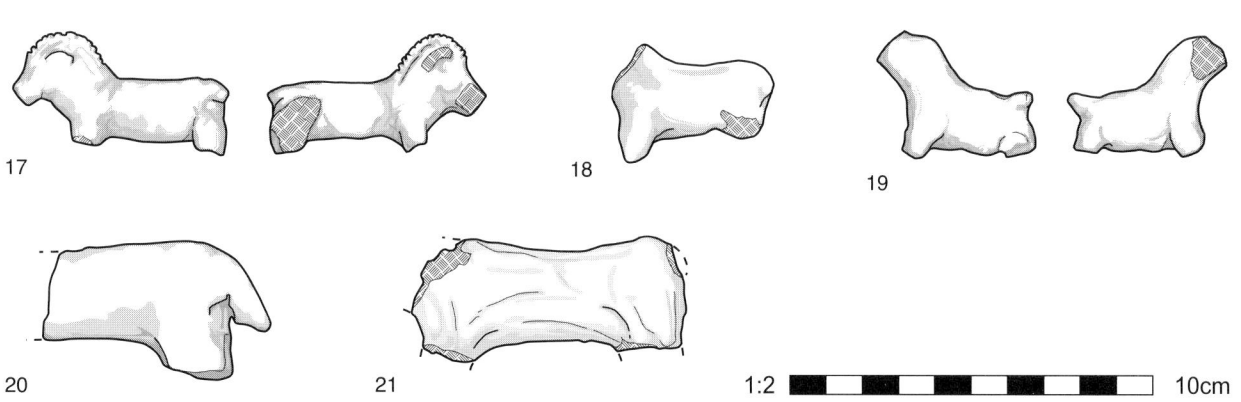

Plate 70: *Animal Figurines–Equids and Cattle*

	CB number	Area and Phase	Loc & Lot No.	Description, dimensions
1	CB 2956	A, Phase II	L. 81.2 F 35.2	Rear half only, legs missing. Buff clay, sparse chaff temper, incised line along top of back. 5.7 cm long, 3.7 cm high, 4.7 cm wide.
2	CB 2368	A, Phase III	L. 61.4 E 198.3	Legs missing. Buff clay. 6.3 cm long, 5.4 cm high, 3.1 cm wide.
3	CB 1826	G, Phase II/1	L. 4.4 E 66.1	Head only. Pale buff clay entirely covered with fugitive brown-red paint, no visible temper. 3.6 cm long, 2.8 cm high, 1.8 cm wide.
4	CB 1942	G, Phase II/1	L. 11.1 E 74.1	Rear half only. Brown core, brown-black surface, fine sand temper. 5.3 cm long, 4.0 cm high, 3.2 m wide.
5	CB 2048	G, Phase II/1	L. 55.3 E 97.3	Head and left legs missing. Greenish-buff clay, sparse chaff and sand temper. 7.0 cm long, 4.5 cm high, 2.5 cm wide.
6	CB 2614	G, Phase II/1	L. 14.1 E 83.2	Head and three legs missing. Buff clay, common medium chaff temper, red-brown paint. Painted harness–three parallel lines along back, one line encircling neck, traces of reins on neck. 6.6 cm long, 5.0 cm high, 2.4 cm wide.
7	CB 2114	G, Phase II/2	L. 54.3 E 105.1	Neck and torso only, probably equid. Pale greenish buff clay, medium chaff temper, laterally pierced (at least twice) through mane. 4.3 cm long, 5.7 cm high, 4.0 cm wide.
8	CB 2625	G, Phase II/2	L. 62.3 E 117.1	Head and legs missing, possible equid. Buff clay, fine chaff temper. 3.9 cm long, 1.8 cm high, 1.7 cm wide.
9	CB 2921	G, Phase II/2	L. 54.10 F 210.1	Rear half only, legs missing, species indeterminate. Red-buff clay, fine grit temper. 4.8 cm long, 3.6 cm high, 3.4 cm wide.
10	CB 2999	G Phase II/2	L. 54.10 F 210.3	Rear half only. Large grey grit temper. 4.6 cm long, 2.7 cm high, 2.9 cm wide.
11	CB 1949	A, Phase IA	L. 67.1 E 29.1	Head only, horns broken. 3.8 cm high, 3.3 cm long, 2.4 cm wide.
12	CB 780	A, Phase II	L. 13.1 D 57	Head only. Buff core, buff-pink surface, fine sparse lime temper/ inclusions. 3.5 cm high, 3.6 cm wide, 3.1 cm long
13	CB 2050	A, Phase II	L. 54.4 E 28.1	Horn only. Greenish-buff clay, sparse sand temper. 4.0 cm long, 1.4 cm max wide, 1.1 cm max thick.
14	CB 2958	A, Phase II	L. 81.1 F 35.2	Head only, cow or bull, red paint stripes on face and neck. 5.6 cm long, 3.9 cm high, 5.2 cm wide.

ANIMAL FIGURINES–EQUIDS

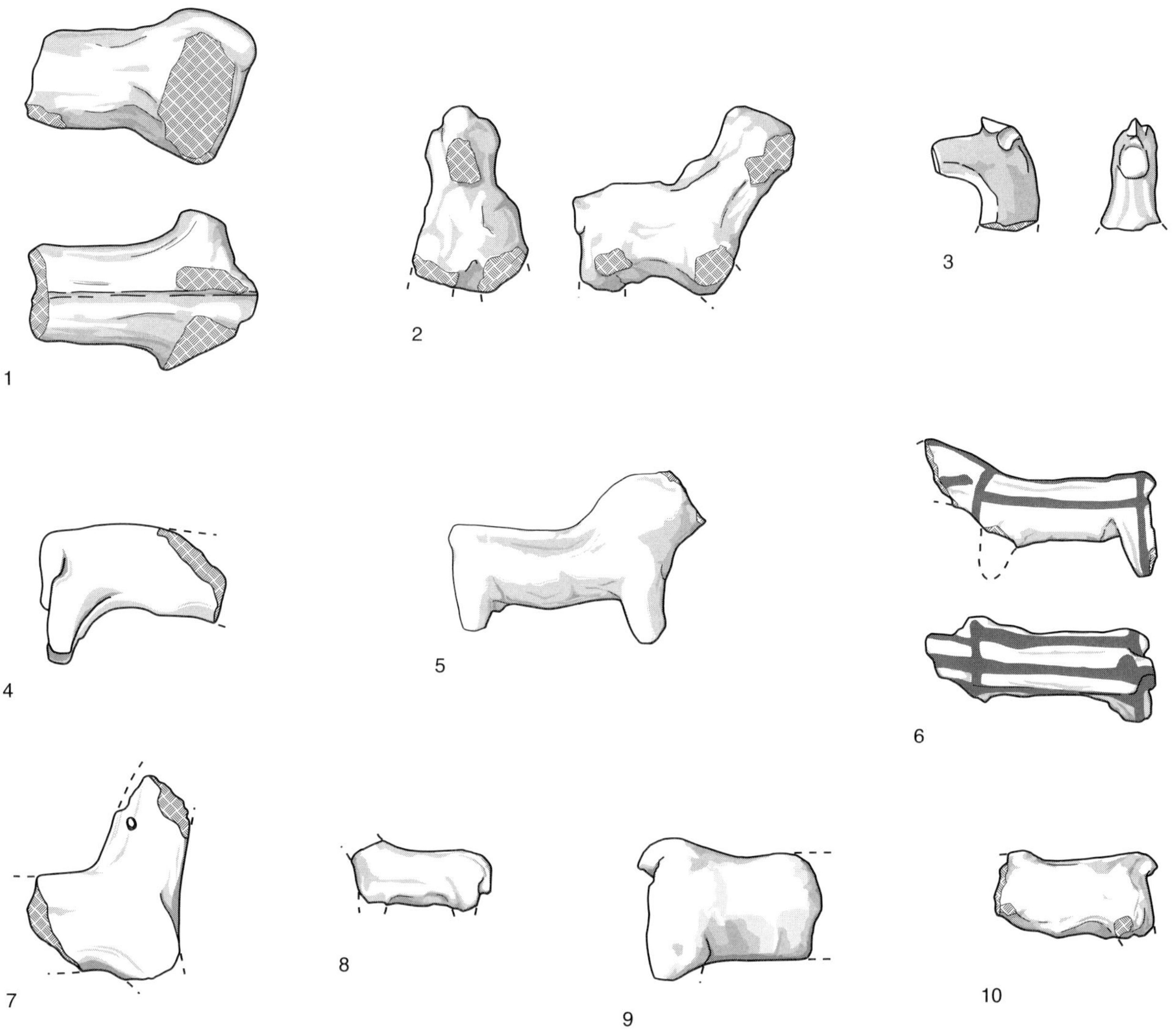

PLATE 70

ANIMAL FIGURINES–CATTLE

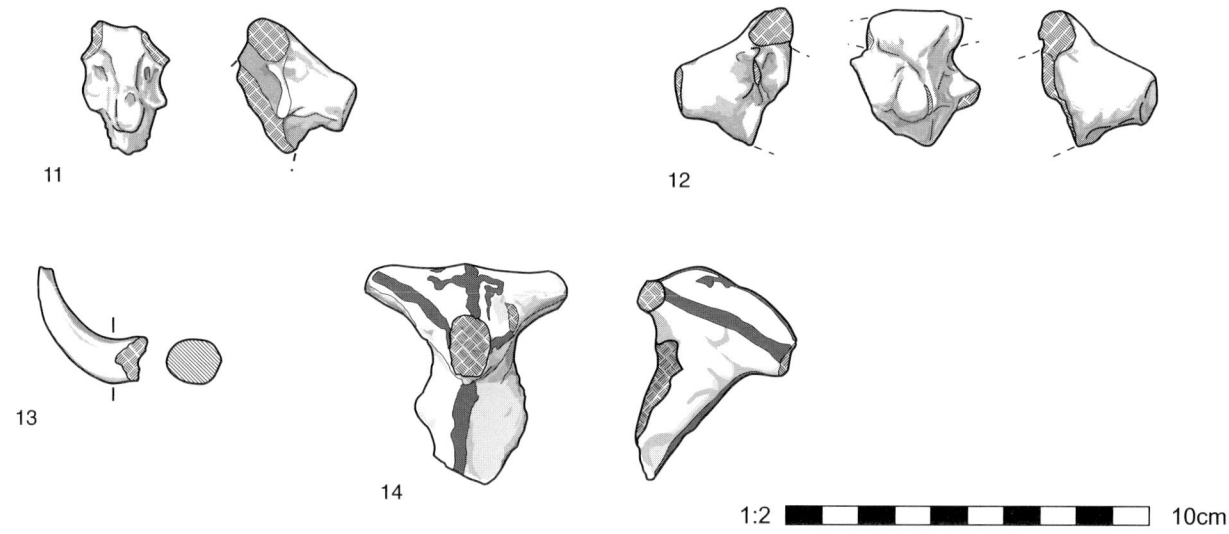

1:2 10cm

Plate 71: *Animal Figurines–Miscellaneous*

	CB number	Area and Phase	Loc & Lot No.	Description, dimensions
1	CB 913	A, Phase IA	L. 32.1 D 366	Head and shoulders only. Dark grey-brown clay, fine light chaff-temper. 2.8 cm long, 2.8 cm high, 1.4 cm wide.
2	CB 2415	A, Phase IA	L. 67.7 E 271.1	Most of head and legs missing. Brown un-tempered clay. 5.2 cm long, 3.3 cm high, 2.2 cm wide.
3	CB 2801	A, Phase I	L. 76.1 F 4.2	Torso and head only, pendent ears (or horns?). Dark grey clay (10YR 4/4), no visible temper. 3.4 cm long, 3.0 cm high, 1.7 cm wide.
4	CB 1897	A, Phase II	L. 62.1 E 21.1	Legs and tail missing. 5.0 cm long, 3.1 cm high, 2.0 cm wide.
5	CB 1943	G, Surface	L. 57.1 E 99.1	Pale buff surface, medium chaff temper. Surface very abraded. 4.7 cm long, 3.0 cm high, 1.9 cm wide.
6	CB 4216	G, Phase III	L. 79.1 F 467.1	Legs missing. Black clay, 7.5 YR 2.5/1, sparse fine chaff temper. 6.6 cm long, 3.7 cm high, 2.6 cm wide.
7	CB 1916	A, Phase II	L. 61.1 E 22.2	Head only, unusually small. 1.5 cm high, 1.7 cm long, 1.3 cm wide.
8	CB 1807	G, Surface	L. 1 E 61.2	Unusually small, lightly baked, possible dog from short tail and high-set ears. One leg missing, nose chipped. Brown clay, no visible temper. 3.2 cm long, 2.3 cm high, 1.0 cm wide.
9	CB 1823	G, Surface	L. 1 E 61.3	Unusually small animal figurine, surface abraded, legs, tail and nose missing. Grey clay, fine sand temper. 3.7 cm long, 2.5 cm high, 1.3 cm wide.
10	CB 2106	G, Phase II/1	L. 4.1 E 86.1	Unusually small, torso and rear legs only. Black-brown clay, sparse grey grit temper. 2.3 cm long, 1.3 cm high, 1.2 cm wide.
11	CB 1804	A, Phase II	L. 54.1 E 7.1	Possible leg of animal figurine. Pale buff clay, no visible temper. 3.4 cm high, 1.75 cm max diameter.
12	CB 2289	A, Phase III	L. 61.4 E 198.2	Leg (?). 2.7 cm high, 2.4 cm wide, 1.4 cm th.
13	CB 2418	A, Phase III	L. 61.5 E 207.3	Leg only. Dark brown-grey clay, no visible temper. 2.5 cm high, 2.3 cm wide, 1.9 cm thick.
14	CB 1940	G, Phase II/1	L. 55.1 E 97.1	Hind end of animal figurine, detailed male genitalia. Orange core, pale orange surface, no visible temper. 4.0 cm long, 2.7 cm high, 3.1 cm wide.
15	CB 3938	G, Phase II/2	L. 34.5 F 454.1	Torso segment of figurine. 1.4 cm long, 3.5 cm high, 2.7 cm wide.
16	CB 2592	A, Phase II	L. 47.2 E 229.2	Head and three legs missing, traces of incised mane, long cylindrical body. Medium buff clay, medium chaff temper. 8.2 cm long, 5.0 cm high, 3.2 cm wide.
17	CB 2115	G, Phase II/1A	L. 59.1 E 101.1	Pinched and flattened face, flattened base, battered and abraded. Pale buff un-tempered clay, fugitive black paint over entire surface. 3.8 cm high, 1.8 cm wide, 1.6 cm thick.
18	CB 2212	G, Phase II/2	L. 2.3 E 102.1	Hollow spherical body, pierced through nose and top of back, fugitive pale red paint stripes along body. Greenish-buff clay, fine sparse chaff and fine sparse lime temper. 5.2 cm long, 3.7 cm high, 3.1 cm wide.

ANIMAL FIGURINES–MISCELLANEOUS   PLATE 71

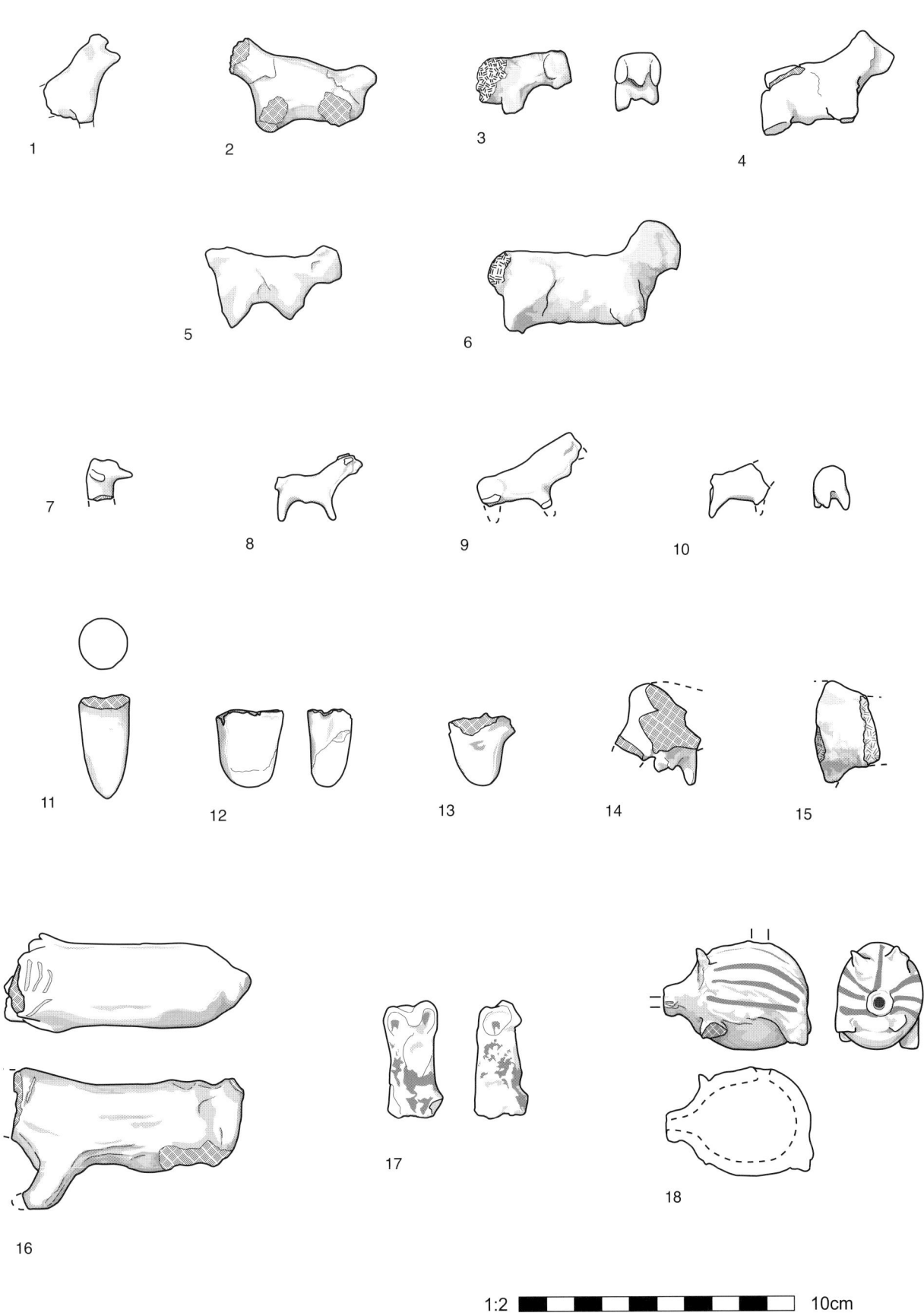

Plate 72: *Model Wheels*

	CB number	Area and Phase	Locus and Lot Number	Description, dimensions
1	CB 2419	A, Phase I A	L. 67.7 E 271.1	Badly chipped around edges. Dark grey-brown clay, sparse chaff temper. 4.7 cm diam., 2.2 cm thick at hub.
2	CB 68	A, Phase I	L. 9.1 D 26	Approximately 2/3 preserved, red-orange clay with sparse chaff temper, scarlet red paint cross-hatched lines on one side, curved lines on the other. 7.8 cm diam., 3.4 cm thick at hub.
3	CB 721	A, Phase I	L. 17.2 D 340	Buff- buff orange clay with light chaff temper. Small off-centre perforation. 4.2 cm diam., 2.4 cm thick at hub.
4	CB 1849	G, Surface	L. 1 E 64.2	Unusual toothed edge, buff core, buff-red surface, medium chaff temper. 5.8 cm diam., 2.9 cm thick at hub.
5	CB 1948	G, Phase II/1	L. 13.1 E 75.1	Red-brown paint outlining hub on each side. Orange-brown core and surface, medium chaff and sand temper. C. 8 cm diam., 5.0 cm thick at hub.
6	CB 2613	G, Phase II/1	L. 14.1 E 83.2	Badly chipped around edges. Grey core, orange surface, common medium chaff temper. 4.1-4.6 cm diam., 2.6 cm thick at hub.
7	CB 2107	G, Phase II/1	L. 9.2 E 77.1	Hub only, smaller than average. Dark grey-brown clay, no visible temper. 2.0 cm wide, 2.4 cm thick at hub.
8	CB 2624	G, Phase II/2	L. 16.5 E 249.2	Just over half preserved, larger than average. Buff clay, medium chaff temper. 10.3 cm diam., 5.6 cm thick at hub.
9	CB 2621	G, Phase II/2	L.9.8 E 250.1	Just under one-half preserved. Pale brown-grey clay, medium chaff temper. 3.9 cm diam., 2.2 cm thick at hub.
10	CB 3779	G, Phase II/2	L. 54.10 F 210.5	Badly chipped around edges. Light brown-buff clay, 7.5YR 6/3, medium chaff temper. C. 5 cm diam., 3.5 cm thick at hub.
11	CB 3946	G, Phase II/2	L. 46.1 F 86.2	Badly chipped around edges. 5.1 cm long, 4.2 cm wide, 4.2 cm thick at hub.
12	CB 3880	G, Phase III	L. 37.4 F 222.1	Almost complete, larger than average. Light grey clay, 2.5Y 7/2, common large chaff temper. C. 8 cm diam., 3.4 cm thick at hub.

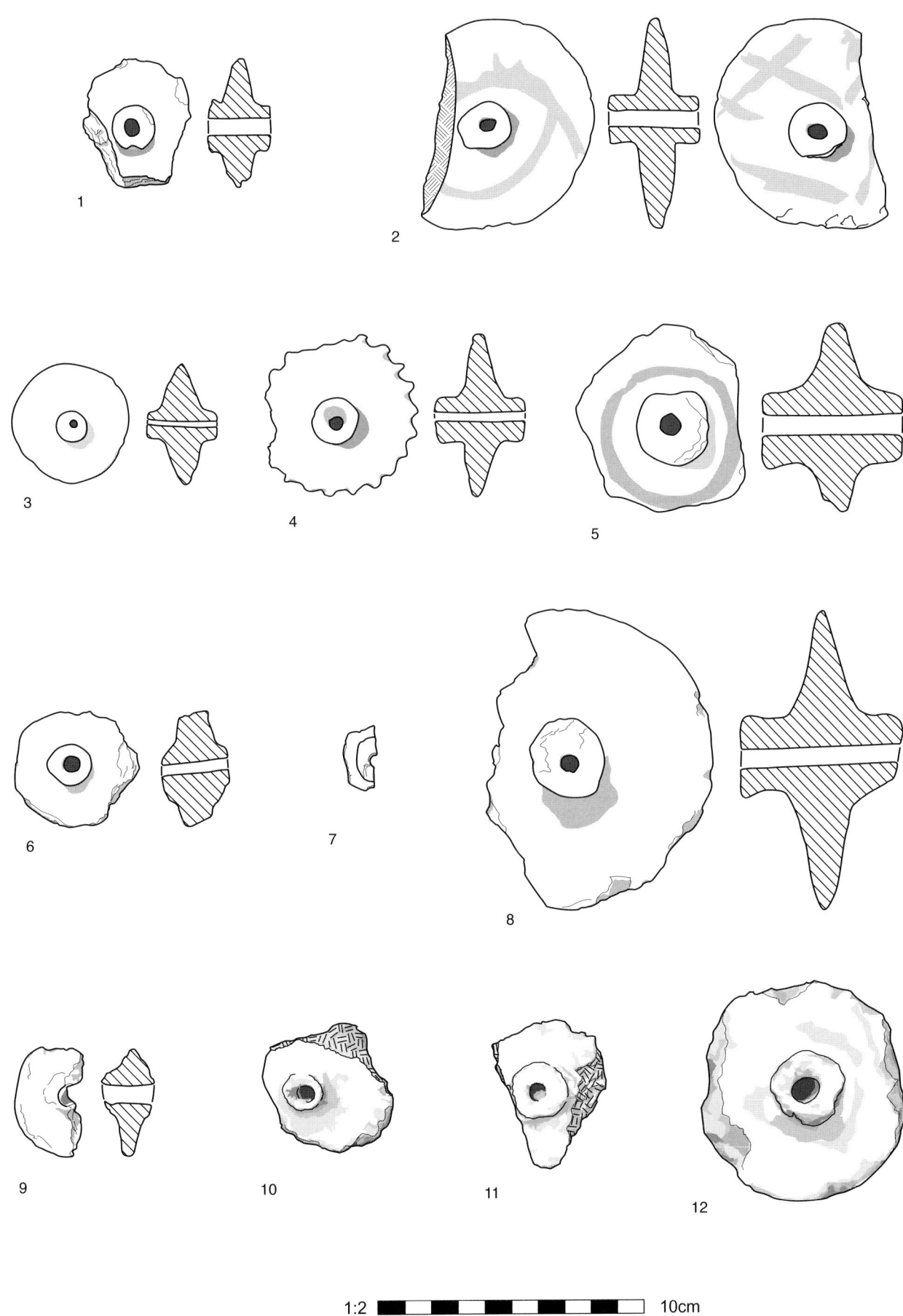

PLATE 72

Plate 73: *Model wagons and Human Figurines*

	CB number	Area and Phase	Locus & Lot no.	Description, dimensions
1	CB 788	A, Phase II	L. 16.2 D 261	Large baked clay wagon or chariot. Buff-orange core and paler buff surface, medium-heavy chaff and fine sparse lime temper. 8.5 cm long, 12.0 cm wide, 5.2 cm high.
2	CB 2590	A, Phase II	L. 47.2 E 229.2	Small baked clay chariot or wagon, part of base with one axle and beginning of curve up to front preserved. Pink core, pale buff surface, occasional fine chaff and common fine lime temper. 6.1 cm long, 4.3 cm wide, 2.0 cm high.
3	CB 4233	G, Phase III	L. 37.5 F 226.2	Corner of model chariot or wagon, horizontal and vertical incised lines and punctate decoration. 4.2 cm long, 3.7 cm wide, 4.3 cm high.
4	CB 3954	G, Phase IV	L.75.1 F 224.1	Chariot or wagon, base and part of sides, incised horizontal lines on sides. Light yellowish-brown clay, 10YR 6/4. 7.0 cm long, 5.5 cm high, 5.9 cm wide.
5	CB 1777	A, Phase IA	L. 32.1 E 40.1	Head only, tall head-dress, mould-made, back smoothed and left plain. Orange clay, fine grit and chaff temper. 5.1 cm high, 3.2 cm wide, 2.2 cm thick.
6	CB 384	A, Phase II	L. 19.1 D 66	Central section of plaque, mould-made, torso of nude frontal female, hands clasped below breasts. Reverse flat. Orange-buff clay with buff-greenish surface (2.5YR 8/3), light chaff temper. 3.8 cm high, 3.8 cm wide, 1.8 cm thick.
7	CB 2417	A, Phase II	L. 61.2 E 194.1	Very schematic human figurine, torso only, applied belt, vestigial arms, legs and head missing. Green-buff clay, sparse sand and lime temper. 3.4 cm high, 2.7 cm wide, 1.7 cm thick.
8	CB 2596	A, Phase II	L. 21.1 E 221.2	Very schematic human figurine, torso only. Pale buff clay. 4.8 cm high, 3.2 cm wide, 2.2 cm thick.
9	CB 1933	A, Phase II	L. 64.1 E 24.1	Lightly baked, very schematic possible human figurine, roughly conical, pinched nose, asymmetrical punctate eyes. Dark brown clay, fine chaff temper. 2.9 cm high, 1.7 cm max diam.
10	CB 2062	A, Phase II	L. 55.1 E 12.8	Very schematic possible human figurine, pointed cone, flat base, face area damaged. Brown clay, no visible temper. 2.7 cm high, 1.6 cm max diam.
11	CB 2061	G, Phase II/1	L. 2.2 E 95.3	Very schematic possible human figurine, cone with flat base, pinched nose and punctate eyes. Brown-grey clay, no visible temper. 2.6 cm high, 1.5 cm max diam.
12	CB 1918	G, Phase II/1	T.11 shaft E 67.2	Possible very schematic human figurine. Cylindrical, one end flattened, opposite end broken. 3.4 cm high, 1.6 cm max diam.
13	CB 3000	G, Phase II/1	L. 34.3 F 67.1	Schematic human figurine, head missing, arms and legs broken. 3.2 cm high, 3.0 cm wide, 1.2 cm thick.
14	CB 2974	G, Phase II/2	L. 54.10 F 210.2	Female figurine, flat base, head and one arm broken. Pale red clay, medium sand temper. 6.0 cm high, 5.6 cm wide.
15	CB 2975	G, Phase II/2	L. 54.10 F 210.2	Halaf figurine head, schematic, no features indicated, irregular rounded top, concave sides. 1.5 cm high, 1.0 cm max diam.
16	CB 2976	G, Phase II/2	L. 54.10 F 210.2	Schematic human figurine, oblong broken at one base, with applied projecting cone-like arm. 4.0 cm high, 2.8 cm wide, 1.8 cm thick.
17	CB 4214	G, Phase III	L. 50.1 F 470.1	Upper body of female figurine, head missing, arms bent and hands on chest, vestigial breasts applied to shoulders, applied bracelet on each wrist, rows of circular impressions on back across shoulders and down centre. Pale olive clay, 5Y 6/4, medium chaff temper. 4.7 cm high, 5.9 cm wide, 2.6 cm thick.

PLATE 73

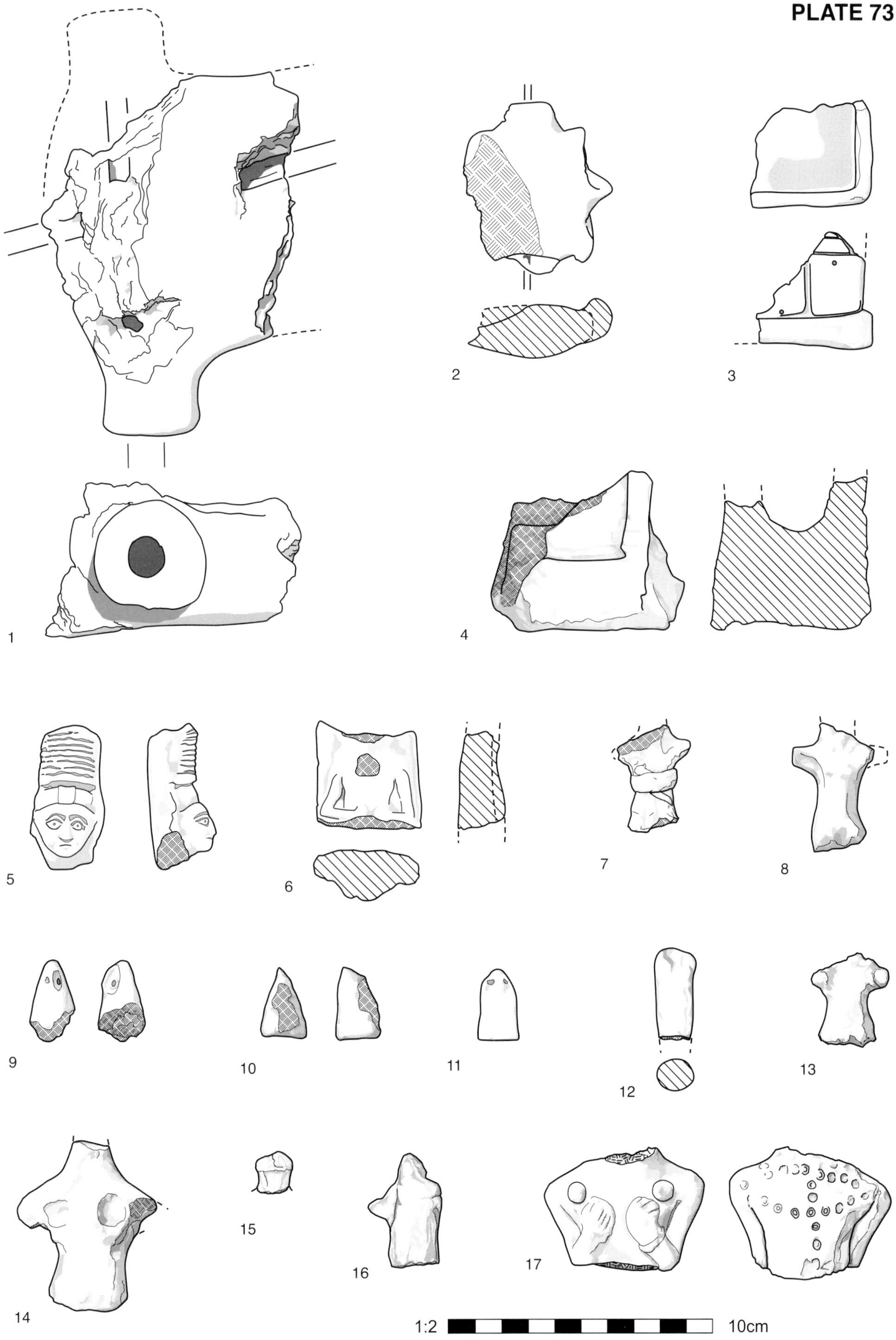

1:2 ▇▇▇▇▇▇ 10cm

Plate 74: *Grinding Stones, Hammer-stones*

	CB number	Area and Phase	Locus & Lot number	Description, dimensions
1	CB 43	A, Surface	L. 1.2 D 12	Pear-shaped basalt pestle. 6.1 cm high, 5.1 cm max diam. at base.
2	CB 327	A, Phase II	99-6 D 54	Pear-shaped basalt pestle, flattened on two sides. 5.7 cm high, 4.5 cm wide, 3.4 cm thick
3	CB 747	A, Phase II	L. 29.1 D 349	Cuboid limestone grindstone. All surfaces slightly battered and abraded. 6.0 x 5.6 x 5.5 cm.
4	CB 789	A, Phase II	L. 16.2 D 361	Squat pear-shaped basalt pestle. 4.5 cm high, 4.5 cm max diam.
5	CB 1839	G, Phase II/IA	L. 3.1 E 63.2	Cuboid basalt grindstone, all surfaces smoothed. 4.1 cm high, 4.1 cm wide, 3.6 cm thick. Found in association with pear-shaped pestle CB 1840.
6	CB 1840	G, Phase II/1A	L. 3.1 E 63.2	Faceted pear-shaped basalt pestle, flattened on two sides. 3.9 cm high, 5.4 cm wide, 3.6 cm thick. Found in association with cuboid CB 1839.
7	CB 2826	G, Phase II/1A	L. 31.2 F 57.1	Squat cylindrical basalt pestle, smoothed on one end from use. 6.6 cm high, ca. 5.3 cm diam.
8	CB 2538	G, Phase II/2	L. 54.4 E 108.3	Squat pear-shaped basalt pestle. 5.1 cm high, 5.1 cm max. diam.
9	CB 2790	A, Phase II	L. 75.1 F 27.1	Cylindrical grindstone/ hammer-stone, fine-grained dark grey stone, chipped and polished on both ends, slight polish on one side. 6.3 cm long, 3.2 cm wide, 2.9 cm thick.
10	CB 2984	A, Phase II	L. 81.2 F 35.3	Oblong hammer-stone, one end flattened and chipped from use, opposite end rounded, oval cross-section. 7.5 cm long, 4.8 cm wide, 2.9 cm thick.
11	CB 2051	A, Phase II	L. 54.4 E 28.1	Conical basalt pestle, wide shallow groove around circumference, near base, both ends polished from use. 12.0 cm high, 7.5 cm max diam.

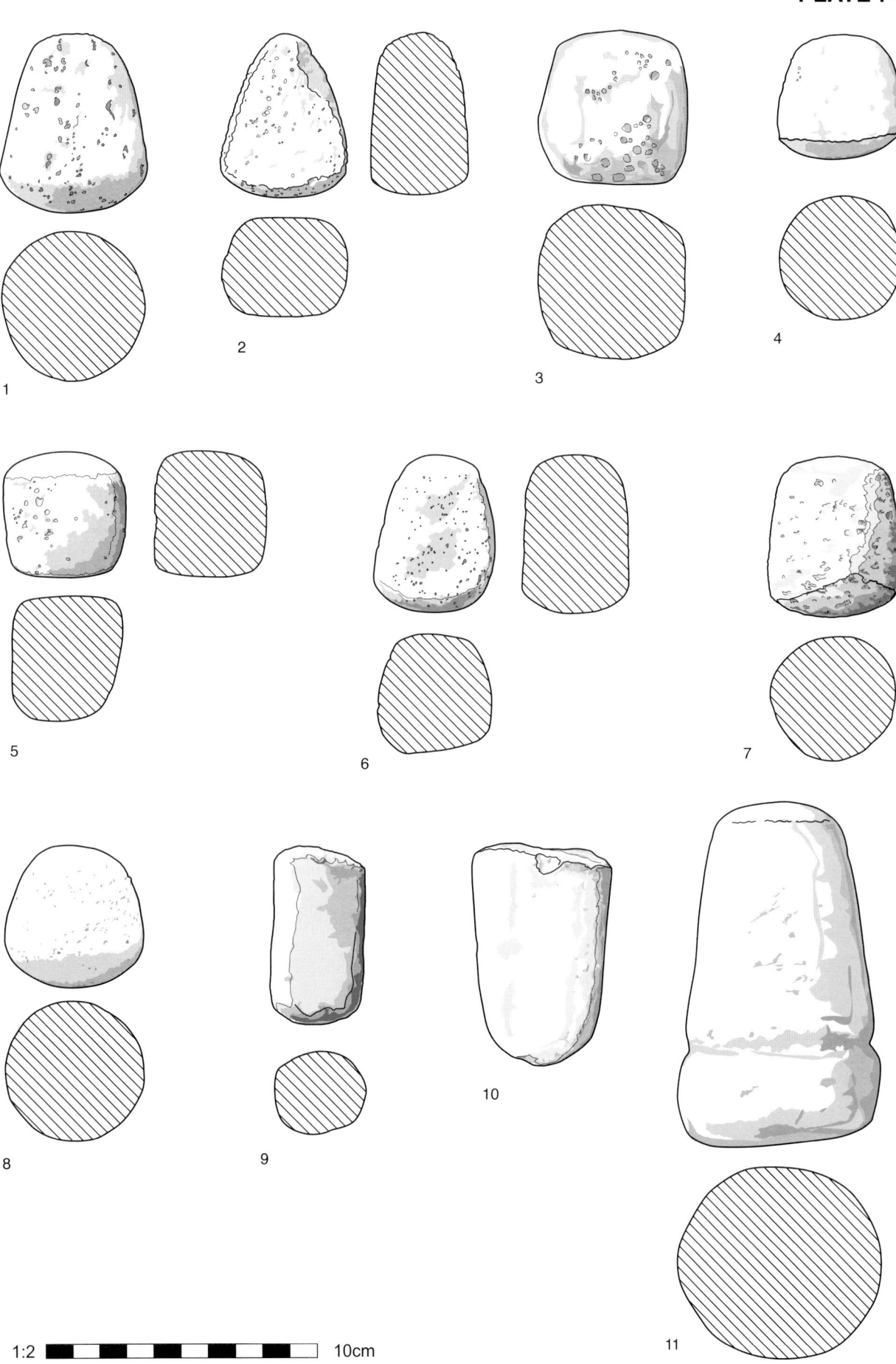

PLATE 74

Plate 75: *Grinding Stones, hammer-stones*

	CB number	Area and Phase	Locus & Lot number	Description, dimensions
1	CB 1944	G, Phase II/1	L. 12.1 E 71.1	Approximately half of cylindrical grindstone/ whetstone. Joins to CB 1945, but each was used as a separate tool. Flattened/broken end battered and chipped, rounded end ground slightly. Dense heavy sandy sedimentary stone. Found with CB 1945, 1946 and 1947. 17 cm long, 10.3 cm wide, 9.5 cm thick.
2	CB 1945	G, Phase II/1	L. 12.1 E 71.1	Approximately half of cylindrical grindstone/ whetstone. Joins to CB 1944, but each was used as a separate tool. Flattened/broken end battered and chipped, rounded end ground slightly. Dense heavy sandy sedimentary stone. Found with CB 1944, 1946 and 1947. 19.5 cm long, 10.0 cm wide, 9.3 cm thick.
3	CB 1946	G, Phase II/1	L. 12.1 E 71.1	Roughly oblong basalt grinding and pounding stone, both ends chipped and battered, two sides slightly flattened and polished from use. Found with CB 1944, 1945 and 1947. 15.3 cm long, 5.5 cm wide. 4.8 cm thick.
4	CB 1947	G, Phase II/1	L.12.1 E 71.1	Roughly cuboid pestle, opposing ends rounded and polished from use, dense fine-grained brown stone. Found with CB 1944, 1945 and 1946. 7.3 cm long, 5.8 cm wide, 4.7 cm thick.
5	CB 16	A, IA	L. 1.2 D 5	Disk-shaped basalt grinding stone, slightly tapered cross-section. 10.3 cm diam., 3.0-4.3 cm thick.
6	CB 2864	G, Phase III	L. 27.2 F 205.1	Sub-rectangular grinding stone, flattened on all six sides, somewhat irregular. Coarse-textured basalt. 8.0 cm long, 6.5 cm wide, 5.0 cm thick.

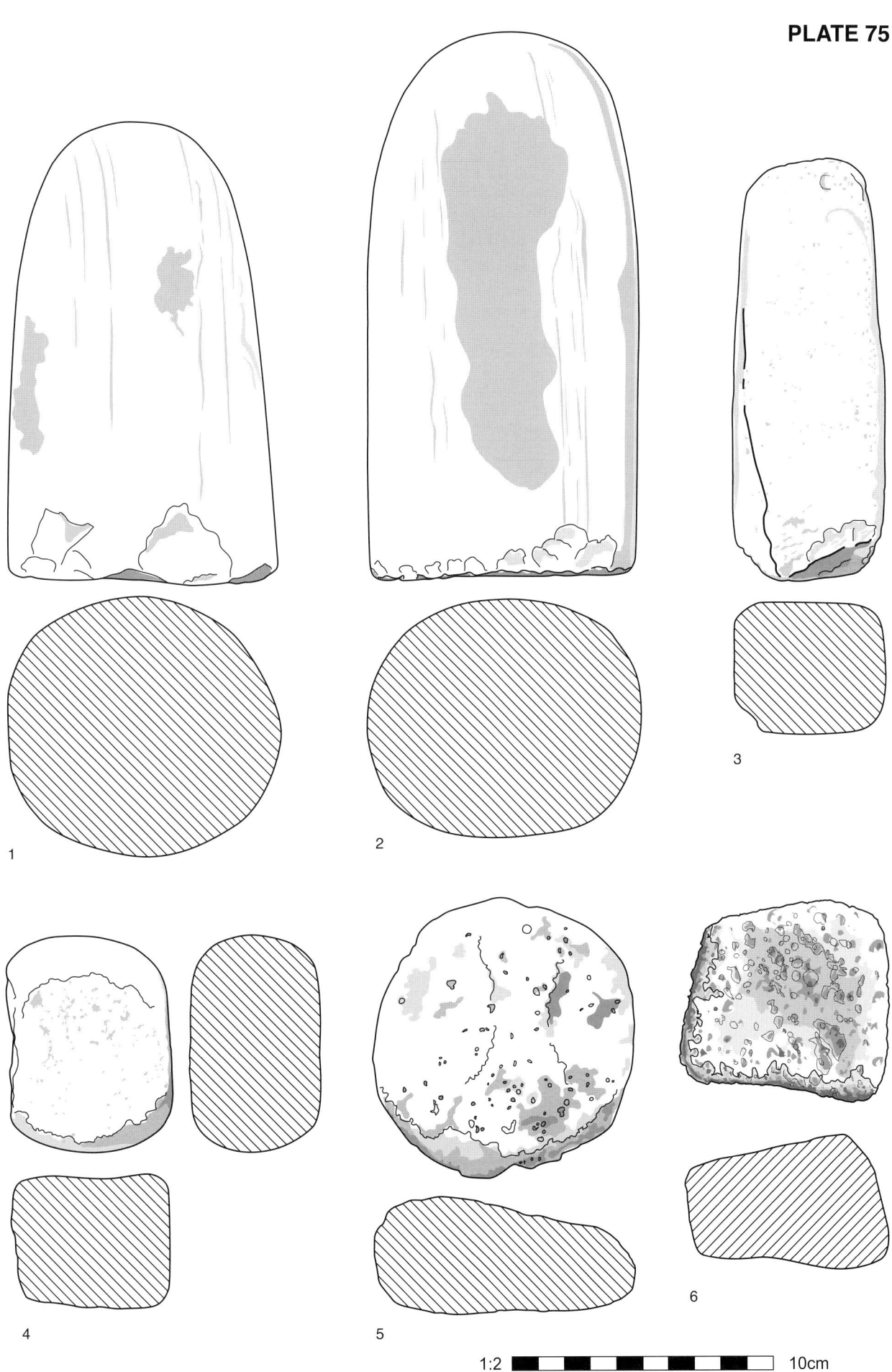

PLATE 75

1:2 10cm

Plate 76: *Stone mortars, grinding stones and bowls*

	CB number	Area and Phase	Locus & Lot number	Description, dimensions
1	CB 1778	A, Phase II	L. 39.1 E 31.1	Approximately 3/4 of basalt bowl or mortar, plain rim, shallow, conical, three low feet. C. 17 cm diam., 7.1 cm high.
2	CB 2116	G, Phase II/2	L. 52.1 E 94.1	Approximately 1/4 of basalt bowl, hemispherical, plain rim, three low rounded feet (one preserved). C. 19 cm diam., 10.0 cm high.
3	CB 2863	G, Phase III	L. 27.2 F 205.1	Just over one-half of basalt bowl, plain rim, hemispherical, slightly flattened base. C. 21 cm diam., 12 cm high.
4	CB 4217	G, Phase III	L. 79.1 F 467.2	Approximately one-half basalt mortar, rounded square in plan, plain rim, flat base, near-vertical sides, very smooth interior. Concave base, as if base was also used for grinding at one point. 17.2 cm wide, 10.3 cm long, 7.2 cm high, 13.5 cm diam. interior hollow.
5	CB 2630	G, Phase II/2	L. 16.4 E 247.1	"Bathtub"-shaped basalt mortar or vessel.. C. 23 cm long, 11.5 cm high, 17.0 cm wide.
6	CB 4220	G, Phase II/1A	L. 67.1 F 75.1	Oblong basalt grinding stone, plano-convex cross-section and extended plano-convex profile. Damaged on both sides and one end. 29.8 cm long, 11.3 cm wide, 4.4 cm high.
7	CB 3899	G, Phase III	L. 44.3 F 215.1	Oblong basalt grinding stone, plano-convex cross-section and extended plano-convex profile. 32.5 cm long, 13.0 cm wide, 5.0 cm high.
8	CB 1876	A, Phase II	L. 52.1 E 4.4	Rim-to-base profile fragment of shallow basalt bowl, flattened rim, rounded sides, low disk base. C. 11 cm diam,. c. 4. cm high.
9	CB 3769	G, Phase III	L. 37.3 F 213.3	Rim sherd of small stone bowl, plain thick rim, white and red veined marble. C. 7 cm diam., 3.9 cm high as preserved.

PLATE 76

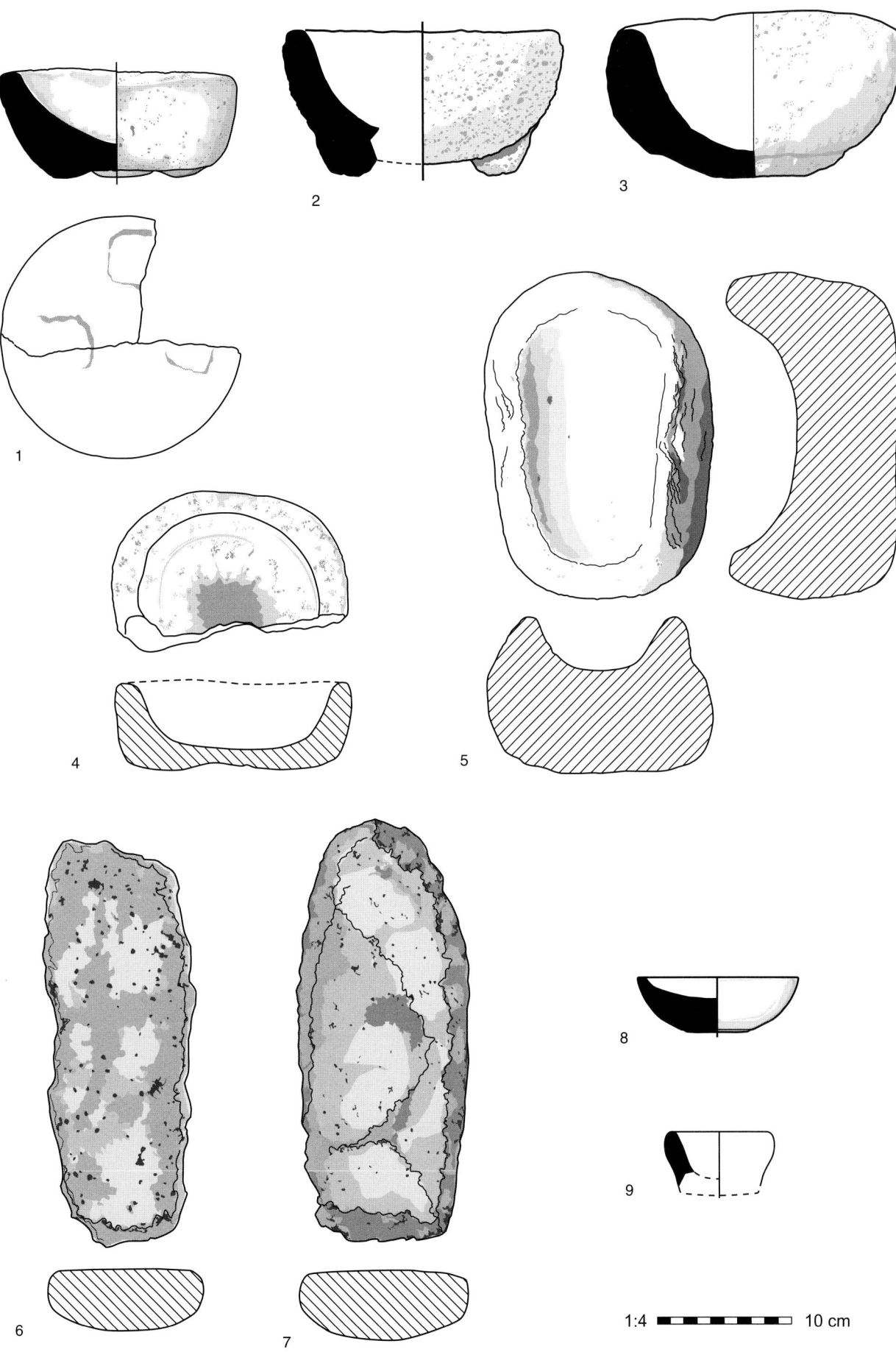

Plate 77: *Whetstones, Burnishing Tools*

	CB number	Area and Phase	Locus & Lot number	Description, dimensions
1	CB 2818	A, Phase I	L. 76.5 F 5.6	Sub-rectangular flat whetstone, both sides have grooves from use, both ends have a rounded notch. Pale pink-red sandstone. 5.7 cm long, 4.5 cm wide, 1.5 cm thick.
2	CB 3046	A, Phase I	L. 78.1 F 7.1	Ovoid burnishing stone, slightly flattened at ends, circular cross-section. Yellow-brown stone. 4.9 cm long, 3.1 cm max. diam.
3	CB 2957	A, Phase II	L. 81.2 F 35.2	Roughly square, worked, fine-grained whetstone, rounded rectangular cross-section. 4.7 cm long, 4.1 cm wide, 2.5 cm thick.
4	CB 2052	A, Phase III	L. 44.1 E 58.1	One end of an oblong whetstone, oval cross-section, fine-grained dense dark grey stone, pierced near end by drilling from both sides, polish around hole from suspension on a string. 3.2 cm long, 1.9 cm wide, 0.9 cm thick.
5	CB 2825	G, Phase I	L. 29.1 F 55.1	Whetstone (?) or burnishing tool, irregular 3-sided pyramidal stone, smooth polished faces with occasional striations, attempt made to pierce through tapered top, left unfinished. Dark red and black conglomerate stone. 5.1 cm high, 3.8 cm wide, 3.5 cm thick.
6	CB 2109	G, Phase II/1	L. 9.4 E 85.1	Rectangular whetstone, flat base, slightly tapered, pierced through smaller end, rectangular cross-section, dense sandy dark grey stone. 3.8 cm high, 2.6 cm wide, 1.6 cm thick.
7	CB 2542	G, Phase II/1	L. 55.3 E 109.1	Sub-rectangular whetstone, dense fine-grained pale brown stone, plano-convex cross-section, edges bevelled from use. 5.4 cm long, 8.5 cm wide, 3.5 cm thick.
8	CB 3001	G, Phase II/1	L. 34.1 F 64.1	Roughly triangular whetstone, grey-brown fine-grained stone, oval cross-section, edges bevelled from use. 7.3 cm long, 5.3 cm wide, 2.1 cm thick.
9	CB 3002	G, Phase II/1	L. 34.1 F 64.1	Possible whetstone, tapering, square-sectioned, horizontal groove near one end, rounded head, opposite end broken. Fine-grained greenish-buff stone. 7.0 cm high, 2.7 cm wide, 2.4 cm thick.
10	CB 3094	G, Phase III	L. 40.3 F 69.1	Trapezoidal celt, smooth, polished, mottled dark green, dense fine-grained stone. 5.9 cm long, 5.1 cm wide, 1.5 cm thick.
11	CB 2060	G, Phase II/1	L. 55.1 E 97.1	Small shallow stone plate, fine-grained soft dark grey-green stone, interior shows heavy use as a cutting surface, exterior shows occasional use. Irregular edges, ground to shape from a larger piece. C 3.6 cm diam., 0.6 cm high.
12	CB 3427	G, Phase III	L. 40.2 F 68.2	Bi-conical hammer-stone, chipped on both ends, fine dense stone. 7.5 cm long, 4.3 cm max. diam.

PLATE 77

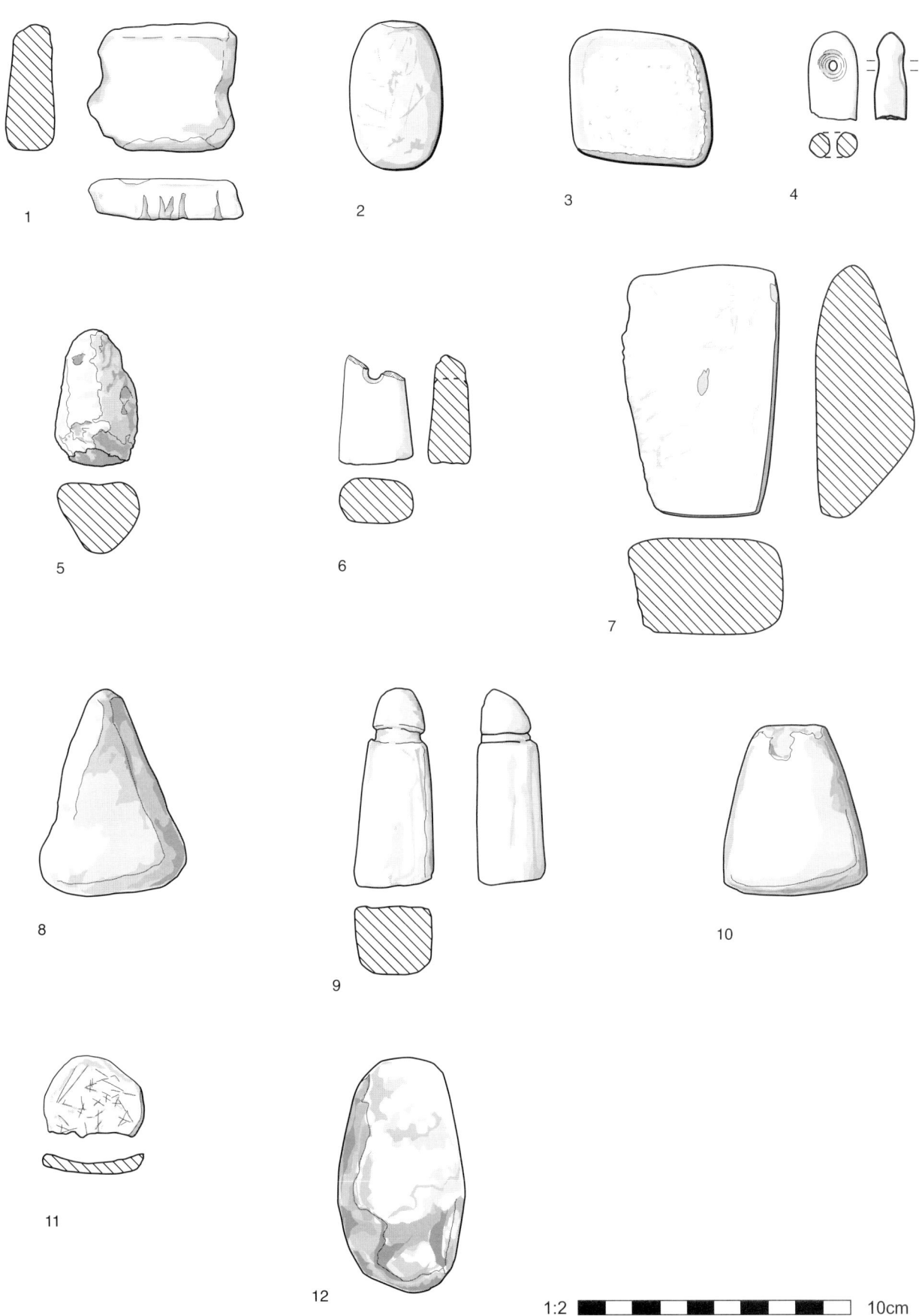

Plate 78: *Spindle Whorls and Loom Weights*

	CB number	Area and Phase	Locus & Lot number	Description, dimensions
1	CB 911	A, Phase IA	L. 32.1 D 366	Approximately half, baked clay spindle whorl, plano-convex in cross-section, central piercing. Dense heavy dark grey (2.5YR 7/2) un-tempered clay. 4.0 cm diam., 1.7 cm high
2	CB 2615	G, Phase II/2	L. 9.6 E 241.1	Baked clay bi-conical pierced spindle whorl. Buff clay, sparse fine chaff temper. 2.6 cm diam., 1.2 cm thick.
3	CB 2816	A, Phase I	L. 76.5 F 5.5	Lightly baked clay bi-conical pierced spindle whorl, c 2/3 preserved. Grey (7.5YR 5/1) clay, fine lime temper. 2.6 cm diam., 1.9 cm thick.
4	CB 2909	A, Phase II	L. 81.2 F 35.1	Approximately one half pierced limestone ring, plano-convex cross-section. Might be net weight, loom weight or spindle whorl. 5.5 cm diam., 2.2 cm thick.
5	CB 917	A, Phase II	L. 21.2 D 370	Flat stone disk, fine-grained dark grey stone (slate?), beginning of drilled piercing on either side, which would not have met evenly. Possible net weight. 4.6-5.0 cm diam., 0.9 cm thick.
6	CB 2620	G, Phase II/1	L. 9.4 E 85.2	Just over one-half stone disk, grey marble. 3.0 cm diam., 0.65 cm thick.
7	CB 2792	G, Phase I	L. 26.2 F 53.2	One-half of base of pottery vessel, broken and worked into disk, hole bored into centre. Red-buff clay, fine lime temper. C. 5.0 cm diam., 1.2 cm thick.
8	CB 3878	G, Phase III	L. 69.1 F 219.2	Baked clay possible loom weight, irregular faceted surface. Pale yellow clay, 2.5Y 7.3, common chaff temper. 4.0 cm high, 4.1 cm wide, 3.5 cm thick. 1.6 cm diam. hole.
9	CB 912	A, Phase IA	L. 32.1 D 366	Approximately half of a baked clay oblong object, tapered at one end, near-vertical piercing, possible loom weight. Pale buff core and surface (10YR 3/3), medium chaff temper. 5.0 cm long, 3.2 cm wide, 3.4 cm high.
10	CB 2047	A, Phase II	L. 61.2 E 25.3	Irregular cobble of dense white stone. Pierced off-centre; hole appears to be from a natural flaw on one side but was drilled and grooved on the other. One side polished, opposite side battered and chipped from use. 6.6 cm long, 6.0 cm wide, 4.6 cm th.
11	CB 3770	G, Phase II/2	L. 54.10 F 210.5	Approximately one-half pierced limestone ring, plano-convex cross-section. C. 5.5 cm diam., 5.1 cm thick.
12	CB 370	A, Phase I	99-11 D 75	Basalt ring-shaped object, possible door-socket or loom weight, plano-convex cross-section. 17 cm diam, 6.5 cm thick
13	CB 997	A, Phase III	L. 34.1 D 384	Approximately one-fourth of large basalt ring, centrally-pierced, smoothed. Door-socket or loom weight. C. 13 cm original diam., 6.2 cm high.

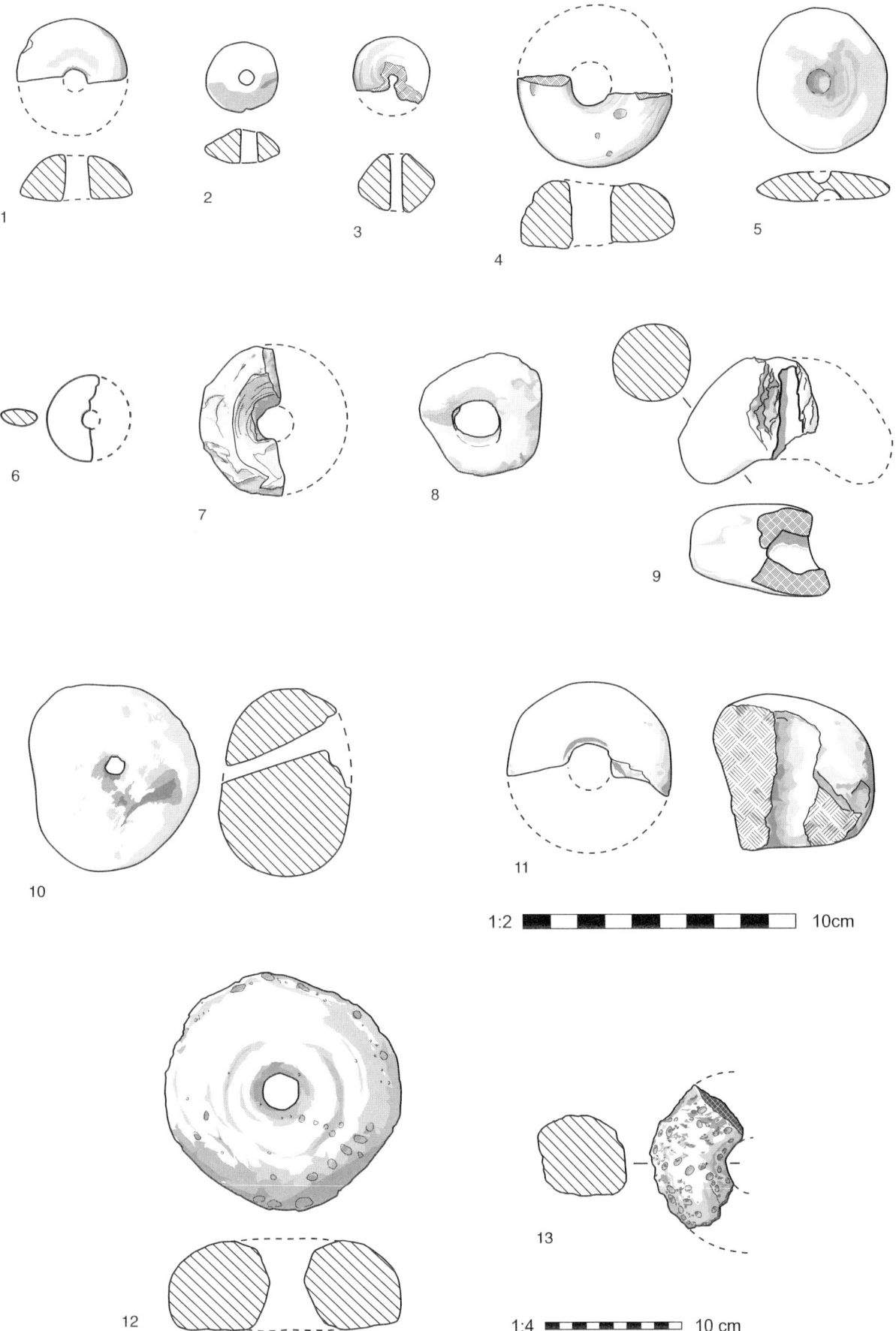

PLATE 78

Plate 79: *Bone Weaving Tools*

	CB number	Area and Phase	Locus & Lot number	Description, dimensions
1	CB 988	A, Phase II	T. 4 D 397	Bone weaving needle, pierced laterally through triangular-sectioned head, tapers to circular-sectioned point, polished at point from use. 15.7 cm long, 0.7 cm max wide, 0.9 cm max thick. One of pair, near to neck of skeleton.
2	CB 991	A, Phase II	T. 4 D 397	Bone weaving needle, pierced vertically through triangular-sectioned head, tapers to circular-sectioned point, polished at point from use. 15.4 cm long, 0.65 max wide, 0.9 cm max thick. One of pair, close to face of skeleton.
3	CB 986	A, Phase II	T. 4 D 397	Plano-convex bone disk, vertically pierced. Shape would seem to indicate spindle whorl, but it is small and light for this purpose, with no traces of wear. A "model" of a spindle whorl? 2.7-2.9 cm diam., 0.8 cm high.
4	CB 2827	G, Phase II/1A	L. 30.1 F 56.1	Bone weaving needle, slightly curved, laterally pierced through triangular-sectioned head, tapers to circular-sectioned point, polished from use. 11.4 cm long, 1.5 cm max wide.
5	CB 2824	A, Phase I	L. 76.5 F 5.6	End of bone awl or needle, circular cross-section, polished from use at tip. 4.5 cm long, 0.5 cm diam.
6	CB 2202	G, Phase II/1	L. 54.1 E 96.2	Tapered tip from bone awl or weaving needle, circular cross-section, polished from use. 2.1 cm long, 0.4 cm wide, 0.25 cm thick.
7	CB 2920	G, Phase II/2	L. 54.10 F 210.1	Point of bone awl or needle, polished from use, circular cross-section. 3.4 cm long, 0.4 cm max. diam.
8	CB 2981	A, Phase II	L. 81.2 F 35.3	Bone tool, flat cross-section, tapered to extremely fine sharp point at one end. 5.1 cm long, 0.9 cm wide, 0.2 cm thick.
9	CB 2866	G, Phase II/2	L. 54.9 F 26.1	Point of bone awl (?) or weaving tool, one side and both edges polished. 4.4 cm long, 1.4 cm wide, 0.35 cm max. thick.

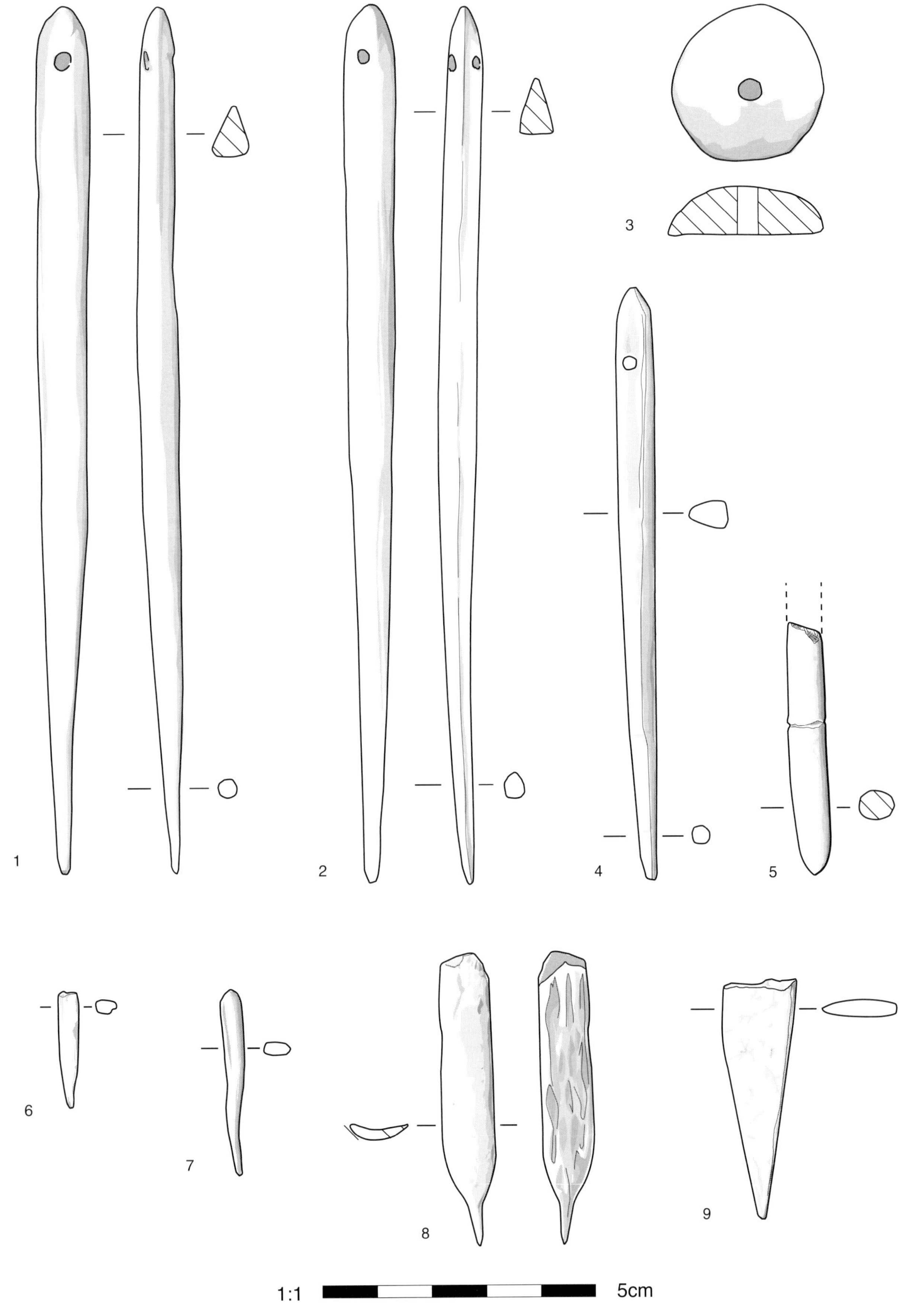

Plate 80: *Seals & sealings*

	CB number	Area and Phase	Locus & Lot number	Description, dimensions
1	CB 1836	A, Phase I	L. 1 near pit L. 39 E 40.3	Baked clay cylinder seal, schematic scene, gouged manufacturing style. Two human figures standing, facing left with right arms raised. Unclear vertical object (stylized altar?) in front of each figure. Reddish-brown core, dark brown surface, no temper. Incised lines at top and bottom. 1.9 cm high, 0.95 cm diam.
2 a & b	CB 2802	A, Phase II	Drain 01-9 F 30.1	Lightly baked clay seal impression, irregular outline. Obverse has single rolling of a south Mesopotamian introduction scene, three standing figures facing right approaching a seated figure on the right. All three figures have their right hands raised, as does the seated figure. Reverse has impressions of three strands of string and a knot. Grey clay (GLEY1 5/N) with lime inclusions. Fingerprints on sides. 3.9 cm long, 2.9 cm wide, 0.8 cm thick.
3	CB 72	A, Phase I	L. 5.1 D 18	Flattened oval lump of fired clay with loosely-woven textile impression on one side, irregular depressions on the other. 4.7 cm long, 3.7 cm wide, 1.8 cm thick
4 a & b	CB 3032	A, Phase II	L. 81.2 F 35.3	Burned clay sealing. Obverse has impressions of two fingerprints, reverse is plain. Triangular cross-section preserves the strongly-angled rim of a jar. 3.8 cm long, 2.0 cm wide, 1.2 cm thick.
5	CB 3765	A, Phase II	L. 81.2 F 35.6	Lightly baked clay sealing. Multiple fingerprints on obverse, reverse has impression of three separate strings and possible reed basket. Light reddish brown 5YR 6/4. 4.7 cm long, 2.9 cm wide, 2.1 cm thick.

PLATE 80

1

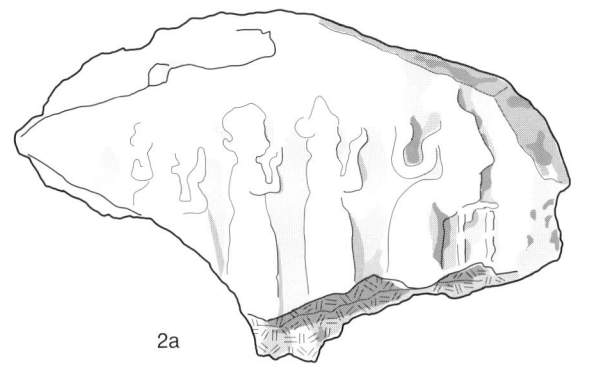

2a

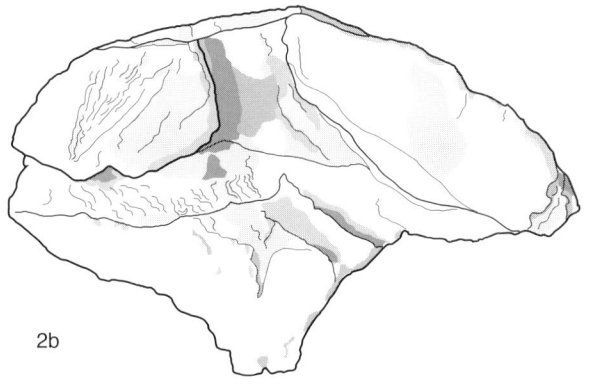

2b

2:1 5 cm

3

4a

4b

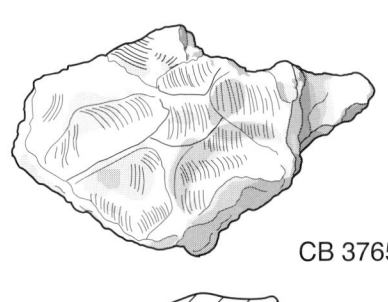

CB 3765

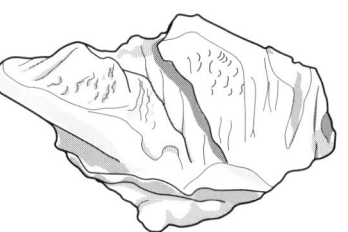

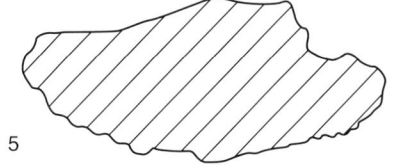

5

1:1 5cm

Plate 81: *Seals and Tallies*

	CB number	Area and Phase	Locus & Lot number	Description, dimensions
1	CB 1806	A, Phase II	L. 41.1 E 39.1	Conical lightly baked (?) clay stamp seal with concentric circles engraved on flat base. Dark brown clay with sparse medium-sized chaff temper. 3.9 cm high, 4.0 cm max diam.
2	CB 2791	A, Phase II	L. 54.5 F 29.1	Conical baked clay stamp seal with concentric circles engraved on slightly convex base. Reddish clay (2.5YR 5/6) with sparse fine chaff temper. 5.4 cm high, 3.8 cm max diam.
3	CB 2211	A, Phase II	L. 16.3 E 216.1	Baked clay disk, approximately 2/3 preserved, incised on one surface–circle near edge and X across the centre, reverse plain. Brown-black clay, sparse fine chaff temper. 5.8 cm diam., 1.7 cm thick.
4	CB 2414	A, Phase II	L. 41.1 E 38.13	Lightly baked clay oblong, tapered at one end, incised central line and multiple lines perpendicular to it on obverse, single possibly random line across reverse. Dark grey-brown clay, sparse chaff temper. 5.5 cm long, 3.1 cm wide, 1.6 cm thick.
5	CB 1879	A, Phase II	L. 56.1 E 8.2	Baked clay disk, plano-convex cross-section, lower surface flat, upper domed surface covered with rows of shallow indentations or punctates in two sizes. Brown-dark grey clay, sand temper. 4.2 cm diam., 1.5 cm high.
6	CB 1829	G, Phase II/1A	L. 3.2 E 63.4	Irregular baked clay object, flat base, rounded upper surface with incised central line and areas of random punctate decoration to each side. Dark brown-black un-tempered clay. 2.7 cm long, 2.9 cm wide, 1.0 cm high.
7	CB 2908	A, Phase II	Drain 01-9 F 30.4	Lightly baked clay oblong with pinched "tail", sub-rectangular cross-section, plain surfaces. 3.6 cm long, 2.0 cm wide, 0.6 cm thick.
8	CB 3767	A, Phase II	L. 81.2 F 35.6	Piece of deliberately squeezed clay, originally square/rectangular. Has the morphology of a tablet, but no signs are visible on either side. Erased and squashed? Light reddish brown, 5YR 6/4. 3.9 cm long, 3.7 cm wide, 2.1 cm thick.

PLATE 81

1:1　5cm

Plate 82: *Sealings, Tokens and Seal*

	CB number	Area and Phase	Locus & Lot number	Description, dimensions
1	CB 40	A, Surface	L. 1.3 D 10	Approximately half of an un-baked un-tempered clay sealing for small rectangular container, roughly rectangular in both plan and cross-section. Laterally-pierced by small stick, longitudinal string holes. Dark grey 10YR 5/2. 2.9 cm long, 3.5 cm wide, 2.0 cm thick. No seal impression.
2	CB 3766	A, Phase II	L. 81.2 F 35.6	Lightly baked clay sealing, just over half preserved, disk shaped, convex obverse, pressed over circular, slightly convex object. Dark grey GLEY1 4/N. 2.9 cm diam., 1.1 cm thick.
3	CB 1779	A, Phase II	00-4 E 3.1	Brown veined haematite date-shaped weight, one end chipped. 2.56 cm long, 0.96 cm max diam.
4	CB 2918	G, Phase II/2	L. 54.10 F 210.1	Conical baked clay token or "game piece", pierced laterally through top. Brownish-grey clay, no visible temper. 3.0 cm high, 2.3 cm max. diam.
5	CB 2944	G, Phase II/2	L 28.1 F 77.5	Squat conical baked clay token or "game piece", pierced vertically through top. C 3.2 cm diam., 2.3 cm high.
6	CB 2945	G, Phase II/2	L. 28.1 F 77.5	Conical baked clay token or "game piece", concave sides. 1.9 cm high, ca. 1.9 cm max. diam.
7	CB 2058	G, Phase II/1	L. 10.1 E 73.4	Unbaked or lightly baked clay cylinder with slightly concave sides, fingerprints on surface from manufacture, no use wear visible. Dark brown un-tempered clay. 3.2 cm high, 2.3 cm max diam.
8	CB 2201	G, Phase II/2	L. 54.4 E 108.1	Baked clay token, flattened circular base, tapering towards broken top. Pale brown un-tempered clay. 1.4 cm high, 2.0-2.1 cm diam.
9	CB 1941	G, Phase II/1	L. 55.1 E 97.1	Worked bone object, possible pendant or token, spherical body, narrow "neck" and domed disk top. 1.5 cm high, 1.05 cm max diam.
10	CB 2056	G, Phase II/1	L. 55.1 E 97.1	Lightly baked clay sphere, possible 'token'. Dark brown clay, sparse fine chaff temper. 1.5-1.7 cm diam.
11	CB 2057	G, Phase II/1	L. 54.1 E 96.1	Lightly baked clay sphere, possible 'token'. Dark buff clay, sparse fine sand temper. 1.5-1.7 cm diam.
12	CB 2059	G, Phase II/1	L. 55.1 E 97.1	Lightly baked clay sphere, possible 'token'. Dark brown clay, sparse fine sand temper, slightly chipped. 2.2 cm diam.
13	CB 1828	G, Phase II/1	L. 51.1 E 91.2	Approximately one-half of square white stone stamp seal, laterally pierced. Geometric design of excised X and triangles. Probably Late Chalcolithic. 2.25 cm long, 1.4 cm wide, 0.85 cm thick.

PLATE 82

Plate 83: *Metal Objects*

	CB number	Area and Phase	Locus and Lot	Description, dimensions
1	CB 751	A, Phase II	L. 29.1 D 349	Lead ingot, circular cross-section, straight shaft tapered at one end to thin wire formed into a loop, end wrapped around shaft. Part of loop broken, rodent tooth damage over entire length. 9.1 cm long, 0.65 max diam.
2	CB 2203	A, Phase III	L. 44.2 E 213.1	Fragmentary and corroded lead ingot, circular cross section, coiled and wrapped at end, as CB 751. C 4.5 cm long, 0.6 cm diam.
3	CB 2597	A, Phase II	L. 38.1 E 224.1	Short bent segment of fine lead wire, circular cross-section. C 2.2 cm total length, 0.1 cm diam. wire.
4	CB 2982	A, Phase II	L. 81.2 F 35.3	Two segments of lead wire, circular cross-section. 6.1 cm total length, 0.2 cm wire diam.
5	CB 1880	G, Phase II/1	L. 2.2 E 68.1	Partial loop of thick lead wire, circular cross-section. 2.2 cm long, 1.7 cm wide, wire diam 0.4 cm.
6	CB 2083	G, Phase II/1	T. 13 E 82.1	Lead ingot, straight shaft, circular cross-section, warped and corroded, head disintegrated. 6.5 cm long, 0.6 cm diam shaft
7	CB 2196	G, Phase II/1	L. 9.2 E 77.1	Lead ingot, plain head, circular cross-section, probably originally straight, now bent nearly to a right angle. Originally 10.5 cm long, 0.6 cm max diam.
8	CB 2872	G, Phase II/1	L. 32.2 F 59.3	Fragment of lead wire, slightly bent, tapering, oval cross-section. 3.0 cm long, 0.3 cm max. diam.
9	CB 2200	G, Phase II/2	L. 54.4 E 108.1	Lead ingot, plain head, circular cross-section, looped head, currently bent and broken, originally straight. Originally ca. 13 cm long, 0.6 cm max diam.
10	CB 2424	G, Phase II/2	L. 9.6 E 241.2	Lead ingot, circular cross-section, straight shaft tapered at one end to thin wire formed into a loop, with end wrapped around stem 1.5 times. 8.1 cm long, 0.45 cm max. diam.
11	CB 2622	G, Phase II/2	L. 4.7 E 76.3	Curved segment of fine lead wire, circular cross-section. C 2.4 cm total length, 0.15 cm diam. wire.
12	CB 4154	G, Phase IV	L. 74.1 F 228.2	Lead ingot, circular cross-section, originally straight, now bent to an S-curve, one end drawn out into thin wire and wrapped in a knot around shaft, other end blunt. 8.2 cm long, 0.5 cm diam.
13	CB 992	A, Phase II	T. 4 D 397	Silver pin, circular cross-section, pierced near one end, badly corroded, possibly ca. one-half missing. 5.0 cm long, 0.5 cm diam. Found in front of face of skeleton.
14	CB 2084	G, Phase II/1	T. 13 E 82.1	Bronze tweezers (?), folded-over flat strip of metal, rectangular cross-section. 4.0 cm long, 1.1 cm max wide, 0.3 cm thick
15	CB 2085	G, Phase II/1	T. 13 E 82.1	Two-part clasp or ornament, silver. One piece of coiled wire (a), one flattened metal strip with rounded ends, raised boss at the centre of each end (b). (a) 1.65 cm long, 0.7 cm wide, 0.2 cm thick. (b) 3.5 cm long, 1.0 cm wide, 0.15 cm thick.
16	CB 2623	G, Phase II/2	L. 62.2 E 116.1	Very corroded flat irregular bronze object, possible pendant. 2.5 cm high, 2.3 cm wide, 0.5 cm thick.

PLATE 83

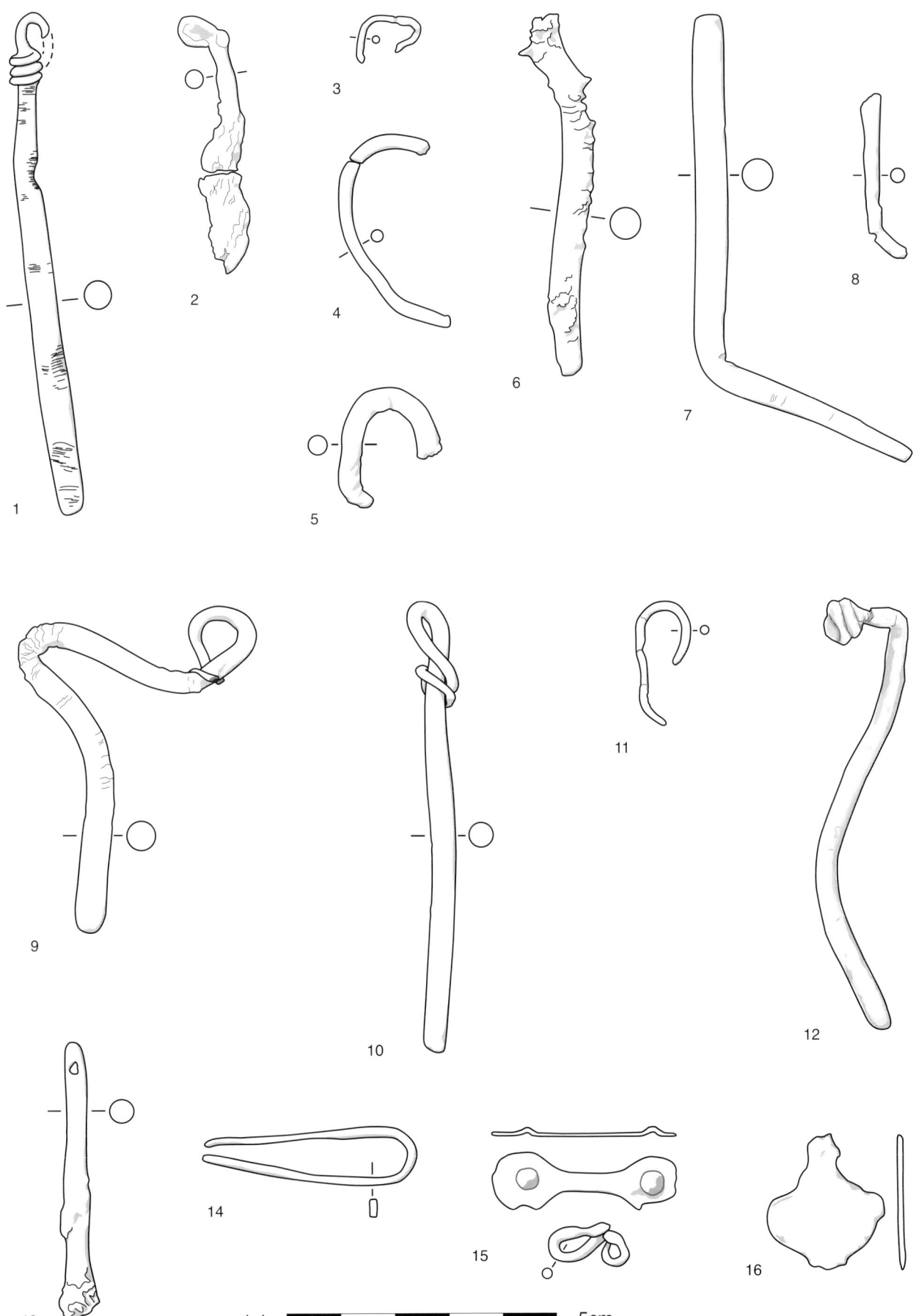

Plate 84: *Metal Objects*

	CB number	Area and Phase	Locus and Lot	Description, dimensions
1	CB 907	A, Phase IA	L. 32.1 D 367	Bronze pin, straight shaft, circular cross-section, possibly widened and flattened at ends, complete but badly corroded. 9.8 cm long, 0.7 cm max diam, 0.4 cm shaft diam.
2	CB 2970	A, Phase I	L. 78.1 F 7.1	Bronze pin, short tang, square-sectioned tang and shaft, incised herringbone lines near top of shaft. 13.4 cm long, 0.5 cm max. wide.
3	CB 3047	A, Phase I	01-1 F 9.1	Point of bronze pin or needle, circular cross-section, corroded. 1.8 cm long, 0.2 max. diam.
4	CB 2416	A, Phase II	L. 30.1 E 217.1	Flattened head of bronze pin, circular cross-section shaft, corroded and broken. 2.2 cm long, 1.0 cm max diam.
5	CB 2980	A, Phase II	L. 81.2 F 35.3	Two bronze pin fragments, straight segments, one with square cross-section, one circular. 3.1 cm long, 0.4 cm wide; 2.9 cm long, 0.4 cm diam.
6	CB 2423	A, Phase III	L. 61.7 E 216.1	Shaft of straight bronze pin, circular cross-section, head missing (?). 7.6 cm long, 0.25 cm diam.
7	CB 2198	G, Phase II/1A	L. 59.2 E 107.1	Bronze pin, straight, plain head, circular cross-section, corroded. 8.7 cm long, 0.5 cm max diam.
8	CB 2080	G, Phase II/1	T. 13 E 82.1	Bronze cloak pin, spherical fluted head, straight shaft with circular cross-section, incised lines around shaft just below head, lateral hole mid-shaft, traces of string (brown organic material) wrapped around tapered end. 13.1 cm long, 1.3 cm diam head
9	CB 2081	G, Phase II/1	T. 13 E 82.1	Bronze pin, straight shaft, flattened head, square-sectioned shaft tapering to circular section. 12.2 cm long, 0.8 cm wide.
10	CB 2199	G, Phase II/2	L. 54.4 E 108.1	Segment of bronze pin, square cross-section. 3.9 cm long, 0.75 cm wide, 0.7 cm thick.
11	CB 2205	G, Phase II/2	L. 54.3 E 105.1	Corroded tip of bronze pin, circular cross-section. 3.0 cm long, 0.6 cm max diam.
12	CB 2927	A, Phase I	L. 76.5 F 5.6	Segment of bronze blade, oval cross-section, corroded and warped. 4.7 cm long, 2.3 cm wide, 0.35 cm max. thick. Possibly part of same object as CB 2928.
13	CB 2928	A, Phase I	L. 76.5 F 5.6	Long tang and one shoulder of possible knife, bronze, corroded. 5.1 cm long, 3.2 cm wide. Possibly part of same object as CB 2927.
14	CB 3098	G, Phase II/2	01-4, 01-5 F 85.1	Short segment of bronze, square cross-section, corroded. 2.3 cm long, 1 cm wide, 1 cm thick.

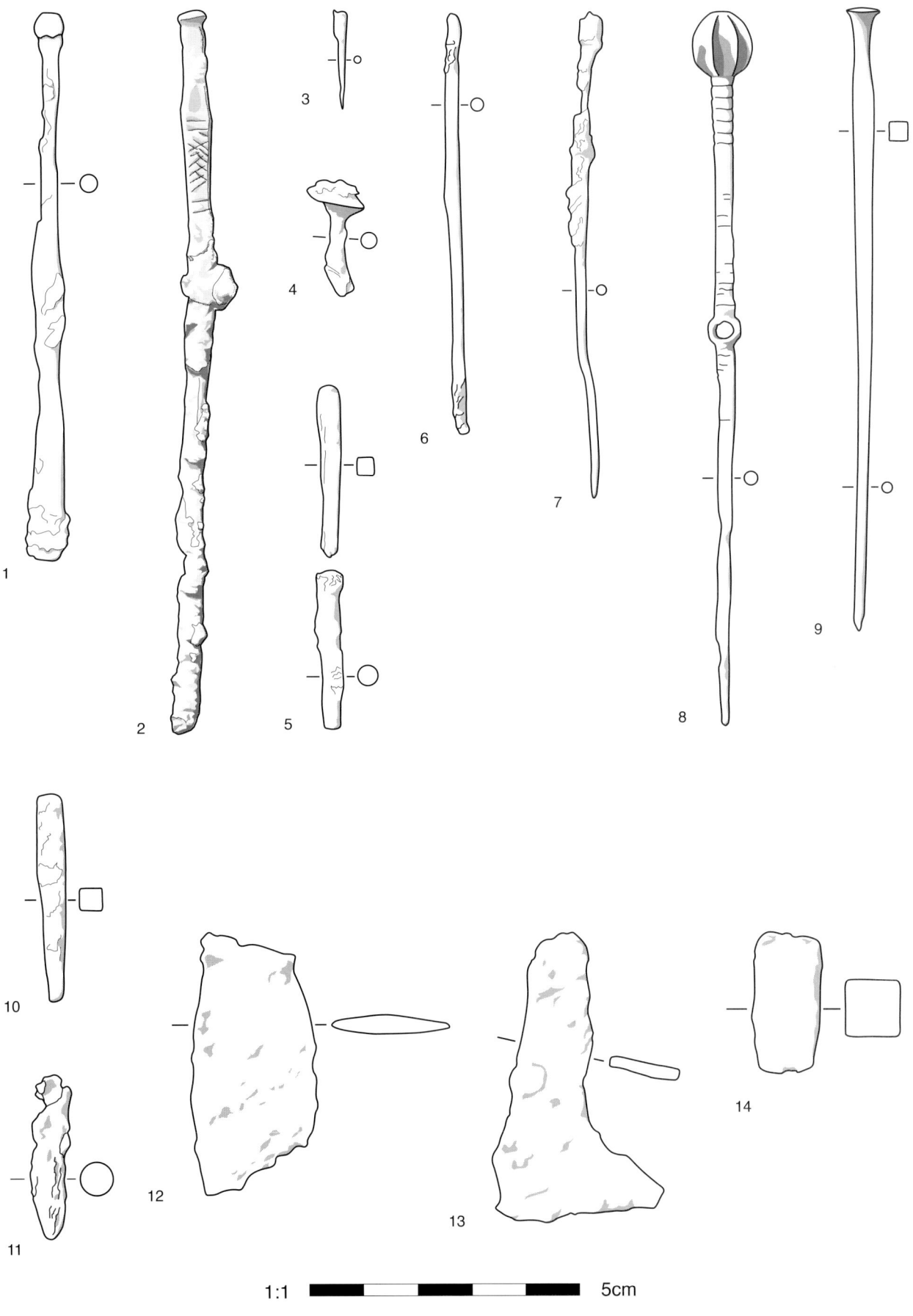

PLATE 84

Plate 85: *Metal Objects*

	CB number	Area and Phase	Locus and Lot	Description, dimensions
1	CB 2788	A, Phase IA	L. 67.8 F 26.1	Ring of bronze wire, single loop, ends slightly overlapping, circular cross-section. Corroded. C 2 cm diam., 0.35 cm diam wire.
2	CB 3104	A, Phase I	T. 41 F 21.1	Badly corroded and broken small, bronze bracelet in four fragments, single loop of wire with ends not quite overlapping, circular cross-section. Possibly slightly thicker at centre. C 3.5 cm diam., 0.3 cm wire diam.
3	CB 3105	A, Phase I	T. 41 F 21.1	Corroded bronze wire loop, very small bracelet or large ring, ends overlapping (probably post-deposition), circular cross-section. 3.4 cm long, 2.4 cm wide, 0.3 cm wire diam.
4	CB 3106	A, Phase I	T. 41 F 21.1	Corroded and broken bronze bracelet in two fragments, single loop with ends slightly overlapping, circular cross-section. C 4.0 cm diam., 0.3 cm wire diam.
5	CB 725	A, Phase II	L. 14.1 D 333	Small corroded bronze ring, single loop of wire, ends not quite closed, circular cross-section. 1.6 cm approximate diam, 0.4 cm wire diam.
6	CB 2204	A, Phase II	00-34 E 214.1	Fragmentary and corroded bronze ring, single loop, ends not quite closed, circular cross-section. C 1.8 cm diam, 0.5 cm thick.
7	CB 1831	A, Phase III	L. 53.1 E 5.3	Fragment of curved bronze wire, circular cross-section, large finger ring or small bracelet. 2.3 cm long, 0.4 cm max diam.
8	CB 2082	G, Phase II/1	T. 13 E 82.1	Bronze finger ring, thin strip of flattened metal, single loop, fragmentary and corroded. C 2.0 cm diam, 0.6 cm wide.
9	CB 3097	G, Phase II/2	L. 39.1 F 79.1	Fragment of bronze wire, circular cross-section, corroded. Total length c 6 cm., 0.2 cm diam. wire.
10	CB 985	A, Phase II	T. 4 D 397	Conical bronze beer strainer with reed straw partially preserved, found inside jar CB 990. Badly corroded. Metal cone 6.4 cm high, 7.0 cm high with preserved section of reed, 1.5-1.6 max diam.
11	CB 2066	G, Phase II/1	T. 11 E 79.1	Conical bronze beer strainer with reed straw partially preserved, found inside jar CB 2000. Badly corroded, fibrous material corroded to exterior. Metal cone 7.3 cm high, 10.0 cm high with preserved section of reed, 1.3 max diam.
12	CB 2092	G, Phase II/1	T. 13 E 82.1	Conical bronze beer strainer with reed straw partially preserved, found inside jar CB 2076. Badly corroded, fibrous material corroded to exterior. 6.7 cm high, 1.5 max diam.
13	CB 3090	G, Phase II/2	T. 39 F 71.1	Conical bronze beer strainer for reed straw, corroded, traces of columns of perforations. Found inside jar CB 3093. 7.2 cm high, 1.3 max diam.
14	CB 2626	G, Phase II/1	L. 2.2 E 252.2	Conical bronze beer strainer for reed straw, corroded, two vertical columns of perforations visible. 8.8 cm high, 1.5 max diam.
15	CB 4215	G, Phase III	L. 79.1 F 467.1	Hollow bronze cone made from single sheet of metal, similar in shape to the bronze beer strainers but longer and lacking any indication of perforations. Strainer or possible spear point? 12.1 cm long, 1.9 cm max. diam.

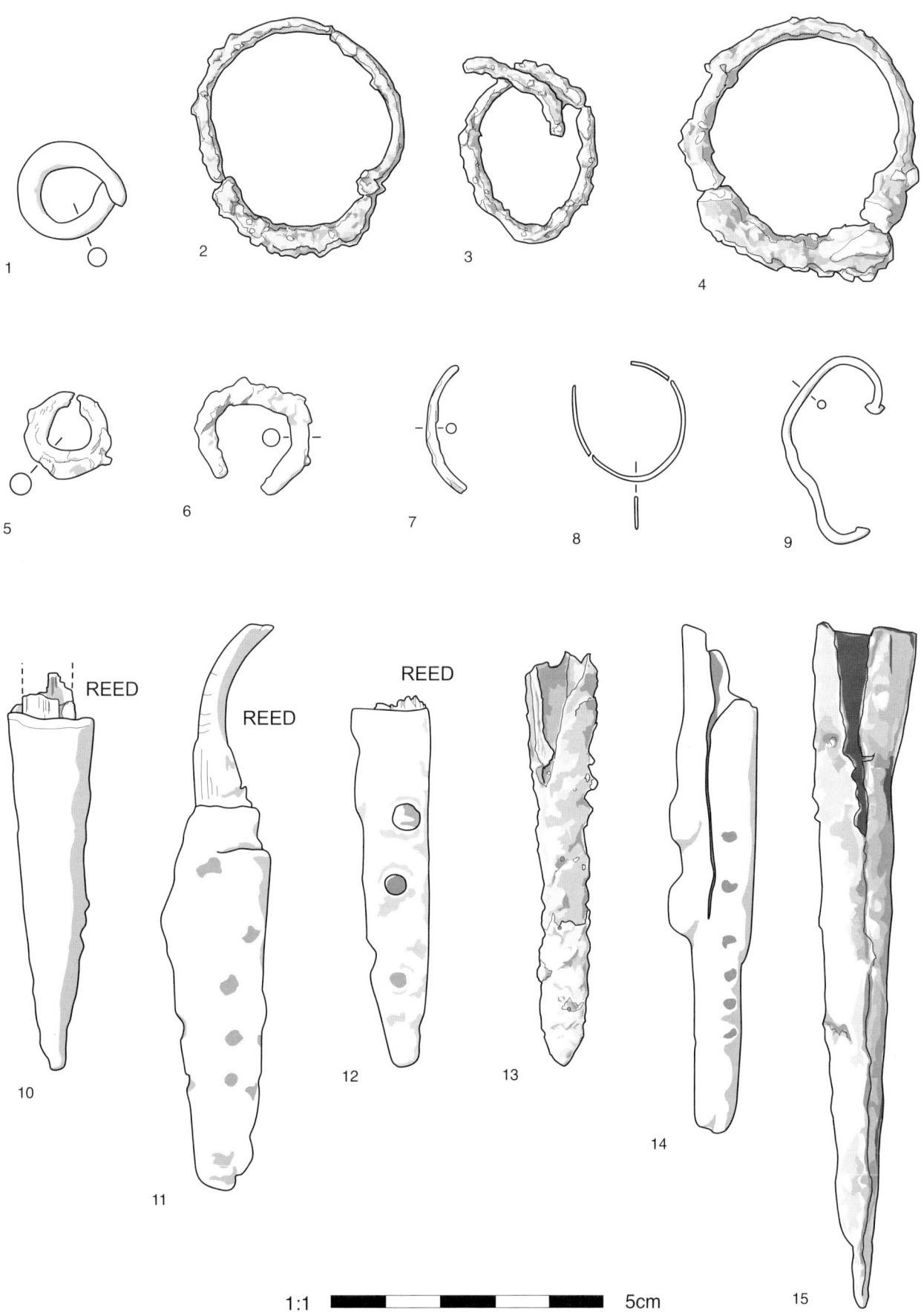

PLATE 85

Plate 86: *Beads*

	CB no.	Area & Phase	Locus & Lot	Description, dimensions
1	CB 4	A, S	L. 1.1 D 1	Cylindrical bead, dark blue stone or frit, surface abraded. 2.0 cm long, 1.0 cm diam.
2	CB 796	A IA	L. 32.1 D 364	Cylindrical bead, fine-grained grey limestone, one end chipped. 2.6 cm long, 1.5 cm diam.
3	CB 1802	A, S	L. 1.1 E 5.1	Pale blue faience bead, faded to white, fluted ring. 1.17 cm diam., 0.98 cm thick.
4	CB 2422	A IA	L. 67.1 E 29.4	One-half ring-shaped clear rock crystal bead. 0.8 cm diam., 0.45 cm thick.
5	CB 1877	A I	L. 58.1 E 13.1	Cylindrical bead, light blue frit, one end broken. 1.4 cm long, 0.8 cm diam.
6	CB 3107	A I	T. 41 F 21.1	Two grey faience hemispherical beads. 0.6 and 0.5 cm diam., 0.5 cm thick.
7	CB 772	A II	L. 29.1 D 357	Barrel-shaped bead, fine-grained white stone. 0.9 cm long, 0.8 cm max diam.
8	CB 1805	A II	L. 54.1 E 7.1	Pendant, curved segment of polished grey marble, triangle cross-section, notches on base/ inner curve, pierced–and broken–at slightly wider end. 3.8 cm long, 0.65 max wide.
9	CB 2420	A II	L. 61.1 E 274.1	Ring-shaped bead, dark green-grey stone, possibly steatite. 0.6 cm diam., 0.3 cm thick.
10	CB 2421	A II	L. 52.2 E 185.2	Slightly irregular bi-conoid bead. Dark brown baked clay. 1.5 cm long, 1.0 cm diam.
11	CB 2540	A II	L. 62.2 E 206.4	Slightly irregular disk-shaped bead, white crystalline stone. 0.8-0.9 cm diam., 0.2 cm thick.
12	CB 2593	A II	L. 49.1 E 227.2	Ring-shaped translucent rock crystal bead. 0.85 cm diam., 0.25 cm thick.
13	CB 2803	A II	01-9 F 30.1	Fragment of worked translucent rock crystal, part of disk or inlay, broken at two ends, bevelled and polished on both sides. 1.3 cm long max., 1.0 cm. wide.
14	CB 2804	A II	L. 77.1 F 31.1	One-half of worked flat shell (mother of pearl) ring. 2.3 cm diam., 0.3 cm max. thick.
15	CB 2959	A II	01-15 F 36.1	Irregular rounded fragment of mother-of-pearl, inlay. 1.4 cm long, 1.1 cm wide, 0.3 cm thick.
16	CB 2960	A II	01-15 F 36.1	Two-thirds of baked clay bi-conical bead. 1.5 cm long, 0.9 cm max. diam.
17	CB 2288	A III	L. 61.4 E 198.2	Cylindrical banded agate bead, translucent white and pale brown, hole off-centre. 1.6 cm long, 0.85 cm max. diam.
18	CB 1825	G, S	L. 1.1 E 64.1	Rounded rectangular bead, yellow-green glass. 0.75 cm long, 0.7 cm wide, 0.65 cm thick.
19	CB 2616	G, S	L. 60.1 E 104.1	Ring-shaped faience or frit bead, grey-blue-white. 0.8 cm diam., 0.6 cm thick.
20	CB 2997	G, S	L. 43.1 F 66.1	Triangular stone inlay or ornament, oval cross-section. 1.2 cm long, 1.0 cm wide, 0.5 cm thick.
21	CB 2197	G II/1A	L. 59.2 E 107.1	One-half of ring-shaped clear rock crystal bead, drilled from both sides. 0.95 cm diam, 0.65 cm thick.
22	CB 1939	G II/1	L. 4.3 E 65.1	Cylindrical bead, white and grey fine-grained marble, one end broken. 0.95 cm long, 0.4 cm diam.
23	CB 2049	G II/1	L. 55 E 97.3	Olive shell (*Olividae*), whole but worn and abraded, pierced through top end as a pendant. 3.6 cm long, 2.2 cm diam.
24	CB 2618	G II/1	L. 63.1 E 111.2	Ring-shaped dark grey stone bead, off-centre piercing. 0.75 cm diam., 0.35 cm thick.

25	CB 1824	G II/2	L. 51.2 E 91.1	Plano-convex bead, pierced vertically and laterally, four incised radial lines on base, dark grey stone. Very worn, loop created by lateral piercing broken away. 0.9 cm diam., 0.5 cm thick.
26	CB 2541	G II/2	L. 62.1 E 115.1	Cylindrical bead, chalky white material, possibly frit. 1.9 cm long, 0.9 cm diam.
27	CB 2617	G II/2	L. 16.1 E 243.3	Disk-shaped shell bead. 0.8 cm diam., 0.15 cm thick.
28	CB 2619	G II/2	L. 4.6 E 84.2	Ring-shaped black stone bead. 1.0 cm diam., 0.35 cm max. thick.
29	CB 2627	G II/2	L. 19.1 E 253.2	Date-shaped brown haematite bead. 1.75 cm long, 0.8 cm diam.
30	CB 2628	G II/2	L. 4.8 E 246.1	Disk-shaped translucent rock crystal bead, roughly chipped edges. 0.8 cm diam., 0.25 cm thick.
31	CB 2917	G II/2	L. 54.10 F 210.1	Shell bead or pendant, possibly natural perforation, polished around edges of hole from string wear. White and brown stripes, Gastropod. 1.4 cm long, 1.0 cm wide, 0.9 cm thick.
32	CB 2973	G II/2	L. 54.10 F 210.2	Ball-shaped carnelian bead. 0.55 cm diam.
33	CB 3877	G II/2	L. 54.10 F 210.6	Ring-shaped carnelian bead. 0.5 cm diam., 0.2 cm thick.
34	CB 3780	G III	L. 37.3 F 213.4	Approximately one-third of ring-shaped carnelian bead. C 0.75 cm diam., 0.7 cm thick.
35	CB 3879	G III	L. 70.1 F 220.1	Bi-conical baked clay bead, dark brown. 1.3 cm long, 1.0 cm max. diam.
36	CB 3955	G III	L. 77.1 F 227.1	Bi-conical baked clay bead, slightly chipped at ends, dark grey, 10YR 4/1. 2.1 cm long, 1.3 cm max. diam.

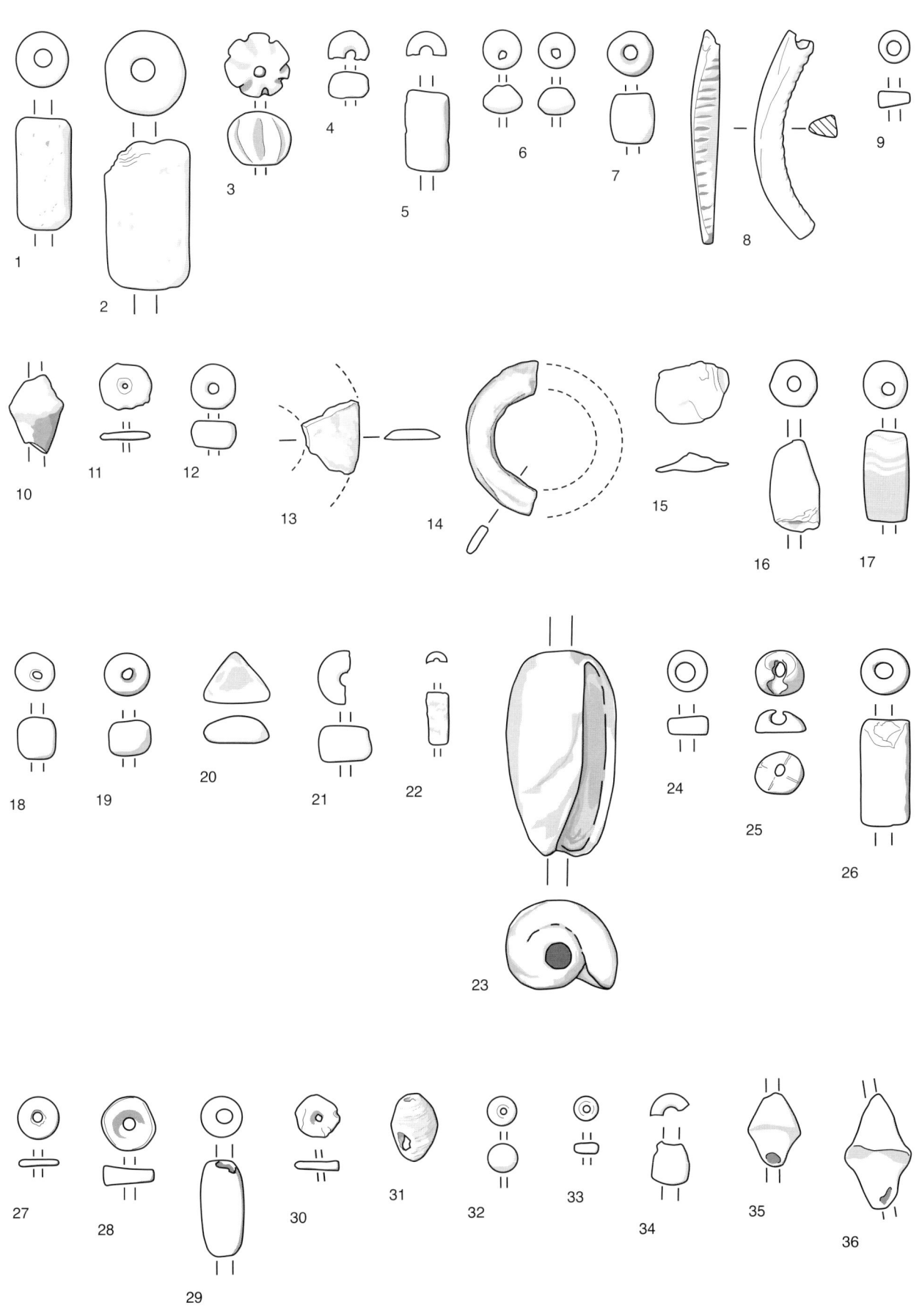

PLATE 86

Plate 87: *Beads and Ornaments*

	CB number	Area and Phase	Locus and Lot	Description, dimensions
1	CB 2086	G, Phase II/1	T. 13 E 82.1	Short string of beads from neck of skeleton. a) Ring-shaped black stone bead, 1.35 cm diam, 0.4 cm thick b) Cylindrical blue-tan frit bead, 1.55 cm long, 0.4 cm diam. c) Cylindrical white faience bead, 1.3 cm long, 0.8 cm diam. d) Rounded rectangular black stone bead, incised groove on one side, worn, 2.3 cm long, 1.9 cm wide Not illustrated) Fragment of cowrie shell pendant, 1.0 cm long, 1.0 cm max diam.
2	CB 2978	G, Phase II/1	T. 33 F 63.1	String of 164 beads, 15 different types, near neck of skeleton. a) 1 slightly irregular oval disk, banded grey and white stone, pierced at one end, 2.0 cm long, 1.5 cm wide, 0.45 cm thick. b) 1 grey faience lion-shaped bead, longitudinally pierced, 1.4 cm long, 0.9 cm high, 0.5 cm thick. c) 1 bi-conical, dark red banded agate, 1.6 cm long, 0.7 cm max. diam. d) 1 cylindrical rock crystal, 1.3 cm long, 0.7 cm diam. e) 1 triangular white stone, notched near base, incised central and oblique lines, pierced laterally through tip, 1.3 cm long, 1.2 cm wide, 0.6 cm thick. f) 1 hemispherical grey faience, 0.8 cm diam., 0.5 cm thick. g) 1 cylinder with hub at each end, grey faience, 1.6 cm long, 0.7 cm diam. (h) 1 cylinder, rounded ends, grey stone, 1.7 cm long, 0.8 cm diam. i) 1 bi-conical pale green faience, 1.1 cm long, 0.6 cm max. diam. j) 1 cylinder, white faience, 0.7 cm long, 0.5 cm diam. (k) 1 flattened trapezoid, pale green faience, 1.5 cm long, 1.25 cm wide, 0.35 cm thick l) 2 ring-shaped white stone, 0.7 cm diam., 0.35 cm thick. m) 5 spherical grey-white faience, 0.7 cm diam., 0.4 cm thick. n) 14 small Gastropod or Cowrie shells o) 132 ring-shaped white faience, 0.25 cm diam., 0.15 cm thick.
3	CB 1767	A, Phase IA	T. 7 E 2.1	Bronze bracelet, single loop with ends not quite meeting, oval cross-section. C 4.5 cm diam (irregular), 0.95 cm max thick.
4	CB 76	A, Surface	L. 1.1 D 30	Bronze Roman coin, abraded and corroded. a) Obv: female head facing right, inscription. b) Rev: Central standard flanked by two standing figures holding spears or standards, inscriptions.

PLATE 87

1 a) b) c) d)

2 a) b) c) d) e) f) g) h) i) j) k) l) m) n) o)

1:1 5cm

3

1:1 5cm

4

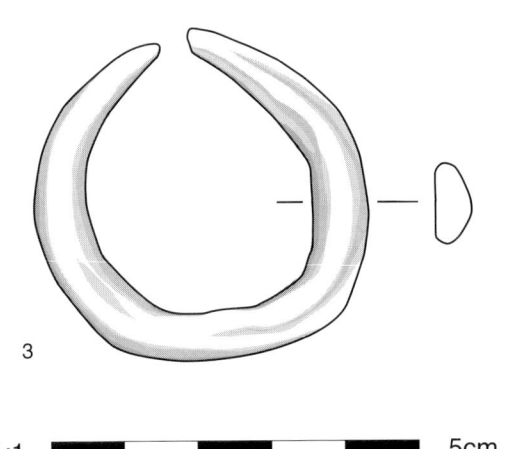

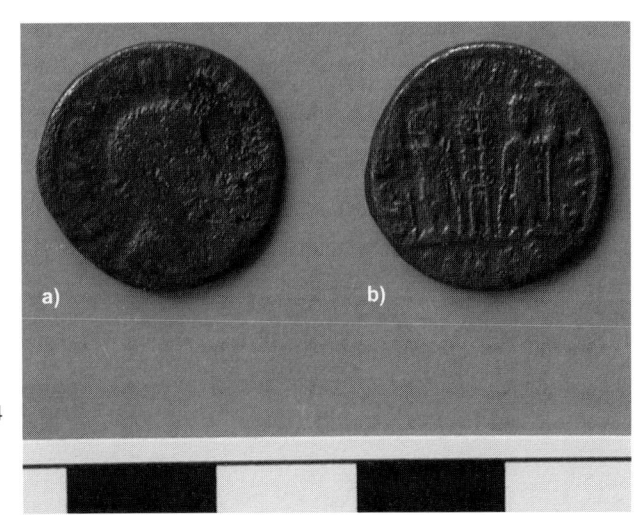

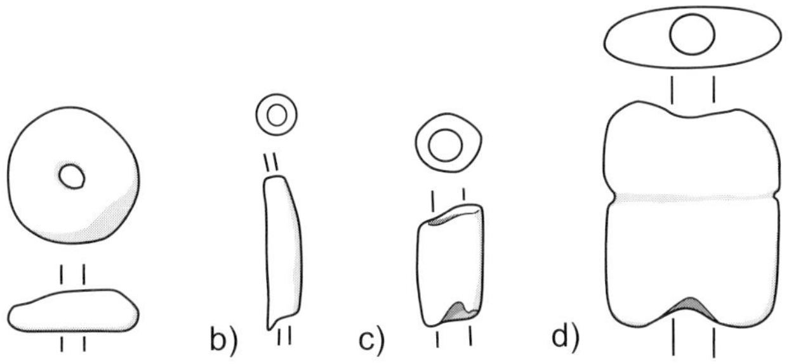

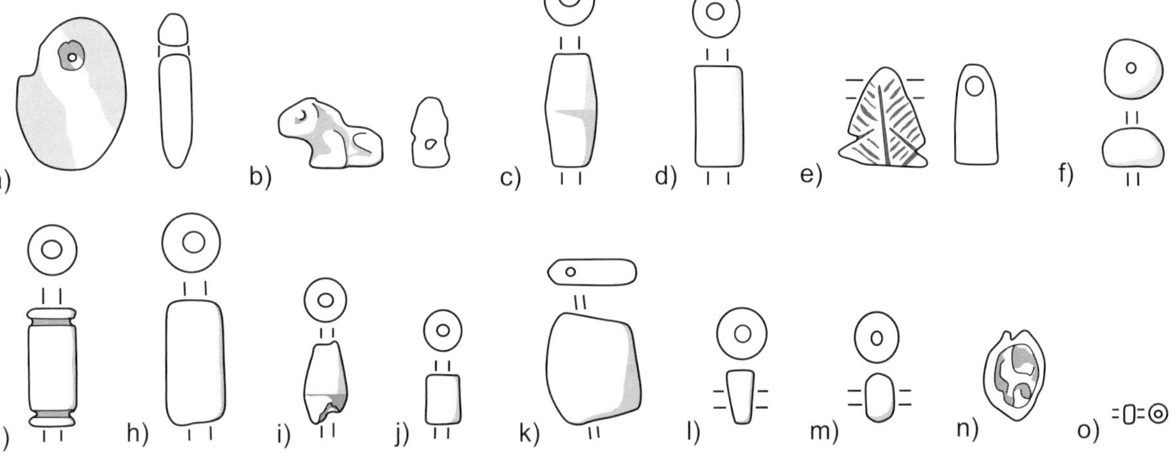

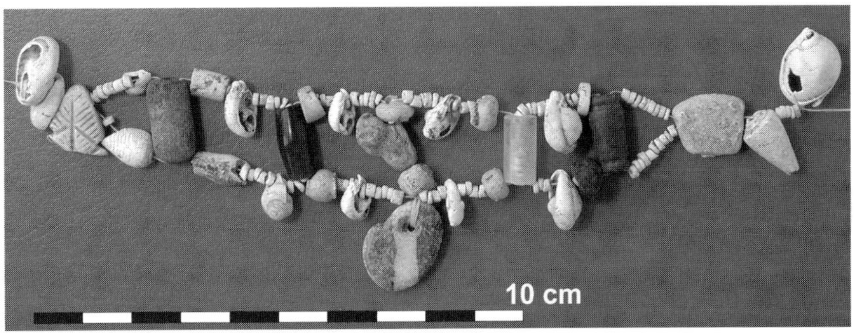

Plate 88: *Miscellaneous objects*

	CB number	Area and Phase	Locus and Lot	Description, dimensions
1	CB 2817	A, Phase I	L. 74.1 F 3.2	Vitrified clay squat cylinder, greenish-grey surface (GLEY1 3/1), black core, crack in one end, slag blob on exterior, one edge chipped. 2.4 cm high, 2.3 cm diam.
2	CB 987	A, Phase II	L. 37.1, T.4 burial pit D 397	Unbaked clay "firedog" or leg of tripod stand, cylindrical cross-section with flared foot. Top broken; deep finger impression in side. Buff clay (7.5YR 6/4), sparse medium chaff and large white grit temper. 6.9 cm high, 6.4 cm max diam.
3	CB 4218	G, Phase III	L. 37.5 F 226.4	Central section of small ceramic stand, part of upper bowl on short neck, part of base, rectangular cross-section, laterally pierced, fugitive black paint stripes around bowl and neck and vertically on base. Light grey clay, 2.5Y 7/2, sparse chaff temper. 7.1 cm high, 5.2 cm wide, 2.6 cm thick, cup diam. ca. 6 cm.
4	CB 3099	G, Phase II/2	L. 54.10 F 210.3	Unbaked clay ovoid 'sling bullet". Brown clay, no visible temper. 4.3 cm long, 2.3 cm max. diam.
5	CB 4219	G, Phase III	L. 37.5 F 226.4	Fragment of triangular unbaked clay "sling bullet". Brown clay, 7.5YR 4/2, no visible temper. 4.2 cm long, 2.8 cm wide, 2.1 cm thick.
6	CB 2209	G, Phase II/1	L. 10.2 E 73.6	Unbaked clay object, handmade, roughly rectangular, trough-like central depression, side and one corner missing, low foot at each corner. No traces of residue or use-wear. Grey core, brown surface, no visible temper. 7.3 cm long, 3.5 cm wide, 2.6 cm high.
7	CB 4192	G, Phase II/2	L. 34.5 F 454.3	Unbaked clay "bottle stopper", tapering cylinder with short "handle", with indentations for a finger-hold. Random fingernail impressions on sides of cylinder, from manufacture (?). Reddish yellow clay, 7.5 YR 7/6, no visible temper. 5.2 cm high, 3.4 cm max diam.
8	CB 3947	G, Phase II/1	L. 33.4 F 458.1	Baked clay model brick, rectangular in plan and cross-section, shallow groove in upper surface, one end missing. Pale brown-light yellowish brown clay, 10YR 6.3-4, common chaff temper. 8.4 cm long, 7.4 cm wide, 3.2 cm thick.
9	CB 34	A, Phase I	L.3.1 D 14	Rectangular basalt door-socket with deep, regular circular depression. One end broken. 17 cm long, 13 cm wide, 10 cm high
10	CB 42	A, Phase I	L. 3.1 D 15	Approximately 1/4 of large limestone door-socket or ring, tall plano-convex cross-section. 27 cm long, max 11.2 cm wide, 7.5 cm th
11	CB 2046	A, Phase II	L. 52.2 E 6.5	Approximately one-half of roughly square slab of basalt, centrally pierced from both sides. Door-socket or loom weight. 12.5 cm long, 7.0 cm wide, 4.0 cm thick.

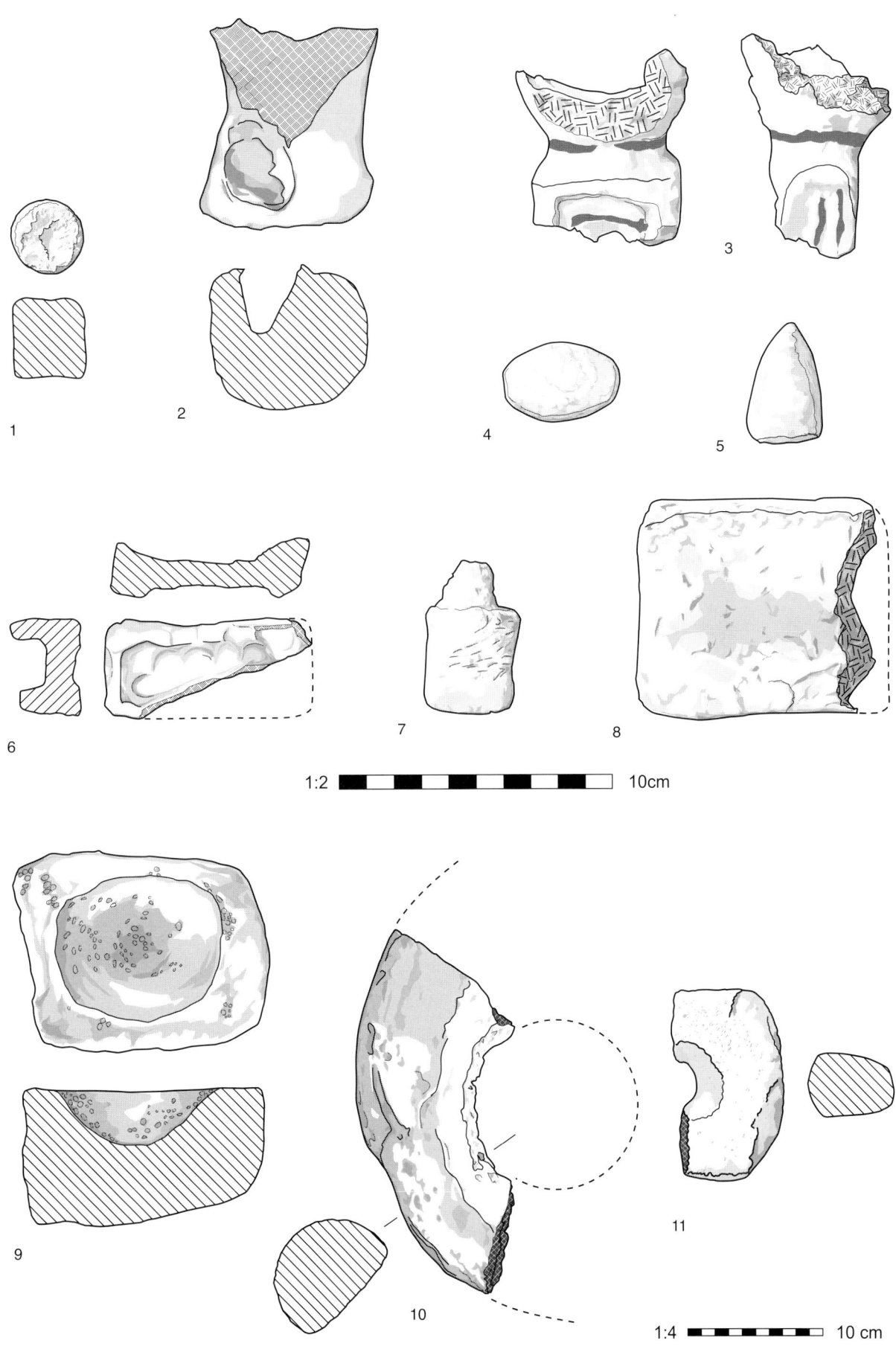

PLATE 88

Summary

Chapter 1 introduces Chagar Bazar, a northern Mesopotamian (NE Syria) site with a long and complex biography. This biography begins in the 6th millennium BC, and its final chapters include the 1930s excavations conducted by Sir Max Mallowan and the recent excavations (since 1999) by the British School of Archaeology in Iraq, the University of Liège, and the Syrian Directorate General of Antiquities & Museums. This study incorporates settlement archaeology and ideas of "place" in exploring the settlement and its internal and external landscapes. We have taken a contextual approach, isolating and integrating different aspects of the settlement's material culture, such as architecture, pottery and objects. Our primary focus is the settlement in the early 2nd millennium BC (Old Babylonian Period, post-Samsi-Addu), its final ancient occupation. The archive recovered by Mallowan in Area TD at Chagar Bazar belongs to the reign of Samsi-Addu, but post-Samsi-Addu political history is well known from archives at Tell Leilan and Mari.

Chapter 2 describes the architecture in Area A, which lies on a well-defined spur of the mound that extends northeast of the site's core and towards the Wadi Khanzir. The centre of this spur is dominated by a large community building, which we propose was the locus of administration for the settlement in the post-Samsi-Addu era. This building has a similar plan to that seen in some contemporary houses, but its scale and construction are far grander. The rooms were relatively clean, and it is distinguished by a baked-brick and cobble-paved courtyard and a large assembly room. It is surrounded by a cluster of houses and possible stables. The detached north-eastern mound location would have meant the buildings here were a prominent landmark to travellers coming along the *wadi* from the north in particular. Traces of architecture below the main phase uncovered indicate that there were similar imposing structures in this area in an earlier phase. The main buildings underwent some minor adaptations during their use and were ultimately abandoned, with the area becoming open space for rubbish disposal and pits.

Chapter 3 explores the architecture exposed in Area G, adjacent to Mallowan's 1930s excavations in Area BD, along the northern ridge of the main mound. Our excavations here allowed reinterpretations of Mallowan's work, including complete excavation of some houses and a correction of plan alignment. Area G provides a useful contrast to Area A, with smaller and more irregular houses lining a 40 meter-long narrow alley. Four phases of architecture belonging to the early 2nd millennium BC were exposed. The houses to the west of the alley most often were possibly single-roomed buildings with substantial courtyards; those houses to the east of the alley, connecting to Mallowan's plans, were more often multi-roomed and more irregular. Phase distinctions entailed re-building of structures on previous alignments and the maintenance of original ground plans, but phase changes also incorporated relocation of doorways, superimposition of multiple occupational floors, and new construction of stone pavements and drains that may indicate shifts in room function. Space use in this portion of the site was intensive, both horizontally and vertically.

Chapter 4 covers the 23 human burials recovered from below the buildings and open spaces in both Areas A and G. Courtyards were the most common location of burials within houses, although infant graves were sometimes found in open areas. Most graves were simple pits, but several shaft and pit graves were exposed, plus one vaulted tomb similar to examples found by Mallowan and also represented at Tell Arbid and Tell Mohammed Diyab. The Chagar Bazar graves are fairly typical of Mesopotamian burial practices in that they are dominated by single interments, often with small numbers of grave goods, primarily pottery vessels and personal ornaments such as beads. The emphasis on treatment of the dead as an individual and the provision of food and drink reflect region-wide ideas of the afterlife best known from southern Mesopotamian texts. The numbers of adults and children were almost equal, but there were some variations in their ratio in the different phases of both areas. The Appendix to Chapter 4 offers a full scientific analysis of the skeletons, including assessments of preservation, sex, age, general health at death and during childhood, plus specific diseases, conditions and deformities.

Chapter 5 discusses the ceramic assemblages from Areas A and G, which have particularly close parallels at contemporary Tell Brak, Tell Leilan and Tell al-Rimah. A typology is developed, comprising both a range of wares (common, fine, burnished grey, cooking pot) and a variety of bowl and jar forms. Close analysis of the bowls in particular indicates an emphasis within the assemblage on vessels for communal eating events, as indicated by their size/volume, decoration and carination. The standardization of form, volume and manufacturing details (such as temper, colour and decoration) in many vessels is high, suggesting that they were produced in semi-specialised or fully-specialised workshops. The exception is found among cooking pots, which have a very different fabric and technique and may have been manufactured within households. Some contrasts could be made in the wares and relative popularity of types found in the two excavated areas, which support the different functions identified on the basis of architectural plans, administrative versus domestic.

Chapter 6 is devoted to the objects recovered from the excavations. Baked clay figurines were the most common object class, but ornaments, metal objects, grinding stones and other stone tools were also frequent. Less common were bone weaving tools, clay sealings and other administrative items. The contexts with the greatest densities of objects (and ceramics and other materials) were the alleys in both Areas A and G, evidence of discard practices; courtyards saw the second-highest density, while most inner rooms remained relatively clean. Clay figurines were dominated by animals, particularly equids and zebu, which may have been equally children's toys or expressions of adult aspirations. Stone grindstones and bone weaving tools are expressive of the primary labour tasks performed within the houses. Administrative items were few but are clustered mainly in Area A; there were no inscribed objects, but sealings, tokens and tallies were present and may have been appropriate for a mostly-illiterate population. Metal objects were most frequently preserved in burials and include the same range of items as recovered by Mallowan in his earlier excavations: pins, rings, beer strainers and occasional ornaments or tools. Strings of beads were also recovered from burials.

Chapter 7 concludes the volume with a summary of the settlement's internal contrasts and role in the larger regional landscape as a meaningful landmark of significant time depth. The architecture and material culture in Area G indicate very little variation among houses and suggest that tightly-networked and easily accessible social and economic systems existed within the settlement. In Area A, the use of a house plan for the community building signified the informality of administration in the post-Samsi-Addu era. Regional surveys around Chagar Bazar indicate that the area was relatively free of permanent settlement, but texts speak to the presence of a substantial nomadic population. The arrangement of buildings within the site, the visibility of certain aspects, and the selection of the mound itself for resettlement after an earlier 2nd millennium BC hiatus, may have been aimed at making a visual impression on both inhabitants and external viewers such as the local nomads.

كالخرز مثلاً . إن التركيز على فردية المتوفى و مرافقته بأواني الطعام و الشراب يعكس انتشار اعتقادات الحياة الأخرى ما بعد الموت و المعروفة جيداً من خلال النصوص الرافدية الجنوبية. تضم القبور عدداً متساوياً تقريباً من الراشدين و الأطفال بشكل عام , ولكن تظهر هنالك بعض الفروقات في هذه المعدلات عند النظر إلى كل سوية بشكل منفرد.

الفصل الرابع مرفق بملحق يضم دراسة تحليلية للهياكل العظمية المكتشفة من حيث درجةِ حفظها و العمر و الجنس و وضع الشخص الصحي عند الوفاة و خلال سنوات الطفولة أيضاً، بالإضافة الى تحديد ما اذا كان يعاني من أمراض أو تشوهات معينة. الفصل الخامس من الكتاب يتناول الفخار المكتشف في كل من المنطقة G و A و الذي يتشابه الى حد كبير مع فخار تل براك و تل ليلان و تل الزماح . لقد قمنا بتطوير طريقة لتصنيف الفخار تتضمن وصف لنوع العجينة (عادية , رقيقة , عجينة أواني الطبخ, مطلية بالخزف), و وصف لتنوع أشكال الأواني كالجرار و الزبادي مثلاً. أظهرت الدراسة المعمقة للأواني الفخارية و جودِ اتجاه لصنع الأواني الكبيرة المعدة للاستخدام الجماعي في مآدب الطعام. تظهر ذلك واضحاً من خلال النظر إلى حجم هذه الأواني و كميتها و طريقة زخرفتها. إن اتباع المواصفات القياسية في صنع هذه الأواني من حيث الشكل و الكمية و تفاصيل الصنعة (المواد المضافة الى الصلصال و اللون و الزخرفة) يدل على أن صناعة الفخار كانت تتم على يد محترفين للمهنة بشكل كامل أو شبه محترفين إن الاستثناء الوحيد لهذه القاعدة هو أواني الطبخ حيث أنها صنعت بطرق مختلفة و بأشكال مختلفة مما يرجح أنها كانت منزلية الصنع. تظهر المقارنة بين أنواع الفخار المكتشف في كل من منطقتي التنقيب إلى وجود اختلاف في كيفية استخدام الأواني بين المنطقتين حيث تسود بعض الأنواع على حساب البعض الآخر مما يؤكد فرضية اختلاف طبيعة المنطقتين, فواحدة كانت مخصصة للمباني السكنية وأخرى للمباني الإدارية.

الفصل السادس من الكتاب مخصص لدراسة اللقى الأثرية المكتشفة. تشكل الدمى الطينية المشوية الصنف الأكثر انتشاراً من هذه اللقى بالإضافة الي كمية جيدة من الحلي والقطع المعدنية وكذالك أدوات الطحن الحجرية. أما اللقى الأقل انتشاراً فتشمل الأدوات العظمية المستخدمة عادة في صناعة النسيج وطبعات الأختام الطينية والأدوات الإدارية عامة. كانت الأزقة في كلتا المنطقتين من أغنى الأماكن باللقى والفخار والعديد من المواد الأثرية، وذلك بسبب رمي الأشياء التي انتهى استخدامها فيها، بينما احتوت باحات الأبنية على ثاني أعلى كمية من اللقى المكتشفة، و خلت الغرف نسبياً من اللقى. بالنسبة إلى الدمى الطينية كان الشكل الغالب هو حيوانات من فصيلة الخيليات والدربانيات والتي ربما كانت تستخدم كدمى للعب الصغار أو كتعبيرات فنية صنعها الكبار. من ناحية أخرى تدل أدوات الطحن الحجرية وأدوات النسيج العظمية علي وجود مهام عمل رئيسية كانت تنفذ في تلك البيوت. أما الأدوات الإدارية فكانت قليلة ومتمركزة في المنطقة A. لم نعثر على لقى تحتوي على كتابات ولكن عثرنا على طبعات أختام طينية وأشكال طينية لعملة رمزية مما يوحي بغلبة السكان الأميين. أما فيما يتعلق باللقى المعدنية والتي وجدت مراراً" في القبور, فإنها تشمل مشابك وخواتم ومصافي الجعة وكمية قليلة من الحلي والأدوات, بالإضافة إلى الأسلاك التي ربما استخدمت كسلال لتعليق الخرز.

الفصل السابع من الكتاب هو عبارة عن خاتمة وملخص لتعدد واختلاف الوظائف الداخلية للمستوطنة وللدور البارز الذي لعبته في محيطها الإقليمي لفترة طويلة ومهمة من الزمن. تشير دلائل العمارة والآثار المادية و الثقافية في المنطقة G على عدم وجود تنوع في البيوت السكنية مما يعكس وجود منظومة اقتصادية واجتماعية ذات علاقات متداخلة ومفتوحة في المستوطنة. أما في المنطقة A فيعتبر استخدام نفس مخطط المنزل العادي عند تشييد المباني العامة انعكاساً للتعامل غير الرسمي في المسائل الإدارية في عصر ما بعد شمشي حدد. تظهر المسوحات الأثرية في محيط شاغار بازار أن المنطقة كانت خالية من المستوطنات المستقرة مما يتوافق مع ما تحدثت عنه النصوص المسمارية من وجود مجموعات كبيرة من البدو الرحل في هذه الفترة. إن توزع الأبنية داخل الموقع و اختياره بالذات لإعادة الاستيطان بعد فترة من الانقطاع في بداية الألف الثاني ق . م , ربما كان هدفه إبهار سكان المستوطنة و الناظرين إليها من البدو المحليين.

خلاصة

الفصل الأول من الكتاب هو عبارة عن تعريف بموقع شاغار بازار الأثري الواقع في شمال بلاد الرافدين (شمال شرق سوريا) ذو التاريخ الطويل والمعقد . بدأ هذا التاريخ في الألف السادس قبل الميلاد, وأما فصوله الأخيرة فتشمل الحفريات التي قام بها السيد ماكس مالوان في ثلاثينيات القرن الماضي, وحتى التنقيبات الحديثة العهد التي قامت بها المدرسة البريطانية للآثار في العراق بالتعاون مع جامعة لياج والمديرية العامة للآثار والمتاحف في سوريا. تقوم هذه الدراسة بربط المستوطنة أثرياً مع فكرة (المكان) بحيث تتضمن البحث في المشهد الأثري الداخلي والخارجي للموقع . لقد قمنا باتباع منهج بحث شامل يعتمد على دراسة جوانب مختلفة للآثار المادية و الثقافية للموقع كالفخار و العمارة و اللقى و الربط بينها. كان اهتمامنا مركزاً على فترة الألف الثاني قبل الميلاد (العهد البابلي القديم , فترة ما بعد شمشي حدد) و التي كانت آخر فترة استيطان للموقع. يعود تاريخ الأرشيف الذي عثر عليه مالوان في المنطقة TD من الموقع إلى فترة حكم شمشي حدد, أما بالنسبة لفترة ما بعد شمشي حدد فهي معروفة من خلال الأرشيف التي عثر عليها في تل ليلان و ماري.

الفصل الثاني من الكتاب مخصص لوصف العمارة في المنطقة A و التي تتوضع في مكان أشبه بالنتوء البارز من التل, يمتد إلى الجهة الشمالية الشرقية من مركز الموقع باتجاه وادي خنزير. بتوسط هذه المنطقة بناء ضخم يبدو أنه للاستخدام العام حيث نرجح أنه المبنى الإداري العام للمستوطنة في الفترة ما بعد شمشي حدد. يتشابه تصميم هذا المبنى مع كثير من مخططات البيوت المعاصرة له في الموقع و لكن بالطبع يختلف عن هذه الأبنية من حيث المساحة و طريقة البناء. غرف هذا المبنى كانت تقريباً خالية من الموجودات, أما الباحة فتميزت بأنها مرصوفة بالآجر و الحصى الكبيرة, و كذلك يحتوي المبنى على غرفة اجتماعات كبيرة و يحيط به تجمع بيوت و ربما إسطبلات. إن موضع التلة الشمالية الشرقية المنفصل عن باقي أجزاء الموقع جعل من الأبنية في هذه المنطقة نقطة علامة للمسافرين العابرين على امتداد الوادي و خصوصاً القادمين من الشمال. تشير بقايا العمارة التي عثر عليها مباشرة تحت السوية الرئيسية سالفة الذكر إلى وجود أبنية أقدم بنية للغاية نقشها وعلى الطريقة نفسها. تبين لنا أنه جرى بعض التعديلات الطفيفة على أبنية السوية الرئيسية خلال فترة استخدامها و لكنها هجرت فيما بعد و تحولت المنطقة برمتها إلى مكب للنفايات و فضاء مفتوح.

الفصل الثالث من الكتاب يتناول العمارة المكتشفة في المنطقة G التي تقع بقرب الحفريات التي قام بها مالوان في الثلاثينيات. لقد ساعدت التنقيبات الجديدة على إعادة تفسير نتائج عمل مالوان و كذلك شملت عملية إعادة تنقيب بعض البيوت المكتشفة سابقاً و تصحيح لمخططاتها القديمة. تقدم المنطقة نموذجاً مختلفاً للعمارة لما هو الحال في المنطقة A, حيث البيوت هنا أصغر و أقل انتظاما و تصطف على جانبي زقاق ضيق. تم تمييز أربعة سويات معمارية يعود تاريخها إلى أوائل الألف الثاني قبل الميلاد. تتألف البيوت الموجودة على الجانب الغربي من الزقاق من غرفة واحدة مع باحة كبيرة. أما البيوت في الجانب الشرقي فغالباً ما تضم أكثر من غرفة و لكن من دون وجود مخطط نظامي. لقد تم تحديد السويات المعمارية بناء على وجود دليل على إعادة كاملة للبناء, حتى و أن كانت هذه الإعادة قد تمت على نفس نسق السوية السابقة. أما التغيرات التي حدثت في نفس السوية فتم تميزها من خلال وجود عدة دلائل منها على سبيل المثال: تغيير أماكن الأبواب أو تعاقب الأرضيات الأثرية أو إضافة الأرصفة الحجرية أو إعادة تمديد مصارف المياه, مما يدل على حدوث تغيير في طريقة استخدام الغرف. تشير كل المعطيات إلى استخدام الفراغ في هذا الجزء من الموقع بشكل مكثف, أفقياً من حيث التغيير و التعديل المستمر على العناصر المعمارية, و عامودياً أي خلال تعاقب الزمن.

الفصل الرابع من الكتاب مخصص لنتائج دراسة 23 قبر و جدت تحت مستوى الأبنية أو في الفضاء المفتوح في كل من المنطقة A و G . كانت باحات الأبنية من أكثر الأماكن استخداماً للدفن ضمن التجمعات السكنية, و لكن عثر على بعض القبور أيضاً في الفضاءات المفتوحة. كانت معظم القبور عبارة عن حفر بسيطة و لكم تم العثور أيضاً على عدة قبور حفرت بحد نظامي. و كذلك عثر على مدفن واحد ذي قبة يتشابه مع تلك المدافن التي اكتشفها مالوان و المعروفة أيضا من تل عربيد و تل محمد ذياب. تعتبر قبور شاغار بازار الأثري من النمط التقليدي للقبور الرافدية, حيث أنها غالياً ما تحتوي معزب واحد و قليل من اللقى الجنائزية التي تضم بشكل أساسي أواني فخارية و بعض الحلي الخاصة بالمتوفى